PROBLEMS
IN PHILOSOPHY:
WEST AND EAST

PROBLEMS IN PHILOSOPHY:
WEST AND EAST

Edited by

R. T. Blackwood
Hamilton College

A. L. Herman
University of Wisconsin at Stevens Point

PRENTICE-HALL, INC., *Englewood Cliffs, N.J.*

Library of Congress Cataloging in Publication Data

BLACKWOOD, RUSSELL THORN,   comp.
  Problems in philosophy, West and East.

    1. Philosophy, Comparative—Collected works.
2. Philosophy—Introductions—Collected works. I. Herman, A. L.,
joint comp. II. Title.
B799.B54   108   75-2330
ISBN 0-13-719708-X

Printed in the United States of America

10 9 8 7 6 5 4 3 2 1

PRENTICE-HALL INTERNATIONAL, INC., *London*
PRENTICE-HALL OF AUSTRALIA, PTY. LTD., *Sydney*
PRENTICE-HALL OF CANADA, LTD., *Toronto*
PRENTICE-HALL OF INDIA PRIVATE LIMITED, *New Delhi*
PRENTICE-HALL OF JAPAN, INC., *Tokyo*

For
Elizabeth and Barbara

CONTENTS

2

PROBLEMS OF EPISTEMOLOGY

3

PROBLEMS OF THEOLOGY

4

PROBLEM OF ETHICS

WHAT MAKES ACTIONS RIGHT?   *392*

IS THE UNIVERSE MORAL?   *436*

PREFACE

Problems in Philosophy: West and East is designed to introduce the beginning student to problems in philosophy by using selections from both Eastern and Western sources. From these sources the student may receive encouragement to go further into Eastern and Western philosophy with the critical and comparative spirit which this text hopes to foster. This book is the result of several decades of collective teaching experience by the editors with students interested in both Eastern and Western philosophy. The text could very well be used, along with supplementary materials, to introduce students to either type of philosophy. But we feel it could be best employed by using the materials from both areas to introduce the beginner to the field of philosophy.

Each instructor has his own particular and peculiar approach to introducing the discipline to students and the suggestions we make concerning the employment of the present text should probably be seen simply as our own peculiar way of working and nothing else. It is fashionable in beginning courses in philosophy to start the students off with a philosophic climax—a climax drawn first from religion and then from ethics, or vice versa. The instructor is thereby assured that students will remain through the arousal and excitement phases at least and then by the time he turns to other philosophic matters the student will have been intellectually seduced and a divorce rendered unthinkable.

This approach, of course, has merits and it can be carried out with this text by beginning with "The Problems of Theology" and continuing from there to "The Problems of Ethics," or by reversing the procedure.

Because each of the four sections of the text—Metaphysics, Epistemology, Theology, and Ethics—is a separate and self-contained unit there is nothing to prevent the instructor from starting and ending where he pleases and as the pedagogical mood strikes. However, the editors have found that there is much philosophic good to be gained by keeping more or less to the serial plan of the sections as listed in the contents. Thus, although the text is designed to be used in any order the instructor sees fit, there is an order the editors have found to be a more logical one than others, i.e., the order laid out in the contents. Thus by first clarifying the philosophic problems and solutions about the real and using what we believe to be exciting and well-written selections to help that clarification, we immediately throw the student into several quite basic philosophical puzzles. There is in addition a kind of natural psychological order to the selections in the section on Metaphysics; by the time the student is beginning to feel the problems and wonder about their solutions, he has begun to search for an answer to the question, Can anything at all be known? Then he is ready for the move into the section on Epistemology, where attempts are made to define knowledge and to hold before the student the possibility of knowledge and the puzzles that can be raised with respect to such a possibility. The Theology and the Ethics sections follow in that order in the text with a foundation already laid in the nature of the real and the way of knowing that real.

Depending on the background and interests of each instructor, the order of the selections in each section can be altered and moved about freely without doing any harm to the individual topics of the section. But once again, we have found that there is much philosophic good to be gained by keeping more or less to the serial plan of the readings as presented in each section. However, time, the interest and excitement of the students, and the personal professional concerns of the instructor will naturally determine what is retained and what is lost among the readings in each of the four sections.

In the preparation of this anthology we have been aided greatly by the librarians of Hamilton College and the University of Wisconsin at Stevens Point. Mrs. Donald M. Jones and Mr. Randall J. Harris have assisted in the preparation of the text. We have also received support from the state of New York by appointment as New York State Faculty Scholars in Oriental Studies. Most importantly, we have been encouraged by our students over many years.

R. T. BLACKWOOD

A. L. HERMAN

PROBLEMS
IN PHILOSOPHY:
WEST AND EAST

GENERAL INTRODUCTION: WHAT IS PHILOSOPHY?

The word "philosophy" comes from two Greek words—*philein,* which means "to love," and *sophos,* which means "wisdom"; hence "philosophy" has come to mean "the love of wisdom" and "philosopher" "the lover of wisdom." This helps very little of course, in understanding what "philosophy" means until we know precisely what "wisdom" means and also what it means to love or to have regard for that wisdom. In pursuing the meaning of philosophy, furthermore, we should take pains to be sure that we do not define it so narrowly that we might exclude many activities that are truly philosophical, nor define it so broadly that we might include many activities that clearly do not belong to the discipline of philosophy. To understand what philosophy is is to understand what philosophers do, and what philosophers do is found in the way that they think about certain kinds of puzzles and problems.

We can most profitably pursue our subject by looking carefully at four things: first, what philosophy meant to the Greeks who invented and used the word. We will do this by seeing what they envisaged the goal of philosophy to be. Second, we will investigate what these same Greeks used as means to reach that goal by examining a methodology that came to be called "the dialectic." Third, we will see what kinds of questions, puzzles, and problems the method of philosophy was meant to be used against by looking at five traditional subfields of philosophy. Finally, we will examine how both this understanding of the goals of philosophy and the way to the goals, together with the five subfields of philosophy, relate to Eastern philosophy. All these preliminaries are simply the occasion for showing that philosophic thinking about philosophic problems and philosophic solutions are and

1

can be generated from very ordinary pursuits and interests—pursuits and interests as elemental as the search for happiness and wisdom through philosophic means.

THE GOAL OF PHILOSOPHY

First, philosophy is most closely associated in Greece with two Athenians, Socrates (469–399 B.C.) and his pupil Plato (427–347 B.C.). Although the word "philosophy" was invented by a semireligious secret brotherhood of ascetic Greeks called "Pythagoreans" who were contemporaries of both Socrates and Plato, it is to these two Athenians rather than to the Pythagoreans that the name "philosopher" has come to apply most aptly. For Socrates made what was perhaps the most important discovery in the history of Western philosophy, and his devoted disciple, Plato, wrote about that discovery with passion and genius in the dialogues that have made both their names immortal. What Socrates discovered was what he called "the soul," or *psyche* in Greek, and what he proclaimed, according to Plato, was that his mission on earth was to teach men to look after and care for their individual souls. In Plato's dialogue *Apology* is Socrates' ringing defense of his life as a philosopher to a jury of Athenians who are seeking to have him put to death for atheism and treason. Socrates says,

> Men of Athens, I honor and love you; but I shall obey God rather than you and while I have life and strength I shall never cease from the practice and teaching of philosophy, exhorting any one whom I meet and saying to him after my manner: you, my friend, a citizen of the great and mighty and wise city of Athens, are you not ashamed of heaping up the greatest amount of money and honor and reputation, and caring so little about wisdom and truth and the greatest improvement of the soul, which you never regard or heed at all? (Apology 29, *The Dialogues of Plato*, transl. B. Jowett.)

Socrates then states what it is that he does that leads to the wisdom that the philosopher is concerned with:

> For I do nothing but go about persuading you all, old and young alike, not to take thought for your persons or your properties, but first and chiefly to care about the greatest improvement of the soul. I tell you that virtue is not given by money, but that from virtue comes money and every other good of man, public as well as private. This is my teaching. (Ibid., Apology 30.)

Socrates' defense of his life and conduct before his Athenian peers was unsuccessful and he was executed for "corrupting the youth of the state" and other alleged crimes. In defining the mission of the philosopher and the aim of philosophy as somehow or other concerned with the improvement of the soul, Socrates set a stamp on the discipline of philosophy which has, for good or ill, been with philosophers and philosophy ever since. For the wisdom that philosophers love is a wisdom that comes from knowing the soul, and the virtue and manliness that make the good life possible come from that wisdom. Thus the wise man is the man who knows himself, who knows his capacities and potentialities, his limitations and shortcomings. And living within these limitations and realizing those potentialities lead to the good life and make happiness possible. Thus philosophy—and thus the love of wisdom and the care for the improvement of the soul—is a significantly practical activity and this practical concern is a characteristic of Greek philosophy that has influenced Western philosophy down to the present day.

THE WAY TO WISDOM: THE DIALECTIC

Although the roots of Western philosophy are Greek and Greek philosophy was indeed fascinated with the self and with happiness, there is yet another side to philosophy and the love of wisdom that is similarly Greek and Platonic in origin. For if the goal of philosophy is that knowledge of the self that we call "wisdom," and if that knowledge produces virtue and happiness and the good life, then we might well ask, How is all this wisdom to be achieved? In other words, what is the method or way by which this self is to be known? The way Socrates and Plato chose to pursue these goals was by dialoguing, by asking careful questions, by employing what came to be called "the dialectic." The dialectical method is simply the technique of using questions and answers in order to arrive at understanding, truth, or wisdom. In place of praying for divine insight or waiting upon a transcendental intuition, one began by getting clear on precisely what it was that one wanted to ask a question about, and generally a teacher or guide might be necessary to initiate and then guide the investigation. Here Socrates was and remains the teacher *par excellence* for the dialectical method in the Western tradition. He claimed that he was but a midwife to assist in the birth of his pupil's ideas, but added that he was barren and bereft of knowledge and ideas himself. Socrates was probably being ironical in saying that he knew nothing himself, for he skillfully guides the pupil through the dialectic to a conclusion that one feels he knew was going to come all along. To this extent Socrates is not different from the philosophic midwives of the Eastern tradition, those gurus and sages of the Upanishads and the Chinese tradition who dialectically led their young pupils along quite similar paths to the understanding of the self. The dialectic, however, whether from East or West, moves from question to answer and to an ever-increasing understanding of both until finally, if the delivery is successful, if the investigation is fruitful, the idea is born or clarified, and understanding and wisdom are the ultimate result.

But the questions and the answers from both the Eastern and Western traditions sound strangely familiar regardless of who asks and who answers them. Who am I? Why was I born? Why was I born now and not ten years ago? or ten years hence? or fifty years hence? Is what I see what there really is? Is the world around me real? or is it an appearance of some other more real entity? How may I see the real? How is liberation from fear and suffering reached? Is there happiness to be found in this world? What must I do to achieve wisdom? Are all my actions condemnable? Am I capable of any right actions at all? Is the self real or an illusion? Why does God permit evil in the world? Can I ever reach certain truth or knowledge?

FIVE SUBFIELDS OF PHILOSOPHY

As time passed these questions and the problems that occasioned them tended to align or group themselves into several common areas of study and concern, and these areas in time became the five subfields of the professional discipline of philosophy. We can illustrate this most clearly by briefly mentioning these subfields together with the kinds of questions that defined them.

METAPHYSICS. The philosopher who is engaged in metaphysics is concerned with questions about the nature of ultimate reality. Traditionally the ultimately real, or the "really real" as opposed to what merely seems real or appears real, was that which was unchanging, perfect, uncreated, and not dependent on anything else for its existence. This traditional notion of the real has altered somewhat over the centuries, but the questions the metaphysician asks have not: What is everything made of? Is that ultimate stuff really real? or was it made or created from some other stuff or being? In other words, if the ultimate building materials of the universe are water, air, fire, and earth, the metaphysician wants to know where they came from and whether they are all reducible to some one or other stuff, such as material atoms (as the metaphysical materialist believes) or immaterial minds, ideas, or a Mind (as the metaphysical idealist believes). What is the origin of the totality that we call the universe? Has it been created by some Superbeing? And if so, what is the nature of such a being? And if not, has the universe always existed and will it always exist? What is the nature of man? What is real in man's nature? Is his soul, that entity that was of such moment to Socrates and Plato, eternal and real? Finally, the metaphysician, that philosopher who is interested in the dialectic relating to the ultimately real, wants to know the meaning of basic words like "real," "ultimately real," "soul," "universe," "existence." For the task of getting clear on precisely what words mean in the questions and answers in which they appear is essential to answering the questions in the first place.

EPISTEMOLOGY. The philosopher who is engaged in epistemology is concerned with questions about the nature of knowledge: When we say that we know something or other, what kind of a claim are we making? Is knowing the same thing as believing? How do they differ? What are the standards or the criteria of knowledge? If one person knows that today is Tuesday can another person also know that today is not Tuesday? What kind of evidence is acceptable for our being able to say that we know something or other? Is knowing how to ride a bicycle the same kind of knowing as knowing that this object over here is a bicycle? Can there be different kinds of knowledge? Finally, the epistemologist, that philosopher who is interested in the dialectic relating to the nature of knowledge and the criteria for knowledge, wants to know what meaning fundamental words like "knowledge," "knowing," "evidence," "belief," "standard," or "criteria" have. For getting clear on the meaning of concepts used in the epistemological dialectic is just as important for the epistemologist as it was previously for the metaphysician.

LOGIC. The philosopher who is engaged in logic is concerned with questions about the nature of inference. Thus if we know that you are a human being, then what else can we infer or conclude by virtue of this first knowing? For if we know that you are a human being we also know by logical inference that you are either male or female, that you have a four-chambered heart, that you have a brain, and that you can reason or draw logical conclusions. Logic is in part the study of the rules that allow us to draw such inferences and to conclude either that those inferences are valid, i.e., the inferences do not violate any logical rules, or that those inferences are invalid, i.e., the inferences do violate some logical rule or other. The logician wishes to catalogue such rules and to study both the formal or artificial systems as well as the informal or natural systems of logic in which such rules of inference are embedded. Finally, the logician, that philosopher who is interested in the dialectic relating to the nature of inference and the standards for valid inference, wants to know what meaning key words in his own discipline have—words like "inference," "valid," "fallacy," "logical system," "formal system." For, obviously once again, getting clear on precisely what these basic words mean is essential to any dialectical session the philosopher may open in the subfield of logic.

ETHICS. The philosopher who is engaged in ethics is concerned with questions about the nature of human conduct insofar as that conduct is called "right" or "wrong," "good" or "bad." When we say that stealing is "wrong," what allows us to so label it? Is stealing always wrong? Who says so, when, and why? Is killing another human being wrong? Presumably so, and yet there are occasions when such killing is deemed right. Is lying wrong? If one lies to save another's life, then is it still wrong to lie? Finally, the moral philosopher, that philosopher who is interested in the dialectic relating to ethical judgments about human conduct, wants to know the meaning of the fundamental words employed in the discipline of ethics, words like "human conduct," "right," and "wrong." Such words as "stealing," "lying," and "killing" need careful explication as well. Thus it is no easy matter to define the conditions under which someone can be said to be telling a lie. Once again, if the dialectic in ethics is to make any sense at all, and if it is going to be fruitful and salutary, then getting clear on what our basic concepts mean is surely essential.

The fifth and final subfield of philosophy is a relatively late invention, for while philosophers since Socrates have been engaged in its implementation and exercise it is only recently that it has come to be recognized as a distinct subfield of the discipline itself. What is involved in this fifth sub-field of philosophy is really the focusing of critical attention on a number of other disciplines of human interest and concern such as art, religion or theology, science, history, education, mathematics, sports, psychology, and even philosophy itself. Because the philosopher is interested in the pursuit of knowledge and truth, and because he is interested in the dialectic that promotes and leads to knowledge and truth, he is going to be interested in these other disciplines that make claims to knowledge and truth. Thus this fifth subfield of philosophy is dependent on these other nonphilosophic areas, except where philosophy itself is the discipline under scrutiny. What is produced as a result of such dependency are philosophies such as the philosophy of art, the philosophy of theology, the philosophy of science, the philosophy of history, and so on. Our interest, however, is in what all of these philosophies have in common. We can treat that topic in the fifth and final subfield of philosophy, which follows.

THE PHILOSOPHY OF X. The philosopher who is engaged in the philosophy of X (where "X" stands for art, theology, science, history, and so on) is concerned about the truth claims and the knowledge claims of each of the several disciplines in which such claims are made. Thus the artist claims to have knowledge about what the beautiful in art is, or he claims to know what the conditions are or must be for the production of the beautiful or the aesthetically interesting. The aesthetician may claim, as many have, that art brings truth and that truth and beauty are one. The philosopher is interested in such claims simply because they form part of that continuing dialectic that is the heart of philosophy. Hence he simply moves his discussion over into the area of art. Such discussion then can be called "the philosophy of art." The philosopher of art wants to know what such basic concepts as "work of art," "beauty," "truth," and "aesthetic experience" mean. He therefore engages the artist and the aesthetician in the dialectic in order to clarify such concepts.

The historian, to take another example, makes claims to have knowledge of the past; he says that past events can be known and that there is value in knowing the past. Naturally, the philosopher is interested once again and "the philosophy of history" is the outcome of that interest. In general, the philosopher of X is simply applying the critical techniques to X that we found the metaphysician, the epistemologist, the logician, and the moral philosopher employing earlier. Just as these four kinds of philosophers asked probing questions about the meanings of basic or fundamental words in their subfields—words like "real," "knowledge," "valid inference," and "right action"—so now the philosopher of X is seeking to clarify the essential concepts in the discipline or disciplines to which he decides to carry the dialectic. The philosophy of X, therefore, can be seen in the light of the following definition of "philosophy": Philosophy involves the analysis and clarification of basic concepts in any discipline that makes truth claims or knowledge claims. Thus insofar as art and history make such claims, they are fair game for the philosopher or they are fair game, for that matter, for the artist or historian playing philosopher. For, on this latter point, there is a clear sense in which we are all philosophers.

In conclusion, then, to the second point being made here about philosophy, let us say this: The goal of philosophy is wisdom, knowledge about the self, and all that such knowledge must entail. The way to that goal, which is what we have been talking about above, is through the dialectic, the asking of serious questions first about reality, then about knowledge, then about reason and inference, then about human moral action, and finally about knowledge and truth in general wherever they occur. And this, in truth, is where Greek philosophy, Western philosophy, now more or less stands.

It remains for us now to speak to a fourth and final point, and that is to relate philosophy West to philosophy East and to address the reasons for this book on problems in philosophy.

PHILOSOPHY WEST AND EAST

Although it is true that "philosophy" was a Greek invention, it is just as true that philosophy was not a Greek invention. That is to say, the word "philosophy," being a Greek word as we have already seen, was a Greek invention, but that need not entail that the critical and dialectical spirit of the discipline of philosophy need be a Greek invention at all. And in fact it wasn't. Centuries before Socrates and Plato began their ruminations on the nature of man and the universe, the Indians of South Asia were reflecting critically on their universe and doing metaphysics, epistemology, and ethics together with a philosophy of theology in much the same way as we have just outlined those subfields. Chinese and Buddhist philosophers who were contemporaries of Socrates also developed an Eastern dialectic of philosophy built on a foundation laid centuries earlier. In many ways the critical reflections of Eastern philosophers are not terribly different from the critical reflections of Western philosophers, for the heart of the philosophic dialectic is the irritation of gnawing doubt wherein seemingly unanswerable questions about man, the universe, God, and reality cluster around certain central problems. It is this ability to share irritation, to seek to erase it by, as Socrates put it, caring about the greatest improvement of the self, that binds us and holds us all together as philosophic brothers. But though a common philosophic humanity, i.e., a caring about general philosophic puzzles and problems, binds all of us together, there are more specific areas of concern in which this common worry about questions of a philosophic sort becomes manifest. Thus it is that metaphysical materialists of West and East can share a common specific irritation about the ways that idealists and transcendentalists comport themselves. And empiricists from both traditions can feel a mutual bond of philosophic unease toward epistemological rationalists from both East and West. But the philosophic brotherhood is built on more than a shared goal like wisdom, or realization, or liberation, and a shared means or way or yoga to that goal. Such a philosophic brotherhood is built on more than the finding of kindred spirits with which to pass a depressingly worrisome philosophical moment or two while feeling that one is not after all alone and isolated in one's materialism or idealism. For what binds philosophers and students of philosophy into this brotherhood is the common belief that, paraphrasing an old saying about studying foreign languages, he who knows only his own philosophic tradition knows little of that. It is this interest, curiosity, and concern that forces the materialist to study the idealist's position, that brings the empiricist to learn the rationalist's position, and it is what brings the Christian to study the Hindu, and the Muslim the Buddhist. It is what has been bringing Eastern and Western philosophers together for over a century now—namely, the feeling that one's own position is best known by seeing it from all possible sides and angles.

And this brings us then to the purpose of this book. Its aim is to introduce the student of philosophy to several of the most basic problems in the subfields of philosophy that have bothered and irritated philosophers from both the Western and the Eastern tradition. But not only does the book raise these central philosophic problems for the student to see and appreciate, but the selections have also been carefully chosen to indicate in most cases what a likely or a possible solution to the problem could be or might be like. The book is meant to serve, therefore, as a device for philosophic dialectic in which the dialogue between authors and reader is meant to inculcate, in a modest way to be sure, the wisdom that seems to be the goal of the brotherhood of philosophers. To this end the book seeks to do four things: First, it seeks to introduce the student to the basic problems of philosophy. In this sense, it constitutes a text for a first course in philosophy. Second, it seeks to introduce the student to both Eastern and Western philosophy by providing selections from the foremost philosophers from both traditions. In this sense, it constitutes a text in what might be called "comparative philosophy." Third, it seeks to demonstrate that there are solutions to philosophic problems which, although they may not be ultimate or final solutions, are in and by themselves worth considering. In this sense, it constitutes a text of solutions to philosophic puzzles that are worth thinking about and poring over. Fourth and finally, it seeks to show that we in the twentieth century are not alone with our philosophic concerns, that for several thousand years men and women from all over the world have spent energy and time being concerned about problems that we are still, as philosophers, concerned about today. In this sense, it shows the abiding universality and significance of man's philosophic life.

Part 1

PROBLEMS
OF METAPHYSICS

INTRODUCTION:
SCIENCE AND METAPHYSICS

It may appear a bit odd to introduce a book of readings in philosophy with the problems of metaphysics. The subject itself is perhaps the most abstruse and puzzling of all the areas of philosophy because it treats "ultimate truths" and "ultimate reals." Whenever we are inclined to think of the "mysteries of the universe"—e.g., Is there a real world of matter or mind? Is there a life after death? Who or what created the universe? Or was it created at all?—we come close to the area designated by philosophers as "metaphysics." Further, in a scientific age that puts a premium on meticulous empirical observation, the kind of armchair philosophizing undertaken by many metaphysicians is anathema. The age is hostile to metaphysics, hostile to its subject matter (talk about ultimates), and hostile to its methodology (armchair, as opposed to laboratory, investigations).

It is hoped that the oddness will disappear, however, in the course of the readings. Metaphysics may talk about ultimates, but it begins with the same sort of homely, particular observations that the scientist employs. If philosophy, as Aristotle says, begins in wonder, then it is this wonder that makes us ask questions, and the questions and the wonder essentially begin with what we experience with our five senses. But not only do both scientist and metaphysician begin essentially with questions about what we see or hear, they are both occupied in thinking about that which could explain what is seen or heard. Both retire to their armchairs to ponder their observations, consider their hypotheses, and think about ways of testing these hypotheses. The scientist and the metaphysician begin in the same place and both make use of the same methodological pondering. If we were to condemn the metaphysician merely for the way he begins philosophizing and for the method he uses in philosophizing, we would have to condemn the scientist as well.

But what makes the scientist and the metaphysician different? For one thing, they ask different kinds of questions about man, the universe, time, space, and the stuff that makes up man, the universe, time, and space. Questions that give the metaphysician sleepless nights do not bother the scientist, or at least they don't bother him as a scientist. For another, the metaphysician and the scientist differ in the way in which they orient themselves to the universe. It is usually said of the metaphysician that he wants a world-view, a macroscopic picture of all time and space. He wants an hypothesis that will explain everything, and not just specific animal or plant behavior. Thus, the metaphysician not only asks different questions, but he expects different answers.

The questions you might keep in mind as you go through the readings in this section are, Would the scientist ask this kind of question? What kind of an answer would the scientist give to such a question? Man is the wondering animal, the animal that asks questions. The kind of questions that he asks and the kind of answers that he accepts determine precisely whether he is a metaphysician or a scientist.

The word "metaphysics" means "beyond physics," and as first employed that was exactly what it meant.[1] The meaning of "metaphysics" is now much more complicated. The best way of indicating this meaning would be to give a brief but traditional definition to the word and then illustrate the use of the definition in the four historical subdivisions of metaphysics.

"Metaphysics" is defined as the study of that which is ultimately real or, if you like, *really* real, as distinguished from that which is only *apparently* real. Men have always been concerned about the distinction between the real and the unreal, the true and the deceptive, the real and the appearance of the real. The philosopher has merely taken a professional interest in a subject that concerns us all, and he has given that interest a name: "Metaphysics."

If "metaphysics" is the investigation of the real, where does it do its investigation, i.e., what kinds of objects does it study in order to discover the real? There are four subdivisions of metaphysics, and each one becomes the arena for investigation into the nature of some aspect of reality. These four subdivisions are ontology, cosmology, rational psychology, and rational theology.

ONTOLOGY

Ontology is concerned primarily with the nature of the stuff of which the world or the universe is made. The kinds of questions asked by the ontolo-

---

[1] Andronicus of Rhodes (70 B.C.), in editing the manuscripts of Aristotle, placed a number of the chapters *after* the section called "Physics," and labeled the new section "Metaphysics." Much of the material in these papers following "Physics" considered "Being as being," and the way in which being is known. Hence the meaning of "metaphysics" changed from designating a chapter heading, an editor's label of convenience, to designating the subject under discussion in that chapter: Being, and how that which is (real) is known.

gist are: What is everything made of? Is consciousness the foundation or basic stuff of the real world, or is that basic stuff material in some sense, e.g., atoms, space, and their compounds? Is the ultimate stuff out of which everything comes one stuff or many stuffs, e.g., are there many basic material things (maybe earth, air, fire, water, and ether), or many different mental things, or just one stuff (fire alone or earth alone, or God's Mind alone or Nature's Mind alone)? Further, how does the basic stuff change and become the different things of an ordinary world? Such questions have bothered the ontologist and they will worry us a bit in the section that follows.

COSMOLOGY

Cosmology, as its etymology indicates, is the "discourse or discussion about the cosmos" or the ordered universe. If we could argue that ontology has a scientific counterpart in physics and chemistry, then cosmology finds its closest counterpart in astronomy. Cosmology is concerned principally with the origin of the universe and the nature of the order found in the universe.

Perhaps the first question that men asked about their environment was asked about the stars or the moon. Mysterious objects such as stars and moons would naturally draw attention; their periodic and ordered paths would perhaps add a touch of awe to that attention; and finally, if these sky-things did not become objects of religious veneration, they might be studied as intently as one would study elephants and men. This study and the attention that leads to it are the essential parts of all cosmologies. The theories they lead to, where the speculation becomes dogmatically hardened, are the public property which other men may look to in order to explain the wonder and the awe at what they feel.

Cosmological speculation may be very simple or extremely complex; it may account for none of the observations or it may account for all. For instance, the Greek myths which account for the origin of Ursa Major and Ursa Minor are quite simple accounts used to explain how the Big and Little Dippers came to be where they are. But these mythical explanations cannot account for the fact that individual stars within these constellations are changing their relative positions, however slightly, nor that some star elements of the constellations mentioned, while appearing to the naked eye as single, are in reality multiple clusters. As our observations are improved by the introduction of new instruments, the old "explanations" just won't do because, for one thing, they accounted merely for old observations. Cosmology, unless it can keep step with the revolutions in astronomy and astrophysics, would appear to be in the precarious position of having to explain the new solely by means of the old.

RATIONAL PSYCHOLOGY

A third division of metaphysics is rational psychology. Rational psychology has man as its principal concern—man as a rational and spiritual being. The questions of rational psychology are, What is the ultimate nature of man? and more particularly, Who are you? For the ancient Greeks as well as for the Hindus, Buddhists, Muslims, Jews, and Christians the problem was a noetic one: Know yourself. The self has been variously identified with the body, the mind or consciousness, and at times with some kind of divine or spiritual substance. Suppose you ask yourself the question, "Who am I?" What kind of answer can you give? If you identify yourself with your body, then you must face the so-called problem of personal identity. That problem, simply stated, is this: Are you the same person today that you were yesterday? And if you are, how do you know that you are? You may answer, "Of course I'm the same person today; I recognized myself in the mirror." But this answer, identifying the self with the body, won't do. Biologists tell us that our body is undergoing constant change at every moment. Your body at this minute is not the same as it was a minute ago, much less yesterday, a week ago, or ten years ago. Common sense certainly urges us to admit that we are the same today as yesterday, yet critical analysis also shows this to be impossible, if the "we" is our material body. Well then, "Who are you?"

Suppose you identify yourself with consciousness, or more particularly with your memories. It certainly makes sense to say that you are you and not I because the things you remember are different from things I remember, and this can be tested by our getting together and comparing our memories. This certainly is one way of showing that you are not I and, silly as the undertaking might seem, it is a very important criterion for distinguishing and identifying people.[2] Thus you know that you are the same person today that you were yesterday because there is a continuity as well as a similarity of memories between yesterday and today. For what you remember now is the sum of what you could remember yesterday plus the memories of the experiences between now and yesterday. And further, the things you remember today are similar to the things you recall remembering yesterday. Hence you are your memories; you are the same person you were yesterday; and you know this because memory can be trusted.

But this won't do either. The answers to the questions raised by the problem of identity rest precisely upon the presupposition that your memory can be trusted. Can it? Much of the time it can, but some of the time it cannot. Does this mean that much of the time you know who you are while some of the time you do not? Thus, if you forget that you performed a particular act three days ago, and if you are to be identified with your memory, it follows that you did not perform the act that you performed. Any argument that leads to such a contradiction just won't do.

If self is not identified with either body or consciousness, what is left? Some philosophers have held that man's self is to be identified with God. When the New Testament speaks of the true light that enlightens every

2 Thus the question might be raised, Is this person standing in front of me, though much changed in physical appearance, my long-lost brother? We test to see what memories his consciousness contains. If his memories are similar to mine the probability is increased that he is my brother. It is often the case that long-lost "Romanov princesses" are shown to be frauds by precisely such methods.

man, or the Hindus say that the atman is identical with Brahman, they both seem to be speaking of an identity of the self (usually written with capital S) with God. Whether or not this solves the problem of the self dealt with by law courts, the self bound up with the business of going to school, eating, and working, is debatable indeed. But it is one way, again, of identifying the person and answering the problem of personal identity.

Another problem involving the self and its nature arises when we attempt to consider the question, Is the self basically good, or evil, or is it neither? An answer to this question presupposes that we can locate or identify the self, for it makes no sense to apply the adjectives *good, evil,* or a neutral word to something we know not what.

If the claim is made that the self is basically evil, what does this claim mean, and what does it entail? For the metaphysician the claim itself may be an ultimate supposition, resting on no prior suppositions nor following from any previous premises. Or the claim may rest on observations of the world. In either case, to say that man is basically evil is to say that in some sense or other he is controlled by a depravity inherent in his nature, and that his actions may or may not be signs of this depravity. It is difficult, if not impossible, to rest this claim merely on empirical observations. To those pessimistic persons who hold to utter depravity on empirical grounds, one can always point to an Albert Schweitzer or a Jane Addams or a Mohandas Gandhi to challenge their conclusions. To those who reject sensory observations and fall back on revelation, personal or public, there is, of course, little that one can say to challenge them.

If the claim is made that the self is basically good, the meaning and implication of this assertion will follow the pattern of the previous discussion. The method of criticizing this claim will also be little different.

The third claim, that man's nature is neither corrupt nor pure, is perhaps more defensible. This claim, an environmentalist doctrine, holds that man becomes what his surroundings are: He is conditioned or made into the kind of being he is; he has no inherent or essential nature.

A final issue involving the self is the so-called "mind-body" problem. The problem is generated whenever one presupposes that that which we call "mind" is different substantially from that which we call "body." The problem is further complicated if one also holds that unlikes cannot interact. Thus, if the mind is one kind of stuff, and if the body is another kind of stuff, then how can thoughts ever be affected by matter (sensation) or matter ever be affected by thoughts (willing and desiring, and putting our willing and desiring to work in the material world)? Metaphysical dualism holds that man is composed of both mind and body. The metaphysical monist, who argues that only matter is ultimately real, or that only mind is ultimately real, does not have to face the mind-body problem. However, new issues emerge which are just as difficult to handle, e.g., if all is matter how can we account for thoughts, or are they matter too? If all is mental or mind-stuff, how does one account for a world in which, to common sense, there do indeed appear to be nonmental things, e.g., elephants and bicycles? These problems involve us more directly in a discussion of ontology and only indirectly in rational psychology.

RATIONAL THEOLOGY

The fourth and final division of of metaphysics is rational theology. Rational theology has as its principal concern divine or supernatural beings—Gods, Angels, Devils, Witches, Wizards, and Warlocks. Rational theology is concerned with the existence of these beings, their nature, and their relation to each other, the world, and especially to men. Do Gods exist? How do you know? Is there a Devil? Is evil a force in the universe? Does man have supernatural ends set for him by God or the Devil? Is man immortal? If so, in what sense? The question of human immortality is yet another area in which two divisions of metaphysics tend to blend with each other; in this instance rational psychology and rational theology merge in discussing the relation of man to the supernatural. Does man "live forever"? Does his soul, if he has one, transmigrate? Does God control man's life after death?

CONCLUSION

In discussing the Divine as a creator, we might find rational theology merging with cosmology. Further, when the nature of the Divine is discussed we again might find ourselves discussing ontology. It is no accident, of course, that such blendings and mergings occur. The metaphysician, at least in his speculative and noncritical state,[3] desires a super-picture of the universe. He is not going to quit once he gets the ontology tacked down. Because he wants a full and complete account of being in itself, as well as an account of creation, man, and God, and because these entities are all interrelated in that whole he is researching, it follows that there will be an overlap and coincidence in the divisions of metaphysics which study the parts of that interrelated whole.

The picture we intend to give in the sections that follow will be of two divisions of metaphysics: ontology and rational psychology. The questions of cosmology and rational theology, while interesting and exciting in themselves, are excluded here because of requirements of space. However, many

[3] Metaphysics is usually distinguished in another sense, in terms of methodology. There are two ways of doing metaphysics and these two methods can be applied to all four of the areas of metaphysics. Here is an illustration: Suppose that we ask you to read the first chapter of Genesis in the Old Testament. Then we ask you what kind of philosophy you've been reading. You reply, correctly, that if it is taken literally it was metaphysics and in particular cosmological metaphysics. We can both agree that Genesis is a cosmological account of the ultimate nature of the world. Suppose we then ask you to read a critical discussion by a philosopher or theologian of the Genesis account. Is it metaphysics? The answer is that it is also metaphysics. And the usual distinction to be drawn between the Genesis account and the commentator's discussion is to say that the former is *speculative* metaphysics and the latter is *critical* metaphysics. Or in another idiom, the former is metaphysical talk, the latter is talk about metaphysics. A similar parallel holds, as we said, in the other three divisions of metaphysics.

of the questions raised by rational theology will be treated in a later section of this book under the title "Problems of Theology."

We turn then to ontology and rational psychology and to the questions posed by these two metaphysical disciplines: What is the nature of that which is ultimately real? And what is the ultimate nature of man?

ONTOLOGY

Suppose we asked you what this book is made of. What would you say? To say that it is made of pages and board covers is in a sense to answer the question, but this is merely an enumeration of the parts. Thus the question answered with this response is not the one posed but rather a different one, i.e., "What is this book composed of?" The question "What is this book made of?" is an odd question, and one that we are likely to interpret, as we have above, as a query about composition in terms of parts and a whole. If we continued our pursuit along this line we would end up by talking about atoms which have protons and electrons as parts, which in turn have still more minute entities called "electrostatic charges" as parts. This tack is satisfactory to the scientist who perhaps has little time for the question we wish to pose. We can make that question clearer by beginning over but with a question about the parts of the atom: "What is the electrostatic charge made of?" The important point here is that once again we are not asking a question about composition of parts. We have reached, we are supposing, the final or ultimately divisible portion of the book; there are no parts to such ultimates. The question makes no sense, then, if it is interpreted as just another question about further reducibility. But it does makes sense if we see the inquiry as one into the nature of the whole, i.e., the whole as a subatomic whole, a molecular whole, or a macroscopic whole. And the ontologist is peculiarly adept at investigating and speaking about such wholes

Traditionally there have been three kinds of answers to such a question as "What is the book made of?" We will take up these answers in the order in which they will be treated in the readings, and will refer to the metaphysical theories behind these answers as Materialism, Idealism, and Transcendentalism.

MATERIALISM

Materialism is the metaphysical position that maintains that only matter is ultimately real. But what is matter? In the history of philosophy matter is usually conceived of as a substance that is extended in space, persistent through time, and impenetrable or resistant to other matters. Further, in the more ancient texts matter is considered to be easily apprehended by the senses. At times, even the ultimate material constituents, like atoms, can be seen by the naked eye as Democritus, the Greek atomist, claims when he sees motes in a beam of sunlight. This criterion, the ready accessibility of the ultimates of reality, has made materialism a public and a more democratic metaphysical theory than the other two ontologies represented below.

Our selections are from the Indian and the Roman traditions. The first is from the work *De Rerum Natura* [On the Nature of Things] by the Roman naturalistic poet-philosopher Lucretius (d. 55 B.C.). In this selection Lucretius, borrowing extensively from the Greek atomistic theory of Leucippus and Democritus (fl. 430 B.C.) and the ethical life philosophy of Epicurus (341–270 B.C.), lays the foundation for his own ethical life theory by postulating a materialistic ontology: All that ultimately exists are atoms and the void.

The second selection is the Indian summary of philosophic materialism called the Sarvadarsánasaṁgraha (ś is pronounced sh). The Indian materialistic school is called "Cārvāka" (pronounced "charvaka"); it is a school that began in about 600 B.C., but it has roots at least 1000 years before that date. Cārvāka denies a future life, holding that only what can be perceived exists and that only matter can be perceived, hence only matter exists. Consciousness and the soul are only modifications of this underlying matter.

IDEALISM

Returning to our previous example of the book, suppose we question the materialist more closely about what he says the book is made of. When he says the book is brown and black and has white pages, what are the objects of these sensory experiences? Quite obviously they are colors. And where are the colors? That is, are the colors in the world and out there in space? The physicist and the neurophysiologist tell us that colors are caused by stimulations of various wavelengths of light bombarding our retinas which in turn stimulate the optic nerves running from the ocular orbit to the occipital lobe of the brain. Now, the sensing of colors is indeed a complicated process; but one thing we can say about this complex process that we call "seeing a color" is that the color we see is not out there in the world. Where are the colors then, if they are not in the material and external world?

One group of philosophers maintains that the objects we sense are all composed of colors of various sorts, and that all colors exist in the mind. They conclude therefore that all objects are mind-dependent and must, if they are real, exist as ideas in some mind or other. This view is called "Idealism." Metaphysical idealism maintains that what is ultimately real can only be minds and their ideas: Reality is mental.

The doctrine of metaphysical idealism is shocking when first presented in this bold way. We want to argue that the book is not "just in our mind," for this seems to give it a kind of private status that common sense would surely reject. But the argument of the idealists is, while apparently uncommon-sensical, extremely difficult if not impossible to refute on rational grounds. If you hold that all the things you see are only colors (or color shades), remembering that shape and size (so-called "primary qualities") and all colors exist only in the mind, then all that you see exists only in your mind: The argument is absurd but irrefutable and will work with a few changes for all the five senses.

The author of Western metaphysical idealism is a comparatively late figure in the history of philosophy, Bishop George Berkeley, an eighteenth-century British philosopher. Berkeley, by very careful arguments, attempts to refute the materialistic doctrine which he considered atheistical and damning of free will, by introducing idealism. Whether his arguments are successful, and whether this absurd but irrefutable doctrine is all we said it was, you will have to judge for yourself.

The second selection is taken from the Buddhist tradition, and is much older than Berkeley's idealism. The *Viṁśatikā* of Vasubandhu (4th century A.D.), represents the idealist wing of Mahāyāna (or Northern) Buddhism. In this selection, Vasubandhu argues with great care and against many serious objections that only consciousness is real, and the external, apparent world is unreal.

TRANSCENDENTALISM

There is no really good name for the third ontological position. We have called it "transcendentalism," others have called it "pantheism" (the view that all of creation is part of the divine substance) or "pan-en-theism" (the view that while all of creation is part of God and hence substantially identical with God or the divine, the creation does not limit God in any sense).[1] Whatever the best term may be, transcendentalism follows from the view that only spirit is ultimately real. The position is usually at great

[1] "Pantheism" is translated generally as "All is God," or "Everything is God." This seems to be a metaphysical position that no one wants to be identified with and, indeed, it is used pejoratively when used at all. It is easily argued that in the history of philosophy, both East and West, there never has been an honest-to-goodness example of pantheism. "Pan-en-theism" is translated as "All in God," i.e., the doctrine contends that while all the created universe is in God, all of God is not exhausted in or inside the creation. Throughout the history of philosophy, it would seem to be pan-en-theism rather than pantheism that the philosophers are talking about.

pains to account for the apparent non-spirit world in some way (e.g., Is this book spirit?). The most frequent way out is to claim that the world is unreal, merely apparent, or just plain illusory. Thus transcendentalism (or transcendental realism) argues that only that which transcends the physical and mental world is real.

To make the position clearer let's look at a problem. Suppose you believe that only spiritual substance (Gods, Satan, nonmental and non-physical Forms, spirits, Ideals, or something of that sort) is real. Suppose further you believe that these Gods or spirits cannot be apprehended by the senses, i.e., you cannot see or touch this real substance. How then do you account for the world of books, elephants, and bicycles that you see about you. Are they God? Or did God create them? If they are God, you have the problem of trying to explain how God can be both a bicycle and an elephant. If they are not God, but are created by God, then you have the problem of assigning some sort of ontological status to the creation. At this point some metaphysicians would argue that the creation when compared to the real is illusory, i.e., it is not really there at all. Other metaphysicians who hold that only the transcendental is real might say that the elephant and the book are not illusions (after all, I do see them), but that they are less real than the transcendent. This account of the apparent world involves an ontological continuum or scale, with pure reality at one end and lesser degrees of reality at the other. A third position might hold that books, elephants, and bicycles are all real. This view holds that the transcendent is even more immanent than the second view mentioned previously, and concludes that, for example, books *are* the transcendent, in some sense.

In the selections that follow we find the first view forcefully presented that the world around us is unreal and that reality is neither in nor of the world, neither in minds as ideas, nor in the world as things. Rather, the ontological real lies beyond mind and matter in a transcendent realm of forms (as argued by Plato) or Brahman, the divine power (as stipulated by the Hindus in the *Upanishads*).

In the *Phaedo* selection, Socrates explains the nature of the true philosopher: He is a man who is "always dying." The world around him means nothing to him in comparison to that which is real, and the real is not apprehended by or through the bodily senses but through the soul. This real that Socrates discusses in the *Phaedo,* the form of justice itself and the form of beauty itself, is not dependent on minds, however (i.e., Plato is not an idealist). The selections from the *Republic,* the myth of the cave and the analogy of the divided line, show clearly that the forms are not the ideas of the idealist, but independent, transcendent entities, which are eternal and unchanging.

The selection from the Indian *Upanishads* argues the same point in a very interesting manner. The *Katha Upanishad* tells the story of the young boy Naciketas who is sent inadvertently to the house of Death when his father loses his temper and shouts at him, "I will give you to Death." Because a brahmin must keep his promise, the boy must go to the land of the dead, where the remainder of the dialogue occurs. The discussion centers around the question "What is existence, being, and the real?" Once again, as with Plato, a transcendent nonnatural, nonmental entity is given as the answer. The dialogue is not only a discourse on the nature of the ultimately real, but it presents in addition a description of the way (yoga) for discovering the real.

Materialism

On the Nature of Things

LUCRETIUS

Lucretius (c. 99–55 B.C.) is perhaps the most famous of the Roman Epicureans and Atomists. His extremely long poem On the Nature of Things *has come down to us nearly complete, lacking nothing but a final revision. The selection is taken from Book I of the poem, in which he lays down the materialistic metaphysics for his moral, psychological, and physical theories to be developed later in the work*

[Lines 159–634]

If things came from nothing, any kind might be born of any thing, nothing would require seed. Men for instance might rise out of the sea, the scaly race out of the earth, and birds might burst out of the sky; horned and other herds, every kind of wild beasts would haunt with changing brood tilth and wilderness alike. Nor would the same fruits keep constant to trees, but would change; any tree might bear any fruit. For if there were not begetting bodies for each, how could things have a fixed unvarying mother? But in fact because things are all produced from fixed seeds, each thing is born and goes forth into the borders of light out of that in which resides its matter and first bodies; and for this reason all things cannot be gotten out of all things, because in particular things resides a distinct power. Again why do we see the rose put forth in spring, corn in the season of heat, vines yielding at the call of autumn, if not because, when the fixed seeds of things have streamed together at the proper time, whatever is born discloses itself, while the due seasons are there and the quickened earth brings its weakly products in safety forth into the borders of light? But if they came from nothing, they would rise up suddenly at uncertain periods and unsuitable times of year, inasmuch as there would be no first-beginnings to be kept from a begetting union by the unpropitious season. No nor would time be required for the growth of things after the meeting of the seed, if they could increase out of nothing. Little babies would at once grow into men and trees in a moment would rise and spring out of the ground. But none of these events it is plain ever comes to pass, since all things grow step by step at a fixed time, as is natural, since they all grow from a fixed seed and in

From *De Rerum Natura* [On the Nature of Things], Book I, transl. H. A. J. Munro.

growing preserve their kind; so that you may be sure that all things increase in size and are fed out of their own matter. Furthermore without fixed seasons of rain the earth is unable to put forth its gladdening produce, nor again if kept from food could the nature of living things continue its kind and sustain life; so that you may hold with greater truth that many bodies are common to many things, as we see letters common to different words, than that any thing could come into being without first-beginnings. Again why could not nature have produced men of such a size and strength as to be able to wade on foot across the sea and rend great mountains with their hands and outlive many generations of living men, if not because an unchanging matter has been assigned for begetting things and what can arise out of this matter is fixed? We must admit therefore that nothing can come from nothing, since things require seed before they can severally be born and be brought out into the buxom fields of air. Lastly since we see that tilled grounds surpass untilled and yield a better produce by the labour of hands, we may infer that there are in the earth first-beginnings of things which by turning up the fruitful clods with the share and labouring the soil of the earth we stimulate to rise. But if there were not such, you would see all things without any labour of ours spontaneously come forth in much greater perfection.

Moreover nature dissolves every thing back into its first bodies and does not annihilate things. For if aught were mortal in all its parts alike, the thing in a moment would be snatched away to destruction from before our eyes; since no force would be needed to produce disruption among its parts and undo their fastenings. Whereas in fact, as all things consist of an imperishable seed, nature suffers the destruction of nothing to be seen, until a force has encountered it sufficient to dash things to pieces by a blow or to pierce through the void places within them and break them up. Again if time, whenever it makes away with things through age, utterly destroys them eating up all their matter, out of what does Venus bring back into the light of life the race of living things each after its kind, or, when they are brought back, out of what does earth manifold in works give them nourishment and increase, furnishing them with food each after its kind? Out of what do its own native fountains and extraneous rivers from far and wide keep full the sea? Out of what does ether feed the stars? For infinite time gone by and lapse of days must have eaten up all things which are of mortal body. Now if in that period of time gone by those things have existed, of which this sum of things is composed and recruited, they are possessed no doubt of an imperishable body, and cannot therefore any of them return to nothing. Again the same force and cause would destroy all things without distinction, unless everlasting matter held them together, matter more or less closely linked in mutual entanglement: a touch in sooth would be sufficient cause of death, inasmuch as any amount of force must of course undo the texture of things in which no parts at all were of an everlasting body. But in fact, because the fastenings of first-beginnings one with the other are unlike and matter is everlasting, things continue with body uninjured, until a force is found to encounter them strong enough to overpower the texture of each. A thing therefore never returns to nothing, but all things after disruption go back into the first bodies of matter. Lastly rains die, when father ether has tumbled them into the lap of mother earth; but then goodly crops spring up and boughs are green with leaves upon the trees, trees themselves grow and are laden with fruit; by them in turn our race and the race of wild beasts are fed, by them we see glad towns teem with children and the leafy forests ring on all sides with the song of new birds; through them cattle wearied with their load of fat lay their bodies down about the glad pastures and the white milky stream pours from the distended udders; through them a new brood with weakly limbs frisks and gambols over the soft grass, rapt in their young hearts with the pure new milk. None of the things therefore which seem to be lost is utterly lost, since nature replenishes one thing out of another and does not suffer any thing to be begotten, before she has been recruited by the death of some other.

Now mark me: since I have taught that things cannot be born from nothing, cannot when begotten be brought back to nothing, that you may not haply yet begin in any shape to mistrust my words, because the first-beginnings of things cannot be seen by the eyes, take moreover this list of bodies which you must yourself admit are in the number of things and cannot be seen. First of all the force of the wind when aroused beats on the harbours and whelms huge ships and scatters clouds; sometimes in swift whirling eddy it scours the plains and straws them with large trees and scourges the mountain summits with forest-rending blasts: so fiercely does the wind rave with a shrill howling and rage with threatening roar. Winds therefore sure enough are unseen bodies which sweep the seas, the lands, ay and the clouds of heaven, tormenting them and catching them up in sudden whirls. On they stream and spread destruction abroad in just the same way as the soft liquid nature of water, when all at once it is borne along in an overflowing stream, and a great downfall of water from the high hills augments it with copious rains, flinging together fragments of forests and entire trees; nor can the strong bridges sustain the sudden force of coming water: in such wise turbid with much rain the river dashes upon the piers with mighty force: makes havoc with loud noise and rolls

under its eddies huge stones: wherever aught opposes its waves, down it dashes it. In this way then must the blasts of wind as well move on, and when they like a mighty stream have borne down in any direction, they push things before them and throw them down with repeated assaults, sometimes catch them up in curling eddy and carry them away in swift-circling whirl. Wherefore once and again I say winds are unseen bodies, since in their works and ways they are found to rival great rivers which are of a visible body. Then again we perceive the different smell of things, yet never see them coming to our nostrils; nor do we behold heats nor can we observe cold with the eyes nor are we used to see voices. Yet all these things must consist of a bodily nature, since they are able to move the senses; for nothing but body can touch and be touched. Again clothes hung up on a shore which waves break upon become moist, and then get dry if spread out in the sun. Yet it has not been seen in what way the moisture of water has sunk into them nor again in what way this has been dispelled by heat. The moisture therefore is dispersed into small particles which the eyes are quite unable to see. Again after the revolution of many of the sun's years a ring on the finger is thinned on the under side by wearing, the dripping from the eaves hollows a stone, the bent ploughshare of iron imperceptibly decreases in the fields, and we behold the stone-paved streets worn down by the feet of the multitude; the brass statues too at the gates show their right hands to be wasted by the touch of the numerous passers by who greet them. These things then we see are lessened, since they have been thus worn down; but what bodies depart at any given time the nature of vision has jealously shut out our seeing. Lastly the bodies which time and nature add to things by little and little, constraining them to grow in due measure, no exertion of the eyesight can behold;

and so too wherever things grow old by age and decay, and when rocks hanging over the sea are eaten away by the gnawing salt spray, you cannot see what they lose at any given moment. Nature therefore works by unseen bodies.

And yet all things are not on all sides jammed together and kept in by body: there is also void in things. To have learned this will be good for you on many accounts; it will not suffer you to wander in doubt and be to seek in the sum of things and distrustful of our words. If there were not void, things could not move at all; for that which is the property of body, to let and hinder, would be present to all things at all times; nothing therefore could go on, since no other thing would be the first to give way. But in fact throughout seas and lands and the heights of heaven we see before our eyes many things move in many ways for various reasons, which things, if there were no void, I need not say would lack and want restless motion: they never would have been begotten at all since matter jammed on all sides would have been at rest. Again however solid things are thought to be, you may yet learn from this that they are of rare body: in rocks and caverns the moisture of water oozes through and all things weep with abundant drops; food distributes itself through the whole body of living things; trees grow and yield fruit in season, because food is diffused through the whole from the very roots over the stem and all the boughs. Voices pass through the walls and fly through houses shut, stiffening frost pierces to the bones. Now if there are no void parts, by what way can the bodies severally pass? You would see it to be quite impossible. Once more, why do we see one thing surpass another in weight though not larger in size? For if there is just as much body in a ball of wool as there is in a lump of lead, it is natural it should weigh the same, since the property

of body is to weigh all things downwards, while on the contrary the nature of void is ever without weight. Therefore when a thing is just as large, yet is found to be lighter, it proves sure enough that it has more of void in it; while on the other hand that which is heavier shows that there is in it more of body and that it contains within it much less of void. Therefore that which we are seeking with keen reason exists sure enough, mixed up in things; and we call it void.

And herein I am obliged to forestall this point which some raise, lest it draw you away from the truth. The waters they say make way for the scaly creatures as they press on, and open liquid paths, because the fish leave room behind them, into which the yielding waters may stream; thus other things too may move and change place among themselves, although the whole sum be full. This you are to know has been taken up on grounds wholly false. For on what side I ask can the scaly creatures move forwards, unless the waters have first made room? again on what side can the waters give place, so long as the fish are unable to go on? Therefore you must either strip all bodies of motion or admit that in things void is mixed up from which every thing gets its first start in moving. Lastly if two broad bodies after contact quickly spring asunder, the air must surely fill all the void which is formed between the bodies. Well, however rapidly it stream together with swift-circling currents, yet the whole space will not be able to be filled up in one moment; for it must occupy first one spot and then another, until the whole is taken up. But if haply any one supposes that, when the bodies have started asunder, that result follows because the air condenses, he is mistaken; for a void is then formed which was not before, and a void also is filled which existed before; nor can the air condense in such a way, nor supposing it could, could it methinks without void draw into itself and bring its parts together.

Wherefore, however long you hold out by urging many objections, you must needs in the end admit that there is a void in things. And many more arguments I may state to you in order to accumulate proof on my words; but these slight footprints are enough for a keen-searching mind to enable you by yourself to find out all the rest. For as dogs often discover by smell the lair of a mountain-ranging wild beast though covered over with leaves, when once they have got on the sure tracks, thus you in cases like this will be able by yourself alone to see one thing after another and find your way into all dark corners and draw forth the truth. But if you lag or swerve a jot from the reality, this I can promise you, Memmius, without more ado: such plenteous draughts from abundant wellsprings my sweet tongue shall pour from my richly furnished breast, that I fear slow age will steal over our limbs and break open in us the fastnesses of life, ere the whole store of reasons on any one question has by my verses been dropped into your ears.

But now to resume the thread of the design which I am weaving in verse: all nature then, as it exists by itself, is founded on two things: there are bodies and there is void in which these bodies are placed and through which they move about. For that body exists by itself the general feeling of mankind declares; and unless at the very first belief in this be firmly grounded, there will be nothing to which we can appeal on hidden things in order to prove anything by reasoning of mind. Then again, if room and space which we call void did not exist, bodies could not be placed anywhere nor move about at all to any side; as we have demonstrated to you a little before. Moreover there is nothing which you can affirm to be at once separate from all body and quite distinct from void, which would so

to say count as the discovery of a third nature. For whatever shall exist, this of itself must be something or other. Now if it shall admit of touch in however slight and small a measure, it will, be it with a large or be it with a little addition, provided it do exist, increase the amount of body and join the sum. But if it shall be intangible and unable to hinder any thing from passing through it on any side, this you are to know will be that which we call empty void. Again whatever shall exist by itself, will either do something or will itself suffer by the action of other things, or will be of such a nature as things are able to exist and go on in. But no thing can do and suffer without body, nor aught furnish room except void and vacancy. Therefore beside void and bodies no third nature taken by itself can be left in the number of things, either such as to fall at any time under the ken of our senses or such as any one can grasp by the reason of his mind.

For whatever things are named, you will either find to be properties linked to these two things or you will see to be accidents of these things. That is a property which can in no case be disjoined and separated without utter destruction accompanying the severance, such as the weight of a stone, the heat of fire, the fluidity of water. Slavery on the other hand, poverty and riches, liberty, war, concord, and all other things which may come and go while the nature of the thing remains unharmed, these we are wont, as it is right we should, to call accidents. Time also exists not by itself, but simply from the things which happen the sense apprehends what has been done in time past, as well as what is present and what is to follow after. And we must admit that no one feels time by itself abstracted from the motion and calm rest of things. So when they say that the daughter of Tyndarus was ravished and the Trojan nations were subdued in war, we must mind that they do not force us to admit that these things are by themselves, since those generations of men, of whom these things were accidents, time now gone by has irrevocably swept away. For whatever shall have been done may be termed an accident in one case of the Teucran people, in another of the countries simply. Yes for if there had been no matter of things and no room and space in which things severally go on, never had the fire, kindled by love of the beauty of Tyndarus' daughter, blazed beneath the Phrygian breast of Alexander and lighted up the famous struggles of cruel war, nor had the timber horse unknown to the Trojans wrapt Pergama in flames by its night-issuing brood of sons of the Greeks; so that you may clearly perceive that all actions from first to last exist not by themselves and are not by themselves in the way that body is, nor are terms of the same kind as void is, but are rather of such a kind that you may fairly call them accidents of body and of the room in which they severally go on.

Bodies again are partly first-beginnings of things, partly those which are formed of a union of first-beginnings. But those which are first-beginnings of things no force can quench: they are sure to have the better by their solid body. Although it seems difficult to believe that aught can be found among things with a solid body. For the lightning of heaven passes through the walls of houses, as well as noise and voices; iron grows red-hot in the fire and stones burn with fierce heat and burst asunder; the hardness of gold is broken up and dissolved by heat; the ice of brass melts vanquished by the flame; warmth and piercing cold ooze through silver, since we have felt both, as we held cups with the hand in due fashion and the water was poured down into them. So universally there is found to be nothing solid in things. But yet because true reason and the nature of things constrains,

attend until we make clear in a few verses that there are such things as consist of solid and everlasting body, which we teach are seeds of things and first-beginnings, out of which the whole sum of things which now exists has been produced.

First of all then since there has been found to exist a two-fold and widely dissimilar nature of two things, that is to say of body and of place in which things severally go on, each of the two must exist for and by itself and quite unmixed. For wherever there is empty space which we call void, there body is not; wherever again body maintains itself, there empty void no wise exists. First bodies therefore are solid and without void. Again since there is void in things begotten, solid matter must exist about this void, and no thing can be proved by true reason to conceal in its body and have within it void, unless you choose to allow that that which holds it in is solid. Again that can be nothing but a union of matter which can keep in the void of things. Matter therefore, which consists of a solid body, may be everlasting, though all things else are dissolved. Moreover if there were no empty void, the universe would be solid; unless on the other hand there were certain bodies to fill up whatever places they occupied, the existing universe would be empty and void space. Therefore sure enough body and void are marked off in alternate layers, since the universe is neither of a perfect fullness nor a perfect void. There are therefore certain bodies which can vary void space with full. These can neither be broken in pieces by the stroke of blows from without nor have their texture undone by aught piercing to their core nor give way before any other kind of assault; as we have proved to you a little before. For without void nothing seems to admit of being crushed in or broken up or split in two by cutting, or of taking in wet or permeating cold or penetrating fire, by which all things are destroyed. And the more anything contains within it of void, the more thoroughly it gives way to the assault of these things. Therefore if first bodies are as I have shown solid and without void, they must be everlasting. Again unless matter had been eternal, all things before this would have utterly returned to nothing and whatever things we see would have been born anew from nothing. But since I have proved above that nothing can be produced from nothing, and that what is begotten cannot be recalled to nothing, first-beginnings must be of an imperishable body into which all things can be dissolved at their last hour, that there may be a supply of matter for the reproduction of things. Therefore first-beginnings are of solid singleness, and in no other way can they have been preserved through ages during infinite time past in order to reproduce things.

Again if nature had set no limit to the breaking of things, by this time the bodies of matter would have been so far reduced by the breaking of past ages that nothing could within a fixed time be conceived out of them and reach its utmost growth of being. For we see that anything is more quickly destroyed than again renewed; and therefore that which the long, the infinite duration of all bygone time had broken up demolished and destroyed, could never be reproduced in all remaining time. But now sure enough a fixed limit to their breaking has been set, since we see each thing renewed, and at the same time definite periods fixed for things each after its kind to reach the flower of their age. Moreover while the bodies of matter are most solid, it may yet be explained in what way all things which are formed soft, as air, water, earth, fires, are so formed and by what force they severally go on, since once for all there is void mixed up in things. But on the other hand if the first-beginnings of things be soft, it cannot be explained out of what enduring

basalt and iron can be produced; for their whole nature will utterly lack a first foundation to begin with. First-beginnings therefore are strong in solid singleness, and by a denser combination of these all things can be closely packed and exhibit enduring strength.

Again if no limit has been set to the breaking of bodies, nevertheless the several bodies which go to things must survive from eternity up to the present time, not yet assailed by any danger. But since they are possessed of a frail nature, it is not consistent with this that they could have continued through eternity harassed through ages by countless blows. Again too since a limit of growing and sustaining life has been assigned to things each after its kind, and since by the laws of nature it stands decreed what they can each do and what they cannot do, and since nothing is changed, but all things are so constant that the different birds all in succession exhibit in their body the distinctive marks of their kind, they must sure enough have a body of unchangeable matter also. For if the first-beginnings of things could in any way be vanquished and changed, it would then be uncertain too what could and what could not rise into being, in short on what principle each thing has its power defined, its deepest boundary mark; nor could the generations reproduce so often each after its kind the nature habits, way of life and motions of the parents.

Then again since there is ever a bounding point to bodies, which appears to us to be a least, there ought in the same way to be a bounding point the least conceivable to that first body which already is beyond what our senses can perceive: that point sure enough is without parts and consists of a least nature and never has existed apart by itself and will not be able in future so to exist, since it is in itself a part of that other; and so a first and single part and then other and other similar parts in succession fill up in close serried mass the nature of the first body; and since these cannot exist by themselves, they must cleave to that from which they cannot in any way be torn. First-beginnings therefore are of solid singleness, massed together and cohering closely by means of least parts, not compounded out of a union of those parts, but, rather, strong in everlasting singleness. From them nature allows nothing to be torn, nothing further to be worn away, reserving them as seeds for things. Again unless there shall be a least, the very smallest bodies will consist of infinite parts, inasmuch as the half of the half will always have a half and nothing will set bounds to the division. Therefore between the sum of things and the least of things what difference will there be? There will be no distinction at all; for how absolutely infinite soever the whole sum is, yet the things which are smallest will equally consist of infinite parts. Now since on this head true reason protests and denies that the mind can believe it, you must yield and admit that there exist such things as are possessed of no parts and are of a least nature. And since these exist, those first bodies also you must admit to be solid and everlasting. Once more, if nature creatress of things had been wont to compel all things to be broken up into least parts, then too she would be unable to reproduce anything out of those parts, because those things which are enriched with no parts cannot have the properties which begetting matter ought to have, I mean the various entanglements, weights, blows, clashings, motions, by means of which things severally go on.

[Lines 921–1117]

Now mark and learn what remains to be known and hear it more distinctly. Nor does my mind fail to perceive how dark the things are; but the great hope of praise has smitten my heart with sharp thyrsus, and at the same time has struck into my breast sweet love of the Muses, with which now inspired I traverse in blooming thought the pathless haunts of the Pierides never yet trodden by sole of man. I love to approach the untasted springs and to quaff, I love to cull fresh flowers and gather for my head a distinguished crown from spots whence the Muses have yet veiled the brows of none; first because I teach of great things and essay to release the mind from the fast bonds of religious scruples, and next because on a dark subject I pen such lucid verses o'erlaying all with the Muses' charm. For that too would seem to be not without good grounds: just as physicians when they purpose to give nauseous wormwood to children, first smear the rim round the bowl with the sweet yellow juice of honey, that the unthinking age of children may be fooled as far as the lips, and meanwhile drink up the bitter draught of wormwood and though beguiled yet not be betrayed, but rather by such means recover health and strength; so I now, since this doctrine seems generally somewhat bitter to those by whom it has not been handled, and the multitude shrinks back from it in dismay, have resolved to set forth to you our doctrine in sweet-toned Pierian verse and o'erlay it as it were with the pleasant honey of the Muses, if haply by such means I might engage your mind on my verses, till you clearly perceive the whole nature of things, its shape and frame.

But since I have taught that most solid bodies of matter fly about forever unvanquished through all time, mark now, let us unfold whether there is or is not any limit to their sum; likewise let us clearly see whether that which has been found to be void, or room and space, in which things severally go on, is all of it altogether finite or stretches without limits and to an unfathomable depth.

Well then the existing universe is

bounded in none of its dimensions; for then it must have had an outside. Again it is seen that there can be an outside of nothing, unless there be something beyond to bound it, so that that is seen, farther than which the nature of this our sense does not follow the thing. Now since we must admit that there is nothing outside the sum, it has no outside, and therefore is without end and limit. And it matters not in which of its regions you take your stand; so invariably, whatever position any one has taken up, he leaves the universe just as infinite as before in all directions. Again if for the moment all existing space be held to be bounded, supposing a man runs forward to its outside borders, and stands on the utmost verge and then throws a winged javelin, do you choose that when hurled with vigorous force it shall advance to the point to which it has been sent and fly to a distance, or do you decide that something can get in its way and stop it? for you must admit and adopt one of the two suppositions; either of which shuts you out from all escape and compels you to grant that the universe stretches without end. For whether there is something to get in its way and prevent its coming whither it was sent and placing itself in the point intended, or whether it is carried forward, in either case it has not started from the end. In this way I will go on and, wherever you have placed the outside borders, I will ask what then becomes of the javelin. The result will be that an end can nowhere be fixed, and that the room given for flight will still prolong the power of flight. Lastly one thing is seen by the eyes to end another thing; air bounds off hills, and mountains air, earth limits sea and sea again all lands; the universe however there is nothing outside to end.

Again if all the space of the whole sum were enclosed within fixed borders and were bounded, in that case the store of matter by its solid weights would have streamed together from all sides to the lowest point nor could anything have gone on under the canopy of heaven, no nor would there have been a heaven nor sunlight at all, inasmuch as all matter, settling down through infinite time past, would lie together in a heap. But as it is, sure enough no rest is given to the bodies of the first-beginnings, because there is no lowest point at all, to which they might stream together as it were, and where they might take up their positions. All things are ever going on in ceaseless motion on all sides and bodies of matter stirred to action are supplied from beneath out of infinite space. Therefore the nature of room and the space of the unfathomable void are such as bright thunderbolts cannot race through in their course though gliding on through endless tract of time, no nor lessen one jot the journey that remains to go by all their travel: so huge a room is spread out on all sides for things without any bounds in all directions round.

Again nature keeps the sum of things from setting any limit to itself, since she compels body to be ended by void and void in turn by body, so that either she thus renders the universe infinite by this alternation of the two, or else the one of the two, in case the other does not bound it, with its single nature stretches nevertheless immeasurably. But void I have already proved to be infinite; therefore matter must be infinite; for if void were infinite, and matter finite neither sea nor earth nor the glittering quarters of heaven nor mortal kind nor the holy bodies of the gods could hold their ground one brief passing hour; since forced asunder from its union the store of matter would be dissolved and borne along the mighty void, or rather I should say would never have combined to produce any thing, since scattered abroad it could never have been brought together. For verily not by design did the first-beginnings of things station themselves each in its right place guided by keen intelligence, nor did they bargain sooth to say what motions each should assume, but because many in number and shifting about in many ways throughout the universe they are driven and tormented by blows during infinite time past, after trying motions and unions of every kind at length they fall into arrangements such as those out of which this our sum of things has been formed, and by which too it is preserved through many great years when once it has been thrown into the appropriate motions, and causes the streams to replenish the greedy sea with copious river waters and the earth, fostered by the heat of the sun, to renew its produce, and the race of living things to come up and flourish, and the gliding fires of ether to live: all which these several things could in no wise bring to pass, unless a store of matter could rise up from infinite space, out of which store they are wont to make up in due season whatever has been lost. For as the nature of living things when robbed of food loses its substance and wastes away, thus all things must be broken up, as soon as matter has ceased to be supplied, diverted in any way from its proper course. Nor can blows from without hold together all the sum which has been brought into union. They can, it is true, frequently strike upon and stay a part, until others come and the sum can be completed. At times however they are compelled to rebound and in so doing grant to the first-beginnings of things room and time for flight, to enable them to get clear away from the mass in union. Wherefore again and again I repeat many bodies must rise up; nay for the blows themselves not to fail, there is need of an infinite supply of matter on all sides.

And herein, Memmius, be far from believing this, that all things as they say press to the centre of the sum, and that for this reason the nature of the world

stands fast without any strokes from the outside and the uppermost and lowest parts cannot part asunder in any direction, because all things have been always pressing towards the centre (if you can believe that anything can rest upon itself); or that the heavy bodies which are beneath the earth all press upwards and are at rest on the earth, turned topsy-turvy, just like the images of things we see before us in the waters. In the same way they maintain that living things walk head downwards and cannot tumble out of earth into the parts of heaven lying below them any more than our bodies can spontaneously fly into the quarters of heaven; that when those see the sun, we behold the stars of night; and that they share with us time about the seasons of heaven and pass nights equal in length to our days. But groundless error has devised such dreams for fools, because they have embraced false principles of reason. For there can be no centre where the universe is infinite; no nor, even if there were a centre, could anything take up a position there any more on that account than for some quite different reason be driven away. For all room and space, which we term void, must through centre, through no-centre alike give place to heavy bodies, in whatever directions their motions tend. Nor is there any spot of such a sort that when bodies have reached it, they can lose their force of gravity and stand upon void; and that again which is void must not serve to support anything, but must, as its nature craves, continually give place. Things cannot therefore in such a way be held in union, o'ermastered by love of a centre.

Again since they do not suppose that all bodies press to the centre, but only those of earth, and those of water, both such as descend to the earth in rain and those which are held in by the earth's body, so to say, the fluid of the sea and great waters from the mountains; while on the other hand they teach that the subtle element of air and hot fires at the same time are carried away from the centre and that for this reason the whole ether round bickers with signs and the sun's flame is fed throughout the blue of heaven, because heat flying from the centre all gathers together there, and that the topmost boughs of trees could not put forth leaves at all, unless from time to time nature supplied food from the earth to each throughout both stem and boughs, their reasons are not only false, but they contradict each other. Space I have already proved to be infinite; and space being infinite matter as I have said must also be infinite lest after the winged fashion of flames the walls of the world should suddenly break up and fly abroad along the mighty void, and all other things follow for like reasons and the innermost quarters of heaven tumble in from above and the earth in an instant withdraw from beneath our feet and amid the commingled ruins of things in it and of heaven, ruins unloosing the first bodies, should wholly pass away along the unfathomable void, so that in a moment of time not a wrack should be left behind, nothing save untenanted space and viewless first-beginnings. For on whatever side you shall first determine first bodies to be wanting, this side will be the gate of death for things, through this the whole crowd of matter will fling itself abroad.

If you will thoroughly con these things, then carried to the end with slight trouble you will be able by yourself to understand all the rest. For one thing after another will grow clear and dark night will not rob you of the road and keep you from surveying the utmost ends of nature: in such wise things will light the torch for other things.

Sarvadarśanasaṁgraha

MĀDHAVA

Mādhava, the author of the Sarvadarśanasaṁgraha *(1380 A.D.), provides the reader of this fascinating text with a sketch of some sixteen philosophic systems of ancient and medieval India. The book is, consequently, a history of classical Indian Philosophy, but it is a history with a bias, culminating and climaxing, as it does, in the sixteenth of the systems,* advaita *Vedānta, which has captured the author's attention and allegiance. As a result, the description which he offers of Cārvāka (pronounced "charvaka"), the school of metaphysical materialism here under discussion, is a description written by a man hostile to the school he is depicting. The fragments which he quotes directly from the Cārvāka, however, are invaluable to us, for they undoubtedly are taken verbatim from extant tests, written by these Indian materialists, texts which are now, unfortunately, lost to us. Hence the summaries and the quotations he offers give a fairly adequate picture of this ancient school (which probably dates from the seventh century B.C.), which still has its modern Indian adherents. The Cārvāka bears a close resemblance to the Epicurean philosophy of ancient Rome in that both identify the "soul" with bodily matter and both stress the importance of worldly pleasures as the aim of life.*

The efforts of Cārvāka are indeed hard to be eradicated, for the majority of living beings hold by the current refrain—

While life is yours, live joyously;
None can escape Death's searching eye:
When once this frame of ours they burn,
How shall it e'er again return?

The mass of men, in accordance with the Śāstras of policy and enjoyment, considering wealth and desire the only ends of man and denying the existence of any object belonging to a future world, are found to follow only the doctrine of Cārvāka. Hence another name for that school is Lokāyata, a name well accordant with the thing signified.

In this school the four elements, earth, etc., are the original principles; from these alone, when transformed into the body, intelligence is produced, just as the inebriating power is developed from the

The Sarvadarśanasaṁgraha, by Mādhava Āchārya, transl. E. F. Cowell and E. E. Gough; London, Kegan Paul, Trench, Trübner & Co., Ltd., 1904.

mixing of certain ingredients; and when these are destroyed, intelligence at once perishes also. They quote the *śruti* [Vedic text] for this [*Brhadāraṇyaka Upaniṣad* II.IV.12]: "Springing forth from these elements, itself solid knowledge, it is destroyed when they are destroyed—after death no intelligence remains." Therefore the soul is only the body distinguished by the attribute of intelligence, since there is no evidence for any self distinct from the body, as such cannot be proved, since this school holds that perception is the only source of knowledge and does not allow inference, etc.

The only end of man is enjoyment produced by sensual pleasures. Nor may you say that such cannot be called the end of man as they are always mixed with some kind of pain, because it is our wisdom to enjoy the pure pleasure as far as we can, and to avoid the pain which inevitably accompanies it; just as the man who desires fish takes the fish with their scales and bones, and having taken as many as he wants, desists; or just as the man who desires rice, takes the rice, straw and all, and having taken as much as he wants, desists. It is not therefore for us, through a fear of pain, to reject the pleasure which our nature instinctively recognizes as congenial. Men do not refrain from sowing rice, because forsooth there are wild animals to devour it; nor do they refuse to set the cooking-pots on the fire, because forsooth there are beggars to pester us for a share of the contents. If any one were so timid as to forsake a visible pleasure, he would indeed be foolish like a beast, as has been said by the poet—

The pleasure which arises to men from
    contact with sensible objects,
Is to be relinquished as accompanied by
    pain—such is the reasoning of fools;
The berries of paddy, rich with the
    finest white grains,
What man, seeking his true interest,

would fling away because covered with husk and dust?

If you object that, if there be no such thing as happiness in a future world, then how should men of experienced wisdom engage in the *Agnihotra*[1] and other sacrifices, which can only be performed with great expenditure of money and bodily fatigue, your objection cannot be accepted as any proof to the contrary, since the *Agnihotra*, etc., are only useful as means of livelihood, for the Veda is tainted by the three faults of untruth, self-contradiction, and tautology; then again the impostors who call themselves Vaidic [or Vedic] pandits are mutually destructive, as the authority of the *jñāna-kāṇḍa* (section on knowledge) is overthrown by those who maintain that of the *karma-kāṇḍa* (section on action), while those who maintain the authority of the *jñāna-kāṇḍa* reject that of the *karma-kāṇḍa;* and lastly, the three Vedas themselves are only the incoherent rhapsodies of knaves, and to this effect runs the popular saying—

The *Agnihotra*, the three Vedas, the
    ascetic's three staves, and smearing
    oneself with ashes—
Brhaspati says these are but means of
    livelihood for those who have no
    manliness nor sense.

Hence it follows that there is no other hell than mundane pain produced by purely mundane causes, as thorns, etc.; the only Supreme is the earthly monarch whose existence is proved by all the world's eyesight; and the only liberation is the dissolution of the body. By holding the doctrine that the soul is identical with the body, such phrases as "I am thin," "I am black," etc., are at once intelligible, as the attributes of thinness, etc., and self-consciousness will reside in the same subject (the body); and the use of the phrase "my

[1] Sacrificial offering to fire.

body" is metaphorical like "the head of Rāhu" [Rāhu being really *all head.*]

All this has been thus summed up—
In this school there are four elements, earth, water, fire, and air;
And from these four elements alone is intelligence produced,
Just like the intoxicating power from *kiṇva*,[2] etc., mixed together;
Since in "I am fat," "I am lean," these attributes abide in the same subject,
And since fatness, etc., reside only in the body, it alone is the soul and no other,
And such phrases as "my body" are only significant metaphorically.

* * *

. . . But an opponent will say, if you thus do not allow *adṛṣṭa*,[3] the various phenomena of the world become destitute of any cause. But we cannot accept this objection as valid, since these phenomena can all be produced spontaneously from the inherent nature of things. Thus it has been said—

The fire is hot, the water cold, refreshing cool the breeze of morn;
By whom came this variety? from their own nature was it born.
And all this has been also said by Bṛhaspati—
There is no heaven, no final liberation, nor any soul in another world,
Nor do the actions of the four castes, orders, etc., produce any real effect.
The *Agnihotra,* the three Vedas, the ascetic's three staves, and smearing oneself with ashes,
Were made by Nature as the livelihood of those destitute of knowledge and manliness.

If a beast slain in the *Jyotiṣṭoma rite*[4] will itself go to heaven,
Why then does not the sacrificer forthwith offer his own father?
If the *Śrāddha*[5] produces gratification to beings who are dead,
Then here, too, in the case of travellers when they start, it is needless to give provisions for the journey.
If beings in heaven are gratified by our offering the *Śrāddha* here,
Then why not give the food down below to those who are standing on the housetop?
While life remains let a man live happily, let him feed on ghee[6] even though he runs in debt;
When once the body becomes ashes, how can it ever return again?
If he who departs from the body goes to another world,
How is it that he comes not back again, restless for love of his kindred?
Hence it is only as a means of livelihood that *brāhmins* have established here
All these ceremonies for the dead—there is no other fruit anywhere.
The three authors of the Vedas were buffoons, knaves, and demons.
All the well-known formulas of the pandits, *jarpharī, turpharī,* etc.
And all the obscene rites for the queen commanded in the *Aśvamedha,*[7]
These were invented by buffoons, and so all the various kinds of the presents to the priests,
While the eating of flesh was similarly commanded by night-prowling demons.

Hence in kindness to the mass of living beings must we fly for refuge to the doctrine of Cārvāka. Such is the pleaant consummation.

---

[2] An intoxicating herb.
[3] The unseen force.
[4] A Vedic sacrifice.

[5] Oblations to the dead.
[6] Clarified butter.
[7] A sacrificial ritual.

Idealism

Of the Principles of Human Knowledge

GEORGE BERKELEY

George Berkeley (pronounced Bárklee) (1685–1753) was born in Ireland and educated at Trinity College in Dublin. The book from which the following selection is taken was published in 1710 and is by far his most popular work. The idealist philosophy championed by Berkeley is most carefully developed throughout the entire work.

It is evident to anyone who takes a survey of the objects of human knowledge, that they are either ideas (1) actually imprinted on the senses, or else such as are (2) perceived by attending to the passions and operations of the mind, or lastly (3) ideas formed by help of memory and imagination, either compounding, dividing, or barely representing those originally perceived in the aforesaid ways. By sight I have the ideas of lights and colors, with their several degrees and variations. By touch I perceive hard and soft, heat and cold, motion and resistance, and of all these more and less either as to quantity or degree. Smelling furnishes me with odors, the palate with tastes, and hearing conveys sounds to the mind in all their variety of tone and composition. And as several of these are observed to accompany each other, they come to be marked by one name, and so to be reputed as one thing. Thus, for example, a certain color, taste, smell, figure, and consistence, having been observed to go together, are accounted one distinct thing, signified by the name "apple." Other collections of ideas constitute a stone, a tree, a book, and the like sensible things; which, as they are pleasing or disagreeable, excite the passions of love, hatred, joy, grief, and so forth.

2. But besides all that endless variety of ideas or objects of knowledge, there is likewise something which knows or perceives them, and exercises divers operations, as willing, imagining, remembering, about them. This perceiving, active being is what I call *mind, spirit, soul,* or *myself.* By which words I do not denote any one of my ideas, but a thing entirely distinct from them wherein they exist, or, which is the same thing, whereby they are perceived; for the existence of an idea consists in being perceived.

3. That neither our thoughts, nor passions, nor ideas formed by the imagination,

From *Of the Principles of Human Knowledge*, Sections 1–10.

exist without the mind, is what everybody will allow. And it seems no less evident that the various sensations or ideas imprinted on the sense, however blended or combined together (that is, whatever objects they compose), cannot exist otherwise than in a mind perceiving them. I think an intuitive knowledge may be obtained of this by anyone that shall attend to what is meant by the term "exist" when applied to sensible things. The table I write on I say exists—that is, I see and feel it; and if I were out of my study I should say it existed—meaning thereby that if I was in my study I might perceive it, or that some other spirit actually does perceive it. There was an odor, that is, it was smelt; there was a sound, that is, it was heard; a color or figure, and it was perceived by sight or touch. This is all that I can understand by these and the like expressions. For as to what is said of the absolute existence of unthinking things without any relation to their being perceived, that seems perfectly unintelligible. Their *esse* is *percipi,* nor is it possible they should have any existence out of the minds or thinking things which perceive them.

4. It is indeed an opinion strangely prevailing amongst men, that houses, mountains, rivers, and in a word all sensible objects, have an existence, natural or real, distinct from their being perceived by the understanding. But with how great an assurance and acquiescence soever this principle may be entertained in the world, yet whoever shall find in his heart to call it in question may, if I mistake not, perceive it to involve a manifest contradiction. For what are the forementioned objects but the things we perceive by sense? and what do we perceive *besides our own ideas or sensations?* and is it not plainly repugnant that any one of these, or any combination of them, should exist unperceived?

5. If we thoroughly examine this tenet it will perhaps be found at bottom to depend on the doctrine of *abstract ideas.* For can there be a nicer strain of abstraction than to distinguish the existence of sensible objects from their being perceived, so as to conceive them existing unperceived? Light and colors, heat and cold, extension and figures—in a word the things we see and feel—what are they but so many sensations, notions, ideas, or impressions on the sense? And is it possible to separate, even in thought, any of these from perception? For my part, I might as easily divide a thing from itself. I may, indeed, divide in my thoughts, or conceive apart from each other, those things which perhaps I never perceived by sense so divided. Thus I imagine the trunk of a human body without the limbs, or conceive the smell of a rose without thinking on the rose itself. So far, I will not deny, I can abstract, if that may properly be called abstraction which extends only to the conceiving separately such objects as it is possible may really exist or be actually perceived asunder. But my conceiving or imagining power does not extend beyond the possibility of real existence or perception. Hence, as it is impossible for me to see or feel anything without an actual sensation of that thing, so it is impossible for me to conceive in my thoughts any sensible thing or object distinct from the sensation or perception of it.

6. Some truths there are so near and obvious to the mind that a man need only open his eyes to see them. Such I take this important one to be, to wit, that all the choir in heaven and furniture of the earth, in a word all those bodies which compose the mighty frame of the world, have not any subsistence without a mind, that their *being* is to be perceived or known; that consequently so long as they are not actually perceived by me, or do not exist in my mind or that of any other created spirit, they must either have no existence at all, or else subsist in the mind of some Eternal Spirit; it being perfectly unintelli-

gible, and involving all the absurdity of abstraction, to attribute to any single part of them an existence independent of a spirit. To be convinced of which, the reader need only reflect and try to separate in his own thoughts the *being* of a sensible thing from its *being perceived.*

7. From what has been said it follows there is not any other substance than *spirit,* or that which perceives. But for the fuller proof of this point, let it be considered the sensible qualities are color, figure, motion, smell, taste, etc.—that is, the ideas perceived by sense. Now, for an idea to exist in an unperceiving thing is a manifest contradiction, for to have an idea is all one as to perceive; that therefore wherein color, figure, and the like qualities exist must perceive them; hence it is clear there can be no unthinking substance or *substratum* of those ideas.

8. But, say you, though the ideas themselves do not exist without the mind, yet there may be things *like* them, whereof they are copies or resemblances, which things exist without the mind in an unthinking substance. I answer, an idea can be like nothing but an idea; a color or figure can be like nothing but another color or figure. If we look but never so little into our thoughts, we shall find it impossible for us to conceive a likeness except only between our ideas. Again, I ask whether those supposed originals or external things, of which our ideas are the pictures or representations, be themselves perceivable or no? If they are, then they are ideas and we have gained our point; but if you say they are not, I appeal to anyone whether it be sense to assert a color is like something which is invisible; hard or soft, like something which is intangible; and so of the rest.

9. Some there are who make a distinction betwixt *primary* and *secondary* qualities. By the former they mean extension, figure, motion, rest, solidity or impenetrability, and number; by the latter they denote all other sensible qualities, as colors, sounds, tastes, and so forth. The ideas we have of these they acknowledge not to be the resemblances of anything existing without the mind, or unperceived, but they will have our ideas of the primary qualities to be patterns or images of things which exist without the mind, in an unthinking substance which they call *matter.* By *matter,* therefore, we are to understand an inert, senseless substance, in which extension, figure, and motion do actually subsist. But it is evident from what we have already shown, that extension, figure, and motion are only ideas existing in the mind, and that an idea can be like nothing but another idea, and that consequently neither they nor their archetypes can exist in an unperceiving substance. Hence, it is plain that the very notion of what is called *matter,* or *corporeal substance,* involves a contradiction in it.

10. They who assert that figure, motion, and the rest of the primary or original qualities do exist without the mind in unthinking substances, do at the same time acknowledge that color, sounds, heat, cold, and suchlike secondary qualities, do not; which they tell us are sensations existing in the mind alone, that depend on and are occasioned by the different size, texture, and motion of the minute particles of matter. This they take for an undoubted truth, which they can demonstrate beyond all exception. Now, if it be certain that those original qualities are inseparably united with the other sensible qualities, and not, even in thought, capable of being abstracted from them, it plainly follows that they exist only in the mind. But I desire anyone to reflect and try whether he can, by any abstraction of thought, conceive the extension and motion of a body without all other sensible qualities. For my own part, I see evidently that it is not in my power to frame an idea of a body extended and moving, but I must withal give it some color or other

sensible quality which is acknowledged to exist only in the mind. In short, extension, figure, and motion, abstracted from all other qualities, are inconceivable. Where therefore the other sensible qualities are, there must these be also, to wit, in the mind and nowhere else.

Viṁśatikā

VASUBANDHU

Vasubandhu (4th century A.D.*) is the leading representative of the Yogācāra or Vijñānavāda school of Buddhist thought. The Vijñānavādins argue that the objects in the external world depend for their existence on consciousness (independency being a mark of the real).*

In the *Mahāyāna* it is established that the three worlds are representation-only. According to the scriptures it is said that the three worlds are only mind. Mind, thought, consciousness, discernment are different names. What is here spoken of as mind includes mental activities also in its meaning. "Only" excludes external objects; it does not do away with mental associates. When inner representations arise, seemingly external objects appear, as persons having bad eyes see hairs and flies. . . .

To this doctrine there are supposed objections. . . .

I. If representations are without real objects,
   Then their spatial and temporal determination,

The indetermination of the perceiving stream of consciousness
And their action must be unfounded.

II. Place and time are determined as in a dream;
   The selves are not determined, just as the ghosts [in their abode]
   Together behold the same river of pus etc., [and]
   As in dreams there is function in the loss of [semen].

That is, as in a dream although there are no real objects, yet it is in a certain place that such things as a village, a garden, a man, or a woman are seen, not in all places, and in this place it is at a certain time that this village, garden, etc., are seen, not at all times. . . .

From *Viṁśatikā, Wei Shih Er Shih Lun* [The treatise in twenty stanzas on representation-only], transl. Clarence H. Hamilton; New Haven, American Oriental Series, XIII, American Oriental Society, 1938. Reprinted by permission of the American Oriental Society.

That is, just as the hungry ghosts through ripening the same kind of deeds assemble together as many selves and all see the pus river, in this it is not determined that only one sees. . . . From this [we see that] though there are no real objects apart from consciousness, yet the principle of the indetermination of the stream which perceives is explained.

Again as in dream, although the objects are unreal, they yet have function such as the loss of semen, etc. . . .

III. All [are exemplified] as [those] in hell
Together behold the infernal guards, etc.,
And their ability to inflict torments;
Therefore the four principles are still established.

IV. As the animals in heaven
Those in hell are not, indeed;
For the asserted animals and ghosts
Suffer not that bitterness.

V. If you grant that from the force of deeds
Special elements are born
Which produce such transformations,
Why not admit [the process to be] consciousness?

VI. The impression of the deed is in one place;
You assert its fruit to be in another;
That the consciousness which is impressed has the fruit
You deny. What is the reason?

[Objector] . . . if it is only consciousness which appears as if colored, etc., and there is no separate colored, etc., object, then the Buddha ought not to have said that there are "bases" of cognition, visual, and so on.

[Answer] This teaching is not a reason, for it has a different meaning. . . .

VII. Conforming to the creatures to be converted
The World-honored One with secret intention
Said there are bases of cognition, visual, etc.,
Just as there are beings of apparitional birth.

. . . he did not say that creatures of apparitional birth really exist, because he said, "There is neither creature nor self but only elements and causes." . . . The bases are not really existent apart.

[Question] In accordance with what inner meaning does he speak of ten bases, visual, etc.? . . .

VIII. [Perceptive] consciousness is born from its own seed
And develops into an apparent object aspect.
To establish the distinction of inner and outer bases of cognition,
Buddha says there are ten of these.

[Question] What advantage is there in this teaching of an inner meaning?

IX. By reason of this teaching one enters into
[The doctrine of] the egolessness of the individual:
The asserted non-substantiality of elements
One enters again by reason of the remainder of the teaching,

[Objection] If by knowing that all elements of every kind are non-existent we enter into the insubstantiality of elements, then representation-only is also, in the end, non-existent. How can representation-only be sustained?

[Answer] It is not the man who knows that all elements of every kind are non-existent who obtains the name of having "entered the insubstantiality of elements"; but he who penetrates the insubstantiality of the elements of the "self-natures" and the "special characters" conceived by the imagination of the ignorant, is thus named him who has "entered the insubstantiality of elements." . . .

[Question] Again, how do we know that Buddha intended such an inner meaning when he said there are bases of sense cognition? Are there not separate, really existing outer elements, having color-and-form, etc., which become severally the objects of visual, etc. consciousness?

x. That real is neither one [thing],
  Nor is it many atoms;
  Again, it is not an agglomeration, etc.,
  Because the atom is not proved.

. . . the external object cannot logically be one, because we cannot grasp the substance of the whole apart from the parts. Also it logically is not many, because we cannot apprehend the atoms separately. . . .

xi. One atom joined with six others
  Must consist of six parts.
  If it is in the same place with six
  The aggregate must be as one atom.

If one atom on each of its six sides joins with another atom it must consist of six parts, because the place of one does not permit of being the place of the others. If there are six atoms in one atom's place then all the aggregates must be as one atom in quantity, because though revolving in mutual confrontation they do not exceed that quantity; and so aggregates also must be invisible.

xii. Since [it is stated that] atoms do not join,
  Of what, then, is the joining of the aggregates?
  If joining is not proved [of the latter]
  It is not because they have no spatial divisions.

If you . . . say that aggregates also do not join one another, then you should not say that atoms are without combination because of having no spatial divisions. Aggregates have spatial divisions, and yet you do not grant their combination. Therefore the non-combining of atoms is not due to their lack of spatial division. For this reason the single real atom is not proved. Whether atomic combination is or is not admitted, the mistake is still as we have said. Whether spatial division of atoms is or is not admitted, both views are greatly in error. . . .

xiii. If the atom has spatial divisions,
  It logically should not make a unity.
  If it has none, there should be neither shadow nor occultation;
  Aggregates being no different would likewise be without these two.

. . . The fault of multiplicity is as explained before. Unity also is irrational.

xiv. Assuming unity, there must be no walking progressively,
  At one time, no grasping and not grasping,
  And no plural, disconnected condition;
  Moreover, no scarcely perceptible, tiny things.

. . . if one step is taken it reaches everywhere . . . a unitary thing cannot at one time be both obtained and not obtained. A single place, also, ought not to contain disconnected things such as elephants, horses, etc. If the place contains one, it also contains the rest. How can we say that one is distinguished from another? Granting two [things present], how comes it that in one place there can be both occupancy and non-occupancy, that there can be a seeing of emptiness between? . . .

[Question] The existence or non-existence of anything is determined by means of proof. Among all means of proof immediate perception is the most excellent. If there are no external objects how is there this awareness of objects such as are now immediately evident to me? . . .

xv. Immediate awareness is the same as in dreams, etc.
At the time when immediate awareness has arisen,
Seeing and its object are already non-existent;
How can it be admitted that perception exists?

[According to] those who hold the doctrine of momentariness, at the time when this awareness arises the immediate objects, visible [tangible, audible] etc. are already destroyed. How can you admit that at this time there is immediate perception? . . .

If you wish thus to prove the existence of external objects from "first experiencing, later remembering," this theory also fails. . . .

xvi. [first part] As has been said, the apparent object is a representation.
It is from this that memory arises.

[Question] If, in waking time as well as in a dream, representations may arise although there are no true objects, then, just as the world naturally knows that dream objects are non-existent, why is it not naturally known of the objects in waking time? . . .

xvi. [second part] Before we have awakened we cannot know
That what is seen in the dream does not exist.

After this, the purified knowledge of the world which is obtained takes precedence; according to the truth it is clearly understood that those objects are unreal. The principle is the same.

[Objection] If for all sentient beings representations arise as apparent objects because of transformation and differentiation in their own streams of consciousness, and are not born from external things acting as objects, then how explain the fact that those sentient beings through contact with good or evil friends, or through hearing true or false doctrines, are determined to two kinds of representation since there are neither friends nor teaching? . . .

xvii. [first part] By the power of reciprocal influence
The two representations become determined.

That is to say, because a distinct representation in one stream of consciousness occasions the arising of a distinct representation in another stream of consciousness, each becomes determined, but not by external objects. . . .

xvii. [second part] The mind by sleep is weakened:
Dream and waking retributions are not the same.

[Question] If only representations exist . . . how are sheep, etc., killed by anybody?

xviii. Because of transformation in another's representation
The act of killing and injuring occurs;
Just as the mental power of a demon, etc.,
Causes another to lose his memory.

xix. The emptiness of Daṇḍaka forest, etc.,
How [came it] from a ṛṣi's anger?
"Mental punishment is a great crime."
How again can this be proved?

[Question] If only representations exist, does knowledge of another's mind know another's mind or not? . . .

If it cannot know, why speak of knowledge of another's mind? If it can know,
representation-only is of necessity not
proved.

[Answer] Although it knows the mind
of another it does not know it exactly. . . .

> xx. How does knowledge of another's
>   mind
>   Know its object inexactly?
>   Just as the knowledge in knowing
>   one's own mind
>   Does not know [it] as the Buddha's
>   object.

[Question] Why is this knowledge of
one's own mind not an exact knowing of
its object?

[Answer] Because of ignorance. Both
knowledges of the object, because each is
covered over and darkened by ignorance,
do not know it as the ineffable object
reached by the pure knowledge of a Buddha. These two, in their objects, do not
know exactly because of the false appearing of seemingly external objects; and because the distinction between what is apprehended and the apprehender is not
yet discontinued.

[Conclusion]

The doctrines and implications of
representation-only are of kinds infinitely
diverse for decision and selection; difficult
is it to fathom their profundities. Without
being a Buddha, who is able to comprehend their total extent?

> xxi. I, according to my ability,
>   Have briefly demonstrated the
>   principles of representation-only;
>   Among these all [other] kinds,
>   Difficult to think, are reached by
>   Buddhas [alone].

Transcendentalism

Phaedo and *The Republic*

PLATO

Plato (428-7 B.C.–348-7 B.C.) has been called the founder of Western philosophic thought. His numerous dialogues and letters provide us not only with a picture of classical Greek life, but they contain the germ of almost every major philosophical school represented since his time. The main speaker in the selections presented below is Socrates, Plato's famous teacher and the spokesman for Plato's own views in many of the dialogues. In the Phaedo *selection Socrates is awaiting death in an Athenian jail and presents his views on the nature of the real. In the* Republic *selection Socrates presents by analogy and myth further reflections on the nature of reality.*

FROM PHAEDO

And now, O my judges, I desire to prove to you that the real philosopher has reason to be of good cheer when he is about to die, and that after death he may hope to obtain the greatest good in the other world. And how this may be, Simmias and Cebes, I will endeavour to explain. For I deem that the true votary of philosophy is likely to be misunderstood by other men; they do not perceive that he is always pursuing death and dying; and if this be so, and he has had the desire of death all his life long, why when his time comes should he repine at that which he has been always pursuing and desiring?

Simmias said laughingly: Though not in a laughing humour, you have made me laugh, Socrates; for I cannot help thinking that the many when they hear your words will say how truly you have described philosophers, and our people at home will likewise say that the life which philosophers desire is in reality death, and that they have found them out to be deserving of the death which they desire.

And they are right, Simmias, in thinking so, with the exception of the words "they have found them out"; for they have not found out either what is the nature of that death which the true philosopher deserves, or how he deserves or desires death. But enough of them—let us discuss the matter among ourselves. Do we believe that there is such a thing as death?

To be sure, replied Simmias.

From the Jowett translation of *Phaedo* and *The Republic*.

45

Is it not the separation of soul and body? And to be dead is the completion of this; when the soul exists in herself, and is released from the body and the body is released from the soul, what is this but death?

Just so, he replied.

There is another question, which will probably throw light on our present enquiry if you and I can agree about it— Ought the philosopher to care about the pleasures—if they are to be called pleasures —of eating and drinking?

Certainly not, answered Simmias.

And what about the pleasures of love— should he care for them?

By no means.

And will he think much of the other ways of indulging the body for example, the acquisition of costly raiment, or sandals, or other adornments of the body? Instead of caring about them, does he not rather despise anything more than nature needs? What do you say?

I should say that the true philosopher would despise them.

Would you not say that he is entirely concerned with the soul and not with the body? He would like, as far as he can, to get away from the body and to turn to the soul.

Quite true.

In matters of this sort philosophers, above all other men, may be observed in every sort of way to dissever the soul from the communion of the body.

Very true.

Whereas, Simmias, the rest of the world are of opinion that to him who has no sense of pleasure and no part in bodily pleasure life is not worth having; and that he who is indifferent about them is as good as dead.

That is also true.

What again shall we say of the actual acquirement of knowledge?—is the body, if invited to share in the enquiry, a hinderer or a helper? I mean to say, have sight and hearing any truth in them? Are they not, as the poets are always telling us, inaccurate witnesses? and yet, if even they are inaccurate and indistinct, what is to be said of the other senses?—for you will allow that they are the best of them?

Certainly, he replied.

Then when does the soul attain truth? —for in attempting to consider anything in company with the body she is obviously deceived.

True.

Then must not true existence be revealed to her in thought, if at all?

Yes.

And thought is best when the mind is gathered into herself and none of these things trouble her—neither sounds nor sights nor pain nor any pleasure—when she takes leave of the body, and has as little as possible to do with it, when she has no bodily sense or desire, but is aspiring after true being?

Certainly.

And in this the philosopher dishonours the body; his soul runs away from his body and desires to be alone and by herself?

That is true.

Well, but there is another thing, Simmias: Is there or is there not an absolute justice?

Assuredly there is.

And an absolute beauty and absolute good?

Of course.

But did you ever behold any of them with your eyes?

Certainly not.

Or did you ever reach them with any other bodily sense?—and I speak not of these alone, but of absolute greatness, and health, and strength, and of the essence or true nature of everything. Has the reality of them ever been perceived by you through the bodily organs? or rather, is not the nearest approach to the knowledge of their several natures made by him who so orders his intellectual vision as to have the most exact conception of the essence of each thing which he considers?

Certainly.

And he attains to the purest knowledge of them who goes to each with the mind alone, not introducing or intruding in the act of thought sight or any other sense together with reason, but with the very light of the mind in her own clearness searches into the very truth of each; he who has got rid, as far as he can, of eyes and ears and, so to speak, of the whole body, these being in his opinion distracting elements which when they infect the soul hinder her from acquiring truth and knowledge—who, if not he, is likely to attain to the knowledge of true being?

What you say has a wonderful truth in it, Socrates, replied Simmias.

And when real philosophers consider all these things, will they not be led to make a reflection which they will express in words something like the following? "Have we not found," they will say, "a path of thought which seems to bring us and our argument to the conclusion, that while we are in the body, and while the soul is infected with the evils of the body, our desire will not be satisfied? and our desire is of the truth. For the body is a source of endless trouble to us by reason of the mere requirement of food; and is liable also to diseases which overtake and impede us in the search after true being: it fills us full of loves, and lusts, and fears, and fancies of all kinds, and endless foolery, and in fact, as men say, takes away from us the power of thinking at all. Whence come wars, and fightings, and factions? whence but from the body and the lusts of the body? Wars are occasioned by the love of money, and money has to be acquired for the sake and in the service of the body; and by reason of all these impediments we have no time to give to philosophy; and, last and worst of all, even if we are at leisure and betake ourselves

to some speculation, the body is always breaking in upon us, causing turmoil and confusion in our enquiries, and so amazing us that we are prevented from seeing the truth. It has been proved to us by experience that if we would have pure knowledge of anything we must be quit of the body—the soul in herself must behold things in themselves: and then we shall attain the wisdom which we desire, and of which we say that we are lovers; not while we live, but after death; for if while in company with the body, the soul cannot have pure knowledge, one of two things follows—either knowledge is not to be attained at all, or, if at all, after death. For then, and not till then, the soul will be parted from the body and exist in herself alone. In this present life, I reckon that we make the nearest approach to knowledge when we have the least possible intercourse or communion with the body, and are not surfeited with the bodily nature, but keep ourselves pure until the hour when God himself is pleased to release us. And thus having got rid of the foolishness of the body we shall be pure and hold converse with the pure, and know of ourselves the clear light everywhere, which is no other than the light of truth." For the impure are not permitted to approach the pure. These are the sort of words, Simmias, which the true lovers of knowledge cannot help saying to one another, and thinking. You would agree; would you not?

Undoubtedly, Socrates.

But, O my friend, if this be true, there is great reason to hope that, going whither I go, when I have come to the end of my journey, I shall attain that which has been the pursuit of my life. And therefore I go on my way rejoicing, and not I only, but every other man who believes that his mind has been made ready and that he is in a manner purified.

Certainly, replied Simmias.

And what is purification but the separation of the soul from the body, as I was saying before; the habit of the soul gathering and collecting herself into herself from all sides out of the body; the dwelling in her own place alone, as in another life, so also in this, as far as she can—the release of the soul from the chains of the body?

Very true, he said.

And this separation and release of the soul from the body is termed death?

To be sure, he said.

And the true philosophers, and they only, are ever seeking to release the soul. Is not the separation and release of the soul from the body their especial study?

That is true.

And, as I was saying at first, there would be a ridiculous contradiction in men studying to live as nearly as they can in a state of death, and yet repining when it comes upon them.

Clearly.

And the true philosophers, Simmias, are always occupied in the practice of dying, wherefore also to them least of all men is death terrible. Look at the matter thus: if they have been in every way the enemies of the body, and are wanting to be alone with the soul, when this desire of theirs is granted, how inconsistent would they be if they trembled and repined, instead of rejoicing at their departure to that place where, when they arrive, they hope to gain that which in life they desired—and this was wisdom—and at the same time to be rid of the company of their enemy. Many a man has been willing to go to the world below animated by the hope of seeing there an earthly love, or wife, or son, and conversing with them. And will he who is a true lover of wisdom, and is strongly persuaded in like manner that only in the world below he can worthily enjoy her, still repine at death? Will he not depart with joy? Surely he will, O my friend, if he be a true philosopher. For he will have a firm conviction that there, and there only, he can find wisdom in her purity. And if this be true, he would be very absurd, as I was saying, if he were afraid of death.

He would indeed, replied Simmias.

And when you see a man who is repining at the approach of death, is not his reluctance a sufficient proof that he is not a lover of wisdom, but a lover of the body, and probably at the same time a lover of either money or power, or both?

Quite so, he replied.

FROM THE REPUBLIC

Book VI

. . . If you will only give such an explanation of the good as you have already given of justice and temperance and the other virtues, we shall be satisfied.

Yes, my friend, and I shall be at least equally satisfied, but I cannot help fearing that I shall fail, and that my indiscreet zeal will bring ridicule upon me. No, sweet sirs, let us not at present ask what is the actual nature of the good, for to reach what is now in my thoughts would be an effort too great for me. But of the child of the good who is likest him, I would fain speak, if I could be sure that you wished to hear—otherwise, not.

By all means, he said, tell us about the child, and you shall remain in our debt for the account of the parent.

I do indeed wish, I replied, that I could pay, and you receive, the account of the parent, and not, as now, of the offspring only; take, however, this latter by way of interest, and at the same time have a care that I do not render a false account, although I have no intention of deceiving you.

Yes, we will take all the care that we can: proceed.

Yes, I said, but I must first come to an understanding with you, and remind you of what I have mentioned in the course of this discussion, and at many other times.

What?

The old story, that there is a many beautiful and a many good, and so of other things which we describe and define; to all of them "many" is applied.

True, he said.

And there is an absolute beauty and an absolute good, and of other things to which the term "many" is applied there is an absolute; for they may be brought under a single idea, which is called the essence of each.

Very true.

The many, as we say, are seen but not known, and the ideas are known but not seen.

Exactly.

And what is the organ with which we see the visible things?

The sight, he said.

And with the hearing, I said, we hear, and with the other senses perceive the other objects of sense?

True.

But have you remarked that sight is by far the most costly and complex piece of workmanship which the artificer of the senses ever contrived?

No, I never have, he said.

Then reflect: has the ear or voice need of any third or additional nature in order that the one may be able to hear and the other to be heard?

Nothing of the sort.

No, indeed, I replied; and the same is true of most, if not all, the other senses—you would not say that any of them requires such an addition?

Certainly not.

But you see that without the addition of some other nature there is no seeing or being seen?

How do you mean?

Sight being, as I conceive, in the eyes, and he who has eyes wanting to see; colour being also present in them, still unless

there be a third nature specially adapted to the purpose, the owner of the eyes will see nothing and the colours will be invisible.

Of what nature are you speaking?

Of that which you term light, I replied.

True, he said.

Noble, then, is the bond which links together sight and visibility, and great beyond other bonds by no small difference of nature; for light is their bond, and light is no ignoble thing?

Nay, he said, the reverse of ignoble.

And which, I said, of the gods in heaven would you say was the lord of this element? Whose is that light which makes the eye to see perfectly and the visible to appear?

You mean the sun, as you and all mankind say.

May not the relation of sight to this deity be described as follows?

How?

Neither sight nor the eye in which sight resides is the sun?

No.

Yet of all the organs of sense the eye is the most like the sun?

By far the most like.

And the power which the eye possesses is a sort of effluence which is dispensed from the sun?

Exactly.

Then the sun is not sight, but the author of sight who is recognized by sight.

True, he said.

And this is he whom I call the child of the good, whom the good begat in his own likeness, to be in the visible world, in relation to sight and the things of sight, what the good is in the intellectual world in relation to mind and the things of mind.

Will you be a little more explicit? he said.

Why, you know, I said, that the eyes, when a person directs them towards objects on which the light of day is no longer shining, but the moon and stars only, see dimly, and are nearly blind; they seem to have no clearness of vision in them?

Very true.

But when they are directed towards objects on which the sun shines, they see clearly and there is sight in them?

Certainly.

And the soul is like the eye: when resting upon that on which truth and being shine, the soul perceives and understands and is radiant with intelligence; but when turned towards the twilight of becoming and perishing, then she has opinion only, and goes blinking about, and is first of one opinion and then of another, and seems to have no intelligence?

Just so.

Now, that which imparts truth to the known and the power of knowing to the knower is what I would have you term the idea of good, and this you will deem to be the cause of science, and of truth in so far as the latter becomes the subject of knowledge; beautiful too, as are both truth and knowledge, you will be right in esteeming this other nature as more beautiful than either; and, as in the previous instance, light and sight may be truly said to be like the sun, and yet not to be the sun, so in this other sphere, science and truth may be deemed to be like the good, but not the good; the good has a place of honour yet higher.

What a wonder of beauty that must be, he said, which is the author of science and truth, and yet surpasses them in beauty; for you surely cannot mean to say that pleasure is the good?

God forbid, I replied; but may I ask you to consider the image in another point of view?

In what point of view?

You would say, would you not, that the sun is not only the author of visibility in all visible things, but of generation and nourishment and growth, though he himself is not generation?

Certainly.

In like manner the good may be said to be not only the author of knowledge to all things known, but of their being and essence, and yet the good is not essence, but far exceeds essence in dignity and power.

Glaucon said, with a ludicrous earnestness: By the light of heaven, how amazing!

Yes, I said, and the exaggeration may be set down to you; for you made me utter my fancies.

And pray continue to utter them; at any rate let us hear if there is anything more to be said about the similitude of the sun.

Yes, I said, there is a great deal more.

Then omit nothing, however slight.

I will do my best, I said; but I should think that a great deal will have to be omitted.

You have to imagine, then, that there are two ruling powers, and that one of them is set over the intellectual world, the other over the visible. I do not say heaven, lest you should fancy that I am playing upon the name (οὐρανός, ὁρατός). May I suppose that you have this distinction of the visible and intelligible fixed in your mind?

I have.

Now take a line which has been cut into two unequal parts, and divide each of them again in the same proportion, and suppose the two main divisions to answer, one to the visible and the other to the intelligible, and then compare the subdivisions in respect of their clearness and want of clearness, and you will find that the first section in the sphere of the visible consists of images. And by images I mean, in the first place, shadows, and in the second place, reflections in water and in solid, smooth and polished bodies and the like: Do you understand?

Yes, I understand.

Imagine, now, the other section, of

which this is only the resemblance, to include the animals which we see, and everything that grows or is made.

Very good.

Would you not admit that both the sections of this division have different degrees of truth, and that the copy is to the original as the sphere of opinion is to the sphere of knowledge?

Most undoubtedly.

Next proceed to consider the manner in which the sphere of the intellectual is to be divided.

In what manner?

Thus: There are two subdivisions, in the lower of which the soul uses the figures given by the former division as images; the enquiry can only be hypothetical, and instead of going upwards to a principle descends to the other end; in the higher of the two, the soul passes out of hypotheses, and goes up to a principle which is above hypotheses, making no use of images as in the former case, but proceeding only in and through the ideas themselves.

I do not quite understand your meaning, he said.

Then I will try again; you will understand me better when I have made some preliminary remarks. You are aware that students of geometry, arithmetic, and the the kindred sciences assume the odd and the even and the figures and three kinds of angles and the like in their several branches of science; these are their hypotheses, which they and every body are supposed to know, and therefore they do not deign to give any account of them either to themselves or others; but they begin with them, and go on until they arrive at last, and in a constant manner, at their conclusion?

Yes, he said, I know.

And do you not know also that although they make use of the visible forms and reason about them, they are thinking not of these, but of the ideals which they resemble; not of the figures which they draw, but of the absolute square and the absolute diameter, and so on—the forms which they draw or make, and which have shadows and reflections in water of their own, are converted by them into images, but they are really seeking to behold the things themselves, which can only be seen with the eye of the mind?

That is true.

And of this kind I spoke as the intelligible, although in the search after it the soul is compelled to use hypotheses; not ascending to a first principle, because she is unable to rise above the region of hypothesis, but employing the objects of which the shadows below are resemblances in their turn as images, they having in relation to the shadows and reflections of them a greater distinctness, and therefore a higher value.

I understand, he said, that you are speaking of the province of geometry and the sister arts.

And when I speak of the other division of the intelligible, you will understand me to speak of that other sort of knowledge which reason herself attains by the power of dialectic, using the hypotheses not as first principles, but only as hypotheses—that is to say, as steps and points of departure into a world which is above hypotheses, in order that she may soar beyond them to the first principle of the whole; and clinging to this and then to that which depends on this, by successive steps she descends again without the aid of any sensible object, from ideas, through ideas, and in ideas she ends.

I understand you, he replied; not perfectly, for you seem to me to be describing a task which is really tremendous; but, at any rate, I understand you to say that knowledge and being, which the science of dialectic contemplates, are clearer than the notions of the arts, as they are termed, which proceed from hypotheses only: these are also contemplated by the understanding, and not by the senses: yet, because they start from hypotheses and do not ascend to a principle, those who contemplate them appear to you not to exercise the higher reason upon them, although when a first principle is added to them they are cognizable by the higher reason. And the habit which is concerned with geometry and the cognate sciences I suppose that you would term understanding and not reason, as being intermediate between opinion and reason.

You have quite conceived my meaning, I said; and now, corresponding to these four divisions, let there be four faculties in the soul—reason answering to the highest, understanding to the second, faith (or conviction) to the third, and perception of shadows to the last—and let there be a scale of them, and let us suppose that the several faculties have clearness in the same degree that their objects have truth.

I understand, he replied, and give my assent, and accept your arrangement.

Book VII

And now, I said, let me show in a figure how far our nature is enlightened or unenlightened: Behold! human beings living in an underground den, which has a mouth open towards the light and reaching all along the den; here they have been from their childhood, and have their legs and necks chained so that they cannot move, and can only see before them, being prevented by the chains from turning round their heads. Above and behind them a fire is blazing at a distance, and between the fire and the prisoners there is a raised way; and you will see, if you look, a low wall built along the way, like the screen which marionette players have in front of them, over which they show the puppets.

I see.

And do you see, I said, men passing along the wall carrying all sorts of vessels, and statues and figures of animals made of wood and stone and various materials, which appear over the wall? Some of them are talking, others silent.

You have shown me a strange image, and they are strange prisoners.

Like ourselves, I replied; and they see only their own shadows, or the shadows of one another, which the fire throws on the opposite wall of the cave?

True, he said; how could they see anything but the shadows if they were never allowed to move their heads?

And of the objects which are being carried in like manner they would only see the shadows?

Yes, he said.

And if they were able to converse with one another, would they not suppose that they were naming what was actually before them?

Very true.

And suppose further that the prison had an echo which came from the other side, would they not be sure to fancy when one of the passers-by spoke that the voice which they heard came from the passing shadow?

No question, he replied.

To them, I said, the truth would be literally nothing but the shadows of the images.

That is certain.

And now look again, and see what will naturally follow if the prisoners are released and disabused of their error. At first, when any of them is liberated and compelled suddenly to stand up and turn his neck round and walk and look towards the light, he will suffer sharp pains; the glare will distress him, and he will be unable to see the realities of which in his former state he had seen the shadows; and then conceive some one saying to him, that what he saw before was an illusion, but that now, when he is approaching nearer to being and his eye is turned towards more real existence, he has a clearer vision —what will be his reply? And you may further imagine that his instructor is pointing to the objects as they pass and requiring him to name them—will he not be perplexed? Will he not fancy that the shadows which he formerly saw are truer than the objects which are now shown to him?

Far truer.

And if he is compelled to look straight at the light, will he not have a pain in his eyes which will make him turn away to take refuge in the objects of vision which he can see, and which he will conceive to be in reality clearer than the things which are now being shown to him?

True, he said.

And suppose once more, that he is reluctantly dragged up a steep and rugged ascent, and held fast until he is forced into the presence of the sun himself, is he not likely to be pained and irritated? When he approaches the light his eyes will be dazzled, and he will not be able to see anything at all of what are now called realities.

Not all in a moment, he said.

He will require to grow accustomed to the sight of the upper world. And first he will see the shadows best, next the reflections of men and other objects in the water, and then the objects themselves; then he will gaze upon the light of the moon and the stars and the spangled heaven; and he will see the sky and the stars by night better than the sun or the light of the sun by day?

Certainly.

Last of all he will be able to see the sun, and not mere reflections of him in the water, but he will see him in his own proper place, and not in another; and he will contemplate him as he is.

Certainly.

He will then proceed to argue that this is he who gives the season and the years, and is the guardian of all that is in the visible world, and in a certain way the cause of all things which he and his fellows have been accustomed to behold?

Clearly, he said, he would first see the sun and then reason about him.

And when he remembered his old habitation, and the wisdom of the den and his fellow-prisoners, do you not suppose that he would felicitate himself on the change, and pity them?

Certainly, he would.

And if they were in the habit of conferring honour among themselves on those who were quickest to observe the passing shadows and to remark which of them went before, and which followed after, and which were together; and who were therefore best able to draw conclusions as to the future, do you think that he would care for such honours and glories, or envy the possessors of them? Would he not say with Homer,

Better to be the poor servant of a poor master.

and to endure anything, rather than think as they do and live after their manner?

Yes, he said, I think that he would rather suffer anything than entertain these false notions and live in this miserable manner.

Imagine once more, I said, such an one coming suddenly out of the sun to be replaced in his old situation; would he not be certain to have his eyes full of darkness?

To be sure, he said.

And if there were a contest, and he had to compete in measuring the shadows with the prisoners who had never moved out of the den, while his sight was still weak, and before his eyes had become steady (and the time which would be needed to acquire this new habit of sight might be very considerable), would he not be ridiculous? Men would say of him that up he went and down he came without his eyes; and that it was better not even to think of ascending; and if any one tried to loose another and lead him up to the light, let them only catch the offender, and they would put him to death.

No question, he said.

This entire allegory, I said, you may now append, dear Glaucon, to the previous argument; the prison-house is the world of sight, the light of the fire is the sun, and you will not misapprehend me if you interpret the journey upwards to be the ascent of the soul into the intellectual world according to my poor belief, which, at your desire, I have expressed— whether rightly or wrongly God knows. But, whether true or false, my opinion is that in the world of knowledge the idea of good appears last of all, and is seen only with an effort; and, when seen, is also inferred to be the universal author of all things beautiful and right, parent of light and of the lord of light in this visible world, and the immediate source of reason and truth in the intellectual; and that this is the power upon which he who would act rationally either in public or private life must have his eye fixed.

I agree, he said, as far as I am able to understand you.

Moreover, I said, you must not wonder that those who attain to this beatific vision are unwilling to descend to human affairs; for their souls are ever hastening into the upper world where they desire to dwell; which desire of theirs is very natural, if our allegory may be trusted.

Yes, very natural.

And is there anything surprising in one who passes from divine contemplations to the evil state of man, misbehaving himself in a ridiculous manner; if, while his eyes are blinking and before he has become accustomed to the surrounding darkness, he is compelled to fight in courts of law, or in other places, about the images or the shadows of images of justice, and is endeavouring to meet the conceptions of those who have never yet seen absolute justice?

Anything but surprising, he replied.

Any one who has common sense will remember that the bewilderments of the eyes are of two kinds, and arise from two causes, either from coming out of the light or from going into the light, which is true of the mind's eye, quite as much as of the bodily eye; and he who remembers this when he sees any one whose vision is perplexed and weak, will not be too ready to laugh; he will first ask whether that soul of man has come out of the brighter life, and is unable to see because unaccustomed to the dark, or having turned from darkness to the day is dazzled by excess of light. And he will count the one happy in his condition and state of being, and he will pity the other; or, if he have a mind to laugh at the soul which comes from below into the light, there will be more reason in this than in the laugh which greets him who returns from above out of the light into the den.

That, he said, is a very just distinction.

But then, if I am right, certain professors of education must be wrong when they say that they can put a knowledge into the soul which was "not there before," like sight into blind eyes.

They undoubtedly say this, he replied.

Whereas, our argument shows that the "power and capacity" of learning exists in the soul already; and that just as the eye was unable to turn from darkness to light without the whole body, so too the instrument of knowledge can only by the movement of the whole soul be turned from the world of becoming into that of being, and learn by degrees to endure the sight of being, and of the brightest and best of being, or in other words, of the good.

Very true.

And must there not be some art which will effect conversion in the easiest and quickest manner; not implanting the faculty of sight, for that exists already, but has been turned in the wrong direction, and is looking away from the truth?

Yes, he said, such an art may be presumed.

And whereas the other so-called virtues of the soul seem to be akin to bodily qualities, for even when they are not originally innate they can be implanted later by habit and exercise, the virtue of wisdom more than anything else contains a divine element which always remains, and by this conversion is rendered useful and profitable; or, on the other hand, hurtful and useless. . . .

Katha Upanishad

The Katha Upanishad *has been called the most philosophical of the* Upanishads. *The work is pre-Buddhist and belongs to the seventh or sixth century* B.C. *"Upanishad" means literally "to sit down near" and probably refers to the method of sitting and learning at the feet of a teacher. "Katha" is the name of a Vedic school. The* Katha Upanishad *is really a dialogue between a Brahmin boy, Naciketas, and the Lord of the Dead, Yama. Naciketas has been sent to Yama as a consequence of the anger of Naciketas' father, Vājaśravasa. The latter had given away, as religious gifts, all of his worldly possessions when suddenly his son, Naciketas, seeing everything being thus sacrificed, asks his father, "Father, to whom will you give me?" Receiving no reply, he again asks the same question and then, when his father still remains silent, he finally asks him a third time, "Father, to whom will you give me?" The father in anger cries out, "I will give you to Death." Because a Brahmin is obedient as well as truthful, the unfortunate Naciketas must now, in response to his father's directive, journey to the house of Yama, the Lord of the Dead. The translation that follows is cast as a dialogue in which some dramatic license has been taken, putting the* Upanishad *into the form of a short play. The lines spoken by the servant and the response to him are not part of the original text but otherwise the translation is a fair and faithful rendering of this very early and very influential* Upanishad.

SCENE I

The house of Yama, King of the Dead. Naciketas is seated on the floor. The walls are hung in black, a servant enters and bows to Naciketas.

SERVANT: You are brave indeed to journey thus to this house. Yama, the Lord of the Dead, was not expecting you.

NACIKETAS: I have waited. I will wait longer.

SERVANT: Again I ask you, why have you come here? Why have you waited these three days for my master?

The translation is by A. L. Herman.

NACIKETAS: I come to fulfill my father's command.

SERVANT: Three days I have wanted to speak to you. Please tell me why you have come; and come so unexpectedly. My master will be angry that he was not here to receive a Brahmin youth. Expected or not, the laws of hospitality decree that the host should be here. I can do nothing for you until he returns.

NACIKETAS: I am patient. I have nowhere else to go, now that I have done the deed that sent me here.

SERVANT: But why? Tell me why you have come? My master will be so angry that he was not here to receive you that first day.

NACIKETAS: I look back and I see men come hither and I see them no more. I look ahead and I see that all must finally come here. Mortal man withers and dies like the grasses of the field. But like that grass he will be born again. I wait patiently.

SERVANT: But why have you come? All unannounced, all unprepared are we here. Three days you wait. Oh my master will be vexed.

NACIKETAS: (*Rising and moving about rubbing his legs.*) My father has renounced the world. Full of sorrow and fear he has given me to death. Full of anger he sent me forth.

SERVANT: And you came? But how? How could you find this dreaded place, young sir?

NACIKETAS: Among many who will some day die I go as the first. Among many who are dying now I go with them. (*He turns.*) What will Yama do to me who came in this way, dead by his own hand?

SERVANT: But why? A youth to this house, a Brahmin youth, young sprouting seedling, hardly ripe for dooming yet. Why have you come here?

NACIKETAS: My father in haste and anger sent me here. Upon my asking him, as he gave away his goods, he sent me here. Three times I asked to whom he would send me. And then but once he said, "To death." To death have I come, to Yama have I come.

SERVANT: But why, why, young sir?

NACIKETAS: A Brahmin is ever truthful. Holding fast to truth he never swerves from promises made. To keep my father's word, to obey my father's command, to make my father's truth, here I have come. (*Walks about rubbing his hands and arms.*) What will Yama do with me?

SERVANT: He will be angry that he was not here to greet a truth-protecting Brahmin youth. Oh, he will be vexed. (*Exits.*)

NACIKETAS: How cold the earth is here. How warm and sweet the sun that I miss. Death's house is not my home. And though he is not here I fear the moment when he shall return. What is it that Yama will do to me this day?

[*Enter Yama bearing a bowl of water. He is agitated and upset at not having been present when his guest arrived.*

YAMA: Welcome my young Brahmin. (*Offering water to Naciketas.*)

The Brahmin who enters a house as a
    guest
Is like holy fire in the houses of men.
Such a guest should be greeted with
    the gift of water.
Welcome, my young Brahmin.
(*Offers the bowl to Naciketas.*)

NACIKETAS: Sir, I am honored. (*He moistens his lips with the water.*)
YAMA:

It is well said in the holy scriptures,
That should a Brahmin dwell in the house of an inhospitable man who neglects his guest, then that foolish host shall lose his hopes and expectations, his possessions and his heavenly merit, his friendships and his loves. Such a one shall have his sons, his cattle, everything torn pitilessly from him.

Even I, Yama, am subject to this law. Therefore welcome to my house.

NACIKETAS: My lord, it was not intended that . . . I am an unexpected guest, my lord.

YAMA:

Nonetheless I am the absent host.
  Three nights you have spent in this
  my house, without hospitality's food
  or comfort.
You are, Oh Brahmin, a guest most
  worthy of reverence.
Having neglected you thus for three
  days, let me do you honor now.

NACIKETAS: If you so wish, my Lord, let it be thus.

YAMA: And let it be thus as you desire three times. To make amends, to honor you aright I grant you three boons, three wishes as you see fit.

NACIKETAS: My lord Yama, most dreadful of the holy Gods. I know not . . . three boons . . . my Lord . . .
(He is at a loss for words.)

YAMA: Three boons to repair my tardiness, to honor you. Come, choose. Choose rightly three times.

NACIKETAS:

Three days have I been in this your
  house, Oh Yama
Three days in darkness, cold and
  gloom.
I who came here by his own choice, his
  own hand.
I miss the sun my Lord,
  I miss the sweet warm earth, my
  father, and my life.

YAMA: Yes, choose, go on, choose now rightly.

NACIKETAS:

Oh Death, as the first of my wishes, I choose to be returned to my father: let him be free from anger towards me; let his warm face and his gentle smile greet me as the sweet sun shall also greet me.

This I would wish, Oh Death, to be thus returned to earth, to father and to life.

YAMA: You will find your father as before, but cheerful, warm, and loving. His passions departed, his anger flown, he will greet you full well as you return from this cold, lifeless realm, to earth, to father and to life. Granted. Now choose the second. Come, choose wisely.

NACIKETAS: *(Warming to his two remaining wishes as the possibilities unfold.)* My Lord Yama. There is a second wish that I would press.

YAMA: Say it. Say it.

NACIKETAS: It is said, my Lord, that in heaven there is no fear at all, no anxiety, no pain or sorrow. There in that world there is no old age to fear, no hunger, no thirst, no pain and torment of impending death. There in that realm one has gone beyond all these, but especially has one gone beyond old age and death.

YAMA: That is true. You declare the heavenly world well and truly.

NACIKETAS: Oh Yama, the way to that heavenly world, that world beyond sorrow and death, the way to that happiness is by understanding the great fire sacrifice.

YAMA: The fire sacrifice and the understanding of that great rite is truly the way to immortality. You speak the truth once again, my young Brahmin.

NACIKETAS: Then I would have you teach to me the fire sacrifice, the knowing of which brings immortality and freedom. Teach me that fire wisdom, that is my second wish.

YAMA: To you I will declare the fire sacrifice, and you shall learn it and have the understanding of the fire which shall lead to immortality. Granted. Now choose the third. Come, choose wisely once again.

NACIKETAS: Oh Yama, Lord of the Dead, for my third boon I would choose the most difficult knowledge of all.

YAMA: Go on. Choose. I have promised

you three boons. You have chosen well for two, first earth and then heaven. Say on, what is your third wish?

NACIKETAS: Oh Yama, this is my third wish. Among men there is doubt about what happens to a man when he dies.

YAMA: Ah, but careful, now, good Brahmin.

NACIKETAS: Some say a man exists when dead, others that he exists not. This I would know, Oh Death, when a man dies what then? What happens to a man when dead?

YAMA: My good Naciketas. Even the Gods themselves have not understood this matter. It is not easy to comprehend. The truth of it is subtle and difficult. So come choose another boon, choose another.

NACIKETAS: I would know that, my Lord.

YAMA: Oh Naciketas, do not press me here. Let me off that boon. Choose another, any other, please.

NACIKETAS: My Lord, I would know that. What happens to a man when his body dies. Does he yet live?

YAMA: (Agitated, moving about.) Naciketas, choose another, I urge you. Choose sons and grandsons who shall live a hundred years, choose herds of cattle, elephants, gold and horses. Choose any of these, choose all of these.

NACIKETAS: My Lord, I would know about man.

YAMA: Choose all the wide and open earth; choose that and live as long as your mind and heart desire. Choose that!

NACIKETAS: My Lord, I have chosen.

YAMA: Choose any other boon; choose wealth and long life. Be King, if you wish, of the entire earth! I will make you an enjoyer of all desires! Think of that, Oh Naciketas, any desire you wish I will grant. Any desire.

NACIKETAS: My Lord . . .

YAMA: Whatever is hard to get in the mortal world, think on it, Naciketas, that will I get for you. Tell me what you would have. Lovely maidens, together with char-

iots and sweet musical sounds—such lovely ones are never to be obtained by mortals. But you, Naciketas, you can have them all. They will wait on your every desire. Choose them, I beg of you. But do not question me about dying.

NACIKETAS: These things and all that you have mentioned come to an end. Whatever power and vigor and manliness one possesses, all that passes away, all that ends some day. For you, Oh Yama, *you* are these chariots, *you* are these lovely maidens, *you* are their dancing, their music, their singing.

Man is not to be satisfied with wealth and riches and life. Shall we these possess when we meet finally with you? Shall we live and taste pleasure when we meet finally with you. No, Lord Yama. Only that boon, that choice that I have made, only that is what I have chosen, nothing else.

YAMA: You are difficult to be put off. For one so young you are truly difficult.

NACIKETAS: What use, Oh Lord of Death, is this slowly decaying body dwelling on this unhappy earth, when one knows that the ageless Gods are free from death and decay. How then can I take delight in a long life and the pleasures that come from beauty and love and pleasure.

YAMA: Yes, you have understood after all.

NACIKETAS: Then, Lord Yama, tell me what I would know. Tell me what there is in the great Hereafter for man, tell me I pray you the secret that lies even now hidden from me. This boon I would have, my Lord, and nothing else.

YAMA: (Resigned.) Naciketas, it is granted.

SCENE II

We are in the house of Vājaśravasa, Naciketas' father. This is not immediately evident as the scene opens, however, but as the conversation progresses it becomes gradually obvious. Further, Yama, who carries on the dialogue with Naciketas, slowly reveals himself as Vājaśravasa, until by the end of the scene Vājaśravasa and not Yama stands before Naciketas. At the same time the servant changes from Yama's servant to Vājaśravasa's.

YAMA: Naciketas, you have seen already the difference between that which is merely pleasant and that which is truly best.

NACIKETAS: Explain this to me. I know it but I seem not to understand it.

YAMA: Both pleasure and the good bind a man to deeds and to this world. Both call forth rebirth. But of the two, the good is the best. That man fails who simply chooses the pleasanter thing.

NACIKETAS: And I have chosen the best, the good, and the right?

YAMA: By renouncing the things and materials of this world, the cattle, the elephants, the lovely maidens, the chariots, the wealth and the riches, by renouncing all these for the sake of knowledge of man, you have chosen the best, indeed.

NACIKETAS: But is knowledge not also binding? Have you not said that both the pleasant and the good bind the soul and bring one back to this world, one dreary round following one dreary round. Tell me truly now?

YAMA: And tell you I shall. But slowly . . . very slowly. You must see that between knowledge and ignorance, between the good and the pleasant there is a wide chasm indeed. For those who abide in the midst of ignorance, self-wise, puffed up with thinking themselves learned, stumbling about and turning hither and thither are they, going about deluded in company with many others just as deluded, they go like blind men led by the blind.

[*Servant enters, goes up to Yama and bows.*]

YAMA: For those deluded in this way in this world, for those charmed by wealth and ignorance and pleasures, for those thinking that this is the only world, that this life is the only life, that there is no other—again and again that one comes under my control.

SERVANT: My Lord Yama, you are needed elsewhere. Too long have you stayed.

YAMA: (*Waving the servant aside.*) To one thus deluded, with wealth, the world, there is no way out of the cycle of torments and rebirths. And you, beloved Naciketas, you have come to me for instruction in this matter. You have seen through the world's delusions and you have come to me, your teacher, to be taught not only the good and the best, but that which stands even beyond that and before that and is not binding nor enthralling.

NACIKETAS: I know that what is best excels what is pleasant. But now is there another that stands beyond the best?

YAMA: There is indeed. Beyond the right and the good there is another. Beyond the law, beyond religion, beyond God there is another that does not bind. That does not hold one to this world, nor to my world, nor to heaven.

NACIKETAS: But then doing the right, obeying the holy law of dharma is that not enough to set one forever free?

YAMA: It is not. Both good and evil come from desire. Desiring good is forever binding, just as is desiring the evil. Knowledge is just as binding as ignorance. Desiring knowledge is just as binding as desiring to remain ignorant. The best is just as binding as the pleasant. Desiring the best, the right, is just as binding as desiring the pleasant. All bind, all come from desire, all hold one to heaven, to my world, or to earth. But for the truly wise man these are not enough.

NACIKETAS: But what way out is there then? How can I escape rebirth if not by seeking knowledge, if not by obeying the holy commandments, if not by attending to the priestly sacrifices and holy rites? What way out is there then, Oh my teacher.

[*The servant comes forward again and bows.*]

YAMA:

Him who is hard to see,
Him who is hidden, set in the secret
    place of the heart
Him who is dwelling in the depths
    of you
Him who is really God, your true
    teacher
Him who through yoga-study one comes
    to see,
Him one finally comes to by leaving
    both joy and sorrow, good and evil,
    the best and the pleasant, and knowl-
    edge and ignorance behind. By aban-
    doning all these.

NACIKETAS: But what is the way, then, Lord Yama, to this hidden and secret place?

YAMA: *(Seeming not to hear.)* Apart from the right and the unright, apart from what has been done and will be done, apart from what has been and what will be, apart from all these, in your heart, look . . . look now, right now . . . and declare what you see.

NACIKETAS: I am unable to answer, my Lord. I am overwhelmed, and stopped.

YAMA: Listen and I will declare it to you.

SERVANT: My Lord Yama, you are needed at once, my Lord. Too long have you been here now.

YAMA: Yes, yes I know. A bit longer.

SERVANT: My Lord, now. You are needed now.

YAMA: A moment more.

[*He waves the servant aside. Servant retires to the right.*]

The goal as well as the origin that all our sacred scriptures glorify, that our holy men go in search of, and for the hearing of which all men practice the holy life, that goal I will tell you in one word.

NACIKETAS: What word, my Lord?

YAMA: That source, that goal, that sacred sound is OM.

NACIKETAS: I don't understand. What does it mean?

YAMA:

That syllable is Brahman,
the spiritual power, the
holy power of the universe.
Knowing OM whatever one
    desires is his.
OM is the chief and only
    support of the universe
Knowing that support one
    becomes great in the
    world of Brahman.

NACIKETAS: But where is that world, where does it lie?

YAMA:

That OM dwells in you
Naciketas.
It is not born, It does not
    die
It has not come from anywhere,
    It has not become anyone.
Unborn, constant, eternal, the
    first and the last.
It dies not when the body dies.
That is what you searched for.

NACIKETAS: I do not yet see what this is to be. What is this Brahman, this OM? What does It do? What happens to It?

YAMA: My dear Naciketas, listen to me.

YAMA:

If the slayer thinks that he slays
If the slain thinks himself slain
Both of these understand not.
This One neither slays nor
    is It slain.

Smaller than the smallest,
    greater than the greatest
Is this Brahman, this OM,
    this Atman that is set in
    the heart of every creature here.
When once one is freed from
    sorrow and joy, from
    pain and pleasure,
    from all binding desire,

Then and then only can one
perceive this Atman, this
OM, this true Self.

NACIKETAS:

But tell me, what is the
way to this, my true Self.
How may I behold It, loosening
all desire, giving up
all joys and sorrows.

Tell me what I must do?

YAMA: This true Self, this Atman is not to be obtained by instruction, nor by intellect, nor by learning. He is to be obtained only by those whom He chooses. Only to such a person, through His own favor is He to be seen, felt and understood.
[*The servant of Yama is now seen as the servant of Vājaśravasa, and at the same time Yama is seen as Vājaśravasa. The servant approaches.*]
SERVANT: My Lord, there are more things to do. Other guests are coming. There are other tasks to perform. You must be brief, my Lord.
YAMA-VĀJAŚRAVASA: Yes, yes, I am coming. But a moment more, now.

Naciketas, my dearest, this Atman is not known by him who has become attached to bad conduct, nor to good conduct. But he who, through the practice of yoga, has a tranquil mind, who is inwardly peaceful, only that one can behold Him.

Only when you perceive priests and princes as food for Death's eating, as all alike, indifferently, similar to one another at the banquet Yama has set for himself—
Only then will you see the
Truth, the OM, the Brahman.

NACIKETAS: I can only dimly see.
VĀJAŚRAVASA:

Arise, Naciketas!
Awake Naciketas! Seek further the answers to your question! Understand those answers!
This path is like the sharpened edge of a glistening razor.
It is hard to traverse, a path impossible to travel, the poets say.
What is soundless, touchless, formless and imperishable,
What is without taste, without odor, ever constant, ever abiding
What is without beginning, without end, higher than the highest,
By seizing that, you shall be liberated from the mouth of death.

SERVANT: My Lord, Vājaśravasa, you must come. There are things to be distributed to the people. The wooden stool is still on the porch and awaits your choice of a new owner. The crowd of seekers and guests grows. You must come.
VĀJAŚRAVASA: Yes, I have finished here. (Rising). I am coming, too.
                [End]

RATIONAL PSYCHOLOGY

THE PROBLEM OF THE NATURE OF MAN

In the history of philosophy perhaps the most perennial problem for man has been the problem of identity: Who is man? What is it to be a man? Where does man's real nature lie, and what is that nature like? The psalmist declares to his Lord:

> What is man that thou art
>   mindful of him,
> And the son of man that thou
>   dost care for him?

and Sophocles, in the same rhapsodic tones, has the chorus in Antigone speak as if to answer the psalmist:

> Many the things that mighty be,
> And nought is mightier than Man.
> For he can cross the foaming ocean, . . .
> Steering amid the mantling waves that roar around him . . .
> Man, full of ingenuity . . .
> Language and lofty thought . . .
> With plans for all things,
> Planless in nothing, meets he the future!
> Of death alone the avoidance
> No foreign aid will bring.

Wise in his craft of art
Beyond the bounds of expectation
The while to good he goes, the while to evil.

That the interest in the nature of man was of concern to both Hebrew and Greek is significant of the perplexity and universality of the question.

The problem of the nature of man can be treated in two distinct ways. First, we may inquire directly into the qualities of man's nature with respect to his goodness, his corruptness, or his potentiality for either one or the other in terms of a blending or compounding of good with evil. Or, secondly, we could ask what it is in man that possesses or holds this nature together? Of this last question most men have assumed that it is the self, the ego, the person, or something making up or composing the individual as distinct from the species, that makes man what he is, i.e., makes him wholly good, or wholly evil, or a blending of good and evil. We will treat these two topics separately, and very briefly, and then go on to discuss the readings in relation to these topics.

The first metaphysical question regarding man is, What is the essential nature of man? This question begs the further question, Does man have a nature? Both of these questions, however, belong within the discipline of rational psychology. The metaphysician who answers "no" to the second question is bound to engage in an explanation as to why or on what grounds man, *qua* man, is without a nature. In recent years it has fallen to the existentialists to make this argument clear, while in ancient times the sophist and the skeptic had been prone to defend the view that men—but not man—have a nature. The existentialist in his nihilistic denial of all essences has necessarily overthrown natures as well. Each man, he argues, creates himself and consequently a man becomes individually and distinctly what he creates.

The Greeks, as we have seen from the quotation from *Antigone,* were necessarily optimistic about man's powers and capabilities: "The while to good he goes, the while to evil." Man's nature is not burdened by any kind of basic good nor basic evil; nonetheless, "nought is mightier than man." Furthermore, the gloomy oracular forebodings in Greek tragedy in general can always be interpreted and summed up as "For evil done, expect evil in return." [1]

To the psalmist's question, What is man? the existentialist argues that man possesses no essential and innate nature, but creates himself; the Greek may be interpreted as holding a similar view: Man is mighty because there is no nature to hold him back. But the Greek's view is stronger yet, it can be argued. Of the undertakings man is best known for—philosophy, languages, exploration, art—all are expressions of some seeming inherent goodness in man. That is to say, the Greek is optimistic (despite parts of *Antigone* and *Oedipus Rex*), while the existentialist is known, widely, for his pessimism.

[1] The classic case is Sophocles' *Oedipus Rex*. In seeking to avoid the oracle's prophecy (and such avoidance was considered an evil act), the penalty was evil returned; in this case by fate and in a most horrible manner.

The Hebrew psalmist who first asked the question continues on to give an answer:

> Yet thou hast made him little less than God,
> And dost crown him with glory and honor.
> Thou hast given him dominion over the works of thy hands;
> Thou hast put all things under his feet,
> All sheep and oxen and also the beasts of the field,
> The birds of the air, and the fish of the sea,
> Whatever passes along the paths of the sea.

The response is not unlike that of Sophocles. To generalize on the basis of one or two passages and speak for an entire religion is dangerous. All we can do is to note that these are answers to the question, What is man? and pass on to others. The characteristic optimism that flows through both the psalm and the *Antigone* passages can give us a reason for arguing that, at the very least, the assertions do not hold that man is inherently evil; and, in comparison with the existentialist view, perhaps it can even be argued that man to the Jew and the Greek was basically capable of more good than the existentialist would be willing to admit.

In juxtaposition to these views there is the opinion that man is base and corrupt by nature. The argument usually begins by an appeal to experience: Look around you at the wars, the filth of our cities and the destruction of human decency and dignity, the traffic in degradation exemplified in the unnatural use of narcotics, the slavery in human prostitution and the horrors of man's inhuman relations to himself and the world around him. Thomas Hobbes, looking upon the evils of English political life in the seventeenth century, proclaimed the life of man as "nasty, mean, brutish and short." The argument may lead then to a statement about the nature of man's soul, an argument supported, it is said, by the appeal to experience. The statement about man's soul, its corrupt and sinful nature, usually ends the matter.

But the interpretation of man's nature is not exhausted by these three basic positions. There may be many combinations of the positions. For example, although man may be initially corrupt—e.g., "All have sinned and fall short of the glory of God," as St. Paul has said—there may be a way in which we can be saved from the consequences of our corrupt selves. In St. Paul's case, the way is that of religious discipline. Thus, combined with the initial pessimism of the sinfulness of man, there may be a final and ultimate reason for optimism. Most religions hold out such a final promise to man.

In the selections that follow various kinds of answers are given to the first of our questions, What is the nature of man?

The Chinese philosopher Hsüntze argues that man's fundamental nature is evil and that whatever good his behavior demonstrates is the result of training and discipline. He argues, rather effectively, against a compatriot, Mencius (Mengtze), who maintained that man's basic nature was good and that vicious behavior represented a sliding away from the natural. Both Hsüntze and Mencius base their arguments on observations of man in the world. St. Augustine, on the other hand, bases his arguments primarily on divine revelation regarding the sinful nature of man (such as that quoted above from St. Paul) and then turns to his own childhood and adulthood in order to find evidence for his beliefs. The anguish of the sick-souled saint who begins with revelation and documents that revelation with personal experience makes an interesting contrast to the rather healthy-minded pessimism of the empirically oriented Chinese sage.

The view that the basic strategy of Hsüntze and St. Augustine, and Mencius for that matter, is fundamentally wrong-headed is advanced by Jean-Paul Sartre. Sartre is bitterly opposed to those philosophies and theologies which would lay out, as if by fiat, man's nature, thereby placing arbitrary limitations on man's potentialities. Such limitation is slavery and the search for such a nature evidence of bad faith.

THE PROBLEM OF PERSONAL IDENTITY

The argument over the nature of human nature might well be aided by consideration of the other central question in rational psychology: Does man have a nature? Or more particularly, Does he have a soul or a self? And, Is that which makes up the self locatable or identifiable? And, If so in what way? The questions can all be distilled into one major problem mentioned previously in the introduction to this section, the problem of personal identity. Briefly, we can recapitulate the issues involved. The question to be answered is simply: Who am I? The answer involves a plethora of subsidiary questions that make this particular question clearer: How do I know I am me? Is there really a self which endures through time? What is that self? How do I know it? One can see that bound up with these questions is the question dealt with in the previous section, What is the nature of man?

In the selections that follow, the clearest outline of the problem is presented by John Locke, a late seventeenth-century English philosopher. Locke is concerned with the question, Who am I? And in order to answer it he asks, How do I know I am the same person today that I was yesterday? And, What is the seat of this self that is the same and endures through time? Locke's answer is that my memory or consciousness guarantees that I am the same person today that I was yesterday; the self, therefore, is a compound of all those memories that one has had. Although this answer is not very satisfactory for reasons already mentioned in our introduction, it is still the best common-sense answer that we have to the question, and it is philosophically the best introduction to the problem in the literature.

A second "answer" to the question is the assertion that there is really no question at all because there is no self. The Buddhist philosopher Vasubandhu states in his fourth-century A.D. work, the *Abhidharmakosha,* that the self is illusory. This doctrine, the doctrine of *anatta* (*an*—no; *atta*—self), is the cornerstone of Buddhist philosophy, and it is in direct contrast to the Personalist thesis, which dates back to about 300 B.C. in India, that there is in addition to mental events or consciousness, something or someone who has these experiences. The selection provided is a lively argument: it is a discussion between Vasubandhu and one of these Personalists.

The Nature of Man

The Nature of Man Is Evil

HSÜNTZE

Hsüntze (fl. 298–238 B.C.) argues that man's nature is basically evil, and that only through law and social pressure can that nature be controlled. His works on law have been used extensively to justify authoritarian control in political matters, and his "tough-minded" attitude toward man and society can be directly traced to his philosophy of the nature of man.

The nature of man is evil; his goodness is only acquired training. The original nature of man to-day is to seek for gain. If this desire is followed, strife and rapacity results, and courtesy dies. Man originally is envious and naturally hates others. If these tendencies are followed, injury and destruction follows; loyalty and faithfulness are destroyed. Man originally possesses the desires of the ear and eye; he likes praise and is lustful. If these are followed, impurity and disorder results, and the rules of proper conduct (Li) and justice (Yi) and etiquette are destroyed. Therefore to give rein to man's original nature, to follow man's feelings, inevitably results in strife and rapacity, together with violations of etiquette and confusion in the proper way of doing things, and reverts to a state of violence. Therefore the civilizing influence of teachers and laws, the guidance of the rules of proper conduct (Li) and justice (Yi) is absolutely necessary. Thereupon courtesy results; public and private etiquette is observed; and good government is the consequence. By this line of reasoning it is evident that the nature of man is evil and his goodness is acquired.

Crooked wood needs to undergo steaming and bending to conform to the carpenter's rule; then only is it straight. Blunt metal needs to undergo grinding and whetting; then only is it sharp. The original nature of man to-day is evil, so he needs to undergo the instruction of teachers and laws, then only will he be upright. He needs the rules of proper conduct (Li) and justice (Yi), then only will there be good government. But man to-day is without good teachers and laws; so he is selfish, vicious, and unrighteous. He is without the rules of proper conduct (Li) and justice (Yi), so there is rebellion, dis-

From *The Works of Hsüntze*, transl. Homer H. Dubs; London, Arthur Probsthain, 1928. Reprinted by permission of Arthur Probsthain, London.

order, and no good government. In ancient times the Sage-Kings knew that man's nature was evil, selfish, vicious, unrighteous, rebellious, and of itself did not bring about good government. For this reason they created the rules of proper conduct (*Li*) and justice (*Yi*); they established laws and ordinances to force and beautify the natural feelings of man, thus rectifying them. They trained to obedience and civilized men's natural feelings, thus guiding them. Then good government arose and men followed the right Way (*Tao*). Now the people who are influenced by good teachers and laws, who accumulate literature and knowledge, who are led by the rules of proper conduct (*Li*) and justice (*Yi*) become superior men. Those who give rein to their natural feelings, who take joy in haughtiness, and break the rules of proper conduct (*Li*) and justice (*Yi*), become small-minded men. By this line of reasoning it is evident that the original nature of man is evil, and his goodness is acquired.

Mencius says, "The fact that men are teachable shows that their original nature is good." I reply: This is not so. This is not understanding the nature of man, nor examining the original nature of man, nor the part played by acquired elements. Whatever belongs to original nature is the gift of Nature. It cannot be learned. It cannot be worked for. The Sage-Kings brought forth the rules of proper conduct (*Li*) and justice (*Yi*). Men learn them and gain ability; they work for them and obtain results in the development of character. What cannot be learned and cannot be worked for, what is in the power of Nature only is what is meant by original nature. That which can be learned and which gives men ability, which can be worked for and which brings results in the development of character, whatever is in the power of man is what is meant by acquired character. This is the distinction between original nature and acquired

character. Now according to the nature of man, the eye has the power of seeing and the ear has the power of hearing. However, when a person sees a thing, his quickness of sight is not outside of his eye; when he hears, his quickness of hearing is not outside of his ear. It is evident that quickness of sight and quickness of hearing cannot be learned. Mencius says: Now the original nature of man is good; all have lost and destroyed their original nature, hence it is evil. I reply: When he says this, he is greatly mistaken. Now considering the nature of man, as soon as he is born, he would already have grown away from his first estate, he would already have grown from his natural disposition. He would already have lost and destroyed it. By this line of reasoning it is evident that the original nature of man is evil and his goodness is acquired.

The doctrine that man's original nature is good implies that without growing away from his first estate, he becomes admirable; without growing away from his natural disposition, he becomes beneficial. To say that man's original nature is admirable, his heart and thoughts are good, is the same as to say that the power of seeing is not apart from the eye and the power of hearing is not apart from the ear. So we say, if there is an eye, there is the power of seeing; if there is an ear, there is the power of hearing. Now the nature of man is that when he is hungry, he desires repletion; when he is cold, he desires warmth; when he labours, he seeks rest. This is man's natural feeling. But now when a man is hungry and sees food, he dares not rush in ahead of others, instead the eater yields to others. When working, he dares not seek rest, instead he works for others. The son yielding precedence to his father, the younger brother yielding to his older brother; the son working for his father, the younger brother working for his older brother—these two kinds of actions are contrary to original nature and antagonistic to natural feeling. Nevertheless there is the doctrine (*Tao*) of filial piety, the etiquette of the rules of proper conduct (*Li*) and justice (*Yi*). If a person follows his natural feelings, he has no courtesy; if he has courtesy, then it is antagonistic to his natural feelings. By this line of reasoning it is evident that man's original nature is evil and his goodness is acquired.

A questioner may say: If man's original nature is evil, then whence come the rules of proper conduct (*Li*) and justice (*Yi*)? In answer I say: All rules of proper conduct (*Li*) and justice (*Yi*) come from the acquired training of the Sage, not from man's original nature. The potter pounds and moulds the clay and makes the vessel—but the vessel comes from the potter's acquired skill, not from the potter's innate character. The workman hews a piece of wood and makes a vessel; but the vessel comes from the workman's acquired training, not from his innate character. The Sage gathers together ideas and thoughts, and becomes skilled by his acquired training, so as to bring forth the rules of proper conduct (*Li*) and justice (*Yi*), and originate laws and regulations. So the rules of proper conduct (*Li*), justice (*Yi*), laws and regulations come from the acquired knowledge of the Sage, not from man's original nature.

The eye desires colour, the ear desires sound, the mouth desires flavours, the heart desires gain, the body desires pleasure and ease: these all come from man's original nature and feelings. Give man a stimulus and they come forth of their own accord; they do not need to be taught to man before they can come forth. But if a man is stimulated and the virtue we are seeking cannot of itself come forth, if it needs to wait to be taught and then only can come forth—this is what is meant by an acquired characteristic. This is the distinction between original nature and acquired characteristics, the evidence of their dissimilarity. So the Sages influenced men's nature and established acquired training. When acquired training had arisen, the rules of proper conduct (*Li*) and justice (*Yi*) were evolved, laws and regulations were made. Hence the rules of proper conduct (*Li*), justice (*Yi*), laws, and regulations were brought forth by the Sages. The Sage has his original nature in common with ordinary people; he is not different from ordinary people in this respect. He is different and superior to ordinary people in his acquired training.

It is the original nature and tendency of man to desire gain and to seek to obtain it. If brothers have property and are to divide it, if they follow their original nature and feelings of desiring gain and seeking to obtain it, thus they will mutually thwart each other and endeavour to seize the property. But reform them by the etiquette of the rules of proper conduct (*Li*) and justice (*Yi*), and they will be willing to yield to outsiders. So by following the original nature and feelings, brothers will quarrel; influence them by the rules of proper conduct (*Li*) and justice (*Yi*), and they will yield to strangers. Every man's desire to be good is because his nature is evil. So if he is mean, he wants to be generous; if he is in circumscribed circumstances he wants unhampered circumstances; if he is poor, he wants to be rich; if he is in a low social position, he wishes to be in an honourable position; if he has it not within himself, he inevitably seeks it from without. For if he were rich, he would not desire wealth; if he were in a high position, he would not want more power. If he has it within his power, he would certainly not seek it from without. By this line of reasoning we see that men's desire to be good comes from his original nature being evil.

Now the original nature of man is

really without the rules of proper conduct (*Li*) and justice (*Yi*), hence he strives to learn and seeks to have it. By his original nature he does not know the rules of proper conduct (*Li*) and justice (*Yi*), hence he thinks and reflects, and seeks to learn these principles. Then only are they developed. So man is naturally without the rules of proper conduct (*Li*) and justice (*Yi*), he does not know the rules of proper conduct (*Li*) and justice (*Yi*). If man is without the rules of proper conduct (*Li*) and justice (*Yi*), there is disorder; if he does not know the rules of proper conduct (*Li*) and justice (*Yi*), there is rebellion. So these virtues are evolved. Then rebellion and disorder are within man himself. By this line of reasoning it is evident that the original nature of man is evil and his goodness is an acquired characteristic.

Mencius says, "The nature of man is good." I reply: This is not so. In whatever age or place on earth, in ancient times or in the present, men have meant by goodness true principles and just government. They have meant by evil partiality, a course bent on evil, rebellion, and disorder. This is the distinction between goodness and evil. Now if we sincerely consider the nature of man, is it firmly established in true principles and just government? If so, then what use are the Sage-Kings? What use are the rules of proper conduct (*Li*) and justice (*Yi*)? Although there were Sage-Kings, the rules of proper conduct (*Li*) and justice (*Yi*), what could they add to true principles and just government?

Now that is not the situation. Man's nature is evil. Anciently the Sage-Kings knew that man's nature was evil, that it was partial, bent on evil, and corrupt, rebellious, disorderly, without good government, hence they established the authority of the prince to govern man; they set forth clearly the rules of proper conduct (*Li*) and justice (*Yi*) to reform him; they es-

tablished laws and government to rule him; they made punishments severe to warn him; and so they caused the whole country to come to a state of good government and prosperity, and to accord with goodness. This is the government of the Sage-Kings, the reforming influence of the rules of proper conduct (*Li*) and justice (*Yi*).

Now suppose we try to remove the authority of the prince, and be without the reforming influence of the rules of proper conduct (*Li*) and justice (*Yi*); suppose we try to remove the beneficent control of the laws and the government, and be without the restraining influence of punishments. Let us stand and see how the people of the whole country would behave. If this were the situation, then the strong would injure the weak and rob him; the many would treat cruelly the few and rend them. The whole country would be in a state of rebellion and disorder. It would not take an instant to get into this condition. By this line of reasoning, it is evident that the nature of man is evil and that his goodness is acquired.

The man who is versed in the ancient times certainly sees its evidences in the present; he who is versed in the principles of Nature can certainly give evidence of their effect upon man. Every debater prizes distinctions and has evidence to support them. So he can sit down and discuss them; he can rise and establish them; he can act and exhibit them. Now Mencius says: Man's nature is good. This is without discrimination or evidence. A person can sit and discuss it, but he cannot rise and establish it; he cannot act and exhibit it. Isn't this extraordinarily erroneous? For if man's nature were good, then we could do away with the Sage-Kings; we would put an end to the rules of proper conduct (*Li*) and justice (*Yi*). But if man's nature is evil, then we should follow the Sage-Kings and prize the rules of proper conduct (*Li*) and justice (*Yi*). For the carpenter's square and rule are produced because there is crooked wood; the plumb-line arose because things were not straight; princes were established, the rules of proper conduct (Li) and justice (Yi) became evident because man's nature is evil. By this line of reasoning, it is evident that the nature of man is evil and his goodness is acquired.

Straight wood does not need to undergo the action of the carpenter's rule in order to be straight; its nature is straight. Crooked wood does need to undergo the action of the carpenter's rule; it needs to be steamed and then only will it be straight, because its nature is crooked. Now the nature of man is evil; he needs to undergo the government of the Sage-Kings, the reforming action of the rules of proper conduct (Li) and justice (Yi), then good government and order will issue, and actions will accord with virtue. By this line of reasoning it is evident that the nature of man is evil and his goodness is acquired.

A questioner may say: Even if the rules of proper conduct (Li) and justice (Yi) are accumulated acquired training, they are from man's nature. For the Sage-Kings could bring them forth. In reply I say: This is not so. The potter pounds and moulds the clay and brings the piece of pottery into being; then from clay there comes to be pottery. Can it be that this is the potter's naure? The workman hews a piece of wood and brings a vessel into being; thus from wood there comes to be a vessel. Can it be that this is the workman's original nature? Now the relation of the Sage to the rules of proper conduct (Li) and justice (Yi) is the same as that of the potter and the clay; he brings them into being; thus the rules of proper conduct (Li) and justice (Yi) are accumulated acquired training. How can they be the original nature of man? The nature of all men, of Yao and Shun, of Ch'ie and Chih is the same. The nature of the superior

man and of the little-minded man is the same. Now do we use the rules of proper conduct (Li) and justice (Yi) to make men's nature; do we accumulate acquired training for that purpose? Then why do we prize Yao and Yu? Why do we honour the superior man? What we prize in Yao, Yu, and the superior man is that they could reform their original nature and create acquired training. When their acquired training was created, they brought forth the rules of proper conduct (Li) and justice (Yi). Thus the relation of the Sage to the rules of proper conduct (Li) and justice (Yi) and accumulated acquired training is the same as that of the potter and the clay: he brings the pottery into being. By this line of reasoning how can the rules of proper conduct (Li) and justice (Yi) and accumulated acquired training be of man's nature? What was low about Ch'ie, Chih and the little-minded man was that they followed their nature and acted according to their inclinations: they took joy in haughtiness and the result was that they were avaricious for gain, striving and grasping. Hence it is evident that the nature of man is evil and his goodness is acquired.

Heaven was not partial to Tsen, Ch'ien, and Hsiao Yi, nor did it neglect the common multitude. Then why are Tsen, Ch'ien, and Hsiao Yi alone truly and perfectly filial, and why do they alone have the name of special filiality? The reason is that they observed the rules of proper conduct (Li) and justice (Yi) to the utmost extent. Heaven was not partial to the people of Ts'i and Lu, nor did it neglect the people of Ts'in. But the people of Ts'in are not as good in the righteous relation between father and son and in the proper reserve between husband and wife, as are the people of Ts'i and Lu in filial piety and reverential respect. Why is this? The reason is that the people of Ts'in follow their feelings and original nature, take pleasure in haughtiness, and are remiss in observing the rules of proper conduct (*Li*) and justice (*Yi*). How can it be that their nature could be different?

"The man on the street can become a Yu"—how about that? What gave Yu the qualities of Yu was that he carried into practice benevolence (*Jen*), justice (*Yi*), obedience to the laws, and uprightness. If so, then there is the means of knowing and practising benevolence (*Jen*), justice (*Yi*), obedience to law, and uprightness. Moreover, every man on the street has the nascent ability of knowing the principles of benevolence (*Jen*), justice (*Yi*), obedience to law, and uprightness, and the means whereby he can carry out the principles of benevolence (*Jen*), justice (*Yi*), obedience to law, and uprightness. Thus it is evident that he can become a Yu.

Now are the qualities of benevolence (*Jen*), justice (*Yi*), obedience to law, and uprightness definitely without the possibility of being known or of being carried out? If so, then even Yu could not have known benevolence (*Jen*), justice (*Yi*), obedience to law and uprightness, nor could he have been able to be benevolent (*Jen*), just (*Yi*), law-abiding, or upright. Then is the man on the street definitely without the power of knowing benevolence (*Jen*), justice (*Yi*), obedience to law, and uprightness, and definitely without the ability to be benevolent (*Jen*), just (*Yi*), law-abiding, and upright? Then the man on the street, on the one hand, could not know the righteous relation between father and son, nor on the other hand could he know the standard of correctness of prince and minister. Now that is not so. Every man on the street can on the one hand know the righteous relation between father and son, and on the other hand he can know the standard of uprightness of prince and minister. Thus it is evident that the man on the street possesses the power of knowing and the ability to practise these virtues. Now if the man on the street uses his power of knowledge and his ability of acting on the nascent ability of knowing benevolence (*Jen*) and justice (*Yi*) and the means of becoming so, then it is clear that he can become a Yu; if he concentrates his mind on one purpose, if he thinks and studies and investigates thoroughly, daily adding to his knowledge and retaining it long, if he accumulates goodness and does not stop, then he will become as wise as the gods, a third with Heaven and Earth. For the Sage is the man who has attained to that state by accumulative effort.

A person may say: The Sage attains to that stage by cumulative effort, but not everyone can cumulate his efforts: why is that? I reply, He has the capability, but he does not use it. For the small-minded man can become a superior man, but he is not willing to become a superior man; the superior man can become a small-minded man, but he is not willing to become a small-minded man. It is not impossible for the small-minded man and the superior man to exchange places; nevertheless they do not exchange places. There is the possibility, but they do not use it. For it is true that the man on the street can become a Yu, but it is probably not true that the man on the street has the ability to become a Yu. Although he does not have the ability to make himself a Yu, that does not destroy the possibility that he could become a Yu. It is perfectly possible that he could govern the whole country, yet he may never have the ability to govern the whole country. It is never an impossibility that the labourer, the artisan, the farmer, and the merchant might exchange professions, yet they never can exchange professions. By this line of reasoning a person could probably not be able to be so and so; yet although he could not, it does not remove the possibility of his becoming so and so. Then there is a great difference between whether a person has the ability and whether he has the possibility of being so and so. Thus the impossibility for them to exchange places is evident. . . .

*   *   *

Yao asked Shun, "How are the passions of man?" Shun answered, "The passions of man are far from beautiful. Why do you ask? When a man has a wife and children, his filial duty to his parents decreases; when sensual desires are satisfied, then faithfulness between friends decreases; when his desire for noble title and high salary is satisfied, then his faithfulness towards his prince decreases. Man's passions! Man's passions are far from beautiful! Why do you ask? Only the Worthy is not thus. . . ."

*   *   *

There are those who have the knowledge of the Sage; there are those who have the knowledge of the scholar or superior man; there are those who have the knowledge of the small-minded man, and there are those who have the knowledge of the menial. To be able to speak much, polished and in order, to discuss a matter for a whole day; through a thousand turns and changes, altogether to be discussing only one subject—this is the wisdom of the Sage. To speak little, but to the point and sparingly, coherently, and according to rule, as if a thread ordered the speech—this is the wisdom of the scholar or superior man. His speech is flattering, and his actions are rebellious, his actions and doings are far wrong—this is the knowledge of the little-minded man. With sharp retorts and triflingly clever, but without concatenation, with great cleverness in out of the way knowledge, but without real usefulness, practised in quickly making many distinctions but not going to the point, not caring for right or wrong, not considering error or truth, having for an object to overcome his opponent—this is the knowledge of a menial.

There is superior courage, mediocre courage, and inferior courage. He who dares to stand erect for the best Way there is in the world, who dares to act out the meaning of the Way (Tao) of the former Kings, who on the one hand will not follow a prince who governs wrongly and on the other hand will not follow a people who would govern wrongly; who when there is benevolence (Jen) will not consider poor emolument a bar, nor when there is no benevolence (Jen) will he consider riches an attraction, who when the country recognizes his talents, desires only that the country should rejoice with him, and who when the country does not recognize him, he will stand alone between Heaven and Earth and not fear—he is a man of superior courage. Respectful of the rules of proper conduct (Li) and of few desires, stressing the attainment of fidelity and laying no store by goods or wealth; when a worthy man comes, being willing to resign and advance him; but when an unworthy man is in office, daring to expel and remove him—this is courage of medium grade. Laying no store by his character but thinking wealth important, rejoicing in trouble and spreading it widely, evading the consequences of his actions, not caring for right or wrong, unstable in character, having for his object getting the best of others—this is courage of inferior character. . . .

*   *   *

Fan-jo and Chü-shu were famous bows of antiquity. But if they had not been put in frames for straightening, they could not have been straight of themselves. The Ts'ung of Duke Huan, the Ch'ueh of Duke T'ai, the Lu of King Wen, the Fu of Prince Chuang, Ho-lü's Kan-chiang, Mo-hsie, Chü-ch'ueh, P'i-lu: these were renowned swords of ancient times. But if they had not been ground, they could not have become sharp; if somebody had not laboured on them, they could not have cut. Hua, Liu, Ch'i, Chi, Hsien-li, Lu-er: these were all famous horses of antiquity. But on the one hand they needed the control of a bit and reins, and on the other they needed the fear of the whip. Add to that the driving of Ts'ao-fu and then they could do the thousand *li* in one day. Thus although a man has fine natural qualities and knows how to discuss, he needs to seek a virtuous teacher and serve him as a disciple; he needs to pick out good friends and attach himself to them. When he obtains a virtuous teacher and serves him as a disciple, then what he hears is the Way (*Tao*) of Yao, Shun, Yu, and T'ang. When he obtains good friends and attaches himself to them, then what he sees is conduct according to loyalty, faithfulness, reverence, and humility. His character daily advances in benevolence (*Jen*) and justice (*Yi*), and unconsciously he grows like those people. Now if he should live with people who are not virtuous, then what he would hear would be cheating, maliciousness, falseness, and hypocrisy. What he would see would be impurity, boasting, excesses, erroneous doctrine, and conduct that is avaricious of gain. His character would advance towards deserving capital punishment, and unconsciously he would become like these people. It is said: If you do not know a person, look at his friends. If you do not know the prince of a state, look to the right and left. Follow that and it will be sufficient! Follow that and it will be sufficient!

The Confessions and The City of God

ST. AUGUSTINE

St. Aurelius Augustine (354–430) began his intellectual career as a Manichaean, and not until his thirty-fourth year did he become a Christian. He became Bishop of Hippo in North Africa in 395, and died there as the barbarians from the north were laying siege to its walls.

THE CONFESSIONS, BOOK ONE

Chapter VII

Hearken, O God! Alas for the sins of men! Man saith this, and Thou dost have mercy on him; for Thou didst create him, but didst not create the sin that is in him. Who bringeth to my remembrance the sin of my infancy? For before Thee none is free from sin, not even the infant which has lived but a day upon the earth. Who bringeth this

From *The Confessions*, trans. J. G. Pilkington, and *The City of God*, trans. M. Dods.

to my remembrance? Doth not each little one, in whom I behold that which I do not remember of myself? In what, then, did I sin? Is it that I cried for the breast? If I should now so cry—not indeed for the breast, but for the food suitable to my years—I should be most justly laughed at and rebuked. What I then did deserved rebuke; but as I could not understand those who rebuked me, neither custom nor reason suffered me to be rebuked. For as we grow we root out and cast from us such bad habits. I have not seen any one who is wise, when purging anything cast away the good. Or was it good, even for a time, to strive to get by crying that which, if given, would be hurtful—to be bitterly indignant that those who were free and its elders, and those to whom it owed its being, besides many others wiser than it, who would not give way to the nod of its good pleasure, were not subject to it—to endeavor to harm, by struggling as much as it could, because those commands were not obeyed which only could have been obeyed to its hurt? Then, in the weakness of the infant's limbs, and not in its will, lies its innocency. I myself have seen and known an infant to be jealous though it could not speak. It became pale, and cast bitter looks on its foster-brother. Who is ignorant of this? Mothers and nurses tell us that they appease these things by I know not what remedies; and may this be taken for innocence, that when the fountain of milk is flowing fresh and abundant, one who has need should not be allowed to share it, though needing that nourishment to sustain life? Yet we look intently on these things, not because they are not faults, nor because the faults are small, but because they will vanish as age increases. For although you may allow these things now, you could not bear them with equanimity if found in an older person.

Thou, therefore, O Lord my God, who gavest life to the infant, and a frame which, as we see, Thou hast endowed with senses, compacted with limbs, beautified with form, and, for its general good and safety, hast introduced all vital energies— Thou commandest me to praise Thee for these things, to give thanks unto the Lord, and to sing praise unto Thy name, O Most High; for Thou art a God omnipotent and good, though Thou hadst done nought but these things, which none other can do but Thou, who alone madest all things, O Thou most fair, who madest all things fair, and orderest all according to Thy law. This period, then, of my life, O Lord, of which I have no remembrance, which I believe on the word of others, and which I guess from other infants, it displeases me—true though the guess be— to add it to this life of mine which I lead in this world; inasmuch as, in the darkness of my forgetfulness, it is like that which I passed in my mother's womb. But if I was conceived in iniquity, and in sin did my mother nourish me in the womb, where, I pray thee, O my God, where, Lord, or when was I, Thy servant, innocent? But behold, I pass by that time, for what have I to do with that, the memories of which I cannot recall?

Chapter X

And yet I erred, O Lord God, the Creator and Disposer of all things in Nature— but of sin the Disposer only—I erred, O Lord my God, in doing contrary to the wishes of my parents and of those masters; for this learning which they (no matter for what motive) wished me to acquire, I might have put to good account afterwards. For I disobeyed them not because I had chosen a better way, but from a fondness for play, loving the honor of victory in the matches, and to have my ears tickled with lying fables, in order that they might itch the more furiously—the same curiosity beaming more and more in my eyes for the shows and sports of my elders. Yet those who give these entertainments are held in such high repute, that almost all desire the same for their children, who they are still willing should be beaten, if these same games keep them from the studies by which they desire them to arrive at being the givers of them. Look down upon these things, O Lord, with compassion, and deliver us who now call upon Thee; deliver those also who do not call upon Thee, that they may call upon Thee, and that Thou mayest deliver them.

Chapter XI

Even as a boy I had heard of eternal life promised to us through the humility of the Lord our God condescending to our pride, and I was signed with the sign of the cross, and was seasoned with His salt even from the womb of my mother, who greatly trusted in Thee. Thou sawest, O Lord, how at one time, while yet a boy, being suddenly seized with pains in the stomach, and being at the point of death— Thou sawest, O my God, for even then Thou wast my keeper, with what emotion of mind and with what faith I solicited from the piety of my mother, and of Thy Church, the mother of us all, the baptism of Thy Christ, my Lord and my God. On which, the mother of my flesh being much troubled—since she, with a heart pure in Thy faith, travailed in birth more lovingly for my eternal salvation—would, had I not quickly recovered, have without delay provided for my initiation and washing by Thy life-giving sacraments, confessing Thee, O Lord Jesus, for the remission of sins. So my cleansing was deferred, as if I must needs, should I live, be further polluted; because, indeed, the guilt contracted by sin would, after baptism, be greater and more perilous. Thus I at that time believed with my mother and the whole house, except my father; yet he did not overcome the influence of my mother's piety in me so as to prevent my

believing in Christ, as he had not yet believed in Him. For she was desirous that Thou, O my God, shouldest be my Father rather than he; and in this Thou didst aid her to overcome her husband, to whom, though the better of the two, she yielded obedience, because in this she yielded obedience to Thee, who dost so command.

I beseech Thee, my God, I would gladly know, if it be Thy will, to what end my baptism was then deferred? Was it for my good that the reins were slackened, as it were, upon me for me to sin? Or were they not slackened? If not, whence comes it that it is still dinned into our ears on all sides, "Let him alone, let him act as he likes, for he is not yet baptized"? But as regards bodily health, no one exclaims, "Let him be more seriously wounded, for he is not yet cured!" How much better, then, had it been for me to have been cured at once; and then, by my own and my friends' diligence, my soul's restored health had been kept safe in Thy keeping, who gavest it! Better, in truth. But how numerous and great waves of temptation appeared to hang over me after my childhood! These were foreseen by my mother; and she preferred that the unformed clay should be exposed to them rather than the image itself.

BOOK TWO

Chapter IV

Theft is punished by Thy law, O Lord, and by the law written in men's hearts, which iniquity itself cannot blot out. For what thief will suffer a thief? Even a rich thief will not suffer him who is driven to it by want. Yet had I a desire to commit robbery, and did so, compelled neither by hunger, nor poverty, but through a distaste for well-doing, and a lustiness of iniquity. For I pilfered that of which I had already sufficient, and much better. Nor did I desire to enjoy what I pilfered, but the theft and sin itself. There was a pear-tree close to our vineyard, heavily laden with fruit, which was tempting neither for its color nor its flavor. To shake and rob this some of us wanton young fellows went, late one night (having, according to our disgraceful habit, prolonged our games in the streets until then), and carried away great loads, not to eat ourselves, but to fling to the very swine, having only eaten some of them; and to do this pleased us all the more because it was not permitted. Behold my heart, O my God; behold my heart, which Thou hadst pity upon when in the bottomless pit. Behold, now, let my heart tell Thee what it was seeking there, that I should be gratuitously wanton, having no inducement to evil but the evil itself. It was foul, and I loved it. I loved to perish. I loved my own error—not that for which I erred, but the error itself. Base soul, falling from Thy firmament to utter destruction—not seeking aught through the shame but the shame itself!

Chapter V

There is a desirableness in all beautiful bodies, and in gold, and silver, and all things; and in bodily contact sympathy is powerful, and each other sense has its proper adaptation of body. Worldly honor has also its glory, and the power of command, and of overcoming; whence proceeds also the desire for revenge. And yet to acquire all these, we must not depart from Thee, O Lord, nor deviate from Thy law. The life which we live here has also its peculiar attractiveness, through a certain measure of comeliness of its own, and harmony with all things here below. The friendships of men also are endeared by a sweet bond, in the oneness of many souls. On account of all these, and such as these, is sin committed; while through

an inordinate preference for these goods of a lower kind, the better and higher are neglected—even Thou, our Lord God, Thy truth, and Thy law. For these meaner things have their delights, but not like unto my God, who hath created all things; for in Him doth the righteous delight, and He is the sweetness of the upright in heart.

When, therefore, we inquire why a crime was committed, we do not believe it, unless it appear that there might have been the wish to obtain some of those which we designated meaner things, or else a fear of losing them. For truly they are beautiful and comely, although in comparison with those higher and celestial goods they are abject and contemptible. A man murdered another; what was his motive? He desired his wife or his estate; or would steal to support himself; or he was afraid of losing something of the kind by him; or, being injured, he was burning to be revenged. Would he commit murder without a motive, taking delight simply in the act of murder? Who would credit it? For as for that savage and brutal man, of whom it is declared that he was gratuitously wicked and cruel, there is yet a motive assigned. "Lest through idleness," he says, "hand or heart should grow inactive."[1] And to what purpose? Why, even that, having once got possession of the city through that practice of wickedness, he might attain honors, empire, and wealth, and be exempt from the fear of the laws, and his difficult circumstances from the needs of his family, and the consciousness of his own wickedness. So it seems that even Catiline himself loved not his own villainies, but something else, which gave him the motive for committing them.

Chapter VI

What was it, then, that I, miserable one, so doted on in thee, thou theft of mine,

---

[1] Sallust, *De Bello Catil.* c. 9.

thou deed of darkness, in that sixteenth year of my age? Beautiful thou wert not, since thou wert theft. But art thou anything, that so I may argue the case with thee? Those pears that we stole were fair to the sight, because they were Thy creation, Thou fairest of all, Creator of all, Thou good God—God, the highest good, and my true good. Those pears truly were pleasant to the sight; but it was not for them that my miserable soul lusted, for I had abundance of better, but those I plucked simply that I might steal. For, having plucked them, I threw them away, my sole gratification in them being my own sin, which I was pleased to enjoy. For if any of these pears entered my mouth, the sweetener of it was my sin in eating it. And now, O Lord my God, I ask what it was in that theft of mine that caused me such delight; and behold it has no beauty in it—not such, I mean, as exists in justice and wisdom; nor such as is in the mind, memory, senses, and animal life of man; nor yet such as is the glory and beauty of the stars in their courses; or the earth, or the sea, teeming with incipient life, to replace, as it is born, that which decays; nor, indeed, that false and shadowy beauty which pertains to deceptive vices.

For thus pride imitates high estate, whereas Thou alone art God, high above all. And what does ambition seek but honors and renown, whereas Thou alone art to be honored above all, and renowned for evermore? The cruelty of the powerful wishes to be feared; but who is to be feared but God only, out of whose power what can be forced away or withdrawn—when, or where, or whither, or by whom? The enticements of the wanton would fain be deemed love; and yet is naught more enticing than Thy charity, nor is aught loved more healthfully than that, Thy truth, bright and beautiful above all. Curiosity affects a desire for knowledge, whereas it is Thou who supremely knowest all things. Ignorance and foolishness themselves are concealed under the names of ingenuousness and harmlessness, because nothing can be found more ingenuous than Thou; and what is more harmless, since it is a sinner's own works by which he is harmed? And sloth seems to long for rest; but what sure rest is there besides the Lord? Luxury would fain be called plenty and abundance; but Thou art the fulness and unfailing plenteousness of unfading joys. Prodigality presents a shadow of liberality; but Thou art the most lavish giver of all good. Covetousness desires to possess much; and Thou art the Possessor of all things. Envy contends for excellence; but what so excellent as Thou? Anger seeks revenge; who avenges more justly than Thou? Fear starts at unwonted and sudden chances which threaten things beloved, and is wary for their security; but what can happen that is unwonted or sudden to Thee? or who can deprive Thee of what Thou lovest? or where is there unshaken security save with Thee? Grief languishes for things lost in which desire had delighted itself, even because it would have nothing taken from it, as nothing can be from Thee.

Thus the soul commits fornication when she turns away from Thee, and seeks without Thee what she cannot find pure and untainted until she returns to Thee. Thus all pervertedly imitate Thee who separate themselves far from Thee and raise themselves up against Thee. But even by thus imitating Thee they acknowledge Thee to be the Creator of all nature, and so that there is no place whither they can altogether retire from Thee. What, then, was it that I loved in that theft? And wherein did I, even corruptedly and pervertedly, imitate my Lord? Did I wish, if only by artifice, to act contrary to Thy law, because by power I could not, so that, being a captive, I might imitate an imperfect liberty by doing with impunity things which I was not allowed to do, in obscured likeness of

Thy omnipotency? Behold this servant of Thine, fleeing from his Lord, and following a shadow! O rottenness! O monstrosity of life and profundity of death! Could I like that which was unlawful only because it was unlawful?

Chapter VII

What shall I render unto the Lord, that while my memory recalls these things my soul is not appalled at them? I will love Thee, O Lord, and thank Thee, and confess unto Thy name, because Thou hast put away from me these so wicked and nefarious acts of mine. To Thy grace I attribute it, and to Thy mercy, that Thou hast melted away my sin as it were ice. To Thy grace also I attribute whatsoever of evil I have not committed; for what might I not have committed, loving as I did the sin for the sin's sake? All I confess to have been pardoned me, both those which I committed by my own perverseness, and those which, by Thy guidance, I committed not. Where is he who, reflecting upon his own infirmity, dares to ascribe his chastity and innocency to his own strength, so that he should love Thee the less, as if he had been in less need of Thy mercy, whereby Thou dost forgive the transgressions of those that turn to Thee? For whosoever, called by Thee, obeyed Thy voice, and shunned those things which he reads me recalling and confessing of myself, let him not despise me, who, being sick, was healed by that same Physician by whose aid it was that he was not sick, or rather was less sick. And for this let him love Thee as much, even all the more, since by whom he sees me to have been restored from so great a feebleness of sin, by Him he sees himself from a like feebleness to have been preserved.

Chapter VIII

What fruit had I then, wretched one, in those things which, when I remember them, cause me shame—above all in that theft, which I loved only for the theft's sake? And as the theft itself was nothing, all the more wretched was I who loved it. Yet by myself alone I would not have done it—I recall what my heart was—alone I could not have done it. I loved, then, in it the companionship of my accomplices with whom I did it. I did not, therefore, love the theft alone—rather, it was that alone that I loved, for the companionship was nothing. What is the fact? Who is it that can teach me, but He who illuminateth mine heart and searcheth out the dark corners thereof? What is it that has come into my mind to inquire about, to discuss, and to reflect upon? For had I at that time loved the pears I stole, and wished to enjoy them, I might have done so alone, if I could have been satisfied with the mere commission of the theft by which my pleasure was secured; nor needed I have provoked that itching of my own passions, by the encouragement of accomplices. But as my enjoyment was not in those pears, it was in the crime itself, which the company of my fellow-sinners produced.

THE CITY OF GOD, BOOK THIRTEEN

Chapter XIV

For God, the author of natures, not of vices, created man upright; but man, being of his own will corrupted, and justly condemned, begot corrupted and condemned children. For we all were in that one man, since we all were that one man, who fell into sin by the woman who was made from him before the sin. For not yet was the particular form created and distributed to us, in which we as individuals were to live, but already the seminal nature was there from which we were to be propagated; and this being vitiated by sin, and bound by the chain of death, and justly condemned, man could not be born of man in any other state. And thus, from the bad use of free will, there originated the whole train of evil, which, with its concatenation of miseries, convoys the human race from its depraved origin, as from a corrupt root, on to the destruction of the second death, which has no end, those only being excepted who are freed by the grace of God.

Chapter XV

It may perhaps be supposed that because God said, "Ye shall die the death," and not "deaths," we should understand only that death which occurs when the soul is deserted by God, who is its life; for it was not deserted by God, and so deserted Him, but deserted Him, and so was deserted by Him. For its own will was the originator of its evil, as God was the originator of its motions towards good, both in making it when it was not, and in remaking it when it had fallen and perished. But though we suppose that God meant only this death, and that the words, "In the day ye eat of it ye shall die the death," should be understood as meaning, "In the day ye desert me in disobedience, I will desert you in justice," yet assuredly in this death the other deaths also were threatened, which were its inevitable consequence. For in the first stirring of the disobedient motion which was felt in the flesh of the disobedient soul, and which caused our first parents to cover their shame, one death indeed is experienced, that, namely, which occurs when God forsakes the soul. (This was intimated by the words He uttered, when the man, stupefied by fear, had hid himself, "Adam, where art thou?"—words which He used not in ignorance of inquiry, but warning him to consider where he was, since God was not with him.) But when the soul itself forsook the body, corrupted and decayed with age, the other death was ex-

perienced of which God had spoken in pronouncing man's sentence, "Earth thou art, and unto earth shalt thou return." And of these two deaths that first death of the whole man is composed. And this first death is finally followed by the second, unless man be freed by grace. For the body would not return to the earth from which it was made, save only by the death proper to itself, which occurs when it is forsaken of the soul, its life. And therefore it is agreed among all Christians who truthfully hold the Catholic faith, that we are subject to the death of the body, not by the law of nature, by which God ordained no death for man, but by His righteous infliction on account of sin; for God, taking vengeance on sin, said to the man, in whom we all then were, "Dust thou art, and unto dust shalt thou return."

BOOK FOURTEEN

Chapter I

We have already stated in the preceding books that God, desiring not only that the human race might be able by their similarity of nature to associate with one another, but also that they might be bound together in harmony and peace by the ties of relationship, was pleased to derive all men from one individual, and created man with such a nature that the members of the race should not have died, had not the two first (of whom the one was created out of nothing, and the other out of him) merited this by their disobedience; for by them so great a sin was committed, that by it human nature was altered for the worse, and was transmitted also to their posterity, liable to sin and subject to death. And the kingdom of death so reigned over men, that the deserved penalty of sin would have hurled all headlong even into the second death, of which there is no end, had not the undeserved grace of God saved some therefrom. And thus it has come to pass, that though there are very many and great nations all over the earth, whose rites and customs, speech, arms, and dress, are distinguished by marked differences, yet there are no more than two kinds of human society, which we may justly call two cities, according to the language of our Scriptures. The one consists of those who wish to live after the flesh, the other of those who wish to live after the spirit; and when they severally achieve what they wish, they live in peace, each after their kind.

Chapter IV

When, therefore, man lives according to man, not according to God, he is like the devil. Because not even an angel might live according to an angel, but only according to God, if he was to abide in the truth, and speak God's truth and not his own lie. And of man, too, the same apostle says in another place, "If the truth of God hath more abounded through my lie"—"my lie," he said, and "God's truth." When, then, a man lives according to the truth, he lives not according to himself, but according to God; for He was God who said, "I am the truth." When, therefore, man lives according to himself—that is, according to man, not according to God—assuredly he lives according to a lie; not that man himself is a lie, for God is his author and creator, who is certainly not the author and creator of a lie, but because man was made upright, that he might not live according to himself, but according to Him that made him—in other words, that he might do His will and not his own; and not to live as he was made to live, that is a lie. For he certainly desires to be blessed even by not living so that he may be blessed. And what is a lie if this desire be not? Wherefore it is

not without meaning said that all sin is a lie. For no sin is committed save by that desire or will by which we desire that it be well with us, and shrink from it being ill with us. That, therefore, is a lie which we do in order that it may be well with us, but which makes us more miserable than we were. And why is this, but because the source of man's happiness lies only in God, whom he abandons when he sins, and not in himself, by living according to whom he sins?

In enunciating this proposition of ours, then, that because some live according to the flesh and others according to the spirit, there have arisen two diverse and conflicting cities, we might equally well have said, "because some live according to man, others according to God." For Paul says very plainly to the Corinthians, "For whereas there is among you envying and strife, are ye not carnal, and walk according to man?" So that to walk according to man and to be carnal are the same; for by *flesh,* that is, by a part of man, man is meant. For before he said that those same persons were animal whom afterwards he calls carnal, saying, "For what man knoweth the things of a man, save the spirit of man which is in him? even so the things of God knoweth no man, but the Spirit of God. Now we have received not the spirit of this world, but the Spirit which is of God; that we might know the things which are freely given to us of God. Which things also we speak, not in the words which man's wisdom teacheth, but which the Holy Ghost teacheth; comparing spiritual things with spiritual. But the animal man perceiveth not the things of the Spirit of God; for they are foolishness unto him." It is to men of this kind, then, that is, to animal men, he shortly after says, "And I, brethren, could not speak unto you as unto spiritual, but as unto carnal." And this is to be interpreted by the same usage, a part being taken for the whole. For both the soul and the flesh, the component parts of man, can be used to signify the whole man; and so the animal man and the carnal man are not two different things, but one and the same thing, viz., man living according to man. In the same way it is nothing else than men that are meant either in the words, "By the deeds of the law there shall no *flesh* be justified;" or in the words, "Seventy-five *souls* went down into Egypt with Jacob." In the one passage, "no flesh" signifies "no man"; and in the other, by "seventy-five souls" seventy-five men are meant. And the expression, "not in words which man's wisdom teacheth," might equally be "not in words which fleshly wisdom teacheth;" and the expression, "ye walk according to man," might be "according to the flesh." And this is still more apparent in the words which followed: "For while one saith, I am of Paul, and another, I am of Apollos, are ye not men?" The same thing which he had before expressed by "ye are animal," "ye are carnal," he now expresses by "ye are men"; that is, ye live according to man, not according to God, for if you lived according to Him, you should be gods.

Existentialism

JEAN-PAUL SARTRE

Jean-Paul Sartre (b. 1905) is perhaps the most famous living existentialist thinker and writer. A novelist, dramatist, essayist, and philosopher, Sartre has contributed greatly to both France's and the world's literature. In 1964 he refused the Nobel prize in literature. The question Sartre considers in this essay is: If there is no human nature for me to depend on, and if in consequence I am totally free, then what are the implications for my own person, myself, of this absolute freedom?

. . . What is meant by the term *existentialism?*

Most people who use the word would be rather embarrassed if they had to explain it, since, now that the word is all the rage, even the work of a musician or painter is being called existentialist. A gossip columnist in *Clartés* signs himself *The Existentialist,* so that by this time the word has been so stretched and has taken on so broad a meaning, that it no longer means anything at all. It seems that for want of an advance-guard doctrine analogous to surrealism, the kind of people who are eager for scandal and flurry turn to this philosophy which in other respects does not at all serve their purposes in this sphere.

Actually, it is the least scandalous, the most austere of doctrines. It is intended

From *Existentialism*, transl. Bernard Frechtman; New York, Philosophical Library, 1947, pp. 14–38.

strictly for specialists and philosophers. Yet it can be defined easily. What complicates matters is that there are two kinds of existentialist; first, those who are Christian, among whom I would include Jaspers and Gabriel Marcel, both Catholic; and on the other hand the atheistic existentialists, among whom I class Heidegger, and then the French existentialists and myself. What they have in common is that they think that existence precedes essence, or, if you prefer, that subjectivity must be the starting point.

Just what does that mean? Let us consider some object that is manufactured, for example, a book or a paper-cutter: here is an object which has been made by an artisan whose inspiration came from a concept. He referred to the concept of what a paper-cutter is and likewise to a known method of production, which is part of the concept, something which is, by and large, a routine. Thus, the paper-cutter is at once an object produced in a certain way and, on the other hand, one having a specific use; and one can not postulate a man who produces a paper-cutter but does not know what it is used for. Therefore, let us say that, for the paper-cutter, essence—that is, the ensemble of both the production routines and the properties which enable it to be both produced and defined—precedes existence. Thus, the presence of the paper-cutter or book in front of me is determined. Therefore, we have here a technical view of the world whereby it can be said that production precedes existence.

When we conceive God as the Creator, He is generally thought of as a superior sort of artisan. Whatever doctrine we may be considering, whether one like that of Descartes or that of Leibnitz, we always grant that will more or less follows understanding or, at the very least, accompanies it, and that when God creates He knows exactly what He is creating. Thus, the concept of man in the mind of God is comparable to the concept of paper-cutter in the mind of the manufacturer, and, following certain techniques and a conception, God produces man, just as the artisan, following a definition and a technique, makes a paper-cutter. Thus, the individual man is the realisation of a certain concept in the divine intelligence.

In the eighteenth century, the atheism of the *philosophes* discarded the idea of God, but not so much for the notion that essence precedes existence. To a certain extent, this idea is found everywhere; we find it in Diderot, in Voltaire, and even in Kant. Man has a human nature; this human nature, which is the concept of the human, is found in all men, which means that each man is a particular example of a universal concept, man. In Kant, the result of this universality is that the wildman, the natural man, as well as the bourgeois, are circumscribed by the same definition and have the same basic qualities. Thus, here too the essence of man precedes the historical existence that we find in nature.

Atheistic existentialism, which I represent, is more coherent. It states that if God does not exist, there is at least one being in whom existence precedes essence, a being who exists before he can be defined by any concept, and that this being is man, or, as Heidegger says, human reality. What is meant here by saying that existence precedes essence? It means that, first of all, man exists, turns up, appears on the scene, and, only afterwards, defines himself. If man, as the existentialist conceives him, is indefinable, it is because at first he is nothing. Only afterward will he be something, and he himself will have made what he will be. Thus, there is no human nature, since there is no God to conceive it. Not only is man what he conceives himself to be, but he is also only what he wills himself to be after this thrust toward existence.

Man is nothing else but what he makes

of himself. Such is the first principle of existentialism. It is also what is called subjectivity, the name we are labeled with when charges are brought against us. But what do we mean by this, if not that man has a greater dignity than a stone or table? For we mean that man first exists, that is, that man first of all is the being who hurls himself toward a future and who is conscious of imagining himself as being in the future. Man is at the start a plan which is aware of itself, rather than a patch of moss, a piece of garbage, or a cauliflower; nothing exists prior to this plan; there is nothing in heaven; man will be what he will have planned to be. Not what he will want to be. Because by the word "will" we generally mean a conscious decision, which is subsequent to what we have already made of ourselves. I may want to belong to a political party, write a book, get married; but all that is only a manifestation of an earlier, more spontaneous choice that is called "will." But if existence really does precede essence, man is responsible for what he is. Thus, existentialism's first move is to make every man aware of what he is and to make the full responsibility of his existence rest on him. And when we say that a man is responsible for himself, we do not only mean that he is responsible for his own individuality, but that he is responsible for all men.

The word subjectivism has two meanings, and our opponents play on the two. Subjectivism means, on the one hand, that an individual chooses and makes himself; and, on the other, that it is impossible for man to transcend human subjectivity. The second of these is the essential meaning of existentialism. When we say that man chooses his own self, we mean that every one of us does likewise; but we also mean by that that in making this choice he also chooses all men. In fact, in creating the man that we want to be, there is not a single one of our acts which does not

at the same time create an image of man as we think he ought to be. To choose to be this or that is to affirm at the same time the value of what we choose, because we can never choose evil. We always choose the good, and nothing can be good for us without being good for all.

If, on the other hand, existence precedes essence, and if we grant that we exist and fashion our image at one and the same time, the image is valid for everybody and for our whole age. Thus, our responsibility is much greater than we might have supposed, because it involves all mankind. If I am a workingman and choose to join a Christian trade-union rather than be a communist, and if by being a member I want to show that the best thing for man is resignation, that the kingdom of man is not of this world, I am not only involving my own case—I want to be resigned for everyone. As a result, my action has involved all humanity. To take a more individual matter, if I want to marry, to have children; even if this marriage depends solely on my own circumstances or passion or wish, I am involving all humanity in monogamy and not merely myself. Therefore, I am responsible for myself and for everyone else. I am creating a certain image of man of my own choosing. In choosing myself, I choose man.

This helps us understand what the actual content is of such rather grandiloquent words as anguish, forlornness, despair. As you will see, it's all quite simple.

First, what is meant by anguish? The existentialists say at once that man is anguish. What that means is this: the man who involves himself and who realizes that he is not only the person he chooses to be, but also a law-maker who is, at the same time, choosing all mankind as well as himself, can not help escape the feeling of his total and deep responsibility. Of course, there are many people who are not anxious; but we claim that they are hiding their anxiety, that they are fleeing from it. Certainly, many people believe that when they do something, they themselves are the only ones involved, and when someone says to them, "What if everyone acted that way?" they shrug their shoulders and answer, "Everyone doesn't act that way." But really, one should always ask himself, "What would happen if everybody looked at things that way?" There is no escaping this disturbing thought except by a kind of double-dealing. A man who lies and makes excuses for himself by saying "not everybody does that," is someone with an uneasy conscience, because the act of lying implies that a universal value is conferred upon the lie.

Anguish is evident even when it conceals itself. This is the anguish that Kierkegaard called the anguish of Abraham. You know the story: an angel has ordered Abraham to sacrifice his son; if it really were an angel who has come and said, "You are Abraham, you shall sacrifice your son," everything would be all right. But everyone might first wonder, "Is it really an angel, and am I really Abraham? What proof do I have?"

There was a madwoman who had hallucinations; someone used to speak to her on the telephone and give her orders. Her doctor asked her, "Who is it who talks to you?" She answered, "He says it's God." What proof did she really have that it was God? If an angel comes to me, what proof is there that it's an angel? And if I hear voices, what proof is there that they come from heaven and not from hell, or from the subconscious, or a pathological condition? What proves that they are addressed to me? What proof is there that I have been appointed to impose my choice and my conception of man on humanity? I'll never find any proof or sign to convince me of that. If a voice addresses me, it is always for me to decide that this is the angel's voice; if I consider that such

an act is a good one, it is I who will choose to say that it is good rather than bad.

Now, I'm not being singled out as an Abraham, and yet at every moment I'm obliged to perform exemplary acts. For every man, everything happens as if all mankind had its eyes fixed on him and were guiding itself by what he does. And every man ought to say to himself, "Am I really the kind of man who has the right to act in such a way that humanity might guide itself by my actions?" And if he does not say that to himself, he is masking his anguish.

There is no question here of the kind of anguish which would lead to quietism, to inaction. It is a matter of a simple sort of anguish that anybody who has had responsibilities is familiar with. For example, when a military officer takes the responsibility for an attack and sends a certain number of men to death, he chooses to do so, and in the main he alone makes the choice. Doubtless, orders come from above, but they are too broad; he interprets them, and on this interpretation depend the lives of ten or fourteen or twenty men. In making a decision he can not help having a certain anguish. All leaders know this anguish. That doesn't keep them from acting; on the contrary, it is the very condition of their action. For it implies that they envisage a number of possibilites, and when they choose one, they realize that it has value only because it is chosen. We shall see that this kind of anguish, which is the kind that existentialism describes, is explained, in addition, by a direct responsibility to the other men whom it involves. It is not a curtain separating us from action, but is part of action itself.

When we speak of forlornness, a term Heidegger was fond of, we mean only that God does not exist and that we have to face all the consequences of this. The existentialist is strongly opposed to a certain kind of secular ethics which would like to abolish God with the least possible expense. About 1880, some French teachers tried to set up a secular ethics which went something like this: God is a useless and costly hypothesis; we are discarding it; but, meanwhile, in order for there to be an ethics, a society, a civilization, it is essential that certain values be taken seriously and that they be considered as having an *a priori* existence. It must be obligatory, *a priori,* to be honest, not to lie, not to beat your wife, to have children, etc., etc. So we're going to try a little device which will make it possible to show that values exist all the same, inscribed in a heaven of ideas, though otherwise God does not exist. In other words—and this, I believe, is the tendency of everything called reformism in France—nothing will be changed if God does not exist. We shall find ourselves with the same norms of honesty, progress, and humanism, and we shall have made of God an outdated hypothesis which will peacefully die off by itself.

The existentialist, on the contrary, thinks it very distressing that God does not exist, because all possibility of finding values in a heaven of ideas disappears along with Him; there can no longer be an *a priori* Good, since there is no infinite and perfect consciousness to think it. Nowhere is it written that the Good exists, that we must be honest, that we must not lie; because the fact is we are on a plane where there are only men. Dostoievsky said, "If God didn't exist, everything would be possible." That is the very starting point of existentialism. Indeed, everything is permissible if God does not exist, and as a result man is forlorn, because neither within him nor without does he find anything to cling to. He can't start making excuses for himself.

If existence really does precede essence, there is no explaining things away by reference to a fixed and given human nature. In other words, there is no determinism, man is free, man is freedom. On the other hand, if God does not exist, we find no values or commands to turn to which legitimize our conduct. So, in the bright realm of values, we have no excuse behind us, nor justification before us. We are alone, with no excuses.

That is the idea I shall try to convey when I say that man is condemned to be free. Condemned, because he did not create himself, yet, in other respects is free; because, once thrown into the world, he is responsible for everything he does. The existentialist does not believe in the power of passion. He will never agree that a sweeping passion is a ravaging torrent which fatally leads a man to certain acts and is therefore an excuse. He thinks that man is responsible for his passion.

The existentialist does not think that man is going to help himself by finding in the world some omen by which to orient himself. Because he thinks that man will interpret the omen to suit himself. Therefore, he thinks that man, with no support and no aid, is condemned every moment to invent man. Ponge, in a very fine article, has said, "Man is the future of man." That's exactly it. But if it is taken to mean that this future is recorded in heaven, that God sees it, then it is false, because it would really no longer be a future. If it is taken to mean that, whatever a man may be, there is a future to be forged, a virgin future before him, then this remark is sound. But then we are forlorn.

To give you an example which will enable you to understand forlornness better, I shall cite the case of one of my students who came to see me under the following circumstances: his father was on bad terms with his mother, and, moreover, was inclined to be a collaborationist; his older brother had been killed in the German offensive of 1940, and the young man, with somewhat immature but generous feelings, wanted to avenge him. His mother lived alone with him, very much upset by the half-treason of her husband and the death of her older son; the boy was her only consolation.

The boy was faced with the choice of leaving for England and joining the Free French Forces—that is, leaving his mother behind—or remaining with his mother and helping her to carry on. He was fully aware that the woman lived only for him and that his going-off—and perhaps his death—would plunge her into despair. He was also aware that every act that he did for his mother's sake was a sure thing, in the sense that it was helping her to carry on, whereas every effort he made toward going off and fighting was an uncertain move which might run aground and prove completely useless; for example, on his way to England he might, while passing through Spain, be detained indefinitely in a Spanish camp; he might reach England or Algiers and be stuck in an office at a desk job. As a result, he was faced with two very different kinds of action: one, concrete, immediate, but concerning only one individual; the other concerned an incomparably vaster group, a national collectivity, but for that very reason was dubious, and might be interrupted en route. And, at the same time, he was wavering between two kinds of ethics. On the one hand, an ethics of sympathy, of personal devotion; on the other, a broader ethics, but one whose efficacy was more dubious. He had to choose between the two.

Who could help him choose? Christian doctrine? No. Christian doctrine says, "Be charitable, love your neighbor, take the more rugged path, etc., etc." But which is the more rugged path? Whom should he love as a brother? The fighting man or his mother? Which does the greater good, the vague act of fighting in a group, or the concrete one of helping a particular hu-man being to go on living? Who can decide *a priori*? Nobody. No book of ethics can tell him. The Kantian ethics says, "Never treat any person as a means, but as an end." Very well, if I stay with my mother, I'll treat her as an end and not as a means; but by virtue of this very fact, I'm running the risk of treating the people around me who are fighting, as means; and, conversely, if I go to join those who are fighting, I'll be treating them as an end, and, by doing that, I run the risk of treating my mother as a means.

If values are vague, and if they are always too broad for the concrete and specific case that we are considering, the only thing left for us is to trust our instincts. That's what this young man tried to do; and when I saw him, he said, "In the end, feeling is what counts. I ought to choose whichever pushes me in one direction. If I feel that I love my mother enough to sacrifice everything else for her—my desire for vengeance, for action, for adventure—then I'll stay with her. If, on the contrary, I feel that my love for my mother isn't enough, I'll leave."

But how is the value of a feeling determined? What gives his feeling for his mother value? Precisely the fact that he remained with her. I may say that I like so-and-so well enough to sacrifice a certain amount of money for him, but I may say so only if I've done it. I may say "I love my mother well enough to remain with her" if I have remained with her. The only way to determine the value of this affection is, precisely, to perform an act which confirms and defines it. But, since I require this affection to justify my act, I find myself caught in a vicious circle.

On the other hand, Gide has well said that a mock feeling and a true feeling are almost indistinguishable; to decide that I love my mother and will remain with her, or to remain with her by putting on an act, amount somewhat to the same thing. In other words, the feeling is formed by the acts one performs; so, I can not refer to it in order to act upon it. Which means that I can neither seek within myself the true condition which will impel me to act, nor apply to a system of ethics for concepts which will permit me to act. You will say, "At least, he did go to a teacher for advice." But if you seek advice from a priest, for example, you have chosen this priest; you already knew, more or less, just about what advice he was going to give you. In other words, choosing your adviser is involving yourself. The proof of this is that if you are a Christian, you will say, "Consult a priest." But some priests are collaborating, some are just marking time, some are resisting. Which to choose? If the young man chooses a priest who is resisting or collaborating, he has already decided on the kind of advice he's going to get. Therefore, in coming to see me he knew the answer I was going to give him, and I had only one answer to give: "You're free, choose, that is, invent." No general ethics can show you what is to be done; there are no omens in the world. The Catholics will reply, "But there are." Granted—but, in any case, I myself choose the meaning they have.

When I was a prisoner, I knew a rather remarkable young man who was a Jesuit. He had entered the Jesuit order in the following way: he had had a number of very bad breaks; in childhood, his father died, leaving him in poverty, and he was a scholarship student at a religious institution where he was constantly made to feel that he was being kept out of charity; then, he failed to get any of the honors and distinctions that children like; later on, at about eighteen, he bungled a love affair; finally, at twenty-two, he failed in military training, a childish enough matter, but it was the last straw.

This young fellow might well have felt that he had botched everything. It was a sign of something, but of what? He might have taken refuge in bitterness or despair.

But he very wisely looked upon all this as a sign that he was not made for secular triumphs, and that only the triumphs of religion, holiness, and faith were open to him. He saw the hand of God in all this, and so he entered the order. Who can help seeing that he alone decided what the sign meant?

Some other interpretation might have been drawn from this series of setbacks; for example, that he might have done better to turn carpenter or revolutionist. Therefore, he is fully responsible for the interpretation. Forlornness implies that we ourselves choose our being. Forlornness and anguish go together.

As for despair, the term has a very simple meaning. It means that we shall confine ourselves to reckoning only with what depends upon our will, or on the ensemble of probabilities which make our action possible. When we want something, we always have to reckon with probabilities. I may be counting on the arrival of a friend. The friend is coming by rail or street-car; this supposes that the train will arrive on schedule, or that the street-car will not jump the track. I am left in the realm of possibility; but possibilities are to be reckoned with only to the point where my action comports with the ensemble of these possibilities, and no further. The moment the possibilities I am considering are not rigorously involved by my action, I ought to disengage myself from them, because no God, no scheme, can adapt the world and its possibilities to my will. When Descartes said, "Conquer yourself rather than the world," he meant essentially the same thing.

The Marxists to whom I have spoken reply, "You can rely on the support of others in your action, which obviously has certain limits because you're not going to live forever. That means: rely on both what others are doing elsewhere to help you, in China, in Russia, and what they will do later on, after your death, to

carry on the action and lead it to its ful-
fillment, which will be the revolution.
You even *have* to rely upon that, otherwise
you're immoral." I reply at once that I
will always rely on fellow-fighters insofar
as these comrades are involved with me in
a common struggle, in the unity of a party
or a group in which I can more or less
make my weight felt; that is, one whose
ranks I am in as a fighter and whose movements I am aware of at every moment. In
such a situation, relying on the unity and
will of the party is exactly like counting
on the fact that the train will arrive on
time or that the car won't jump the track.
But, given that man is free and that there
is no human nature for me to depend on,
I can not count on men whom I do not
know by relying on human goodness or
man's concern for the good of society. I
don't know what will become of the Russian revolution; I may make an example
of it to the extent that at the present time
it is apparent that the proletariat plays a
part in Russia that it plays in no other
nation. But I can't swear that this will
inevitably lead to a triumph of the proletariat. I've got to limit myself to what
I see.

Given that men are free and that to-
morrow they will freely decide what man
will be, I can not be sure that, after my
death, fellow-fighters will carry on my

work to bring it to its maximum perfection. Tomorrow, after my death, some
men may decide to set up Fascism, and the
others may be cowardly and muddled
enough to let them do it. Fascism will
then be the human reality, so much the
worse for us.

Actually, things will be as man will
have decided they are to be. Does that
mean that I should abandon myself to
quietism? No. First, I should involve myself; then, act on the old saw, "Nothing
ventured, nothing gained." Nor does it
mean that I shouldn't belong to a party,
but rather that I shall have no illusions
and shall do what I can. For example, suppose I ask myself, "Will socialization, as
such, ever come about?" I know nothing
about it. All I know is that I'm going to
do everything in my power to bring it
about. Beyond that, I can't count on anything. Quietism is the attitude of people
who say, "Let others do what I can't do."
The doctrine I am presenting is the very
opposite of quietism, since it declares,
"There is no reality except in action."
Moreover, it goes further, since it adds,
"Man is nothing else than his plan; he
exists only to the extent that he fulfills
himself; he is therefore nothing else than
the ensemble of his acts, nothing else than
his life."

Personal Identity

An Essay Concerning Human Understanding

JOHN LOCKE

John Locke (1632–1704) was the first of the great British empiricists. The selection that follows is from his famous An Essay Concerning Human Understanding, *first published in 1690. Locke had a fascinating life, living close to the heads of state—in favor and out, depending on how the political wind was blowing. Trained to be a doctor, he turned instead to writing and tutoring, where he made both his fame and a modest income.*

OF IDENTITY AND DIVERSITY

Another occasion the mind often takes of comparing, is the very being of things, when, considering *anything as existing at any determined time and place,* we compare it with *itself existing at another time,* and thereon form the ideas of *identity* and *diversity.* When we see anything to be in any place in any instant of time, we are sure (be it what it will) that it is that very thing, and not another which at that same time exists in another place, how like and undistinguishable soever it may be in all other respects: and in this consists *identity,* when the ideas it is attributed to vary not at all from what they were that moment wherein we consider their former existence, and to which we compare the present. For we never finding, nor conceiving it possible, that two things of the same kind should exist in the same place at the same time, we rightly conclude, that, whatever exists anywhere at any time, excludes all of the same kind, and is there itself alone. When therefore we demand whether anything be the *same* or no, it refers always to something that existed such a time in such a place, which it was certain, at that instant, was the same with itself, and no other. From whence it follows, that one thing cannot have two beginnings of existence, nor two things one beginning; it being impossible for two things of the same kind to be or exist in the same instant, in the very same place; or one and the same thing in different places. That, therefore, that had one beginning, is the same thing; and that which had a different beginning in time and place from that, is not the same, but diverse. That which has made the diffi-

From *An Essay Concerning Human Understanding.* Book II, Chapter XXVII.

culty about this relation has been the little care and attention used in having precise notions of the things to which it is attributed.

We have the ideas but of three sorts of substances: 1. *God.* 2. *Finite intelligences.* 3. *Bodies.*

First, *God* is without beginning, eternal, unalterable, and everywhere, and therefore concerning his identity there can be no doubt.

Secondly, *Finite spirits* having had each its determinate time and place of beginning to exist, the relation to that time and place will always determine to each of them its identity, as long as it exists.

Thirdly, The same will hold of every *particle of matter,* to which no addition or subtraction of matter being made, it is the same. For, though these three sorts of substances, as we term them, do not exclude one another out of the same place, yet we cannot conceive but that they must necessarily each of them exclude any of the same kind out of the same place: or else the notions and names of identity and diversity would be in vain, and there could be no such distinctions of substances, or anything else one from another. For example: could two bodies be in the same place at the same time; then those two parcels of matter must be one and the same, take them great or little; nay, all bodies must be one and the same. For, by the same reason that two particles of matter may be in one place, all bodies may be in one place: which, when it can be supposed, takes away the distinction of identity and diversity of one and more, and renders it ridiculous. But it being a contradiction that two or more should be one, identity and diversity are relations and ways of comparing well founded, and of use to the understanding.

All other things being but modes or relations ultimately terminated in substances, the identity and diversity of each particular existence of them too will be by

the same way determined: only as to things whose existence is in succession, such as are the actions of finite beings, v. g. *motion* and *thought,* both which consist in a continued train of succession, concerning *their* diversity there can be no question: because each perishing the moment it begins, they cannot exist in different times, or in different places, as permanent beings can at different times exist in distant places; and therefore no motion or thought, considered as at different times, can be the same, each part thereof having a different beginning of existence.

From what has been said, it is easy to discover what is so much inquired after, the *principium individuationis;* and that, it is plain, is existence itself; which determines a being of any sort to a particular time and place, incommunicable to two beings of the same kind. This, though it seems easier to conceive in simple substances or modes; yet, when reflected on, is not more difficult in compound ones, if care be taken to what it is applied: v.g. let us suppose an atom, i.e. a continued body under one immutable superficies, existing in a determined time and place; it is evident, that, considered in any instant of its existence, it is in that instant the same with itself. For, being at that instant what it is, and nothing else, it is the same, and so must continue as long as its existence is continued; for so long it will be the same, and no other. In like manner, if two or more atoms be joined together into the same mass, every one of those atoms will be the same, by the foregoing rule: and whilst they exist united together, the mass, consisting of the same atoms, must be the same mass, or the same body, let the parts be ever so differently jumbled. But if one of these atoms be taken away, or one new one added, it is no longer the same mass or the same body. In the state of living creatures, their identity depends not on a mass of the same particles, but on something else. For in them the variation of great parcels of matter alters not the identity: an oak growing from a plant to a great tree, and then lopped, is still the same oak; and a colt grown up to a horse, sometimes fat, sometimes lean, is all the while the same horse: though, in both these cases, there may be a manifest change of the parts; so that truly they are not either of them the same masses of matter, though they be truly one of them the same oak, and the other the same horse. The reason whereof is, that, in these two cases—a *mass of matter* and a *living body*—identity is not applied to the same thing.

We must therefore consider wherein an oak differs from a mass of matter, and that seems to me to be in this, that the one is only the cohesion of particles of matter any how united, the other such a disposition of them as constitutes the parts of an oak; and such an organization of those parts as is fit to receive and distribute nourishment, so as to continue and frame the wood, bark, and leaves, etc., of an oak, in which consists the vegetable life. That being then one plant which has such an organization of parts in one coherent body, partaking of one common life, it continues to be the same plant as long as it partakes of the same life, though that life be communicated to new particles of matter vitally united to the living plant, in a like continued organization conformable to that sort of plants. For this organization, being at any one instant in any one collection of matter, is in that particular concrete distinguished from all other, and *is* that individual life, which existing constantly from that moment both forwards and backwards, in the same continuity of insensibly succeeding parts united to the living body of the plant, it has that identity which makes the same plant, and all the parts of it, parts of the same plant, during all the time that they exist united in that continued organization, which is fit to con-

vey that common life to all the parts so united.

The case is not so much different in *brutes* but that any one may hence see what makes an animal and continues it the same. Something we have like this in machines, and may serve to illustrate it. For example, what is a watch? It is plain it is nothing but a fit organization or construction of parts to a certain end, which, when a sufficient force is added to it, it is capable to attain. If we would suppose this machine one continued body, all whose organized parts were repaired, increased, or diminished by a constant addition or separation of insensible parts, with one common life, we should have something very much like the body of an animal; with this difference, That, in an animal the fitness of the organization, and the motion wherein life consists, begin together, the motion coming from within; but in machines the force coming sensibly from without, is often away when the organ is in order, and well fitted to receive it.

This also shows wherein the identity of the same *man* consists; viz. in nothing but a participation of the same continued life, by constantly fleeting particles of matter, in succession vitally united to the same organized body. He that shall place the identity of man in anything else, but like that of other animals, in one fitly organized body, taken in any one instant, and from thence continued, under one organization of life, in several successively fleeting particles of matter united to it, will find it hard to make an embryo, one of years, mad and sober, the *same* man, by any supposition, that will not make it possible for Seth, Ismael, Socrates, Pilate, St. Austin, and Cæsar Borgia, to be the same man. For if the identity of *soul alone* makes the same *man;* and there be nothing in the nature of matter why the same individual spirit may not be united to different bodies, it will be possible that those men, living in distant ages, and of different tempers, may have been the same man: which way of speaking must be from a very strange use of the word man, applied to an idea out of which body and shape are excluded. And that way of speaking would agree yet worse with the notions of those philosophers who allow of transmigration, and are of opinion that the souls of men may, for their miscarriages, be detruded into the bodies of beasts, as fit habitations, with organs suited to the satisfaction of their brutal inclinations. But yet I think nobody, could he be sure that the *soul* of Heliogabalus were in one of his hogs, would yet say that hog were a *man* or *Heliogabalus.*

It is not therefore unity of substance that comprehends all sorts of identity, or will determine it in every case; but to conceive and judge of it aright, we must consider what idea the word it is applied to stands for: it being one thing to be the same *substance,* another the same *man,* and a third the same *person,* if *person, man,* and *substance,* are three names standing for three different ideas—for such as is the idea belonging to that name, such must be the identity; which, if it had been a little more carefully attended to, would possibly have prevented a great deal of that confusion which often occurs about this matter, with no small seeming difficulties, especially concerning *personal* identity, which therefore we shall in the next place a little consider.

An animal is a living organized body; and consequently the same animal, as we have observed, is the same continued *life* communicated to different particles of matter, as they happen successively to be united to that organized living body. And whatever is talked of other definitions, ingenious observation puts it past doubt, that the idea in our minds, of which the sound man in our mouths is the sign, is nothing else but of an animal of such a certain form. Since I think I may be con-

fident, that, whoever should see a creature of his own shape or make, though it had no more reason all its life than a cat or a parrot, would call him still a *man;* or whoever should hear a cat or a parrot discourse, reason, and philosophize, would call or think it nothing but a *cat* or a *parrot;* and say, the one was a dull irrational man, and the other a very intelligent rational parrot. A relation we have in an author of great note, is sufficient to countenance the supposition of a rational parrot. His words are:

"I had a mind to know, from Prince Maurice's own mouth, the account of a common, but much credited story, that I had heard so often from many others, of an old parrot he had in Brazil, during his government there, that spoke, and asked, and answered common questions, like a reasonable creature: so that those of his train there generally concluded it to be witchery or possession; and one of his chaplains, who lived long afterwards in Holland, would never from that time endure a parrot, but said they all had a devil in them. I had heard many particulars of this story, and assevered by people hard to be discredited, which made me ask Prince Maurice what there was of it. He said, with his usual plainness and dryness in talk, there was something true, but a great deal of false of what had been reported. I desired to know of him what there was of the first. He told me short and coldly, that he had heard of such an old parrot when he had been at Brazil; and though he believed nothing of it, and it was a good way off, yet he had so much curiosity as to send for it: that it was a very great and a very old one; and when it came first into the room where the prince was, with a great many Dutchmen about him, it said presently, *What a company of white men are here!* They asked it, what it thought that man was, pointing to the prince. It answered, *Some General or other.* When they brought it close to him, he asked it, *D'où venez-vous?* It answered, *De Marinnan*. The Prince, *A qui estes-vous?* The parrot, *A un Portugais*. The Prince, *Que fais-tu là?* Parrot, *Je garde les poulles*. The Prince laughed, and said, *Vous gardez les poulles?* The parrot answered, *Qui, moi; et je sçai bien faire;* and made the chuck four or five times that people use to make to chickens when they call them. I set down the words of this worthy dialogue in French, just as Prince Maurice said them to me. I asked him in what language the parrot spoke, and he said in Brazilian. I asked whether he understood Brazilian; he said No, but he had taken care to have two interpreters by him, the one a Dutchman that spoke Brazilian, and the other a Brazilian that spoke Dutch; that he asked them separately and privately, and both of them agreed in telling him just the same thing that the parrot had said. I could not but tell this odd story, because it is so much out of the way, and from the first hand, and what may pass for a good one; for I dare say this Prince at least believed himself in all he told me, having ever passed for a very honest and pious man: I leave it to naturalists to reason, and to other men to believe, as they please upon it; however, it is not, perhaps, amiss to relieve or enliven a busy scene sometimes with such digressions whether to the purpose or no."

I have taken care that the reader should have the story at large in the author's own words, because he seems to me not to have thought it incredible; for it cannot be imagined that so able a man as he, who had sufficiency enough to warrant all the testimonies he gives of himself, should take so much pains, in a place where it had nothing to do, to pin so close, not only a man whom he mentions as his friend, but on a Prince in whom he acknowledges very great honesty and piety, a story which, if he himself thought incredible, he could not but also think ridiculous. The Prince, it is plain, who vouches this story, and our author, who relates it from him, both of them call this talker a parrot: and I ask any one else who thinks such a story fit to be told, whether, if this parrot, and all of its kind, had always talked, as we have a prince's word for it this one did—whether, I say, they would not have passed for a race of *rational animals;* but yet, whether, for all that, they would have been allowed to be men, and not *parrots?* For I presume it is not the idea of a thinking or rational being alone that makes the *idea of a man* in most people's sense: but of a body, so and so shaped, joined to it; and if that be the idea of a man, the same successive body not shifted all at once, must, as well as the same immaterial spirit, go to the making of the same man.

This being premised, to find wherein personal identity consists, we must consider what *person* stands for—which I think, is a thinking intelligent being, that has reason and reflection, and can consider itself as itself, the same thinking thing, in different times and places; which it does only by that consciousness which is inseparable from thinking, and, as it seems to me, essential to it: it being impossible for any one to perceive without *perceiving* that he does perceive. When we see, hear, smell, taste, feel, meditate, or will anything, we know that we do so. Thus it is always as to our present sensations and perceptions: and by this every one is to himself that which he calls *self*—it not being considered, in this case, whether the same self be continued in the same or divers substances. For, since consciousness always accompanies thinking, and it is that which makes every one to be what he calls self, and thereby distinguishes himself from all other thinking things, in this alone consists personal identity, i.e., the sameness of a rational being: and as far as this consciousness can be extended backwards to any past action or thought, so far reaches the identity of that person; it is the same self now it was then; and it is by the same self with this present one that now reflects on it, that that action was done.

But it is further inquired, whether it be the same identical substance. This few would think they had reason to doubt of, if these perceptions, with their consciousness, always remained present in the mind, whereby the same thinking thing would be always consciously present, and, as would be thought, evidently the same to itself. But that which seems to make the difficulty is this, that this consciousness being interrupted always by forgetfulness, there being no moment of our lives wherein we have the whole train of all our past actions before our eyes in one view, but even the best memories losing the sight of one part whilst they are viewing another; and we sometimes, and that the greatest part of our lives, not reflecting on our past selves, being intent on our present thoughts, and in sound sleep having no thoughts at all, or at least none with that consciousness which remarks our waking thoughts—I say, in all these cases, our consciousness being interrupted, and we losing the sight of our past selves, doubts are raised whether we are the same thinking thing, i.e., the same *substance* or no. Which, however reasonable or unreasonable, concerns not *personal* identity at all. The question being what makes the same person; and not whether it be the same identical substance, which always thinks in the same person, which, in this case, matters not at all: different substances, by the same consciousness (where they do partake in it) being united into one person, as well as different bodies by the same life are united into one animal, whose identity is preserved in that change of substances by the unity of one continued life. For, it being the same consciousness that makes a man be himself to himself, personal identity depends on that only, whether it be annexed solely to one individual substance, or can be continued in a succession of several substances. For as far as any intelligent being *can* repeat the idea of any past action with the same consciousness it had of it at first, and with the same consciousness it has of any present action; so far it is the same personal self. For it is by the consciousness it has of its present thoughts and actions, that it is *self to itself* now, and so will be the same self, as far as the same consciousness can extend to actions past or to come; and would be by distance of time, or change of substance, no more two persons, than a man be two men by wearing other clothes to-day than he did yesterday, with a long or a short sleep between: the same consciousness uniting those distant actions into the same person, whatever substances contributed to their production.

That this is so, we have some kind of evidence in our very bodies, all whose particles, whilst vitally united to this same thinking conscious self, so that *we feel* when they are touched, and are affected by, and conscious of good or harm that happens to them, are a part of ourselves; i.e., of our thinking conscious self. Thus, the limbs of his body are to every one a part of himself; he sympathizes and is concerned for them. Cut off a hand, and thereby separate it from that consciousness he had of its heat, cold, and other affections, and it is then no longer a part of that which is himself, any more than the remotest part of matter. Thus, we see the *substance* whereof personal self consisted at one time may be varied at another, without the change of personal identity; there being no question about the same person, though the limbs which but now were a part of it, be cut off.

But the question is, Whether if the same substance which thinks be changed, it can be the same person; or, remaining the same, it can be different persons?

And to this I answer: First, This can be no question at all to those who place thought in a purely material animal constitution, void of an immaterial substance. For, whether their supposition be true or no, it is plain they conceive personal identity preserved in something else than identity of substance; as animal identity is preserved in identity of life and not of substance. And therefore those who place thinking in an immaterial substance only, before they can come to deal with these men, must show why personal identity cannot be preserved in the change of immaterial substances, or variety of particular immaterial substances, as well as animal identity is preserved in the change of material substances, or variety of particular bodies: unless they will say, it is one immaterial spirit that makes the same life in brutes, as it is one immaterial spirit that makes the same person in men; which the Cartesians at least will not admit, for fear of making brutes thinking things too.

But next, as to the first part of the question, Whether, if the same thinking substance (supposing immaterial substances only to think) be changed, it can be the same person? I answer, that cannot be resolved but by those who know what kind of substances they are that do think; and whether the consciousness of past actions can be transferred from one thinking substance to another. I grant were the same consciousness the same individual action it could not: but it being a present representation of a past action, why it may not be possible, that that may be represented to the mind to have been which really never was, will remain to be shown. And therefore how far the consciousness of past actions is annexed to any individual agent, so that another cannot possibly have it, will be hard for us to determine, till we know what kind of action it is that cannot be done without a reflex act of perception accompanying it, and how performed by thinking substances, who cannot think without being conscious of it. But that which we call the

same consciousness, not being the same individual act, why one intellectual substance may not have represented to it, as done by itself, what *it* never did, and was perhaps done by some other agent—why, I say, such a representation may not possibly be without reality of matter of fact, as well as several representations in dreams are, which yet whilst dreaming we take for true—will be difficult to conclude from the nature of things. And that it never is so, will by us, till we have clearer views of the nature of thinking substances, be best resolved into the goodness of God; who, as far as the happiness or misery of any of his sensible creatures is concerned in it, will not, by a fatal error of theirs, transfer from one to another that consciousness which draws reward or punishment with it. How far this may be an argument against those who would place thinking in a system of fleeting animal spirits, I leave to be considered. But yet, to return to the question before us, it must be allowed, that, if the same consciousness (which, as has been shown, is quite a different thing from the same numerical figure or motion in body) can be transferred from one thinking substance to another, it will be possible that two thinking substances may make but one person. For the same consciousness being preserved, whether in the same or different substances, the personal identity is preserved.

As to the second part of the question, Whether the same immaterial substance remaining, there may be two distinct persons; which question seems to me to be built on this—Whether the same immaterial being, being conscious of the action of its past duration, may be wholly stripped of all the consciousness of its past existence, and lose it beyond the power of ever retrieving it again: and so as it were beginning a new account from a new period, have a consciousness that *cannot* reach beyond this new state. All those who hold pre-existence are evidently of this mind; since they allow the soul to have no consciousness of what it did in that pre-existent state, either wholly separate from body, or informing any other body; and if they should not, it is plain experience would be against them. So that personal identity, reaching no further than consciousness reaches, a pre-existent spirit not having continued so many ages in a state of silence, must needs make different persons. Suppose a Christian Platonist or a Pythagorean should, upon God's having ended all his works of creation the seventh day, think his soul hath existed ever since; and should imagine it has revolved in several human bodies; as I once met with one, who was persuaded his had been the *soul* of Socrates (how reasonably I will not dispute; this I know, that in the post he filled, which was no inconsiderable one, he passed for a very rational man, and the press has shown that he wanted not parts or learning)—would any one say, that he, being not conscious of any of Socrates's actions or thoughts, could be the same *person* with Socrates? Let any one reflect upon himself, and conclude that he has in himself an immaterial spirit, which is that which thinks in him, and, in the constant change of his body keeps him the same: and is that which he calls *himself:* let him also suppose it to be the same soul that was in Nestor or Thersites, at the Siege of Troy (for souls being, as far as we know anything of them, in their nature indifferent to any parcel of matter, the supposition has no apparent absurdity in it), which it may have been, as well as it is now the soul of any other man: but he now having no consciousness of any of the actions either of Nestor or Thersites, does or can he conceive himself the same person with either of them? Can he be concerned in either of their actions? attribute them to himself, or think them his own, more than the actions of any other men that ever existed? So that this consciousness, not

reaching to any of the actions of either of those men, he is no more one *self* with either of them than if the soul or immaterial spirit that now informs him had been created, and began to exist, when it began to inform his present body; though it were never so true, that the same *spirit* that informed Nestor's or Thersites' body were numerically the same that now informs his. For this would no more make him the same person with Nestor, than if some of the particles of matter that were once a part of Nestor were now a part of this man; the same immaterial substance, without the same consciousness, no more making the same person, by being united to any body, than the same particle of matter, without consciousness, united to any body, makes the same person. But let him once find himself conscious of any of the actions of Nestor, he then finds himself the same person with Nestor.

And thus may we be able, without any difficulty, to conceive the same person at the resurrection, though in a body not exactly in make or parts the same which he had here—the same consciousness going along with the soul that inhabits it. But yet the soul alone, in the change of bodies, would scarce to any one but to him that makes the soul the man, be enough to make the same man. For should the soul of a prince, carrying with it the consciousness of the prince's past life, enter and inform the body of a cobbler, as soon as deserted by his own soul, every one sees he would be the same *person* with the prince, accountable only for the prince's actions: but who would say it was the same *man?* The body too goes to the making the man, and would, I guess, to everybody determine the man in this case, wherein the soul, with all its princely thoughts about it, would not make another man: but he would be the same cobbler to every one besides himself. I know that, in the ordinary way of speaking, the same person, and the same man, stand for one and the same thing. And indeed every one will always have a liberty to speak as he pleases, and to apply what articulate sounds to what ideas he thinks fit, and change them as often as he pleases. But yet, when we will inquire what makes the same *spirit, man,* or *person,* we must fix the ideas of spirit, man, or person in our minds; and having resolved with ourselves what we mean by them, it will not be hard to determine, in either of them, or the like, when it is the same, and when not.

But though the same immaterial substance or soul does not alone, wherever it be, and in whatsoever state, make the same *man;* yet it is plain, consciousness, as far as ever it can be extended—should it be to ages past—unites existences and actions very remote in time into the same *person,* as well as it does the existences and actions of the immediately preceding moment: so that whatever has the consciousness of present and past actions, is the same person to whom they both belong. Had I the same consciousness that I saw the ark and Noah's flood, as that I saw an overflowing of the Thames last winter, or as that I write now, I could no more doubt that I who write this now, that saw the Thames overflowed last winter, and that viewed the flood at the general deluge, was the same *self,* place that self in what *substance* you please—than that I who write this am the same *myself* now whilst I write (whether I consist of all the same substances, material or immaterial, or no) that I was yesterday. For as to this point of being the same self, it matters not whether this present self be made up of the same or other substances—I being as much concerned, and as justly accountable for any action that was done a thousand years since, appropriated to me now by this self-consciousness, as I am for what I did the last moment.

Self is that conscious thinking thing—whatever substance made up of (whether spiritual or material, simple or compounded, it matters not)—which is sensible or conscious of pleasure and pain, capable of happiness or misery, and so is concerned for itself, as far as that consciousness extends. Thus every one finds that, whilst comprehended under that consciousness, the little finger is as much a part of himself as what is most so. Upon separation of this little finger, should this consciousness go along with the little finger, and leave the rest of the body, it is evident the little finger would be the person, the same person; and self then would have nothing to do with the rest of the body. As in this case it is the consciousness that goes along with the substance, when one part is separate from another, which makes the same person, and constitutes this inseparable self: so it is in reference to substances remote in time. That with which the consciousness of this present thinking thing *can* join itself, makes the same person, and is one self with it, and with nothing else; and so attributes to itself, and owns all the actions of that thing, as its own, as far as that consciousness reaches, and no further; as every one who reflects will perceive.

In this personal identity is founded all the right and justice of reward and punishment; happiness and misery being that for which every one is concerned for *himself,* and not mattering what becomes of any *substance,* not joined to, or affected with that consciousness. For, as it is evident in the instance I gave but now, if the consciousness went along with the little finger when it was cut off, that would be the same self which was concerned for the whole body yesterday, as making part of itself, whose actions then it cannot but admit as its own now. Though, if the same body should still live, and immediately from the separation of the little finger have its own peculiar consciousness, whereof the little finger knew nothing, it would not at all be concerned for it, as a part of itself, or could own any of its actions, or have any of them imputed to him.

This may show us wherein personal identity consists: not in the identity of substance, but, as I have said, in the identity of consciousness, wherein if Socrates and the present mayor of Queinborough agree, they are the same person: if the same Socrates waking and sleeping do not partake of the same consciousness, Socrates waking and sleeping is not the same person. And to punish Socrates waking for what sleeping Socrates thought, and waking Socrates was never conscious of, would be no more of right, than to punish one twin for what his brother-twin did, whereof he knew nothing, because their outsides were so like, that they could not be distinguished; for such twins have been seen.

But yet possibly it will still be objected, Suppose I wholly lose the memory of some parts of my life, beyond a possibility of retrieving them, so that perhaps I shall never be conscious of them again; yet am I not the same person that did those actions, had those thoughts that I once was conscious of, though I have now forgot them? To which I answer, that we must here take notice what the word *I* is applied to; which, in this case, is the *man* only. And the same man being presumed to be the same person, I is easily here supposed to stand also for the same person. But if it be possible for the same man to have distinct incommunicable consciousness at different times, it is past doubt the same man would at different times make different persons; which, we see, is the sense of mankind in the solemnest declaration of their opinions, human laws not punishing the mad man for the sober man's actions, nor the sober man for what the mad man did—thereby making them two persons: which is somewhat explained by our way of speaking in English when we say such an one is "not himself," or is "beside himself"; in which

phrases it is insinuated, as if those who now, or at least first used them, thought that self was changed; the self-same person was no longer in that man.

But yet it is hard to conceive that Socrates, the same individual man, should be two persons. To help us a little in this, we must consider what is meant by Socrates, or the same individual *man*.

First, it must be either the same individual, immaterial, thinking substance; in short, the same numerical soul, and nothing else.

Secondly, or the same animal, without any regard to an immaterial soul.

Thirdly, or the same immaterial spirit united to the same animal.

Now, take which of these suppositions you please, it is impossible to make personal identity to consist in anything but consciousness; or reach any further than that does.

For, by the first of them, it must be allowed possible that a man born of different women, and in distant times, may be the same man. A way of speaking which, whoever admits, must allow it possible for the same man to be two distinct persons, as any two that have lived in different ages without the knowledge of one another's thoughts.

By the second and third, Socrates, in this life and after it, cannot be the same man any way, but by the same consciousness; and so making human identity to consist in the same thing wherein we place personal identity, there will be no difficulty to allow the same man to be the same person. But then they who place human identity in consciousness only, and not in something else, must consider how they will make the infant Socrates the same man with Socrates after the resurrection. But whatsoever to some men makes a man, and consequently the same individual man, wherein perhaps few are agreed, personal identity can by us be placed in nothing but consciousness (which is that alone which makes what we call *self*) without involving us in great absurdities.

But is not a man drunk and sober the same person? why else is he punished for the fact he commits when drunk, though he be never afterwards conscious of it? Just as much the same person as a man that walks, and does other things in his sleep, is the same person, and is answerable for any mischief he shall do in it. Human laws punish both, with a justice suitable to *their* way of knowledge; because, in these cases, they cannot distinguish certainly what is real, what counterfeit: and so the ignorance in drunkenness or sleep is not admitted as a plea. For, though punishment be annexed to personality, and personality to consciousness, and the drunkard perhaps be not conscious of what he did, yet human judicatures justly punish him; because the fact is proved against him, but want of consciousness cannot be proved for him. But in the Great Day, wherein the secrets of all hearts shall be laid open, it may be reasonable to think, no one shall be made to answer for what he knows nothing of; but shall receive his doom, his conscience accusing or excusing him.

Nothing but consciousness can unite remote existences into the same person: the identity of substance will not do it; for whatever substance there is, however framed, without consciousness there is no person: and a carcass may be a person, as well as any sort of substance be so, without consciousness.

Could we suppose two distinct incommunicable consciousnesses acting the same body, the one constantly by day, the other by night; and, on the other side, the same consciousness, acting by intervals, two distinct bodies: I ask, in the first case, whether the day and the night—man would not be two as distinct persons as Socrates and Plato? And whether, in the second case, there would not be one person in two distinct bodies, as much as one man is the same in two distinct clothings? Nor is it at all material to say, that this same, and this distinct consciousness, in the cases above mentioned, is owing to the same and distinct immaterial substances, bringing it with them to those bodies; which, whether true or no, alters not the case: since it is evident the personal identity would equally be determined by the consciousness, whether that consciousness were annexed to some individual immaterial substance or no. For, granting that the thinking substance in man must be necessarily supposed immaterial, it is evident that immaterial thinking thing may sometimes part with its past consciousness, and be restored to it again: as appears in the forgetfulness men often have of their past actions; and the mind many times recovers the memory of a past consciousness, which it had lost for twenty years together. Make these intervals of memory and forgetfulness to take their turns regularly by day and night, and you have two persons with the same immaterial spirit, as much as in the former instance two persons with the same body. So that self is not determined by identity or diversity of substance, which it cannot be sure of, but only by identity of consciousness.

Abhidharmakosha

VASUBANDHU

Vasubandhu (4th century A.D.) argues in the dialogue that follows that there is no self. This so-called "Personalist controversy" is taken from the famous fourth-century work by Vasubandhu, the Abhidharmakosha. *Personalism, at the time of the writing of that work, was a flourishing sect in India claiming approximately 60,000 adherents out of a total of 200,000 Buddhist monks in India.*

THE PERSONALIST CONTROVERSY

Is final deliverance then possible outside this Dharma, and can it be won on the basis of non-Buddhist doctrines? No, it cannot, for all other teachings are corrupted by false ideas about a "self." Instead of taking it as a mere conventional term applied to a series of impersonal processes, they believe in a self which is a substance independent of the Skandhas. But the mere belief in such a self must of necessity generate defilements. Those who hold it will be forced to pursue life in the Samsaric world, and will be unable to free themselves completely from it.

The Personalist thesis, first part: But is it not true that a Buddhist school, the Personalists, speak of a Person who is neither identical with the Skandhas, nor different from them? And is not this Person a kind of self? And yet, as Buddhists they should be able to win deliverance!

We must ask ourselves whether this Person exists as a *real entity*, i.e., as one of the separate elements of existence, like the elementary sight-objects, sounds, and so on, which careful analysis reveals; or whether it has a *merely nominal existence*, which denotes a combination of simple elements, as "milk" is a combination of sights, smells, tastes and touchables.

THE PERSONALIST: Why should not either assumption be true?

VASUBANDHU: If the Person is a real entity with a nature of its own, it must be different from the elementary data, just as these are different from one another. It must then be either produced by causes, or unconditioned. In the first case it is not eternal, as you maintain, and you must be able to state its conditions in detail. In the second case you adopt a clearly non-Buddhistic doctrine, and, in addition, your Person could not do anything, and would be a rather useless hypothesis. The Person is therefore unlikely to be a real entity. But if you regard it as a mere designation, then your view does not differ in the least from ours.

THE PERSONALIST: We claim that there is a Person; but we do not say that he is an entity. Nor do we believe that he exists merely as a designation for the Skandhas. What we say is that the word "Person" denotes a kind of structural unity which is found in correlation with the Skandhas of one individual, i.e. with those elements which are actually present, internal to him, and appropriated by him.

The Personalist thesis, second part: The Personalist also teaches that the Person is "ineffable," that his relation to the elements cannot be defined, that he is neither identical nor non-identical with them. He distinguishes five kinds of cognizable things—the first three are the conditioned dharmas, i.e., those past, future and present; the fourth is the Unconditioned; and the fifth is the "ineffable," and refers to the Person. But if the Person were quite ineffable, if nothing at all could be stated about it, then one could not say of it either that it is the fifth category or that it is not!

THE PERSONALIST: It is perfectly true that the Person is not an object of consciousness.

VASUBANDHU: Very well, but then one can never be aware of it; if unaware of it, one cannot cognize it; if it cannot be an object of cognition, how can its existence ever be established? And if one cannot do that, your system falls to pieces. *(Vasubandhu then quotes a number of canonical texts, of which I give three here.)* The *Bimbisarasutra* says: "The foolish ignorant common people, putting their trust in words, imagine that there is such a thing as a self. But there is neither "I" nor "mine." There are only dharmas, ill at ease, future, present and past." In the *Kshudragama* the Buddha says to the Brahmin Badari: "Badari, one who has heard the four holy truths, he can free himself from all bonds: thought alone de-

files, thought alone purifies. The self has, in fact, not the nature of a self. To think that there is a self is a perverted view. There is nowhere here a living being, there is no self; dharmas alone together with their causes do exist. No person can be found in all the Skandhas when examined. And, having seen that a person is inwardly empty, you must also see the outside world as empty. Even those who meditate on emptiness cannot be said to exist." And another *Sutra* says: "Five calamities result from a belief in a self: wrong opinions about the actual status of a self, an individual, a soul; non-distinction from non-Buddhists; one goes astray on a wrong road; thought does not leap forward into emptiness, finds no serenity in it, does not abide in it, does not resolve upon it; one will never be sufficiently purified to win the qualities of a saint."

THE PERSONALIST: These texts have no authority for us. They do not form part of our Scriptures.

VASUBANDHU: What then is the authority behind your system—your sect or the word of the Buddha? How can you claim the Buddha as your Teacher, how can you be Shakyamuni's sons, if you do not accept all the Buddha's words as binding on you?

THE PERSONALIST: The texts you have just quoted are not the Buddha's own words, and they are not in the Scriptures of our school.

VASUBANDHU: That is not very convincing. For all the other schools accept these texts, and they are not in conflict either with other Sutras, or with the Dharma. This is therefore sheer effrontery on your part. And how then, incidentally, do you explain the Sutra which says: "To mistake for a self that which is not a self, that is a perverted notion, a perverted idea, a perverted opinion."

THE PERSONALIST: The Sutra only says that it is a perversion to mistake a not-self for a self; but it does not say that it is a perversion to recognize a self as a self. And also: According to your doctrines the Lord could not possibly be omniscient. You say that all thoughts and mental activities change incessantly, and that each mental act lasts only for one moment. How then can it know all the dharmas? Only an abiding Person can be omniscient.

VASUBANDHU: May I point out that then your Person would be eternal, and that contradicts your statements that we cannot say whether he is eternal or not. And this is how we account for the Buddha's omniscience: For us the word "Buddha" is a term denoting a series of momentary events. We do not believe that in one single moment he just knows all the dharmas simultaneously. The unique feature of his series of momentary mental actions lies in the fact that, by the mere act of turning his mind on anything, there arises immediately a correct and unperverted knowledge of any object whatever, if there should be at the same time the desire to know it. That is the sense in which we speak of "omniscience."

THE PERSONALIST: Why then, if the word "person" means nothing but the five Skandhas which form the range of grasping, did the Lord teach the "Burden Sutra," which says: "I will teach you the burden, its taking up, its laying down, and the bearer of the burden. The five Skandhas, which are the range of grasping, are the burden. Craving takes up the burden. The renunciation of craving lays it down. The bearer of the burden is the person: this venerable man, with such and such a name, born so and so, of such and such a clan, who sustains himself on this or that food, experiences these pleasures and pains, lives for just so long, stays here for just so long, terminates his life-span in just this way." For, if "person" were only another name for the Skandhas, if "person" and Skandhas were actually identical, then the burden would carry itself, and that is absurd.

VASUBANDHU: You have misunderstood the message of this Sutra. The Lord speaks of a "person" here only in order to conform to the usage of the world. In fact this so-called "personality" is nothing but a series of consecutive impersonal momentary events, all of them linked to suffering. But the processes which have taken place in the past cause suffering in those which succeed them. The preceding Skandhas are therefore called the "burden," the subsequent ones its "bearer."

THE PERSONALIST: Moreover, another Sutra says: "One person, when he arises, when he is born in the world, is born for the weal of the many. Who is that one person? It is the Tathagata."

VASUBANDHU: Here again the Lord just conforms to the usage of the world. For that reason he treats here as a unit that which is in fact a complex; it is quite usual for people to speak of a "word," although it is in fact a compound of syllables, or of a heap of rice, although it obviously comprises a multiplicity of grains. In addition, this Sutra says of the person that "he arises," and that, contrary to your teaching, makes him into something conditioned.

THE PERSONALIST: The term "arises" has one meaning when applied to the dharmas, another when applied to the Person. A dharma is said to "arise" because it exists now after not having existed before. A person, however, is said to "arise," or to "be born" when, on rebirth in a certain form, he takes up, or acquires, certain constituents, which make him into "this man," "this animal," "this ghost," and so on. It is quite usual to say of a man who has acquired a knowledge of grammar that "a grammarian is born," or "a grammarian has arisen," but that does not mean that he has come from nothing. The person "arises" in the sense that he acquires at a certain time a certain series of attributes, in the above quotation those of a Buddha.

VASUBANDHU: This explanation has

been expressly condemned by the Lord. For He has said: "There is action, and there is the retribution of action. But apart from the causally linked sequence of impersonal dharmas there is no one who acts, there is no one who gives up one set of Skandhas, and takes up others instead." In consequence there is no person who gives up his Skandhas at death and takes up others at rebirth.

THE PERSONALIST: Nevertheless, the Person is real, for it has been said: "To say that the self does not exist, in truth and in reality, is a wrong view."

VASUBANDHU: This is no proof, for it has also been said that to affirm the existence of a self is a wrong view. We Abhidharmists believe that both the general affirmation and the general negation of a self are extremist views, in accordance with the well-known saying of the *Vatsogotra-sutra*: "Those, Ananda, who affirm a self fall into the extreme of the belief in its eternal continuation; those who deny it fall into the extreme of the belief in its eventual annihilation."

THE PERSONALIST: If the Person does not exist, who then is it that wanders about in Samsara? It is difficult to see how the Samsara itself can wander about.

VASUBANDHU: The correct explanation is, however, quite simple: When a flame burns a piece of wood, one says that it wanders along it; nevertheless there is nothing but a series of flame-moments. Likewise there is a continuous series of processes which incessantly renews itself, and which is falsely called a living being. Impelled by craving, this series is said to "wander" in Samsara.

THE PERSONALIST: If the momentary processes alone exist, how can you explain these words of the Lord, when he said, on recalling one of his former lives: "This sage Sunetra, who existed in the past, that Sunetra was I." All the psycho-physical elements have changed, and it can therefore only be the "person" that makes the Buddha and Sunetra identical.

VASUBANDHU: What in fact is it that the Lord thinks of when he speaks here of "I"? If, as you say, he means the "person," then the past "I" is identical with the present "I," and your "person" will be permanent, as against your intentions. For us, however, the Lord only meant to say that his actually present dharmas are parts of the same continuous series of dharmas as those of Sunetra. As one says: "This fire has burned its way to here." In any case, you assert the existence of a real self, which is of a nature so subtle and elusive, that the Tathagatas alone can see it. In that case, the Buddhas would become believers in "I" and "mine," with all its pernicious consequences for the spiritual life. They will form an attachment to that part of the universe which they come to consider as their own, and in that way they will be far removed from deliverance!

THE PERSONALIST: It is only when, as is the habit of non-Buddhists, something which is not the true Self is mistaken for the true Self, that one will feel affection for that pretended self. If, however, one sees, as the Buddhas do, the Ineffable Person as the true self, then, because that actually is the true self, no affection for it is thereby engendered.

Part 2

PROBLEMS
OF EPISTEMOLOGY

INTRODUCTION:
WHAT IS EPISTEMOLOGY?

"Epistemology" is a compound Greek word formed from two simpler parts, *epistemé,* which means "knowledge," and the Greek word *logos,* which means "discourse." Hence, "epistemology" means "a discourse on the nature of knowledge." The epistemologist is thus interested in questions like, What is knowledge? or, What are the criteria of knowledge? How does one know or come to know anything at all? And, finally and most importantly, the epistemologist wants to know, How does one know that one knows anything? This last question is most important, for it gets the philosopher into a discussion of the grounds of knowledge, i.e., the ways, or means, of knowing, and it is in discussions of these ways and their validity or efficacy that philosophy has been most useful.

KNOWING, KNOWLEDGE, AND TRUE BELIEF

Philosophers have generally distinguished between two general kinds of knowing, and the distinction seems to make plausible sense. The distinction is between knowing *how* and knowing *that,* i.e., between knowing how to do something-or-other like tie my shoelaces, and knowing that my shoelaces are untied. The first kind of knowing is called *practical knowledge* and the second kind of knowing is called *theoretical knowledge* or *propositional knowledge,* and the two, as can be seen, are quite distinct. Thus I can have all kinds of theoretical knowledge about bicycle riding, shoelace tying, swimming, mountain climbing, and so on, but at the same time be totally inept at bicycle riding, shoelace tying, swimming, mountain climbing, and so on. Knowing how involves a skill. A practical expertise and ability are necessary in successfully accomplishing or doing something: and the actual doing itself may be totally unrelated to knowing that a set of statements is true.

On the other hand, there may be some occasions in which theoretical knowledge leads directly to practical knowledge, i.e., where knowing *that* leads easily and comfortably to knowing *how.* Thus, in knowing that plants need both water and sunshine in order to grow, I would as a consequence know how, in a loose sense of that word, to raise plants properly. Other examples might easily spring to mind wherein theoretical knowledge about the truth of a set of propositions makes practical knowledge possible, or easier, or even inevitable. And yet the distinction is important, and not the least of the reasons is that in the West professional philosophers in general have been notoriously interested only in propositional knowledge. Western philosophy on the whole has been concerned primarily with knowledge-claims involving statements that purport to be true. Non-Western philosophy is not, in the main, oriented to this same theoretical approach to knowledge. Rather, the purpose of knowledge as well as the purpose of philosophy and even life generally, is and has been wholly practical. The commitment that most non-Western philosophy makes to man, life, and the world is not unlike the commitment made by the defenders of the so-called "liberal arts" in the heyday of that progressive educational philosophy in Western universities. The apologists and defenders of this liberal education maintained that education should aim at the liberation and freedom of the mind of man from ignorance, sloth, and the general depradations of youth. The educated man was the free and happy man, hence education, it might well have been argued, led to that *eudaimonia,* happiness, that the Greeks made so much of. The liberal arts of the Renaissance—nameiy, astronomy, arithmetic, geometry, music, rhetoric, grammar, and logic—all led to this happy liberation, and thus liberal education and the liberal arts had, curiously enough, the most practical aim possible. This aim was not simply knowledge for knowledge's sake, nor did this education lead to a vocation or occupation in society, but rather the liberal arts led instead to the cessation of mental enslavement: Much non-Western philosophy is set upon that same road; the knowledge that it discovers has the same happy effect of freedom or liberation.

KNOWLEDGE AS JUSTIFIED TRUE BELIEF

When I say, "I know that p" (where p stands for any meaningful English sentence, i.e., any expression that is either true or false), certainly one of the first things that I am saying is that p is true. It would undoubtedly sound odd to say, "I know that Sanskrit is an Indo-European language but it's not true that Sanskrit is an Indo-European language." Therefore, we say that what I know—truly know, that is—must be true. I cannot be said to know the false or that which is false. Now I may know that a particular proposition is false, but then what I know is that it is true that that particular false proposition is false, i.e., I know the true or that which is true. I know that it is false that the Indus Valley civilization flourished in the fifth century of the Christian era, so what I know to be true is that that statement about that date of the Indus Valley civilization is false. Hence, the *truth* of what I know, the *truth* of the proposition that I know, is part of the definition of knowledge, for I could not really know something unless it were true.

In technical terms we say that the truth of p is a *necessary condition,* but not a *sufficient condition,* for knowledge. To say that a condition is necessary—i.e., to say that "p is true" is a necessary condition for knowing that p—is to say two things: first, that without this necessary condition to knowing that p, knowledge could not occur, it would be impossible; second, that this condition of knowing that p, alone and by itself, is not sufficient or enough to bring knowledge into being. The latter point is significant, for it means, among other things, that something else, some other remaining necessary conditions, must be found to bring about the knowledge that we are attempting to define. What we are searching for is that set of necessary conditions which, when taken together, will form the sufficient condition that will bring knowledge about. In calling this truth-condition "necessary" we simply indicate, then, that it must be present if knowledge is to occur, but that it alone and by itself is not a sufficient condition for the production of knowledge. Thus, to repeat, the truth of p is a first and necessary condition for knowing that p. Only true propositions are known.

When I say, "I know that p," certainly one of the second things that I am saying is that I believe p. It would, again, probably sound odd indeed to say, "I know that Sanskrit is a highly inflected language but I don't believe that it is highly inflected." It is not only odd, it is self-contradictory, and no one wants to be guilty of committing the intellectual sin of self-contradiction. Therefore, we say that what is known must be believed. Thus all knowledge has a belief component that serves to ground knowledge, existentially, in a knower, such that in order to be a knower in relation to a known one must first of all be a believer of that which is known. In other words, if there were no human beings, and they are after all the only terrestrial creatures capable of believing anything, knowledge would be impossible, i.e., there would be no knowledge. Thus, to summarize, the belief that p or the belief in p by the knower is a second and necessary condition for knowing that p. Only believed propositions are known.

But although the belief component of knowledge is necessary for knowledge, it must seem, nonetheless, a little odd to talk about belief in this way. Does one just believe a statement p? What sense does it make to say, "I believe that p"? Believing is the sort of thing that demands an object, a proper object, and p is not strictly speaking a proper object for believing. What one believes about p is what is important here. Merely believing in God doesn't make much sense—it is rather what one believes *about* God and *about* p that is important. Thus to say, "I believe in God," is really shorthand for saying, "I believe the following *truths* about God: He is real, He is good, He is all-knowing, etc.," or, "I trust in God." To say, "I believe that p," is really shorthand for saying, "I believe that p is true." Thus when I say that I believe that by *samsāra* or rebirth I will be carried on to another body when this one dies, I am really saying that I believe that it is true that by *samsāra* I will move on to another body when this one dies. Our two necessary conditions for knowledge—namely, belief and the truth of that which is believed—are now oddly combined into a single necessary condition for knowledge—namely, true belief.

But true belief is not yet sufficient for knowledge, as a little reflection will show. For if a person cannot give an account or justification for what he believes truly, then we usually don't say that he really knows. We say that such a believer is lucky, or a good guesser, or something like that. Suppose that everything that I believe, for example, always turns out to be true. Suppose I believe that the temperature will be 75 degrees tomorrow and the temperature is, curiously enough, 75 degrees tomorrow. Suppose I believe that the amount of money you have on your person is $5 and the amount you have is, indeed, $5. Further, suppose that every prediction I thus make about temperature and money turns out to be true. Suppose now you ask me, How do you do it? Now from the hypothesis we are working with here, it is supposed that I can give no account or justification for my true beliefs about future or present events regarding temperatures and money in people's pockets or purses. I just don't know how or why I believe that these things will happen in the way that I believe they will happen. And because I don't know, it follows that I really don't know; that is to say, without an account, a justification, or evidence, my true belief is just that—a true belief—and it is not knowledge. Thus true belief still stands as a necessary but not a sufficient condition for knowledge. What is needed to carry true belief out of the clutches of good guesses or lucky hunches is a third and final necessary condition for knowledge—namely, an account or justification for what one believes truly.

When I say, "I know that p," undoubtedly then, one of the third and final things that I am saying is that I have evidence for believing that p, or rather that I have a justification for what I believe and claim to know. It would certainly sound odd, once more, to say, "I know that the Aryans drove chariots but I have no evidence for this." It might sound all right to say, "I believe that the Aryans drove chariots but I have no evidence for this"; but this serves, once more, to underscore the basic difference between belief, true or otherwise, and knowledge. What separates true belief from knowledge is that knowledge entails a justification of that which is known and belief does not. Thus we say that justification or evidence forms the third and final necessary condition for knowledge. Thus, to summarize, the evidence for p is a necessary but not, once again, a sufficient condition for knowledge.

But then we have three necessary conditions for knowledge of p—namely, p is true, the belief that p, and the evidence for p. So in summary we can say that when I say, "I know that p," it is sufficient for that knowledge that p be true, and that I believe p, and that I have evidence for p. In other words, knowledge for the epistemologist is simply justified true belief.[1]

TRUTH

Pilate's question, "What is truth?", surely is freighted with much dramatic significance when it is presented in the Gospel according to John. Yet in a more pedestrian way it must be addressed by every inquirer and addressed most meticulously by the epistemologist. If knowledge has to do with justified true belief then we must not only look at what counts to show a belief to be true but we must also be quite clear about just what we mean when we say that it is true.

The many attempts to define the nature of truth seem to be grouped into three families. The *correspondence* theory holds that a proposition is true

[1] For an expanded treatment of this entire topic, see John Hospers, *An Introduction to Philosophical Analysis* (Englewood Cliffs, N.J.: Prentice-Hall, Inc., 1967), pp. 143–49.

if it corresponds to what the facts are. Thus, the proposition, "The earth is round," is a true proposition because the earth in fact is round. The *coherence* theory claims that a proposition is true if it is necessitated by other propositions known to be true. Thus, the proposition, "Vertical angles are equal," is a true proposition because it is necessitated by, or coheres with, other true propositions including "equals subtracted from equals leave equals," "angles equal to a straight line are equal to each other," etc. The *pragmatic* theory of truth states that a proposition is true insofar as the holding to it or the acceptance of it produces satisfactory or successful consequences in our experience. Had he been an epistemologist as well as a sailor, Columbus might have resorted to something like the pragmatic theory of truth in urging his men to sail westward.

Finally, it may be that we are not always consistent in adopting a single theory of truth. It may be that we are quite fickle in our allegiance and trade off our theories to suit our purposes. Or, as suggested in one of the following selections, the three theories may not be quite as opposed as they at first seem. (A more complete elucidation of the three theories of truth will be found in the article on the Nyāya theory of knowledge by Satischandra Chatterjee, which appears below.)

Knowledge as Justified True Belief

Theaetetus

PLATO

Plato's dialogue, Theaetetus, is a classic in the tradition of Socratic inquiry, for it represents an attempt to get at the roots of knowledge by analyzing and displaying the separate elements that must stand as necessary conditions of all real knowledge. The dialogue steers in the direction of answering the question, What is knowledge? by arguing that knowledge must be true opinion together with an account. Along the route to this "conclusion" we are witness to one of the finest philosophic exchanges in the Western tradition, an exchange between Socrates and the youth, Theaetetus.

[The text following represents the latter part of the dialogue.]

SOCRATES: Then, once more, what shall we say that knowledge is? for we are not going to lose heart as yet.

THEAETETUS: Certainly, I shall not lose heart, if you do not.

SOCRATES: What definition will be most consistent with our former views?

THEAETETUS: I cannot think of any but our old one, Socrates.

SOCRATES: What was it?

THEAETETUS: Knowledge was said by us to be true opinion; and true opinion is surely unerring, and the results which follow from it are all noble and good.

SOCRATES: He who led the way into the river, Theaetetus, said "The experiment will show"; and perhaps if we go forward in the search, we may stumble upon the thing which we are looking for; but if we stay where we are, nothing will come to light.

THEAETETUS: Very true; let us go forward and try.

SOCRATES: The trail soon comes to an end, for a whole profession is against us.

THEAETETUS: How is that, and what profession do you mean?

SOCRATES: The profession of the great wise ones who are called orators and lawyers; for these persuade men by their art and make them think whatever they like, but they do not teach them. Do you imagine that there are any teachers in the world so clever as to be able to convince others of the truth about acts of robbery or violence, of which they were not eye-witnesses, while a little water is flowing in the clepsydra?

From the Jowett translation of *Theaetetus*.

THEAETETUS: Certainly not, they can only persuade them.

SOCRATES: And would you not say that persuading them is making them have an opinion?

THEAETETUS: To be sure.

SOCRATES: When, therefore, judges are justly persuaded about matters which you can know only by seeing them, and not in any other way, and when thus judging of them from report they attain a true opinion about them, they judge without knowledge and yet are rightly persuaded, if they have judged well.

THEAETETUS: Certainly.

SOCRATES: And yet, O my friend, if true opinion in law courts and knowledge are the same, the perfect judge could not have judged rightly without knowledge; and therefore I must infer that they are not the same.

THEAETETUS: That is a distinction, Socrates, which I have heard made by some one else, but I had forgotten it. He said that true opinion, combined with reason, was knowledge, but that the opinion which had no reason was out of the sphere of knowledge; and that things of which there is no rational account are not knowable—such was the singular expression which he used—and that things which have a reason or explanation are knowable.

SOCRATES: Excellent; but then, how did he distinguish between things which are and are not "knowable"? I wish that you would repeat to me what he said, and then I shall know whether you and I have heard the same tale.

THEAETETUS: I do not know whether I can recall it; but if another person would tell me, I think that I could follow him.

SOCRATES: Let me give you, then, a dream in return for a dream: Methought that I too had a dream, and I heard in my dream that the primeval letters or ele-

ments out of which you and I and all other things are compounded, have no reason or explanation; you can only name them, but no predicate can be either affirmed or denied of them, for in the one case existence, in the other nonexistence is already implied, neither of which must be added, if you mean to speak of this or that thing by itself alone. It should not be called itself, or that, or each, or alone, or this, or the like; for these go about everywhere and are applied to all things, but are distinct from them; whereas, if the first elements could be described, and had a definition of their own, they would be spoken of apart from all else. But none of these primeval elements can be defined; they can only be named, for they have nothing but a name, and the things which are compounded of them, as they are complex, are expressed by a combination of names, for the combination of names is the essence of a definition. Thus, then, the elements or letters are only objects of perception, and cannot be defined or known; but the syllables or combinations of them are known and expressed, and are apprehended by true opinion. When, therefore, any one forms the true opinion of anything without rational explanation, you may say that his mind is truly exercised, but has no knowledge; for he who cannot give and receive a reason for a thing, has no knowledge of that thing; but when he adds rational explanation, then, he is perfected in knowledge and may be all that I have been denying of him. Was that the form in which the dream appeared to you?

THEAETETUS: Precisely.

SOCRATES: And you allow and maintain that true opinion, combined with definition or rational explanation, is knowledge?

THEAETETUS: Exactly.

SOCRATES: Then may we assume, Theaetetus, that to-day, and in this casual manner, we have found a truth which in former times many wise men have grown old and have not found?

THEAETETUS: At any rate, Socrates, I am satisfied with the present statement.

SOCRATES: Which is probably correct—for how can there be knowledge apart from definition and true opinion? And yet there is one point in what has been said which does not quite satisfy me.

THEAETETUS: What was it?

SOCRATES: What might seem to be the most ingenious notion of all: That the elements or letters are unknown, but the combination or syllables known.

THEAETETUS: And was that wrong?

SOCRATES: We shall soon know; for we have as hostages the instances which the author of the argument himself used.

THEAETETUS: What hostages?

SOCRATES: The letters, which are the elements; and the syllables, which are the combinations—he reasoned, did he not, from the letters of the alphabet?

THEAETETUS: Yes; he did.

SOCRATES: Let us take them and put them to the test, or rather, test ourselves: What was the way in which we learned letters? and, first of all, are we right in saying that syllables have a definition, but that letters have no definition?

THEAETETUS: I think so.

SOCRATES: I think so too; for, suppose that some one asks you to spell the first syllable of my name: Theaetetus, he says, what is SO?

THEAETETUS: I should reply S and O.

SOCRATES: That is the definition which you would give of the syllable?

THEAETETUS: I should.

SOCRATES: I wish that you would give me a similar definition of the S.

THEAETETUS: But how can any one, Socrates, tell the elements of an element? I can only reply, that S is a consonant, a mere noise, as of the tongue hissing; B, and most other letters, again, are neither

vowel-sounds nor noises. Thus letters may be most truly said to be undefined; for even the most distinct of them, which are the seven vowels, have a sound only, but no definition at all.

SOCRATES: Then, I suppose, my friend, that we have been so far right in our idea about knowledge?

THEAETETUS: Yes; I think that we have.

SOCRATES: Well, but have we been right in maintaining that the syllables can be known, but not the letters?

THEAETETUS: I think so.

SOCRATES: And do we mean by a syllable two letters, or if there are more, all of them, or a single idea which arises out of the combination of them?

THEAETETUS: I should say that we mean all the letters.

SOCRATES: Take the case of the two letters S and O, which form the first syllable of my own name; must not he who knows the syllable, know both of them?

THEAETETUS: Certainly.

SOCRATES: He knows, that is, the S and O?

THEAETETUS: Yes.

SOCRATES: But can he be ignorant of either singly and yet know both together?

THEAETETUS: Such a supposition, Socrates, is monstrous and unmeaning.

SOCRATES: But if he cannot know both without knowing each, then if he is ever to know the syllable, he must know the letters first; and thus the fine theory has again taken wings and departed.

THEAETETUS: Yes, with wonderful celerity.

SOCRATES: Yes, we did not keep watch properly. Perhaps we ought to have maintained that a syllable is not the letters, but rather one single idea framed out of them, having a separate form distinct from them.

THEAETETUS: Very true; and a more likely notion than the other.

SOCRATES: Take care; let us not be

cowards and betray a great and imposing theory.

THEAETETUS: No, indeed.

SOCRATES: Let us assume then, as we now say, that the syllable is a simple form arising out of the several combinations of harmonious elements—of letters or of any other elements.

THEAETETUS: Very good.

SOCRATES: And it must have no parts.

THEAETETUS: Why?

SOCRATES: Because that which has parts must be a whole of all the parts. Or would you say that a whole, although formed out of the parts, is a single notion different from all the parts?

THEAETETUS: I should.

SOCRATES: And would you say that all and the whole are the same, or different?

THEAETETUS: I am not certain; but, as you like me to answer at once, I shall hazard the reply, that they are different.

SOCRATES: I approve of your readiness, Theaetetus, but I must take time to think whether I equally approve of your answer.

THEAETETUS: Yes; the answer is the point.

SOCRATES: According to this new view, the whole is supposed to differ from all?

THEAETETUS: Yes.

SOCRATES: Well, but is there any difference between all [in the plural] and the all [in the singular]? Take the case of number—when we say one, two, three, four, five, six; or when we say twice three, or three times two, or four and two, or three and two and one, are we speaking of the same or of different numbers?

THEAETETUS: Of the same.

SOCRATES: That is of six?

THEAETETUS: Yes.

SOCRATES: And in each form of expression we spoke of all the six?

THEAETETUS: True.

SOCRATES: Again, in speaking of all [in the plural], is there not one thing which we express?

THEAETETUS: Of course there is.

SOCRATES: And that is six?

THEAETETUS: Yes.

SOCRATES: Then in predicating the word "all" of things measured by number, we predicate at the same time a singular and a plural?

THEAETETUS: Clearly we do.

SOCRATES: Again, the number of the acre and the acre are the same; are they not?

THEAETETUS: Yes.

SOCRATES: And the number of the stadium in like manner is the stadium?

THEAETETUS: Yes.

SOCRATES: And the army is the number of the army; and in all similar cases, the entire number of anything is the entire thing?

THEAETETUS: True.

SOCRATES: And the number of each is the parts of each?

THEAETETUS: Exactly.

SOCRATES: Then as many things as have parts are made up of parts?

THEAETETUS: Clearly

SOCRATES: But all the parts are admitted to be the all, if the entire number is the all?

THEAETETUS: True.

SOCRATES: Then the whole is not made up of the parts, for it would be the all, if consisting of all the parts?

THEAETETUS: That is the inference.

SOCRATES: But is a part a part of anything but the whole?

THEAETETUS: Yes, of the all.

SOCRATES: You make a valiant defense, Theaetetus. And yet is not the all that of which nothing is wanting?

THEAETETUS: Certainly.

SOCRATES: And is not a whole likewise that from which nothing is absent? but that from which anything is absent is neither a whole nor all—if wanting in anything, both equally lose their entirety of nature.

THEAETETUS: I now think that there is no difference between a whole and all.

SOCRATES: But were we not saying that when a thing has parts, all the parts will be a whole and all?

THEAETETUS: Certainly.

SOCRATES: Then, as I was saying before, must not the alternative be that either the syllable is not the letters, and then the letters are not parts of the syllable, or that the syllable will be the same with the letters, and will therefore be equally known with them?

THEAETETUS: You are right.

SOCRATES: And, in order to avoid this, we suppose it to be different from them?

THEAETETUS: Yes.

SOCRATES: But if letters are not parts of syllables, can you tell me of any other parts of syllables, which are not letters?

THEAETETUS: No, indeed, Socrates; for if I admit the existence of parts in a syllable, it would be ridiculous in me to give up letters and seek for other parts.

SOCRATES: Quite true, Theaetetus, and therefore, according to our present view, a syllable must surely be some indivisible form?

THEAETETUS: True.

SOCRATES: But do you remember, my friend, that only a little while ago we admitted and approved the statement, that of the first elements out of which all other things are compounded there could be no definition, because each of them when taken by itself is uncompounded; nor can one rightly attribute to them the words "being" or "this," because they are alien and inappropriate words, and for this reason the letters or elements were indefinable and unknown?

THEAETETUS: I remember.

SOCRATES: And is not this also the reason why they are simple and indivisible? I can see no other.

THEAETETUS: No other reason can be given.

SOCRATES: Then is not the syllable in the same case as the elements or letters, if it has no parts and is one form?

THEAETETUS: To be sure.

SOCRATES: If, then, a syllable is a whole, and has many parts or letters, the letters as well as the syllable must be intelligible and expressible, since all the parts are acknowledged to be the same as the whole?

THEAETETUS: True.

SOCRATES: But if it be one and indivisible, then the syllables and the letters are alike undefined and unknown, and for the same reason?

THEAETETUS: I cannot deny that.

SOCRATES: We cannot, therefore, agree in the opinion of him who says that the syllable can be known and expressed, but not the letters.

THEAETETUS: Certainly not; if we may trust the argument.

SOCRATES: Well, but will you not be equally inclined to disagree with him, when you remember your own experience in learning to read?

THEAETETUS: What experience?

SOCRATES: Why, that in learning you were kept trying to distinguish the separate letters both by the eye and by the ear, in order that when you heard them spoken or saw them written, you might not be confused by their position.

THEAETETUS: Very true.

SOCRATES: And is the education of the harp-player complete unless he can tell what string answers to a particular note; the notes, as every one would allow, are the elements or letters of music?

THEAETETUS: Exactly.

SOCRATES: Then, if we argue from the letters and syllables which we know to other simples and compounds, we shall say that the letters or simple elements as a class are much more certainly known than the syllables, and much more indispensable to a perfect knowledge of any subject; and if some one says that the syllable is known and the letter unknown, we shall consider that either intentionally or unintentionally he is talking nonsense?

THEAETETUS: Exactly.

SOCRATES: And there might be given other proofs of this belief, if I am not mistaken. But do not let us in looking for them lose sight of the question before us, which is the meaning of the statement, that right opinion with rational definition or explanation is the most perfect form of knowledge.

THEAETETUS: We must not.

SOCRATES: Well, and what is the meaning of the term "explanation"? I think that we have a choice of three meanings.

THEAETETUS: What are they?

SOCRATES: In the first place, the meaning may be, manifesting one's thought by the voice with verbs and nouns, imaging an opinion in the stream which flows from the lips, as in a mirror or water. Does not explanation appear to be of this nature?

THEAETETUS: Certainly; he who so manifests his thought, is said to explain himself.

SOCRATES: And every one who is not born deaf or dumb is able sooner or later to manifest what he thinks of anything; and if so, all those who have a right opinion about anything will also have right explanation; nor will right opinion be anywhere found to exist apart from knowledge.

THEAETETUS: True.

SOCRATES: Let us not, therefore, hastily charge him who gave this account of knowledge with uttering an unmeaning word; for perhaps he only intended to say, that when a person was asked what was the nature of anything, he should be able to answer his questioner by giving the elements of the thing.

THEAETETUS: As for example, Socrates . . . ?

SOCRATES: As, for example, when Hesiod says that a waggon is made up of a hundred planks. Now, neither you nor I could describe all of them individually; but if any one asked what is a waggon, we should be content to answer, that a wag-gon consists of wheels, axle, body, rims, yoke.

THEAETETUS: Certainly.

SOCRATES: And our opponent will probably laugh at us, just as he would if we professed to be grammarians and to give a grammatical account of the name of Theaetetus, and yet could only tell the syllables and not the letters of your name —that would be true opinion, and not knowledge; for knowledge, as has been already remarked, is not attained until, combined with true opinion, there is an enumeration of the elements out of which anything is composed.

THEAETETUS: Yes.

SOCRATES: In the same general way, we might also have true opinion about a waggon; but he who can describe its essence by an enumeration of the hundred planks, adds rational explanation to true opinion, and instead of opinion has art and knowledge of the nature of a waggon, in that he attains to the whole through the elements.

THEAETETUS: And do you not agree in that view, Socrates?

SOCRATES: If you do, my friend; but I want to know first, whether you admit the resolution of all things into their elements to be a rational explanation of them, and the consideration of them in syllables or larger combinations of them to be irrational—is this your view?

THEAETETUS: Precisely.

SOCRATES: Well, and do you conceive that a man has knowledge of any element who at one time affirms and at another time denies that element of something, or thinks that the same thing is composed of different elements at different times?

THEAETETUS: Assuredly not.

SOCRATES: And do you not remember that in your case and in that of others this often occurred in the process of learning to read?

THEAETETUS: You mean that I mistook the letters and misspelt the syllables?

SOCRATES: Yes.

THEAETETUS: To be sure; I perfectly remember, and I am very far from supposing that they who are in this condition have knowledge.

SOCRATES: When a person at the time of learning writes the name of Theaetetus, and thinks that he ought to write and does write *Th* and *e;* but, again, meaning to write the name of Theodorus, thinks that he ought to write and does write *T* and *e* —can we suppose that he knows the first syllables of your two names?

THEAETETUS: We have already admitted that such a one has not yet attained knowledge.

SOCRATES: And in like manner he may enumerate without knowing them the second and third and fourth syllables of your name?

THEAETETUS: He may.

SOCRATES: And in that case, when he knows the order of the letters and can write them out correctly, he has right opinion?

THEAETETUS: Clearly.

SOCRATES: But although we admit that he has right opinion, he will still be without knowledge?

THEAETETUS: Yes.

SOCRATES: And yet he will have explanations, as well as right opinion, for he knew the order of the letters when he wrote; and this we admit to be explanation.

THEAETETUS: True.

SOCRATES: Then, my friend, there is such a thing as right opinion united with definition or explanation, which does not as yet attain to the exactness of knowledge.

THEAETETUS: It would seem so.

SOCRATES: And what we fancied to be a perfect definition of knowledge is a dream only. But perhaps we had better not say so as yet, for were there not three explanations of knowledge, one of which must, as we said, be adopted by him who maintains knowledge to be true opinion combined with rational explanation? And very likely there may be found some one who will not prefer this but the third.

THEAETETUS: You are quite right; there is still one remaning. The first was the image or expression of the mind in speech; the second, which has just been mentioned, is a way of reaching the whole by an enumeration of the elements. But what is the third definition?

SOCRATES: There is, further, the popular notion of telling the mark or sign of difference which distinguishes the thing in question from all others.

THEAETETUS: Can you give me any example of such a definition?

SOCRATES: As, for example, in the case of the sun, I think that you would be contented with the statement that the sun is the brightest of the heavenly bodies which revolve about the earth.

THEAETETUS: Certainly.

SOCRATES: Understand why—the reason is, as I was just now saying, that if you get at the difference and distinguishing characteristic of each thing, then, as many persons affirm, you will get at the definition or explanation of it; but while you lay hold only of the common and not of the characteristic notion, you will only have the definition of those things to which this common quality belongs.

THEAETETUS: I understand you, and your account of definition is in my judgment correct.

SOCRATES: But he, who having right opinion about anything, can find out the difference which distinguishes it from other things will know that of which before he had only an opinion.

THEAETETUS: Yes; that is what we are maintaining.

SOCRATES: Nevertheless, Theaetetus, on a nearer view, I find myself quite disappointed; the picture, which at a distance was not so bad, has now become altogether unintelligible.

THEAETETUS: What do you mean?

SOCRATES: I will endeavour to explain: I will suppose myself to have true opinion of you, and if to this I add your definition, then I have knowledge, but if not, opinion only.

THEAETETUS: Yes.

SOCRATES: The definition was assumed to be the interpretation of your difference.

THEAETETUS: True.

SOCRATES: But when I had only opinion, I had no conception of your distinguishing characteristics.

THEAETETUS: I suppose not.

SOCRATES: Then I must have conceived of some general or common nature which no more belonged to you than to another.

THEAETETUS: True.

SOCRATES: Tell me, now—How in that case could I have formed a judgment of you any more than of any one else? Suppose that I imagine Theaetetus to be a man who has nose, eyes, and mouth, and every other member complete; how would that enable me to distinguish Theaetetus from Theodorus, or from some outer barbarian?

THEAETETUS: How could it?

SOCRATES: Or if I had further conceived of you, not only as having nose and eyes, but as having a snub nose and prominent eyes, should I have any more notion of you than of myself and others who resemble me?

THEAETETUS: Certainly not.

SOCRATES: Surely I can have no conception of Theaetetus until your snub-nosedness has left an impression on my mind different from the snub-nosedness of all others whom I have ever seen, and until your other peculiarities have a like distinctness; and so when I meet you to-morrow the right opinion will be re-called?

THEAETETUS: Most true.

SOCRATES: Then right opinion implies the perception of differences?

THEAETETUS: Clearly.

SOCRATES: What, then, shall we say of adding reason or explanation to right opinion? If the meaning is, that we should form an opinion of the way in which something differs from another thing, the proposal is ridiculous.

THEAETETUS: How so?

SOCRATES: We are supposed to acquire a right opinion of the differences which distinguish one thing from another when we have already a right opinion of them, and so we go round and round—the revolution of the scytal, or pestle, or any other rotary machine, in the same circles, is as nothing compared with such a requirement; and we may be truly described as the blind directing the blind; for to add those things which we already have, in order that we may learn what we already think, is like a soul utterly benighted.

THEAETETUS: Tell me; what were you going to say just now, when you asked the question?

SOCRATES: If, my boy, the argument, in speaking of adding the definition, had used the word to "know," and not merely "have an opinion" of the difference, this which is the most promising of all the definitions of knowledge would have come to a pretty end, for to know is surely to acquire knowledge.

THEAETETUS: True.

SOCRATES: And so, when the question is asked, What is knowledge? this fair argument will answer "Right opinion with knowledge"—knowledge, that is, of difference, for this, as the said argument maintains, is adding the definition.

THEAETETUS: That seems to be true.

SOCRATES: But how utterly foolish, when we are asking what is knowledge, that the reply should only be, right opinion with knowledge of difference or of anything! And so, Theaetetus, knowledge is neither sensation nor true opinion, nor yet definition and explanation accompanying and added to true opinion?

THEAETETUS: I suppose not.

SOCRATES: And are you still in labour

and travail, my dear friend, or have you brought all that you have to say about knowledge to the birth?

THEAETETUS: I am sure, Socrates, that you have elicited from me a good deal more than ever was in me.

SOCRATES: And does not my art show that you have brought forth wind, and that the offspring of your brain are not worth bringing up?

THEAETETUS: Very true.

SOCRATES: But if, Theaetetus, you should ever conceive afresh, you will be all the better for the present investigation, and if not, you will be soberer and humbler and gentler to other men, and will be too modest to fancy that you know what you do not know. These are the limits of my art; I can no further go, nor do I know aught of the things which great and famous men know or have known in this or former ages. The office of a midwife I, like my mother, have received from God; she delivered women, and I deliver men; but they must be young and noble and fair.

And now I have to go to the porch of the King Archon, where I am to meet Meletus and his indictment. To-morrow morning, Theodorus, I shall hope to see you again at this place.

Truth

The Nyāya Theory of Knowledge

SATISCHANDRA CHATTERJEE

Satischandra (S. C.) Chatterjee was born in West Bengal in 1893 and received his education at Nyayaratna Institution, Ripon College, Scottish Church College, and the University of Calcutta. He has been Premchand Roychand Scholar Lecturer at Calcutta as well as head of the Department of Philosophy at that institution. In examining Indian and Western theories of truth, Professor Chatterjee demonstrates the Nyāya theory, a view that is generated by one of the six great orthodox philosophical systems of medieval India. The Nyāya theory of truth, as described by Chatterjee, is an interesting synthesis of the three classical theories of truth known in the West as the correspondence theory, the coherence theory, and the pragmatic theory. What Nyāya and Chatterjee do with these three separate theories makes interesting and challenging reading.

INDIAN AND WESTERN THEORIES OF TRUTH

Here we propose to examine the Indian theories of truth . . . in the light of parallel Western theories. With regard to truth there are two main questions, namely, how truth is constituted, and how truth is known. The first question relates to the nature of truth and the answers to it give us the definitions of truth. The second question refers to the ascertainment of truth and the answers to it give us the tests or criteria of truth.

With regard to these two questions there seem to be two possible answers.

Thus it may be said that truth is a self-evident character of all knowledge. Every knowledge is true and known to be true by its very nature. Knowledge does not depend on any external conditions either to be made true or to be known as true. This is the theory of the intrinsic validity *(svataḥ prāmāṇya)* of knowledge as advocated by the Sāṅkhya, Mīmāṃsā and Advaita Vedānta systems of Indian Philosophy. According to the last two schools, the truth of knowledge consists just in its being uncontradicted *(abādhita)*. The absence of contradiction, however, is not a positive but a negative condition of truth. Knowledge is both made true and known

From *The Nyāya Theory of Knowledge*, Calcutta, University of Calcutta, 1950.

to be true by its own internal conditions. It is only falsehood that is externally conditioned. So truth is self-evident, while falsity requires to be evidenced by external grounds. The Sāṅkhya goes further than this. It maintains that both truth and falsehood are internally conditioned and immediately known, *i.e.,* are self-evident.

There is no exact parallel to the above theory of truth in Western philosophy. It is true that in modern European philosophy knowledge, in the strict sense, is always taken to mean true belief. But truth or validity is not regarded as intrinsic to all knowledge, independently of all external conditions. It is in the writings of Professor L. A. Reid, a modern realist who owes no allegiance to the current schools of realism, that we find some approach to the view that truth is organic to knowledge. But even Reid makes it conditional on knowledge efficiently fulfilling its function, namely, the apprehension of reality as it is. He thinks that truth is nothing else but knowledge doing its job. Thus he says: "Truth is, indeed, simply, . . . the quality of knowledge perfectly fulfilling its functions." Again he observes: "If knowledge were not transitive, if we were not in direct contact with reality, then all our tests, coherence, correspondence, and the rest, would be worthless." Here truth is admitted to be a natural function of knowledge, but not as inherent and self-evident in all knowledge. In the theory of intuitionism, we find a close approach to the view of self-evident validity. To the question "How do we know that a belief is true or valid?" intuitionism has a simple answer to give, namely, that we know it immediately to be such. As Hobhouse puts the matter: "Intuitionism has a royal way of cutting this, and indeed most other knots: for it has but to appeal to a perceived necessity, to a clear idea, to the inconceivability of the opposite, all of which may be known

by simply attending to our own judgment, and its task is done." Among intuitionists, Lossky has made an elaborate attempt to show that truth and falsity are known through an immediate consciousness of their objectivity and subjectivity respectively. For him, truth is the objective and falsity the subjective appearance of the object. But how do we know that the one is objective and the other is subjective? The answer given by Lossky as also by Lipps is that we have "an immediate consciousness of subjectivity" and "an immediate consciousness of objectivity." To quote Lossky's own words: "It is in this consciousness of objectivity and subjectivity, and not . . . in the laws of identity, contradiction, and excluded middle, that our thought has a real and immediate guide in its search for truth."

It should be remarked here that the above theories of self-evident truth or intrinsic validity give us a rather jejune and untenable solution of the logical problem of truth. They leave no room for the facts of doubt and falsehood in the sphere of knowledge. But any theory of truth which fails to explain its correlate, namely, falsehood, becomes so far inadequate. Further, it makes a confusion between psychological belief and logical certainty. Psychologically a wrong belief may be as firm as a right one. But this does not mean that there is no distinction between the two. Subjective certitude, as such, cannot be accepted as a test of truth. It is true that the theory of intrinsic validity does not appeal to any test of truth other than the truth itself. It assumes that the truth of knowledge is self-evident, and that we cannot think of the opposite. In fact, however, there is no such self-evident truth. It is only in the case of the self that we can speak of self-evidence in this sense. The self is a self-manifesting reality. It is manifest even in any doubt or denial of its reality. Hence self-evidence belongs really to the self only. It is on the analogy of the self that we speak of the self-evidence of any other truth. A truth is self-evident in so far as it has the evidence of the self or is evident like the self. But as we have just said, there is no such self-evident truth other than the self itself. In the case of any other truth, we can always think of the opposite in a sensible way. That "two and two make five" is not as nonsensical as "abracadabra." Even if the opposite of a certain belief be inconceivable, it does not follow that the belief is infallible. What was once inconceivable is now not only conceivable but perfectly true. Hence we cannot say that self-evident validity is intrinsic to all knowledge.

The second answer to the question "How is truth constituted and known?" leads us to the theory of extrinsic validity *(paratah prāmāṇya).* According to this, the truth of any knowledge is both constituted and known by certain external conditions. As a general rule, the validity of knowledge is due to something that is not inherent in it. So also the knowledge of validity depends on certain extraneous tests. Validity is thus assigned to one knowledge on the ground of some other knowledge. This is the theory of extrinsic validity as advocated by the Nyāya and the Buddhist systems. In Western philosophy, the correspondence, the coherence and the pragmatist theories of truth all come under the doctrine of extrinsic validity. In each of them the truth of knowledge is made to depend on certain external conditions other than the knowledge itself. According to almost all realists, old and new, it is correspondence to facts that constitutes both the nature and the test of truth. Of course, some realists differ from this general position and hold a different view of the matter. Thus Alexander makes coherence the ground of truth. But in speaking of coherence as determined by reality, he accepts indirectly the theory of correspondence. Reid, on the other hand, treats correspondence to the given

only as a test of truth. Russell defines truth in terms of correspondence and accepts coherence as a test of some truths, while others are said to be self-evident. In the philosophy of objective idealism, coherence in the sense of the systematic unity of all experiences is made both the ground and the test of truth. The truth consists in the coherence of all experiences as one self-maintaining and all-inclusive system. It is in this sense that Bosanquet says that "the truth is the whole and it is its own criterion. Truth can only be tested by more of itself." Hence any particular knowledge is true in so far as it is consistent with the whole system of experience. On this view, the truth of human knowledge becomes relative, since coherence as the ideal of the completed system of experience is humanly unattainable. For pragmatism, truth is both constituted and known by practical utility. The truth of knowledge consists in its capacity to produce practically useful consequences. So also the method of ascertaining truth is just to follow the practical consequences of a belief and see if they have any practical value. With this brief statement of the realistic, the idealistic and the pragmatist theories of truth, we proceed to examine the Buddhist and the Nyāya theories of extrinsic validity.

From what we have said before it is clear that the Buddhists adopt the pragmatist theory of truth and reality. For them, practical efficiency is the test of both truth and reality. The real is what possesses practical efficiency *(arthakriyā)* and the true is the useful and so practically efficient *(arthakriyāsāmarthya).* But the pragmatic conception of truth is embarrassed by serious difficulties. The Nyāya criticism of the Buddhist conception of *pramāṇa* has brought out some of these difficulties. Here we may note that to reduce the true to the useful is to make it almost meaningless. It is by no means the case that truth is only a matter of practical utility. The atomic and the electron theories of matter make very little difference in our practical life. Similarly, the different theories of truth involve no great difference in their practical consequences. But in the absence of any other test than that of practical utility we cannot say which one is true and which is false. Further, there are certain beliefs which are admittedly wrong but which are otherwise useful for certain purposes of life. But no one would claim any truth for a wrong belief on account of its practical utility. Hence the Buddhist and the pragmatist theories of truth cannot be accepted as sound and satisfactory.

The Nyāya theory of truth, it will be seen, combines the correspondence, the coherence and the pragmatist theories with certain modifications. According to it, the truth of knowledge consists in its correspondence with objective facts, while coherence and practical utility are the tests of truth in such cases in which we require a test. It defines the truth of all knowledge as a correspondence of relations *(tadvati tatprakāraka)*. To know a thing is to judge it as having such-and-such a character. This knowledge of the thing will be true if the thing has really such-and-such a character; if not, it will be false. The Nyāya view of correspondence is thus different from the new realistic idea of structural correspondence or indentity of contents. That knowledge corresponds to some object does not, for the Naiyāyika, mean that the contents of the object bodily enter into consciousness and become its contents. When, for example, I know a table, the table as a physical existent does not figure in my consciousness. This means only that I *judge* something as having the attribute of "tableness" which really belongs to it. There is a subjective cognition of a physical object. The one corresponds to the other, because it *determines* the object as it is, and does not itself become what it is. If it so became the ob-

ject itself, there would be nothing left on the subjective side that might correspond to the physical object. Nor again does the Nyāya follow the critical realist's idea of correspondence between character-complexes, referred to the object by the knowing mind, and the characters actually belonging to the object. When we know anything we do not first apprehend a certain logical essence or a character-complex and then refer it to the thing known. Our knowledge is in direct contact with the object. In knowing the object we judge it as having a relation to certain characters or attributes. Our knowledge will be true if there is correspondence between the relation asserted in knowledge, and that existing among facts. Thus my knowledge of a conch-shell as white is true because there is a real relation between the two corresponding to the relation affirmed by me. On the other hand, the perception of silver in a shell is false because it asserts a relation between the two, which does not correspond to a real relation between them.

While truth consists in correspondence, the criterion of truth is, for the Nyāya, coherence in a broad sense *(saṃvāda)*. But coherence does not here mean anything of the kind that objective idealism means by it. The Nyāya coherence is a practical test and means the harmony between cognitive and conative experiences *(pravṛttisāmarthya)* or between different kinds of knowledge *(tajjātīyatva)*. That there is truth in the sense of correspondence cannot, as a general rule, be known directly by intuition. We know it indirectly from the fact that the knowledge in question coheres with other experiences of the same object as also with the general system of our knowledge. Thus the perception of water is known to be valid when different ways of reaction or experiment give us experience of the same water. It is this kind of coherence that Alexander accepts as a test of truth when he says: "If truth is tested by reference to other propositions, the test is not one of correspondence to reality but of whether the proposition tested is consistent or not with other propositions." Hobhouse also means the same thing by "consilience" as a measure of validity. According to him, validity belongs to judgments as forming a consilient system. Of course, he admits that such validity is relative and not absolute, since the ideal of a complete system of consilient judgments is unattainable. The Nyāya idea of *samvāda* or coherence may be better explained as a combination of Reid's methods of correspondence and coherence. If we take the judgment "that is the light of a ship," we can test its truth by what Reid calls the correspondence method "of approaching the light and seeing a ship." This is exactly what the Nyāya means by *pravṛttisāmarthya* or successful activity. Or, we can employ, so says Reid, the cheaper coherence method "of comparing this knowledge with other kinds of knowledge and see if it is consistent with them." In this we have the Nyāya method of testing one knowledge by reference to some other valid knowledge *(tajjātīyatva)*. But the Nyāya goes further than this and accepts practical utility also as a test of truth. Thus the validity of the perception of water may be known from correspondence and coherence in the above sense. But it may be further known from the satisfaction of our practical needs or the fulfilment of our practical purposes in relation to water, such as drinking, bathing, washing, etc. But the Nyāya never admits the pragmatist contention that the truth of any knowledge is constituted by its utility or serviceableness. Knowledge is made true by its correspondence to some reality or objective fact. It is true not because it is useful, but it is useful because it is already true. Hence truth consists in correspondence and is tested by coherence and practical efficiency.

But from the standpoint of the modern Nyāya, all truths do not require to be tested. Some truths are known as such without any test or confirmation. These are manifestly necessary and so self-evident truths. Here the Nyāya view has some affinity with Russell's theory of truth. In both, truth is defined by correspondence to fact, but in different ways. Although truth is thus externally conditioned, some truths are admitted by both to be self-evident. For the Nyāya, however, such truths are only necessary truths or what Russell calls *a priori* principles. Of the different kinds of knowledge by acquaintance—sensation, memory, introspection, etc.—which are admitted by Russell to have self-evident truth, it is only introspection or self-consciousness *(anuvyavasāya)* that is admitted by the Nyāya as having self-evident validity. The validity of self-consciousness is self-evident because there is a necessary relation between consciousness and its contents. When I become conscious of a desire for food, I find that my consciousness is necessarily related to the desire, it is the desire itself as it becomes explicit. Here I not only know something, but know that I am knowing it, *i.e.*, the truth of my knowledge is self-evident.

The different theories of truth discussed above may be shown to supplement one another and be reconciled as complementary aspects of a comprehensive theory. The first requisite of such a theory is the independent existence of a world of objects. If there were no such world, there would be no ground for the distinction between truth and falsehood. Some of our beliefs are true or false according as they are or are not borne out by independent objects or facts. It is because there are certain independent objects, to which our beliefs may or may not conform, that we distinguish between truth and error. Hence we say that truth consists in the correspondence of our knowledge with independent objects or facts. The difficulty on this view, it is generally remarked, is that if the objects are independent of knowledge, we cannot know whether our knowledge corresponds with them or not. How can we know what is outside and beyond knowledge, and see that true knowledge agrees with it? The reply to this is that in the case of external objects, physical things and other minds, we cannot straightway know the correspondence between our knowledge and its objects. Still, we cannot deny the reality of these external objects. But for the independent existence of other things and minds we cannot explain the order and uniformity of our experiences and the similarity of the experiences that different individuals may have under similar circumstances. That some of our experiences represent the real qualities of things may then be known from the fact that they are given in the same way to different persons, or to the same persons through different senses. As Professor Price has shown, "sense-data cohere together in families, and families are coincident with physical occupants." On the other hand, some of our experiences are not taken to represent the qualities of things, because they do not cohere with other experiences of the same individual or of different individuals. The first kind of experiences is considered to be true and objective, while the second is judged to be false and subjective. Similarly, our knowledge of other minds is true when it correctly represents the contents of those minds. It will be false, if what we impute to them forms no part of their actual contents. This shows that it is correspondence to facts that constitutes the nature of truth, although we cannot directly *know* such correspondence in the case of physical things and other minds. To know this we have to consider if one knowledge coheres with others or the whole body of human knowledge, and also consider if we can successfully act on our knowledge. What is true works, although whatever works is not true. Thus

we know the correspondence of knowledge with facts from its coherence and pragmatic value. But to know that a certain knowledge corresponds with facts is to *know* its truth. It does not constitute its truth. The knowledge becomes true if, and only if, it corresponds with facts. We know or test its truth when we find that it is coherent with other parts of our knowledge and our practical activities. So truth is constituted by correspondence with facts and is tested by coherence and practical activity.

The Vedānta view of truth as uncontradicted experience logically implies the coherence theory of truth. That some experience is uncontradicted means that it is different from the contradicted. But to be different from the contradicted means to belong to the body of coherent knowledge. We do not and cannot rightly judge an experience to be uncontradicted unless we relate it to other experiences and find that it is congruous with them. A dream experience is wrongly judged by the dreamer to be uncontradicted and true, because he cannot relate it to his waking experiences. It cannot be said that a dream experience is true for the time being and becomes false afterwards. What is once true is always true. A dream experience may sometimes be *judged* to be true, but it is really false for all time. And its falsity appears from its incoherence with waking experience. Hence we are to say that an experience is really uncontradicted when it is related to other experiences and is found to be coherent with them.

It may be urged against the above view that truth consists in correspondence and is tested by coherence, that it either assumes the truth of the testing knowledge, or must go on testing knowledge *ad infinitum*. If knowledge is true when it corresponds with facts, and if the correspondence cannot be directly known, then the truth of every knowledge must be tested by its coherence with others. This, however, means that there can be no end of the process of proving knowledge and, therefore, no final proof of any knowledge. To solve this difficulty we must admit that there is at least one case in which knowledge is, by itself, known to be true. We have such a case in self-consciousness. While the truth of all other knowledge is to be tested by coherence, the truth of self-consciousness is self-evident and requires no extraneous test. The self is a self-manifesting reality. Hence the contents of our mind or the self are manifested by themselves. They are at once existent facts and contents of consciousness. To become conscious of the contents of one's mind is just to make them explicit. What we are here conscious of are not outside or beyond consciousness. Mental contents not only *are,* but are conscious of themselves. The state of knowledge and the object of knowledge being identical, we cannot strictly speak of a correspondence of the one with the other. Or, if we speak of a correspondence between them, we are to say that it is directly known and so need not be known or tested in any other way.

When we feel pain, or know something, or resolve to do anything, we may be conscious of feeling it, or knowing it, or resolving to do it. What we are here conscious of as objects are the objects themselves as they become explicit or conscious of themselves. Similarly, necessary truths and *a priori* principles like the laws of thought, logical and mathematical truths seem to have self-evident validity. The reason for this is that these truths are or express the forms and contents of our own consciousness. They are inherent in or arise out of the nature of our own thought and consciousness, and in knowing them consciousness knows itself, *i.e.* its own forms. They are at once modes and objects of consciousness. In any judgment or knowledge of them, the content and object of consciousness are the same and directly known to be the same. Such knowledge is, therefore, not only true, but also known to be true by itself. Hence we admit that the truth of self-consciousness is self-evident, while all other truths are evidenced by external tests like coherence and pragmatic utility or verification.

THE SIX JUSTIFICATIONS
OF TRUE BELIEF

The six traditional justifications of true belief in the West are sensation, inference, intuition, revelation, authority, and faith. We will briefly discuss each in the critical spirit of the epistemologist, and offer at least one major difficulty which each one encounters in attempting to be a ground of knowledge.

SENSATION

Sense experience is surely the chief way in which most of us justify our beliefs about the world around us. We know that cobras love milk, that Delhi is the capital of India, that Wisconsin is cold in the winter, that the Plover River is a haven for game fish, and so on, by sensory observation. We live, work, breed, and die with sensory experience guiding us, warning us, depressing us, and consoling us all the way. Probably three-fourths of all the knowledge we have is based upon the evidence of the senses. In order to test the truth or falsity of certain statements we simply resort to looking and seeing, smelling, tasting, hearing, and touching. The five sense organs—the eyes, nose, tongue, ears, and body surfaces—deliver information to the brain which the brain labels, catalogues, and judges. This information is usually called *the data from the senses* or *sense data* (or *sense datum*, singular). Thus right now thousands of bits of information are bombarding your senses: from the book you receive visual sense data, perhaps of white and black; from your nose you receive olfactory sense data: from your tongue you receive gustatory sense data; from your ears you receive auditory

129

sense data; and, finally, from your various body surfaces you receive tactile sense data—perhaps pressures on your back, bottom, and legs right now. All that we know about the world around us at this moment comes from these sense data that we receive in these ways. We make judgments, form beliefs and, finally, corroborate those beliefs by sense experience.

But there are two other sets of data that the brain works with in addition to sense data. One of these sets is called *somatic data*—information from inside the body, e.g., aches, pains, gurgles. The other set is called *hallucinatory data*—information from within the brain alone, e.g., dreams, both the day and the night variety, curious imaginings, seeings and hearings of what just isn't there. Somatic data can be pleasant, amusing, unpleasant, and/or interesting, while hallucinatory data can be pleasurable, terrifying, and even unpredictable, and it will cause all sorts of problems for the empiricist who says that the senses alone can give us knowledge or justify our beliefs about the external world.

For example, the critic of empiricism will invariably ask the empiricist, How do you know when you are having *veridical data*, i.e., real physical object sense data? And, How can you be sure you're not having an hallucination right now? Put into a more familiar form, the question becomes, How do you know you aren't dreaming right now? That is to say, How do you know that you didn't dream that you came into this room, opened this book, sat down, and that right now you're *dreaming* that you're reading (receiving dream data) and not really reading (receiving veridical or physical object sense data)? The empiricist who places so much trust in the justification of true belief through sensation or sense experience or sense data must provide a defensible criterion for distinguishing false hallucinatory or dream experience from true, veridical experience. And this, the critic says, the empiricist cannot do. In examining the historical philosophic battles between the realists, supported by the empiricists, and the rationalists and idealists, supported by the critics, we will have occasion in the readings below to return to this matter once again.

If sensation cannot provide a sure and certain grounding for knowledge, perhaps we will have better luck with the second of the kinds of justification for true belief: Inference.

INFERENCE

If I know that this book contains 100 pages, then it follows that something else is also knowable, and this something else that I can know is known by what is called *inference*. Thus, from the knowledge that the length of this book is 100 pages, I can correctly infer that the book has 50 pages plus 50 pages, or that the book is either made of paper or not made of paper, or even that it has 100 pages; and all three of these latter propositions will be true in virtue of the first statement about the 100 pages being true and in virtue of certain rules of inference being accepted. Thus one kind of inference allows me to deduce that something is *absolutely true* from the fact that something else is true. It is called *deductive* inference. A second kind of inference allows me to induce, rather than deduce, that something is *probably true* from the fact that a whole lot of other things are true. Thus if I observe that a certain man is a professor and that he is pedantic and stuffy, and that another man is a professor and that he too is pedantic and stuffy, and if I make a great many observations of other professors and discover that each one that I have observed is, oddly enough, pedantic and stuffy, then I might very well conclude by induction from all my previous particular observations that it is quite probably true that all professors are pedantic and stuffy. This conclusion, which I might claim as something that I know, is arrived at and justified by what is called *inductive inference.*

Thus we have two kinds of inference that can be used to justify true beliefs. These two kinds of inference were exemplified by the two propositions, that the book has 50 pages plus 50 pages, and that all professors are pedantic and stuffy. The former proposition was justified by deductive inference, and the latter by inductive inference.

But, in the examples that we have given, the use of both types of inference depended on certain other judgments being true. In the case of deductive inference, the proposition that the book has 50 pages plus 50 pages was known to be true only if the proposition that the book contains 100 pages was known to be true. But that latter proposition, if not known by inference itself, was very probably known by or justified by sensation—that is, someone simply counted the pages. And in the case of inductive inference, the proposition that all professors are pedantic and stuffy was known to be true only if my previous propositions about pedantic, stuffy professors I have met were known to be true. But those previous propositions were also, I am assuming, known by or justified by sensation, i.e., I simply saw a correlation between being professorial and being pedantic and stuffy. If all this is the case, then it turns out that both deductive inference and inductive inference, at least insofar as cases like the above are concerned, rest upon sensation. That is to say, the conclusions thus drawn by either deduction or induction are only as good as the truth of the assumptive propositions they deduce or induce from. And because those assumptive propositions rely upon sensation, then those deductive and inductive conclusions, in effect, rely upon sensation as well. Consequently, the problems that we have met already with respect to sensation as a justification for knowledge would seem now to have infected inference as well.

However, inference might well be grounded in one or another of the other types of justifications of knowledge and not simply in sensation. Our final verdict regarding inference, therefore, will not be in until we examine the other four ways of knowing. Hence, we pass on to the third kind of justification for true belief: Intuition.

INTUITION

Propositions that are justified by intuition are said, by some philosophers, to be known immediately and with certainty to be true. Philosophers who claim legitimacy for intuitive knowledge are called *rationalists,* while those who deny the possibility of such knowledge and claim instead that the only legitimate ground for knowledge is sensation are called *empiricists.* Thus the empiricists claim that all our knowledge comes from sensation, while the rationalist simply claims that at least one, maybe more, true beliefs can be justified, not by sensation, but by what they generally call *intuition.* Hence to prove the empiricist's case false, the rationalist has merely to show that one true belief is known, immediately, i.e., without recourse to other propositions or to other ways of knowledge. He must also show that it is known with certainty, i.e., that its truth is indubitable and necessary. If he can do these two things, empiricism will be shown to be false and rationalism will be shown to be true. The rationalist believes that he has a number of such propositions which are both certain but not logically, i.e., deductively, certain as are the judgments of the mathematician, and known *a priori,* that is to say, known independently of sense experience. The judgments of the rationalist, therefore, are called *synthetic a priori* judgments: Synthetic (rather than an *analytic* judgment) because they are about things in space and time, physical objects, objective entities, and not simply about meanings of words; and *a priori* (rather than *a posteriori*) because they are justified independently of the data of the senses.

Philosophers since the time of Immanuel Kant (1724–1804) have made this distinction between these two types of judgments or statements and between these two types of evidence or justification. Thus synthetic judgments and analytic judgments differ, the defenders of this dichotomy claim, in that analytic judgments are all trivially true simply by virtue of the meanings of the words involved in the judgment. One of the terms of the judgment, called the *predicate term,* simply analyzes or repeats all or part of the other term of the judgment, called the *subject term.* For example, these analytic judgments follow that pattern: "All brown desks (the subject term) are brown desks (the predicate term)"; "All black turkeys are black"; "All triangles have three sides"; and so on. But synthetic judgments, on the contrary, are not trivially true, and their predicate terms do not merely analyze or repeat or define the subject terms of the judgment. For example, these synthetic judgments follow that pattern: "All brown desks (the subject term) are wooden" (the predicate term)—which is both synthetic and false, as it turns out; "All black turkeys are noisy"; "All triangles are small"; and so on. *A priori* and *a posteriori,* as we have stated, relate to whether or not the justification of the judgment comes from sensory experience: *a priori* indicates it does not, and *a posteriori* indicates that it does.

Finally, one last distinction between analytic and synthetic judgments can be made. A rather interesting and useful test can be applied to all putative, or supposedly, analytic propositions to determine whether they are really analytic or not. Thus it is claimed that the denial of an analytic proposition is self-contradictory; so in our test for analyticity we simply deny or negate a putative analytic proposition and if it becomes logically self-contradictory, then the original judgment was plainly analytic. Take, for example, these four supposedly analytic judgments: "2 + 2 = 4"; "All yogis are yogis";

"All black cobras are cobras"; and *"Mokṣa* means 'liberation'" (which is the definition of "liberation" in Sanskrit). By denying each of these judgments we obtain these four patently self-contradictory judgments: "2 + 2 ≠ 4"; "Not all yogis are yogis"; "Some black cobras are not cobras"; and *"Mokṣa* does not mean 'liberation.'" Hence, because these latter four judgments are self-contradictory, the initial four judgments must have been analytic judgments. Or to put the matter in a slightly different way, because all of the latter four judgments are necessarily or logically false, the initial four judgments must have been necessarily or logically true, i.e., analytic.

All synthetic judgments, on the other hand, can be denied without self-contradiction resulting. Take for example these four supposedly synthetic judgments: "Two tigers plus two tigers equals four tigers"; "All yogis worship Lord Vishnu"; "All black cobras are vicious"; and *"Mokṣa* is the goal of human existence." By denying each of these judgments we obtain these four non-self-contradictory judgments which may be either true or false but not logically or necessarily either true or false, simply because they are judgments known *a posteriori* and not *a priori:* "Two tigers plus two tigers does not equal four tigers" (it could happen); "Not all yogis worship Lord Vishnu"; "Some black cobras are not vicious"; and *"Mokṣa* is not always the goal of human existence." Thus, because these latter four judgments are not self-contradictory, the initial four judgments must have been synthetic judgments, i.e., they were either synthetically true or synthetically false.

The quarrels that have come to the fore in the history of philosophy have tended to center around the question as to whether or not there are synthetic *a priori* judgments, and it is here that the rationalist (who says there are) and the empiricist (who says there are not) lock horns.

Here is an example that the rationalist might use to justify his contention that synthetic *a priori* judgments are possible. Take this statement, which you must utter to yourself in order to get the full synthetic *a priori* flavor: "I exist," or "I am alive," or even just plain "I am." Apply the test of self-contradictoriness, mentioned above, by denying the judgment in order to determine whether or not it is analytic. Say aloud, "I do not exist," or "I am not alive." Plainly, the rationalist would argue, it is weird, odd, and curiously strange to say this, but it is not, certainly, self-contradictory. Therefore, it is plainly not analytic; hence it must be synthetic. Next, how does one know whether the judgment, "I exist," is true or not? Not by the data of the senses, surely a rationalist might continue, and not, it would seem, by logically deducing the judgment from some set of prior propositions or assumptions. But then the judgment is not dependent for its truth on sensation or inference. And if it is not dependent on sensation, but rather is known immediately and intuitively, then we say that the judgment is known or justified *a priori,* hence we have a genuine synthetic *a priori* judgment on our hands. At least the rationalist is sure of this. The rationalist contends or might contend then, that such propositions as, "I exist" and/ or "God exists"; "Everything that is colored is spread out or extended"; "Promise keeping and truth telling are always right"; *"Brahman* is identical with *Ātman"* and/or "The law of karma is universal," are all synthetic *a priori* judgments because each one is certain, indubitable, and immediately, intuitively known.

The critics of rationalism, of whom the empiricists are in the majority, are quick to point out that each one of the examples of putative synthetic *a priori* judgments are either *a posteriori* if they are synthetic, or analytic if they are *a priori,* and that under no circumstances can they be both synthetic and necessary as the rationalists contend. And there the battle is joined and the controversy rages.

Other philosophic critics of both rationalism and intuitionism have pointed out that intuition, although it may be a way or means of knowing, can never be a justification for knowledge. The rationale for this distinction between a means of knowing and a justification for knowledge is extremely important and rather straightforward, as a little reflection should show. Thus I may arrive at a belief by a sudden and blinding illumination of insight that at the moment of intuition must seem both immediate and certain. We all have those sudden "Aha!" feelings from time to time, when reason penetrates to the very core of a problem or puzzle and the solution is immediately and indubitably laid before us. We say in the presence of this sudden illumination of our previous difficulty, "How could I ever have missed it?" But this rather common experience of piercing illumination or intuition is simply a means to the clearing up of the problem or puzzle. The intuition is the vehicle of the solution, not the solution itself. For that solution, whatever it is, is the justification for whatever true belief is revealed by the intuition, and that solution may involve further sensory investigation of the true belief, inference, or whatever.

Thus, suppose that I can't remember where I put a particularly important paper I have written. I look high and low for it, lose sleep over it, and am really overwrought at not being able to find the wretched thing. Suddenly it hits me! Perhaps the insight or intuition occurs in a dream or meditative state of mind, but suddenly, with clarity, sureness, immediacy, and certainty I believe—not know, but believe—I know where the paper was placed. Now it is intuition that is the means to the belief, the strong or certain belief; but the belief is not corroborated, really certain, really true, until the mere psychological state of certainty has been vindicated or substantiated by finding the paper in the place indicated by the sudden intuition. Now, what I formerly simply believed very strongly, that the paper was in such and such a place, has been turned into knowledge, for the justification of the true belief has been provided by sensation. Hence, the critic of intuitionism reminds the rationalists that intuition is at best a means or way to knowledge and never a justification for true belief. So we turn next to the fourth attempt to justify true belief: Revelation.

REVELATION

Revelation is used by many persons to justify all manner of beliefs. Thus, by revelation one can know, it is said, that God exists, that there are devils, ogres, nymphs, ghosts, spirits and sprites, that the world was created in 4004 B.C., that the soul is immortal, that there is a heaven and a hell, that man cannot swim or fly, that killing atheists and heretics is right, that the sun is 10 miles away and the moon is larger than the sun, that my religious beliefs are superior to yours, that if you don't believe as I do you will be damned and, finally, that if you don't believe as I do, I have a duty to assassinate you.

"Revelation" can mean two things: Either the process by which God's mind is made known to man or the product of a particular revelation, i.e., a text or pronouncement of some sort. Those who believe in revelation as a justification for true belief hold that both kinds of revelation, process and product, are necessary in order to justify true belief. Thus revelationists contend that there is a God or communicator who communicates (process) and an auditor who hears the communication. But the route of the revelation does not stop there. The auditor in general must pass on what he hears to other auditors—and this passing on is usually in the form of an utterance (product), as with the Delphic priestess of Apollo, or in the form of some written tablet or text (product). In the Indian tradition these texts are referred to as *śruti*—i.e., what is heard and passed on by a beginningless unbroken chain or *ṛṣis* or sages of the religion, as opposed to another set of texts called *smṛti*—i.e., what is remembered in the tradition of the religion. The sacred revelations of *śruti,* for example, comprise the four *Vedas* and the two hundred or so *Upanishads,* while the *smṛti* include such texts as the *Bhagavad Gītā*. In the West, of course, the *Old Testament* for the Jews, the *Old* and *New Testaments* for the Christians, and the *Koran* for the Muslims constituted sacred revelation or *śruti;* while the established and respected books of commentaries on these texts, the writings of the church fathers, the saints, the martyrs, and the mystics, though not constitutive of revelation, might perhaps be easily likened to the Indian *smṛti*.

There are a number of problems that are bound to crop up in attempting to use revelation to justify true belief and turn it into knowledge. We will mention two: First, examine once again the route of revelation as it travels from God or the Divine source or communicator to the first auditor (if there is a first) and then to the second auditor or audience. We want to focus on the possibility of error when the message, call it "M," travels from God or communicator through the first auditor to the second auditor. To begin with, the message from God or communicator, call it "MG," reaches the heart or mind of the first auditor. He "hears," and then interprets what he hears, and then passes on what he thinks he hears as a text or as a verbal pronouncement to the second auditor. Note that he might even be the second auditor himself. Now at any one of these three moments—the hearing moment, the interpreting moment, and/or the passing-on moment—MG could become distorted, and during these three moments of hearing, interpreting, and the passing on of MG, the use of revelation to justify true belief as knowledge could be called into question.

Second, there is a vicious circularity present for anyone who attempts to use revelation to justify any knowledge claim. Suppose I claim that God exists, and you ask me, "How do you know this?" Suppose I answer that I know it because the Bible says so. You then ask, "Why should I believe the Bible?", whereupon I answer, "Because it was written by God." You are bound to ask me, "How do you know it was written by God?", and I answer, "Because the Bible says so." Again you ask, "Why should I believe the Bible?", and I come up with the same answer as before, "Because it was written by God." And we are off and running, chasing our own logical tail. The Bible cannot be used to substantiate itself, for it then assumes the very point at issue, i.e., that God exists. No revelation, the critics say, can be used to substantiate any knowledge claim, for scripture purchases what authority it has in virtue of this appeal to special omniscience, and one ends up in the worst possible trivial assumption, namely, that it is true because it says so, or it is right because it says it is: Self-justifying assertion is hardly the best foundation on which to build knowledge. Thus, because of the circularity and question-begging inherent in all arguments that use scripture, *per se,* to ground knowledge claims, the employment of revelation to justify knowledge claims is once again called into question. I say *"per se,"* above, for scriptures do contain a great deal of factual information: historical, anthropological, sociological, and cultural information about peoples and civilizations. But while scripture, as an historical account, can be a source of knowledge of this sort, it cannot *as revelation, as scripture,* be a justification for knowledge. Or so the critics say.

We turn next to the fifth of the kinds of justification for true belief: Authority.

AUTHORITY

Authority may be of one or two kinds. When the word is spelled with an initial upper-case letter "A," as "Authority," it is not at all distinct from revelation where the Author being referred to is God. But there is a second kind of authority that is new and that is used as a justification for true belief, and this authority is regarded by many persons as a fifth way, or means, of justification for some knowledge claims.

Much of the factual information that we receive from magazines, newspapers, television, radio, and the mass media in general are grounded in authority. We know that the temperature in New Delhi was 85° F yesterday, and we know it because Radio India reported it, and they passed it on to us from an expert, a meteorologist perhaps—i.e., an authority. The information that students receive from their professors and textbooks that is purely factual has its justification, and therefore counts as knowledge from that source—namely, the expert, the specialist, the authority. Thus we know that ethyl alcohol or ethanol is accurately symbolized by the molecular formula C_2H_5OH, and we know that ethanol has certain observable properties. Most of us know these things not because we have seen and tested out these properties for ourselves, but because a chemist has observed them, and we know that we can trust this chemist. How do we know he is to be trusted? Because all *bona fide* authorities are reliable—that is simply what we mean by the word "authority." How do we know Chemist Jones is reliable and a *bona fide* authority on chemistry? Because we know something about his background, training, degrees, and reputation. Suppose Chemist Jones tells us authoritatively all about ethanol, and then says that drinking ethanol will make one tipsy and it is wrong to get tipsy. Do we now know two things based on the authority of Chemist Jones? Not at all. But do we know that drinking ethanol will make me tipsy or drunk because Jones says it will? Yes, we can base the truth of this factual statement on the authority of Chemist Jones. But do we also know that getting tipsy or drunk is wrong because Jones says it is wrong? Not at all. There is nothing factual about the latter statement, rather it is a normative judgment or a value judgment and not factual at all. There are no authorities in matters of value, unless one returns again to Authority and revelation to justify such value judgments. But as far as authority in value judgments is concerned, each man and each woman, it would seem, is his or her own authority; which is to say, that there are no authorities or experts in matters of the ultimate sources of value and normative judgments. And sentences that talk overtly or covertly about "right" and "wrong," "good" and "bad," "beautiful" and "ugly," and the like, are, generally speaking, value judgments.

When Professor Jones the chemist says that ethanol has a molecular formula of C_2H_5OH we believe him because he is an authority. But if we ask Professor Jones, "How do you know this? How do you know that C_2H_5OH is the same as ethanol?" he might reply, "Why Professor von Werner said so!" And so we ask Professor von Werner how he knows this and if he refers us to another authority we ask the same question of him. But at some place along the chemical trail we're going to meet the final authority, the man who answers something like this: "I know ethanol is C_2H_5OH because by quantitative and qualitative analysis of ethanol I have proved or empirically shown that its molecular formula must be C_2H_5OH." But the end of this trial of experts, then, has landed us back with sensation, the first of the justifications of true belief dealt with above. The final authority knows what he knows, then, not by authority at all, but by sensation. The other authorities could, if it were demanded of them, repeat the same experiment as the final authority and come up with the same set of observations and proofs if it were asked of them: That is what makes them authorities too. If the statement which is accepted on authority is factual and not normative then it is backed up or justified ultimately not by authority, but by sensation in the physical and natural sciences, or by deductive inference in the logical and mathematical disciplines. In either case, justification by authority, the critics say, must reduce to either justification by sensation or justification by inference. Because we have already dealt with these two ways of justification previously, together with their attendant problems, we shall pass on to the sixth and final justification of true belief treated by the epistemologist: Faith.

FAITH

Faith is regarded by many persons as a justification of true beliefs in the area of the religious life, in certain medical practices, and even in grounding certain kinds of assertions made day to day by the ordinary man. Thus we hear people say, "You've got to have faith," or "My life would be nothing without my faith," or "If you have faith you will be helped," or "My faith took away my warts," or "Those who have faith know that God or man or their neighbor or themselves or what-have-you are this or that or something or other." Let's see if we can find out what's going on when this word "faith" is used in these ways.

"Faith" has at least three senses. First it can mean a religious sect or group, as in saying, "I belong to the Roman Catholic faith." This is not the epistemological sense of the word that we wish to pursue here. Second, it can mean simply "strong belief" or "powerful feeling," as in, "I have faith that my Redeemer liveth." This sense of "faith" is psychological, and just wishing, hoping, or desiring that a belief be true won't, obviously, make it true. This second sense of "faith" is, consequently, not really different from belief, and as we have already noted, beliefs are not the same as knowledge. Nor can faith, in the sense of "strong belief," be used to turn belief into knowledge; that is to say, a belief plus strong belief doesn't equal knowledge. However, there is a third sense of "faith" that is neither sect nor psychological but epistemological, and it is this sense that we are interested in here. This third sense of faith involves the attempt to justify the truth of certain propositions, usually theological in origin, by an appeal to the notion of faith.

When someone says, "I have faith in God," this assertion is usually opaque as it stands—i.e., when one looks closely at the assertion it makes no sense whatever. Thus when someone says, "I have faith in God," this is usually shorthand or an abbreviation for, "I have faith that something or other involving God or about God is the case or true or certain."

In other words, "having faith in," alone and by itself, doesn't make much sense. What is demanded, then, is an interpretation that will make sense out of this opaque assertion, that will bring light and render the statement translucent. We suggest a translation device for all utterances that go, "I have faith in . . ." or "I have faith for . . ." or "I have faith about . . ." What is meant or intended in all such cases is really, "I have faith that, . . ." and this in turn has as its translation, "I have a strong belief that. . . ." In other words, an utterance of the form, "I have faith in God," is really intending or saying, "I have a strong belief that something or other about God is the case"—for example, either that God exists or that God is good, or that God will be merciful to me, or that God is omniscient, omnipotent, beneficent, or benevolent. The point, again, is that "having faith in" God is not clear as it stands but that it can always be reduced or translated out. So also can the other examples of "faith for" and "faith about" be translated into talk about assenting to the truth of certain propositions that are clear.

However, as must appear plain by now, this third or epistemological sense of "faith," the critics say, simply reduces by the above analysis to the second or psychological sense of faith mentioned previously. In other words, the epistemological sense of faith is merely a reiteration of faith as strong belief in the truth of certain propositions about God. And just as previously we couldn't justify one belief by adding a strong belief to it in order to call the first belief "knowledge," so also now we are bound once again to be frustrated, the critics say, in the attempt to turn faith, in the epistemological sense, into a justification of true belief for the simple reason that there is no real epistemological sense of faith but only a covert psychological one. But see the selections below for a defense of "faith."

We will conclude this brief excursion into epistemology by reminding the reader what the excursion has all been about. We have been attempting to explicate the concept of knowledge, and part of that explication has been to find a ground, reason, or justification for propositions that we claimed to know. For if "knowledge" is defined, as we have assumed it was, as "justified true belief," the major epistemological battle becomes one of finding a justification for those true beliefs. The six kinds of justifications we examined, however, all seemed to have serious problems. Thus sensation and synthetic *a posteriori* judgments might not yield sure or certain grounds for knowledge, and because inductive inference and authority were both shown to be species of sensation, they, too, shared in the uncertainties of sensation. We showed, further, that although deductive, inference, and analytic judgments were certain, they might be only trivially true, as the example, "All black turkeys are turkeys," shows. Intuition and synthetic *a priori* judgments, furthermore, prove to be problematic to say the least, and all of them share the same skeptical fate as faith, which seemed to be merely another name for strong belief. Thus all six grounds of true belief may fail to measure up to the standard which epistemologists have set as the ideal for a justification for knowledge: a ground that would be both certain and nontrivial. Whether one or more of the attempts at justification can be revised to meet the critics is the continuing challenge to the epistemologist.

Sensation

Meditations on the First Philosophy

RENÉ DESCARTES

René Descartes (1596–1650) was a genius and a polymath of the first order. Born in Touraine, France, he was educated at the Jesuit school at La Fleche and later studied law at the University of Poitiers. His interests ranged from science to mathematics (for which he invented or discovered analytic geometry) to theology, ethics, and philosophy. If Aristotle was, as is said, the last man who knew everything, then Descartes must surely rank as the man who knew almost everything. In this selection from his Meditations, *Descartes asks the simple questions, What things can I successfully doubt? and What things can I indubitably know? The answers to both questions launch him into epistemological issues with which philosophers East and West are still wrestling.*

MEDITATION I

Of the things which may be brought within the sphere of the doubtful.

It is now some years since I detected how many were the false beliefs that I had from my earliest youth admitted as true, and how doubtful was everything I had since constructed on this basis; and from that time I was convinced that I must once for all seriously undertake to rid myself of all the opinions which I had formerly accepted, and commence to build anew from the foundation, if I wanted to establish any firm and permanent structure in the sciences. But as this enterprise appeared to be a very great one, I waited until I had attained an age so mature that I could not hope that at any later date I should be better fitted to execute my design. This reason caused me to delay so long that I should feel that I was doing wrong were I to occupy in deliberation the time that yet remains to me for action. To-day, then, since very opportunely for the plan I have in view I have delivered my mind from every care [and am happily agitated by no passions] and since I have procured for myself an assured leisure in a peaceable retirement, I shall at last seriously and freely address myself to the general upheaval of all my former opinions.

Now for this object it is not necessary that I should show that all of these are

From *Meditations on the First Philosophy,* in the *Philosophical Works of Descartes,* transl. E. S. Haldane and G. R. T. Ross; Cambridge, Cambridge University Press, 1911.

false—I shall perhaps never arrive at this end. But inasmuch as reason already persuades me that I ought no less carefully to withhold my assent from matters which are not entirely certain and indubitable than from those which appear to me manifestly to be false, if I am able to find in each one some reason to doubt, this will suffice to justify my rejecting the whole. And for that end it will not be requisite that I should examine each in particular, which would be an endless undertaking; for owing to the fact that the destruction of the foundations of necessity brings with it the downfall of the rest of the edifice, I shall only in the first place attack those principles upon which all my former opinions rested.

All that up to the present time I have accepted as most true and certain I have learned either from the senses or through the senses; but it is sometimes proved to me that these senses are deceptive, and it is wiser not to trust entirely to any thing by which we have once been deceived.

But it may be that although the senses sometimes deceive us concerning things which are hardly perceptible, or very far away, there are yet many others to be met with as to which we cannot reasonably have any doubt, although we recognise them by their means. For example, there is the fact that I am here, seated by the fire, attired in a dressing gown, having this paper in my hands and other similar matters. And how could I deny that these hands and this body are mine, were it not perhaps that I compare myself to certain persons, devoid of sense, whose cerebella are so troubled and clouded by the violent vapours of black bile, that they constantly assure us that they think they are kings when they are really quite poor, or that they are clothed in purple when they are really without covering, or who imagine that they have an earthenware head or are nothing but pumpkins or are made of glass. But they are mad, and I should not

be any the less insane were I to follow examples so extravagant.

At the same time I must remember that I am a man, and that consequently I am in the habit of sleeping, and in my dreams representing to myself the same things or sometimes even less probable things, than do those who are insane in their waking moments. How often has it happened to me that in the night I dreamt that I found myself in this particular place, that I was dressed and seated near the fire, whilst in reality I was lying undressed in bed! At this moment it does indeed seem to me that it is with eyes awake that I am looking at this paper; that this head which I move is not asleep, that it is deliberately and of set purpose that I extend my hand and perceive it; what happens in sleep does not appear so clear nor so distinct as does all this. But in thinking over this I remind myself that on many occasions I have in sleep been deceived by similar illusions, and in dwelling carefully on this reflection I see so manifestly that there are no certain indications by which we may clearly distinguish wakefulness from sleep that I am lost in astonishment. And my astonishment is such that it is almost capable of persuading me that I now dream.

Now let us assume that we are asleep and that all these particulars, e.g., that we open our eyes, shake our head, extend our hands, and so on, are but false delusions; and let us reflect that possibly neither our hands nor our whole body are such as they appear to us to be. At the same time we must at least confess that the things which are represented to us in sleep are like painted representations which can only have been formed as the counterparts of something real and true, and that in this way those general things at least, i.e., eyes, a head, hands, and a whole body, are not imaginary things, but things really existent. For, as a matter of fact, painters, even when they study with the greatest skill to represent sirens and satyrs by forms the most strange and extraordinary, cannot give them natures which are entirely new, but merely make a certain medley of the members of different animals; or if their imagination is extravagant enough to invent something so novel that nothing similar has ever before been seen, and that then their work represents a thing purely fictitious and absolutely false, it is certain all the same that the colours of which this is composed are necessarily real. And for the same reason, although these general things, to wit [a body], eyes, a head, hands, and such like, may be imaginary, we are bound at the same time to confess that there are at least some other objects yet more simple and more universal, which are real and true; and of these just in the same way as with certain real colours, all these images of things which dwell in our thoughts, whether true and real or false and fantastic, are formed.

To such a class of things pertains corporeal nature in general, and its extension, the figure of extended things, their quantity or magnitude and number, as also the place in which they are, the time which measures their duration, and so on.

That is possibly why our reasoning is not unjust when we conclude from this that Physics, Astronomy, Medicine and all other sciences which have as their end the consideration of composite things, are very dubious and uncertain; but that Arithmetic, Geometry and other sciences of that kind which only treat of things that are very simple and very general, without taking great trouble to ascertain whether they are actually existent or not, contain some measure of certainty and an element of the indubitable. For whether I am awake or asleep, two and three together always form five, and the square can never have more than four sides, and it does not seem possible that truths so clear and apparent can be suspected of any falsity [or uncertainty].

Nevertheless I have long had fixed in my mind the belief that an all-powerful God existed by whom I have been created such as I am. But how do I know that He has not brought it to pass that there is no earth, no heaven, no extended body, no magnitude, no place, and that nevertheless [I possess the perceptions of all these things and that] they seem to me to exist just exactly as I now see them? And, besides, as I sometimes imagine that others deceive themselves in the things which they think they know best, how do I know that I am not deceived every time that I add two and three, or count the sides of a square, or judge of things yet simpler, if anything simpler can be imagined? But possibly God has not desired that I should be thus deceived, for He is said to be supremely good. If, however, it is contrary to His goodness to have made me such that I constantly deceive myself, it would also appear to be contrary to His goodness to permit me to be sometimes deceived, and nevertheless I cannot doubt that He does permit this.

There may indeed be those who would prefer to deny the existence of a God so powerful, rather than believe that all other things are uncertain. But let us not oppose them for the present, and grant that all that is here said of a God is a fable; nevertheless in whatever way they suppose that I have arrived at the state of being that I have reached—whether they attribute it to fate or to accident, or make out that it is by a continual succession of antecedents, or by some other method—since to err and deceive oneself is a defect, it is clear that the greater will be the probability of my being so imperfect as to deceive myself ever, as is the Author to whom they assign my origin the less powerful. To these reasons I have certainly nothing to reply, but at the end I feel constrained to confess that there is nothing in all that I formerly believed to be true, of which I cannot in some measure doubt, and that not merely through want of thought or through levity, but for reasons which are very powerful and maturely considered; so that henceforth I ought not the less carefully to refrain from giving credence to these opinions than to that which is manifestly false, if I desire to arrive at any certainty [in the sciences].

But it is not sufficient to have made these remarks, we must also be careful to keep them in mind. For these ancient and commonly held opinions still revert frequently to my mind, long and familiar custom having given them the right to occupy my mind against my inclination and rendered them almost masters of my belief; nor will I ever lose the habit of deferring to them or of placing my confidence in them, so long as I consider them as they really are, i.e., opinions in some measure doubtful, as I have just shown, and at the same time highly probable, so that there is much more reason to believe in than to deny them. That is why I consider that I shall not be acting amiss, if, taking of set purpose a contrary belief, I allow myself to be deceived, and for a certain time pretend that all these opinions are entirely false and imaginary, until at last, having thus balanced my former prejudices with my latter [so that they cannot divert my opinions more to one side than to the other], my judgment will no longer be dominated by bad usage or turned away from the right knowledge of the truth. For I am assured that there can be neither peril nor error in this course, and that I cannot at present yield too much to distrust, since I am not considering the question of action, but only of knowledge.

I shall then suppose not that God who is supremely good and the fountain of truth, but some evil genius not less powerful than deceitful, has employed his whole energies in deceiving me; I shall consider that the heavens, the earth, colours, figures, sound, and all other external things are nought but the illusions and dreams of which this genius has availed himself in order to lay traps for my credulity; I shall consider myself as having no hands, no eyes, no flesh, no blood, nor any senses, yet falsely believing myself to possess all these things; I shall remain obstinately attached to this idea, and if by this means it is not in my power to arrive at the knowledge of any truth, I may at least do what is in my power [i.e., suspend my judgment], and with firm purpose avoid giving credence to any false thing, or being imposed upon by this arch deceiver, however powerful and deceptive he may be. But this task is a laborious one, and insensibly a certain lassitude leads me into the course of my ordinary life. And just as a captive who in sleep enjoys an imaginary liberty, when he begins to suspect that his liberty is but a dream, fears to awaken, and conspires with these agreeable illusions that the deception may be prolonged, so insensibly of my own accord I fall back into my former opinions, and I dread awakening from this slumber, lest the laborious wakefulness which would follow the tranquility of this repose should have to be spent not in daylight, but in the excessive darkness of the difficulties which have just been discussed.

MEDITATION II

Of the Nature of the Human Mind; and that it is more easily known than the Body.

The Meditation of yesterday filled my mind with so many doubts that it is no longer in my power to forget them. And yet I do not see in what manner I can resolve them; and, just as if I had all of a sudden fallen into very deep water, I am so disconcerted that I can neither make certain of setting my feet on the bottom, nor can I swim and so support myself on the surface. I shall nevertheless make an effort and follow anew the same path as that on which I yesterday entered, i.e., I shall proceed by setting aside all that in which the least doubt could be supposed to exist, just as if I had discovered that it was absolutely false; and I shall ever follow in this road until I have met with something which is certain, or at least, if I can do nothing else, until I have learned for certain that there is nothing in the world that is certain. Archimedes, in order that he might draw the terrestrial globe out of its place, and transport it elsewhere, demanded only that one point should be fixed and immovable; in the same way I shall have the right to conceive high hopes if I am happy enough to discover one thing only which is certain and indubitable.

I suppose, then, that all the things that I see are false; I persuade myself that nothing has ever existed of all that my fallacious memory represents to me. I consider that I possess no senses; I imagine that body, figure, extension, movement and place are but the fictions of my mind. What, then, can be esteemed as true? Perhaps nothing at all, unless that there is nothing in the world that is certain.

But how can I know there is not something different from those things that I have just considered, of which one cannot have the slightest doubt? Is there not some God, or some other being by whatever name we call it, who puts these reflections into my mind? That is not necessary, for is it not possible that I am capable of producing them myself? I myself, am I not at least something? But I have already denied that I had senses and body. Yet I hesitate, for what follows from that? Am I so dependent on body and senses that I cannot exist without these? But I was persuaded that there was nothing in all the world, that there was no heaven, no earth, that there were no minds, nor any bodies: was I not then likewise persuaded that I

did not exist? Not at all; of a surety I myself did exist since I persuaded myself of something [or merely because I thought of something]. But there is some deceiver or other, very powerful and very cunning, who ever employs his ingenuity in deceiving me. Then without doubt I exist also if he deceives me, and let him deceive me as much as he will, he can never cause me to be nothing so long as I think that I am something. So that after having reflected well and carefully examined all things, we must come to the definite conclusion that this proposition: I am, I exist, is necessarily true each time that I pronounce it, or that I mentally conceive it.

But I do not yet know clearly enough what I am, I who am certain that I am; and hence I must be careful to see that I do not imprudently take some other object in place of myself, and thus that I do not go astray in respect of this knowledge that I hold to be the most certain and most evident of all that I have formerly learned. That is why I shall now consider anew what I believed myself to be before I embarked upon these last reflections; and of my former opinions I shall withdraw all that might even in a small degree be invalidated by the reasons which I have just brought forward, in order that there may be nothing at all left beyond what is absolutely certain and indubitable.

What then did I formerly believe myself to be? Undoubtedly I believed myself to be a man. But what is a man? Shall I say a reasonable animal? Certainly not; for then I should have to inquire what an animal is, and what is reasonable; and thus from a single question I should insensibly fall into an infinitude of others more difficult; and I should not wish to waste the little time and leisure remaining to me in trying to unravel subtleties like these. But I shall rather stop here to consider the thoughts which of themselves spring up in my mind, and which were not inspired by anything beyond my own nature alone when I applied myself to the consideration of my being. In the first place, then, I considered myself as having a face, hands, arms, and all that system of members composed of bones and flesh as seen in a corpse which I designated by the name of body. In addition to this I considered that I was nourished, that I walked, that I felt, and that I thought, and I referred all these actions to the soul: but I did not stop to consider what the soul was, or if I did stop, I imagined that it was something extremely rare and subtle like a wind, a flame, or an ether, which was spread throughout my grosser parts. As to body I had no manner of doubt about its nature, but thought I had a very clear knowledge of it; and if I had desired to explain it according to the notions that I had then formed of it, I should have described it thus: By the body I understand all that which can be defined by a certain figure: something which can be confined in a certain place, and which can fill a given space in such a way that every other body will be excluded from it; which can be perceived either by touch, or by sight, or by hearing, or by taste, or by smell: which can be moved in many ways not, in truth, by itself, but by something which is foreign to it, by which it is touched [and from which it receives impressions]: for to have the power of self-movement, as also of feeling or of thinking, I did not consider to appertain to the nature of body: on the contrary, I was rather astonished to find that faculties similar to them existed in some bodies.

But what am I, now that I suppose that there is a certain genius which is extremely powerful, and, if I may say so, malicious, who employs all his powers in deceiving me? Can I affirm that I possess the least of all those things which I have just said pertain to the nature of body? I pause to consider, I revolve all these things in my mind, and I find none of which I can say that it pertains to me. It would be tedious to stop to enumerate them. Let us pass to the attributes of soul and see if there is any one which is in me? What of nutrition or walking [the first mentioned]? But if it is so that I have no body it is also true that I can neither walk nor take nourishment. Another attribute is sensation. But one cannot feel without body, and besides I have thought I perceived many things during sleep that I recognised in my waking moments as not having been experienced at all. What of thinking? I find here that thought is an attribute that belongs to me; it alone cannot be separated from me. I am, I exist, that is certain. But how often? Just when I think; for it might possibly be the case if I ceased entirely to think, that I should likewise cease altogether to exist. I do not now admit anything which is not necessarily true: to speak accurately I am not more than a thing which thinks, that is to say a mind or a soul, or an understanding, or a reason, which are terms whose significance was formerly unknown to me. I am, however, a real thing and really exist; but what thing? I have answered: a thing which thinks.

And what more? I shall exercise my imagination [in order to see if I am not something more]. I am not a collection of members which we call the human body: I am not a subtle air distributed through these members, I am not a wind, a fire, a vapour, a breath, nor anything at all which I can imagine or conceive; because I have assumed that all these were nothing. Without changing that supposition I find that I only leave myself certain of the fact that I am somewhat. But perhaps it is true that these same things which I supposed were non-existent because they are unknown to me, are really not different from the self which I know. I am not sure about this, I shall not dispute about it now; I can only give judgment on things that are known to me. I know that I exist, and I inquire what I am, I whom I know to exist. But it is very certain that the knowledge of my existence taken in its precise significance does not depend on things whose existence is not yet known to me; consequently it does not depend on those which I can feign in imagination. And indeed the very term *feign* in imagination proves to me my error, for I really do this if I image myself a something, since to imagine is nothing else than to contemplate the figure or image of a corporeal thing. But I already know for certain that I am, and that it may be that all these images, and, speaking generally, all things that relate to the nature of body are nothing but dreams [and chimeras]. For this reason I see clearly that I have as little reason to say, "I shall stimulate my imagination in order to know more distinctly what I am," than if I were to say, "I am now awake, and I perceive somewhat that is real and true: but because I do not yet perceive it distinctly enough, I shall go to sleep of express purpose, so that my dreams may represent the perception with greatest truth and evidence." And, thus, I know for certain that nothing of all that I can understand by means of my imagination belongs to this knowledge which I have of myself, and that it is necessary to recall the mind from this mode of thought with the utmost diligence in order that it may be able to know its own nature with perfect distinctness.

But what then am I? A thing which thinks. What is a thing which thinks? It is a thing which doubts, understands [conceives], affirms, denies, wills, refuses, which also imagines and feels.

Certainly it is no small matter if all these things pertain to my nature. But why should they not so pertain? Am I not that being who now doubts nearly everything, who nevertheless understands certain things, who affirms that one only is true, who denies all the others, who desires to know more, is averse from being deceived, who imagines many things, some-

times indeed despite his will, and who perceives many likewise, as by the intervention of the bodily organs? Is there nothing in all this which is as true as it is certain that I exist, even though I should always sleep and though he who has given me being employed all his ingenuity in deceiving me? Is there likewise any one of these attributes which can be distinguished from my thought, or which might be said to be separated from myself? For it is so evident of itself that it is I who doubts, who understands, and who desires, that there is no reason here to add anything to explain it. And I have certainly the power of imagining likewise; for although it may happen (as I formerly supposed) that none of the things which I imagine are true, nevertheless this power of imagining does not cease to be really in use, and it forms part of my thought. Finally, I am the same who feels, that is to say, who perceives certain things, as by the organs of sense, since in truth I see light, I hear noise, I feel heat. But it will be said that these phenomena are false and that I am dreaming. Let it be so; still it is at least quite certain that it seems to me that I see light, that I hear noise and that I feel heat. That cannot be false; properly speaking it is what is in me called feeling; and used in this precise sense that is no other thing than thinking.

From this time I begin to know what I am with a little more clearness and distinction than before; but nevertheless it still seems to me, and I cannot prevent myself from thinking, that corporeal things, whose images are framed by thought, which are tested by the senses, are much more distinctly known than that obscure part of me which does not come under the imagination. Although really it is very strange to say that I know and understand more distinctly these things whose existence seems to me dubious, which are unknown to me, and which do not belong to me, than others of the truth of which I am convinced, which are known to me and which pertain to my real nature, in a word, than myself. But I see clearly how the case stands: my mind loves to wander, and cannot yet suffer itself to be retained within the just limits of truth. Very good, let us once more give it the freest rein, so that, when afterwards we seize the proper occasion for pulling up, it may the more easily be regulated and controlled.

Let us begin by considering the commonest matters, those which we believe to be the most distinctly comprehended, to wit, the bodies which we touch and see; not indeed bodies in general, for these general ideas are usually a little more confused, but let us consider one body in particular. Let us take, for example, this piece of wax: it has been taken quite freshly from the hive, and it has not yet lost the sweetness of the honey which it contains; it still retains somewhat of the odour of the flowers from which it has been culled; its colour, its figure, its size are apparent; it is hard, cold, easily handled, and if you strike it with the finger, it will emit a sound. Finally all the things which are requisite to cause us distinctly to recognise a body are met with in it. But notice that while I speak and approach the fire what remained of the taste is exhaled, the smell evaporates, the colour alters, the figure is destroyed, the size increases, it becomes liquid, it heats, scarcely can one handle it, and when one strikes it, no sound is emitted. Does the same wax remain after this change? We must confess that it remains; none would judge otherwise. What then did I know so distinctly in this piece of wax? It could certainly be nothing of all that the senses brought to my notice, since all these things which fall under taste, smell, sight, touch, and hearing, are found to be changed, and yet the same wax remains.

Perhaps it was what I now think, viz. that this wax was not that sweetness of honey, nor that agreeable scent of flowers, nor that particular whiteness, nor that figure, nor that sound, but simply a body which a little while before appeared to me as perceptible under these forms, and which is now perceptible under others. But what, precisely, is it that I imagine when I form such conceptions? Let us attentively consider this, and, abstracting from all that does not belong to the wax, let us see what remains. Certainly nothing remains excepting a certain extended thing which is flexible and movable. But what is the meaning of flexible and movable? Is it not that I imagine that this piece of wax being round is capable of becoming square and of passing from a square to a triangular figure? No, certainly it is not that, since I imagine it admits of an infinitude of similar changes, and I nevertheless do not know how to compass the infinitude by my imagination, and consequently this conception which I have of the wax is not brought about by the faculty of imagination. What now is this extension? Is it not also unknown? For it becomes greater when the wax is melted, greater when it is boiled, and greater still when the heat increases; and I should not conceive [clearly] according to truth what wax is, if I did not think that even this piece that we are considering is capable of receiving more variations in extension than I have ever imagined. We must then grant that I could not even understand through the imagination what this piece of wax is, and that it is my mind alone which perceives it. I say this piece of wax in particular, for as to wax in general it is yet clearer. But what is this piece of wax which cannot be understood excepting by the [understanding or] mind? It is certainly the same that I see, touch, imagine, and finally it is the same which I have always believed it to be from the beginning. But what must particularly be observed is that its perception is neither an act of vision, nor of touch, nor of imagination, and has never been such although it may have appeared formerly to be so, but only an intuition of the mind, which may be imperfect and confused as it was formerly, or clear and distinct as it is at present, according as my attention is more or less directed to the elements which are found in it, and of which it is composed.

Yet in the meantime I am greatly astonished when I consider [the great feebleness of mind] and its proneness to fall [insensibly] into error; for although without giving expression to my thoughts I consider all this in my own mind, words often impede me and I am almost deceived by the terms of ordinary language. For we say that we see the same wax, if it is present, and not that we simply judge that it is the same from its having the same colour and figure. From this I should conclude that I knew the wax by means of vision and not simply by the intuition of the mind; unless by chance I remember that, when looking from a window and saying I see men who pass in the street, I really do not see them, but infer that what I see is men, just as I say that I see wax. And yet what do I see from the window but hats and coats which may cover automatic machines? Yet I judge these to be men. And similarly solely by the faculty of judgment which rests in my mind, I comprehend that which I believed I saw with my eyes.

A man who makes it his aim to raise his knowledge above the common should be ashamed to derive the occasion for doubting from the forms of speech invented by the vulgar; I prefer to pass on and consider whether I had a more evident and perfect conception of what the wax was when I first perceived it, and when I believed I knew it by means of the external senses or at least by the common sense as it is called, that is to say by the imaginative faculty, or whether my present conception is clearer now that I have most carefully examined what it is, and in what

way it can be known. It would certainly be absurd to doubt as to this. For what was there in this first perception which was distinct? What was there which might not as well have been perceived by any of the animals? But when I distinguish the wax from its external forms, and when, just as if I had taken from it its vestments, I consider it quite naked, it is certain that although some error may still be found in my judgment, I can nevertheless not perceive it thus without a human mind.

But finally what shall I say of this mind, that is, of myself, for up to this point I do not admit in myself anything but mind? What then, I who seem to perceive this piece of wax so distinctly, do I not know myself, not only with much more truth and certainty, but also with much more distinctness and clearness? For if I judge that the wax is or exists from the fact that I see it, it certainly follows much more clearly that I am or that I exist myself from the fact that I see it. For it may be that what I see is not really wax, it may also be that I do not possess eyes with which to see anything; but it cannot be that when I see, or (for I no longer take account of the distinction) when I think I see, that I myself who think am nought. So if I judge that the wax exists from the fact that I touch it, the same thing will follow, to wit, that I am; and if I judge that my imagination, or some other cause, whatever it is, persuades me that the wax exists, I shall still conclude the same. And what I have here remarked of wax may be applied to all other things which are external to me [and which are met with outside of me]. And further, if the [notion or] perception of wax has seemed to me clearer and more distinct, not only after the sight or the touch, but also after many other causes have rendered it quite manifest to me, with how much more [evidence] and distinctness must it be said that I now know myself, since all the reasons which contribute to the knowledge of wax, or any other body whatever, are yet better proofs of the nature of my mind! And there are so many other things in the mind itself which may contribute to the elucidation of its nature, that those which depend on body such as these just mentioned, hardly merit being taken into account.

But finally here I am, having insensibly reverted to the point I desired, for, since it is now manifest to me that even bodies are not properly speaking known by the senses or by the faculty of imagination, but by the understanding only, and since they are not known from the fact that they are seen or touched, but only because they are understood, I see clearly that there is nothing which is easier for me to know than my mind. But because it is difficult to rid oneself so promptly of an opinion to which one was accustomed for so long, it will be well that I should halt a little at this point, so that by the length of my meditation I may more deeply imprint on my memory this new knowledge.

An Essay Concerning Human Understanding

JOHN LOCKE

John Locke *(1632–1704) has set, in his* Essay, *the foundation for the epistemological theory called* empiricism. *In his search for the origin of our knowledge he concludes that there is nothing in the understanding that was not first in the senses. Thus, the epistemological program which Locke establishes amounts essentially to this: For every idea you have, hunt down the sensation and the thing that gave it birth. If you cannot find the sensation that caused the idea, then you may reasonably be sure that the idea is spurious.*

FROM QUALITIES AND POWERS OF BODIES

7. To discover the nature of our *ideas* the better, and to discourse of them intelligibly, it will be convenient to distinguish them *as they are ideas or perceptions in our minds; and as they are modifications of matter in the bodies that cause such perceptions in us:* that so we may not think (as perhaps usually is done) that they are exactly the images and resemblances of something inherent in the subject; most of those of sensation being in the mind no more the likeness of something existing without us, than the names that stand for them are the likeness of our ideas, which yet upon hearing they are apt to excite in us.

8. Whatsoever the mind perceives *in itself,* or is the immediate object of percep-

From *An Essay Concerning Human Understanding.* Book II, Chapter XXVII.

tion, thought, or understanding, that I call *idea;* and the power to produce any idea in our mind, I call *quality* of the subject wherein that power is. Thus a snowball having the power to produce in us the ideas of white, cold, and round—the power to produce those ideas in us, as they are in the snowball, I call qualities; and as they are sensations or perceptions in our understandings, I call them ideas; which *ideas,* if I speak of sometimes as in the things themselves, I would be understood to mean those qualities in the objects which produce them in us.

9. Qualities thus considered in bodies are,

First, such as are utterly inseparable from the body, in what state soever it be; and such as in all the alterations and changes it suffers, all the force can be used upon it, it constantly keeps; and such as sense constantly finds in every particle of matter which has bulk enough to be perceived; and the mind finds inseparable from every particle of matter, though less than to make itself singly be perceived by our senses: v.g., Take a grain of wheat, divide it into two parts; each part has still solidity, extension, figure, and mobility: divide it again, and it retains still the same qualities; and so divide it on, till the parts become insensible; they must retain still each of them all those qualities. For division (which is all that a mill, or pestle, or any other body, does upon another, in reducing it to insensible parts) can never take away either solidity, extension, figure, or mobility from any body, but only makes two or more distinct separate masses of matter, of that which was but one before; all which distinct masses, reckoned as so many distinct bodies, after division, make a certain number. These I call *original* or *primary qualities* of body, which I think we may observe to produce simple ideas in us, viz., solidity, extension, figure, motion or rest, and number.

10. *Secondly,* such qualities which in

truth are nothing in the objects themselves but powers to produce various sensations in us by their primary qualities, i.e., by the bulk, figure, texture, and motion of their insensible parts, as colours, sounds, tastes, etc. These I call *secondary qualities.* To these might be added a *third* sort, which are allowed to be barely powers; though they are as much real qualities in the subject as those which I, to comply with the common way of speaking, call qualities, but for distinction, secondary qualities. For the power in fire to produce a new colour, or consistency, in *wax* or *clay*—by its primary qualities, is as much a quality in fire, as the power it has to produce in *me* a new idea or sensation of warmth or burning, which I felt not before—by the same primary qualities, viz., the bulk, texture, and motion of its insensible parts.

11. The next thing to be considered is, how bodies produce ideas in us; and that is manifestly by impulse, the only way which we can conceive bodies to operate in.

12. If then external objects be not united to our minds when they produce ideas therein; and yet we perceive these *original* qualities in such of them as singly fall under our senses, it is evident that some motion must be thence continued by our nerves, or animal spirits, by some parts of our bodies, to the brains or the seat of sensation, there to produce in our minds the particular ideas we have of them. And since the extension, figure, number, and motion of bodies of an observable bigness, may be perceived at a distance by the sight, it is evident some singly imperceptible bodies must come from them to the eyes, and thereby convey to the brain some motion; which produces these ideas which we have of them in us.

13. After the same manner that the ideas of these original qualities are produced in us, we may conceive that the ideas of *secondary* qualities are also pro-

duced, viz., by the operation of insensible particles on our senses. For, it being manifest that there are bodies and good store of bodies, each whereof are so small, that we cannot by any of our senses discover either their bulk, figure, or motion—as is evident in the particles of the air and water, and others extremely smaller than those; perhaps as much smaller than the particles of air and water, as the particles of air and water are smaller than peas or hail-stones; let us suppose at present that the different motions and figures, bulk and number, of such particles, affecting the several organs of our senses, produce in us those different sensations which we have from the colours and smells of bodies; v.g., that a violet, by the impulse of such insensible particles of matter, of peculiar figures and bulks, and in different degrees and modifications of their motions, causes the ideas of the blue colour, and sweet scent of that flower to be produced in our minds. It being no more impossible to conceive that God should annex such ideas to such motions, with which they have no similitude, than that he should annex the idea of pain to the motion of a piece of steel dividing our flesh, with which that idea hath no resemblance.

14. What I have said concerning colours and smells may be understood also of tastes and sounds, and other the like sensible qualities; which, whatever reality we by mistake attribute to them, are in truth nothing in the objects themselves, but powers to produce various sensations in us; and depend on those primary qualities, viz., bulk, figure, texture, and motion of parts.

15. From whence I think it easy to draw this observation—that the ideas of primary qualities of bodies are resemblances of them, and their patterns do really exist in the bodies themselves, but the ideas produced in us by these secondary qualities have no resemblance of them at all. There is nothing like our ideas, existing in the bodies themselves. They are, in the bodies we denominate from them, only a power to produce those sensations in us; and what is sweet, blue, or warm in idea, is but the certain bulk, figure, and motion of the insensible parts, in the bodies themselves, which we call so.

16. Flame is denominated hot and light; snow, white and cold; and manna, white and sweet, from the ideas they produce in us. Which qualities are commonly thought to be the same in those bodies that those ideas are in us, the one the perfect resemblance of the other, as they are in a mirror, and it would by most men be judged very extravagant if one should say otherwise. And yet he that will consider that the same fire that, at one distance produces in us the sensation of warmth, does, at a nearer approach, produce in us the far different sensation of pain, ought to bethink himself what reason he has to say—that this idea of warmth, which was produced in him by the fire, is *actually in the fire;* and his idea of pain, which the same fire produced in him the same way, is *not* in the fire. Why are whiteness and coldness in snow, and pain not, when it produces the one and the other idea in us; and can do neither, but by the bulk, figure, number, and motion of its solid parts?

17. The particular bulk, number, figure, and motion of the parts of fire or snow are really in them—whether any one's senses perceive them or no: and therefore they may be called *real* qualities, because they really exist in those bodies. But light, heat, whiteness, or coldness, are no more really in them than sickness or pain is in manna. Take away the sensation of them; let not the eyes see light or colours, nor the ears hear sounds; let the palate not taste, nor the nose smell, and all colours, tastes, odours, and sounds, *as they are such particular ideas,* vanish and cease, and are reduced to their causes, i.e., bulk, figure, and motion of parts.

OF OUR COMPLEX IDEAS
OF SUBSTANCES

1. The mind being, as I have declared, furnished with a great number of the simple ideas, conveyed in by the senses as they are found in exterior things, or by reflection on its own operations, takes notice also that a certain number of these simple ideas go constantly together; which being presumed to belong to one thing, and words being suited to common apprehensions, and made use of for quick dispatch, are called, so united in one subject, by one name; which, by inadvertency, we are apt afterward to talk of and consider as one simple idea, which indeed is a complication of many ideas together: because, as I have said, not imagining how these simple ideas *can* subsist by themselves, we can accustom ourselves to suppose some *substratum* wherein they do subsist, and from which they do result, which therefore we call *substance*.

2. So that if any one will examine himself concerning his notion of pure substance in general, he will find he has no other idea of it at all, but only a supposition of he knows not what *support* of such qualities which are capable of producing simple ideas in us; which qualities are commonly called accidents. If any one should be asked, what is the subject wherein colour or weight inheres, he would have nothing to say, but the solid extended parts; and if he were demanded, what is it that solidity and extension adhere in, he would not be in a much better case than the Indian . . . who, saying that the world was supported by a great elephant, was asked what the elephant rested on; to which his answer was—a great tortoise: but being again pressed to know what gave support to the broad-backed tortoise, replied—*something, he knew not what*. And thus here, as in all other cases where we use words without having clear and distinct ideas, we talk like children:

who, being questioned what such a thing is, which they know not, readily give this satisfactory answer, that it is *something*: which in truth signifies no more, when so used, either by children or men, but that they know not what; and that the thing they pretend to know, and talk of, is what they have no distinct idea of at all, and so are perfectly ignorant of it, and in the dark. The idea then we have, to which we give the *general* name substance, being nothing but the supposed, but unknown, support of those qualities we find existing, which we imagine cannot subsist *sine re substante,* without something to support them, we call that support *substantia;* which, according to the true import of the word, is, in plain English, standing under or upholding.

3. An obscure and relative idea of *substance in general* being thus made we come to have the ideas of *particular sorts of substances,* by collecting *such* combinations of simple ideas as are, by experience and observation of men's senses, taken notice of to exist together; and are therefore supposed to flow from the particular internal constitution, or unknown essence of that substance. Thus we come to have the ideas of a man, horse, gold, water, etc.; of which substances, whether any one has any other *clear* idea, further than of certain simple ideas co-existent together, I appeal to every one's own experience. It is the ordinary qualities observable in iron, or a diamond, put together, that make the true complex idea of those substances, which a smith or a jeweller commonly knows better than a philosopher; who, whatever *substantial forms* he may talk of, has no other idea of those substances, than what is framed by a collection of those simple ideas which are to be found in them: only we must take notice, that our complex ideas of substances, besides all those simple ideas they are made up of, have always the confused idea of something to which they belong, and in which they subsist: and

therefore when we speak of any sort of substance, we say it is a thing having such or such qualities; as body is a thing that is extended, figured, and capable of motion; spirit, a thing capable of thinking; and so hardness, friability, and power to draw iron, we say, are qualities to be found in a loadstone. These, and the like fashions of speaking, intimate that the substance is supposed always *something besides* the extension, figure, solidity, motion, thinking, or other observable ideas, though we know not what it is.

4. Hence, when we talk or think of any particular sort of corporeal substances, as horse, stone, etc., though the idea we have of either of them be but the complication or collection of those several simple ideas of sensible qualities, which we used to find in the thing called horse or stone; yet, *because we cannot conceive how they should subsist alone, nor one in another,* we suppose them existing in and supported by some common subject; which support we denote by the name substance, though it be certain we have no clear or distinct idea of that thing we suppose a support.

Commentary on the Vedānta Sūtras

ŚAṀKARA

Śaṁkara (pronounced "shängkärə") (788–820 A.D.) has been justifiably called "The St. Thomas Aquinas of Hinduism." At a time when Hinduism was under heavy philosophic attack from the Buddhist idealists, Śaṁkara marshalled the forces of Hindu realism in order to do battle with the Buddhists and to set straight other philosophers and theologians who seemed set on going down strange, heterodox paths. The number of books and tracts attributed to him is enormous; from magnificent commentaries on the several Upanishads *and the* Bhagavad Gītā *to extraordinary discussions of the* Vedānta Sūtras *of Bādarāyana, from which discussions our selection is taken. The 555* sūtras, *or short, pithy aphorisms that Bādarāyana is thought to have composed, are nearly unintelligible without a commentary. What emerges in Śaṁkara's commentary is the essence of his entire* advaita (*nondualistic*) Vedānta *philosophy—namely, a metaphysical monism that makes room, nonetheless, for an interesting kind of epistemological realism. Śaṁkara defends this realism against the attacks of the Buddhist idealists in the passages that follow, and concludes his defense with a slashing* ad hominem *diatribe against the person of Gautama Buddha.*

FROM BOOK TWO

Chapter II

28. The non-existence (of external things) cannot be maintained, on account of (our) consciousness (of them).*

There having been brought forward, in what precedes, the various objections which lie against the doctrine of the reality of the external world (in the Buddhist sense), such as the impossibility of account-

* This is the sūtra; now comes the commentary—EDS.

ing for the existence of aggregates, etc., we are now confronted by those Buddhists who maintain that only cognitions (or ideas, vijñāna) exist. The doctrine of the reality of the external world was indeed propounded by Buddha conforming himself to the mental state of some of his disciples whom he perceived to be attached to external things; but it does not represent his own true view according to which cognitions alone are real.

According to this latter doctrine the process, whose constituting members are the act of knowledge, the object of knowl-

From *The Vedānta Sūtras with the Commentary of Śaṅkarācārya*, transl. George Thibaut; *Sacred Books of the East*, Vol. XXXIV, F. Müller, ed., London, Oxford University Press, 1896.

edge, and the result of knowledge,[1] is an altogether internal one, existing in so far only as it is connected with the mind (buddhi). Even if external things existed, that process could not take place but in connexion with the mind. If, the Buddhists say, you ask how it is known that that entire process is internal and that no outward things exist apart from consciousness, we reply that we base our doctrine on the impossibility of external things. For if external things are admitted, they must be either atoms or aggregates of atoms such as posts and the like. But atoms cannot be comprehended under the ideas of posts and the like, it being impossible for cognition to represent (things as minute as) atoms. Nor, again, can the outward things be aggregates of atoms such as pillars and the like, because those aggregates can neither be defined as different nor as non-different from the atoms.[2] In the same way we can show that the external things are not universals and so on.

Moreover, the cognitions—which are of a uniform nature only in so far as they are states of consciousness—undergo, according to their objects, successive modifications, so that there is presented to the mind now the idea of a post, now the idea of a wall, now the idea of a jar, and so on. Now this is not possible without some distinction on the part of the ideas themselves, and hence we must necessarily admit that the ideas have the same forms as

their objects. But if we make this admission, from which it follows that the form of the objects is determined by the ideas, the hypothesis of the existence of external things becomes altogether gratuitous. From the fact, moreover, of our always being conscious of the act of knowledge and the object of knowledge simultaneously it follows that the two are in reality identical. When we are conscious of the one we are conscious of the other also; and that would not happen if the two were essentially distinct, as in that case there would be nothing to prevent our being conscious of one apart from the other. For this reason also we maintain that there are no outward things. Perception is to be considered as similar to a dream and the like. The ideas present to our minds during a dream, a magical illusion, a mirage and so on, appear in the twofold form of subject and object, although there is all the while no external object; hence we conclude that the ideas of posts and the like which occur in our waking state are likewise independent of external objects; for they also are simply ideas. If we be asked how, in the absence of external things, we account for the actual variety of ideas, we reply that that variety is to be explained from the impressions left by previous ideas.[3] In the beginningless saṁsāra ideas and mental impressions succeed each other as causes and effects, just as the plant springs from the seed and seeds are again produced from the plant, and there exists therefore a sufficient reason for the variety of ideas actually experienced. That the variety of ideas is solely due to the impressions left on the mind by past ideas follows, moreover, from the following affirmative and negative judgments: we both (the Vedāntins as well as the Buddhists) admit that in dreams, etc. there presents

---

[1] According to the Vijñānavādin the cognition specialised by its various contents, such as, for instance, the idea of blue colour is the object of knowledge; the cognition in so far as it is consciousness (avabhāsa) is the result of knowledge; the cognition in so far as it is power is māna, knowledge; in so far as it is the abode of that power it is pramātri, knowing subject.

[2] If they are said to be different from the atoms they can no longer be considered as composed of atoms; if they are non-different from atoms they cannot be the cause of the mental representations of gross non-atomic bodies.

[3] Vāsanā, above translated by mental impression, strictly means any member of the infinite series of ideas which precedes the present actual idea.

itself a variety of ideas which arise from mental impressions, without any external object; we (the Buddhists) do not admit that any variety of ideas can arise from external objects, without mental impressions. Thus we are again led to conclude that no outward things exist.

To all this we (the Vedāntins) make the following reply. The non-existence of external things cannot be maintained because we are conscious of external things. In every act of perception we are conscious of some external thing corresponding to the idea, whether it be a post or a wall or a piece of cloth or a jar, and that of which we are conscious cannot but exist. Why should we pay attention to the words of a man who, while conscious of an outward thing through its approximation to his senses, affirms that he is conscious of no outward thing, and that no such thing exists, any more than we listen to a man who while he is eating and experiencing the feeling of satisfaction avers that he does not eat and does not feel satisfied? If the Buddhist should reply that he does not affirm that he is conscious of no object but only that he is conscious of no object apart from the act of consciousness, we answer that he may indeed make any arbitrary statement he likes, but that he has no arguments to prove what he says. That the outward thing exists apart from consciousness, has necessarily to be accepted on the ground of the nature of consciousness itself. Nobody when perceiving a post or a wall is conscious of his perception only, but all men are conscious of posts and walls and the like as objects of their perceptions. That such is the consciousness of all men, appears also from the fact that even those who contest the existence of external things bear witness to their existence when they say that what is an internal object of cognition appears like something external. For they practically accept the general consciousness, which testifies to the existence of an external world, and being at the same time anxious to refute it they speak of the external things as "like something external." If they did not themselves at the bottom acknowledge the existence of the external world, how could they use the expression "like something external?" No one says, "Vishnumitra appears like the son of a barren mother." If we accept the truth as it is given to us in our consciousness, we must admit that the object of perception appears to us as something external, not like something external. But—the Buddhist may reply—we conclude that the object of perception is only like something external because external things are impossible. This conclusion we rejoin is improper, since the possibility or impossibility of things is to be determined only on the ground of the operation or non-operation of the means of right knowledge; while on the other hand, the operation and non-operation of the means of right knowledge are not to be made dependent on preconceived possibilities or impossibilities. Possible is whatever is apprehended by perception or some other means of proof; impossible is what is not so apprehended. Now the external things are, according to their nature, apprehended by all the instruments of knowledge; how then can you maintain that they are not possible, on the ground of such idle dilemmas as that about their difference or non-difference from atoms? Nor, again, does the non-existence of objects follow from the fact of the ideas having the same form as the objects; for if there were no objects the ideas could not have the forms of the objects, and the objects are actually apprehended as external. For the same reason (i.e., because the distinction of thing and idea is given in consciousness) the invariable concomitance of idea and thing has to be considered as proving only that the thing constitutes the means of the idea, not that the two are identical. Moreover, when we are conscious first of a pot and then of a piece of cloth, consciousness remains the same in the two acts while what varies are merely the distinctive attributes of consciousness; just as when we see at first a black and then a white cow, the distinction of the two perceptions is due to the varying blackness and whiteness while the generic character of the cow remains the same. The difference of the one permanent factor (from the two—or more—varying factors) is proved throughout by the two varying factors, and vice versa the difference of the latter (from the permanent factor) by the presence of the one (permanent factor). Therefore thing and idea are distinct. The same view is to be held with regard to the perception and the remembrance of a jar; there also the perception and the remembrance only are distinct while the jar is one and the same; in the same way as when conscious of the smell of milk and the taste of milk we are conscious of the smell and taste as different things but of the milk itself as one only.

Further, two ideas which occupy different moments of time and pass away as soon as they have become objects of consciousness cannot apprehend—or be apprehended by—each other. From this it follows that certain doctrines forming part of the Buddhist system cannot be upheld; so the doctrine that ideas are different from each other; the doctrine that everything is momentary, void, etc.; the doctrine of the distinction of individuals and classes; the doctrine that a former idea leaves an impression giving rise to a later idea; the doctrine of the distinction, owing to the influence of ignorance, of the attributes of existence and non-existence; the doctrine of bondage and release (depending on absence and presence of right knowledge).[4]

[4] For all these doctrines depend on the comparison of ideas which is not possible unless there be a permanent knowing subject in addition to the transitory ideas.

Further, if you say that we are conscious of the idea, you must admit that we are also conscious of the external thing. And if you rejoin that we are conscious of the idea on its own account because it is of a luminous nature like a lamp, while the external thing is not so; we reply that by maintaining the idea to be illuminated by itself you make yourself guilty of an absurdity no less than if you said that fire burns itself. And at the same time you refuse to accept the common and altogether rational opinion that we are conscious of the external thing by means of the idea different from the thing! Indeed a proof of extraordinary philosophic insight! It cannot, moreover, be asserted in any way that the idea apart from the thing is the object of our consciousness; for it is absurd to speak of a thing as the object of its own activity. Possibly you (the Buddhist) will rejoin that, if the idea is to be apprehended by something different from it, that something also must be apprehended by something different and so on ad infinitum. And, moreover, you will perhaps object that as each cognition is of an essentially illuminating nature like a lamp, the assumption of a further cognition is uncalled for; for as they are both equally illuminating the one cannot give light to the other. But both these objections are unfounded. As the idea only is apprehended, and there is consequently no necessity to assume something to apprehend the Self which witnesses the idea (is conscious of the idea), there results no regressus ad infinitum. And the witnessing Self and the idea are of an essentially different nature, and may therefore stand to each other in the relation of knowing subject and object known. The existence of the witnessing Self is self-proved and cannot therefore be denied. Moreover, if you maintain that the idea, lamplike, manifests itself without standing in need of a further principle to illuminate it, you maintain thereby that ideas exist which are not apprehended by any of the means of knowledge, and which are without a knowing being; which is no better than to assert that a thousand lamps burning inside some impenetrable mass of rocks manifest themselves. And if you should maintain that thereby we admit your doctrine, since it follows from what we have said that the idea itself implies consciousness; we reply that, as observation shows, the lamp in order to become manifest requires some other intellectual agent furnished with instruments such as the eye, and that therefore the idea also, as equally being a thing to be illuminated, becomes manifest only through an ulterior intelligent principle. And if you finally object that we, when advancing the witnessing Self as self-proved, merely express in other words the Buddhist tenet that the idea is self-manifested, we refute you by remarking that your ideas have the attributes of originating, passing away, being manifold, and so on (while our Self is one and permanent). We thus have proved that an idea, like a lamp, requires an ulterior intelligent principle to render it manifest.

29. And on account of their difference of nature (the ideas of the waking state) are not like those of a dream.

We now apply ourselves to the refutation of the averment made by the Buddhist, that the ideas of posts, and so on, of which we are conscious in the waking state, may arise in the absence of external objects, just as the ideas of a dream, both being ideas alike. The two sets of ideas, we maintain, cannot be treated on the same footing, on account of the difference of their character. They differ as follows. The things of which we are conscious in a dream are negated by our waking consciousness. "I wrongly thought that I had

a meeting with a great man; no such meeting took place, but my mind was dulled by slumber, and so the false idea arose." In an analogous manner the things of which we are conscious when under the influence of a magic illusion, and the like, are negated by our ordinary consciousness. Those things, on the other hand, of which we are conscious in our waking state, such as posts and the like, are never negated in any state. Moreover, the visions of a dream are acts of remembrance, while the visions of the waking state are acts of immediate consciousness; and the distinction between remembrance and immediate consciousness is directly cognised by every one as being founded on the absence or presence of the object. When, for instance, a man remembers his absent son, he does not directly perceive him, but merely wishes so to perceive him. As thus the distinction between the two states is evident to every one, it is impossible to formulate the inference that waking consciousness is false because it is mere consciousness, such as dreaming consciousness; for we certainly cannot allow would-be philosophers to deny the truth of what is directly evident to themselves. Just because they feel the absurdity of denying what is evident to themselves, and are consequently unable to demonstrate the baselessness of the ideas of the waking state from those ideas themselves, they attempt to demonstrate it from their having certain attributes in common with the ideas of the dreaming state. But if some attribute cannot belong to a thing on account of the latter's own nature, it cannot belong to it on account of the thing having certain attributes in common with some other thing. Fire, which is felt to be hot, cannot be demonstrated to be cold, on the ground of its having attributes in common with water. And the difference of nature between the waking and the sleeping state we have already shown.

30. The existence (of mental impressions) is not possible (on the Buddhist view) on account of the absence of perception (of external things).

We now proceed to that theory of yours, according to which the variety of ideas can be explained from the variety of mental impressions, without any reference to external things, and remark that on your doctrine the existence of mental impressions is impossible, as you do not admit the perception of external things. For the variety of mental impressions is caused altogether by the variety of the things perceived. How, indeed, could various impressions originate if no external things were perceived? The hypothesis of a beginningless series of mental impressions would lead only to a baseless regressus ad infinitum, sublative of the entire phenomenal world, and would in no way establish your position. The same argument, i.e., the one founded on the impossibility of mental impressions which are not caused by external things, refutes also the positive and negative judgments, on the ground of which the denier of an external world above attempted to show that ideas are caused by mental impressions, not by external things. We rather have on our side a positive and a negative judgment whereby to establish our doctrine of the existence of external things, viz., "the perception of external things is admitted to take place also without mental impressions," and "mental impressions are not admitted to originate independently of the perception of external things." Moreover, an impression is a kind of modification, and modifications cannot, as experience teaches, take place unless there is some substratum which is modified. But, according to your doctrine, such a substratum of impressions does not exist, since you say that it cannot be cognised through any means of knowledge.

31. And on account of the momentariness (of the ālayavijñāna, it cannot be the abode of mental impressions).

If you maintain that the so-called internal cognition (ālayavijñāna [5]) assumed by you may constitute abode of the mental impressions, we deny that, because that cognition also being admittedly momentary, and hence non-permanent, cannot be the abode of impressions any more than the quasi-external cognitions (pravritti-vijñāna). For unless there exists one continuous principle equally connected with the past, the present, and the future,[6] or an absolutely unchangeable (Self) which cognises everything, we are unable to account for remembrance, recognition, and so on, which are subject to mental impressions dependent on place, time, and cause. If, on the other hand, you declare your ālayavijñāna to be something permanent, you thereby abandon your tenet of the ālayavijñāna as well as everything else being momentary. Or (to explain the Sūtra in a different way) as the tenet of general momentariness is characteristic of the systems of the idealistic as well as the realistic Buddhists, we may bring forward against the doctrines of the former all those arguments dependent on the principle of general momentariness which we have above urged against the latter.

We have thus refuted both nihilistic doctrines, viz., the doctrine which maintains the (momentary) reality of the ex-

[5] The vijñānaskandha comprises vijñānas of two different kinds, the ālayavijñāna and the pravrittivijñāna. The ālayavijñāna comprises the series of cognitions or ideas which refer to the ego; the pravrittivijñāna comprises those ideas which refer to apparently external objects, such as colour and the like. The ideas of the latter class are due to the mental impressions left by the antecedent ideas of the former class.

[6] Viz., in the present case the principle that what presents itself to consciousness is not non-existent.

ternal world, and the doctrine which asserts that ideas only exist. The third variety of Buddhist doctrine, viz., that everything is empty (i.e., that absolutely nothing exists), is contradicted by all means of right knowledge, and therefore requires no special refutation. For this apparent world, whose existence is guaranteed by all means of knowledge, cannot be denied, unless some one should find out some new truth (based on which he could impugn its existence)—for a general principle is proved by the absence of contrary instances.

32. And on account of its general deficiency in probability.

No further special discussion is in fact required. From whatever new points of view the Buddhist system is tested with reference to its probability, it gives way on all sides, like the walls of a well dug in sandy soil. It has, in fact, no foundation whatever to rest upon, and hence the attempts to use it as a guide in the practical concerns of life are mere folly. Moreover, Buddha by propounding the three mutually contradictory systems, teaching respectively the reality of the external world, the reality of ideas only, and general nothingness, has himself made it clear either that he was a man given to make incoherent assertions, or else that hatred of all beings induced him to propound absurd doctrines by accepting which they would become thoroughly confused. So that—and this the Sūtra means to indicate—Buddha's doctrine has to be entirely disregarded by all those who have a regard for their own happiness.

Nyāyakanikā

VĀCASPATIMIŚRA

Vācaspatimiśra (pronounced "vächäspätee-mishrə") (10th century A.D.) was a universal genius of the Indian medieval period. He wrote commentaries on Indian philosophies as diverse as Nyāya (the Indian system of logic), advaita Vedānta (the Indian version of metaphysical monism and epistemological pluralism), and Sāṁkhya * (the Indian system of metaphysical dualism). The selection below has Vācaspati ingeniously pitting two Buddhists against one another on the question, Is there an external world? Is there a world that uniquely corresponds to the images or ideas that we are said to have in perception? The Yogācāra represents the idealist who, like Berkeley, maintains that all we ever know are our own ideas; while the Sautrāntika, by way of a discussion of the nature of judgment, represents the realist who, rather like Locke and Śaṁkara, maintains that external objects are "real" and known. For ease in reading, simply ignore all the brackets.

3. CONTEST WITH EXTREME IDEALISM. SENSE PERCEPTION DOES NOT WARRANT THE EXISTENCE OF AN EXTERNAL WORLD.

THE YOGĀCĀRA: All this is wrong! Because, indeed, if you maintain that images are inherent in our knowledge and they refer to [external] reality, we shall ask [how do you come to know this?] Do you know it by direct evidence or by inference?

First of all, you cannot invoke direct awareness, because your awareness testifies to the presence in you of the image of

something blue, this image is locked up in its own self [it cannot make a step beyond, in order] to grasp another blue thing [the blue object]. Indeed the reflected image is one blue thing, not two blue things [the image and the object]. And we have already called attention to the fact that it is impossible to be at once [out of the cognition and in the cognition], to be a separate thing [from knowledge and to be cognized by it as] its object.

SAUTRĀNTIKA: Let it be so! However the object of cognition is double, the *prima facie* apprehended [in sensation], and the distinctly settled [in a perceptual judgment]. Now, in respect to sense-perception what is immediately seized [in a sensation] is only one single moment, but

* Sometimes transliterated Sāṅkhya.

From Vācaspatimiśra, *Nyāyakaṇikā*, in F. Th. Stcherbatsky, *Buddhist Logic*, Vol. II; Leningrad, Bibliotheca Buddhica XXVI, 1932.

what is distinctly settled [in a perceptual judgment] is a compact chain of moments, [the constructed thing], the object of our purposive action. If that were not so, cognition could not guide the actions of those who act in pursuit of definite aims. [When we speak of] knowledge guiding our actions and leading to successful attainment of aims, we only mean that knowledge points to an object of a possible [successful] action. Now, the moment of sensation is not the moment of action, since the latter does not exist any more when the action takes place. But the chain of moments [the continuity of the object] can be [the aim of purposive action]. However [a chain of moments] cannot be grasped directly [in sensation], and therefore we must admit [the importance and conditioned reality] of the constructed [chains of moments].

The same applies to an inferential judgment. The object it is *prima facie* intent upon is a Universal [an absent thing constructed in imagination], whose essence is to represent a contrast with some other things. But the [corresponding] judgment refers that Universal to [some particular point of reality], which becomes the object of our purposive action and is capable of being successfully attained. Both these ways of cognition [direct perception proceeding from the particular to the general and inference proceeding from the general to the particular], are right means of cognition only in respect of successful purposive action, as has been stated [by Dignāga], "a man who has distinctly delineated his object by these two modes of cognition in a judgment, takes action, and is not lead astray." Thus it is that the external [real object] is not accessible to our direct knowledge, but being indirectly ascertained [in a judgment] it is an object [of cognition nevertheless].

YOGĀCĀRA: All this is wrong! You do not know at all what a judgment is!

SAUTRĀNTIKA: A judgment is a mental construction [of the form "this is blue"].

Indirect cognition [or inference], because in its essence it is nothing but constructive thought, is conterminous with [judgment]. Direct cognition [or sense-perception] is also a judgment because it calls forth a thought-construction.

YOGĀCĀRA: But a construction also, since it is intent upon the image [produced by it and cannot make a step beyond it], how can it judge [or execute constructions regarding external reality]?

SAUTRĀNTIKA: [This is however possible], if you accept [the following explanation]. The image [which a man feels inwardly present in his mind] is his own. It is not something [artificially] constructed [by combining in thought]. On the contrary, it is something intimately and directly felt. Indeed, a mental construction is something arranged [by our mind's initiative]. The true essence of a thing is never an arrangement. It is always [something unique], something not standing in any relation to whatsoever [something unutterable], something that cannot be designated by a [connotative] name. It is [also something concrete and vivid], a glaring reflex [non-operated upon by the mind]. Thus it is that images are not mental arrangements [for a consciousness which feels their immediate presence] in itself. But the mind projects the inward reflex into the external world and guides the purposive actions of those who are desirous of dealing with these external objects, in directing them towards this or towards that thing. Nor are the people [who are thus guided by images projected into the external world] deceived [in their aims, since experience does not contradict them], because indirectly [these images, although themselves subjective and notional], are produced by external [reality]; and since they are related to reality, the real aims are successfully reached. Accordingly, it has been stated [by Dharmottara] [judgment or inference guides the purposive actions of men], because "the course it takes consists in having *prima facie* to deal with mental contents of a [general] unreal character and in ascertaining through them some real fact."

YOGĀCĀRA: Please explain what is meant by the words "[knowledge] constructs [in a perceptual judgment a kind] of reality out of that unreality which is the image present to it."

SAUTRĀNTIKA: Does it not mean that it imagines a real object [i.e., some efficient point-instant producing a possible sensation]?

YOGĀCĀRA: What is the essence of constructive thought? Is it an imagined sensation or some other function? The first is impossible! [An imagined sensation is indeed a *contradictio in adjecto.*] Sensation and imagination being the one passive and the other active [the one non-constructive and the other constructive, imaginative sensation] would be as it were a liquid solid stuff. [Constructive thought or imagination] is a function different [from sensation]. The question is whether it operates after [sensation] or simultaneously with it? The first is impossible, because cognition being a momentary flash cannot operate by degrees. Even those schools who deny Universal Momentariness, even they maintain that thought, as well as motion, cannot operate intermittently and therefore [sensation and imagination], cannot operate alternately [when something is felt and imagined at the same time]. But if you assume that sensation and imagination work simultaneously, we can admit this, with the proviso that the object is immanent in cognition; because if we suppose that what we feel is [not in us], but out of us, the term "feeling" will loose itself every intelligible meaning.

And thus, what is really immediately felt in us is the [double] subject-object aspect of our knowledge, and what is constructed in imagination is the [external] object. Our own self, what we internally feel in us, is not something constructed in imagination [on the other hand the external] object, since it is constructed in imagination, is not the thing actually felt in sensation. [We cannot know] whether the [external] object exists or does not exist, but [what we call] construction [of an object] is nothing but the [imagined] "grasping" [aspect of its idea]. It has been already mentioned that to "grasp" something external to our knowledge is impossible.

SAUTRĀNTIKA: [We also assume a kind of] imputed externality [viz.], our images [coalesce with external objects in that sense] that we are not conscious of the difference, and that is why our purposive actions [when guided by our judgments], are directed towards external objects [and are successful].

YOGĀCĀRA: But [when they coalesce], is the external object also cognized at that time or not? The first is excluded, according to what we have just said, viz., that [real] "grasping" is an impossibility. But if no external object is really apprehended and we simply don't feel the difference [between the external thing and an imagined idea], this undiscrimination alone could not guide our purposive actions towards a definite aim, since [undiscriminated from our image will be not exclusively one definite object, but all] others will be also undiscriminated at that time, and the consequence will be that [our image] could direct us not towards the definite object to which it corresponds, but to another one.

Thus it is that our immediate feeling cannot be relied upon as a proof of the reality of an external world.

4. IMPOSSIBILITY TO PROVE THE REALITY OF AN EXTERNAL WORLD BY RATIOCINATION.

YOGĀCĀRA: Neither can [the reality of the external world] be established by inference. It has been, indeed, sufficiently explained that, just as simple awareness, inference cannot seize the external object neither directly, nor indirectly. There is no fact from which its existence could be deduced with logical necessity. [If such a fact exists], it must be either an effect [of external reality from which the existence of the cause could be necessarily deduced] or a fact possessing externality as its inherent property [the existence of this property could then be deduced analytically]. There are no such facts.

SAUTRĀNTIKA: However there is one! Yourself, you the Yogācāra, deny Solipsism, and you admit the influence of a foreign stream of thought upon my stream of thought. When the perceptions of walking and speaking arise in my mind [and they do not refer to my own walking and speaking because they] are not preceded by my own will to walk and to speak, [we assume the existence of another person who walks and speaks]. We then can throw the argument in the following syllogistic form],

Major premise: If something appears accidentally in a combination otherwise constant, it must depend upon a special cause.

Example: Just as my perceptions of external purposive movements and of [foreign] speech, which depend upon the presense of another personality.

Minor premise: Such are the perceptions of external objects, the subject of our controversy.

Conclusion: [They are due to a special cause.]

This is an analytical judgment, [since the predicate, the necessary existence of a special cause, is an inherent property of the subject, the occasional change in our stream of thought]. And this special cause lying outside our subjective stream of thought is the external object.

YOGĀCĀRA: [The external object is superfluous, there is an internal] Biotic Force which accidentally becomes mature and evokes an idea; this idea is also accidental [and changing concomitantly with a change in its cause].

SAUTRĀNTIKA: But is not your Biotic Force [in this case simply] the force of subjective thought, contained in one continuous stream, the force to produce out of itself corresponding objective thoughts. Its [so called] maturity is its [perfect development and] readiness immediately to produce its effect. Its cause is the preceding moment of the same stream, because you [the Yogācāra] do not admit [in this case] causality between different streams. But then, either every [moment] in the subjective stream of thought will be a "cause of maturity," or not a single one, because [as moments of subjective thought all are in this respect] equal. They are equal, because if you, according to your intention, chose in the subjective stream one moment as ready [to produce out of itself a given objective thought], all other moments will be just in the same position!

YOGĀCĀRA: [No!], because every new moment has a different force. Since the moments change, their effects are also changing.

SAUTRĀNTIKA: But then [if every moment is different], there will be only one moment capable of producing the image of a blue patch or capable of arousing it from [its dormant condition in the store-consciousness]. No other moment will be able to do it [the image of the blue patch will then never recur in the same individual]. Or, if [other moments] will also be [able to do it], how is it that every moment [is supposed] to have a different efficiency? [If it is not different], then all the moments of the stored up subjective stream of consciousness [uninfluenced by external objects, being in the same position], will have the same capacity; and, since an efficient cause being present, cannot postpone its action [all the moments will then produce just the same image of a blue patch].

If all our ideas have the same origin in the subjective stream of thought, they must be always the same [since their cause is always the same]. But this [constancy] is incompatible with the [actual] changing character of our ideas.

[If there were no external cause], there would be unchanging constancy of thought, which excludes change. [But change exists, and] is thus proved to depend upon an external cause. Thus it is that an invariable concomitance [between the change of thought and its external cause] is established. Neither do you, Idealists, admit all our knowledge of the external world to be produced by the influence on us of other minds, you admit it only [in order to avoid Solipsism] in regard of some of our [external] perceptions [viz.], the perceptions of external purposive movements and of [another man's] speech. Moreover, even assuming [for the sake of argument, that every occasional external perception] is produced by the influence of a foreign personality, the effect cannot be changing, since such a personality is constantly present. [You cannot maintain that the other personality is sometimes present and sometimes absent], because the chain of moments constituting the personality is quite compact and cannot be occasionally relegated to a remote place, since according to [your] Idealism, space as an external entity does not exist. And because thought is not physical [the foreign personality which is only] thought, never does occupy a definite place. [Nor can a stream of thought be occasionally present] in respect of the time [of its appearance], since you do not admit the appearance of something [new, of something] that did not previously exist. Therefore our syllogism proves the existence of external [physical] objects.

YOGĀCĀRA: This is wrong! Although [in our opinion] the origin of all our external perceptions is exclusively to be found in our internal stream of thought, there is nevertheless an occasional variety of perceptions. The reason [in your syllogism] is fallacious, it is uncertain, its absence in contrary cases is uncertain [since the change of our perceptions can be explained from within]. . . . Moreover, when you maintain that to be an object of knowledge means to be (1) [a point of reality] producing cognition, and (2) to be coordinated with the respective image [by the sense of sameness] [we will object that all the other causes and conditions of our knowledge are also to a certain extent coordinated with it through a sense of sameness, viz.] when a perception of colour is produced the sense of vision produces the limitation [of it to the visual sphere], light produces the distinctness [of the image], the previous moment of consciousness produces the following one. Since all these causes are coordinated with their respective results by [special kinds of] coordinations, and since they are the causes [of our perception of a blue patch of colour], they [according to your definition] must be also objects [not only causes], just as the blue patch [is an object, because it is a cause]. And if you maintain that the object is absolutely the same [as its image], and that that is it what makes it an object, then [we will answer] that the preceding conscious moment, the moment preceding our perception of the blue, possesses still more sameness than the [external] blue object, and that it consequently [will fall under your definition and] constitute an object of our image of the blue patch! [Hence your "coordination" explains nothing!]

SAUTRĀNTIKA: To be an object of our knowledge does not only mean to be [a point of reality] producing it and coordinated with its image, but it also means to be established as such by a perceptual judgment ["this is the blue"]. This judgment refers just to an external thing, not to something else. [The sensation or feeling is purely internal, but in the following moment we have constructed an image, projected it into the external world and identified it with a point of external reality, i.e., we have judged].

YOGĀCĀRA: No! We have already answered this. We have proved above [that neither by immediate awareness nor by inference can the reality of the external world be established].

An Enquiry Concerning Human Understanding

DAVID HUME

David Hume (1711–1776), Scottish-born and educated, stands as the leading British empiricist of the eighteenth century. This reputation rests principally on two works: A Treatise of Human Nature, *begun while the author was only 23 and published in two volumes in 1739, with a third and final volume in 1740; and* An Enquiry Concerning Human Understanding, *published in 1748. The* Treatise *was an instant disaster and failed to bring its young author the recognition he felt he deserved. The secod work was really a popularized restatement of the subject of Book I of the earlier* Treatise; *along with a number of other moral and political essays and a lengthy history of England, it finally earned for Hume the literary and philosophical acclaim he truly deserved.*

The selection that follows is taken from the Enquiry, *and it lays out not only Hume's empiricism but a very modern empirical epistemology for those who have chosen to accept Hume's arguments.*

Part I

. . . I need not insist upon the more trite topics, employed by the sceptics in all ages, against the evidence of *sense;* such as those which are derived from the imperfection and fallaciousness of our organs, on numberless occasions; the crooked appearance of an oar in water; the various aspects of objects, according to their different distances; the double images which arise from the pressing one eye; with many other appearances of a like nature. These sceptical topics, indeed, are only sufficient to prove, that the senses alone are not implicitly to be depended on; but that we must correct their evidence by reason, and by considerations, derived from the nature of the medium, the distance of the object, and the disposition of the organ, in order to render them, within their sphere, the proper *criteria* of truth and falsehood. There are other more profound arguments against

From *An Enquiry Concerning Human Understanding,* Section XII.

the senses, which admit not of so easy a solution.

It seems evident, that men are carried, by a natural instinct or prepossession, to repose faith in their senses; and that, without any reasoning, or even almost before the use of reason, we always suppose an external universe, which depends not on our perception, but would exist, though we and every sensible creature were absent or annihilated. Even the animal creation are governed by a like opinion, and preserve this belief of external objects, in all their thoughts, designs, and actions.

It seems also evident, that, when men follow this blind and powerful instinct of nature, they always suppose the very images, presented by the senses, to be the external objects, and never entertain any suspicion, that the one are nothing but representations of the other. This very table, which we see white, and which we feel hard, is believed to exist, independent of our perception, and to be something external to our mind, which perceives it. Our presence bestows not being on it; our absence does not annihilate it. It preserves its existence uniform and entire, independent of the situation of intelligent beings, who perceive or contemplate it.

But this universal and primary opinion of all men is soon destroyed by the slightest philosophy, which teaches us, that nothing can ever be present to the mind but an image or perception, and that the senses are only the inlets, through which these images are conveyed, without being able to produce any immediate intercourse between the mind and the object. The table, which we see, seems to diminish, as we remove farther from it; but the real table, which exists independent of us, suffers no alteration: it was, therefore, nothing but its image, which was present to the mind. These are the obvious dictates of reason; and no man, who reflects, ever doubted, that the existences, which we consider, when we say, *this house* and *that tree,* are nothing but perceptions in the mind, and fleeting copies or representations of other existences, which remain uniform and independent.

So far, then, are we necessitated by reasoning to contradict or depart from the primary instincts of nature, and to embrace a new system with regard to the evidence of our senses. But here philosophy finds herself extremely embarrassed, when she would justify this new system, and obviate the cavils and objections of the sceptics. She can no longer plead the infallible and irresistible instinct of nature: for that led us to a quite different system, which is acknowledged fallible and even erroneous. And to justify this pretended philosophical system, by a chain of clear and convincing argument, or even any appearance of argument, exceeds the power of all human capacity.

By what argument can it be proved, that the perceptions of the mind must be caused by external objects, entirely different from them, though resembling them (if that be possible) and could not arise either from the energy of the mind itself, or from the suggestion of some invisible and unknown spirit, or from some other cause still more unknown to us? It is acknowledged, that, in fact, many of these perceptions arise not from anything external, as in dreams, madness, and other diseases. And nothing can be more inexplicable than the manner, in which body should so operate upon mind as ever to convey an image of itself to a substance, supposed of so different, and even contrary a nature.

It is a question of fact, whether the perceptions of the senses be produced by external objects, resembling them: how shall this question be determined? By experience surely; as all other questions of a like nature. But here experience is, and must be entirely silent. The mind has never anything present to it but the perceptions, and cannot possibly reach any experience of their connection with objects. The supposition of such a connection is, therefore, without any foundation in reasoning.

To have recourse to the veracity of the supreme Being, in order to prove the veracity of our senses, is surely making a very unexpected circuit. If his veracity were at all concerned in this matter, our senses would be entirely infallible; because it is not possible that he can ever deceive. Not to mention, that, if the external world be once called in question, we shall be at a loss to find arguments, by which we may prove the existence of that Being or any of his attributes.

This is a topic, therefore, in which the profounder and more philosophical sceptics will always triumph, when they endeavor to introduce an universal doubt into all subjects of human knowledge and inquiry. Do you follow the instincts and propensities of nature, may they say, in assenting to the veracity of sense? But these lead you to believe that the very perception or sensible image is the external object. Do you disclaim this principle, in order to embrace a more rational opinion, that the perceptions are only representations of something external? You here depart from your natural propensities and more obvious sentiments; and yet are not able to satisfy your reason, which can never find any convincing argument from experience to prove, that the perceptions are connected with any external objects.

There is another sceptical topic of a like nature, derived from the most profound philosophy; which might merit our attention, were it requisite to dive so deep, in order to discover arguments and reasonings, which can so little serve to any serious purpose. It is universally allowed by modern inquirers, that all the sensible qualities of objects, such as hard, soft, hot, cold, white, black, etc. are merely sec-

ondary, and exist not in the objects themselves, but are perceptions of the mind, without any external archetype or model, which they represent. If this be allowed, with regard to secondary qualities, it must also follow, with regard to the supposed primary qualities of extension and solidity; nor can the latter be any more entitled to that denomination than the former. The idea of extension is entirely acquired from the senses of sight and feeling; and if all the qualities, perceived by the senses, be in the mind, not in the object, the same conclusion must reach the idea of extension, which is wholly dependent on the sensible ideas or the ideas of secondary qualities. Nothing can save us from this conclusion, but the asserting, that the ideas of those primary qualities are attained by *abstraction,* an opinion, which, if we examine it accurately, we shall find to be unintelligible, and even absurd. An extension, that is neither tangible nor visible, cannot possibly be conceived; and a tangible or visible extension, which is neither hard nor soft, black or white, is equally beyond the reach of human conception. Let any man try to conceive a triangle in general, which is neither *isosceles* nor *scalenum,* nor has any particular length or proportion of sides; and he will soon perceive the absurdity of all the scholastic notions with regard to abstraction and general ideas.[1]

[1] This argument is drawn from Dr. Berkeley; and indeed most of the writings of that very ingenious author form the best lessons of scepticism, which are to be found either among the ancient or modern philosophers, Bayle not excepted. He professes, however, in his title-page (and undoubtedly with great truth) to have composed his book against the sceptics as well as against the atheists and free-thinkers. But that all his arguments, though otherwise intended, are, in reality, merely sceptical, appears from this, *that they admit of no answer and produce no conviction.* Their only effect is to cause that momentary amazement and irresolution and confusion, which is the result of scepticism.

Thus the first philosophical objection to the evidence of sense or to the opinion of external existence consists in this, that such an opinion, if rested on natural instinct, is contrary to reason, and if referred to reason, is contrary to natural instinct, and at the same time carries no rational evidence with it, to convince an impartial inquirer. The second objection goes farther, and represents this opinion as contrary to reason; at least, if it be a principle of reason, that all sensible qualities are in the mind, not in the object. Bereave matter of all its intelligible qualities, both primary and secondary, you in a manner annihilate it, and leave only a certain unknown, inexplicable *something*, as the cause of our perceptions; a notion so imperfect, that no sceptic will think it worth while to contend against it.

Part II

It may seem a very extravagant attempt of the sceptics to destroy *reason* by argument and ratiocination; yet is this the grand scope of all their inquiries and disputes. They endeavor to find objections, both to our abstract reasonings, and to those which regard matter of fact and existence.

The chief objection against all *abstract* reasonings is derived from the ideas of space and time; ideas, which, in common life and to a careless view, are very clear and intelligible, but when they pass through the scrutiny of the profound sciences (and they are the chief object of these sciences) afford principles, which seem full of absurdity and contradiction. No priestly *dogmas*, invented on purpose to tame and subdue the rebellious reason of mankind, ever shocked common sense more than the doctrine of the infinite divisibility of extension, with its consequences; as they are pompously displayed by all geometricians and metaphysicians, with a kind of triumph and exultation. A

real quantity, infinitely less than any finite quantity, containing quantities infinitely less than itself, and so on *in infinitum;* this is an edifice so bold and prodigious, that it is too weighty for any pretended demonstration to support, because it shocks the clearest and most natural principles of human reason.[2] But what renders the matter more extraordinary, is that these seemingly absurd opinions are supported by a chain of reasoning, the clearest and most natural; nor is it possible for us to allow the premises without admitting the consequences. Nothing can be more convincing and satisfactory than all the conclusions concerning the properties of circles and triangles; and yet, when these are once received, how can we deny, that the angle of contact between a circle and its tangent is infinitely less than any rectilineal angle, that as you may increase the diameter of the circle *in infinitum,* this angle of contact becomes still less, even *in infinitum,* and that the angle of contact between other curves and their tangents may be infinitely less than those between any circle and its tangent, and so on, *in infinitum?* The demonstration of these principles seems as unexceptionable as that which proves the three angles of a triangle to be equal to two right ones, though the latter opinion be natural and easy, and the former big with contradiction and absurdity. Reason here seems to be thrown into a kind of amazement and suspense, which, without the suggestions

2 Whatever disputes there may be about mathematical points, we must allow that there are physical points; that is, parts of extension, which cannot be divided or lessened, either by the eye or imagination. These images, then, which are present to the fancy or senses, are absolutely indivisible, and consequently must be allowed by mathematicians to be infinitely less than any real part of extension; and yet nothing appears more certain to reason, than that an infinite number of them composes an infinite extension. How much more an infinite number of those infinitely small parts of extension, which are still supposed infinitely divisible.

of any sceptic, gives her a diffidence of herself, and of the ground on which she treads. She sees a full light, which illuminates certain places; but that light borders upon the most profound darkness. And between these she is so dazzled and confounded, that she scarcely can pronounce with certainty and assurance concerning any one object.

The absurdity of these bold determinations of the abstract sciences seems to become, if possible, still more palpable with regard to time than extension. An infinite number of real parts of time, passing in succession, and exhausted one after another, appears so evident a contradiction, that no man, one should think, whose judgment is not corrupted, instead of being improved, by the sciences, would ever be able to admit of it.

Yet still reason must remain restless, and unquiet, even with regard to that scepticism, to which she is driven by these seeming absurdities and contradictions. How any clear, distinct idea can contain circumstances, contradictory to itself, or to any other clear, distinct idea, is absolutely incomprehensible; and is, perhaps, as absurd as any proposition, which can be formed. So that nothing can be more sceptical, or more full of doubt and hesitation, than this scepticism itself, which arises from some of the paradoxical conclusions of geometry or the science of quantity.[3]

[3] It seems to me not impossible to avoid these absurdities and contradictions, if it be admitted, that there is no such thing as abstract or general ideas, properly speaking; but that all general ideas are, in reality, particular ones, attached to a general term, which recalls, upon occasion, other particular ones, that resemble, in certain circumstances, the idea, present to the mind. Thus when the term *horse* is pronounced, we immediately figure to ourselves the idea of a black or a white animal, of a particular size or figure: but as that term is also usually applied to animals of other colors, figures and sizes, these ideas, though not actually present to the imagination, are easily recalled; and our reasoning and conclusion pro-

The sceptical objections to *moral* evidence, or to the reasonings concerning matter of fact, are either *popular* or *philosophical*. The popular objections are derived from the natural weakness of human understanding; the contradictory opinions, which have been entertained in different ages and nations; the variations of our judgment in sickness and health, youth and old age, prosperity and adversity; the perpetual contradiction of each particular man's opinions and sentiments; with many other topics of that kind. It is needless to insist farther on this head. These objections are but weak. For as, in common life, we reason every moment concerning fact and existence, and cannot possibly subsist, without continually employing this species of argument, any popular objections, derived from thence, must be insufficient to destroy that evidence. The great subverter of *Pyrrhonism* or the excessive principles of scepticism is action, and employment, and the occupations of common life. These principles may flourish and triumph in the schools; where it is, indeed, difficult, if not impossible, to refute them. But as soon as they leave the shade, and by the presence of the real objects, which actuate our passions and sentiments, are put in opposition to the more powerful principles of our nature, they vanish like smoke, and leave the most determined sceptic in the same condition as other mortals.

The sceptic, therefore, had better keep

ceed in the same way, as if they were actually present. If this be admitted (as seems reasonable) it follows that all the ideas of quantity, upon which mathematicians reason, are nothing but particular, and such as are suggested by the senses and imagination, and consequently, cannot be infinitely divisible. It is sufficient to have dropped this hint at present, without prosecuting it any farther. It certainly concerns all lovers of science not to expose themselves to the ridicule and contempt of the ignorant by their conclusions; and this seems the readiest solution of these difficulties.

within his proper sphere, and display those *philosophical* objections, which arise from more profound researches. Here he seems to have ample matter of triumph; while he justly insists, that all our evidence for any matter of fact, which lies beyond the testimony of sense or memory, is derived entirely from the relation of cause and effect; that we have no other idea of this relation than that of two objects, which have been frequently *conjoined* together; that we have no argument to convince us, that objects, which have, in our experience, been frequently conjoined, will likewise, in other instances, be conjoined in the same manner; and that nothing leads us to this inference but custom or a certain instinct of our nature; which it is indeed difficult to resist, but which, like other instincts, may be fallacious and deceitful. While the sceptic insists upon these topics, he shows his force, or rather, indeed, his own and our weakness; and seems, for the time at least, to destroy all assurance and conviction. These arguments might be displayed at greater length, if any durable good or benefit to society could ever be expected to result from them.

For here is the chief and most confounding objection to *excessive* scepticism, that no durable good can ever result from it; while it remains in its full force and vigor. We need only ask such a sceptic, *What his meaning is? And what he proposes by all these curious researches?* He is immediately at a loss, and knows not what to answer. A Copernican or Ptolemaic, who supports each his different system of astronomy, may hope to produce a conviction, which will remain constant and durable, with his audience. A Stoic or Epicurean displays principles, which may not be durable, but which have an effect on conduct and behavior. But a Pyrrhonian cannot expect, that his philosophy will have any constant influence on the mind: or if it had, that its influence

would be beneficial to society. On the contrary, he must acknowledge, if he will acknowledge anything, that all human life must perish, were his principles universally and steadily to prevail. All discourse, all action would immediately cease; and men remain in a total lethargy, till the necessities of nature, unsatisfied, put an end to their miserable existence. It is true; so fatal an event is very little to be dreaded. Nature is always too strong for principle. And though a Pyrrhonian may throw himself or others into a momentary amazement and confusion by his profound reasonings; the first and most trival event in life will put to flight all his doubts and scruples, and leave him the same, in every point of action and speculation, with the philosophers of every other sect, or with those who never concerned themselves in any philosophical researches. When he awakes from his dream, he will be the first to join in the laugh against himself, and to confess, that all his objections are mere amusement, and can have no other tendency than to show the whimsical condition of mankind, who must act and reason and believe; though they are not able, by their most diligent inquiry, to satisfy themselves concerning the foundation of these operations, or to remove the objections, which may be raised against them.

Part III

There is, indeed, a more *mitigated* scepticism or *academical* philosophy, which may be both durable and useful, and which may, in part, be the result of this Pyrrhonism, or *excessive* scepticism, when its undistinguished doubts are, in some measure, corrected by common sense and reflection. The greater part of mankind are naturally apt to be affirmative and dogmatical in their opinions; and while they see objects only on one side, and have no idea of any counterpoising argument, they throw themselves precipitately into the principles, to which they are inclined; nor have they any indulgence for those who entertain opposite sentiments. To hesitate or balance perplexes their understanding, checks their passion, and suspends their action. They are, therefore, impatient till they escape from a state, which to them is so uneasy: and they think, that they could never remove themselves far enough from it, by the violence of their affirmations and obstinacy of their belief. But could such dogmatical reasoners become sensible of the strange infirmities of human understanding, even in its most perfect state, and when most accurate and cautious in its determinations; such a reflection would naturally inspire them with more modesty and reserve, and diminish their fond opinion of themselves, and their prejudice against antagonists. The illiterate may reflect on the disposition of the learned, who, amidst all the advantages of study and reflection, are commonly still diffident in their determinations: and if any of the learned be inclined, from their natural temper, to haughtiness and obstinacy, a small tincture of Pyrrhonism might abate their pride, by showing them, that the few advantages, which they may have attained over their fellows, are but inconsiderable, if compared with the universal perplexity and confusion, which is inherent in human nature. In general, there is a degree of doubt, and caution, and modesty, which, in all kinds of scrutiny and decision, ought forever to accompany a just reasoner.

Another species of *mitigated* scepticism which may be of advantage to mankind, and which may be the natural result of the Pyrrhonian doubts and scruples, is the limitation of our inquiries to such subjects as are best adapted to the narrow capacity of human understanding. The *imagination* of man is naturally sublime,

delighted with whatever is remote and extraordinary, and running, without control, into the most distant parts of space and time in order to avoid the objects, which custom has rendered too familiar to it. A correct *judgment* observes a contrary method, and avoiding all distant and high inquiries, confines itself to common life, and to such subjects as fall under daily practice and experience; leaving the more sublime topics to the embellishment of poets and orators, or to the arts of priests and politicians. To bring us to so salutary a determination, nothing can be more serviceable, than to be once thoroughly convinced of the force of the Pyrrhonian doubt, and of the impossibility, that anything, but the strong power of natural instinct, could free us from it. Those who have a propensity to philosophy, will still continue their researches; because they reflect, that, besides the immediate pleasure, attending such an occupation, philosophical decisions are nothing but the reflections of common life, methodized and corrected. But they will never be tempted to go beyond common life, so long as they consider the imperfection of those faculties which they employ, their narrow reach, and their inaccurate operations. While we cannot give a satisfactory reason, why we believe, after a thousand experiments, that a stone will fall, or fire burn; can we ever satisfy ourselves concerning any determination, which we may form, with regard to the origin of worlds, and the situation of nature, from, and to eternity?

This narrow limitation, indeed, of our inquiries, is, in every respect, so reasonable, that it suffices to make the slightest examination into the natural powers of the human mind and to compare them with their objects, in order to recommend it to us. We shall then find what are the proper subjects of science and inquiry.

It seems to me, that the only objects

of the abstract science or of demonstration are quantity and number, and that all attempts to extend this more perfect species of knowledge beyond these bounds are mere sophistry and illusion. As the component parts of quantity and number are entirely similar, their relations become intricate and involved; and nothing can be more curious, as well as useful, than to trace, by a variety of mediums, their equality or inequality, through their different appearances. But as all other ideas are clearly distinct and different from each other, we can never advance farther, by our utmost scrutiny, than to observe this diversity, and, by an obvious reflection, pronounce one thing not to be another. Or if there be any difficulty in these decisions, it proceeds entirely from the undeterminate meaning of words, which is corrected by juster definitions. That *the square of the hypothenuse is equal to the squares of the other two sides,* cannot be known, let the terms be ever so exactly defined, without a train of reasoning and inquiry. But to convince us of this proposition, *that where there is no property, there can be no injustice,* it is only necessary to define the terms, and explain injustice to be a violation of property. This proposition is, indeed, nothing but a more imperfect definition. It is the same case with all those pretended syllogistical reasonings, which may be found in every other branch of learning, except the sciences of quantity and number; and these may safely, I think, be pronounced the only proper objects of knowledge and demonstration.

All other inquiries of men regard only matter of fact and existence; and these are evidently incapable of demonstration. Whatever *is* may *not be.* No negation of a fact can involve a contradiction. The non-existence of any being, without exception, is as clear and distinct an idea as its existence. The proposition, which affirms it not to be, however false, is no less conceivable and intelligible, than that which affirms it to be. The case is different with the sciences, properly so called. Every proposition, which is not true, is there confused and unintelligible. That the cube root of 64 is equal to the half of 10, is a false proposition, and can never be distinctly conceived. But that Caesar, or the angel Gabriel, or any being never existed, may be a false proposition, but still is perfectly conceivable, and implies no contradiction.

The existence, therefore, of any being can only be proved by arguments from its cause or its effect; and these arguments are founded entirely on experience. If we reason *a priori,* anything may appear able to produce anything. The falling of a pebble may, for aught we know, extinguish the sun; or the wish of a man control the planets in their orbits. It is only experience, which teaches us the nature and bounds of cause and effect, and enables us to infer the existence of one object from that of another.[4] Such is the foundation of moral reasoning, which forms the greater part of human knowledge, and is the source of all human action and behavior.

Moral reasonings are either concerning particular or general facts. All deliberations in life regard the former; as also all disquisitions in history, chronology, geography, and astronomy.

The sciences, which treat of general facts, are politics, natural philosophy, physics, chemistry, etc., where the qualities, causes and effects of a whole species of objects are inquired into.

[4] That impious maxim of the ancient philosophy, *Ex nihilo, nihil fit,* by which the creation of matter was excluded, ceases to be a maxim, according to this philosophy. Not only the will of the supreme Being may create matter; but, for aught we know *a priori,* the will of any other being might create it, or any other cause, that the most whimsical imagination can assign.

Divinity or Theology, as it proves the existence of a Deity, and the immortality of souls, is composed partly of reasonings concerning particular, partly concerning general facts. It has a foundation in *reason*, so far as it is supported by experience. But its best and most solid foundation is *faith* and divine revelation.

Morals and criticism are not so properly objects of the understanding as of taste and sentiment. Beauty, whether moral or natural, is felt, more properly than perceived. Or if we reason concerning it, and endeavor to fix its standard, we regard a new fact, to wit, the general tastes of mankind, or some such fact, which may be the object of reasoning and inquiry.

When we run over libraries, persuaded of these principles, what havoc must we make? If we take in our hand any volume; of divinity or school metaphysics, for instance; let us ask, *Does it contain any abstract reasoning concerning quantity or number?* No. *Does it contain any experimental reasoning concerning matter of fact and existence?* No. Commit it then to the flames: for it can contain nothing but sophistry and illusion.

A Refutation of Solipsism
(An Annotated Translation of Saṃtānāntarasiddhi)

DHARMAKĪRTI and HIDENORI KITAGAWA

Dharmakīrti (7th century A.D.) was a Buddhist logician and an outstanding defender of the school of Buddhist idealism. One of the immediate dangers for the epistemological idealist is that this position can easily lead to solipsism (self-alone-ism), an impractical, uncommon-sensical conclusion with which few idealists are prepared to live. Dharmakīrti took upon himself the defense of the Buddhist idealist position against the realist's charge that idealism led to solipsism, and he produced the tract from which the following translation is taken. The translation, along with a brief commentary, is by a contemporary scholar of the Tibetan language, Hidenori Kitagawa; the translation is from the Tibetan, the only language in which Dharmakīrti's Sanskrit text now survives, and we reprint below the first half of this translation.

Samtānāntarasiddhi is one of the seven principal works ascribed to Dharmakīrti, a great Buddhist logician of India who lived around the middle of the seventh century. Saṃtānāntarasiddhi is a dialogue between the Realists and the Idealists on the problem of solipsism. The Realists attack the Idealists claiming that it is impossible for the Idealists to avoid solipsism. Dharmakīrti, being one of the leading polemics of the Yogācārins, a school representing idealist thought in Buddhism, refutes the Realists' charge, claiming that not only is it possible for the Idealists to avoid solipsism, but also that it is more reasonable to believe in idealism than in realism. Most of Dharmakīrti's works deal with logic; Saṃtānāntarasiddhi is especially important because it presents the metaphysical and the epistemological backgrounds of his system of logic.

The Sanskrit text of this book is lost, and we have no Chinese translations. We do have Tibetan translations; according to Tohoku Catalogue these are as follows:

No. 4219: Rgyud gshan grub-pa shes-bya-baḥi rab-tu-byed-pa (Saṃtānāntarasiddhi-nāma-prakaraṇa).

No. 4238: Rgyud gshan grub-paḥi ḥgrel-bśad (Saṃtānāntarasiddhiṭīkā).

The first is the work of Dharmakīrti

From "A Refutation of Solipsism," an annotated translation of *Samtānāntarasiddhi*, by Hidenori Kitagawa, *Greater India Society Journal*; Calcutta, Vol. 14, Number 1, 1955, pp. 55–73.

himself and the second is the commentary by Vinītadeva. In addition to these there is another Tibetan commentary, Mkhas-paḥi yid ḥphrog, written by a Mongolian monk, Ṅag-dbaṅ-bstan-dar. Th. Stcherbatsky has prepared a critical edition of all these three works and has translated the first two into Russian.

"Saṃtānāntarasiddhi" means literally the proof of the existence of another stream. More explicitly, "Saṃtānā" means the stream of psychological activities; so Dharmakīrti uses "Saṃtānāntarasiddhi" to mean the proof of the existence of another person. The Buddhists define the person in terms of the stream of psychological activities and not in terms of the soul in the sense of an unchangeable and eternal entity; they did not believe that such a soul exists. Therefore, the question of the existence of the soul of another person is of no concern to Dharmakīrti. His defence of idealism is directed towards a proof of the existence of a stream of psychological activities other than one's own. [Note: Since the style of Saṃtānāntarasiddhi is very compact—one śloka and ninety four sūtras—I have had to translate it freely together with some explanations. Whenever I supplied words in order to make my translation intelligible, I used square brackets. But when these words were substituted for a pronoun, I left them outside the brackets and put them in italics; the words which were substituted for other brief expressions than pronouns, however, were simply left outside the brackets without using italics. . . .]

According to the commentaries "the Realists" in Saṃtānāntarasiddhi refers to the Sautrāntikas except in Sūtras 34 to 39 (both inclusive) where it refers to the Vaibhāṣikas. Of course, the word "the Idealists" refers to the Yogācārins of whom Dharmakīrti is the spokesman.

REALISTS: [We infer the existence of the movement of another mind on the following grounds. First,] we observe in ourselves that [our bodily] actions and speech are preceded by a movement of [our] mind; then we observe *bodily actions and speech* in another person, and on the ground of these observations we infer [the existence of] a movement [of mind in others. If there existed nothing but the mind, as you insist, then bodily actions and speech would not exist and we could not infer the existence of the movement of another mind] (first part of Sūtra 1).

IDEALISTS: Even [if we stand] on the side of idealism, we can use the same reasoning; therefore, we—who claim that there exists nothing but the mind—are also able to infer [the existence of] another mind (second part of S. 1). [For,] *we* do not admit that those representations which appear as the signifier [of the existence of another mind] can occur in the absence of a certain movement of that person's mind. [In other words, we claim that nothing exists except mind, but we do not mean that everything is of the imagination and can be created or altered without any cause] (S. 2).

REALISTS: [You may say that the representations are not of the imagination but have a cause; but] in so far as we do not perceive the very causal relationship between our representations and the movement of another mind, we cannot infer [the existence of] intelligence in another person (first part of S. 3).

IDEALISTS: You cannot blame us for that, [even if you maintain that bodily actions and speech really exist,] the same difficulty confronts you (second part of S. 3). In so far as you never observe that *the bodily actions and speech of another* are [necessarily] preceded by the movement of his mind, [the existence of] *another mind* will not be known even by means of them (S. 4).

REALISTS: We can know [the existence

of] another mind: since one's own mind cannot be the efficient cause of the bodily actions and speech of another, [the only plausible explanation is that a mind other than one's own is the efficient cause of these action] (first part of S. 5).

IDEALISTS: Why cannot [one's own mind be the efficient cause of the bodily actions and speech of another]? (second part of S. 5).

REALISTS: [First,] we never feel the mind-cause [—the mind as a cause of the bodily actions and speech of others—] in our own [saṃtāna; in other words, if there is a mind which is the cause of the bodily actions and speech of another person, it should be outside of our saṃtāna] (S. 6). Second, [those actions] which are caused by our own mind are [always] found in our own [saṃtāna] (S. 7). If, [therefore,] *the actions and speech of another* were also caused by our own mind, they should be perceived in the same way as *our own actions* [which, we know, are caused by our own mind. In other words, they should be found in our own saṃtāna] (S. 8). But we know by experience that such is not the case. Therefore, we cannot but admit that the actions of another have their own efficient cause [outside of our saṃtāna] (S. 9).

IDEALISTS: Certainly, we agree with you that we do not feel in our own [saṃtāna] the mind-cause [as a cause of the bodily actions and speech of others] (S. 10). [But from our point of view, the rest of your argument should be as follows: All] the representations, which appear as the signifiers [of the existence of mind] and have a movement of one's own mind as their efficient cause, appear to us as our own [bodily actions and speech]. Therefore, those [representations] which appear as external things must have been caused by another efficient cause [than one's own mind] (S. 11).

REALISTS: Could it not be that those representations which appear as external things do not have [the movement of mind as their] efficient cause at all? (S. 12).

[It seems that the Realists are tacitly assuming that the representations which appear as external things result from mechanical causation rather than mental activity.]

IDEALISTS: If [we admit that] they do not have the movement of mind as their efficient cause, we may be led to admit that nothing has [the movement of mind as its] efficient cause (S. 13). [Certainly,] there is a distinction between those representations which appear as things separated from us and those which appear as things connected to us. But the distinction of these [two types of] representations does not depend on whether or not the representations have a movement of mind as their efficient cause (S. 14). Consequently, even those [representations] which appear as things connected to us may not have [a movement of mind as their] efficient cause, because no distinction, [in terms of their having or not having efficient cause,] is possible [between these two types of representations] (S. 15). Therefore, we cannot admit that only those special [representations of bodily actions and speech] which appear as things connected to us are [causally] preceded by the movement of mind (S. 16).

REALISTS: Why not? (first part of S. 17).

IDEALISTS: [First, because some representations] which appear as a certain kind of actions are definitely [preceded by the movement of mind] even if [they appear as things] separated from us (second part of S. 17). [For instance,] the arrows and stones shot [into the air] have the movement of the mind of the person having shot them as their efficient cause. The actions of a machine are caused by a movement of the mind of the operator; likewise the speech of a phantom or the psychological activities of one who is under the magical influence of another, have a movement of the mind of the magician as their efficient cause. And all these are the representations which appear as things separated from us (S. 18). [Secondly,] the movements [of our mind are the representations which appear as things most closely] connected to us. But when these movements are caused by another person, they are not [causally] preceded *by the movement of our own mind* (S. 19). In view of these facts, it is [more] reasonable [to assume] that we cognize [the existence of] the movement [of mind] simply through [the representations of] certain kinds of actions, [namely, the bodily actions and speech,] regardless of [whether or not these representations refer to the actions connected to us or separated from us] (S. 20). [Thus,] there is no distinction [between these two types of representations in terms of their efficient cause]. Therefore, if one of *these two types of representations* is not preceded [by the movement of mind as its efficient cause,] the other [type of representations] may also not be preceded *by the movement of mind* (S. 21). To sum up: certain kinds of the movement [of mind, namely, the will of speaking, walking etc.,] are cognized through certain kinds of actions regardless of [whether or not these actions appear as things connected to us or separated from us. But we] cannot [cognize] whether [these movements of mind are of greed or anger or stupidity] (S. 22). *You Realists* cognize [the existence of] the movement of another [person's mind] on the ground that you do not experience any movement [of mind] in yourself when you perceive his actions; so do we. But [we claim that] one perceives [the representations] which appear as the actions [of another, while you say that he perceives the actions of another] (S. 23). [Once you refuted us on the grounds that those repre-sentations which appear as external objects may not have the movement of mind as their efficient cause. But] we do not believe that you yourself admit that the speech and [bodily] actions of another person do not have [mental activity as their] efficient cause. [For if you admit this, you must lose the grounds on which you can prove the existence of another mind. Therefore, you have] the same [fault which you have pointed out in the method of our reasoning] (S. 24). To conclude, [both of us] should declare that both [speech and bodily actions, whether we consider them representations or entities,] undoubtedly have a movement [or mind] as their efficient cause and, therefore, they will not occur when there is no *movement of mind* (S. 25). [It is clear, then, that practically] there is no difference between us [in the method of reasoning] because we may [infer the existence of another mind] from the representations *of actions* as [you do] from *the actions per se.* (S. 26).

REALISTS: You claim that [all of our] representations *of the bodily actions and speech* are efficiently caused by the movement [of mind.] Then, why don't you claim [that the representations] in our dreams also [have the movement of mind as their efficient cause]? (S. 27).

IDEALISTS: [Yes, we do. Fundamentally,] both cases are the same (S. 28). Why don't you [agree with us and] say that the [bodily] actions and speech of another person which we perceive in our dreams have the movement [of his mind] as their efficient cause? (S. 29).

REALISTS: [No, we do not;] because they do not really exist (S. 30).

IDEALISTS: [But] why do they not exist? We perceive [them in dreams] just as we do when *we are awake* (S. 31).

REALISTS: Since a man is overcome by sleep, consciousness empty of reality will occur [in dreams] (S. 32).

IDEALISTS: Precisely for this same reason, it is possible for us too to allow that the consciousness empty of the support of another person's [mental activity] occur [in our dreams] (S. 33).

[The Idealists, for the sake of consistency, maintain that even those actions and speech which we perceive in dreams should have the mind of another as the efficient cause just as do those representations one experiences when he is awake. But they also allow, as an exception, that some of the representations in dreams occur during a state of mental paralysis and are not necessarily caused by the movement of another mind. It should be noticed that according to the Idealists even in the case of dreams the state of mental paralysis is theoretically an exceptional one. For, the Idealists believe that some dreams are actually caused by the movement of another mind. (To be treated in Sūtras: 37–39).

According to both of the commentators the argument set forth above were against the Sautrāntikas. The following is against the Vaibhāṣikas, the most radical of the realist schools in Buddhism. The Vaibhāṣikas are concerned with the same problem, i.e., dreams, but they approach it from a different view-point.]

VAIBHĀṢIKAS: In so far as you have admitted that even in dreams the representations are not empty of reality, [you hold the same view with us;] all [the persons] we perceive in dreams are other saṃtānas [and, consequently, real] (S. 34).

[The Vaibhāṣikas contend that even the bodily actions and speech which we perceive in dreams have real existence; the Sautrāntikas claim that only the actions and speech which we perceive while we are awake really exist. Against the opinions expressed by both of these groups of Realists, the Idealists proclaim that everything whether it is perceived in dreams or not is representations and not real. The Sautrāntikas have tried to point out errors in the argument of the Idealists which admits no distinction between the representations of the state of waking and that of sleeping. The Vaibhāṣikas are, on the other hand, trying to win the Idealists to their own side, pointing out that in so far as there is no distinction between these two kinds of representations and even the representations in dreams are not empty of reality, whatever we perceive, whether we are dreaming or awake, must be real. The Idealists answer the Vaibhāṣikas as follows.]

IDEALISTS: Since you argue only for the sake of arguing, you have strayed from the teaching of the Buddha and from right reasoning. So, your argument is groundless. By no means we are to be pursuaded [by you] that *all bodily actions and speech which occur in dreams* must be supported by another person's [mental activity and consequently are real] (S. 35).

[Then the Idealists present their own case.]

IDEALISTS: [Certainly,] we are the ones who claim that all representations of bodily actions and speech are caused by the samtāna of another person. But the difference [between the state of waking and that of sleeping is that in the former case we get most of those representations through] direct perception [while in the latter case they arise mostly from] memories (S. 36). [Actually,] sometimes we do perceive real beings even in a dream, and [in this instance] we must admit that [the representations] are caused [directly] by another person's samtāna [apart from the medium of memories] (S. 37). [For example, sometimes] we see real dreams by the grace of gods etc. (S. 38). Therefore, *our argument* [—fundamentally, everything is the same in dreams as when we are awake—] is not groundless (S. 39).

[Since by now the Idealists feel that they have successfully refuted the Realists, they try to take the offensive. According to the commentators their opponents are again the Sautrāntikas.]

IDEALISTS: By the way, even if [bodily] actions [and speech] are real entities, how can you cognize the existence of another mind by means of them? (S. 40).

REALISTS: Because they are the effects of [the movement of] mind (S. 41).

IDEALISTS: [Your reasoning, i.e., the reasoning from] the effects [to their cause,] is just as applicable to [our proof of the existence of] another mind. Why can one not cognize [the existence of another mind through the representations of bodily actions and speech]? (S. 42).

REALISTS: [The representations of the bodily actions and speech are not necessarily required when we cognize the existence of mind. For,] one can cognize his own saṃtāna on the basis of the mere existence of his [bodily] actions (second part of S. 43).

Even if [the answer of the Realists is as above, the Idealists reply as follows:] (first part of S. 43).

IDEALISTS: Then, [you must admit that] even those who do not perceive [the bodily actions of another person] would be able to cognize another saṃtāna (third part of S. 43).

REALISTS: [No, those who do not perceive] cannot [cognize the existence of another saṃtāna]. For, indicators must be [perceived and] represented [in our mind] (S. 44).

IDEALISTS: *If you admit that the possibility of cognition turns upon the presence of the representations of bodily actions and speech and not upon the existence of bodily actions and speech as separate entities,* it is unnecessary to insist on [such a complicated] process [of cognition] that from [the movement of] another person's mind the [bodily] actions [occur,] from the [bodily] actions the representations [occur,] through these representations we cognize [the existence of] *another mind* (S. 45). In fact, we cognize [the existence of another mind] only by means of the representations of [bodily] actions, which are caused by [the movement of] another mind (S. 46). For, this is the crucial factor which makes the cognition of another mind possible. [To assume the necessity of an intermediate step—the existence of real bodily actions—between the movement of another mind and the representations present to the cognizer is absurd] (S. 47).

[Having thus criticized the view of the Realists, the Idealists briefly outline their method of proving the existence of another mind.]

IDEALISTS: The movement [of mind,] whether of [one's own mind or of another person's mind] is the cause of the representations of [bodily] actions and speech either of [one's self or of another]. Therefore, we can cognize the cause [—the movement of mind in general—] through the effects [—the representations of any bodily action] (S. 48). Among *these representations,* those which are efficiently caused by a movement of one's own [mind] are experienced as our own [bodily actions,] while the representations caused by other persons are experienced as external things. [Therefore, we infer the existence of another mind through the latter type of representations.] But this distinction holds only for the majority of the cases; [there are exceptions, such as the flying arrows and those movements of one's own mind which are caused by other minds] (S. 49).

[Now the Idealists again consider the problem of dreams in order to prove the validity of their epistemology.]

IDEALISTS: Even in the state of dreaming, the causal relation *between the movement of another mind and the representations of the bodily actions and speech resulting therefrom* is the same as in the state of waking (S. 50). But in the state of illusion, [the representations which appear as the bodily actions and speech of other persons] are under the control of a certain additional condition, [namely coma,] just as [the representations of] one's own [bodily actions and speech in dreams] are. Therefore, it is possible in the illusory state of mind that the subconscious residue (vāsanā) deposited in our consciousness, the efficient cause of which is the movement of another person's mind, sometimes will start to work even after a [considerable] lapse of time from [the moment when the actual] movement of another person's mind took place. But it will never start to work in the complete absence of the movement [of another mind] (S. 51). Therefore, in any state [of mind, whether we be in the state of waking or dreaming,] we can definitely infer the movement of mind through the signifier—[the representations of bodily] actions and speech (S. 52).

[Having thus explained their position on the problem of dream phenomena, the Idealists continue their refutation of realism.]

IDEALISTS: [You say that] one takes cognizance of the movement [of another mind] by means of [an indicator—] the [actual bodily] actions: [even] if this is

the case, you must admit that he is able to cognize [another mind] in the state of sleeping as well as in the state of waking, [because we see bodily actions in both cases]. But, if you do not like to admit this, [you must know that the cognition of another mind is] utterly impossible (S. 53). For, [you are now denying your previous argument and are claiming that] the perception of [bodily] actions can occur even when there is no movement of another [mind] (S. 54).

REALISTS: [Of course,] perception may occur even in the absence of [actual bodily] actions. [For, in an illusory state of mind, perception is produced by our fancy without there being any real objects, but bodily actions never take place without the movement of mind preceding them. But according to our theory,] one cognizes the movement [of another mind not by means of the representations of bodily actions, but] by means of the [bodily] actions [themselves]. In the state of illusion, [such as a dream,] there are no [actual bodily] actions; [what] occurs [there are merely] the representations empty of reality, [and from these we cannot infer the movement of another mind]. Therefore, [our assertion that we cognize the movement of another mind only while we are awake and only by means of bodily actions, which really exist,] does not present the difficulty [as pointed out by you] (S. 55).

IDEALISTS: But upon what basis can you make that distinction between the state of dreams which comprise mere representations empty of reality and the state of waking in which real entities are involved? Do we not call those which you term "dream representations" and "real entities" by the same name, viz., "bodily actions"? (S. 56).

REALISTS: Because of [the additional condition—] coma etc. [—the situation] in the state [of illusion] is [entirely] different [from that of the normal state of mind; the representations in dreams are empty of reality while those in the state of waking are not] (S. 57).

IDEALISTS: If you think so, it is precisely because you are confused by avidyā [ignorance] (S. 58).

[According to Vinītadeva, Sūtra 58 is to be paraphrased as follows: If you admit that due to the mental derangement the situation in the state of illusion is different from that of the normal state of mind and, therefore, the representations in the state of dreams are empty of reality, then you must also admit that all of our representations, including even the representations in the state of waking, are empty of reality; for, they are all due to avidyā—the lord of mental derangement. Avidyā is one of the most fundamental concepts of Buddhism. According to the Buddhist philosophy, man is deceived by avidyā, when he believes that something is a real entity.

Thus the Idealists charge the Realists on two counts: (1) In so far as you have admitted the influence of mental derangement on the state of illusion, you must also admit the influence of avidyā even on the so-called normal state of mind. Therefore, (2) all of our representations, whether of the state of illusion or not, are empty of reality and there is no distinction between the representations in dreams and in the state of waking. The Idealists are now triumphant.]

IDEALISTS: Thus, [your theory,] which claims [the reality of] objects apart [from the mind,] has been refuted. Not having been able to conceal your several errors, you are now in a great trouble. With our single answer, [i.e., "It is precisely because you are confused by avidyā," your whole position] is definitely undermined (S. 59).

[Here the main part of Saṃtānāntara-siddhi comes to a close.]

The Critique of Pure Reason

IMMANUEL KANT

Immanuel Kant (1724–1804) was surely the most influential German philosopher of the eighteenth century. Born, reared, and educated in Königsberg, East Prussia, he spent his entire life in that illustrious university town. His most famous work, The Critique of Pure Reason, was published in 1781, and Western philosophy, both the British empiricist tradition and the Continental rationalist tradition, has never since been quite the same. In the Critique Kant attempted to define the limits of human knowledge within the boundaries of his great discovery that though all knowledge begins with experience (an empiricist thesis), what is known is organized and ordered by human reason (a rationalist thesis). Thus Kant emerges as the great epistemological synthesizer of these two disparate positions. In the selection which follows Kant introduces his technical distinction between analytic and synthetic judgments, and a priori and a posteriori evidence.

I. Of the Difference Between Pure and Empirical Knowledge

That all our knowledge begins with experience there can be no doubt. For how is it possible that the faculty of cognition should be awakened into exercise otherwise than by means of objects which affect our senses, and partly of themselves produce representations, partly rouse our powers of understanding into activity, to compare, to connect, or to separate these, and so to convert the raw material of our sensuous impressions into a knowledge of objects, which is called experience? In respect of time, therefore, no knowledge of ours is antecedent to experience, but begins with it.

But, though all our knowledge begins with experience, it by no means follows that all arises out of experience. For, on the contrary, it is quite possible that our empirical knowledge is a compound of that which we receive through impressions, and that which the faculty of cognition supplies from itself (sensuous impressions giving merely the *occasion*), an addition which we cannot distinguish from the original element given by sense, till long practice has made us attentive to, and skilful in separating it. It is, therefore, a question which requires close investigation, and is not to be answered at first sight—whether there exists a knowledge altogether independent of experience, and even of all sensuous impressions?

From Parts I–V of the Introduction to *The Critique of Pure Reason*. The translation is by J. M. D. Meiklejohn.

Knowledge of this kind is called *à priori*, in contradistinction to empirical knowledge, which has its sources *à posteriori*, that is, in experience.

But the expression, *"à priori,"* is not as yet definite enough adequately to indicate the whole meaning of the question above started. For, in speaking of knowledge which has its sources in experience, we are wont to say, that this or that may be known *à priori*, because we do not derive this knowledge immediately from experience, but from a general rule, which, however, we have itself borrowed from experience. Thus, if a man undermined his house, we say, "he might know *à priori* that it would have fallen"; that is, he needed not to have waited for the experience that it did actually fall. But still, *à priori*, he could not know even this much. For, that bodies are heavy, and, consequently, that they fall when their supports are taken away, must have been known to him previously, by means of experience.

By the term "knowledge *à priori*," therefore, we shall in the sequel understand, not such as is independent of this or that kind of experience, but such as is absolutely so of *all* experience. Opposed to this empirical knowledge, or that which is possible only *à posteriori*, that is, through experience. Knowledge *à priori* is either pure or impure. Pure knowledge *à priori* is that with which no empirical element is mixed up. For example, the proposition, "Every change has a cause," is a proposition *à priori*, but impure, because change is a conception which can only be derived from experience.

II. *The Human Intellect, Even in an Unphilosophical State, is in Possession of Certain Cognitions* à Priori

The question now is as to a *criterion*, by which we may securely distinguish a pure from an empirical cognition. Experience no doubt teaches us that this or that object is constituted in such and such a manner, but not that it could not possibly exist otherwise. Now, in the first place, if we have a proposition which contains the idea of necessity in its very conception, it is a judgment *à priori*; if, moreover, it is not derived from any other proposition, unless from one equally involving the idea of necessity, it is absolutely *à priori*. Secondly, an empirical judgment never exhibits strict and absolute, but only assumed and comparative universality (by induction); therefore, the most we can say is—so far as we have hitherto observed, there is no exception to this or that rule. If, on the other hand, a judgment carries with it strict and absolute universality, that is, admits of no possible exception, it is not derived from experience, but is valid absolutely *à priori*.

Empirical universality is, therefore, only an arbitrary extension of validity, from that which may be predicated of a proposition valid in most cases, to that which is asserted of a proposition which holds good in all; as, for example, in the affirmation, "all bodies are heavy." When, on the contrary, strict universality characterizes a judgment, it necessarily indicates another peculiar source of knowledge, namely, a faculty of cognition *à priori*. Necessity and strict universality, therefore, are infallible tests for distinguishing pure from empirical knowledge, and are inseparably connected with each other. But as in the use of these criteria the empirical limitation is sometimes more easily detected than the contingency of the judgment, or the unlimited universality which we attach to a judgment is often a more convincing proof than its necessity, it may be advisable to use the criteria separately, each being by itself infallible.

Now, that in the sphere of human cognition, we have judgments which are necessary, and in the strictest sense universal, consequently pure *à priori,* it will be an easy matter to show. If we desire an example from the sciences, we need only take any proposition in mathematics. If we cast our eyes upon the commonest operations of the understanding, the proposition, "every change must have a cause," will amply serve our purpose. In the latter case, indeed, the conception of a cause so plainly involves the conception of a necessity of connection with an effect, and of a strict universality of the law, that the very notion of a cause would entirely disappear, were we to derive it, like Hume, from a frequent association of what happens with that which precedes, and the habit thence originating of connecting representations—the necessity inherent in the judgment being therefore merely subjective. Besides, without seeking for such examples of principles existing *à priori* in cognition, we might easily show that such principles are the indispensable basis of the possibility of experience itself, and consequently prove their existence *à priori.* For whence could our experience itself acquire certainty, if all the rules on which it depends were themselves empirical, and consequently fortuitous? No one, therefore, can admit the validity of the use of such rules as first principles. But, for the present, we may content ourselves with having established the fact, that we do possess and exercise a faculty of pure *à priori* cognition; and, secondly, with having pointed out the proper tests of such cognition, namely, universality and necessity.

Not only in judgments, however, but even in conceptions, is an *à priori* origin manifest. For example, if we take away by degrees from our conceptions of a body all that can be referred to mere sensuous experience—color, hardness or softness, weight, even impenetrability—the body will then vanish; but the space which it occupied still remains, and this it is utterly impossible to annihilate in thought. Again, if we take away, in like manner, from our empirical conception of any object, corporeal or incorporeal, all properties which mere experience has taught us to connect with it, still we cannot think away those through which we cogitate it as substance, or adhering to substance, although our conception of substance is more determined than that of an object. Compelled, therefore, by that necessity with which the conception of substance forces itself upon us, we must confess that it has its seat in our faculty of cognition *à priori.*

III. Philosophy Stands in Need of a Science which Shall Determine the Possibility, Principles, and Extent of Human Knowledge à Priori

Of far more importance than all that has been above said, is the consideration that certain of our cognitions rise completely above the sphere of all possible experience, and by means of conceptions, to which there exists in the whole extent of experience no corresponding object, seem to extend the range of our judgments beyond its bounds. And just in this transcendental or supersensible sphere, where experience affords us neither instruction nor guidance, lie the investigations of *Reason,* which, on account of their importance, we consider far preferable to, and as having a far more elevated aim than, all that the understanding can achieve within the sphere of sensuous phenomena. So high a value do we set upon these investigations, that even at the risk of error, we persist in following them out, and permit neither doubt nor disregard nor indifference to restrain us from the pursuit. These unavoidable problems of mere pure reason are God, Freedom (of will) and Immortality. The science which, with all its preliminaries, has for its especial object the solution of these problems is named metaphysics—a science which is at the very outset dogmatical, that is, it confidently takes upon itself the execution of this task without any previous investigation of the ability or inability of reason for such an understanding.

Now the safe ground of experience being thus abandoned, it seems nevertheless natural that we should hesitate to erect a building with the cognitions we possess, without knowing whence they come, and on the strength of principles, the origin of which is undiscovered. Instead of thus trying to build without a foundation, it is rather to be expected that we should long ago have put the question, how the understanding can arrive at these à priori cognitions, and what is the extent, validity and worth which they may possess? We say, this is natural enough, meaning by the word natural that which is consistent with a just and reasonable way of thinking; but if we understand by the term, that which usually happens, nothing indeed could be more natural and more comprehensible than that this investigation should be left long unattempted. For one part of our pure knowledge, the science of mathematics, has been long firmly established, and thus leads us to form flattering expectations with regard to others, though these may be of quite a different nature. Besides, when we get beyond the bounds of experience, we are of course safe from opposition in that quarter; and the charm of widening the range of our knowledge is so great, that unless we are brought to a standstill by some evident contradiction, we hurry on undoubtingly in our course. This, however, may be avoided, if we are sufficiently cautious in the construction of our fictions, which are not the less fictions on that account.

Mathematical science affords us a brilliant example, how far, independently of all experience, we may carry our à priori knowledge. It is true that the mathematician occupies himself with objects and cognitions only in so far as they can be represented by means of intuition. But this circumstance is easily overlooked, because the said intuition can itself be given à priori, and therefore is hardly to be distinguished from a mere pure conception. Deceived by such a proof of the power of reason, we can perceive no limits to the extension of our knowledge. The light dove cleaving in free flight the thin air, whose resistance it feels, might imagine that her movements would be far more free and rapid in airless space. Just in the same way did Plato, abandoning the world of sense because of the narrow limits it sets to the understanding, venture upon the wings of ideas beyond it, into the void space of pure intellect. He did not reflect that he made no real progress by all his efforts; for he met with no resistance which might serve him for a support, as it were, whereon to rest, and on which he might apply his powers, in order to let the intellect acquire momentum for its progress. It is, indeed, the common fate of human reason in speculation, to finish the imposing edifice of thought as rapidly as possible, and then for the first time to begin to examine whether the foundation is a solid one or no. Arrived at this point, all sorts of excuses are sought after, in order to console us for its want of stability, or rather indeed, to enable us to dispense altogether with so late and dangerous an investigation. But what frees us during the process of building from all apprehension or suspicion, and flatters us into the belief of its solidity, is this. A great part, perhaps the greatest part, of the business of our reason consists in the analyzation of the conceptions which we already possess of objects. By this means we gain a multitude of cognitions, which, although really nothing more than elucidations or explanations of that which (though in a confused manner) was already thought in our conceptions, are, at least in respect of their form, prized as new introspections; while, so far as regards their matter or content, we have really made no addition to our conceptions, but only disinvolved them. But as this process does furnish real *à priori* knowledge, which has a sure progress and useful results, reason, deceived by this, slips in, without being itself aware of it, assertions of a quite different kind; in which, to given conceptions it adds others, *à priori* indeed, but entirely foreign to them, without our knowing how it arrives at these, and, indeed, without such a question ever suggesting itself. I shall therefore at once proceed to examine the difference between these two modes of knowledge.

IV. Of the Difference Between Analytical and Synthetical Judgments

In all judgments wherein the relation of a subject to the predicate is cogitated (I mention affirmative judgments only here; the application to negative will be very easy), this relation is possible in two different ways. Either the predicate B belongs to the subject A, as somewhat which is contained (though covertly) in the conception A; or the predicate B lies completely out of the conception A, although it stands in connection with it. In the first instance, I term the judgment analytical, in the second, synthetical. Analytical judgments (affirmative) are therefore those in which the connection of the predicate with the subject is cogitated through identity; those in which this connection is cogitated without identity, are called synthetical judgments. The former may be called *explicative,* the latter *augmentative* judgments; because the former add in the predicate nothing to the conception of the subject, but only analyze it into its constituent conceptions, which were thought already in the subject, although in a confused manner; the latter add to our conceptions of the subject a predicate which was not contained in it, and which

no analysis could ever have discovered therein. For example, when I say, "all bodies are extended," this is an analytical judgment. For I need not go beyond the conception of *body* in order to find extension connected with it, but merely analyze the conception, that is, become conscious of the manifold properties which I think in that conception, in order to discover this predicate in it: it is therefore an analytical judgment. On the other hand, when I say, "all bodies are heavy," the predicate is something totally different from that which I think in the mere conception of a body. By the addition of such a predicate therefore, it becomes a synthetical judgment.

Judgments of experience, as such, are always synthetical. For it would be absurd to think of grounding an analytical judgment on experience, because in forming such a judgment, I need not go out of the sphere of my conceptions, and therefore recourse to the testimony of experience is quite unnecessary. That "bodies are extended" is not an empirical judgment, but a proposition which stands firm *à priori.* For before addressing myself to experience, I already have in my conception all the requisite conditions for the judgment, and I have only to extract the predicate from the conception, according to the principle of contradiction, and thereby at the same time become conscious of the necessity of the judgment, a necessity which I could never learn from experience. On the other hand, though at first I do not at all include the predicate of weight in my conception of body in general, that conception still indicates an object of experience, a part of the totality of experience, to which I can still add other parts; and this I do when I recognize my observation that bodies are heavy. I can cognize beforehand by analysis the conception of body through the characteristics of extension, impenetrability, shape, etc., all which are cogitated in this conception. But now I extend my knowledge, and looking back on experience from which I had derived this conception of body, I find weight at all times connected with the above characteristics, and therefore I synthetically add to my conceptions this as a predicate, and say, "All bodies are heavy." Thus it is experience upon which rests the possibility of the synthesis of the predicate of weight with the conception of body, because both conceptions, although the one is not contained in the other, still belong to one another (only contingently, however), as parts of a whole, namely, of experience, which is itself a synthesis of intuitions.

But to synthetical judgments *à priori*, such aid is entirely wanting. If I go out of and beyond the conception A, in order to recognize another B as connected with it, what foundation have I to rest on, whereby to render the synthesis possible? I have here no longer the advantage of looking out in the sphere of experience for what I want. Let us take, for example, the proposition. "Everything that happens has a cause." In the conception of *something that happens,* I indeed think of an existence which a certain time antecedes, and from this I can derive analytical judgments. But the conception of a cause lies quite out of the above conception, and indicates something entirely different from "that which happens," and is consequently not contained in that conception. How then am I able to assert concerning the general conception—"that which happens" —something entirely different from that conception, and to recognize the conception of cause although not contained in it, yet as belonging to it, and even necessarily? What is here the unknown = X, upon which the understanding rests when it believes it has found, out of the conception A a foreign predicate B, which it nevertheless considers to be connected with it? It cannot be experience, because the principle adduced annexes the two

representations, cause and effect, to the representation existence, not only with universality, which experience cannot give, but also with expression of necessity, therefore completely *à priori* and from pure conceptions. Upon such synthetical, that is augmentative propositions depends the whole aim of our speculative knowledge *à priori;* for although analytical judgments are indeed highly important and necessary, they are so only to arrive at that clearness of conceptions which is requisite for a sure and extended synthesis, and this alone is a real acquisition.

V. In All Theoretical Sciences of Reason, Synthetical Judgments à Priori Are Contained as Principles

1. Mathematical judgments are always synthetical. Hitherto this fact, though incontestably true and very important in its consequences, seems to have escaped the analysts of the human mind, nay, to be in complete opposition to all their conjectures. For as it was found that mathematical conclusions all proceed according to the principle of contradiction (which the nature of every apodictic certainty requires), people became persuaded that the fundamental principles of the science also were recognized and admitted in the same way. But the notion is fallacious; for although a synthetical proposition can certainly be discerned by means of the principle of contradiction, this is possible only when another synthetical proposition precedes, from which the latter is deduced, but never of itself.

Before all, be it observed, that proper mathematical propositions are always judgments *à priori,* and not empirical, because they carry along with them the conception of necessity, which cannot be given by experience. If this be demurred to, it matters not; I shall then limit my assertion to *pure* mathematics, the very conception of which implies that it consists of knowledge altogether non-empirical and *à priori*.

We might, indeed, at first suppose that the proposition 7 + 5 = 12, is a merely analytical proposition, following (according to the principle of contradiction), from the conception of the sum of seven and five. But if we regard it more narrowly, we find that our conception of the sum of seven and five contains nothing more than the uniting of both sums into one, whereby it cannot at all be cogitated what this single number is which embraces both. The conception of twelve is by no means obtained by merely cogitating the union of seven and five; and we may analyze our conception of such a possible sum as long as we will, still we shall never discover in it the notion of twelve. We must go beyond these conceptions, and have recourse to an intuition which corresponds to one of the two—our five fingers, for example, or like Segner in his "Arithmetic," five points, and so by degrees, add the units contained in the five given in the intuition, to the conception of seven. For I first take the number 7, and, for the conception of 5 calling in the aid of the fingers of my hand as objects of intuition, I add the units, which I before took together to make up the number 5, gradually now by means of the material image my hand, to the number 7, and by this process, I at length see the number 12 arise. That 7 should be added to 5, I have certainly cogitated in my conception of a sum = 7 + 5, but not that this sum was equal to 12. Arithmetical propositions are therefore always synthetical, of which we may become more clearly convinced by trying large numbers. For it will thus become quite evident, that, turn and twist our conceptions as we may, it is impossible, without having recourse to intuition, to arrive at the sum total or product by means of the mere analysis of our conceptions. Just as little is any principle of pure geometry analytical. "A straight line between two points is the shortest," is a synthetical proposition. For my conception of *straight,* contains no notion of *quantity,* but is merely *qualitative.* The conception of the *shortest* is therefore wholly an addition, and by no analysis can it be extracted from our conception of a straight line. Intuition must therefore here lend its aid, by means of which and thus only, our synthesis is possible.

Some few principles preposited by geometricians are, indeed, really analytical, and depend on the principle of contradiction. They serve, however, like identical propositions, as links in the chain of method, not as principles—for example, *a* = *a*, the whole is equal to itself, or (*a* + *b*) > *a*, the whole is greater than its part. And yet even these principles themselves, though they derive their validity from pure conceptions, are only admitted in mathematics because they can be presented in intuition. What causes us here commonly to believe that the predicate of such apodictic judgments is already contained in our conception, and that the judgment is therefore analytical, is merely the equivocal nature of the expression. We must join in thought a certain predicate to a given conception, and this necessity cleaves already to the conception. But the question is, not what we must join in thought to the given conception, but what we really think therein, though only obscurely, and then it becomes manifest, that the predicate pertains to these conceptions, necessarily indeed, yet not as thought in the conception itself, but by virtue of an intuition, which must be added to the conception.

2. The science of Natural Philosophy (Physics) contains in itself synthetical judgments *à priori,* as principles. I shall adduce two propositions. For instance, the proposition, "In all changes of the material world, the quantity of matter remains unchanged"; or, that, "in all communication of motion, action and reaction must always be equal." In both of these, not only is the necessity, and therefore their origin, *à*

priori clear, but also that they are synthetical propositions. For in the conception of matter, I do not cogitate its permanency, but merely its presence in space, which it fills. I therefore really go out of and beyond the conception of matter, in order to think on to it something *à priori,* which I did not think in it. The proposition is therefore not analytical, but synthetical, and nevertheless conceived *à priori;* and so it is with regard to the other propositions of the pure part of natural philosophy.

3. As to Metaphysics, even if we look upon it merely as an attempted science, yet, from the nature of human reason, an indispensable one, we find that it must contain synthetical propositions *à priori.* It is not merely the duty of metaphysics to dissect, and thereby analytically to illustrate, the conceptions which we form *à priori* of things; but we seek to widen the range of our *à priori* knowledge. For this purpose, we must avail ourselves of such principles as add something to the original conception—something not identical with, nor contained in it, and by means of synthetical judgments *à priori,* leave far behind us the limits of experience; for example, in the proposition, "the world must have a beginning," and such like. Thus metaphysics, according to the proper aim of the science, consists merely of synthetical propositions *à priori.*

Inference

Posterior Analytics

Aristotle (384–322 B.C.) was born in Stagyra in Thrace, where his father was a physician to the King of Macedonia. At the age of about eighteen he went to Athens, where he became a pupil at Plato's Academy and remained as such for about twenty years. Eventually he became a tutor to Alexander of Macedonia, and later, from 355 until 323, he conducted his own school at Athens, the Lyceum. In 323 Alexander died and Athens revolted against Alexander's leaders, and indicted Aristotle for impiety. Aristotle fled the city and died the following year in exile. Aristotle founded the Western study of logic, and from one of his very important works on that subject we take the following selection. In this selection, Aristotle investigates the nature of so-called demonstrative knowledge, seeking its foundations or beginnings, as well as its relation to other kinds of knowledge.

Book I

1 All instruction given or received by way of argument proceeds from pre-existent knowledge. This becomes evident upon a survey of all the species of such instruction. The mathematical sciences and all other speculative disciplines are acquired in this way, and so are the two forms of dialectical reasoning, syllogistic and inductive; for each of these latter makes use of old knowledge to impart new, the syllogism assuming an audience that accepts its premises, induction exhibiting the universal as implicit in the clearly known particular. Again, the persuasion exerted by rhetorical arguments is in principle the same, since they use either example, a kind of induction, or enthymeme, a form of syllogism.

The pre-existent knowledge required is of two kinds. In some cases admission of the fact must be assumed, in others comprehension of the meaning of the term used, and sometimes both assumptions are essential. Thus, we assume that every

"Posterior Analytics," trans. G. R. G. Mure, in *The Oxford Translation of Aristotle*, Vol. 1, ed. W. D. Ross (Oxford, Eng.: The Clarendon Press, 1928); and in *The Basic Works of Aristotle*, ed. Richard McKeon (New York: Random House, Inc., 1941). Reprinted by permission of The Clarendon Press, Oxford, and Random House.

predicate can be either truly affirmed or truly denied of any subject, and that "triangle" means so and so; as regards "unit" we have to make the double assumption of the meaning of the word and the existence of the thing. The reason is that these several objects are not equally obvious to us. Recognition of a truth may in some cases contain as factors both previous knowledge and also knowledge acquired simultaneously with that recognition—knowledge, this latter, of the particulars actually falling under the universal and therein already virtually known. For example, the student knew beforehand that the angles of every triangle are equal to two right angles; but it was only at the actual moment at which he was being led on to recognize this as true in the instance before him that he came to know "this figure inscribed in the semicircle" to be a triangle. For some things (viz., the singulars finally reached which are not predicable of anything else as subject) are only learnt in this way, i.e., there is here no recognition through a middle of a minor term as subject to a major. Before he was led on to recognition or before he actually drew a conclusion, we should perhaps say that in a manner he knew, in a manner not:

If he did not in an unqualified sense of the term *know* the existence of this triangle, how could he *know* without qualification that its angles were equal to two right angles? No: clearly he *knows* not without qualification but only in the sense that he *knows* universally. If this distinction is not drawn, we are faced with the dilemma in the *Meno:* [1] either a man will learn nothing or what he already knows; for we cannot accept the solution which some people offer. A man is asked, "Do you, or do you not, know that every pair is even?" He says he does know it. The questioner then produces a particular pair, of the existence, and so *a fortiori* of the even-

ness, of which he was unaware. The solution which some people offer is to assert that they do not know that every pair is even, but only that everything which they know to be a pair is even: yet what they know to be even is that of which they have demonstrated evenness, i.e., what they made the subject of their premiss, viz., not merely every triangle or number which they know to be such, but any and every number or triangle without reservation. For no premiss is ever couched in the form "every number which you know to be such," or "every rectilinear figure which you know to be such": the predicate is always construed as applicable to any and every instance of the thing. On the other hand, I imagine there is nothing to prevent a man in one sense knowing what he is learning, in another not knowing it. The strange thing would be, not if in some sense he knew what he was learning, but if he were to know it in that precise sense and manner in which he was learning it.

2 We suppose ourselves to possess unqualified scientific knowledge of a thing, as opposed to knowing it in the accidental way in which the sophist knows, when we think that we know the cause on which the fact depends, as the cause of that fact and of no other, and, further, that the fact could not be other than it is. Now that scientific knowing is something of this sort is evident—witness both those who falsely claim it and those who actually possess it, since the former merely imagine themselves to be, while the latter are also actually, in the condition described. Consequently the proper object of unqualified scientific knowledge is something which cannot be other than it is.

There may be another manner of knowing as well—that will be discussed later. What I now assert is that at all events we do know by demonstration. By demonstration I mean a syllogism productive of scientific knowledge, a syllogism, that is, the

1 Plato, *Meno*, 80 E.

grasp of which is *eo ipso* such knowledge. Assuming then that my thesis as to the nature of scientific knowing is correct, the premisses of demonstrated knowledge must be true, primary, immediate, better known than and prior to the conclusion, which is further related to them as effect to cause. Unless these conditions are satisfied, the basic truths will not be "appropriate" to the conclusion. Syllogism there may indeed be without these conditions, but such syllogism, not being productive of scientific knowledge, will not be demonstration. The premisses must be true: for that which is non-existent cannot be known—we cannot know, e.g., that the diagonal of a square is commensurate with its side. The premisses must be primary and indemonstrable; otherwise they will require demonstration in order to be known, since to have knowledge, if it be not accidental knowledge, of things which are demonstrable, means precisely to have a demonstration of them. The premisses must be the causes of the conclusion, better known than it, and prior to it; its causes, since we possess scientific knowledge of a thing only when we know its cause; prior, in order to be causes; antecedently known, this antecedent knowledge being not our mere understanding of the meaning, but knowledge of the fact as well. Now "prior" and "better known" are ambiguous terms, for there is a difference between what is prior and better known in the order of being and what is prior and better known to man. I mean that objects nearer to sense are prior and better known to man; objects without qualification prior and better known are those further from sense. Now the most universal causes are furthest from sense and particular causes are nearest to sense, and they are thus exactly opposed to one another. In saying that the premisses of demonstrated knowledge must be primary, I mean that they must be the "appropriate" basic truths, for I identify primary premiss and basic truth. A "basic truth" in a demonstration is an immediate proposition. An immediate proposition is one which has no other proposition prior to it. A proposition is either part of an enunciation, i.e., it predicates a single attribute of a single subject. If a proposition is dialectical, it assumes either part indifferently; if it is demonstrative, it lays down one part to the definite exclusion of the other because that part is true. The term "enunciation" denotes either part of a contradiction indifferently. A contradiction is an opposition which of its own nature excludes a middle. The part of a contradiction which conjoins a predicate with a subject is an affirmation; the part disjoining them is a negation. I call an immediate basic truth of syllogism a "thesis" when, though it is not susceptible of proof by the teacher, yet ignorance of it does not constitute a total bar to progress on the part of the pupil: one which the pupil must know if he is to learn anything whatever is an axiom. I call it an axiom because there are such truths and we give them the name of axioms *par excellence.* If a thesis assumes one part or the other of an enunciation, i.e. asserts either the existence or the non-existence of a subject, it is a hypothesis; if it does not assert, it is a definition. Definition *is* a "thesis" or a "laying something down," since the arithmetician lays it down that to be a unit is to be quantitatively indivisible; but it is not a hypothesis, for to define what a unit is is not the same as to affirm its existence.

Now since the required ground of our knowledge—i.e., of our conviction—of a fact is the possession of such a syllogism as we call demonstration, and the ground of the syllogism is the facts constituting its premisses, we must not only know the primary premisses—some if not all of them—beforehand, but know them better than the conclusion: for the cause of an attribute's inherence in a subject always itself inheres in the subject more firmly than that attribute; e.g., the cause of our loving anything is dearer to us than the object of our love. So since the primary premises are the cause of our knowledge—i.e., of our conviction—it follows that we know them better—that is, are more convinced of them—than their consequences, precisely because our knowledge of the latter is the effect of our knowledge of the premises. Now a man cannot believe in anything more than in the things he knows, unless he has either actual knowledge of it or something better than actual knowledge. But we are faced with this paradox if a student whose belief rests on demonstration has not prior knowledge; a man must believe in some, if not in all, of the basic truths more than in the conclusion. Moreover, if a man sets out to acquire the scientific knowledge that comes through demonstration, he must not only have a better knowledge of the basic truths and a firmer conviction of them than of the connexion which is being demonstrated: more than this, nothing must be more certain or better known to him than these basic truths in their character as contradicting the fundamental premises which lead to the opposed and erroneous conclusion. For indeed the conviction of pure science must be unshakable.

3   Some hold that, owing to the necessity of knowing the primary premises, there is no scientific knowledge. Others think there is, but that all truths are demonstrable. Neither doctrine is either true or a necessary deduction from the premises. The first school, assuming that there is no way of knowing other than by demonstration, maintain that an infinite regress is involved, on the ground that if behind the prior stands no primary, we could not know the posterior through the prior (wherein they are right, for one cannot traverse an infinite series): if on the other hand—they say—the series terminates and there are primary premises, yet these are unknowable because incapable of demonstration, which according to them is the only form of knowledge. And since thus one cannot know the primary premises, knowledge of the conclusions which follow from them is not pure scientific knowledge nor properly knowing at all, but rests on the mere supposition that the premises are true. The other party agree with them as regards knowing, holding that it is only possible by demonstration, but they see no difficulty in holding that all truths are demonstrated, on the ground that demonstration may be circular and reciprocal.

Our own doctrine is that not all knowledge is demonstrative: on the contrary, knowledge of the immediate premises is independent of demonstration. (The necessity of this is obvious; for since we must know the prior premises from which the demonstration is drawn, and since the regress must end in immediate truths, those truths must be indemonstrable.) Such, then, is our doctrine, and in addition we maintain that besides scientific knowledge there is its originative source which enables us to recognize the definitions.

Now demonstration must be based on premises prior to and better known than the conclusion; and the same things cannot simultaneously be both prior and posterior to one another: so circular demonstration is clearly not possible in the unqualified sense of "demonstration," but only possible if "demonstration" be extended to include that other method of argument which rests on a distinction between truths prior to us and truths without qualification prior, i.e., the method by which induction produces knowledge. But if we accept this extension of its meaning, our definition of unqualified knowledge will prove faulty; for there seem to be two kinds of it. Perhaps, however, the second form of demonstration, that which proceeds from truths better known to us, is not demonstration in the unqualified sense of the term.

The advocates of circular demonstration are not only faced with the difficulty we have just stated: in addition their theory reduces to the mere statement that if a thing exists, then it does exist—an easy way of proving anything. That this is so can be clearly shown by taking three terms, for to constitute the circle it makes no difference whether many terms or few or even only two are taken. Thus by direct proof, if A is, B must be; if B is, C must be; therefore if A is, C must be. Since then—by the circular proof—if A is, B must be, and if B is, A must be, A may be substituted for C above. Then "if B is, A must be" = "if B is, C must be," which above gave the conclusion "if A is, C must be": but C and A have been identified. Consequently the upholders of circular demonstration are in the position of saying that if A is, A must be—a simple way of proving anything. Moreover, even such circular demonstration is impossible except in the case of attributes that imply one another, viz., "peculiar" properties.

Now, it has been shown that the positing of one thing—be it one term or one premiss—never involves a necessary consequent: two premisses constitute the first and smallest foundation for drawing a conclusion at all and therefore *a fortiori* for the demonstrative syllogism of science. If, then, A is implied in B and $C,$ and B and C are reciprocally implied in one another and in $A,$ it is possible, as has been shown in my writings on the syllogism, to prove all the assumptions on which the original conclusion rested, by circular demonstration in the first figure. But it has also been shown that in the other figures either no conclusion is possible, or at least none which proves both the original premisses. Propositions the terms of which are not convertible cannot be circularly demonstrated at all, and since convertible terms occur rarely in actual demonstrations, it is clearly frivolous and impossible to say that demonstration is reciprocal and that therefore everything can be demonstrated. . . .

6 Demonstrative knowledge must rest on necessary basic truths; for the object of scientific knowledge cannot be other than it is. Now attributes attaching essentially to their subjects attach necessarily to them: for essential attributes are either elements in the essential nature of their subjects, or contain their subjects as elements in their own essential nature. (The pairs of opposites which the latter class includes are necessary because one member or the other necessarily inheres.) It follows from this that premisses of the demonstrative syllogism must be connexions essential in the sense explained: for all attributes must inhere essentially or else be accidental, and accidental attributes are not necessary to their subjects.

We must either state the case thus, or else premise that the conclusion of demonstration is necessary and that a demonstrated conclusion cannot be other than it is, and then infer that the conclusion must be developed from necessary premisses. For though you may reason from true premisses without demonstrating, yet if your premisses are necessary you will assuredly demonstrate—in such necessity you have at once a distinctive character of demonstration. That demonstration proceeds from necessary premisses is also indicated by the fact that the objection we raise against a professed demonstration is that a premiss of it is not a necessary truth—whether we think it altogether devoid of necessity, or at any rate so far as our opponent's previous argument goes. This shows how naive it is to suppose one's basic truths rightly chosen if one starts with a proposition which is (1) popularly accepted and (2) true, such as the sophists' assumption that to know is the same as to possess knowledge. For (1) popular acceptance or rejection is no criterion of a basic truth, which can only be the primary law of the genus constituting the subject matter of the demonstration; and (2) not *all* truth is "appropriate."

A further proof that the conclusion must be the development of necessary premises is as follows. Where demonstration is possible, one who can give no account which includes the cause has no scientific knowledge. If, then, we suppose a syllogism in which, though A necessarily inheres in C, yet B, the middle term of the demonstration, is not necessarily connected with A and C, then the man who argues thus has no reasoned knowledge of the conclusion, since this conclusion does not owe its necessity to the middle term; for though the conclusion is necessary, the mediating link is a contingent fact. Or again, if a man is without knowledge now, though he still retains the steps of the argument, though there is no change in himself or in the fact and no lapse of memory on his part; then neither had he knowledge previously. But the mediating link, not being necessary, may have perished in the interval; and if so, though there be no change in him nor in the fact, and though he will still retain the steps of the argument, yet he has not knowledge, and therefore had not knowledge before. Even if the link has not actually perished but is liable to perish, this situation is possible and might occur. But such a condition cannot be knowledge.

When the conclusion is necessary, the middle through which it was proved may yet quite easily be non-necessary. You can in fact infer the necessary even from a non-necessary premiss, just as you can infer the true from the not true. On the other hand, when the middle is necessary the conclusion must be necessary; just as true premisses always give a true conclusion. Thus, if A is necessarily predicated of B and B of C, then A is necessarily predicated of C. But when the conclusion is non-necessary the middle cannot be necessary either. Thus: let A be predicated non-necessarily of C but necessarily of B, and let B be a necessary predicate of C;

then A too will be a necessary predicate of C, which by hypothesis it is not.

To sum up, then: demonstrative knowledge must be knowledge of a necessary nexus, and therefore must clearly be obtained through a necessary middle term; otherwise its possessor will know neither the cause nor the fact that his conclusion is a necessary connexion. Either he will mistake the non-necessary for the necessary and believe the necessity of the conclusion without knowing it, or else he will not even believe it—in which case he will be equally ignorant, whether he actually infers the mere fact through middle terms or the reasoned fact and from immediate premisses.

Of accidents that are not essential according to our definition of essential there is no demonstrative knowledge; for since an accident, in the sense in which I here speak of it, may also not inhere, it is impossible to prove its inherence as a necessary conclusion. A difficulty, however, might be raised as to why in dialectic, if the conclusion is not a necessary connexion, such and such determinate premisses should be proposed in order to deal with such and such determinate problems. Would not the result be the same if one asked any questions whatever and then merely stated one's conclusion? The solution is that determinate questions have to be put, not because the replies to them affirm facts which necessitate facts affirmed by the conclusion, but because these answers are propositions which if the answerer affirm, he must affirm the conclusion—and affirm it with truth if they are true.

Since it is just those attributes within every genus which are essential and possessed by their respective subjects as such that are necessary, it is clear that both the conclusions and the premisses of demonstrations which produce scientific knowledge are essential. For accidents are not necessary: and, further, since accidents are not necessary one does not necessarily have reasoned knowledge of a conclusion drawn from them (this is so even if the accidental premises are invariable but not essential, as in proofs through signs; for though the conclusion be actually essential, one will not know it as essential nor know its reason); but to have reasoned knowledge of a conclusion is to know it through its cause. We may conclude that the middle must be consequentially connected with the minor, and the major with the middle.

7 It follows that we cannot in demonstrating pass from one genus to another. We cannot, for instance, prove geometrical truths by arithmetic. For there are three elements in demonstration: (1) what is proved, the conclusion—an attribute inhering essentially in a genus; (2) the axioms, i.e., axioms which are premises of demonstration; (3) the subject-genus whose attributes, i.e., essential properties, are revealed by the demonstration. The axioms which are premises of demonstration may be identical in two or more sciences: but in the case of two different genera such as arithmetic and geometry you cannot apply arithmetical demonstration to the properties of magnitudes unless the magnitudes in question are numbers. How in certain cases transference is possible I will explain later.

Arithmetical demonstration and the other sciences likewise possess, each of them, their own genera; so that if the demonstration is to pass from one sphere to another, the genus must be either absolutely or to some extent the same. If this is not so, transference is clearly impossible, because the extreme and the middle terms must be drawn from the same genus: otherwise, as predicated, they will not be essential and will thus be accidents. That is why it cannot be proved by geometry that opposites fall under one science, nor even that the product of two cubes is a cube. Nor can the theorem of any one

science be demonstrated by means of another science, unless these theorems are related as subordinate to superior (e.g., as optical theorems to geometry or harmonic theorems to arithmetic). Geometry again cannot prove of lines any property which they do not possess *qua* lines, i.e., in virtue of the fundamental truths of their peculiar genus: it cannot show, for example, that the straight line is the most beautiful of lines or the contrary of the circle; for these qualities do not belong to lines in virtue of their peculiar genus, but through some property which it shares with other genera.

8 It is also clear that if the premises from which the syllogism proceeds are commensurately universal, the conclusion of such demonstration—demonstration, i.e., in the unqualified sense—must also be eternal. Therefore no attribute can be demonstrated nor known by strictly scientific knowledge to inhere in perishable things. The proof can only be accidental, because the attribute's connexion with its perishable subject is not commensurately universal but temporary and special. If such a demonstration is made, one premiss must be perishable and not commensurately universal (perishable because only if it is perishable will the conclusion be perishable; not commensurately universal, because the predicate will be predicable of some instances of the subject and not of others); so that the conclusion can only be that a fact is true at the moment—not commensurately and universally. The same is true of definitions, since a definition is either a primary premiss or a conclusion of a demonstration, or else only differs from a demonstration in the order of its terms. Demonstration and science of merely frequent occurrences—e.g., of eclipse as happening to the moon—are, as such, clearly eternal: whereas so far as they are not eternal they are not fully commensurate. Other subjects too have properties attaching to them in the

same way as eclipse attaches to the moon.
9 It is clear that if the conclusion is to
show an attribute inhering as such, nothing can be demonstrated except from its
"appropriate" basic truths. Consequently
a proof even from true, indemonstrable,
and immediate premisses does not constitute knowledge. Such proofs are like
Bryson's method of squaring the circle; for
they operate by taking as their middle a
common character—a character, therefore,
which the subject may share with another
—and consequently they apply equally to
subjects different in kind. They therefore
afford knowledge of an attribute only as
inhering accidentally, not as belonging to
its subject as such: otherwise they would
not have been applicable to another genus.

Our knowledge of any attribute's connexion with a subject is accidental unless
we know that connexion through the
middle term in virtue of which it inheres,
and as an inference from basic premisses
essential and "appropriate" to the subject
—unless we know, e.g., the property of
possessing angles equal to two right angles
as belonging to that subject in which it inheres essentially, and as inferred from basic premisses essential and "appropriate"
to that subject: so that if that middle term
also belongs essentially to the minor, the
middle must belong to the same kind as
the major and minor terms. The only exceptions to this rule are such cases as
theorems in harmonics which are demonstrable by arithmetic. Such theorems are
proved by the same middle terms as arithmetical properties, but with a qualification
—the fact falls under a separate science (for
the subject genus is separate), but the reasoned fact concerns the superior science,
to which the attributes essentially belong.
Thus, even these apparent exceptions show
that no attribute is strictly demonstrable
except from its "appropriate" basic truths,
which, however, in the case of these sciences have the requisite identity of character.

It is no less evident that the peculiar
basic truths of each inhering attribute are
indemonstrable; for basic truths from
which they might be deduced would be
basic truths of all that is, and the science
to which they belonged would possess universal sovereignty. This is so because he
knows better whose knowledge is deduced
from higher causes, for his knowledge is
from prior premisses when it derives from
causes themselves uncaused: hence, if he
knows better than others or best of all,
his knowledge would be science in a higher
or the highest degree. But, as things are,
demonstration is not transferable to another genus, with such exceptions as we
have mentioned of the application of geometrical demonstrations to theorems in
mechanics or optics, or of arithmetical
demonstrations to those of harmonics.

It is hard to be sure whether one knows
or not; for it is hard to be sure whether
one's knowledge is based on the basic
truths appropriate to each attribute—the
differentia of true knowledge. We think
we have scientific knowledge if we have
reasoned from true and primary premisses.
But that is not so: the conclusion must be
homogeneous with the basic facts of the
science.
10 I call the basic truths of every genus
those elements in it the existence of which
cannot be proved. As regards both these
primary truths and the attributes dependent on them the meaning of the name is
assumed. The fact of their existence as
regards the primary truths must be assumed; but it has to be proved of the remainder, the attributes. Thus we assume
the meaning alike of unity, straight, and
triangular; but while as regards unity and
magnitude we assume also the fact of their
existence, in the case of the remainder
proof is required.

Of the basic truths used in the demonstrative sciences some are peculiar to each
science, and some are common, but common only in the sense of analogous, being

of use only in so far as they fall within the genus constituting the province of the science in question.

Peculiar truths are, e.g., the definitions of line and straight; common truths are such as "take equals from equals and equals remain." Only so much of these common truths is required as falls within the genus in question: for a truth of this kind will have the same force even if not used generally but applied by the geometer only to magnitudes, or by the arithmetician only to numbers. Also peculiar to a science are the subjects the existence as well as the meaning of which it assumes, and the essential attributes of which it investigates, e.g., in arithmetic units, in geometry points and lines. Both the existence and the meaning of the subjects are assumed by these sciences; but of their essential attributes only the meaning is assumed. For example arithmetic assumes the meaning of odd and even, square and cube, geometry that of incommensurable, or of deflection or verging of lines, whereas the existence of these attributes is demonstrated by means of the axioms and from previous conclusions as premises. Astronomy too proceeds in the same way. For indeed every demonstrative science has three elements: (1) that which it posits, the subject genus whose essential attributes it examines; (2) the so-called axioms, which are primary premises of its demonstration; (3) the attributes, the meaning of which it assumes. Yet some sciences may very well pass over some of these elements; e.g., we might not expressly posit the existence of the genus if its existence were obvious (for instance, the existence of hot and cold is more evident than that of number); or we might omit to assume expressly the meaning of the attributes if it were well understood. In the same way the meaning of axioms, such as "Take equals from equals and equals remain," is well known and so not expressly assumed. Nevertheless in the nature of the case the essential elements of demonstration are three: the subject, the attributes, and the basic premises.

That which expresses necessary self-grounded fact, and which we must necessarily believe, is distinct both from the hypotheses of a science and from illegitimate postulate—I say "must believe," because all syllogism, and therefore a fortiori demonstration, is addressed not to the spoken word, but to the discourse within the soul, and though we can always raise objections to the spoken word, to the inward discourse we cannot always object. That which is capable of proof but assumed by the teacher without proof is, if the pupil believes and accepts it, hypothesis, though only in a limited sense hypothesis—that is, relatively to the pupil; if the pupil has no opinion or a contrary opinion on the matter, the same assumption is an illegitimate postulate. Therein lies the distinction between hypothesis and illegitimate postulate: the latter is the contrary of the pupil's opinion, demonstrable, but assumed and used without demonstration.

The definitions—viz., those which are not expressed as statements that anything is or is not—are not hypotheses: but it is in the premises of a science that its hypotheses are contained. Definitions require only to be understood, and this is not hypothesis—unless it be contended that the pupil's hearing is also an hypothesis required by the teacher. Hypotheses, on the contrary, postulate facts on the being of which depends the being of the fact inferred. Nor are the geometer's hypotheses false, as some have held, urging that one must not employ falsehood and that the geometer is uttering falsehood in stating that the line which he draws is a foot long or straight, when it is actually neither. The truth is that the geometer does not draw any conclusion from the being of the particular line of which he speaks, but from what his diagrams symbolize. A further distinction is that all hypotheses and illegitimate postulates are either universal or particular, whereas a definition is neither. . . .

31 Scientific knowledge is not possible through the act of perception. Even if perception as a faculty is of "the such" and not merely of a "this somewhat," yet one must at any rate actually perceive a "this somewhat," and at a definite present place and time: but that which is commensurately universal and true in all cases one cannot perceive, since it is not "this" and it is not "now"; if it were, it would not be commensurately universal—the term we apply to what is always and everywhere. Seeing, therefore, that demonstrations are commensurately universal and universals imperceptible, we clearly cannot obtain scientific knowledge by the act of perception: nay, it is obvious that even if it were possible to perceive that a triangle has its angles equal to two right angles, we should still be looking for a demonstration—we should not (as some say) possess knowledge of it; for perception must be of a particular, whereas scientific knowledge involves the recognition of the commensurate universal. So if we were on the moon, and saw the earth shutting out the sun's light, we should not know the cause of the eclipse: we should perceive the present fact of the eclipse, but not the reasoned fact at all, since the act of perception is not of the commensurate universal. I do not, of course, deny that by watching the frequent recurrence of this event we might, after tracking the commensurate universal, possess a demonstration, for the commensurate universal is elicited from the several groups of singulars.

The commensurate universal is precious because it makes clear the cause; so that in the case of facts like these which have a cause other than themselves universal knowledge is more precious than sense-perceptions and than intuition. (As regards primary truths there is of course a different account to be given.) Hence it is clear that knowledge of things demonstrable cannot be acquired by perception, unless the term perception is applied to the possession of scientific knowledge through demonstration. Nevertheless certain points do arise with regard to connexions to be proved which are referred for their explanation to a failure in sense-perception: there are cases when an act of vision would terminate our inquiry, not because in seeing we should be knowing, but because we should have elicited the universal from seeing; if, for example, we saw the pores in the glass and the light passing through, the reason of the kindling would be clear to us because we should at the same time see it in each instance and intuit that it must be so in all instances.

F. Th. Stcherbatsky

F. Th. Stcherbatsky (1868–1942) was one of the finest Indo-logical scholars to come out of the Soviet Union in the twentieth century. Stcherbatsky lived, worked, and taught in Leningrad at the prestigious Academy of Sciences of the USSR from where his translations, books, and articles emerged in a rather steady stream throughout the 1920s and 1930s. The selection that follows is taken from the monumental work on Buddhist logic in which Stcherbatsky explores the nature of inference and the various problems that Buddhist and non-Buddhist scholars and logicians have found with it.

1. JUDGMENT AND INFERENCE

From the perceptual judgment or judgment proper, we must distinguish another variety of judgment, the inferential one. Since all real cognition, i.e., all cognition of reality, reduces to judgments, i.e., to interpretation of sensations in concepts, and since cognition can be distinguished as a direct and indirect one, the judgment can also be divided in a direct and an indirect one. The direct one is perception, the indirect one is inference. The direct one, we saw, is a synthesis between a sensation and a conception, the indirect one is a synthesis between a sensation and two concepts. The direct one has two terms, the indirect one has three terms. The direct one reduces to the form "this is blue" or "this is smoke." The indirect one can be reduced to the form "this is smoke produced by fire," or "there is some fire, because there is smoke." The smoke is perceived, the judgment "this is smoke" is perceptual and direct. The fire is hidden, the judgment "there is here fire" is inferential and indirect. All things may be divided in perceived and unperceived. The cognition of a non-perceived through a perceived is called inference. It is an indirect cognition, a cognition, so to speak, round the corner, a cognition of an object through its "mark." The hidden object has a mark, and this mark is, in its turn, the characteristic, or the mark of a point of reality. The cognition of a point of reality, as possessing the double mark, as possessing the mark of its mark, is inference—*nota notae est nota rei ipsius.* In a perceptual judgment we cognize the object X through its symbol which is the conception A. In an inferential judgment

From *Buddhist Logic*, Leningrad, Bibliotheca Buddhica XXVI, 1932.

we cognize the object X through its double symbol A and B.

The symbols A and B are related as reason and consequence. When one of them, the element A, is cognized, the cognition of the other, of the element B, necessarily follows. Since the element X, the Substratum of the Qualities A and B, or the Subject of both these Predicates, is indefinite, always the same, its expression can be dropped; its presence will be necessarily understood without any formal expression. In that case the two interrelated elements or qualities A and B will represent the whole inference or the whole inferential judgment. This judgment will then apparently consist of two conceptions only, but related as reason and consequence, the one being the necessary ground for predicating the other.

The inferential judgment will then become a judgment of concomitance. Inference, or the object cognized in an inference, says Dharmottara, is either "a complex idea of the substratum together with its inferred property, or, when the invariable concomitance between the reason and the inferred attribute is considered [abstractly], then the inferred fact appears as this attribute [taken in its concomitance with the reason]." In the first case we just have an inferential judgment, in the second case a judgment of concomitance. The first corresponds to a combination of the minor premise with the conclusion, the second corresponds to the major premise of the Aristotelian syllogism.[1] Indian logic treats them as essen-

tially "one cognition," the cognition, e.g., of the fire as inferred through its mark.

The judgment "fire produces smoke" or "wherever there is smoke there is fire," or "there is no smoke without fire," just as the judgments "the *śiṃśapā* is a tree," or "the blue is a colour," "the cow is an animal," so far they are cognitions of the real and have a hold in reality, must be reduced to the form "there is *here* a fire, because there is smoke," "*this* is blue which is a colour," "*this* is a tree because it is a *śiṃśapā*," "*this* is an animal, since it is a cow," etc. Without the element "this" or "here," either expressed or understood, they would not be cognitions of reality.

However not every cognition containing three terms of which one is the substratum for the two others, will be an inference. Only such a combination of them, where the two attributes are necessarily interrelated, the one deducible from the other, represents an inference. The judgment "there is a fiery hill" contains three terms, however they are not necessarily interrelated. But the judgment "there is here a fire, because there is smoke" "there is no smoke without a fire" are inferential, since smoke is represented as necessarily connected with its cause, the fire.[2]

---

[1] It is clear that those European logicians who explain the relation of subject and predicate in a normal judgment as the relation of reason and consequence, like Herbart and others, especially N. O. Lossky, reduce the normal judgment to a judgment of concomitance. But it is also clear that the judgment of concomitance belongs rather to inference, than to judgment proper, it is the major premise according to the first figure. The subject of such judgments is always the reason of the inference. The judgment "smoke is pro-

duced by fire" is reduced in India to the form "wheresoever there is smoke, there necessarily is some fire," the judgment, "the *śiṃśapā* is a tree" means "if something is characterized as *śiṃśapā* it is necessarily also characterized as a tree," etc. They are hypothetical judgments.

[2] The difference between a judgment of perception and a judgment of inference is, to a certain extent, similar to the difference which Kant draws between a judgment of perception and a judgment of experience. . . . The observation that the "sun warms a stone" is not yet a judgment of experience. But the universal and necessary synthesis between sun's rays and the calefaction of the stone is what Kant calls experience. It is an inference of the form "this stone is warm, because it is sunlit," or "whatsoever is sunlit becomes warmed." Generally speaking it seems better logic

Of what kind this necessary relation is —will be told later on.

2. THE THREE TERMS

Every inference therefore contains three terms which are the logical Subject, the logical Predicate and, between them, the Reason or Mark, which unites them.

The Subject can be the ultimately real Subject or the metaphorical one. The ultimately real is always nothing but a point-instant of pure reality. It represents that substratum of reality which must underlie all thought-construction. It is the element "this," that "thisness" which we already know from the theory of the perceptual judgment. It is the non-subsistent substance with regard to which all other categories are qualities.

The metaphorical or secondary Subject is itself an inferred entity, a quality, with regard to the ultimate subject. But it serves as a sub-stratum for further inference, and appears therefore as an enduring thing possessing qualities, as a substitute for the ultimately real Subject. In the inference "this [place] possesses fire, because it possesses smoke," the element "this" represents the real Subject. In the inference "the mountain possesses fire, because it possesses smoke," the subject "mountain" replaces the real subject or substratum, it is itself partly inferred.

"The subject of such inferences," remarks Dharmottara, "consists of a particular place actually perceived and of an unperceived [inferred] part. It is a complex of something cognized directly and

something invisible [something inferred]. . . . The word 'here' [or 'this'] points to the visible part." The subject [or the substratum] of an inference is thus a combination of a part perceived directly and a part not actually perceived also in all cases where the conclusion represents not a singular, but a universal judgment. E.g., when it is being deduced that all sound represents a compact series of momentary existences, only some particular sound can be directly pointed to, others are not actually perceived. . . . The subject of an inference represents a substratum, an underlying reality, upon which a conception corresponding to the predicate is grafted and this has been shown to consist [sometimes] of a part directly perceived and a part unperceived [i.e., inferred].

Thus the subject of an inference corresponds to Aristotle's Minor Term. As ultimate Subject it corresponds ontologically, to his First Substance or First Essence, "which is a Subject only; it never appears as a predicate of anything else. As *Hic Aliquis* or *Hoc Aliquid* it lies at the bottom [either expressed or implied] of all the work of predication."

According to Dignāga, says Vācaspatimiśra, sense-perception [the true voucher of reality] does not refer to an extended place upon which the smoke is situated. According to his theories, there is no such thing called mountain as a whole consisting of parts [having extension]. Such a mountain is a construction of our imagination. Therefore the true or ultimate Subject in every inference, whether expressed or merely understood, just as in every perceptual judgment, is "thisness," the point-instant, the First Essence, the *Hoc Aliquid*, which is the Subject by its essence, and never can be a Quality or a Predicate.

The second Term of an inference is the logical Predicate otherwise called the *probandum* or the logical Consequence. It represents that quality of the subject which

---

to treat cognition under the heads of perception and inference, or sensibility and understanding, than to treat it under the heads of judgment and syllogism, as the Aristotelian tradition does. A judgment of concomitance surely belongs much more to the process of inference—it is its major premise—than to the process of simple judgments.

is cognized through the inference, the quality which is inferred. It may be expressed as a substantive by itself, e.g., "fire," but with respect to the subject it is its quality, the "fireness" of a given place. Together with the subject this quality represents the "object" cognized through the inference. Dharmottara says, that the object cognized through the inference may be (1) either the substratum whose quality it is intended to cognize or (2) the substratum together with that quality, or (3) that quality alone, when its relation to the logical reason, from which it is deduced, is considered abstractly, e.g., "wheresoever there is smoke, there also is fire," or, more precisely, "wheresoever there is smokeness, there also is fireness." "All inferential relation," says Dignāga, "is based upon a substance-to-quality relation, it is constructed by our understanding, it does not represent ultimate reality."

Indeed the Reason as well as the Consequence must be regarded in respect of their substratum of ultimate reality as its constructed qualities.[3] Taken abstractly the quality deduced through inference, or the logical Predicate, corresponds to Aristotle's Major Term.

The third term is the logical Mark of the Reason already mentioned. It is also a Quality or a mark of the Subject and is itself marked off by the Predicate. It corresponds to the Middle Term of Aristotle and represents the most important part of the inference. The inference can thus be represented in the formula "S is P, because of M," "here there is fire, because there is smoke," "here there are trees, because there are śiṃśapās. It has been al-

ready mentioned that in common life the expression of the real subject is usually omitted and these inferences appear in the form of judgments of concomitance, such as "the śiṃśapā is a tree," "the presence of smoke means presence of fire," or "smoke is produced by fire."

3. THE VARIOUS DEFINITIONS OF INFERENCE

Thus inference can be defined as a cognition of an object through its mark. "This definition," says Dharmottara, "is a definition not of the esssence of an inference, but of its origin. The cognition of the concealed fire is revealed by its mark. The mark produces the cognition of the object which it is the mark of. The origin of the cognition lies in its mark."

Another definition takes inference from the objective side. Inference is the cognition of an inferred, i.e., invisible, concealed object. All objects can be divided in present and absent. The present are cognized by perception, the absent by inference.

A third definition lays stress upon the inseparable connexion which unites the mark with the inferred object and defines inference as a consequence or an application of an inseparable connexion between two facts by a man who has previously noticed that connexion. Thus in our example, the cognition of the concealed fire is a consequence of that inseparable causal tie, which unites smoke with its cause, the fire, and which has been cognized in experience.

A further definition takes it as the most characteristic feature the fact that inference cognizes the general, whereas the object of sense-perception is always the particular.

This is, in a certain respect, the most

---

[3] . . . the categorical judgment S–P (which is also the conclusion of inference), "attributes S–P, directly or indirectly, to the ultimate reality," whereas the major premise which expresses a necessary connection is hypothetical, "it is necessary when it is, *because* of something else." Necessity is always hypothetical.

fundamental definition, since Dignāga opens his great treatise by the statement that there are only two sources of knowledge, perception and inference, and, corresponding to them, only two classes of objects, the particular and the universal. The universal is thus cognized by inference, whereas the particular is grasped by the senses.

However it is clear that the fire whose presence is inferred is as much a particular fire as the one whose presence is perceived by vision. Without the general features which constitute the object fire and are the property of all fires in the world, the particular fire never would have been cognized as fire. Nor would the inferred fire without having been referred in imagination to a certain point-instant of reality ever been cognized as a reality. But still, there is a difference in the generality of the features which are attended to in ratiocination and the particularity of the object which is present to the senses.

According to Dharmottara, inference has an imagined object, e.g., an imagined fire, as its own object, since inference is a cognition of an absent thing which cannot be grasped, which only can be imagined. But its procedure consists in referring this imagined object to a real point and thus its final result is just the same as in sense-perception, the cognition of a point of reality through a constructed symbol. The difference consists in the movement of thought which is the one the opposite of the other. In perception cognition grasps the particular and constructs the symbol. In inference it grasps the symbol and constructs the particular. In this sense only is the general the object of inference, and the particular the object of sense-perception. Otherwise there is no difference in this respect between a perceptual and an inferential judgment. Both, as the Buddhist says, are "one cognition," representing a synthesis "of sensation and non-sensation, conception and non-conception,

imagination and non-imagination." That is to say, it contains a sensible core and its interpretation by the understanding. The difference between sense-perception and inference at this depth of Buddhist investigation is the same as between sensibility and understanding. We are told that there are two sources of knowledge, perception and inference. But the deeper meaning is that the two sources are a sensuous one and a non-sensuous one. It is clear from what has been said that inference is not regarded as a deduction of a proposition or judgment, out of two other propositions or judgments, but as a method of cognizing reality which has its origin in the fact of its having a mark. What really is inferred in an inference is a point of reality as possessing a definite symbol, e.g., a mountain as possessing the unperceived, inferred fire. "There are some," says Dignāga, "who think that the inferred thing is the new property discovered in some place, because of its connection with a perceived mark of that property. Others again maintain that it is not this property itself, but its connection with the substratum that is cognized in inference. Why not assume that the inferred part consists in the substratum itself as characterized by the inferred quality?" That is to say, the thing cognized in an inference is neither the major term nor the connection of the major with the minor, but it is that point of reality which is characterized by its deduced symbol. The definition is the same for Dignāga and Dharmakīrti. The definition of Vasubandhu is not materially different, but its phrasing in the Vādavidhi is severely criticized by Dignāga.

4. INFERRING AND INFERENCE

Since inference is represented as one of the sources of our knowledge, we are again faced by the problem of a difference between a source and its outcome, between the act of cognition and its content. What is the difference between inferring as the act, or the process, of cognition and inference as its result? Just as in sense-perception the Buddhist denies the difference. It is the same thing differently viewed. Inference means cognition of an object through its mark. This cognition is "one cognition," i.e., one act of efficient knowledge which can be followed by a successful action; on analysis it contains an image and its objective reference. Just as in sense-perception there is "conformity" or correspondence between the subjective image and the objective reality. We may, if we like, consider the fact of this conformity as the nearest cause producing knowledge. Conformity will then be the source of cognition and its application to a given point of reality the result. But the conformity of knowledge and knowledge itself are just the same thing, only regarded from different standpoints.

The realistic schools admitted no images and consequently no conformity between the image and external reality. The act of cognition, as every act, is inseparable from an agent, an object, an instrument, its method of procedure, and a result. In inference the result is the conclusion. The procedure and the instrument, according to one party, consist in the knowledge of concomitance between the Reason and the Consequence. According to others, it consists in the cognition of the Mark as present on the Subject of the inference. This step coincides partly with the Minor Premise. It contains more, since it is described as containing the concomitant mark, i.e., a combination of the minor with the major premises. It is the step upon which the conclusion immediately follows. According to Uddyotakara, both these steps represent the act of inferring, they are both the immediately preceding, proximate cause producing the conclusion. The Bud-

dhist, of course, does not deny the existence and importance of these premises. But for him they are cognitions by themselves. What he denies is the difference of *noëma* and *noësis* inside every knowledge. The intentness of knowledge upon its object and the knowledge of this object are the same thing. Dharmottara says that supposing we have cognized through an inference the presence somewhere of a patch of blue colour, the result in this respect will be the same as if we had cognized it through sense-perception. "This [imagined] image of the blue," says he "arises [at first indefinitely]; it is then settled as a definite self-conscious idea of a blue patch [by the way of its contrast with other colours which are not blue]. Thus the coordination of the blue [its contrast with other colours which are not blue, may be regarded] as the source of such a [definitely circumscribed image], and the imagined distinct representation will then appear as its result, because it is through coordination [and contrast] that the definite image of the blue is realized."

Thus "the blue" and "the coordination of the blue" are just the same thing. The blue means similarity with all the things blue in the universe and it means also dissimilarity with all the things not-blue in the universe. Both these similarity and dissimilarity constitute the intentness of our knowledge upon the blue and the cognition of the blue. Whether the presence of the blue patch is perceived or inferred, that makes no difference. There is no difference between the act and the content of knowledge.

5. HOW FAR IS INFERENCE TRUE KNOWLEDGE?

A source of knowledge has been here defined as a first moment of a new cognition which does not contradict experience. It must therefore be free from every subjective, mnemic or imaginative feature. We have seen that in sense-perception only its first moment, which is pure sensation, satisfies to that condition. But such sensation alone, since it is quite indefinite, cannot guide our purposeful actions. Therefore imagination steps in and imparts definiteness to the crude material of sensation.

The perceptual judgment is thus a mixed product of new and old cognition, of objective reality and subjective interpretation. It assumes the dignity or a source of right new cognition, although, strictly speaking, it has not the full right to do it. Inference is still more remote from pure sensation. If the perceptual judgment is not quite new cognition, inference has still lesser rights to pose as a source of right knowledge. Dharmottara therefore exclaims, "Inference is illusion! It deals with non-entia which are its own imagination and (wrongly) identifies them with reality!"

From that height of abstraction from which pure sensation alone is declared to represent ultimate right knowledge attaining at the Thing-in-Itself, the perceptual judgment is, intermingled as it is with elements mnemic, subjective and imaginative, nothing but half-knowledge. Inference which is still more steeped in thought-constructions—two thirds, so to speak, i.e., two of its three terms being imagination—certainly appears as a kind of transcendental illusion. The fact that Dignāga begins by stating that there are only two sources of knowledge and only two kinds of objects, the particular and the universal, as if the two sources existed in equal rights and the two kinds of objects were real objects, i.e., objective realities, this fact is to be explained only by the might of tradition coming from the Nyāya and Vaiśeṣika schools. For after having made this statement at the begin-

ning of his work, Dignāga is obliged to retract step by step all its implications. The universals are, first of all, no realities at all, but pure imagination and mere names. Inference, obliged to manipulate these constructed conceptions, becomes, not a source of right knowledge, but a source of illusion. Nay, even the perceptual judgment is right only at a half, for although it reaches the Thing-in-Itself directly, it is obliged to stand still, powerless before its incognizability. Men must resort to imagination in order to move in a half-real world. Inference from this point of view is a method subservient to sense-perception and to the perceptual judgment. Its office is to correct obvious mistakes. When, e.g., the momentary character of the sound has been apprehended in sensation and interpreted in a perceptual judgment, the theory of the Mīmāṃsakas must be faced according to which the sounds of speech are enduring substances, manifesting themselves in momentary apparitions. Inference then comes to the front and deduces the instantaneous character of these articulate sounds, first from the general character of Instantaneous Being, and then from the special rule that whatever is the outcome of a conscious effort is not enduring. Thus inference is an indirect source of knowledge when it serves to correct illusion. Dharmakīrti says, "Sensation does not convince anybody. If it cognizes something, it does it in the way of a passive reflex, not in the way of judgment. In that part in which sensation has the power to engender the following right judgment, in that part only does it assume [the dignity] of a right knowledge. But in that part in which it is powerless to do it, owing to causes of error, another source of knowledge begins to operate. It brushes away all wrong imagination and thus we have another source [viz., inference] which then comes to the front."

We find the same train of reasoning with Kamalaśīla.

A source of knowledge has indeed been declared to consist in uncontradicted experience. But from that experience its sensational core has at once been singled out as the true source of the knowledge of ultimate reality. The rest, although representing also uncontradicted experience, appears to be a transcendental illusion. "Although it is uncontradicted [empirically]," says Kamalaśīla, "we do not admit that it represents [ultimate] truth." As soon as a sensation has been produced by an external object which in the sequel will be sensed, conceived and named, as, e.g., a fire, attention is aroused and the understanding, after having determined its place in the time and space order, produces a dichotomy. The whole universe of discourse is divided into two classes of objects, fire-like and fire-unlike. There is nothing in the middle between them, both groups are contradictorily opposed to each another. The laws of Contradiction and Excluded Middle begin to operate. Two judgments are produced at once, a judgment of affirmation and a judgment of negation, viz., "this is fire," "this is not a flower, etc.," i.e., it is not a non-fire.

In inference the operation of the understanding is more complicated. When we infer the presence of fire from the presence of smoke, the universe of discourse is dichotomized in a part where smoke follows on fire and a part where non-smoke follows upon non-fire. Between these two groups there is nothing intermediate, no group where smoke could exist without having been produced by fire.

This dichotomizing activity of the mind belongs to its every essence and we will meet it again when analysing the Buddhist theory of Negation, its theory of Contradiction and its doctrine of Dialectic.

Intuition

Critique of Intuition
According to Scientific Empiricism

Herbert Feigl

Herbert Feigl is emeritus Professor of Philosophy at the University of Minnesota and the recent director of the Minnesota Center for the Philosophy of Science. He has taught and lectured with great success at universities in the United States and abroad, and holds numerous honors and distinctions for his teaching and scholarship. From 1924 to 1930, Feigl was a member of the extremely influential Vienna Circle. He brings to the selection below an empiricist's evaluation of intuition as a justification of knowledge.

"Is there intuitive knowledge?" The answer to this question depends on which meaning we associate with the notoriously ambiguous term "intuition." In what follows I shall first attempt to list and discuss briefly the philosophically more important meanings of "intuition." Once these diverse meanings are differentiated, I shall proceed to assess the possibility and the validity especially of trans-empirical intuitive knowledge in the light of the epistemology of scientific empiricism. I realize fully that this is a typical Western point of view; and, although I have made sincere efforts to understand and to appreciate the roles assigned to intuition in Oriental (as well as in Occidental) philos-ophies, my Western bias and "scientism" will remain all too obvious.

"Divide and conquer" is the maxim of analytic philosophy. However, we are not splitting hairs just for the enjoyment of the exercise. We distinguish between the various uses of the word "intuition" (and of related terms) in order to prevent confusion. And it is not merely clarity of discourse and communication, eminently desirable though it is in itself, which we are seeking. In the present context, just as in most other contexts of philosophy, clarity and univocality are prerequisites for making sure that credit is given only where it is due. If "intuition" in one of its many senses designates a way of knowing, it need

From *Philosophy East and West;* Honolulu, University of Hawaii Press, Vol. VIII, Numbers 1 and 2, April, July, 1958, pp. 1–16. Reprinted by permission of the University Press of Hawaii (formerly the University of Hawaii Press).

not, and indeed does not, designate such a way in some of the other senses. I shall try to show that the claims made for trans-empirical intuition are all too often supported by spurious reasons. These reasons are spurious, and in the end illegitimate, precisely because of shifts in meaning of the word "intuition." These shifts are, of course, made quite unwittingly. But it has always been, and will remain, an indispensable part of the Socratic-analytic technique to focus the spotlight of attention on the ambiguity of terms and the dangers of confusion.

The word "intuition" lends itself easily to shifts in meaning because there is a common core, at least a tenuous one, in all its connotations. If these connotations were as disparate as, e.g., in the case of the word "induction," the likelihood of confusion would be much smaller. The meanings of "induction" in the lingo of the Armed Forces, in the terminology of electrodynamics, and in that of logic are so far apart that only a pedant would insist on affixing subscripts to the word or on inventing new terms for at least two of the meanings.

The common core in the many connotations of "intuition" is, of course, *immediacy*. Intuition has thus been contrasted, traditionally and quite generally, with indirect, mediate, relational, or inferential knowledge. Intuition is often identified with direct insight or immediate apprehension. The metaphors of "apprehending" and "grasping" are as common among the synonyms of "intuition" as are "seeing," "beholding," etc. Directly seeing or grasping does not involve laborious reasoning. The idea of a "royal road" or perhaps of a "short cut" to truth or knowledge has been perennially tempting to one type of philosophers. They have maintained, often with a vengeance, that ordinary, labored, reasoned, discursive knowledge does not even penetrate to the heart of things, and that the essence of

reality can be known only by intuition. But of this I shall have to say more after I have soberly listed, and briefly commented upon, the prominent usages of the word "intuition."

First to be mentioned is awareness (and awareness of awareness) of: simple sensory qualia like, e.g., red and green, hot and cold, rough and smooth; relational and Gestalt patterns such as the configurations in the visual field, or the experienced-sound patterns of music in the auditory field. Similarly "direct" are the images of recollection, and also the images of the creative imagination. We have reports about composers (like, e.g., Mozart) who were able to "hear" internally some of their musical compositions before they wrote them. Similarly with artists in other fields who behold the image of their work before they execute it—more or less along the lines "envisioned" by them. As Thomas Mann put it in his *Death in Venice,* it is a matter of "hot conception" and of (subsequent) "cool production." The essential feature of "intuition" in this first sense is, of course, direct experience. We shall see later that it is imperative not to confuse direct experience as such with propositionally formulated knowledge-claims about it.

Second, there is a strictly philosophical and technical use of the word "intuition" which we owe to Kant, or, rather, to the English translation of Kant, because in German it is *"reine Anschauung"* (i.e., "pure visualization," if I may translate literally, but the customary translation of Kant's German is "pure intuition"). According to Kant, we have a direct apprehension of the forms of space and time. Plato long before Kant had already maintained that we are aware of certain fundamental ideas, forms, or essences. This idea has been revived in many other forms of philosophy, most recently perhaps in the phenomenological school, where vision or apprehension of essences is an alleged method of purely philosophical knowledge. There is not sufficient space to deal critically with all of these in one short essay, but I want to list them at least. Suffice it to note here that the ascription of apodictic truth to judgments of "pure intuition" has been severely criticized, and is in any case open to the charge of "psychologism"—the very mistake that Husserl exposed and opposed so vigorously in his *Logical Investigations*.[1]

Third, there are the alleged judgments of direct knowledge, the "self-evident" truths. Here, again, it is claimed that there is a kind of knowledge that is not labored, that is not derived, that is not proved; it is supposed to be neither in need of proof nor capable of proof because it constitutes the very premises of our reasoning. So, we are told that we have intuitive or direct knowledge of the axioms of logic, of arithmetic, of topology; i.e., of the semi-quantitative structure of space, and even of some of the axioms of geometry such as the parallel axiom. This has been maintained by many philosophers. After the development of the non-Euclidean geometries, however, some of these claims were toned down considerably. Also to be mentioned here are the principles of common-sense knowledge, especially the much-used and often-quoted principles of sufficient reason, of causality, and the related principle of induction, all of which are supposed to be self-evident. In the ethical domain, we are told, there is moral intuition, or the "voice of conscience," which enables us to discriminate between right and wrong, good and bad, or good and evil. There is a whole school of intuitionist philosophers in ethics, with G. E. Moore as a prominent recent representative. The entire trend of empiricist philosophy, beginning with Hume, has cast serious doubt upon the validity of such knowledge by intuition.

[1] Edmund Husserl, *Logische Untersuchungen* (Halle a.d.S.: M. Niemeyer, 1913–22).

Fourth, we occasionally find claims to the effect that there is such a thing as "instinctive knowledge." But it is fairly clear that on the level of Homo sapiens there is precious little that is instinctive in the genuine sense in which the word is used by psychologists and biologists as referring to innate capacities. In human beings, the innate capacities are so quickly overlaid by the products of learning, training, or imitation that only a few reflexes and a few concatenations of reflexes can be said to be instinctive. If we want to use the word "knowledge" in the case of animals, then certainly we could speak of the instinctive capacities of birds knowing how to build nests, of beavers knowing how to build dams, of bees and ants knowing how to communicate with each other in certain ways. But the question is, can we call this knowledge? (The word "knowledge" is, of course, also extremely ambiguous.) In the case of human beings, this is highly questionable. Psychologists have suggested that empathy has an innate component; by the very fact that we are human beings, we understand each other on a rather direct level. Here the Germans have coined the term *"Einfühlung,"* which literally translated would mean "the act of feeling oneself into the other person's mind." (When one person says to another, "I know just how you feel," this is an act of empathy, and the speaker is participating imaginatively in the feelings and sentiments of the other.) To what extent the capacity of direct intuition is innate on the human level remains to be empirically examined. However, that we have the capacity of learning how to interpret certain clues given by behavior, such as voice intonation, posture, facial expression, etc., is granted, of course. The question is whether empathy is not wholly or at least largely a product of learning. I shall take this up further a little later under the "hunch."

Fifth, we have reports of extrasensory

perception, based on a great deal of evidence, but I shall not discuss the merits of the experimental studies at Duke University or the even more spectacular ones conducted in England. I am sufficiently impressed by the evidence to say that here is something that neither psychologists nor philosophers can any longer afford to ignore merely because it disagrees with their prejudices. In other words, I am strenuously going through the motions of an open mind. The point is that there is statistical evidence for the occurrence of clairvoyance, telepathy, and precognition, which cannot be plausibly explained within the traditional scientific framework. It is important to note concerning extrasensory perception, as it has been experimentally and statistically verified, that the individual percipient does not know when he hits the "target"; there is no bell in his mind that rings and says, "Now this time you got it." There is no subjective indicator for the correctness of telepathy or clairvoyance. We certainly need further experimental investigations, and later perhaps an attempt at scientific theories, before we jump to any philosophical, let alone theological, conclusions.

Sixth, we come to the "hunch." I use this word from American slang for the simple reason that I cannot think of any other more expressive term to put this briefly. I could, of course, define it more fully. A social psychologist once gave me such formal definitions as these: "the intuitive process consists of a convergence of as yet unverbalized experiences organically included in a pattern of response below the threshold of critical attention, which pattern may emerge in part and when verbalized serve as a partial explanation of the problem which acted as the original stimulus." (A rather formidable definition.) A little more briefly: "Intuition is a judgment based on the convergence and integration of former impressions or memories into a pattern of explanation or expectation in which perceptual details are not on the threshold of critical attention." This can be elucidated by examples. Recall the older generation of doctors. The doctor enters the room of the patient, sniffs the air, takes the patient's hand, and says, "You have diabetes." How does he know? A clue probably paves the way for his diagnosis. If sniffing the air in a patient's room has, in the past, been a clue to him in acute cases of diabetes, now medical science knows that the breath of such a patient contains acetone, a fruity smelling vapor which the "intuitive" doctor recognizes without actually being aware of what he is doing. Similarly, an experienced engineer might, after one look at a bridge or other structure, say, "This is going to break down fairly soon." If you ask him how he knows, he says, "I just know." The first impression, based implicitly on his rich past experience, is that the structure will not last. Later, perhaps, he could make the reasons for his belief explicit. Also, the experienced geologist in the field may suddenly say, "There is oil underneath here." How does he know? He does not smell it, he does not have clairvoyant capacities, but he has had a great deal of relevant experience. Moreover, clinical psychologists and, for that matter, everybody to some extent practices empathy. This is not necessarily innate, but was probably acquired by learning processes. We project ourselves into the other person's situation. Here, again, it is difficult to describe just what clues we utilize, but it stands to reason that if one does not have telepathic capacities, and if one does not see or hear the other person, one cannot practice this kind of empathy. But, even if we do see and hear the other person, it is very hard to describe the actual aspects or configurations in his facial expression, tone of voice, posture, and so on; but many of us have a certain subtlety in knowing immediately whether we bore our partner in conversation, whether we amuse, flatter, or insult him. However, what actually goes on in a case like this would be extremely difficult to describe. Take graphology, for example. From a philosophical point of view, I do not see why some personality traits or momentary moods might not express themselves in handwriting. I think there is a good deal of scientific evidence that handwriting does express a number of these personality facets. There are some so-called "gifted graphologists" who, with just one glance at a piece of writing, can tell what kind of a character the writer has. These gifted graphologists can read out of handwriting specific character and personality traits. Naturally, we ask how do they do it? We are told: "Well, they have a gift for it, that's all." But this is no answer, of course. An answer would have to be found scientifically. Again, we must ask, what are the clues, perhaps not so much in detail but in the total configuration of the handwriting that triggers the graphologist's judgment. Now, even if we do not have a theory as to how such a graphologist achieves all this, we can glean certain empirical regularities by using him as a guinea pig in an experiment, i.e., by confronting him with a variety of types of handwriting and noting how he reacts and to what. In this way we establish empirical correlations as to what his clues are, as to what stimuli he uses in interpreting handwriting by his "intuitive" procedure. This type of activity clearly falls in the rubric of the "hunch." We can define the "hunch," then, as "a product of learning from past experience, which learning is not made explicit at the moment of the use of judgment." The judgment occurs like a flash of insight and therefore involves what has been rather precariously called "unconscious inference." We can hardly question the fact that in the understanding that we extend to each other in everyday life there is an element of this sort of subconscious learn-

ing. How does the baby know that the mother is friendly? The mother smiles. There is a school of psychologists who maintain that there is something inherent in the configuration of the smile which suggests friendliness. But psychologists have made experiments; they have had frowning and stern-looking mothers approach the baby, give it candy or milk, stroke it, etc., and, of course, the baby took the stern face as an expression of friendliness. Hence, it depends on the pattern that surrounds the experience and not on some innate capacity for the interpretation of facial expressions. Furthermore, there are other aspects of the "hunch," such as in problem-solving. There is the case of the scientific or technological genius who, after a long period of pondering about a problem, suddenly "perceives" a solution. Sometimes this happens even during sleep; the thinker awakes in the morning with the solution of which he had no idea on the previous evening. Minor instances of this sort of problem-solving occur in all of us in various life-situations. The final "clicking" of our mind is similar to that of the genius, and may not be fully intelligible even to ourselves.

Seventh, and last, there is mystical or trans-empirical intuition. Here, in contradistinction to the hunch, the target or object of the intuition is claimed to be something that is absolutely beyond the reach of ordinary experience and reasoning, something which cannot be checked empirically. In sharp contrast, the empirical hunch and extrasensory perception have this much in common: their target, or the object of intuition, is empirical; statements about it can be confirmed or disconfirmed by ordinary observation. For instance, if I were a clairvoyant, I could say, "My house (many miles distant) is on fire now." If you ask me how I know, I might say, "I just know—it came to me in a flash." A house on fire is something we can check; we can go there, call up, find out, and so on. Similarly, if the geologist has a hunch that there is oil somewhere underneath the ground, we can drill for it (it might be expensive or hopeless, of course); we can find out whether the geologist is right or wrong. Likewise, in the case of crystal-gazers, if they have premonitions on the basis of crystal-gazing, we can find out whether or not they are right and in what percentage of cases. The hunch—be it that of the geologist or that of the physician who makes a flash diagnosis of diabetes which can be verified by a laboratory test—can be empirically tested. On the other hand, trans-empirical knowledge-claims, mystical intuitions, as I understand them, cannot be tested empirically. Mysticism, especially religious mysticism, claims to give us knowledge about something which cannot be independently reached through ordinary channels, knowledge which cannot be checked, which cannot be tested in the usual empirical way. In other words, here, supposedly, we have a new and independent way of getting at truth. No doubt, some philosophers have been entranced by the hope of finding a "way of knowing directly" in contrast to the arduous and dusty way of the laboratory. It would be wonderful to get at the Absolute by a flash of insight. Mystical intuition differs from the hunch and extrasensory perception in deliberately and avowedly aiming at a trans-empirical target. With religious mysticism, the target is God; with metaphysical mysticism, it may be the Absolute, as we find it particularly in some Eastern, but also in some Western, philosophies. Of course, not all philosophers try to attain a knowledge of God or the Absolute by intuition; there are some, to be sure, who try to construct rational proofs for the existence of one or the other. I am not talking about these philosophers. Here I am concerned exclusively with those philosophers who do

maintain that we can get a knowledge of the Absolute or of God by intuition.

With the list of the meanings of the word "intuition" now completed, I turn to a critique of the last-mentioned form, i.e., of trans-empirical intuition. In accordance with my bias toward the Western "rationalistic" tradition, I am naturally suspicious of the knowledge claims of trans-empirical intuition. As I often say (perhaps I borrowed this from Bertrand Russell), I prefer the "silent mystic," because, when a mystic begins to speak, he admits that he is not speaking directly, but indirectly; his language does not describe, it circumscribes; he is not really giving an adequate account of what he actually experiences, of what he knows through intuition. The mystic can merely allude to what he has experienced, he can only hint at it; he is, in fact, almost helpless in expressing himself about the great blaze of glory that he beholds.

Now, I think we must admit the occurrence of mystical experiences; there is a great deal of evidence that cannot be ignored. What we may question, however, from a philosophical point of view, is the interpretation of mystical experiences. I do not for a moment doubt that some people have very special, powerful, ecstatic experiences. However, even though such people cannot clearly describe what they experience, they nevertheless maintain that they apprehend the Absolute, or, in the case of the religious mystic especially, that intuitive insight provides a direct avenue to the knowledge of God, which cannot be reached in any other way. Of course, mystical visions differ widely, but, among the religious mystics, there is a large subgroup whose members, no matter how they diverge in detail, do perceive the Deity as a personal being; there is, one may say, a large measure of agreement among these mystics in regard to the apprehension of a personal God. To be sure, there are Eastern as well as Western mystical visions in which a purely impersonal absolute ground or all-embracing unity of reality is apprehended. In the light of the prevalent sequence, manifest in many cultures, from magic, animism, polytheistic mythologies, monotheistic creeds, to more abstract religions, it is not implausible that *Brahman* or the Absolute represents a final stage in the successive depersonalization (demythologization) of historically antecedent highly anthropomorphic deities.

The skeptics throughout the ages have tried to account for mystical experience in a naturalistic way. The mystic's reply to the skeptic is that materialists, rationalists, positivists, empiricists, or whatever, have no justification, have no basis for talking about the knowledge-claims of mysticism, are talking like the blind man about the colors. To this I reply that the blind man can know something about the colors; and I urge that the claims of trans-empirical knowledge be more carefully scrutinized. In order to proceed with this strategy, it is necessary first to review the familiar distinction between "intuitive" and "discursive" knowledge. This distinction has been noted in all ages of philosophy, but more especially in recent times. Among the philosophers of the twentieth century, this distinction is frequently made. William James, for instance, distinguished between "knowledge of" and "knowledge about." While the blind man may know nothing of the colors, he can know something about the colors. If someone does not have a sense of humor, says Eddington, he has no intimate knowledge of what a joke is; this may be reflected in his behavior in that he never laughs when exposed to a joke. However, one may still have a psychological theory about jokes and about the comical, even if he is lacking in the capacity of laughing about them.

In Eddington's terms, the distinction is between "intimate" and "symbolic" knowledge. According to him, psychological theory, just like any scientific account, gives us "merely" symbolic, but not intimate knowledge. Bergson, in a very similar vein, claims "absolute" character for intuitive knowledge, and "relative" character for discursive knowledge.[2] F. S. C. Northrop stresses the fundamental difference between "concepts by intuition" and "concepts by postulation." Important features of his epistemology and philosophy of science are based on this contrast.[3] Bertrand Russell's well-known distinction between "knowledge by acquaintance" and "knowledge by description" seems to aim in the same direction, but it is of the utmost importance not to confuse mere acquaintance, i.e., the *having*, or *living through* of direct experience, with knowing something about it. Moritz Schlick,[4] the leader of the Vienna Circle of Logical Positivists, drew this indispensable distinction with superb clarity. (*"Erleben"* and *"Erkennen"* were his key terms for this contrast.) A description of immediate experience, be it in phenomenological or introspective terms, is genuinely cognitive in that it consists of statements which may be either true or false. But it simply does not make sense to ascribe truth or falsity to immediate experience itself. As merely "had," lived through, enjoyed, or suffered, it makes no truth claim; it does not assert or deny anything. It just occurs. (Mystics, as I understand them, do make knowledge-claims, albeit of a very special kind; and they never restrict these knowledge-claims to a mere description of their direct experience. I shall return later to the prob-

2 See Henri Bergson, *An Introduction to Metaphysics,* T. E. Hulme, trans. (New York and London: G. P. Putnam's Sons, 1912).

3 See F. S. C. Northrop, *The Logic of the Sciences and the Humanities* (New York: The Macmillan Co., 1947).

4 Moritz Schlick, *Allgemeine Erkenntnislehre* (Berlin: Springer, 1918, 1925).

lem of the justification of knowledge-claims transcending direct experience.)

The ambiguity just uncovered thus necessitates the distinction between two meanings of "intuition" to which I briefly referred but which was not as yet spelled out in the first item of the list presented above. But it should be obvious how much, by way of philosophical implications, hinges precisely upon a firm grasp of the difference between acquaintance and knowledge by acquaintance. There are a good many philosophers who have been alert to this difference. If I read John Dewey correctly, he certainly was; similarly, though possibly for different reasons, most of the critical realists emphasized the difference between direct experience and knowledge proper.[5]

We are now ready for the discussion of the blind man and his knowledge about colors. Let us assume that we deal with a congenitally blind person. Let us assume, furthermore, that as a psychological matter of fact (which might be questioned, of course) such a person cannot have images of visual shapes or colors. He gets about in life by tactile and auditory sensations, but is completely lacking in the visual field. Regardless of this handicap, however, such a person could learn something about colors; he cold learn to distinguish between, e.g., red and green, with the help of experimental devices. How is this possible? Is there a genuine substitute? I do not wish to mislead the reader. I am certainly not asserting that knowledge about, or knowledge by description, can be a substitute for immediate experience; by merely getting indirectly at the colors of

physical objects, or of various colored lights, the blind man cannot obtain any direct visual experience. Nevertheless, I do assert that the blind man can know all about the colors. I am arguing that the blind man can know all about the colors, both physically and psychologically, without ever having a color-experience himself. How? A blind man can be equipped with modern electronic apparatus—a spectroscope, a photo-electric cell, an amplifier, earphones, or a loud-speaker—and the light waves that come from luminous sources or are reflected from physical objects may be transformed or "translated" into sounds in the earphones or the loud-speaker. Of course, it would be very misleading to say that he hears the colors, but he does get clues concerning the physical characteristics, such as the wave length, the frequency and intensity, etc., of the radiations impinging upon his apparatus. But it may be urged that this concerns the physical stimuli and not the psychological color-experience. Can the blind man investigate the psychology of colors? Of course he can, if he proceeds in the manner of a behavioristic psychologist. In this case he could experiment with an individual who does have eyesight and hence reacts in a discriminatory way to various stimuli which the blind man establishes independently by means of the photosensitive electronic gadgets at his disposal. These devices may be even more sensitive than the human eye. The blind man, then, could be the psychologist of someone else; thus, while he cannot experience the colors, he can study color-perception in the other person. He does this in the way in which anyone might study the other person's mind in all domains of its experience.

The advantage of the person with visual experience over the congenitally blind person thus consists simply in the greater scope of his acquaintance, and hence a broader basis for his knowledge by ac-

5 More recently Albert Hofstadter, in an article "Does Intuitive Knowledge Exist?" *Philosophical Studies*, VI (1955), 81–87, formulates very clearly two senses of "intuition" as follows: (1) intuition as immediate awareness of an object, content, or subject-matter, and (2) intuition as a mode of knowledge developed on the basis of immediate apprehension.

quaintance. But it should by now be fairly obvious that, while this advantage is great from a practical and pragmatic point of view, it is nevertheless true that as long as one has a "foothold" somewhere in direct experience, any sort of existent may well be accessible through knowledge by description. This, after all, is the only epistemological view which renders plausible our knowledge of unobserved and unobservable entities, as, e.g., in modern physics. In regard to all electromagnetic waves outside the narrow "octave" of visible light, all human beings are "blind."

If we are not to commit the reductive fallacies of phenomenalism, the knowledge of physical fields, atomic and subatomic particles and events, must be reconstructed in terms of highly indirect confirmation. The evidential data of the confirmation may well be identified as the "postanalytically given," i.e., as data of direct acquaintance. But knowledge proper is not limited to a mere description of these data. Common-sense knowledge, and to a much vaster extent scientific knowledge, goes beyond these data. It does so by connecting the data through postulated lawful relationships with inferred entities. For our present purpose, it does not matter much whether we analyze theoretical knowledge of this sort in terms of postulate systems and their empirical interpretation, or represent it more picturesquely in terms of a "nomological net" which is tied down to the data in a few places but includes besides a vast array of unobserved and unobservable entities. As long as these postulated entities are richly connected with each other as well as with various observation bases, the corresponding theoretical terms possess empirical significance as well as scientific "objectivity" (i.e., intersubjectivity).

My main point should by now be fairly obvious. The "private," direct experiences of various persons have a place in the nomological net of science. They can be "triangulated from various, and often quite heterogeneous, areas of evidence. That is to say, the "privacy" of first-person experiences is, at least from the scientific point of view, never absolute. It is the relative, contextual privacy connected with the difference between direct and indirect verification. What one person experiences directly can be known about, i.e., inferred, by another person. That is why and how a congenitally blind person can come to know about the color-experiences of persons equipped with eyesight. The case of mystical vision may prima facie appear analogous, but I shall now argue that it is fundamentally different. The analogy appears plausible at first because mystical vision is regarded as—"in principle"—just as intersubjective as is ordinary vision. It is crucially important, however, to remember that "intersubjectivity" in common life and in science does not mean merely a certain communality of experience. Communality of experience is neither necessary nor sufficient for intersubjectivity. It is not necessary because, as the example of the blind and the seeing person demonstrates, intersubjective knowledge concerning physical objects as well as concerning mental states can be achieved without similar ("communal") evidential data. And it is clearly not sufficient in that common (similar) experiences even of a large number of persons need not at all indicate what they are often believed to indicate. "Forty million Frenchmen *can* be wrong!"

The preceding remarks apply to mysticism if mystical experience, or possibly religious experience generally, is taken as evidence for trans-empirical or "supernaturalistic" knowledge-claims. This puts the mystic within the purview and jurisdiction of the criteria of the inductive or hypothetico-deductive methods. That is to say, the justification of knowledge-claims in this type of metaphysics or theology is conceived in analogy to the "transcendent" hypotheses [6] in scientific theories. Here it is always possible to ask whether these hypotheses are really necessary in order to account for the data of observation. And in the spirit of the well-known story about Laplace the answer may well be: *"Nous n'avons pas besoin de cette hypothese."* Within the framework of scientific method (and this is merely a refinement of the framework of sound common sense) we must ask as to whether certain communalities of direct experience (such as the religious or the mystical) cannot be explained in a perfectly "naturalistic" way. I am quite confident that this can be done. The many significant contributions that have been made toward a psychology of religion make this extremely plausible. I shall utilize here the general lines of argument as presented in the psychoanalytic theory of religious experience. Although I am by no means convinced that Freud (e.g., in his *The Future of an Illusion*) has rendered full justice to religion, and, although I seriously question many of the dogmas of the outlook of Freud and his disciples, I think there are sound and important points in the Freudian view which have not been sufficiently taken into consideration by many philosophers. Very briefly, what I think is valid and sound in these explanations of religious experience is simply that whatever communalities we find are explainable in terms of the nat-

ural condition of man, and do not require anything beyond that. Freud, like many another genius, has put his finger on something obvious that we should have discovered a long time ago, but which apparently was not obvious to philosophers or psychologists. What Freud points out is simply this: the reason so many people, in such varied cultural situations, believe in, or even have the experience of, a personal God, is that they were all helpless infants and children at one time, surrounded by comparatively all-powerful adults on whom they depended, at first for physical sustenance, and later on, very significantly, for moral encouragement and discouragement. No wonder that human beings, when emancipated from their natural parents, need a substitute, and erect God in man's image.

Now, all this may sound quite atheistic, but note that it is only a rejoinder to the argument from religious experience. Thomas Aquinas, for instance, did not pay much attention to this argument; he emphasized the cosmological and the teleological arguments. I am not discussing the issue of theology in general, but simply the fashionable argument from religious experience which maintains that it cannot be mere chance that so many people, under widely differing conditions, have had this sort of experience, and that therefore it must be due to the Deity.

I do not claim that I can demonstrate definitively the invalidity of this argument, but the argument is highly questionable, and the advances in psychology indicate more and more that the father and mother images which play a leading role in many prominent religions of mankind may be explained on a perfectly natural, all-too-obvious human basis.

The point of all this is that while I do not for a moment deny the fact of intuitive experiences, I do question some of their interpretations. I am questioning especially the sort of interpretations for

---

[6] W. Kneale, "Induction, Explanation, and Transcendent Hypotheses," in W. Kneale, *Probability and Induction* (Oxford: The Clarendon Press, 1949), pp. 92–110. Reprinted in H. Feigl and M. Brodbeck, eds., *Readings in the Philosophy of Science* (New York: Appleton-Century-Crofts, 1953), pp. 353–367. L. W. Beck, "Construction and Inferred Entities," *Philosophy of Science*, 17 (1950), 74–86. Reprinted in H. Feigl and M. Brodbeck, eds., *op. cit.*, pp. 368–381. H. Feigl, "Existential Hypotheses: Realistic Versus Phenomenalistic Interpretations," *Philosophy of Science*, 17 (1950), 35–62.

which the "religious realists" have argued. At this point I am usually told that the tables may well be turned on the naturalistic atheist: his refusal to believe, his lack of religious experience, can equally well be explained on psychological or psychoanalytic grounds. His aversion to "father figures" of any sort may well be due to a strong Oedipus complex. To this I reply that if our psychology is to be adequate at all, it should be able to account for the atheist's attitude just as much as for the attitude of the theist (and, *mutatis mutandis,* for the metaphysician's belief in Absolutes, as well as for the positivist's militant repudiation of Absolutes). But this is exactly as it should be. From a scientific point of view, both sorts of attitudes should be explainable on the basis of the same type of psychological premisses. The argument which attempted to "turn the tables" on the naturalist is beside the point; it does not concern the issue under dispute. The question was: can the communalities of religious experience be explained without theological hypotheses? And to this question I have sketched an affirmative reply.

Another counter-argument frequently used by metaphysicians and theologians accuses the naturalist or the scientific empiricist of presupposing a metaphysics of his own—viz., the belief that whatever is real (objectively or intersubjectively existent) can be cognitively attained in more than one way. This is indeed in keeping with the modern naturalist's view of reality (indicated above) as a "nomological net" within which all points can be logically "triangulated" from many different bases. If this be metaphysics, make the least of it! It is certainly not metaphysics in the sense of transcendent speculation which is proof against disproof by being immune to empirical testing of any sort whatever. It is metaphysics—inductive metaphysics if you please—in the rather innocuous sense of a broad and admittedly tentative generalization based on the successes of the scientific method to date. We have come to expect a certain congruence of the epistemology of confirmation with the scientific account of the processes of cognition. This is clearly the case with normal perceptual knowledge. The very view of the world which finds its empirical confirmation in perceptual data contains as one of its parts the physics, psychophysics, and psychophysiology of perception, and thus provides at least in outline an explanation of the ways in which human organisms come to know their physical environment.

Note now the contrast with the "transcendent" metaphysics and theology, Occidental as well as Oriental. Mystical intuition of the Absolute or of the Deity, just as much as revelation, must remain unexplainable mysteries if the objects of such intuitions or revelations are not accessible through any other avenue of evidence. And even if, along the lines of the customary arguments, other evidential avenues are adduced, there are at least sketches of naturalistic-empiricist explanations which explain the alleged evidence more simply and parsimoniously. The principle of parsimony, it should be remembered, is an essential aspect of all justifiable explanations. It is part and parcel of what we all mean by the "rationality" of inductive or hypothetico-deductive inference. The theologian or the metaphysician usually terminates his explanations with the admission of "impenetrable mysteries"; whereas the adherent of the scientific method uses well-confirmed theoretical postulates as the premises of his explanations, and acknowledges unsolved, but not unsolvable, problems, along the path of his advancing inquiries.[7]

---

[7] A discussion of the "riddles of the universe" would take us far beyond the limits of the present paper. Elsewhere I have attempted to show quite comprehensively how the most perplexing of them

Let us consider one more argument in favor of the cognitive significance of mystical intuition. It may be said that in all the preceding discussions we have not considered an essential aspect of intuition, namely, intuition as total or partial identification of the knowing subject with the to-be-known object. Religious mystics speak of "identification" or "direct participation" as the essence of their vision of God. And Bergson—as well as many Asian mystics—refers to intuition as a way of directly knowing the Absolute and similarly describes it as an act of identification or coalescence. But Bergson rather helpfully gives his case away by telling us (in his *Introduction to Metaphysics*): "Metaphysics . . . is the science which claims to dispense with symbols. . . . There is one reality, at least, which we all seize from within, by intuition, and not by simple analysis. It is our own personality in its flowing through time."[8] And, in what follows, Bergson gives us a superb phenomenological description of the stream of consciousness. Let us note two important points. First, and inconsistently with the first pronouncement, this description is given with the help of words and sentences (and these are surely symbolic). Second, the prime illustration for intuition by identification is self-awareness. If "identity" is understood in the strict sense of logical, numerical identity, then identification with one's direct experience can amount to no more than just living through one's experience; and, if our earlier analysis is accepted, this does not by

itself constitute knowledge at all. Even such introspective or phenomenological descriptions as Bergson provides utilize analysis, classification, and symbolization. They are claims of knowledge by acquaintance, but not merely acquaintance in the sense of pure, direct experience.

I conclude that the mystic is misled by the power of his experiences to regard them as genuinely cognitive insights. He thus confuses either raw experience with introspective knowledge concerning it, or he considers the data of mystical vision as evidence for a transcendent reality thus apprehended. If he does the first, he relinquishes the claim of attaining an Absolute that is supposed to exist over and above his personal experience. If he does the latter, he cannot expect his critics to admit mystical visions as self-authenticating; in this case his position is open to the criticisms advanced above, i.e., to the charge that he ignores what in all scientific plausibility his "evidence" indicates. It does seem to indicate, not a transcendent Absolute, God, World-Spirit, or the like, but, rather, that the belief in such overarching realities is one of the fondest illusions of mankind, engendered by wishful thinking on the part of human beings precariously embedded in a universe that they did not make, that they only very incompletely understand, and in which they still seek, like helpless children, some reassurance of superior moral guidance and ultimate salvation. And even if the motivation of wishful thought is completely detached from our moral anxieties and from the hopes or fears of a life after death, the impulse to know and to understand existence as whole may explain, though it does not justify, the belief that intuition can afford a glimpse of absolute reality beyond all appearance. Einstein's "cosmic religion," in which God is identified with the order or "rationality" of Nature, is a good example of this type of thought—on

all, i.e., the mind-body problem, may be disentangled, and that a monistic solution can be defended on epistemological and scientific grounds. See H. Feigl, "The 'Mental' and the 'Physical,'" in *Concepts, Theories and the Mind-Body Problem*, Minnesota Studies in the Philosophy of Science. Vol. II (Minneapolis: University of Minnesota Press, 1958), pp. 370–497.
8 P. 9.

the part of one of the most enlightened scientists that we may ever hope to encounter.

A world view that is in keeping with our new age of enlightenment has been proposed by scientific humanism and empiricism.[9] By contrast, the dogmatic views of many "enlighteners" of the eighteenth century and the equally dogmatic ("negativistic") doctrines of nineteenth- and twentieth-century positivism, such as scientific humanism, should not claim that all problems have been solved by science, or that even the general frame of the present scientific outlook will never change. There may indeed be "more things in heaven and earth than our philosophy has dreamt of." But adopting the policy of the open mind of scientific humanism does not prevent us from criticizing what is fallacious in various philosophical doctrines which consider intuition as a way of justifying knowledge-claims.

In sum, then, intuition in the sense of direct experience is never the finished product of knowledge. It is, rather, either the raw material of knowledge, i.e., the confirmation basis of genuine knowledge-claims, or it is a way of arriving at hypotheses which may or may not be found tenable on the basis of further evidence.

There is no doubt that intuition in the sense of the "hunch" is often helpful in providing suggestions for the solution of problems or for the diagnosis of various physical, and, in the case of empathy, mental, conditions.[10] But no matter how strong the "intuitive conviction" in these cases may be, it does not by itself justify the knowledge-claims which are made. Independent intersubjectively accessible evidence provides the only justification that can be accepted as "rational." Intuition (in the sense of direct experience) is neither rational nor irrational. What must be criticized as irrational is the use of intuitive experience in the justification of genuine knowledge-claims. If intuition provides the raw data of knowledge, then, in addition to it, principles of inference are needed. If "intuition" is taken in the sense of the hunch, then only a statistical study of the truth-frequency of these hunches on the part of a given subject and under given conditions could justify any sort of reliance upon it. And any claims for metaphysical or religious insight obtain their plausibility only by borrowing credit from other, and, as we have seen, very different processes which are unfortunately and indiscriminately also comprehended by the extremely ambiguous term "intuition."

[9] See my article, "The Scientific Outlook: Naturalism and Humanism," in H. Feigl and M. Brodbeck, eds., *op. cit.* Also, H. E. McCarthy, "Science and its Critics," reprinted from *The Humanist*, XII, No. 2 (1952) 49–55, in P. P. Wiener, ed., *Readings in Philosophy of Science* (New York: Charles Scribner's Sons, 1953).

[10] For an incisive and detailed analysis of the problem of clinical intuition in psychology and psychiatry, see Paul E. Meehl, *Clinical vs. Statistical Prediction* (Minneapolis: University of Minnesota Press, 1954). Also, S. R. Hathaway, "Clinical Intuition and Inferential Accuracy," *Journal of Personality*, XXIV, No. 3 (March 1956), 223–250.

Feigl on Intuition

P. T. Raju

P. T. Raju *is one of the most famous contemporary Indian philosophers. He has taught as a professor of philosophy and psychology at the University of Rajputana, and has been a visiting professor of philosophy at universities in the United States and India for many years. In the selection which follows, Professor Raju responds to Professor Feigl's critique of intuitionism presented above.*

Professor Feigl's Critique of intuition [1] is not a rejection of intuitive experience but of its validity as knowledge. Or, rather, it is a rejection of intuition as a form of knowledge. Again, it is the mystic intuition that is rejected along with any philosophy that is based upon it, for intuition has many meanings, such as clairvoyance, hunch, etc., which Feigl accepts. Apparently, Feigl did not read my article, "Intuition as a Philosophical Method in India"; [2] otherwise, the conclusion he arrived at, namely, "it simply does not make sense to ascribe truth or falsity to immediate experience itself," [3] and the statement "intuition (in the sense of direct experience) is neither rational nor irrational," [4] would have been noticed by him as mentioned in my paper, for even those who accept intuition as a form of knowing maintain, as do the Naiyāyikas, that nondiscursive knowledge is neither true nor false.[5] The Naiyāyikas drew a distinction between indeterminate and determinate cognition, which is somewhat similar to the distinction between immediate experience and description of immediate experience or acquaintance and knowledge by acquaintance [6] drawn by Feigl.[7]

[1] Herbert Feigl, "Critique of Intuition According to Scientific Empiricism," *Philosophy East and West*, VIII, Nos. 1 and 2 (April, July, 1958), 1–16, (pp. 209–21, this volume).

[2] In *Philosophy East and West*, II, No. 3 (October, 1952), 187–207.

[3] Feigl, *op. cit.*, p. 9, (p. 215).

[4] Raju, *op. cit.*, p. 195.

[5] *Ibid.*

[6] Feigl, *op. cit.*, p. 9, (p. 215).

[7] I hesitate to accept the view that acquaintance is the same as indeterminate cognition. See L. S. Stebbing, *A Modern Introduction to Logic* (London: Methuen and Company, 1950), p. 24, footnote. Acquaintance is not immediate experience; but indeterminate cognition is. My acquaintance with Mr. Nehru is with an object with a definite form. But a thoroughly unmediated experience is with-

From *Philosophy East and West;* Honolulu, University of Hawaii Press, Vol. VIII, Numbers 3 and 4, October, 1958 and January, 1959; pp. 149–63. Reprinted by permission of the University Press of Hawaii (formerly the University of Hawaii Press).

Further, I contended in my paper that intuition by itself had never been used as a philosophical method in India and could never be so used in the East or the West for building up a metaphysical system. Metaphysical or religious insight,[8] Feigl says, always needs the help of discursive reasoning. Insight is insight into the relationships of a plurality and is relational, rational, and discursive. But I attempted to show that this relational knowledge is permeated by intuitive knowledge also and is based upon it, for even rational insight is insight into the meaning of existential forms. I do not know whether this point is acceptable to Feigl or not; if it is not, then metaphysics for him cannot be a rational insight into what one experiences directly.

However, all this applies to the role of intuition in empirical knowledge. But what is its role in the trans-empirical knowledge of the mystic? Or, does he have no knowledge at all, but only lives his experience?[9] It is here that the mystic takes issue. Feigl says that mystic experience cannot be called knowledge, because it is not descriptive and communicable.

But, first, how is my experience of the pen in front of me communicable? Can my experience be transferred to another person? I can only make him have a similar, but not the same, experience.

In the second place, in some cases I cannot even make him have similar experiences, but can only make him understand. Suppose I have a toothache, but without any external symptom. A boy who has never had a toothache cannot even imagine that experience, though I describe

it. He may understand it by analogy to a stomachache or a headache, and may even have sympathy for me. The case of the boy who is born blind but who understands colors when light waves are transformed into sound waves is similar. He can never be made to experience colors. For him, they are hypothetical entities corresponding to different sounds. He understands them as we understand the letters a, b, c, etc., in algebra. They are only symbolic. But the mystic experience is not symbolic, though the mystic may describe it symbolically, often in negative terms.

In the third place, can I communicate my experience of the pen in front of me if my experience is not conscious? If my acquaintance with it also is conscious, why should we not call it knowledge? Here I am speaking of acquaintance, but not of what the Naiyāyikas call indeterminate perceptual knowledge. When I am acquainted with the pen, my physical body is not in contact with the physical pen; my physical eyeball is not in touch with it either; nor does the acquaintance consist of the mere passing of light rays from the pen into my eye. In this case, also, there is no acquaintance, which is an awareness, a consciousness of the object by my mind. Even if that consciousness is not as definite as "pen" but as mere "something," which is indefinite and indeterminate, it is awareness or knowledge. We say, then, that this knowledge is logically insignificant, because, when I say, "I see "something." But if I say, "It is a man," denial. Even if it is a hallucination, it is "something." But if I say, "Is it a man," there is a possibility of denial, for the object may not be a man, but a pillar or lamp post. But the "something" is always a "something." And my knowledge of "something" is also knowledge. If indeterminate knowledge is knowledge, a fortiori, acquaintance is also knowledge. Does Russell mean by "knowledge by acquaintance" "knowledge by acquaintance

out any form. There have been differences of view on this point even in Indian philosophy. For instance, Rāmānuja thinks that even indeterminate cognition has a definite form; this is really Russell's knowledge by acquaintance. The Advaitins follow the Naiyāyikas.

[8] Feigl, op. cit., p. 16, (p. 220).
[9] Ibid., p. 9, (p. 215).

including description"? For him, also, there can be knowledge by acquaintance without any description.

In the fourth place, we therefore have to ask: If my acquaintance is not knowledge, how can I describe it? I can describe only what is known by me. Of course, what is known by me may also be lived by me. In some cases, what is lived by me is not known by me, for instance, the involuntary processes of my nervous, digestive, and muscular systems, and my unconscious memories. But these processes are not part of my experience. Experiences which are lived by me are also known by me. Acquaintance is such an experience. Hence, to deny that mystic experience is knowledge is not justified.

It may be objected that the above discussion is only about terminology, namely, whether the mystic experience is to be called knowledge or not, and is therefore unimportant. What is important is that it has no connection with other experiences or forms of knowledge, that it cannot be confirmed by other forms of knowledge, as my clairvoyant knowledge that my house at a distance of six hundred miles is on fire can be confirmed by ringing up the fire brigade at that place. Clairvoyant knowledge is true or false, but mystic experience is neither since it cannot be confirmed in that way. Feigl admits the occurrence of mystic experiences,[10] such as clairvoyant experiences, but doubts their interpretation. The aim of his criticism seems to be double-edged. He seems to say that mystic experience, though it occurs, cannot claim to be true knowledge, because it cannot be verified by non-mystic methods, that is, according to him, by methods of scientific empiricism; and also that the philosophical interpretation of mystic intuition to the effect that it gives metaphysical insight into the essential nature of reality is false or at least irra-

tional. I should think that these points are separate, for, if there are mystic experiences, and, if they are had by the same person who has other experiences also, they have to be related philosophically to his total experience; and by this relating he gains insight into the totality of his experience and being. If dream experiences throw light on the mind of the person, as psychoanalysts claim, then much more assuredly does mystic experience throw light on his deeper being. If there is something in our being that is susceptible to mystic experience, then it must belong to our being even though it is not possible to verify it by the methods of scientific empiricism.

But is it a justifiable demand that mystic experience should be capable of being verified by methods of non-mystic scientific empiricism? Empiricism itself is a vague idea. If it means a philosophy of experience, then mystic experience, also being experience, should be capable of being included in it. If it means a philosophy of experience confined to the physical world, then it excludes much that is humanly important. It has been shown that the methods of studying the physical world are not applicable even to the biological world, much less to that of the pychological and the spiritual. Have all psychologists accepted the view that behaviorism has succeeded in explaining thought-processes? Yet, behaviorism wants to be "scientific." One may as well demand —and it has been demanded—that the addition of consciousness to the physical body must make a difference to the weight of the latter!

What does the mystic mean when he says that his knowledge is true? He means that he actually had the experience, that his ordinary being was transformed in it, that he had no possibility of even doubting whether it was true or false, that his personality had a feeling of complete satisfaction, and that in that experience he

---

10 *Ibid.*, p. 7, (p. 213).

had no consciousness of the ordinary world. Mystic experience is an inward experience, not knowledge of an external object the reality of which can be tested by others in other ways. The mystic does not say that his experience cannot be had by others; others can have it, provided they follow the same methods for arousing it. It is true in the sense that it can be had by all who want it. It is true in the sense that it belongs to our deeper inward being. If Freud's psychoanalysis is "rational," then the analysis of our inward being also can be rational. If Freud gives a "rational" explanation of the "irrational," then the philosophy of mysticism can give a rational explanation of the supra-rational. If the meaning of "scientific empiricism" can be made to cover Freud's analysis,[11] then it can be made to cover also the analysis of mystic experience. But to explain it will not be the same as verifying it in other ways or explaining it away as an illusion.

Feigl seems to have overlooked the fact that many mystics do not call God by the name "Father" or "Mother," but describe the experience as inexplicable, indescribable, and so on. He is not clear as to what metaphysical position based upon religious experience he is attacking, for there are many even in the West. He speaks of "religious realists,"[12] but that term also does not convey a definite meaning. He says also that "metaphysical or religious insight" cannot be obtained from mystic intuition.[13] But this term also does not mean anything definite. Had he denied the occurrences of mystical experience, it would have been easy to fix his position. I may interpret him, therefore, as meaning

that mystic experience or intuition is of no use in the obtaining of philosophical insight.

But if mystic experience is admitted and man is capable of having such an experience (as he is of having a clairvoyant experience), should we not say that it belongs to the nature of man? Should we not study it, then, if we are to understand fully the being of man? Will not a philosophy of man that does not consider it be inadequate and incomplete and give an incorrect picture of man? If "scientific humanism" is to make a proper study of clairvoyance, etc., should it not also make a proper study of mystic experience and include it? Or, does the adjective "scientific" exclude mystic experience? If so, science must admit that there are experiences beyond its powers of study.

But the world, even if it is independent of man's experience, must be understood via the medium of his experience. If this is anthropomorphism, then not even the scientist can avoid it. He can explain the natural forces only as man can understand and explain them. Then, for philosophy it is as necessary to explain man's nature in terms of its correlation to the objective world as it is necessary to explain the objective world in terms of the forms of experience man can have. At one extreme, namely, that of atoms, electrons, protons, etc., man's sense experience is transcended, and correlation with his direct experiences is given up. Similarly, at the other extreme of mystic experience, correlation with physical objects is transcended. But if both extremes are developments out of man's experience in two directions, can no philosophical insight be gained into the nature of man by considering both? And is it not necessary to consider both? Psychoanalysts tell us that a perverse unconscious can affect even our ordinary perceptions and therefore our reality attitudes. This means that, for a proper reality attitude, the depths of our mind

---

[11] I do not refer to Freud's explanation of the concept of God as Father or Mother, but only to his theory of the unconscious. For the sake of the present argument, it is not necessary to accept or reject the theory.

[12] Feigl, *op. cit.*, p. 13, (p. 219).

[13] *Ibid.*, p. 16, (p. 221).

should be healthy. Similarly, if the mystic core of our being is actual, as Feigl admits, is it not necessary for us to study it and say when it is healthy and when not? If it is actual, it must be present in every man, whether he is aware of it or not. Then a study of its nature becomes as much a part of philosophy as the study of his other forms of experience. If through the latter forms of experience we decide about the nature of reality, it is important to determine how the mystic form is related to them. If the mystic form is deeper than the others, then the reality attributed to mystic experience may be at the root of the realities attributed to the other experiences.

Perhaps Feigl's difficulty is due to the usual confusing of the mystic experience with arguments like the cosmological and the teleological for the existence of God. If the mystic knows God, and if God is the *causa sui* of the world, does the mystic when he knows God know him as the cause of the world? [14] And does he therefore establish the reality of God as the cause of the world, therein using his intuition for metaphysics? No mystic philosopher in India has done this. Many, e. g., Śaṁkara, did not even accept the usual arguments for the existence of God. Those who accepted them did not confuse them with mysticism. Then, what metaphysical insight did the mystic experience provide? The insights are many. The most important is that the mystic experience at its highest and purest is deeply inward to man and is the ground of all other experiences including sense experience. And it is of the highest value, because at least after death man ought to be one with it if he is to enter into a blessed and blissful state. And because it is the ground of all other experiences, they can be understood best with reference to it. Even if these philosophies are not acceptable, the ex-

perience gives a deeper insight into the being of man as pointed out in the above paragraph.

One special point may be mentioned here about mysticism in Indian philosophy. A distinction is made between true and false mysticism. The mystic gets his experience in trance (*samādhi*). The Sāṁkhya-Yoga, for instance, speaks of absorption in primeval matter (*prakṛti*) Deep sleep undisturbed by dream is also like trance. In both cases, man is not conscious. And even in cases in which man is conscious, there are various stages of trance, in all of which there are mystic experiences. The highest or the deepest of these is the realization of God or the Absolute. But man may mistake any of the others for this. So, the ideas of truth and falsity are applicable to mystic experiences also. In order to know which is true and which is false, mystic literature describes their characteristics. These stages are stages of man's inward being. Can scientific humanism or scientific empiricism, in the narrow sense of the term, test their existence? The methods of objective experience, as the existentialists contend, are not applicable to inward experience. How can what cannot be sensed be tested by sense experience? How can what may not even express itself in sense experience be tested by it? The test can be man's inward experience alone. And the use of mystic experience is man's realization of his inwardness and its freedom.

Feigl says that the experience itself is not irrational. Then, also, the use to which it is put need not be irrational. After all, the selfsame consciousness of man passes through all stages, from the objective empirical to the deepest mystical, and is continuous through them, just as it is continuous through the states of waking, dream, and deep sleep. But the objects of the three states are not continuous. Then, how can the experiences of the one be tested by the experiences of

14 In the Aristotelian sense of the word "cause."

the other? Similarly, when man's consciousness in some of the stages of its inwardness gets detached from the objects of the external world, how can the external world be a test of those inward states? If it cannot be a test, should scientific empiricism reject their reality or their usefulness for a proper understanding of man? As man's consciousness passes through those states, when it returns from them to the ordinary empirical level, he interrelates them, just as he interrelates his dream and sleep states with his waking state. And this act of interrelating is rational, and is the work of his reason.

It may be noted that certain physical effects are observed when a man goes into trance. He can live without food, water, and even air for days at a time. Some of the *yogis* of India have given demonstrations by burying themselves for days. Some have swallowed deadliest poisons without being harmed;[15] they are able to do this by complete control of the involuntary system and by preventing the digestive fluids from coming into contact with the swallowed poisons. This is an indication of the freedom of man's consciousness from the physical and vital systems of the body and is a disproof of consciousness as a quality of the body. Even if one *yogi* can live for a day without air, we have some evidence for the independence of life from matter. These examples are meant to show that so-called scientific empiricism or science as it is now understood is not sufficient to explain man's being and has no right to reject what it cannot explain. On the other hand, these demonstrations are not sufficient to prove that the *yogis* have God-realization. They might have been able to attain some of the lower forms of trance or a certain amount of freedom from the laws of matter and life. Whether this realization is God-realization can be known by the *yogis* themselves if at all, and by others who have that realization. Even in the case of the lower realizations, a few external effects can be tested by scientific methods; what the *yogis* actually experience remains only symbolic to us, and they themselves must tell us what they experience.

Feigl requires that the mystic experience be capable of being tested by empirical methods. But what will these methods test? Let us, for argument's sake, agree that the mystic has an experience of God. Let us also agree that God is the world ground sustaining the universe. But, even after the mystic experience, the world goes on as usual. If my cognition of the pen in front of me does not change the pen, the mystic's knowledge of the world ground does not change the world either. No change occurs in the world after the mystic's realization except in the experience and the outlook of the mystic. The only test, therefore, can be by his own experience. Yet, this experience should not be dismissed as valueless either for man or for philosophy. For man, it provides a new understanding of himself and a new outlook. It gives him an experiential basis for communion with the Divine Spirit. The discovery of the deeper levels of his consciousness clarifies for him the nature of his ethical consciousness,[16] that is, the ability of his conscious being to transcend his egoistic particularity. The so-called mystic practices, if they are truly spiritual, should enable man to reach these levels and be steadfast in them. But, unfortunately, there are all kinds of practices for mystic experiences, for instance, the trance introduced by drugs.

[15] This is not done in trance but in the ordinary waking state. But the case is mentioned in order to show the peculiar nature of our being, which can be made in some ways independent of the laws of physiology.

[16] This point was discussed in my paper, "Religion and Spiritual Values in Indian Thought," contributed to the Third East-West Philosophers' Conference.

If true mystic experience is God-realization, and vice versa, then God has to be explained as the Spirit within the spirit of man; otherwise, communion with God could not have been possible. This is a philosophical insight. Whether the two spirits are one and the same or similar but different is a question about which philosophers have disagreed both in India and the West. But there can be no communion and no mystic experience that can be called divine if God is like the God of Aristotle or the deists, keeping aloof from the world processes he started or created. He must be immanent in man's conscious being if communion is to be possible. Now, making the consciousness of man central to philosophy, several systems have been developed both in India and the West. They have always been more or less idealistic, giving primacy to spirit; and many of them are realistic in epistemology. It is true that this method of approach is not suited to the explanation of the structure of an independent material world. But, equally, we have to note, the method of explanation suited to the material world is not suited to the understanding of the inward being of man. We have to recognize the validity of each and find a way of co-ordinating and correlating them. This can be done through proper co-operation of Eastern and Western philosophers. Matter and consciousness exist as co-ordinated and correlated in man. Mystic experience baffles scientific empiricism and shows its inadequacy.

From the purely outward point of view, for those who do not have mystic experience, the method to be used is not that of scientific testing, but postulational technique. But this can give only plausibility, not direct experience. When direct experience is not had, there can be several speculative philosophies as there can be several hypotheses. Direct experience cannot be produced by the methods of scientific empiricism; and mystic experience cannot

be tested by them, unless the meanings of the words "scientific" and "empiricism" are made wide enough. After all, scientific methods are not to be a priori determined, but must be made suitable to the kind of reality they are to study.

Feigl refers to Einstein's conception of God as the order or rationality of Nature as a good example of his method of approach to intuition.[17] But do we not find it in the Greek conception of the *Logos* and the Indian conception of *Mahān Ātmā* (the Cosmic Person, Cosmic Reason)? Suppose, then, that God as the Divine Spirit is immanent in the order of the totality of Nature. Similarly, the consciousness of the individual, particularly his rationality, is immanent in his physical body and forms with it something like an integral unity. Is there nothing in man, then, that corresponds to Cosmic Reason? If man is part of Nature, if reason in man corresponds to reason in Nature, then has his reason nothing to do with Cosmic Reason? To a man with only a "scientific outlook" these questions may appear only speculative. But to the questioning philosopher as well as to the mystic they are questions about man's existence and its nature.

One difficulty with the so-called "scientific outlook" or "rational outlook" in Western philosophy is that it has never taken man's consciousness seriously, on the ground that our consciousness of objects makes no difference to the objects. But our consciousness of ourselves does make a difference to our existence; for, if we are not conscious of ourselves, we cease to exist, though the objects do not cease to exist even if we are not conscious of them. For man himself, it is his conscious being or the being of his consciousness that matters most. Its importance is directly realized in the empirical world in ethical and aesthetic activities. In pure

[17] Feigl, *op. cit.,* p. 15, (p. 220).

science it is treated like a mirror reflecting objects as they are, and not affecting the nature of their existence. But man's existence also is consciousness. Rāmānuja, an Indian Vedāntin, speaks of two kinds of consciousness, the existential consciousness and the attribute consciousness. I should like to call the latter projective consciousness, because in the mystic experience of one's self, it can be withdrawn into existential consciousness. The distinction is that between consciousness of my existence and the consciousness I possess of external objects. I *am* the former; but I *have* the latter. The latter presents objects as they are and does not transform their nature in the process. It is this consciousness which the scientific philosophers consider and treat as unimportant for scientific purposes. They ignore existential consciousness altogether. And this cannot even be known through scientific methods. It has now asserted its presence with a vengeance in the several forms of European existentialism. Feigl says that he keeps an open mind [18] to these problems. Then he should also keep an open mind about the methods of study, without limiting them to the "scientific" as usually understood. Otherwise, to say that every form of knowledge, if true, must be capable of being tested by other forms of knowledge will be dogmatic. There are experiences which can be so tested, but others which cannot. Experience and knowledge are not limited to one type. If indeterminate knowledge of external objects is useless as a truth, it does not follow that indeterminate knowledge of inward reality is also useless as a truth. Again, if we accept Einstein's idea that God is reason in Nature, and, if God is Spirit, how can scientific tests establish that reason in Nature is Spirit?

The real question is: What is the specific field of intuition and what is that

of reason? In part they overlap.[19] This is due to man's being and having more than one kind of consciousness. In the transcendent objective field of atoms, electrons, etc., everything is posited by reason. Similarly, in the transcendent subjective field everything is experienced intuitively. And philosophy in its epistemology should study at what points and how they overlap and interpenetrate, and at what points they do not. But man's consciousness in one form or another is continuous through all.

Feigl has not examined the psychological and epistemological processes of reason and intuition. Had he done this, he would have seen that the mystic's intuition is not supernatural. Feigl uses the words "naturalism," "rationalism," "scientific humanism" and "scientific empiricism." But if mystic intuition is a fact—as he admits—then it is as natural as any other fact and must be as capable of scientific and rational explanation. But, if we delimit the meanings of the words "natural," "scientific," and "rational," then mystic experience must be treated as supernatural or as a freak of Nature. Then science, dangerously to man, will be narrowed down to the realm of physical objects.

II

After the above comment on Feigl's main contention, I may make a few observations on some of his other incidental views, not necessarily to criticize them, but to clarify them as far as I understand them.

1. How is intuition a way of knowing? Feigl distinguishes between acquaintance and knowledge by acquaintance, and says that, if intuition is only acquaintance, it cannot be knowledge. Here I take the word "intuition" in the sense of acquaint-

18 *Ibid.*, p. 16, (p. 221).

19 See my "Intuition as a Philosophical Method In India."

ance, not in the sense of indeterminate cognition of objects. Let us take the example of clairvoyance. X says: "The house is on fire," and communicates this to Y. X has acquaintance, first, with "the house on fire," and then communicates it by the proposition, "The house is on fire." Then, is this communicable proposition knowledge, but not acquaintance with the "house on fire"? If he has no knowledge at the time of acquaintance, what can he communicate? Suppose he does not want to communicate and does not make the proposition; then does he have no knowledge? Is not knowledge involved in acquaintance itself? Or, does Feigl mean by acquaintance simple awareness of sense-contact without the mind's fixing the object as something definite? But there is no sense-contact in clairvoyance. If mind knows the object directly without the senses by developing the object somehow, then it knows the object as a definite something.

Let us leave out clairvoyance, and take the example of the pen in front of me. I am acquainted with the pen. The object is the pen. This acquaintance, it is said, is not knowledge. If the object is "This is a pen," then it is knowledge, because it can be communicated. But if my acquaintance is not knowledge, how can I make the assertion, "This is a pen"? In this instance, it may be said that during acquaintance my sense of vision is in contact with the object, but my mind is not there. But, if so, my acquaintance could not have been with "the pen" but with "something." Knowledge by acquaintance, Russell says, is with individuals, and so acquaintance must be with individuals. The individual here is "the pen," a fixed determinate object, not a mere "something," not even a mere color. Otherwise, acquaintance will be absolutely indeterminate, and knowledge by acquaintance will be the same as indeterminate knowledge. Nor can we say that, when my eyesight is fixed on the object, my mind is not fixed on it; for then the object cannot be "the pen." I may not even see anything, if the impression is not taken by the mind also. And as long as the mind is fixed on the object, it is not conscious of even the class concept "pen." So, if acquaintance is what Russell wishes it to mean, then it is knowledge, though it may not be propositional and communicable. But this knowledge is later developed into propositional form.

For the sake of information, it may be mentioned that among Indian philosophers Rāmānuja thinks that indeterminate perception gives definite knowledge of definite individuals (vyaktis). And what he means by indeterminate perception is what Russell means by acquaintance. But Rāmānuja adds unnecessarily and wrongly that this kind of knowledge is produced only when we perceive an object for the first time. When an American boy sees an elephant for the first time, he has this knowledge. But when he sees it again or sees another elephant, he has determinate perception. Rāmānuja's reason is this: When we see an object for the first time, the class concept could not have been prior; yet we see it as an object with a definite form. The form as a class concept could not have been detached from the object as yet. This is done later, when we see the same object again or when we see another object of the same class. But Rāmānuja does not see that, even when we see the same object again, during the process of perception itself, the form or class concept is not detached from the object in order to turn the perception into the propositional form, "It is an elephant." It is of the form "the elephant." Psychologically, the detachment takes place only when the mind with the form detaches itself from the object before me. But so long as it is conscious of the form, mind is fixed on the particular object and so cannot have an abstract class concept before it. So we have to say that the propositional form is a later development by our consciousness for purposes of reasoning and communication. Then acquaintance becomes descriptive. Yet, acquaintance also is knowledge, as without it the propositional form could not have been developed. But, indeterminate perception is not knowledge, as I know nothing definite but am only aware that one of my senses is in contact with something.

Then, if mystic intuition is acquaintance, it can be knowledge. In Indian thought it also is wrongly called indeterminate knowledge. Rāmānuja should have called it acquaintance, because God, the object of knowledge here, has personality and individuality. But for Śaṁkara it is indeterminate knowledge, as the Absolute for him has no determinateness. Yet it is knowledge, because consciousness is fully present, though mind is transformed and absorbed. In short, there is no separate individual there to reject the knowledge as unimportant, as in the case of indeterminate sense-perception. Both Śaṁkara and Rāmānuja are mystics.

2. Feigl challenges the view that the essence of reality can be known only by intuition and that reasoned discursive knowledge does not even penetrate into the heart of things.[20] But a philosopher may retort by saying that the man who is born blind but who knows about colors through sounds does not penetrate into the reality of colors but has only symbolic knowledge. Like him, the mystic may say that his inward mystic experience may be symbolically explained through reasoning but cannot be experienced except directly.[21] Bergson meant the same thing when he said that duration is known or

experienced only by living it, and this knowledge is intuition. Time spatialized as a straight line is only a symbolic representation. Even if it is symbolized algebraically, it is not knowledge of time that we get but an analysis. Of course, Bergson used many analogies to explain what he meant, and many arguments to show what time was not. But the main question is: Unless we have direct knowledge of time, how can we frame its symbolic representation? What is the symbolic representation about? Do we know what we are explaining? Or, are we constructing a conceptual fiction called time with the help of a graph or algebra? Is time real or only a conceptual fiction?

3. Corresponding to the distinction between intuition and intellect, Feigl points out a number of other distinctions given by Eddington, Northrop, Bergson, Russell, and Schlick. As Northrop is closely connected with this journal, I should say a little about his distinction. Are concepts by postulation merely descriptive in the sense of Russell's? Or, are they intuitive also? Neither Plato's Ideas nor Aristotle's Forms are merely descriptive. For both, they are objects of rational intuition. Considering Kant's philosophy, one may say that the categories are hypothetical entities postulated for explaining experience. As hypothetical entities they may be called conceptual constructions or epistemological fictions. Vaihinger would call them "as-ifs." But, first, Kant himself treats them as constitutive of experience. And, second, the problem which the categories are postulated to solve is: How is physics possible? In fact, Kant took physics to be actual, not as a possible science. Or, to make the question less wide and more specific, it is: Why do I see the object in front of me as a substance with qualities when actually my senses see qualities only? Kant's answer is: Had our mind not used the category of substance-quality in constructing the object, it would not

20 Feigl, *op. cit.*, pp. 12 ff., (p. 216 ff.).

21 Is my knowledge of the chair on which I am sitting the same as my symbolic knowledge of it as a beehive of electrons and protons? Is my direct perception of this chair knowledge at all, unless verified by the formulae of the physicist?

have seen the object as a substance with qualities. Kant does not construct the category substance-quality, but transfers it from the side of the object to that of mind. And what is constructed is the object. Then Kant's postulation is not conceptual construction, but assigning the category to mind. Then what is postulated need not always be a conceptual construction, but may be an intuition.

Indeed, one may give a different interpretation of Kant or even say that Kant was wrong. But my point is that there is often intuition and then description of the intuited object even in Western thought. Even the mystic can have intuitive knowledge of something and then describe it. We generally think that description is description of something with which we are acquainted. The so-called description of a constructed concept like that of multi-dimensional space is description by metaphor, which may better be called a proposal. But the object of mystic knowledge is not an object proposed. The mystic has a right to describe without being silent. If Russell can hold that we can have knowledge by description without corresponding acquaintance—which is a deliberate product of thought, and he is right there—the mystic can at least have the right to describe, however imperfectly,[22] that with which he is acquainted and also say that he has knowledge of what he describes. What Russell means by pure description without possible acquaintance is only mere conceptual con-

struction, which is not really the description of anything except that of the concept constructed. I wonder whether Kant's categories are such pure conceptual constructions. If they are not, then the distinction between concepts by intuition and concepts by postulation cannot be clear-cut. I do not mean, of course, that there can be no concepts by mere postulation as we have in multi-valued logics and multi-dimensional geometries. We can have concepts by intuition also, such as that of color or man. We have no acquaintance in the former case; but in the latter we have acquaintance, and that also is knowledge. I have knowledge of man, not only when I have the concept of man, but also when I am looking at a man.

4. Feigl seems to suggest that, since the Kantian intuition of space and time, the intuitions of the axioms of Euclidian geometry, and instinctive knowledge [23] are now explained otherwise, they are false. But do we not have those experiences? However it is explained, do we not see Euclidean space? Do we not have parental instincts now? Suppose space is explained symbolically in purely algebraic terms. Are the symbols the same as space or is the experience of those symbols the same as the experience of space? Similarly, in the case of mystic experience, let us for argument's sake agree that it can be explained in other terms. But these other terms do not constitute that experience. The greatest difficulty lies in the mystic's contention that in his experience all distinctions between subject and object vanish: this is at least the contention of many. All say that it is beyond mind and reason. So, we cannot explain mystic experience in terms of Freud's Father-image. There is no image at all. The experience is *sui generis* and cannot be explained in other terms. Even supposing an explanation to be possible, it is no substitute for the orig-

---

22 Russell's theory of "incomplete symbols" and "logically inappropriate expressions" shows that he does not think that even definite description can be a complete substitute for knowledge by acquaintance. So, intuition, if we mean acquaintance by that word, is necessary for complete knowledge. And there is nothing strange in the fact that the mystic's description of his object is an incomplete and inappropriate expression. And neither we nor the mystic need be silent about what is known by acquaintance, as Feigl demands.

23 Feigl., *op. cit.*, p. 3, (p. 211).

inal knowledge. To be able to explain a form of knowledge in terms of another form does not mean that the former is not real. To understand colors in terms of sound does not mean that there are no colors.

5. Feigl's reference to the "nomological net" of naturalism suggests that he has an a priori set of rules and laws, and that he will accept as real whatever is caught by the net and reject whatever escapes. But this is a dogmatism which he introduces, while assailing religious dogmatism. No nomological net can be given to us ready-made and complete. This net in its completeness must be what Einstein calls "reason in Nature." This has to be constructed slowly and patiently, study-

ing every form of reality with "natural piety." A net that can catch physical reality may not be able to catch other forms. What any particular science may safely regard as unimportant and even as nonexistent for its own affairs may have tremendous importance for the affairs of other studies and for man's life. If Kant was wrong in constructing an a priori set of categories on the basis of current logic, then the net of laws constructed by naturalism on the basis of external Nature may not suit inward reality and may suffer from similar inadequacy. The mystic philosopher may say this, and we have to keep an open mind even with regard to methods of study.

Revelation

*Lectures on the Origin and
Growth of Religion*

F. MAX MÜLLER

F. Max Müller (1825–1900) was perhaps the world's most prolific Sanskritist of the nineteenth century. As editor of the great series of translations from Sanskrit into English gathered together as the Sacred Books of the East *and as translator of the Indian* Rig-Veda *and many of the Upanishads, Müller's scholarly output of these and additional books and papers was enormous. Born in Germany, he emigrated to England where he ultimately took up residence as Professor of Comparative Philology at Oxford. It is out of this background and deep acquaintance with the Indian Sanskrit texts that Müller relates a story that describes most graphically the nature of Indian revelation within the context of the* Rig-Veda.

And now let me tell you, what will again sound like a fairy-tale, but is nevertheless a simple fact. That Rig-Veda which, for more than three, or it may be four thousand years, has formed the foundation of the religious and moral life of untold millions of human beings, had never been published; and by a combination of the most fortunate circumstances, it fell to my lot to bring out the first complete edition of that sacred text, together with the most authoritative commentary of Hindu theologians, the commentary of Sāyana Ākārya.

The Rig-Veda consists of 1017 or 1028 hymns, each on an average of ten verses.

The total number of words, if we may trust native scholars, amounts to 153,826.

But how, you may ask, was that ancient literature preserved? At present, no doubt, there are manuscripts of the Veda, but few Sanskrit manuscripts in India are older than 1000 after Christ, nor is there any evidence that the art of writing was known in India much before the beginning of Buddhism, or the very end of the ancient Vedic literature. How then were these ancient hymns, and the Brāhmaṇas, and it may be, the Sūtras too, preserved? Entirely by memory, but by memory kept under the strictest discipline. As far back as we know anything of India, we find

From *Lectures on the Origin and Growth of Religion as Illustrated By the Religions of India,* The Hibbert Lectures, 1878; London, Longmans, Green, and Co., Williams and Norgate, 1878.

that the years which we spend at school and at university, were spent by the sons of the three higher classes, in learning from the mouth of a teacher, their sacred literature. This was a sacred duty, the neglect of which entailed social degradation, and the most minute rules were laid down as to the mnemonic system that had to be followed. Before the invention of writing, there was no other way of preserving literature, whether sacred or profane, and in consequence every precaution was taken against accidents.

It has sometimes been asserted that the Vedic religion is extinct in India, that it never recovered from its defeat by Buddhism; that the modern Brahmanic religion, as founded on the Purānas and Tantras, consists in a belief in Vishṇu, Śiva and Brahma and manifests itself in the worship of the most hideous idols. To a superficial observer it may seem to be so, but English scholars who have lived in India in intimate relations with the natives, or native scholars who now occasionally visit us in England, give a very different account. No doubt, Brahmanism was for a time defeated by Buddhism; no doubt it had, at a later time, to accommodate itself to circumstances, and tolerate many of the local forms of worship, which were established in India, before it was slowly subdued by the Brahmans. Nor did Brahmanism ever possess a state machinery to establish uniformity of religious belief, to test orthodoxy, or to punish heresy over the whole of India. But how was it that, during the late famine, many people would rather die than accept food from unclean hands?[1] Are there any priests in Europe or elsewhere, whose authority would be proof against starvation? The influence of the priests is still enormous in India, and all the greater, because

it is embodied in the influence of custom, tradition, and superstition. Now those men who are, even at the present moment, recognised as the spiritual guides of the people, those whose influence for good or evil is even now immense, are believers in the supreme authority of the Veda. Everything, whether founded on individual opinion, on local custom, on Tantras or Purānas, nay, even on the law-books of Manu, must give way, as soon as it can be proved to be in direct conflict with a single sentence of the Veda. On that point there can be no controversy. But those Brahmans, who even in this Kali age, and during the ascendency of the Mlekkhas, uphold the sacred traditions of the past, are not to be met with in the drawing-rooms of Calcutta. They depend on the alms of the people, and live in villages, either by themselves, or in colleges. They would lose their prestige, if they were to shake hands or converse with an infidel, and it is only in rare cases that they drop their reserve, when brought in contact with Europeans whose knowledge of their own sacred language and literature excites their wonderment, and with a little pressure, opens their heart and their mouth, like a treasure-house of ancient knowledge. Of course, they would not speak English or even Bengali. They speak Sanskrit and write Sanskrit, and I frequently receive letters from some of them, couched in the most faultless language.

And my fairy-tale is not all over yet. These men, and I know it as a fact, know the whole Rig-Veda by heart, just as their ancestors did, three or four thousand years ago; and though they have manuscripts, and though they now have a printed text, they do not learn their sacred lore from them. They learn it, as their ancestors learnt it, thousands of years ago, from the mouth of a teacher, so that the Vedic succession should never be broken.[2] That

[1] It is curious that the popular idea that, even during a famine, food must not be accepted from unclean hands, rests on no sacred authority, nay is flatly contradicted by both Śruti and Smriti.

[2] This oral teaching is carefully described in the Prātiśākhya of the Rig-Veda, i.e., probably

oral teaching and learning became in the eyes of the Brahmans one of the great sacrifices, and though the number of those who still keep it up is smaller than it used to be, their influence, their position, their sacred authority, are as great as ever. These men do not come to England, they would not cross the sea. But some of their pupils, who have been brought up half on the native, and half on the English system, are less strict. I have had visits from natives who knew large portions of the Veda by heart; I have been in correspondence with others who, when they were twelve or fifteen years old, could repeat the whole of it.[3] They learn a few lines every day, repeat them for hours, so that the whole house resounds with the noise, and they thus strengthen their memory to that degree, that when their apprenticeship is finished, you can open them like a book, and find any passage you like, any word, any accent. One native scholar, Shankar Pandurang, is at the present moment collecting various readings for my edition of the Rig-Veda, not from manuscripts but from the oral tradition of Vaidik Śrotriyas. He writes, on the 2nd March, 1877, "I am collecting a few of our walking Rig-Veda manuscripts, taking your text as the basis. I find a good many differences which I shall soon be able to examine more closely, when I may be able to say whether they are various readings, or not. I will, of course, communicate them all to you before making any use of them publicly, if I ever do this at all. As I write, a Vaidik scholar is going over your Rig-Veda text. He has his own manuscript on one side, but does not open it, except occasionally. He knows the whole Saṃhitā and Pada texts by heart. I wish I could send you his photograph, how he is squatting in my tent with his Upavīta (the sacred cord) round his shoulders, and only a Doti round his middle, not a bad specimen of our old Rishis."

Think of that half-naked Hindu, repeating under an Indian sky the sacred hymns which have been handed down for three or four thousand years by oral tradition. If writing had never been invented, if India had never been occupied by England, that young Brahman, and hundreds and thousands of his countrymen, would probably have been engaged just the same in learning and saying by heart the simple prayers first uttered on the Sarasvatī, and the other rivers of the Penjab by Vasishtha, Viśvāmitra, Syāvāśva, and others. And here are we, under the shadow of Westminster Abbey, in the very zenith of the intellectual life of Europe, nay, of the whole world, listening in our minds to the same sacred hymns, trying to understand them (and they are sometimes very difficult to understand), and hoping to learn from them some of the deepest secrets of the human heart, that human heart which is the same everywhere, however widely we ourselves may be separated from each other by space and time, by colour and creed.

This is the story I wished to tell you today. And though it may have sounded to some of you like a fairy-tale, believe me it is truer in all its details than many a chapter of contemporary history.

---

in the fifth or sixth century B.C. It is constantly alluded to in the Brāhmaṇas, but it must have existed even during the earlier periods, for in a hymn of the Rig-Veda (VII, 103), in which the return of the rainy season, and the delight and quacking of the frogs is described, we read: "One repeats the speech of the other, as the pupil (repeats the words) of the teacher." The pupil is called śikshamānah, the teacher śaktah, while siksha, from the same root, is the recognised technical term for phonetics in later times.

[3] "Indian Antiquary," 1878, p. 140. "There are thousands of Brahmans," the editor remarks, "who know the whole of the Rig-Veda by heart, and can repeat it, etc."

Revelation

ELIOT DEUTSCH and
J. A. B. VAN BUITENEN

J. A. B. van Buitenen (b. 1928) was born in The Hague, where he studied and eventually taught at the University of Utrecht. He came to the United States in 1956 and is at present professor of Sanskrit and Indic studies at the University of Chicago.

Eliot Deutsch (b. 1931) has taught at Rensselaer Polytechnic Institute, the University of Chicago, and the University of Hawaii, where he is presently professor of philosophy. Deutsch is also the distinguished editor of the journal Philosophy East and West, a post he has held since 1967.

In this selection, the authors explore the nature and meaning of "revelation" as the word is found and used in the Indian tradition.

If we are to form a proper understanding of the meaning and scope of "Revelation," we do well to forget at once the implications of the term in the Mediterranean religions, Judaism, Christianity, and Islām. Strictly speaking, "revelation" is a misnomer, since ultimately there is no revealer. The Sanskrit term for it is *śruti*, literally "the hearing," which means an erudition acquired by listening to the instruction of a teacher. This instruction itself had been transmitted to the teacher through an uninterrupted series of teachers that stretches to the beginning of creation.

Revelation, therefore, is by no means God's word—because, paradoxically, if it were to derive from a divine person, its credibility would be impugned. It is held to be authorless, for if a person, human or divine, had authored it, it would be vulnerable to the defects inherent in such a person. It is axiomatic that revelation is infallible, and this infallibility can be defended only if it is authorless.

Then from where does it come? The answer is stark and simple: it is given with the world. For some of the Mīmāṁsā (or orthodox, exegetical) thinkers who have addressed themselves to this problem, the world is beginningless and the assumption of a creator is both problematic and unnecessary. And even if a beginning of the world is assumed, as in later Hindu thought when it is held that the universe goes through a pulsating rhythm of origination, existence, and dissolution, it is also held that at the dawn of a new world the revelation reappears to the vision of the seers, who once more begin the transmission.

Revelation, then, comes with the world, and it embodies the laws which regulate the well-being of both world and man. It lays down first and foremost what is our *dharma,* our duty. This duty is more precisely defined as a set of acts which either must be done continuously (*nitya*), or occasionally (*naimittika*), or to satisfy a specific wish (*kāmya*).

While we would be inclined to look upon the Revelation as a more or less continuous series of historic texts, spanning close to a millennium from ca. 1400 B.C. till 500 B.C., orthodoxy looks upon it as eternal and therefore simultaneous. Also, the Mīmāṁsā Exegetes laid down rather rigorous criteria for its authority. Orthodox consensus recognizes three fundamental means of knowledge, each of which has its own scope. Of these means (pramāṇas), sensory perception (*pratyakṣa*) holds the first place, for it is through perception that the world is evident to us. Built upon perception is inference (*anumāna*), in which a present perception combines with a series of past perceptions to offer us a conclusion about a fact which is not perceptibly evident. While these two means of knowledge, perceiving and reasoning, tell us everything about the world that we wish to know, they cannot give us any knowledge about matters that are suprasensory. It is here that the force of Revelation comes in. Revelation, then, is authoritative *only* about matters to which neither perception nor inference gives us access; but then it is fully authoritative. This authority, as pointed out, is primarily concerned with one's duties. To give a contrastive example, the orthodox Exegetes would reject most of the Bible as Revelation: most of it they would classify as *itihāsa* or *purāṇa,*

"stories about things past," describing events which were accessible to perception and hence require only the authority of perception; but, for example, the chapters dealing with the Law in Deuteronomy would be considered Revelation in the true sense, since here rules are laid down and results are set forth which escape human perception and inference.

Led by this principle, the Exegetes classified Revelation under three basic rubrics, "injunction" (*vidhi* or *niyoga,* including prohibition or *niṣedha*), "discussion" (*arthavāda*), and "spell" (*mantra*). Spells comprise the mass of formulae, metric or in prose, which were employed at the execution of the rites. Discussion comprises all the texts which describe, glorify, or condemn matters pertaining to rites. Injunction comprises all the statements, direct or indirect, which lay down that certain rites or acts must be done or must not be done.

The stock example is *svargakāmo jyoti-ṣṭomena yajeta,* "he who wishes for heaven should sacrifice with the soma sacrifice." It is in such statements that the authority of Revelation finally resides. It enjoins an action (offering up a sacrifice), the nature of which escapes human invention, for a purpose (heaven) whose existence neither perception nor inference could have acknowledged, upon a person (the sacrificer) who stands qualified for this action on the basis of the injunction. Declarations which accompany the description of the sacrifice, e.g., "the sacrificial pole is the sun," while strictly speaking untrue and carrying no authority, have a derivative authority insofar as they are subsidiary to and supportive of the injunction, and may be condemnatory or laudatory of facts connected with the rite laid down in the injunction (e.g., the sacrificial pole is compared to the sun in a laudatory fashion for its central function at the rite). The spells accompanying the festive celebration of the rite have their secondary, even tertiary, significance only within the context of the rite laid down in the injunction.

From the exegetical point of view, then, much of what is generally described as Revelation holds little authority. For example, the Four Vedas as we call them, the Veda of the hymns (ṛk), the formulae (yajus), the chants (sāma), and the incantations (atharva), are almost entirely under the rubric of "spell." The large disquisitions of the Brāhmaṇas are almost entirely "discussion," except for the scattered injunctions in them; and the same largely holds for the third layer of texts, the Āraṇyakas. Generally speaking, Vedānta will go along with this view.

It is, however, with the last layer of text (the Vedānta or the Upaniṣads) that Exegetes and Vedāntins come to a parting of ways. For the Exegetes and Upaniṣads are in no way an exception to the rules that govern the Revelation as a whole. Nothing much is enjoined in them nor do they embody marked spells. In fact, they are fundamentally "discussion," specifically discussion of the self; and such discussion certainly has a place in the exegetical scheme of things, for this self is none other than the personal agent of the rites and this agent no doubt deserves as much discussion as, say, the sacrificial pole.

Basically therefore the Exegetes find the Revelation solely, and fully, authoritative when it lays down the Law on what actions have to be undertaken by what persons under what circumstances for which purposes. Vedānta accepts this, but only for that portion of Revelation which bears on ritual acts, the karmakāṇḍa. But to relegate the portion dealing with knowledge, the jñānakāṇḍa, to the same ritual context is unacceptable. It is taken for granted that karmakāṇḍa indeed defines the principle of authority in injunctions of acts to be done, but Vedānta declines on the one hand that the Upaniṣads embody an injunction (e.g., that Brahman or the self must be studied and known, or that the world must be dephenomenalized) and declines on the other hand that if the Upaniṣads bear on no injunction they have simply the limited authoritative standing of a discussion. The consensus of the Vedānta is that in the Upaniṣads significant and authoritative statements are made concerning the nature of Brahman.

From the foregoing it will have become clear that very little of the Revelation literature preceding the Upaniṣads was of systematic interest to the Vedāntins. For example, Śaṁkara quotes less than twenty verses from the entire Rigveda in his commentary on the Brahmasūtras, about fourteen lines from the largest Brāhmaṇa of them all, the Śatapatha Brāhmaṇa, but no less than thirty-four verses from the Muṇḍaka Upaniṣad, a fairly minor and short Upaniṣad. This is not to say that Vedānta rejects the previous literature, but that it considers all the relevant wisdom of the Veda concerning these issues to have been embedded in the Upaniṣads.

Authority

Reason and Nature

MORRIS R. COHEN

Morris R. Cohen (1880–1947) was born in Minsk, Russia, and came to the United States when he was twelve. Deeply steeped in the religious traditions of Judaism, he brought to philosophy an interest in law and religion that grounded his professional interests in logic and the philosophy of science. It was Cohen's deep philosophic conviction that "all natural phenomena depend on material conditions"; and it is from this base of scientific materialism that his critique of authority emerges.

AUTHORITY

The prestige of authority, it is generally recognized, rests most firmly in custom. By increasing the means of travel and communication, and thus making it possible for us to visualize ways other than those under which we have grown up, the Industrial Revolution has been one of the most potent forces in undermining the prestige of the customary. By showing the people of Europe that they could take things into their own hands and change the traditional form of government, laws, and even the system of weights and measures, the French Revolution made the path of the questioning and revolutionary spirit more easy. But it also frightened those impressed with the fact that the basis of civilized society rests on habitual obedience and deference to organized authority. From the latter point of view, modern history is a fall from a social order in which every one knows his place and its duties to a bewildering chaos of conflicting claims without any authoritative guidance. The claims of authority have, therefore, been usually pressed or repelled with more poignancy than philosophic detachment.

In discussing the principle of authority we should distinguish between the necessities of conduct and those of purely theoretic decisions. This distinction is frowned upon in an age which so glorifies practical conduct as to regard purely theoretic contemplation either as impossible or as a sinful waste of human energy. Nevertheless, the distinction is quite clear and important. In matters of conduct, we are frequently compelled to decide at once between exclusive alternatives. We must, for instance, either get married or not, go to church or stay out, accept a given position or else refuse it. In theoretic issues, however, we may avoid either alternative by suspending judgment, e.g., when we realize the inadequacy of our information or evidence. It is true, of course, that most people, after having made a decision, do not like to entertain any doubts as to the adequacy of its theoretic justification. But by no canon of intellectual integrity can dislike of doubt constitute a proof of the truths assumed.

In practice, then, it is often much more important to come to a decision one way or another than to wait for adequate reasons on which to base a right decision. Often, indeed, such waiting is a sheer impossibility. Hence mankind frequently finds it necessary to settle doubts by means that have nothing to do with reason. Among such means are the throwing of a coin or of dice (of which the Urim and Thumin may have been an example), the flight of birds, the character of the entrails in the sacrifice, or the ravings of the smoke-intoxicated priestess of Dodona. Note that not only minor questions, but important ones like war, have been decided that way. The desire to find justifying reasons for adhering to decisions once made may promote the belief that these non-rational ways of terminating issues are controlled by supernatural powers on whom it is safer to rely. But in most cases, the given practice is much older than the various explanations offered for it, and its function in eliminating doubt and bringing about decision is undoubtedly the primary fact. Modern anthropology is making us realize the superficial character of the old rationalism which regarded the claims of all magicians or prophets to supernatural power or inspiration as premeditated fraud. In primitive communities magical

power and the sovereignty which goes with it, are often literally thrust on certain individuals who generally share the prevalent ideas and illusions. We thrust sovereignty on others because most of us are unhappy under the great burden of having to make decisions. We can see this in our own day in the way in which the sovereignty of final or authoritative decision has been imposed in many fields upon our newspapers. Worried by doubts as to the correct dress for her boy of ten at an afternoon party, the anxious mother writes to the newspaper. Wishing to be certain as to what is the proper judgment to be passed on a play or concert, we hasten to consult the next morning's newspaper. The latter thus becomes an authority on dress, on the pronunciation and use of words, on the proper conduct for young women engaged or in love, etc.

Political authority or sovereignty has its basis in just this need to have practical controversies settled. When we are parties to a suit, we are anxious that the issue be settled justly, i.e., in our favour. But there is a general interest on the part of all members of the community in having controversies settled one way or another. Otherwise we fall into a state of perpetual war or anarchy. So important is this, especially to people depending on routine work like agriculture or industry, that mankind has borne the most outrageous tyranny on the part of semi-insane despots, rather than by revolt break the habit of obedience and face the dangers of anarchy before the rebel leader effectively asserts his own tyranny. It was not an Oriental, but the most influential of Occidental philosophers, Aristotle, who argued that even an admittedly bad law ought not to be replaced by a reasonably better one, because changing the law diminishes a prestige which is most effectively based on habitual obedience.

English and American communities are apt to flatter themselves on having eliminated tyranny or despotism by the rational devices of parliamentary or constitutional government. The men of the eighteenth century believed it possible to have a government by laws and not by men. (Some lawyers believe this today, perhaps because they do most of the governing.) It is, doubtless, possible by political devices to minimize certain of the grosser forms of tyranny; and a certain amount of discussion of a more or less rational character may profitably be introduced into the shaping of our laws. But so long as men fall short of perfect knowledge and good will, they will have to obey laws which they find oppressive and unjust—laws made, administered, and interpreted, not by an abstract reason in heaven, nor by a mythical will of all the people, but by ordinary human beings with all their human limitations upon them. If every individual refused to obey any law that seemed to him immoral, the advantages of a state law over anarchy would be lost. This is not to deny that tyranny may go to such excesses as to make the temporary anarchy of revolution preferable. But in the ordinary course of human affairs such occasions must be regarded as exceptional or relatively infrequent. Actually, therefore, though some forms of government may in the long run work more reasonably or more agreeably to the will of its citizens, the principle of authority means that the good citizen will submit to what is in fact the arbitrary will or unwise opinion of some boss, legislator, administrator, or judge. Lawyers and sentimentalists may try to hide this unpleasant fact by such fictions as "the law is nothing but reason, the will of the people, etc." But wilfully to confuse such fictions with the actual facts is to corrupt reason at its source.

The practical necessity for authority does not mean that only an absolute monarchy or an hereditary nobility can guarantee a regime of law and order. Experience has amply shown that a titular abso-

lute king may in fact be helpless in the hands of irresponsible courtiers, and that hereditary nobilities may be unruly as well as selfish—just as democracies may in fact be ruled by natural leaders or well-organized cliques. In practice authoritarians are people who are so afraid of the perils of change that they blind themselves to the absurdities and iniquities of the established order, while reformers and revolutionists are so impressed with the existing evils that they give little heed to the even greater evils which their proposals may generate. The true rationality or wisdom of any course of conduct obviously depends upon a true estimate of all its consequences, and such estimate is avoided both by those who will not hear of any change and by those who think that *any* change is necessarily good (because they identify change with life).

In thus recognizing the unavoidable character of authority in communal life, must our reason also abdicate and declare that whatever we must submit to is also right? That is exactly the position of those who, like Mr. Balfour, argue that since our individual reason is highly fallible, the need of order and morality demands the submission of reason itself to authority —defined as a "group of non-rational causes, moral, social, and educational— which produces its results by psychic processes other than reasoning." Authorities, however, differ and in the end they cannot support themselves without reason.

In the history of the reaction against the rationalism of the Enlightenment, we find three main sources of authority to which individual reason is asked to submit. These are: (a) the church, (b) tradition, and (c) the opinions of our superiors or "betters."

The Church

It would obviously take us far afield to examine all the arguments of those who have urged that our fallible individual reason must submit to the infallible authority of the church. But there is a serious difficulty common to all of them, to wit, the great multiplicity of churches, each claiming to be the one instituted by divine authority for the whole of mankind. In ancient days it was possible for men like Dante to view the Roman Catholic Church as the church of all mankind, and to regard all those outside of it as misled by "schismatics" like Mohammed. When, however, Christianity is the religion of a minor part of the human race, divided into so many sects and shades of opinion that it is difficult to say what it is that is common to all of them, and when, moreover, the authority of all supernaturalism is challenged by an increasing number of educated people, surely the old argument from catholicity, that the teachings of the church have been recognized always and everywhere, has lost its force. De Maistre, the most clear-headed of modern apologists, argues that the Pope must be infallible because practical affairs demand some one supreme arbiter. But he dashes his head in vain against the existence of Protestant countries like England, Prussia, and the United States. Any attempt to prove that the authority of the Roman Church is superior to that, for instance, of the Anglican Church must involve reference to the facts of history. These are at best matters of probability; and it is hardly possible to support a claim of infallibility on the basis of historic probabilities.

There is a popular tendency nowadays for those who think militaristic imperialism to be the logical outcome of the Sermon on the Mount, to justify Christianity on the ground that it has produced the most powerful civilization. But apart from the question how far modern western civilization is due to Christianity, the historic fact quite clearly indicates that it is only in the last three centuries that some of the Christian nations have outstripped all the non-Christian ones in material power. In the course of the last thirteen centuries whole peoples in Asia, Europe, and Africa have been converted from Christianity to Islam, while very few have followed the opposite path. This, of course, is not to the rationalist an argument for Mohammedanism. But it certainly disarms the old argument that the spread of Christianity is itself a miracle testifying to the truth of Christian teachings.

The old rationalistic idea of finding the core of truth in that which is common to all the different religions is now generally abandoned. It is inconsistent with the authoritarian claims of every church to be in exclusive possession of the supreme wisdom. But the view of Santayana, that the diverse conflicting religions differ only as do different languages, involves the even more thoroughgoing abandonment by every church of all claim to the possession of distinctive truth. Such thoroughgoing scepticism may fit in with the complacent orthodoxy and extreme worldliness of the Lord Chancellor who told a delegation of dissenters, "Get your damned church established and I will believe in it." It may even fit in with the popular prejudice that every one ought to adhere to the religion of his fathers. But in the end no church can hope to attract thinking people or keep them unless it makes an effort to substantiate some claims to truth in the court of reason.

Tradition

The second form of the appeal to authority against individual reason is the appeal to traditional belief. This may already be seen in Burke's *Reflections on the French Revolution*. In the political life of England and America, Burke has remained the patron saint of all those who would like to see people act on settled beliefs rather than waste time reasoning as to what *is* the right. What is the use of reasoning at all if it leads not to fixed conclusions? Despite the dubious character of his historical contentions and predictions, Burke's great appeal from the reason of individual philosophers to the cumulative wisdom of the ages has become one of the persistent notes of our intellectual life. An extreme and therefore instructive form of it is seen when pious American lawyers like Judge McClain argue against *any* constitutional change on the ground that the constitution embodies the cumulative wisdom of two thousand years of Anglo-Saxon experience—and who will dare to put his private individual reason against that?

It is, of course, easy enough to meet this with the reply that our ancestors were only human and hence subject to error; and that a good deal of what they have left us, e.g., in medicine, is cumulative foolishness. Moreover, the wisdom in our heritage is largely the result of the ideas of individuals who were innovators in their day, so that the elimination of individual reason would mean the death rather than the growth of vital tradition.

But though the extreme form of the argument for tradition can be shown to be untenable, its essence is not thereby eliminated. The essence of the argument for tradition and authority is the actual inability of any single individual thoroughly to apply the process of reasoning and verification to all the propositions that solicit his attention. To doubt *all* things in the Cartesian fashion until they can be demonstrated is impossible practically and theoretically. It is impossible practically, as Descartes himself admitted, because we cannot postpone the business of living until we have reasoned out everything; and it is impossible theoretically because there cannot be any significant doubt except on the basis of some knowledge. To doubt any proposition, to question whether it is true, involves not only a knowledge of its meaning, but also some

knowledge of what conditions are necessary to remove our doubt. Actually all of us do and must begin with a body of traditional or generally accepted beliefs. For it does not and cannot occur to us to doubt any one proposition unless we see some conflict between it and some other of our accepted beliefs. But when such a conflict is perceived within the body of tradition, the appeal to reason has already manifested itself. It may well be contended that many errors are eliminated by the attrition of time, so that any belief long held by a large group of people has a fair presumption in its favour. Unfortunately, however, errors also strike deep roots. Legends grow and abuses become so well established by tradition that it becomes hopeless to try to eradicate them. The history of long-persistent human error certainly looms large in any fair survey of our past. We may argue that what has stood the test of ages of experience cannot be altogether wrong. But it is also true that what has found favour with large multitudes, though sound in the main, can hardly contain a very high accuracy or discrimination between truth and error.

Expert Opinion

Unless we are to fly in the face of all human experience we must admit that some people are, by aptitude, education, or experience, wiser or better informed than others.

It thus seems unpardonable stupidity to rely on our own frail reason, when we can avail ourselves of the judgment of those better qualified. Unfortunately, however, it is not a simple matter to find out who is actually best qualified to decide a given issue. Since the practical disappearance of the doctrine that kings, because of their divine appointment, can do no wrong and are always entitled to unquestioning obedience, there remains only one class of divinely appointed ex-officio superiors, viz., parents. That the conduct of children should conform to the wishes of their parents in matters affecting the life of the family is highly desirable and unavoidable. Parents not only have the power of enforcing obedience, but, all other things being equal, have more experience and therefore generally sounder judgment. Yet nothing but mischief results when respect for parents is conceived as incompatible with questioning the infallibility of their judgment. The necessity of practical obedience does not justify closing the minds of children to free intellectual inquiry when the latter is in the least possible. An emphatically anti-rational phase of parental authority appears when parents assume the right to dictate to colleges what religious, political, or economic doctrines are too dangerous to put before their sons and daughters supposed to be engaged in finding the truth about these subjects. Parents have no right to prevent children from learning more than they know themselves, or to shut the gates of reason.

The difficulty of finding who in any realm *are* our superiors is brought out most clearly by examining that Utopia of shallow "scientific" reformers, viz., government by experts. A priori, Plato's arguments for government by the competent (as against election of officers by lot or ballot) seem unanswerable. But ecclesiastical, as well as political, history shows that government by experts or bureaucracy, from China to Germany and the medieval church, is no more safe against error and abuse than any other human arrangement. Rigorous training and *esprit de corps* may prevent certain abuses. But they breed a narrow class-pride and a subordination of the general interest to the routine of administration, if not the material interests of the governing group. Against Plato's arguments it is well to remember that the method of electing officials by lot

worked so satisfactorily among the Greeks that they regarded it as essential to free democratic government and never gave it up except when compelled by external force such as that of the Macedonians. It was, indeed, great practical wisdom to adapt the duties of office to the competence of possible officials rather than plan for offices that require unattainable ideal governors. The old doctrine that though people cannot govern they can choose the proper governors, finds serious difficulty when we reflect how little opportunity there is to examine with real care the precise qualifications of the candidates or their actual achievements in office.

Nor is the choice of experts by their own associates free from the limitations of human ignorance. The old homely adage: "Get a reputation as an early riser and you can sleep all day," is true in law, medicine, and other professions. Few experts have extensive opportunity of checking up the work of every other expert; and a great deal of professional prestige is based on meretricious grounds. Reputations may be based on previous achievements which happen to have hit a shining mark by an unusually favourable turn of the wind. Even in science the best work is sometimes done by unknown young men who, by the time their work becomes known and appreciated, have passed the zenith of their natural abilities.

In passing judgment on the work of scientific experts we must discriminate between data, or matters of fact, and logic, or methods of reasoning. Confronted by what seems an error of reasoning on the part of a great master such as Laplace or Maxwell, an ordinary man may well doubt whether it is not his own judgment that is at fault. But the masters *have* committed errors which lesser men have been able to discover. Certainly no scientist can openly abandon his reason and assert that a demonstrable error ceases to be one when uttered by a great master.

When we come to matters of fact, the reasonable deference to those in a better position to know is, of course, greater. This is seen best in the case of history. Here absolute proof is unattainable, and in the weighing of probabilities there is involved an element of trust in certain witnesses. If any one refuses to trust Herodotus and doubts the occurrence of the Battle of Thermopylae, we can only bring in certain corroborative witnesses. But the credibility of these witnesses also involves an element of trust. When the amount of corroborative testimony is as great as it is for the existence of George Washington or Napoleon, one who persists in his doubts and attributes the consensus of our witnesses to conspiracy or common delusion is just as unreasonable as one who should refuse to plant potatoes for fear that they might be transformed into tigers and devour his whole family. Yet, though the refusal of all trust in the testimony of others lands us in a state perilously near the insane, the careful or scientific historian is precisely the one who critically scrutinizes the witnesses on whom he must rely. He must closely question what qualified them to report the given facts and what possible motives may have led them to emphasize one phase of what happened rather than another. In history as in a court of law, therefore, the element of trust in the testimony of others has to submit to a process of weighing credibility by reference to the probabilities of human experience. These probabilities are ultimately subject to the laws of mathematics applied to such experience as every individual may in a greater or smaller measure verify for himself. For this reason large experience is a necessary qualification for the historian. But pure reason, in the form of logic, is indispensable not only in determining the weight of the various probabilities, but also in opening the historian's mind to the various possibilities to which habit blinds us.

Similar considerations hold in respect of the experimental scientist. The laboratory worker cannot go very far if he discards all the observations of others. Not only must he practically rely on the authority of the general conclusions and the observation of others, but he cannot begin his work without differentiating and attaching greater authority to some part of the tradition of science than to some other part. Suppose, for instance, that he wishes to verify the fact of the pressure of light, which is generally accepted on the authority of the mathematics of Maxwell, and the experiments of Lebedev, Nichols, and Hull. If he wishes to test this, he will have to rely on the general laws of optics and mechanics assumed in the very use of his instruments of observation. Yet no single proposition of science is authoritative in the sense that we have no right to question it on the basis of our individual reason. Nineteenth-century mathematics and physics have progressed by leaps and bounds through questioning long-established results glorified with the names of Euclid, Newton, and others.

To be sure, the vast majority of people who are untrained can accept the results of science only on authority. But there is obviously an important difference between an establishment that is open and invites every one to come, study its methods, and suggest improvement, and one that regards the questioning of its credentials as due to wickedness of heart, such as Newman attributed to those who questioned the infallibility of the Bible.

Those elementary considerations show how shallow is the reasoning of those who think we can ever dispense with *all* authority and tradition. Yet rationalism obviously remains justified. Reason must determine the proper use of authority. The fact that we cannot possibly doubt *all* things at once does not privilege *any one* proposition to put itself above all question. The position of reason is analogous to that of the executive head of a great enterprise. He cannot possibly examine the work of all his subordinates, yet he can hold every one accountable. The mere fact that every one is likely to be called to account produces a situation markedly different from what would result if some were put above accountability. An even more apt analogy has been drawn between the principle of authority and the credit which makes modern currency systems possible. Rational science treats its credit notes as always redeemable on demand, while non-rational authoritarianism regards the demand for the redemption of its paper as a disloyal lack of faith.

Authority in Indian Philosophy

S. K. SAKSENA

S. K. Saksena *(1903–1974) was a distinguished representative of contemporary Indian philosophy. He held a doctorate from the University of London, and had been chairman of the Department of Philosophy at Hindu College, Delhi University. In addition, he held visiting professorships at universities in the United States and India. Professor Saksena, in the selection that follows, analyzes the concept of authority as one of the valid means to knowledge.*

One of the distinguishing features of Indian philosophy is that almost all the orthodox schools, in addition to other commonly accepted instruments of knowledge like perception and inference, believe in testimony, i.e., verbal or written authority [1] *(śabda)* as one of the valid means of knowledge *(pramāṇas).* It is sometimes said that it is here that Indian philosophy differs most prominently from Western philosophy. Indian philosophy not only recognizes testimony amongst its sources of knowledge, but sometimes even accords it a higher place of importance, inasmuch as by authority alone are certain facts supposed to be known which are not capable of being revealed by other sources of knowledge. Sometimes, again, perception, inference, etc., are in the last analysis made dependent on agreement with authority. Modern Western philosophy, on the contrary, is founded upon a revolt

[1] The terms "testimony" and "authority" have both been used in this paper to stand for the original Sanskrit term *"śabda,"* which means "the word of a reliable person." Actually, in Indian philosophy, there is no difference in the meaning of the two words, but in view of the difference in modern usage, care has been taken to use here one or the other according to what has appeared more appropriate in the given context.

From *Philosophy East and West;* Honolulu, University of Hawaii Press, Vol. I, Number 3, October, 1951, pp. 38–49. Reprinted by permission of the University Press of Hawaii (formerly the University of Hawaii Press).

against authority. Frequently, the history of Western philosophy impresses upon the reader the fact that, while the medieval period is characterized by belief in the authoritative character of revelation, the history of ancient and modern philosophy constitutes eras of reason and free thought. Modern philosophy is supposed to have banished the appeal to testimony (divine or secular) from rational inquiry. Authority may find recognition in religion, but has no place in philosophical and logical investigation, which recognizes only two sources of valid knowledge, i.e., the immediate source of sense perception and the mediate source of inferential reasoning.

In Western philosophy, therefore, there is supposed to be a kind of antithesis between authority and reason. One may choose to put one's faith in authority or elect to be rational, for belief in authority is not conceived to be rational. In Indian philosophy, however, there is no such antithesis. Belief in reason and belief in authority are both regarded as rational and valid, and hence, not only is there no antithesis between reason and authority, but there is also supposed to be none between philosophy and religion. The subject matter of both is investigated and inquired into by the same mental processes of perceptual knowledge, inferential knowledge, and knowledge derived from the statements of the experts.

Often a great distinction between Indian and Western philosophy is made on the basis of their respective differing emphases on intuition and reason. This distinction is in reality not so well founded as it is often assumed to be. In the Western philosophical tradition, there are too enduring anti-intellectual trends, and even systems of thought, and in Indian philosophy, there is too much analytical, dialectical, and non-intuitional disputation to justify such a sweeping generalization. But the recognition in the Indian philosophical tradition in general of au-

thority as a valid means of knowledge and the neglect of the same in modern Western thought is too clear and genuine to be ignored by students of comparative philosophy. While the various schools of Indian philosophy differ with regard to the exact number of the valid sources of knowledge (numbering from one to six in all, i.e., perception, inference, authority, analogy, presumption [or postulation], and non-existence), the recognition of testimony as a valid means of knowledge is one of the greatest common factors in almost all the orthodox schools of Indian philosophy. And thus, while to an outside observer Indian philosophy appears authority-ridden, so much so that reason is made to play a subservient role, Western philosophy is regarded by an Indian as having deprived itself of an important and legitimate channel of knowledge, through which alone are revealed some of our deepest truths.

The purpose of this paper is, therefore, twofold: first, to determine the exact place of testimony in Indian logic and epistemology, and second, to discuss in general the question as to whether testimony should or should not be recognized as a valid means of knowledge.

But first of all, as a preliminary to our inquiry we should do well to note here one or two special features of Indian philosophical thought and literature. The first, for want of a more suitable term, may be called its historical peculiarity, by which I mean that this literature as we know it today has its roots in centuries of oral tradition. All the philosophers historically known to us were preceded by a vast nameless and authorless compendium of knowledge, closely knit and guarded in cryptic lines safe and suitable for oral transmission from generation to generation. The first task, therefore, of early Indian thinkers was to interpret, explain, and co-ordinate this vast body of knowledge inherited and preserved by tradition rather than to function in a vacuum. This often gives to an outside observer the impression that rational thinking in India is authority-ridden or is nothing more than an interpretation of what is believed to have been already accepted as true, and that there is no original and free rational thinking beyond the sphere of the already given. This is not true, however, for, as will be shown later, while Indian philosophy is by historical circumstances interpretative also, in philosophical contribution, it is no less original or daring than any other. It is not wrong, however, for intellect and reasoning to function in relation to a traditional heritage, the beginnings of which, at least in the case of India, are absolutely unknown.

Second, there is a philosophical fact of infinitely greater importance which follows from the above. Psychologically, knowing itself is defined and understood in India as necessarily involving the three steps of *śravaṇa* (hearing), *manana* (examination of what is heard), and *nididhyāsana* (realization or assimilation of what is thus reflected upon). That the first step in knowing is called *hearing* and not *perceiving* shows the verbal character of early knowledge. If an individual or an age has such a thing as tradition preceding it, one learns first by hearing. If, however, one is devoid of all tradition and has nothing to precede one's own thinking, one must look and see for oneself. But as most knowledge is first acquired by hearing from those who know more, verbal testimony is the inevitable relationship between what is learned and the source of learning. But uncritical acceptance of what is given on testimony is never expected, and that is why *manana* or a critical examination by one's own reason of what is thus learned is invariably recommended as a necessary and a prior step to the final realization of truth on the part of a seeker of true knowledge. It is, therefore, this Indian emphasis on testimony

(due to the existence of traditional wisdom) as the inevitable first step of all knowledge that is also sometimes misunderstood in the West as being synonymous with truth itself in Indian philosophy, because the second and the third steps of critical reflection and final assimilation are largely lost sight of.

To begin with, therefore, we should clear up a misunderstanding which exists widely in the West with regard to the logical status of testimony in Indian philosophy. Because orthodox philosophical literature of India accepts the word of the Vedas as true, and because it accepts testimony, i.e., the word of a reliable person, as an independent source of knowledge different from perception and inference, it is popularly believed that Indian philosophy accepts authority as such as true and dispenses with proof. This, however, is not the case, and we often talk at cross purposes because we do not mean the same thing by authority.

Let us see first what is *not* the place of authority in Indian philosophy.

First, testimony is only a *source* of knowledge and is not, as such, to be believed or regarded as true. If it were, there would be no such thing as belief in a particular testimony (say, of the Vedas) and not in authority in general. Those who quote the words of the Vedas as authority do not accept the words of their opponents as authority. Testimony, therefore, like other valid sources of knowledge, is only the *psychological cause* of knowledge and not the *logical ground* of its truth, which is to be determined on other grounds.

Second, testimony does not annul or replace other sources of knowledge, like perception and inference. No one engaged in philosophical activity maintains that it is not necessary to perceive or reason for oneself in view of the fact that some authority is there already to give us all knowledge. This would negate the rational activity itself. Anyone acquainted with philosophical and speculative activity in India would at once see that just the reverse is the case. Actually, the entire literature of the six orthodox systems of Indian philosophy, comprising the Nyāya theory of objects of knowledge and fallacies, the Vaiśeṣika theory of atoms and numbers, the Sāṁkhya theory of the twenty-four principles, the Yoga psychology of the control of the fluctuations of mind, the Mīmāṁsā theory of the self-illuminacy and self-validity of knowledge, and the different varieties of Vedānta, is all spun out of the speculations of the minds of the different thinkers, and hardly anything more than a few suggestions, concepts, and phrases of these later developments can be made to derive from the *śrutis* (the accepted authority of the Vedas).

What, therefore, is the role of testimony in these speculations? And what constitutes the logical ground of its truth? Testimony is *one of the traditionally admitted sources of knowledge*. It is recognized that verbal or written statements of reliable persons reveal as much of the knowledge of facts to another person as his own perceptions and reasoning do. It is through testimony that a child gets his knowledge from parents or teachers, and adults know of the minds of other men and acquire knowledge of the geography and the history of the world they live in. Does Western philosophy deny that the words of another can and do furnish the dark chamber of the mind with knowledge, in addition to the two windows of sensation and reflection with which Locke furnished the mind of man? This would be contrary to our daily experience. How could Western philosophy discuss the views of other philosophers as true or false, if it did not believe them to be the views of those philosophers? Through what source, if not testimony or authority, do we believe in the records of the historians of Buddha and Christ, or even of

our own contemporaries when their words come to us through other reliable persons? While we do not accept what Aristotle said as true, do we not accept what he said as what *he* said? This is itself knowledge by testimony even when we have the words of the philosophers themselves as our guide. This means that both in India and in the West we believe in testimony as a valid means of knowledge. It is impossible to deny that one believes in signs like "danger ahead," "men at work," or "sharp curve," when one is driving on the road.

When Western philosophy denies testimony, it can mean either of two things: first, that testimony as such (no matter whose) is not the same thing as truth, because it can be false, or, second, that testimony is not an independent source of knowledge but is included in perception or inference. The first is a common ground between authority and any other source of knowledge, such as perception or reasoning, for perception or reasoning also (no matter whose) cannot be regarded as necessarily true. Western philosophy does not claim to believe in all perception and inference as true. If we are to disclaim authority on this score, we might as well not believe in perception and reasoning also for the same reason. Just as all cases of perception and reasoning cannot be true, although some will be true, similarly, while all authority may not be true, some will be. But how to determine which testimony is true and which false? The answer is that the truth of testimony is proved or disproved in the same way in which the truth of any other source of knowledge is proved. Perception or inference is proved true or false by correspondence or coherence or pragmatic tests. The same is the case with the words of authority, whether of a doctor or of a religious teacher. Why not, therefore, believe in authority also along with perception and inference as a valid means of knowledge when the validity of knowledge in any case depends upon other conditions? Indian philosophy does no more than recognize that some authority is true exactly as some cases of reasoning and perception are true.

The question may still be asked, "How can we know that a particular authority is right?" We must know it to be right before we can believe in it. Of course, you must know it to be right before you believe it. This is exactly what is meant by the reliability of "word." That one relies upon authority does not mean that one is called upon to believe in unverified or unverifiable authority. No one maintains that testimony or authority is above verifiability, which is again a common ground between authority and all other sources of knowledge. Authority is rejected when it no longer proves to be true. As Vasiṣṭha, one of the most revered and acknowledged authorities in Indian philosophy, says: "A reasonable statement, even of a child, should be accepted, while unreasonable ones are to be discarded like straw, even though they are made by the Creator Himself. A devotee of Reason should value the words even of ordinary persons, provided they advance knowledge and are logical, and should throw away those of sages, if they are not such." [2] Testimony in philosophy is believed to be already tested and verified exactly as in the case of road signs. No one gets out of his car in order to see whether the bridge is really narrow after reading the sign "narrow bridge ahead." You first believe in your road signs (or in the words of the doctor) and that provides an opportunity for the test or verification of the truth or the falsity of the testimony. Verifiability itself would not be possible if one did not admit these signs and words as valid *sources* of

[2] *Yoga Vasiṣṭha*, II. 18. 2, 3. Quoted by B. L. Atreya, *The Philosophy of the Yoga-Vasiṣṭha* (Adyar, Madras: The Theosophical Publishing House, 1936), p. 581.

knowledge to begin with. While verifiability tests the truth or falsity of knowledge, it does not produce it. What is contended here is that knowledge should first be admitted for the time being as true on testimony before you can verify and accept or reject it as true or false. The validity of belief in authority lies solely and exclusively in its reliability. And it is this reliability of the word of another that is recognized as an independent valid source of knowledge in Indian philosophy. This reliability is based entirely upon verifiability. No orthodox Indian system of philosophy says that the words of the Vedas may be false and yet you should believe in them. The orthodox systems only say that they have been established as true and are hence reliable. If you can prove that they are false, they will not be reliable and hence will not constitute authority. But this will be a disbelief only in the Vedas, i.e., the authoritativeness of a particular testimony, but not disbelief in authority itself as a valid means of knowledge.

Now, what is such a valid means of knowledge that finds such an important place in philosophical discussions in orthodox schools of Indian philosophy? Questions relating to the origin and the validity of knowledge are the core of philosophical discussion, and, ever since the time of Locke, epistemology has been a prolegomena to any serious metaphysics in the West. Indian philosophy bestowed serious attention upon the question of the origin and validity of knowledge much earlier than did philosophy in the West. Both in India and in the West, a distinction has always been drawn between opinion and knowledge, between rumor, hearsay, or the personal whims of an individual and what is regarded as psychologically valid sources of knowledge. Obviously every source of knowledge cannot be recognized as acceptable. The question therefore is asked as to what and how many are those independent sources through which alone we rightly acquire our knowledge of fact. *This question of the valid sources of knowledge is not to be confused with the related question of the truth of the knowledge thus acquired.* The question "How do we know what we know?" and the question "How do we know that what we know is true?" are two entirely different questions, and must be constantly kept apart if the issue of authority as a valid means of knowledge is to be clearly apprehended.

In Western philosophy, sense perception and inference have been regarded as the commonly accepted instruments of knowledge since the beginning of the Renaissance, and Western philosophers have almost unanimously accepted the exhaustiveness of these two sources and have seldom questioned their adequacy. Indian philosophers, on the other hand, recognize that our entire body of knowledge at no period of time could be completely accounted for or explained by sense perception and inference alone. We always know much more than can be accounted for by our own perception or inference. In fact, it is incontestable that at any given time verbal testimony accounts for nine-tenths of our stock of knowledge. The question, therefore, is, "Should authority be recognized as an independent and valid means of knowledge?" To answer this question, we must know, first of all, what authority is and what exactly is meant by testimony? Gautama, as one of the greatest expounders of authority, defines authority or "word" in his *Nyāya-sūtra*—the classical text of the traditional "Logical school" of Indian philosophy—as "the assertion of a reliable person," [3] and this definition stands generally accepted and adopted by all other Indian systems. A reliable person is fur-

ther defined in the *Nyāya-bhāṣya* on the same *sūtra* as one "who possesses the direct and right knowledge of things, who is moved by a desire to make known (to others) the thing as he knows it, and who is fully capable of speaking of it." [4] It is interesting to note here that the Nyāya system does not mean by authority divine revelation or scriptural testimony only, but, contrary to the belief of other schools, adds that such a reliable person may be a sage, any ordinary person, or, in fact, anyone. It is further held that it is not at all necessary that such a person should be completely free from moral defects. What is needed is that he should have no motive to give incorrect information—a fact which accords completely with our modern attitude toward authority or the testimony of experts. Testimony is further subdivided into two kinds: *viz.,* testimony based upon things perceived, and testimony based upon things heard and inferred though not seen. A man may, for instance, speak of what he has himself seen, or he may speak of what he has heard or inferred. Either of these could be an equally valid source of knowledge to others.

Now, with regard to authority as a valid source of knowledge, two questions can be raised immediately. First, "Should authority be accepted at all as a valid source of knowledge?" and, second, "If accepted, what should be its place in relation to other means of knowledge?" Is it just like any other source of information giving valid knowledge, or does it enjoy a greater authoritativeness and a place of privilege over perception, inference, and the rest? As to the latter, it is maintained that there is no such thing as a higher and lower validity of knowledge, for the idea of quantity is not admissible in the concept of validity as such. What distinguishes the different means of valid

---

[3] Ganganatha Jha, *Gautama's Nyāyasūtras* (Poona: Oriental Book Agency, 1939), p. 29, I. i. 7.

[4] *Ibid.,* p. 30; *Nyāya-bhāṣya,* I. i. 7.

length,[6] and it is conclusively established that knowledge by verbal or written testimony cannot be included in the category of sensation and ideation, for it does not possess the differentia of perception or inference. Perception requires that the senses be in contact with an external object, and this is not so in the case of testimony, for, when a word is apprehended, it is the inner meaning and not the outer sound which is the object of knowledge. Similarly, it is contended that, for lack of a middle term and "universal concomitance," testimony cannot be classed as the word of a reliable person which is the chief distinguishing mark of authority. That is why this *pramāṇa* is called *śabda*, or "word," to indicate clearly its differentia. Here, knowledge is acquired not through any universal connection but solely because of the reliability of the word of a certain person. Praśastapāda, one of the Vaiśeṣika objectors to testimony, in his *bhāṣya on the Vaiśeṣika-sūtra*, says, "Words and the rest are also included in inference because they have the same principle," i.e., testimony also functions in the same way as inference. When the Vaiśeṣika system maintains that the knowledge derived from "word" is inferential, what is meant is that words also give knowledge by force of a universal connection just as smoke gives rise to the knowledge of fire.[7] Similarly, the Buddhist logician Diṅnāga in his *Pramāṇa-samuccaya* asks, "What is the significance of the credible word? Does it mean that the person who spoke the word is credible or that the fact he averred is credible?"[8] In either case, the means of knowledge is either inference or perception. We have learned from experience that as a general

rule the statements of reliable persons are true, and we apply this experience to the case of the particular statement. To this the Nyāya reply is that the opponent has not understood the meaning of cognition by verbal indication, and that, as explained above, he means by *pramāṇa* quite another thing. When we consider that the Naiyāyika and the Buddhists both hold that the means of knowledge do not carry their own validity with them but that it must be separately established from some other source, it is difficult to understand how the Buddhists can refuse to admit "word" as a separate *pramāṇa*. This confusion is due to the fact that, while the Nyāya is speaking of "word" as a psychological cause of knowledge, the Buddhist is speaking of knowledge as true or false. "Word" (*śabda*) is thus to be regarded as quite an independent source of knowledge, which is not covered under any one of the other sources of knowledge.

The second objection to authority points out the fact that testimony is often false and contradictory. It therefore cannot be accepted as valid. This argument of the opponents of authority is regarded as based on pure prejudice, for it is obvious that this defect is no peculiarity of authority alone, but is common to perception, inference, and any other source of knowledge which may be regarded as valid. Our perceptions, inferences, and analogies can all be wrong and contradictory and do often turn out to be so when they stand in need of correction, but no one refuses to recognize them on that account as valid means of knowledge. Neither perception, nor inference, nor any other source of knowledge is valid as such, for their validity is to be established independently of their origin, unless, of course, like the *Mīmāṁsakas*, we hold that all cognitions produced from whatever source are valid as such. We are here again confusing sources of knowledge and criteria of their truth or falsity. What is con-

---

[6] Jha, *op. cit.*, pp. 177–184; *Nyāya-sūtra*, II. i. 50–57.

[7] Dr. B. Faddegon, *The Vaiçeṣika-system* (Amsterdam: Johannes Muller, 1918). See pp. 465–474.

[8] S. C. Vidyabhusana, *A History of Indian Logic* (Calcutta: Calcutta University, 1921), p. 288.

knowledge like perception, inference, and authority from one another is not their higher or lower validity but the nature and kind of facts and objects which they reveal. Perceptual knowledge, e.g., reveals the externally and sensuously perceptible world; inference employs a non-sensuous process and applies to the abstract and the remote, and authority helps us to cognize what cannot be known by either of the other sources of knowledge. Any one of these could be equally valid or invalid in its own sphere, and there is no point in saying that one is more valid than the other. That testimony is supposed to reveal knowledge of facts like *dharma, mokṣa,* etc., which are in themselves considered to be of more importance to man than knowledge of facts about the sensible world, or that the scriptures are supposed to contain knowledge which is considered to have been acquired by minds higher than our own, is, however, quite another matter. Here, one may ask, is it not a fact that in Indian philosophy a man's reasoning and conclusions are *ipso facto* invalidated if they are not in agreement with the authority of the Veda and the Upaniṣads—called *śruti?* Does this not undermine the independent validity of other sources of knowledge like inference, etc., and lead to their subordination to authority? No. As Śaṅkara himself says, "Scriptures cannot be acknowledged to refute that which is settled by other means of right knowledge." [5] Besides, the agreement sought here is not between inference

and authority, i.e., between one m
knowledge and another, but betw
reasoning of a higher and a lowe
Even at the level of perception or
ing, we always measure and see
ment between our reasoning and
those better trained and skilled t
selves. We always compare lowei
ing with higher reasoning. We do
correspondence between our i
and those of children, imbec
idiots. Amongst reasonable peo
what is reasonable to one man
to another, and we seek to tall
tional conclusion with those i
to be the most perfect in the fie
is thus no subordination of
authority—but only of lower
higher reason, and it is diffic
how one can object to this disti
practice in general, even thoug
not agree as to the particular
persons who possess a more
perfect mind. Those in India
who deny the authority of th
fuse to believe them as the kr
minds higher than their own.
Cārvākas called the Vedas th
of insane minds. That, how
the same as disbelief in the
reliable person.

As to the recognition of te
means of valid knowledge,
has even seemed to have aris
That we actually know and l
mony is a matter of indubita
thus it is as valid as any
such as perception. The o
raised in India against testim
on the score of its independe
knowledge by testimony is
pendent source of knowlec
variety of perception or inf
is no need, therefore, for tl
of authority as a separate so
edge, and this is the secor
Western philosophy may
thority. This argument i

5 F. Max Müller, tr., *Vedānta-sūtras with Śaṅkara's Commentary*, Part I ("The Sacred Books of the East," Vol. XXXIV; Oxford: Clarendon Press, 1890), p. 318; II. i. 13. Or, "Śruti, if in conflict with other means of right knowledge, has to be bent so as to accord with the latter" (*Ibid.*, p. 229); or again, "Moreover, the scriptural passage, 'He is to be heard, to be thought,' enjoins thought in addition to hearing, and thereby shows that Reasoning also is to be resorted to with regard to Brahman" (*Ibid.*, p. 300).

tended is not that the word of a reliable person is true as such, but that we rightly regard it as such until the contrary is established quite in the same manner as we do our perceptions. Moreover, this objection of the opponent is not against all testimony, but only against a particular testimony, a fact to which all the orthodox Indian philosophers would readily agree. The conclusion is unavoidable, therefore, that testimony is as much a valid source of knowledge as perception or inference. There is thus no reason for not including authority among the valid sources of knowledge.

Granting testimony as an independent source of knowledge, the question may now be asked as to wherein the validity of testimony actually lies. The answer is that it lies in the trustworthiness of the speaker and that this trustworthiness is always as verifiable as that of any other means of knowledge, like the signs on the road or the words of a doctor. The *Nyāya-sūtra* continues: "The Trustworthiness of the Word (of the Veda) is based upon the trustworthiness of the reliable (veracious) expositor, just like the trustworthiness of Incantations and of Medical Scriptures." [9] The *Bhāṣya* again raises the question "In what does the trustworthiness of the Medical Scriptures consist?" and the answer given is that it consists in verification. "It consists in the fact that, when the Medical Scriptures declare that 'by doing this and this one obtains what he desires, and by avoiding this and this he escapes from what is undesirable'—and a person acts accordingly—*the result turns out to be exactly as asserted;* and this shows that the said Scriptures are *true,* not *wrong* in what they assert." [10] What is important for us, however, is to note that it is on the basis of verifiability alone that the Vedas

are believed to be reliable and hence authoritative by the orthodox systems. It is quite another matter, if an opponent regards the same as unreliable as a result of unverifiability, for the ground of belief or disbelief in both cases would be the same.

It is necessary to close the discussion with a final reiteration. In Indian philosophical discussion, the term *pramāṇa* is used in the sense of a psychological cause of knowledge, but it is a logical concept also inasmuch as it limits the validity of such causes to only a few of the many possible causes of knowledge; for instance, rumor or hearsay is not regarded as a valid source of knowledge. Translated into English, *pramāṇa* is rendered as "valid means of knowledge," the term *valid* applying to the *means* and not to the *knowledge.* The *pramāṇas* are not the means of *valid knowledge,* but only *valid means* of knowledge, the validity of which is always to be determined by other means. Thus, when the orthodox Indian systems believe in authority as a valid means of knowledge, they do not imply that all testimony is valid, but only that authority is one of the valid means of knowing. When a Westerner opposes authority, he imposes upon authority a validity which is not intended in the Indian recognition of authority as a *pramāṇa,* or he is imposing extra conditions upon authority's being accepted as valid from which he frees perception and inference. Not to include testimony in the sense of the word of a reliable person in one's list of valid sources of knowledge is to reject *prima facie* a vast body of knowledge from the field of philosophical inquiry, and that is hardly justifiable. For such facts as are necessarily revealed by authority alone cannot openly and without prejudice be investigated unless we accept them as the valid data of our knowledge. To refuse to admit testimony as a means of knowledge because not all testimony is true is to throw away the baby with the bath. It is the

---

[9] Jha, *op. cit.,* p. 191; *Nyāya-sūtra,* II. i. 69.
[10] *Ibid.,* p. 192; *Nyāya-bhāṣya,* II. i. 69. The italics are mine.

sheer prejudice of centuries that has un-reasonably made Western philosophy blindly ignore the value of knowledge by testimony in philosophy, while retaining it in all other fields. To end with another quotation from the *Bhāṣya:* "In ordinary worldly matters also, a large amount of business is carried on on the basis of the assertions of veracious persons; and here also the trustworthiness of the ordinary veracious expositor is based upon the same three conditions—he has full knowledge of what he is saying, he has sympathy for others (who listen to him), and he has the desire to expound things as they really exist—and on the basis of these the assertion of the veracious expositor is regarded as trustworthy." [11]

[11] *Ibid.,* p. 193; *Nyāya-bhāṣya,* II. i. 69.

Faith

Buddist Texts on Faith

Buddhism has traditionally placed great stress on faith as a way, means, or method of arriving at truth and knowledge. The selections below serve to underscore this commitment by offering us a definition of faith, several examples of the object of faith, concluding with a discussion between a Greek King and a Buddhist monk on the mark of faith compared to the other four virtues of Buddhism.

THE DEFINITION OF FAITH [1]

The five faculties are Faith, Vigour, Mindfulness, Concentration and Wisdom. Here what is *Faith?* By this faith one has faith in four dharmas. Which four? He accepts the right view which assumes a transmigration in the world of birth-and-death; he puts his trust in the ripening of karma, and knows that he will experience the fruit of any karma that he may have done; even to save his life he does not do any evil deed. He has faith in the mode of life of a Bodhisattva, and, having taken up this discipline, he does not long for any other vehicle. He believes when he hears all the doctrines which are characterized by the true, clear and profound knowledge of conditioned co-production, by such

terms as lack of self, absence of a being, absence of a soul, absence of a person, and by emptiness, the signless and the wishless. He follows none of the false doctrines, and believes in all the qualities (dharmas) of a Buddha, his powers, grounds of self-confidence and all the rest; and when in his faith he has left behind all doubts, he brings about in himself those qualities of a Buddha. This is known as the virtue of faith. His *vigour* consists in his bringing about (in himself) the dharmas in which he has faith. His *mindfulness* consists in his preventing the qualities which he brings about by vigour from being destroyed by forgetfulness. His *concentration* consists in his fixing his one-pointed attention on these very same qualities. With the faculty of *wisdom* he contemplates

[1] *Sikshāsamuccaya, 316 (Akshayamati Sūtra)*

The first selection is from *Buddhist Texts Through the Ages*, Edward Conze et al., eds.; New York, Harper Torchbooks, Harper & Row, Publishers, 1964. "The Objects of Faith" and "The Five Cardinal Virtues" are from *Buddhist Scriptures*, Edward Conze, ed. (copyright © Edward Conze, 1959); Baltimore, Penguin Books, 1959. Reprinted by permission of Harper and Row, and by permission of Penguin Books, Ltd.

those dharmas on which he has fixed his one-pointed attention, and penetrates to their reality. The cognition of those dharmas which arises in himself and which has no outside condition is called the virtue of wisdom. Thus these five virtues, together, are sufficient to bring forth all the qualities of a Buddha.

THE OBJECTS OF FAITH

The Triple Refuge

To the Buddha for refuge I go; to the Dharma for refuge I go; to the Samgha for refuge I go.

For the second time to the Buddha for refuge I go; for the second time to the Dharma for refuge I go; for the second time to the Samgha for refuge I go.

For the third time to the Buddha for refuge I go; for the third time to the Dharma for refuge I go; for the third time to the Samgha for refuge I go.

The Buddha

This Lord is truly the Arhat, fully enlightened, perfect in his knowledge and conduct, well-gone, world-knower, unsurpassed, leader of men to be tamed, teacher of gods and men, the Buddha, the Lord.

What had to be fully known, that I
    have fully known;
What had to be developed, that I
    have developed;
What was to be forsaken, that I have
    forsaken.
Therefore, O Brahmin, I am the
    Buddha.

The Dharma

Well taught has the Lord the Dharma,

it is verifiable, not a matter of time, inviting all to come and see, leading to Nirvana, to be known by the wise, each one for himself.

Enough, Vakkali, what is there to be seen in this putrid body of mine? Who sees Dharma, he sees me. Who sees me, he sees Dharma. Because it is by seeing Dharma that he sees me, it is by seeing me that he sees Dharma.

The Dharma, incomparably pro-
    found and exquisite,
Is rarely met with, even in hundreds
    of thousands of million of kalpas.
We are now permitted to see it, to
    listen to it, to accept and to hold
    it.
May we truly understand the mean-
    ing of the Tathagata's words!

The Samgha

Well-behaved is the Community of the Lord's disciples, straight in their behaviour, upright and correct. The four pairs of men, the eight persons—these are the Community of the Lord's disciples. Worthy they are of offerings, worthy of hospitality, worthy of gifts, worthy of respectful salutation, they, the world's peerless field of merit.

And for a disciple, rightly delivered, whose thought is calm, there is nothing to be added to what has been done, and naught more remains for him to do. Just as a rock of one solid mass remains unshaken by the wind, even so, neither forms, nor sounds, nor smells, nor tastes, nor contacts of any kind, neither desired nor undesired dharmas, can agitate such a one. Steadfast is his thought, gained is deliverance.

Who understand the skandhas five,
In the good doctrine live their life,
Worthy of praises, righteous men,
These are the Buddha's genuine sons.

THE FIVE CARDINAL VIRTUES

The king said: "Is it through wise attention that people become exempt from further rebirth?"—"Yes, that is due to wise attention, and also to wisdom, and the other wholesome dharmas."—"But is not wise attention the same as wisdom?"—"No, your majesty! Attention is one thing, and wisdom another. Sheep and goats, oxen and buffaloes, camels and asses have attention, but wisdom they have not."—"Well put, Nagasena!"

The king said: "What is the mark of attention, and what is the mark of wisdom?"—"Consideration is the mark of attention, cutting off that of wisdom."—"How is that? Give me a simile!"—"You know barley-reapers, I suppose?"—"Yes, I do."—"How then do they reap the barley?"—"With the left hand they seize a bunch of barley, in the right hand they hold a sickle, and they cut the barley off with that sickle."—"Just so, your majesty, the Yogin seizes his mental processes with his attention, and by his wisdom he cuts off the defilements."—"Well put, Venerable Nagasena!"

The king said: "When you just spoke of 'the other wholesome dharmas,' which ones did you mean?"—"I meant morality, faith, vigour, mindfulness, and concentration."—"And what is the mark of morality?"—"Morality has the mark of providing a basis for all wholesome dharmas, whatever they may be. When based on morality, all the wholesome dharmas will not dwindle away."—"Give me an illustration!"—"As all plants and animals which increase, grow, and prosper, do so with the earth as their support, with the earth as their basis, just so the Yogin, with morality as his support, with morality as his basis, develops the five cardinal virtues, i.e., the cardinal virtues of faith, vigour, mindfulness, concentration, and wisdom."

"Give me a further illustration!"

"As the builder of a city when con-structing a town first of all clears the site, removes all stumps and thorns, and levels it; and only after that he lays out and marks off the roads and cross-roads, and so builds the city. Even so the Yogin develops the five cardinal virtues with morality as his support, with morality as his basis."

The king said: "What is the mark of *faith?*"—"Faith makes serene, and it leaps forward."—"And how does faith make serene?"—"When faith arises it arrests the [five] Hindrances, and the heart becomes free from them, clear, serene and undisturbed."—"Give me an illustration!"—"A universal monarch might on his way, together with his fourfold army, cross over a small stream. Stirred up by the elephants and horses, by the chariots and infantry, the water would become disturbed, agitated and muddy. Having crossed over, the universal monarch would order his men to bring some water for him to drink. But the king would possess a miraculous water-clearing gem, and his men, in obedience to his command, would throw it into the stream. Then at once all fragments of vegetation would float away, the mud would settle at the bottom, the stream would become clear, serene and undisturbed, and fit to be drunk by the universal monarch. Here the stream corresponds to the heart, the monarch's men to the Yogin, the fragments of vegetation and the mud to the defilements, and the miraculous water-clearing gem to faith."

"And how does faith leap forward?"—"When the Yogin sees that the hearts of others have been set free, he leaps forward, by way of aspiration, to the various Fruits of a holy life, and he makes efforts to attain the yet unattained, to find the yet unfound, to realize the yet unrealized."—"Give me an illustration!"—"Suppose that a great cloud were to burst over a hill-slope. The water then would flow down the slope, would first fill all the hill's clefts, fissures, and gullies, and would then run into the river below, making its banks overflow on both sides. Now suppose further that a great crowd of people had come along, and unable to size up either the width or the depth of the river, should stand frightened and hesitating on the bank. But then some man would come along, who, conscious of his own strength and power, would firmly tie on his loincloth and jump across the river. And the great crowd of people, seeing him on the other side, would cross likewise. Even so the Yogin, when he has seen that the hearts of others have been set free, leaps forward, by aspiration, to the various Fruits of the holy life, and he makes efforts to attain the yet unattained, to find the yet unfound, to realize the yet unrealized. And this is what the Lord has said in the *Samyutta Nikaya*:

'By faith the flood is crossed,
By wakefulness the sea;
By vigour ill is passed;
By wisdom cleansed is he.' "

"Well put, Nagasena!" . . .

What Faith Is Not

PAUL TILLICH

Paul Tillich (1886–1965) was born in Germany and emigrated to the United States in 1933. In Germany Tillich had been professor of theology at Marburg and a professor of philosophy at Frankfurt before conflict with the Nazis forced his dismissal. In the United States he taught at Union Theological Seminary for many years and was widely hailed as the new leader of the theological existentialists in America. In the selection that follows, Tillich concentrates his attention on the three distortions of faith, explaining precisely what faith is not. To all these wrong definitions Tillich will later juxtapose his own famous definition of "faith" as "ultimate concern."

THE INTELLECTUALISTIC DISTORTION OF THE MEANING OF FAITH

Our positive description of what faith is implies the rejection of interpretations that dangerously distort the meaning of faith. It is necessary to make these implicit rejections explicit, because the distortions exercise a tremendous power over popular thinking and have been largely responsible for alienating many from religion since

"What Faith Is Not" from *Dynamics of Faith* by Paul Tillich. World Perspectives Series, Volume 10, Ruth Nanda Anshen, ed. Copyright © 1957 by Paul Tillich. Reprinted by permission of Harper & Row Publishers, Inc.

the beginning of the scientific age. It is not only the popular mind which distorts the meaning of faith. Behind it lie philosophical and theological thoughts which in a more refined way also miss the meaning of faith.

The different distorted interpretations of the meaning of faith can be traced to one source. Faith as being ultimately concerned is a centered act of the whole personality. If one of the functions which constitute the totality of the personality is partly or completely identified with faith, the meaning of faith is distorted. Such interpretations are not altogether wrong because every function of the human mind participates in the act of faith. But the element of truth in them is embedded in a whole of error.

The most ordinary misinterpretation of faith is to consider it an act of knowledge that has a low degree of evidence. Something more or less probable or improbable is affirmed in spite of the insufficiency of its theoretical substantiation. This situation is very usual in daily life. If this is meant, one is speaking of *belief* rather than of faith. One believes that one's information is correct. One believes that records of past events are useful for the reconstruction of facts. One believes that a scientific theory is adequate for the understanding of a series of facts. One believes that a person will act in a specific way or that a political situation will change in a certain direction. In all these cases the belief is based on evidence sufficient to make the event probable. Sometimes, however, one believes something which has low probability or is strictly improbable, though not impossible. The causes for all these theoretical and practical beliefs are rather varied. Some things are believed because we have good though not complete evidence about them; many more things are believed because they are stated by good authorities. This is the case whenever we accept the evidence which

others accepted as sufficient for belief, even if we cannot approach the evidence directly (for example, all events of the past). Here a new element comes into the picture, namely, the trust in the authority which makes a statement probable for us. Without such trust we could not believe anything except the objects of our immediate experience. The consequence would be that our world would be infinitely smaller than it actually is. It is rational to trust in authorities which enlarge our consciousness without forcing us into submission. If we use the word "faith" for this kind of trust we can say that most of our knowledge is based on faith. But it is not appropriate to do so. We believe the authorities, we trust their judgment, though never unconditionally, but we do not have faith in them. Faith is more than trust in authorities, although trust is an element of faith. This distinction is important in view of the fact that some earlier theologians tried to prove the unconditional authority of the Biblical writers by showing their trustworthiness as witnesses. The Christian may believe the Biblical writers, but not unconditionally. He does not have faith in them. He should not even have faith in the Bible. For faith is more than trust in even the most sacred authority. It is participation in the subject of one's ultimate concern with one's whole being. Therefore, the term "faith" should not be used in connection with theoretical knowledge, whether it is a knowledge on the basis of immediate, prescientific or scientific evidence, or whether it is on the basis of trust in authorities who themselves are dependent on direct or indirect evidence.

The terminological inquiry has led into the material problem itself. Faith does not affirm or deny what belongs to the prescientific or scientific knowledge of our world, whether we know it by direct experience or through the experience of others. The knowledge of our world (including ourselves as a part of the world) is a matter of inquiry by ourselves or by those in whom we trust. It is not a matter of faith. The dimension of faith is not the dimension of science, history or psychology. The acceptance of a probable hypothesis in these realms is not faith, but preliminary belief, to be tested by scholarly methods and to be changed by every new discovery. Almost all the struggles between faith and knowledge are rooted in the wrong understanding of faith as a type of knowledge which has a low degree of evidence but is supported by religious authority. It is, however, not only confusion of faith with knowledge that is responsible for the world historical conflicts between them; it is also the fact that matters of faith in the sense of ultimate concern lie hidden behind an assumedly scientific method. Whenever this happens, faith stands against faith and not against knowledge.

The difference between faith and knowledge is also visible in the kind of certitude each gives. There are two types of knowledge which are based on complete evidence and give complete certitude. The one is the immediate evidence of sense perception. He who sees a green color sees a green color and is certain about it. He cannot be certain whether the thing which seems to him green is really green. He may be under a deception. But he cannot doubt that he sees green. The other complete evidence is that of the logical and mathematical rules which are presupposed even if their formulation admits different and sometimes conflicting methods. One cannot discuss logic without presupposing those implicit rules which make the discussion meaningful. Here we have absolute certitude; but we have no reality, just as in the case of mere sense perception. Nevertheless, this certitude is not without value. No truth is possible without the material given by sense perception and without the form given by the logical and mathematical rules which express the structure in which all reality stands. One of the worst errors of theology and popular religion is to make statements which intentionally or unintentionally contradict the structure of reality. Such an attitude is an expression not of faith but of the confusion of faith with belief.

Knowledge of reality has never the certitude of complete evidence. The process of knowing is infinite. It never comes to an end except in a state of knowledge of the whole. But such knowledge transcends infinitely every finite mind and can be ascribed only to God. Every knowledge of reality by the human mind has the character of higher or lower probability. The certitude about a physical law, a historical fact, or a psychological structure can be so high that, for all practical purposes, it is certain. But theoretically the incomplete certitude of belief remains and can be undercut at any moment by criticism and new experience. The certitude of faith has not this character. Neither has it the character of formal evidence. The certitude of faith is "existential," meaning that the whole existence of man is involved. It has, as we indicated before, two elements: the one, which is not a risk but a certainty about one's own being, namely, on being related to something ultimate or unconditional; the other, which is a risk and involves doubt and courage, namely, the surrender to a concern which is not really ultimate and may be destructive if taken as ultimate. This is not a theoretical problem of the kind of higher or lower evidence, of probability or improbability, but it is an existential problem of "to be or not to be." It belongs to a dimension other than any theoretical judgment. Faith is not belief and it is not knowledge with a low degree of probability. Its certitude is not the uncertain certitude of a theoretical judgment.

THE VOLUNTARISTIC DISTORTION OF THE MEANING OF FAITH

One can divide this form of the distorted interpretation of faith into a Catholic and a Protestant type. The Catholic type has a great tradition in the Roman Church. It goes back to Thomas Aquinas, who emphasized that the lack of evidence which faith has must be complemented by an act of will. This, first of all, presupposes that faith is understood as an act of knowledge with a limited evidence and that the lack of evidence is made up by an act of will. We have seen that this way of understanding faith does not do justice to the existential character of faith. Our criticism of the intellectualistic distortion of the meaning of faith hits basically also the voluntaristic distortion of the meaning of faith. The former is the basis of the latter. Without a theoretically formulated content the "will to believe" would be empty. But the content which is meant in the will to believe is given to the will by the intellect. For instance, someone has doubts about the so-called "immortality of the soul." He realizes that this assertion that the soul continues to live after the death of the body cannot be proved either by evidence or by trustworthy authority. It is a questionable proposition of theoretical character. But there are motives driving people to this assertion. They decide to believe, and make up in this way for the lack of evidence. If this belief is called "faith," it is a misnomer, even if much evidence were collected for the belief in a continuation of life after death. In classical Roman Catholic theology the "will to believe" is not an act which originates in man's striving, but it is given by grace to him whose will is moved by God to accept the truth of what the Church teaches. Even so, it is not the intellect which is determined by its content to believe, but it is the will which performs what the intellect alone cannot do. This kind of interpretation agrees with the authoritarian attitude of the Roman Church. For it is the authority of the Church which gives the contents, to be affirmed by the intellect under the impact of the will. If the idea of grace mediated by the Church and motivating the will is rejected, as in pragmatism, the will to believe becomes willfulness. It becomes an arbitrary decision which may be supported by some insufficient arguments but which could have gone in other directions with equal justification. Such belief as the basis of the will to believe is certainly not faith.

The Protestant form of the will to believe is connected with the moral interpretation of religion by Protestants. One demands "obedience of faith," following a Paulinian phrase. The term can mean two different things. It can mean the element of commitment which is implied in the state of ultimate concern. If this is meant, one simply says that in the state of ultimate concern all mental functions participate—which certainly is true. Or the term "obedience of faith" can mean subjection to the command to believe as it is given in prophetic and apostolic preaching. Certainly, if a prophetic word is accepted as prophetic, i.e., as coming from God, obedience of faith does not mean anything other than accepting a message as coming from God. But if there is doubt whether a "word" is prophetic, the term "obedience of faith" loses its meaning. It becomes an arbitrary "will to believe." Yet one may describe the situation in a more refined way and point to the fact that we are often grasped by something, e.g., Biblical passages, as expressions of the objectively ultimate concern, but we hesitate to accept them as our subjective ultimate concern for escapist reasons. In such cases, one says, the appeal to the will is justified and does not ask for a willful decision. This is true; but such an act of will does not produce faith—faith as ultimate concern is already given. The demand to be obedient is the demand to be what one already is, namely, committed to the ultimate concern from which one tries to escape. Only if this is the situation can obedience of faith be demanded; but then faith precedes the obedience and is not the product of it. No command to believe and no will to believe can create faith.

This is important for religious education, counseling and preaching. One should never convey the impression to those whom one wants to impress, that faith is a demand made upon them, the rejection of which is lack of good will. Finite man cannot produce infinite concern. Our oscillating will cannot produce the certainty which belongs to faith. This is in strict analogy to what we said about the impossibility of reaching the truth of faith by arguments and authorities, which in the best case give finite knowledge of a more or less probable character. Neither arguments for belief nor the will to believe can create faith.

THE EMOTIONALISTIC DISTORTION OF THE MEANING OF FAITH

The difficulty of understanding faith either as a matter of the intellect or as a matter of will, or of both in mutual support, has led to the interpretation of faith as emotion. This solution was, and partly is, supported from both the religious and the secular side. For the defenders of religion it was a retreat to a seemingly safe position after the battle about faith as a matter of knowledge or will had been lost. The father of all modern Protestant theology, Schleiermacher, has described religion as the feeling of unconditional dependence. Of course, feeling so defined does not mean in religion what it means in

popular psychology. It is not vague and changing, but has a definite content: unconditional dependence, a phrase related to what we have called ultimate concern. Nevertheless, the word "feeling" has induced many people to believe that faith is a matter of merely subjective emotions, without a content to be known and a demand to be obeyed.

This interpretation of faith was readily accepted by representatives of science and ethics, because they took it as the best way to get rid of interference from the side of religion in the processes of scientific research and technical organization. If religion is mere feeling it is innocuous. The old conflicts between religion and culture are finished. Culture goes its way, directed by scientific knowledge, and religion is the private affair of every individual and a mere mirror of his emotional life. No claims for truth can be made by it. No competition with science, history, psychology, politics is possible. Religion, put safely into the corner of subjective feelings, has lost its danger for man's cultural activities.

Neither of the two sides, the religious and the cultural, could keep this well-defined covenant of peace. Faith as the state of ultimate concern claims the whole man and cannot be restricted to the subjectivity of mere feeling. It claims truth for its concern and commitment to it. It does not accept the situation "in the corner" of mere feeling. If the whole man is grasped, all his functions are grasped. If this claim of religion is denied, religion itself is denied. It was not only religion which could not accept the restriction of faith to feeling. It was also not accepted by those who were especially interested in pushing religion into the emotional corner. Scientists, artists, moralists showed clearly that they also were ultimately concerned. Their concern expressed itself even in those creations in which they wanted most radically to deny religion. A keen analysis of most philosophical, scientific and ethical systems shows how much ultimate concern is present in them, even if they are leading in the fight against what they call religion.

This shows the limits of the emotionalist definition of faith. Certainly faith as an act of the whole personality has strong emotional elements within it. Emotion always expresses the involvement of the whole personality in an act of life or spirit. But emotion is not the source of faith. Faith is definite in its direction and concrete in its content. Therefore, it claims truth and commitment. It is directed toward the unconditional, and appears in a concrete reality that demands and justifies such commitment.

Part **3**

PROBLEMS OF THEOLOGY

INTRODUCTION

No doubt every age and every culture has had its religious skeptics. There have always been those to whom the claims of institutional religion have been morally oppressive or intellectually incredible. And no doubt in many of those ages there were men who believed theirs to be history's darkest period for religious faith. Now, whether the decline of faith marks the decline of a civilization or whether it signals a dynamic cultural vitality made possible by escape from old superstitions is an interesting question. In either event, the answer to that question will reflect your view as to whether religion is essentially a conservative or liberating social force.

It is also relevant to observe that religion and religious belief have been notoriously resilient. Although the discovery of the natural origin of lightning may have done damage to the priestly description of Zeus, it surely is not the case that the Greek religious mind was stifled forever. Quite apart from the question of the truth of religious claims, it is this very resiliency which suggests to some that even if there are no gods, men would invent them. On the other hand, it may be that religious behavior has only been an answer to a temporary need in the evolution of man. On this view, it may resemble the appendix.

That such suggestions make sense indicates that ours too is an age of religious questioning. It is not only in American undergraduate colleges that thoughtful people ask whether they should be religious. The young Egyptian, with a rifle to defend the Suez and a shovel to help widen it, wonders whether the *Koran* says anything relevant to his condition. That he hears the scripture broadcast daily on the radio indicates that someone finds it important, but whether *he* can find it important may well be a puzzle. The young Tibetan is told by some that Gautama the Buddha discovered the Enlightenment that is the salvation of all mankind. He is told by others that the so-called Buddha was no more than the instrument of a dominant economic group, foisting off on the oppressed a demonic theory designed to perpetuate that economic and social injustice which is all too apparent. It can hardly be doubted that he wonders about the claims of the religious. And what has Pasteur done to the goddess who cures smallpox? In short, our age—whether in West or East—finds it possible to ask: "Should I be religious?"

This section of the book takes up that question, at least from a philosophic perspective. At the outset, however, it is important to note that many, and perhaps most, religious people hold that a philosophic analysis of religion is trivial, a waste of time. In this they may be right. What has speculative inquiry to do with matters of the heart? No sensible man speaks of metaphysics to his betrothed. No sane, though drowning, man speaks of ontology to the lifeguard. When the Lord speaks who can but prophesy? Why then chop with logic the assurances of a divine reward?

To such questions, of course, the philosopher believes he has a ready answer (whether or not that answer is relevant to the question asked is another issue worth pondering). If, the philosopher says, the religious man is claiming that he knows something that is true, that he is wrestling with something that is real, that he has met something that is good, then his claim must face philosophic examination. What evidence can be put forth that religious belief is true? How can we be certain that the object of that belief is a reality and not an illusion? What proof is there that divine power has anything at all to do with the management of our daily lives? Religion must meet and pass this examination if it is to be philosophically respectable. (Again, it must be noted that many religious men don't care whether or not they are philosophically respectable. If religious behavior is like smiling or sneezing—that is, if it is noncognitive—then there are no philosophic issues involved. But where religion involves cognitive elements, the philosopher is very much interested.)

THE EXISTENCE OF THE GODS

To many men the most perplexing religious question is whether or not there are gods. It is not hard to see that there is an intimate connection between the answer to this question and the answer to the question, Should I be religious? Yet interestingly enough, many men have never questioned the existence of gods. Such a question never occurs. To ask whether gods exist is as absurd as asking whether matter exists. Of course it does; one can see it everywhere. Religious scriptures largely represent this attitude. Although they may be filled with proclamations of what the gods are doing, and admonitions concerning what men should do in view of the presence of divine power, rarely do they present clear and well-organized arguments defending the existence of gods. Nor is it quite correct to say that this is an intellectual assumption on the part of such people, unless one is also willing to say that the existence of matter is an intellectual assumption on the part of the chemist. It is more a *necessary* starting point, *self-evident* to all men who have the power to see.

Nevertheless, many men, many of them deeply religious, have felt it necessary to present a case for the existence of gods. Though to some of their colleagues the effort itself has been hardly short of blasphemous, and to hardened skeptics not less than futile, the arguments have been seen by their supporters as a necessary part of a missionary program and an essential ingredient of intellectual honesty. Nor, they have argued, does this put man ahead of the gods, but it is the inevitable consequence of the divine gift of reason.

On one level at least, to argue for the existence of gods is not much different from arguing for other existents, for example neutrinos, "missing links," or distantly receding galaxies. The conclusion of the argument is essentially a claim, "X exists," and as such is worth no more than you can put up for it. It is this fact that leads some to contend that an argument for the existence of gods makes the gods dependent on men. The answer to this contention is that it is a confusion of logical and ontological priority. The fact that Crusoe's knowledge of Friday's existence depends upon Friday's footprints in the sand does not mean that Friday's existence itself depends on those footprints. Those footprints depend on Friday's existence, although to be sure we come to a knowledge of his existence the other way around. Nonetheless, in spite of this confusion the argument seems credible to some.

If a claim is worth no more than what you can put up for it, it might still be the case that many different currencies are acceptable. For example, one might argue that the gods exist because informed authorities say they do. The difficulty in this approach is not hard to locate: How shall we decide who, among the many claimants, are the "informed authorities"? Has the argument really proved anything, or have we only pushed the issue back to another level? On the other hand, it may well be the case that some people are spiritually sensitive to a degree that we should respect. We are sometimes willing to accept the appeal to authority in matters of aesthetic judgment; perhaps we should accept it here also. Further, it may be that the proof of divine existence appeared some time in the past and only to a select group of people, perhaps as an epiphany. Our problem of proof here might not be much different from that faced by historians inquiring into the historicity of certain past events. Here again, the problem of proof forces us to inquire into the reliability of the witnesses.

A more promising approach may be found in the appeal to present experience. Does nature demonstrate law-like behavior? If so, is it possible for unintelligent nature to exhibit such behavior without external guidance? If not, then surely there must exist a cosmic intelligence. The argument is a valid one, and to many it is conclusive. To others, although validly arranged, the argument depends on false premises. Natural selection, or some more intelligent process, may well account for the seemingly law-like behavior; natural disaster may well suggest that nature's behavior shows no intelligence or order at all. Nonetheless, this has been the most perennially appealing of all the empirical arguments.

One might argue, also on empirical grounds, that every event stands as the effect of a prior cause. Experience reveals a cause-effect series. But surely it cannot be the case that the entire series has no first member. If there were no first member there would be no second, tenth, millionth. Therefore, the fact of a cause-effect series today is evidence that there must have been some First Cause which was not itself the effect of another cause. The argument clearly depends on a particular notion of the nature of a series; whether that notion can be sustained may be dubious.

Finally, we might appeal to moral experience. Is it really possible for men to believe that in some long-run sense, virtue is not coordinate with felicity? Can a man retain his moral sanity without believing that the virtuous are ultimately rewarded, the vicious ultimately condemned? Yet surely it is not the case that virtue brings its own reward. Thus if virtue and felicity are coordinate, there must exist a power which brings about that conjunction. Although in its grosser forms this is the argument by which desperate parents often seek to terrify recalcitrant children, when stated in a careful and humane fashion it may have considerable philosophic worth.

It is clear that arguments for the existence of the gods must be at least as well formed as any other argument. What is even clearer is that the evidence that will count for the truth of the conclusions—i.e., the truth of the premises—may itself be the subject of much dispute.

THE NATURE OF THE GODS

Although many religious men have not been concerned to argue the existence of the gods, it would seem that all of them, except the mystics, have been exercised to describe the nature of divine power. Not many of history's religious battles have been fought between the religious and the irreligious. Turk against Crusader, Shintoist against Buddhist, the charge has been "infidel!" not "atheist!" Quite apart from questions of the gods' existence, the distinctions drawn in explication of their nature have stimulated perennial philosophic interest.

It would be well, however, to distinguish "religious" from "theistic." Presumably all theists (the Deists might be an exception) are religious; but it might be the case that some religious people are not theistic. To many, certain forms of Buddhism, though clearly religious, seem to argue that the gods too are a part of the sham of ordinary existence. For many Hindus it would surely be a mistake to say that Brahman is a personal God, although to be sure Brahman may assume the appearance of gods for certain historical purposes. Even Christianity, though clearly theistic, in its doctrine of the Trinity has complicated that theism to an extent which makes it difficult to classify with less involved forms. Although Western minds are accustomed to contrast "theist" and "atheist," a broader perspective might indicate that a more useful opposition might be found between "religious" and "nonreligious."

The last century has produced scores of interesting definitions of religion. In fact, this is a philosophic field of considerable interest in itself, drawing as it does on the work of anthropologists, sociologists, and psychologists. However, the list will not be added to here except in the most general way. You might consider this: A man is religious if he holds that things are not quite what they seem to be. The difficulty with this definition is that it would apparently include, for example, the subatomic physicist who may or may not be religious. Further, it would seem to exclude those religious people who appear to see without question that the gods are active throughout history. Suppose we supplement our definition to include the stipulation that the explanation of why things are not quite what they seem to be is such that it should waken in us feelings of awe, dependence, and reverence. Surely his qualification will eliminate subatomic physics as a form of religion. Though it might not include the pantheist it would seem to include those other religiously gifted persons who never doubt that it is the gods they are serving. Perhaps the pantheist, if there are pantheists, should be treated as a special case, as indeed he has been treated by many of the traditional religions. Perhaps further, this indicates the difficulty of forming any thoroughgoing definition of religion. What is important, however, is that the "religious" man be distinguished from the "natural" man. Let the "natural" man be the man who says that *all* of existence can be explained in the way that most of us feel most of existence can be explained; the "religious" man says that there is something more to existence and that it commands a unique response.

Even with such a general definition the sources of dispute over the nature of the gods are not difficult to locate. Are the gods in space and time? If so, then surely they must be subject to the laws that control the other spatial and temporal entities; but then they would be thoroughly natural and we would be foolish to revere them. But if they are not in space and time, what have they to do with us, or we with them? Perhaps they are both in and out of space and time, in a way we cannot understand. But does that make sense, much less awaken a spirit of devotion?

THE GODS AND HUMAN AFFAIRS

However one settles these questions, if indeed they can be settled, the religious man must further ask how the existence of the gods has any practical relevance in his everyday life. Perhaps, as has been suggested by the Epicureans, the gods, being divine, are sublimely indifferent to social affairs. They exist and have a specific nature, but that existence and that nature have no practical consequences in human experience. More commonly, however, religious men have felt that the existence of the gods does make a difference. Religious dependence does entail practical consequences which will have social and psychological manifestations.

This conviction would seem to take two not easily separated forms. First, it has been argued that if the gods take an interest in human affairs then that interest has implications for the social order. In its most extreme form this line of argument leads into a theocracy. Whether in the Massachusetts Bay Colony, Mecca, or Lhasa, divine concern can be offered as a reason for specific social legislation. A qualified form of the argument might contend that while the State is largely a secular instrument, it nonetheless has specific responsibilities in view of the divine interest in human affairs. The implications of this argument in pluralistic societies, such as the United States or Japan, have provided interesting moments for both legislators and theologians. A further modification of the argument could contend that while the State is wholly secular, it is composed of men, many of whom are religious. Because the gods are concerned with the social life, it is incumbent on those religious men to bring to bear on their society the exhortations and injunctions which are the result of their faith. Religious belief might then serve as a haven within the social order.

A second form of the conviction that the gods are concerned with human affairs might argue that this concern is limited to the pious man's closet. If the social order be seen as ultimately incorrigible, it might still be the case that the individual must meet practical religious responsibilities and that he can find divine guidance. On this view, social responsibilities are distinguishable from personal, or individual responsibilities. In an extreme form, this argument can lead into religious passivism. More commonly, however, it simply contends that while some things are owed to the State, other things—and presumably the more important—are owed to the gods. The relation of the self to the divine powers frees the individual from bondage to the corrupt and corrupting social order. Clearly the argument here plays back into the discussion of the nature of the gods.

MYSTICISM

To many, the mystic's vision stands behind all religious thought. In contrast to the rather prosaic questions recited in the preceding pages, the claims of the mystics call into question the entire philosophic enterprise. There is, they say, a transcendent Realm of Being utterly inaccessible to human intellect, surpassing in beauty and worth anything dreamt by men's philosophies. It is real in a way in which the items of our ordinary experience are not; yet it is the very Ground of Being from which those items of ordinary experience derive whatever lesser existence they might have. It is of incomparable value, yet it is the ground of whatever values might be found in history. Unknowable, it is the illumination that makes all knowledge possible. Although it cannot be stormed by human effort, in a mystery of self-revelation it is open to any who seek.

Such claims are the source of distress to many philosophers. Indeed, some are reluctant to call the assertions claims at all. If they are claims, where is the evidence? But such a question may well be hasty, for the mystic is prepared to answer, "Come with me, and you too will see." But what does going with the mystic entail? Essentially, it involves giving up our ordinary way of looking at things—that is, our habit of distinguishing subject and object, me and thee, mine and thine. But it is just such distinguishing that makes knowing possible, one is tempted to reply. Yet it is just such distinguishing that shuts you off forever from this experience, replies the mystic. Surely you can never know if Galileo speaks the truth if you refuse to look through his telescope.

Now, the analogy to Galileo's "devilish instrument" may not be quite fair. After all, that astronomer's tormentors were accustomed to looking with their eyes; the request was merely for an artificial extension of their ordinary practice. The mystic is asking us to abandon an essential instrument of the knowing enterprise. He is asking us to follow him into a realm that has no charts and, for all we can see, can never have any.

Whatever your reply to this invitation—and it will probably make little difference to the mystic—his contention is that the loss of the subject-object relationship allows him to become, in some sense, one with Being itself. Some men, he says, are like rocks in the sea; though surrounded by it, they are where they are and find themselves distinct from it. Others, however, are like a grain of salt thrown into the sea: they diffuse throughout it, become one with it, are it.

We have not included in this section on the philosophic problems of theology selections representing divergent forms of mysticism because you have already met what is the most *philosophically* interesting issue in the debate between Feigl and Raju in the section on epistemology. But mysticism is also *religiously* interesting and we urge you to explore the many forms it takes in both West and East. But that is another story and one we cannot tell within the confines of this book.

THE EXISTENCE
OF THE GODS

If one finds it meaningful to ask whether or not the gods exist, he will not have difficulty finding authors prepared to argue the affirmative. Arguments for the existence of the gods, although unfashionable during the past century, are scattered throughout the history of Eastern and Western philosophy. A full catalogue would no doubt include thousands of arguments, each slightly different from the other. Nevertheless the arguments can be grouped into several types, each representing a significantly different approach to the conclusion that the gods exist. The following selections illustrate these types.

A discussion in the *Milindapanha* represents what may be called the "appeal to authority." Although his argument is far from conclusive, the sage Nāgasena contends that the fact that we have not seen the Buddha does not show that he does not exist. The implication is that we ought to believe in his existence on the basis of authoritative reports from the past. Now, one should be careful not to dismiss this argument too quickly. Its flaw is clear enough, yet how often in daily affairs do we use this argument to support belief in the existence of things we have not seen? If we did not trust the reports of others, would not the past be lost entirely and would not our knowledge be limited to our own immediate, present experience? One is surely right in being suspicious of any appeal to authority; but the costs of an outright rejection of the argument might be high indeed.

St. Anselm is the author of the most famous statement of the "ontological argument." It can be contended that his *Proslogium* contains two forms of the argument. The first of these, in Chapter II, argues that the greatest possible being (God) exists because it is greater to exist than not to exist. The argument in Chapter III purports to show God's *necessary* existence as a consequence of His perfection. The traditional reply to Anselm's arguments is that they both take existence as a predicate, and that such a procedure leads into a hopeless logical tangle. Ask yourself whether things "have" or fail to "have" existence in the same way that they "have" or fail to "have" sharp edges. To illumine what the critics have in mind, consider what it would be for an entity—for example, a mermaid—to fail to have existence, when existence is taken as a predicate. In spite of this alleged difficulty, the ontological argument has surely been one of the most durable of all the proofs for the existence of the gods.

The Indian Vaiśeṣika work, *The Padārthadharmasaṁgraha,* contains a clear statement of the "causal argument." Briefly, our experience reveals that the entities we meet are effects of prior causes. No one doubts that where there is a house there must have been a housebuilder, or that where there is any change there must have been a cause of that change. But what of the universe itself? Must it not also stand as the effect of some prior cause? If so, then the gods exist.

A related argument, the teleological argument or "argument from design," is offered in Maimonides' *The Guide for the Perplexed.* For this theologian, it is not so much the existence of the universe as the peculiar order which it reveals that is evidence for the existence of the gods. One can consider Maimonides' argument quite apart from the particular cosmology on which it is based. Quite simply, that argument is this: Our experience of nature reveals combinations and patterns that betray intelligence. Because nature is not intelligent, its apparent design must be attributed to another. Thus, the gods exist. In considering this argument, one might ask whether nature's design is real or apparent. Further, one might ask whether design in fact does require a designer. Might it not be that nature's design arose quite naturally?

In his *Monologium,* St. Anselm produces a second argument demonstrating God's existence. Our experience reveals differences in degrees of perfection: things are more or less good, more or less powerful. One explanation of this comparative difference is that the greater possesses more of the quality—for example, goodness—than the lesser. But if this is the case, then surely that quality, goodness, must exist in its perfect form if it is to be represented in lesser historical forms. Another way to put this is to say that if things possess more or less of a quality, then that quality which they possess must truly exist. This argument has some tricky metaphysical implications, as the history of Platonism has shown. Might the argument not be reversed to demonstrate the existence of the most devilish Devil? Yet we do speak of the Justice which our laws seek to copy, the Beauty which our artists strive to represent. If such struggle is worthwhile, don't we also believe in the full existence of those transcendent qualities?

The final selection, taken from Kant, contends that the traditional arguments fail. In Kant's view there are only three arguments other than his own (an admittedly weak "moral argument") purporting to give a rational demonstration of the existence of the gods. They are the ontological argument, the cosmological argument (which is rather similar to the causal argument and Anselm's argument from the degrees of perfection), and the physico-theological argument (or argument from design). It is Kant's contention that the third argument depends on the second, the second on the first, and that the first fails completely. His conclusion is simply that speculative reason is unable to prove the gods' existence.

Milindapanha

The Milindapanha [*The questions of King Milinda*] *is a Pali work purporting to record the conversations of the Greek king Milinda (Menander) with the Buddhist sage Nāgasena. Milinda ruled a portion of north India in the second century* B.C., *and although this work is not of that era, it should be dated not many centuries later.*

BOOK THREE

Chapter 5

1. The king said: "Have you, Nāgasena, seen the Buddha?"

"No, Sire."

"Then have your teachers seen the Buddha?"

"No, Sire."

"Then, venerable Nāgasena, there is no Buddha!"

"But, great king, have you seen the river Ūhā in the Himālaya mountains?"

"No, Sir."

"Or has your father seen it?"

"No, Sir."

"Then, your Majesty, is there therefore no such river?"

"It is there. Though neither I nor my father has seen it, it is nevertheless there."

"Just so, great king, though neither I nor my teachers have seen the Blessed One, nevertheless there was such a person."

"Very good, Nāgasena!"

2. The king said: "Is the Buddha, Nāgasena, pre-eminent?"

"Yes, he is incomparable."

"But how do you know of one you have never seen that he is pre-eminent."

"Now what do you think, O king? They who have never seen the ocean would they know concerning it: 'Deep, unmeasurable, unfathomable is the mighty ocean. Into it do the five great rivers flow —the Ganges, the Jumna, the Akiravatī, the Sarabhū, and Mahī—and yet is there in it no appearance of being more empty or more full!'?"

"Yes, they would know that."

"Just so, great king, when I think of the mighty disciples who have passed away then do I know that the Buddha is incomparable."

"Very good, Nāgasena!"

3. The king said: "Is it possible, Nāgasena, for others to know how incomparable the Buddha is?"

"Yes, they may know it."

From *The Sacred Books of the East*, F. Max Müller, ed., Vol. XXV; London, Oxford University Press.

"But how can they?"

"Long, long ago, O king, there was a master of writing, by name Tissa the Elder, and many are the years gone by since he has died. How can people know of him?"

"By his writing, Sir."

"Just so, great king, whosoever sees what the Truth is, he sees what the Blessed One was, for the Truth was preached by the Blessed One."

"Very good, Nāgasena!"

4. The king said: "Have you, Nāgasena, seen what the Truth is?"

"Have not we disciples, O king, to conduct ourselves our lives long as under the eye of the Buddha, and under his command?"

"Very good, Nāgasena!"

* * *

10. The king said: "Is there such a person as the Buddha, Nāgasena?"

"Yes."

"Can he then, Nāgasena, be pointed out as being here or there?"

"The Blessed One, O king, has passed away by that kind of passing away in which nothing remains which could tend to the formation of another individual. It is not possible to point out the Blessed One as being here or there."

"Give me an illustration."

"Now what do you think, O king? When there is a great body of fire blazing, is it possible to point out any one flame that has gone out, that it is here or there?"

"No, Sir. The flame has ceased, it has vanished."

"Just so, great king, has the Blessed One passed away by that kind of passing away in which no root remains for the formation of another individual. The Blessed One has come to an end, and it cannot be pointed out of him, that he is here or there. But in the body of his doctrine he can, O king, be pointed out. For the doctrine was preached by the Blessed One."

"Very good, Nāgasena!"

Proslogium

St. Anselm

St. Anselm (1033–1109) was the archbishop of Canterbury during one of the many stormy periods in the relations between Church and State in England. He also was a philosopher and theologian of uncommon clarity and ingenuity. The ontological argument is not original with him, but he is its most famous advocate.

Chapter II

Truly there is a God, although the fool hath said in his heart, There is no God.

And so, Lord, do thou, who dost give understanding to faith, give me, so far as thou knowest it to be profitable, to understand that thou art as we believe; and that thou art that which we believe. And, indeed, we believe that thou art a being than which nothing greater can be conceived. Or is there no such nature, since the fool hath said in his heart, there is no God? (Psalms xiv. 1). But, at any rate, this very fool, when he hears of this being of which I speak—a being than which nothing greater can be conceived—understands what he hears, and what he understands is in his understanding; although he does not understand it to exist.

For, it is one thing for an object to be in the understanding, and another to understand that the object exists. When a painter first conceives of what he will afterwards perform, he has it in his under-

standing, but he does not yet understand it to be, because he has not yet performed it. But after he has made the painting, he both has it in his understanding, and he understands that it exists, because he has made it.

Hence, even the fool is convinced that something exists in the understanding, at least, than which nothing greater can be conceived. For, when he hears of this, he understands it. And whatever is understood, exists in the understanding. And assuredly that, than which nothing greater can be conceived, cannot exist in the understanding alone. For, suppose it exists in the understanding alone: then it can be conceived to exist in reality; which is greater.

Therefore, if that, than which nothing greater can be conceived, exists in the understanding alone, the very being, than which nothing greater can be conceived, is one, than which a greater can be conceived. But obviously this is impossible. Hence, there is no doubt that there exists a being, than which nothing greater can

From the S. N. Deane translation of the *Proslogium*.

be conceived, and it exists both in the understanding and in reality.

Chapter III

God cannot be conceived not to exist. God is that, than which nothing greater can be conceived. That which can be conceived not to exist is not God.

And it assuredly exists so truly, that it cannot be conceived not to exist. For, it is possible to conceive of a being which cannot be conceived not to exist; and this is greater than one which can be conceived not to exist. Hence, if that, than which nothing greater can be conceived, can be conceived not to exist, it is not that, than which nothing greater can be conceived. But this is an irreconcilable contradiction. There is, then, so truly a being than which nothing greater can be conceived to exist, that it cannot even be conceived not to exist; and this being thou art, O Lord, our God.

So truly, therefore, dost thou exist, O Lord, my God, that thou canst not be conceived not to exist; and rightly. For, if a mind could conceive of a being better than thee, the creature would rise above the Creator; and this is most absurd. And, indeed, whatever else there is, except thee alone, can be conceived not to exist. To thee alone, therefore, it belongs to exist more truly than all other beings, and hence in a higher degree than all others. For, whatever else exists does not exist so truly, and hence in a less degree it belongs to it to exist. Why, then, has the fool said in his heart, there is no God (Psalms xiv. 1), since it is so evident, to a rational mind, that thou dost exist in the highest degree of all? Why, except that he is dull and a fool?

Padārthadharmasaṁgraha

PRAŚASTAPĀDA

The Padārthadharmasaṁgraha *is a fourth-century work of the Vaiśeṣika (pronounced "Vaisheshika") school of Indian philosophy. The selection consists of a passage from this text along with an authoritative commentary composed six centuries later.*

OF THE ULTIMATE SUBSTANCES

We are now going to describe the process of the creation and destruction of the four ultimate material substances [earth, water, fire, air]. . . . The four gross elements having thus been brought into existence, there is produced, from the mere thought (mental picturing) of the

From *The Padārthadharmasaṁgraha of Praśastapāda* with the *Nyāyakandalī of Śridhara,* transl. Ganganatha Jha; Allahabad: E. J. Lazarus and Co., 1916, in Radhakrishnan and Moore, *A Source Book in Indian Philosophy,* Princeton, N.J.: Princeton University Press, 1957.

Supreme Lord, the Great egg, from out of the fire-atoms mixed up with the atoms of earth; and in this egg having produced all the worlds and the Four-faced Brahmā, the Grandfather of all creatures; the Supreme Lord assigns to him the duty of producing the various creatures. . . .

Question: "What are the proofs for the existence of God?"

This proof is in the form of scriptural authority and inferential reasoning.

This inferential reasoning is—The four great elementary substances are preceded by someone having a knowledge of them, because they are effects—anything that is an effect is preceded by one having a cognition of it, as, for instance, the jar (which is always preceded by the potter), and the four great elementary substances are effects—hence they must be preceded by one having a knowledge of them.

Objection: "The premiss of this inference (that the elementary substances are effects) is not duly cognised by any means of right knowledge—for instance, the fact of the earth being an effect cannot be regarded as duly established."

Reply: This is not right; as the earth, etc., are made up of parts; and everything that has parts is an effect, as for instance the jar; the earth, etc., have parts—hence they must be effects.

Objection: "An inferential reasoning is operative only when the invariable concomitance (upon which it is based) has been duly recognized; as for the invariable comcomitance of the *character of an effect* and *that of being preceded by one having knowledge* of it, this can never be known from the case of the jar and such other substances; as in the case of the sprouting of the seed we find that the sprouting appears *at the same time* as the cognition of the sprout by the person who had sown the seed; and hence in this case we do not find any *precedence* of the doer with the knowledge of the effect over the appearance of the effect. Nor could the sprout,

etc., be included in the subject of the inference in question; as it is only after the invariable concomitance has been duly cognised, and the inference has begun to operate, that we proceed to distinguish the subject and predicate, etc., of the inference, for the benefit of the opponent; while in the case in question (of the sprout) it is found to be always included in a cognition contrary to the concomitance; and as such, there could be no cognition of the necessary concomitance."

Reply: If there be no recognition of the invariable concomitance simply on account of there being no perception of duality or difference (between the time of the appearance of the sprout and the knowledge thereof by the sower), then, in that case, we could never rightly arrive at the . . . inference of the moving of the Sun, . . . it is merely the fact of the stars, etc., having assumed different positions, and not that of their having *moved,* that is perceived at the same time as the cognition of their other positions preceded by the movement of *Devadatta* (the observer) from one place to another. . . .

Objection: "Then again, does the inferential reasoning establish the creator, or a creator capable of creating the Earth, etc.? If it prove a mere creator, then what is desired is not accomplished. As what you seek to prove is not a mere agent, like ourselves; any such person having a limited vision could not create the Earth, etc. . . ."

Reply: This objection does not apply to the case, as what the inference is sought to prove is not any particular kind of creator. All that the premiss put forward proves is the fact of the substances under consideration being preceded by an intelligent being in general; and this necessarily establishes his particular character in the shape of the capability of creating the Earth, etc.—as the existence of no general entity can be proved without the accompaniment of a particular characteristic

. . . [for example] no universal essence of fire could have an existence apart from a particular fire.

The objector's standpoint may be summed up: ". . . For instance, the inference cannot prove the fact of the effects (earth, etc.) being preceded by a body (of the God); because, if there be a body, it would necessarily contain the sense-organs; and having these organs, the God could not have any knowledge of the material causes (atoms), the accessories (in the shape of the karmic tendencies of selves) and the potencies of various instrumentalities—all of which are supersensuous—in the matter of the creation of Earth etc.; and as such He could not be the creator of these. Then as for the creation not being preceded by a body (of God), it is absolutely impossible to prove this; because, as a matter of fact, we find that what a *doer* (of any act) does is—(1) to ascertain the power or capability of the instruments, (2) to desire to fulfil the particular act by means of those instruments, (3) to put forth an effort, (4) to put the body into action, (5) to supervise over the various causes (material and others), and (6) to do the act; and if he does not *ascertain,* or desire, or put forth his effort, or put his body into action, he does not do the act. And from these affirmative and negative universal instances (of the *acting* with the *ascertaining,* etc.) we conclude that like the intelligence (of God), the body also would be a necessary means to the production of effects, . . .

To the above we make the following reply: Does the nature of the *actor* necessarily consist in being bodied? or does it consist in the character of being the operator of instruments recognised as capable of bringing about the necessary effects? The former alternative could not be accepted; as in that case a person in deep sleep, or one who is not doing anything towards an action, would also have to be regarded as the "actor" (as even in these conditions he would have his body

all the same). We must then accept the second alternative; as it is only when this character is present that we find the effect coming about. This character can belong to a bodiless being also; as we find in the case of the self (which is an immaterial thing) operating towards the moving of the body. It might be argued that the body belongs to the self, who has obtained it through its previous deeds (and as such the operating self cannot be regarded as strictly bodiless). True, the body belongs to the self; but it is not the body that supplies the force impelling itself, as any such impulsion by itself would involve a contradiction. It may be urged that the body may be regarded as the means of impulsion, in as much as it is the object of the impelling. But in the case of God also we have the atom as the object to be impelled or operated upon.

Objection: "The impelling of the self's body is found to be brought about by desire and effort; and not when the body does not exist; and from this we infer that the body is the means or author of its own impelling, through the said desire and effort."

Reply: Not so; as the body can be only accepted as impelling or giving rise to desire and effort (and not to its own operations). After the desire and effort have been brought about, and when these begin to operate towards impelling (the body to a certain course of action), the body ceases to be the impelling agent; as the body being the *object* of this impelling could not, at the same time, be its *doer.* And thus we find that there is no similarity between the action of the self and that of the body. Then again, we often meet with cases where certain inanimate things are moved to action by an intelligent being, merely through his own desire and effort, independently of all actions of the body. On the other hand, we never find any action apart from an intelligent being. All these facts go to establish the existence of God.

The Guide for the Perplexed

MAIMONIDES

Maimonides (1135–1204), the leading medieval Jewish philosopher, held that nature's design is evidence for the existence of nature's Designer. Although the argument is not original with Maimonides, his formulation of it was widely influential throughout the Middle Ages.

Chapter XIX

It has been shown that according to Aristotle, and according to all that defend his theory, the Universe is inseparable from God; He is the cause, and the Universe the effect; and this effect is a necessary one; and as it cannot be explained why or how God exists in this particular manner, namely, being One and incorporeal, so it cannot be asked concerning the whole Universe why or how it exists in this particular way. For it is necessary that the whole, the cause as well as the effect, exist in this particular manner, it is impossible for them not to exist, or to be different from what they actually are. This leads to the conclusion that the nature of everything remains constant, that nothing changes its nature in any way, and that such a change is impossible in any existing thing. It would also follow that the Universe is not the result of design, choice, and desire; for if this were the case, they would have been non-existing before the design had been conceived. We, however, hold that all things in the Universe are the result of design, and not merely of necessity; He who designed them may change them when He changes His design. But not every design is subject to change; for there are things which are impossible, and their nature cannot be altered, as will be explained. Here, in this chapter, I merely wish to show by arguments almost as forcible as real proofs, that the Universe gives evidence of design; but I will not fall into the error in which the Mutakallemim have so much distinguished themselves, namely, of ignoring the existing nature of things or assuming the existence of atoms, or the successive creation of accidents, or any of their propositions which I have tried to explain, and which are intended to establish the principle of Divine selection. You must not, however, think that they understood the principle in the same sense as we do, although they undoubtedly aimed at the same thing, and mentioned the same things which we also will mention, when they treated of Divine Selection. For they do not distinguish between selection in the case of a plant to make it red and not white, or sweet and not bitter, and determination in the case of the heavens

From M. Friedländer's translation of *The Guide for the Perplexed*.

which gave them their peculiar geometrical form and did not give them a triangular or quadrilateral shape. The Mutakallemim established the principle of determination by means of their propositions, which have been enumerated above. I will establish this principle only as far as necessary, and only by philosophical propositions based on the nature of things. But before I begin my argument, I will state the following facts: Matter is common to things different from each other; there must be either one external cause which endows this matter partly with one property, partly with another, or there must be as many different causes as there are different forms of the matter common to all things. This is admitted by those who assume the Eternity of the Universe. After having premised this proposition, I will proceed with the discussion of our theme from an Aristotelian point of view, in form of a dialogue.

WE: You have proved that all things in the sublunary world have one common substance; why then do the species of things vary? why are the *individuals* in each species different from each other?

ARISTOTELIAN: Because the composition of the things formed of that substance varies. For the common substance at first received four different forms, and each form was endowed with two qualities, and through these four qualities the substance was turned into the elements of which all things are formed. The composition of the elements takes place in the following manner: First they are mixed in consequence of the motion of the spheres, and then they combine together; a cause for variation arises then in the variation of the degree of heat, cold, moisture, and dryness of the elements which form the constituent parts of the things. By these different combinations things are variously predisposed to receive different forms; and these in their turn are again prepared to receive other forms, and so on. Each

generic form finds a wide sphere in its substance both as regards quality and quantity; and the individuals of the classes vary accordingly. This is fully explained in Natural Science. It is quite correct and clear to every one that readily acknowledges the truth, and does not wish to deceive himself.

WE: Since the combination of the elements prepares substances and enables them to receive different forms, what has prepared the first substance and caused one part of it to receive the form of fire, another part the form of earth, and the parts between these two the forms of water and of air, since one substance is common to all? Through what has the substance of earth become more fit for the form of earth, and the substance of fire more fit for that of fire?

ARISTOTELIAN: The difference of the elements was caused by their different position; for the different places prepared the same substance differently, in the following way: the portion nearest the surrounding sphere became more rarified and swifter in motion, and thus approaching the nature of that sphere, it received by this preparation the form of fire. The farther the substance is away from the surrounding sphere towards the centre, the denser, the more solid, and the less luminous it is; it becomes earth; the same is the cause of the formation of water and air. This is necessarily so; for it would be absurd to deny that each part of the substance is in a certain place; or to assume that the surface is identical with the centre, or the centre with the surface. This difference in place determined the different forms, i.e., predisposed the substance to receive different forms.

WE: Is the substance of the surrounding sphere, i.e., the heavens, the same as that of the elements?

ARISTOTELIAN: No; the substance is different, and the forms are different. The term "body" is homonymously used of these bodies below and of the heavens, as has been shown by modern philosophers. All this has been demonstrated by proof.

But let now the reader of this treatise hear what I have to say. Aristotle has proved that the difference of forms becomes evident by the difference of actions. Since, therefore, the motion of the elements is rectilinear, and that of the spheres circular, we infer that the substances are different. This inference is supported by Natural Science. When we further notice that substances with rectilinear motion differ in their directions, that some move upward, some downward, and the substances which move in the same direction have different velocities, we infer that their forms must be different. Thus we learn that there are four elements. In the same way we come to the conclusion that the substance of all the spheres is the same, since they all have circular motion. Their forms, however, are different, since one sphere moves from east to west, and another from west to east; and their motions have also different velocities. We can now put the following question to Aristotle: There is one substance common to all spheres; each one has its own peculiar form. Who thus determined and predisposed these spheres to receive different forms? Is there above the spheres any being capable of determining this except God? I will show the profundity and the extraordinary acumen which Aristotle displayed when this question troubled him. He strove very hard to meet this objection with arguments, which, however, were not borne out by facts. Although he does not mention this objection, it is clear from his words that he endeavours to show the nature of the spheres, as he has shown that of the things in the sublunary world. Everything is, according to him, the result of a law of Nature, and not the result of the design of a being that designs as it likes, or the determination of a being that determines

as it pleases. He has not carried out the idea consistently, and it will never be done. He tries indeed to find the cause why the sphere moves from east and not from west; why some spheres move with greater velocity, others with less velocity, and he finds the cause of these differences in their different positions in reference to the uppermost sphere. He further attempts to show why there are several spheres for each of the seven planets, while there is only one sphere for the large number of fixed stars. For all this he endeavours to state the reason, so as to show that the whole order is the necessary result of the laws of Nature. He has not attained his object. For as regards the things in the sublunary world, his explanations are in accordance with facts, and the relation between cause and effect is clearly shown. It can therefore be assumed that everything is the necessary result of the motions and influences of the spheres. But when he treats of the properties of the spheres, he does not clearly show the causal relation, nor does he explain the phenomena in that systematic way which the hypothesis of natural laws would demand. For let us consider the spheres: in one case a sphere with greater velocity is above a sphere with less velocity, in another case we notice the reverse; in a third case there are two spheres with equal velocities, one above the other. There are, besides, other phenomena which speak strongly against the hypothesis that all is regulated by the laws of Nature, and I will devote a special chapter to the discussion of these phenomena. In short, there is no doubt that Aristotle knew the weakness of his arguments in tracing and describing the cause of all these things, and therefore he prefaces his researches on these things as follows: "We will now thoroughly investigate two problems, which it is our proper duty to investigate and to discuss according to our capacity, wisdom, and opinion. This our attempt must not be attributed to presumption and pride, but to our extraordinary zeal in the study of philosophy; when we attempt the highest and grandest problems, and endeavour to offer some proper solution, every one that hears it should rejoice and be pleased." So far Aristotle. This shows that he undoubtedly knew the weakness of his theory. How much weaker must it appear when we bear in mind that the science of Astronomy was not yet fully developed, and that in the days of Aristotle the motions of the spheres were not known so well as they are at present. I think that it was the object of Aristotle in attributing in his *Metaphysics* one Intelligence to every sphere, to assume the existence of something capable of determining the peculiar course of each sphere. Later on I will show that he has not gained anything thereby; but now I will explain the words, "according to our capacity, wisdom, and opinion," occurring in the passage which we quoted. I have not noticed that any of the commentators explain them. The term "our opinion" refers to the principle that everything is the result of natural laws, or to the theory of the Eternity of the Universe. By "our wisdom" he meant the knowledge of that which is clear and generally accepted, viz., that the existence of every one of these things is due to a certain cause, and not to chance. By "our capacity" he meant the insufficiency of our intellect to find the causes of all these things. He only intended to trace the causes for a few of them; and so he did. For he gives an excellent reason why the sphere of the fixed stars moves slowly, while the other spheres move with greater velocity, namely, because its motion is in a different direction [from the uppermost sphere]. He further says that the more distant a sphere is from the eighth sphere the greater is its velocity. But this rule does not hold good in all cases, as I have already explained. More forcible still is the following objection:

There are spheres below the eighth that move from east to west. Of these each upper one, according to this rule, would have a greater velocity than the lower one; and the velocity of these spheres would almost equal that of the ninth sphere. But Astronomy had, in the days of Aristotle, not yet developed to the height it has reached at present.

According to our theory of the Creation, all this can easily be explained; for we say that there is a being that determines the direction and the velocity of the motion of each sphere; but we do not know the reason why the wisdom of that being gave to each sphere its peculiar property. If Aristotle had been able to state the cause of the difference in the motion of the spheres, and show that it corresponded as he thought to their relative positions, this would have been excellent, and the variety in their motions would be explained in the same way as the variety of the elements, by their relative position between the centre and the surface; but this is not the case, as I said before.

There is a phenomenon in the spheres which more clearly shows the existence of voluntary determination; it cannot be explained otherwise than by assuming that some being designed it: this phenomenon is the existence of the stars. The fact that the sphere is constantly in motion, while the stars remain stationary, indicates that the substance of the stars is different from that of the spheres. Abu-nasr has already mentioned the fact in his additions to the *Physics* of Aristotle. He says: "There is a difference between the stars and the spheres; for the spheres are transparent, the stars are opaque; and the cause of this is that there is a difference, however small it may be, between their substances and forms." So far Abu-nasr. But I do not say that there is a small difference, but a very great difference; because I do not infer it from the transparency of the spheres, but from their motions. I am convinced that there are three different kinds of substance, with three different forms, namely: (1) Bodies which never move of their own accord; such are the bodies of the stars; (2) bodies which always move, such are the bodies of the spheres; (3) bodies which both move and rest, such are the elements. Now, I ask, what has united these two bodies, which, according to my opinion, differ very much from each other, though, according to Abu-nasr, only a little? Who has prepared the bodies for this union? In short, it would be strange that, without the existence of design, one of two different bodies should be joined to the other in such a manner that it is fixed to it in a certain place but does not combine with it. It is still more difficult to explain the existence of the numerous stars in the eighth sphere; they are all spherical; some of them are large, some small; here we notice two stars apparently distant from each other one cubit; there a group of ten close together; whilst in another place there is a large space without any star. What determined that the one small part should have ten stars, and the other portion should be without any star? and the whole body of the sphere being uniform throughout, why should a particular star occupy the one place and not another? The answer to these and similar questions is very difficult, and almost impossible, if we assume that all emanates from God as the necessary result of certain permanent laws, as Aristotle holds. But if we assume that all this is the result of design, there is nothing strange or improbable; and the only question to be asked is this: What is the cause of this design? The answer to this question is that all this has been made for a certain purpose, though we do not know it; there is nothing that is done in vain, or by chance. It is well known that the veins and nerves of an individual dog or ass are not the result of chance; their

magnitude is not determined by chance; nor is it by chance, but for a certain purpose, that one vein is thick, another thin; that one nerve has many branches, another has none; that one goes down straight, whilst another is bent; it is well known that all this must be just as it is. How, then, can any reasonable person imagine that the position, magnitude, and number of the stars, or the various courses of their spheres, are purposeless, or the result of chance? There is no doubt that every one of these things is necessary and in accordance with a certain design; and it is extremely improbable that these things should be the necessary result of natural laws, and not that of design.

The best proof for design in the Universe I find in the different motions of the spheres, and in the fixed position of the stars in the spheres. For this reason you find all the prophets point to the spheres and stars when they want to prove that there must exist a Divine Being. Thus Abraham reflected on the stars, as is well known; Isaiah (xl. 26) exhorts to learn from them the existence of God, and says, "Lift up your eyes on high, and behold who hath created these things?" Jeremiah [calls God] "The Maker of the heavens"; Abraham calls Him "The God of the heavens" (Gen. xxiv. 7); [Moses], the chief of the Prophets, uses the phrase explained by us "He who rideth on the heavens" (Deut. xxxiii. 26). The proof taken from the heavens is convincing; for the variety of things in the sublunary world, though their substance is one and the same, can be explained as the work of the influences of the spheres, or the result of the variety in the position of the substance in relation to the spheres, as has been shown by Aristotle. But who has determined the variety in the spheres and the stars, if not the Will of God? To say that the Intelligences have determined it is of no use whatever; for the Intelligences are not corporeal, and have no local relation to the spheres. Why then should the one sphere in its desire to approach the Intelligence, move eastward, and another westward? Is the one Intelligence in the east, the other in the west? or why does one move with great velocity, another slowly? This difference is not in accordance with their distances from each other, as is well known. We must then say that the nature and essence of each sphere necessitated its motion in a certain direction, and in a certain manner, as the consequence of its desire to approach its Intelligence. Aristotle clearly expresses this opinion. We thus have returned to the part from which we started; and we ask, Since the substance of all things is the same, what made the nature of one portion different from another? Why has this sphere a desire which produces a motion different from that which the desire of another sphere produces? This must have been done by an agent capable of determining. We have thus been brought to examine two questions: (1) Is it necessary to assume that the variety of the things in the Universe is the result of Design, and not of fixed laws of Nature, or is it not necessary? (2) Assuming that all this is the result of Design, does it follow that it has been created after not having existed, or does *Creatio ex nihilo* not follow, and has the Being which has determined all this done always so? Some of those who believe in the Eternity of the Universe hold the last opinion. I will now begin the examination of these two questions, and explain them as much as necessary in the following chapters.

Chapter XX

According to Aristotle, none of the products of Nature are due to chance. His proof is this: That which is due to chance does not reappear constantly nor frequently, but all products of Nature reappear either constantly or at least fre-

quently. The heavens, with all that they contain, are constant; they never change, as has been explained, neither as regards their essence nor as regards their place. But in the sublunary world we find both things which are constant and things which reappear frequently [though not constantly]. Thus, e.g., the heat of fire and the downward tendency of a stone are constant properties, whilst the form and life of the individuals in each species are the same in most cases. All this is clear. If the parts of the Universe are not accidental, how can the whole Universe be considered as the result of chance? Therefore the existence of the Universe is not due to chance. The following is, in short, the objection which Aristotle raises against one of the earlier philosophers who assumed that the Universe is the result of chance, and that it came into existence by itself, without any cause. Some assume that the heavens and the whole Universe came into existence spontaneously, as well as the rotation and motion [of the spheres], which has produced the variety of things and established their present order. This opinion implies a great absurdity. They admit that animals and plants do not owe their existence or production to chance, but to a certain cause, be that cause Nature, or reason, or the like; e.g., they do not assume that everything might be formed by chance of a certain seed or semen, but that of a certain seed only an olive-tree is produced, and of a certain semen only a human being is developed. And yet they think that the heavens, and those bodies which appear divine among the rest of bodies, came into existence spontaneously, without the action of any such cause as produces plants and animals. Having thus examined this theory, Aristotle then proceeds to refute it at greater length. It is therefore clear that Aristotle believes and proves that things in real existence are not accidental; they cannot be accidental, because they are essential, i.e., there is a cause which necessitates that they should be in their actual condition, and on account of that cause they are just as they in reality are. This has been proved, and it is the opinion of Aristotle. But I do not think that, according to Aristotle, the rejection of the spontaneous origin of things implies the admission of Design and Will. For as it is impossible to reconcile two opposites, so it is impossible to reconcile the two theories, that of necessary existence by causality, and that of Creation by the desire and will of a Creator. For the necessary existence assumed by Aristotle must be understood in this sense, that for everything that is not the product of work there must be a certain cause that produces it with its properties; for this cause there is another cause, and for the second a third, and so on. The series of causes ends with the Prime Cause, from which everything derives existence, since it is impossible that the series should continue *ad infinitum*. He nevertheless does not mean to say that the existence of the Universe is the necessary product of the Creator, i.e., the Prime Cause, in the same manner as the shadow is caused by a body, or heat by fire, or light by the sun. Only those who do not comprehend his words attribute such ideas to him. He uses here the term necessary in the same sense as we use the term when we say that the existence of the *intellectus* necessarily im-

plies that of the *intellectum,* for the former is the efficient cause of the latter in so far as *intellectum*. Even Aristotle holds that the Prime Cause is the highest and most perfect Intellect; he therefore says that the First Cause is pleased, satisfied, and delighted with that which necessarily derives existence from Him, and it is impossible that He should wish it to be different. But we do not call this "design," and it has nothing in common with design. E.g., man is pleased, satisfied, and delighted that he is endowed with eyes and hands, and it is impossible that he should desire it to be otherwise, and yet the eyes and hands which a man has are not the result of his design, and it is not by his own determination that he has certain properties and is able to perform certain actions. The notion of design and determination applies only to things not yet in existence, when there is still the possibility of their being in accordance with the design or not. I do not know whether the modern Aristotelians understood his words to imply that the existence of the Universe presupposes some cause in the sense of design and determination, or whether, in opposition to him, they assumed design and determination, in the belief that this does not conflict with the theory of the Eternity of the Universe.

Having explained this, I will now proceed to examine the opinions of the modern philosophers.

Monologium

St. Anselm

St. Anselm (1033–1109) gave a theological restatement to the Platonic argument for the real existence of the Forms. This archbishop of Canterbury contended that differences in degree of perfection require the real existence of the fully Perfect.

Chapter I

There is a being which is best, and greatest, and highest of all existing beings.

If any man, either from ignorance or unbelief, has no knowledge of the existence of one Nature which is the highest of all existing beings, which is also sufficient to itself in its eternal blessedness, and which confers upon and effects in all other beings, through its omnipotent goodness, the very fact of their existence, and the fact that in any way their existence is good; and if he has no knowledge of many other things, which we necessarily believe regarding God and his creatures, he still believes that he can at least convince himself of these truths in great part, even if his mental powers are very ordinary, by the force of reason alone.

And, although he could do this in many ways, I shall adopt one which I consider easiest for such a man. For, since all desire to enjoy only those things which they suppose to be good, it is natural that this man should, at some time, turn his mind's eye to the examination of that cause by which these things are good, which he does not desire, except as he judges them to be good. So that, as reason leads the way and follows up these considerations, he advances rationally to those truths of which, without reason, he has no knowledge. And if, in this discussion, I use any argument which no greater authority adduces, I wish it to be received in this way: although, on the grounds that I shall see fit to adopt, the conclusion is reached as if necessarily, yet it is not, for this reason, said to be absolutely necessary, but merely that it can appear so for the time being.

It is easy, then, for one to say to himself: Since there are goods so innumerable, whose great diversity we experience by the bodily senses, and discern by our mental faculties, must we not believe that there is some one thing, through which all goods whatever are good? Or are they good, one through one thing, and another through another? To be sure, it is most certain and clear, for all who are willing to see, that whatsoever things are said to possess any attribute in such a way that in mutual comparison they may be said to possess it in greater, or less, or equal degree, are said to possess it by virtue of

From S. N. Deane's translation of the *Monologium*.

some fact, which is not understood to be one thing in one case and another in another, but to be the same in different cases, whether it is regarded as existing in these cases in equal or unequal degree. For, whatsoever things are said to be *just,* when compared one with another, whether equally, or more, or less, cannot be understood as just, except through the quality of *justness,* which is not one thing in one instance, and another in another.

Since it is certain, then, that all goods, if mutually compared, would prove either equally or unequally good, necessarily they are all good by virtue of something which is conceived of as the same in different goods, although sometimes they seem to be called good, the one by virtue of one thing, the other by virtue of another. For, apparently it is by virtue of one quality, that a horse is called *good,* because he is strong, and by virtue of another, that he is called *good,* because he is swift. For, though he seems to be called good by virtue of his strength, and good by virtue of his swiftness, yet swiftness and strength do not appear to be the same thing.

But if a horse, because he is strong and swift, is therefore good, how is it that a strong, swift robber is bad? Rather, then, just as a strong, swift robber is bad, because he is harmful, so a strong, swift horse is good, because he is useful. And, indeed, nothing is ordinarily regarded as good, except either for some utility—as, for instance, safety is called good, and those things which promote safety—or for some honorable character—as, for instance, beauty is reckoned to be good, and what promotes beauty.

But, since the reasoning which we have observed is in no wise refutable, necessarily, again, all things, whether useful or honorable, if they are truly good, are good through that same being through which all goods exist, whatever that being is. But who can doubt this very being, through which all goods exist, to be a great good? This must be, then, a good through itself, since every other good is through it.

It follows, therefore, that all other goods are good through another being than that which they themselves are, and this being alone is good through itself. Hence, this alone is supremely good, which is alone good through itself. For it is supreme, in that it so surpasses other beings, that it is neither equalled nor excelled. But that which is supremely good is also supremely great. There is, therefore, some one being which is supremely good, and supremely great, that is, the highest of all existing beings.

Chapter II

The same subject continued.

But, just as it has been proved that there is a being that is supremely good, since all goods are good through a single being, which is good through itself; so it is necessarily inferred that there is something supremely great, which is great through itself. But I do not mean physically great, as a material object is great, but that which, the greater it is, is the better or the more worthy—wisdom, for instance. And since there can be nothing supremely great except what is supremely good, there must be a being that is greatest and best, i.e., the highest of all existing beings.

Chapter III

There is a certain Nature through which whatever is exists, and which exists through itself, and is the highest of all existing beings.

Therefore, not only are all good things such through something that is one and the same, and all great things such through something that is one and the same; but whatever is, apparently exists through something that is one and the same. For, everything that is, exists either through something, or through nothing. But nothing exists through nothing. For it is altogether inconceivable that anything should not exist by virtue of something.

Whatever is, then, does not exist except through something. Since this is true, either there is one being, or there are more than one, through which all things that are exist. But if there are more than one, either these are themselves to be referred to some one being, through which they exist, or they exist separately, each through itself, or they exist mutually through one another.

But, if these beings exist through one being, then all things do not exist through more than one, but rather through that one being through which these exist.

If, however, these exist separately, each through itself, there is, at any rate, some power or property of existing through self (*existendi per se*), by which they are able to exist each through itself. But, there can be no doubt that, in that case, they exist through this very power, which is one, and through which they are able to exist, each through itself. More truly, then, do all things exist through this very being, which is one, than through these, which are more than one, which, without this one, cannot exist.

But that these beings exist mutually through one another, no reason can admit; since it is an irrational conception that anything should exist through a being on which it confers existence. For not even beings of a relative nature exist thus mutually, the one through the other. For, though the terms *master* and *servant* are used with mutual reference, and the men thus designated are mentioned as having mutual relations, yet they do not at all exist mutually, the one through the other, since these relations exist through the subjects to which they are referred.

Therefore, since truth altogether excludes the supposition that there are more beings than one, through which all things exist, that being, through which all exist, must be one. Since, then, all things that are exist through this one being, doubtless this one being exists through itself. Whatever things there are else, then, exist through something other than themselves, and this alone through itself. But whatever exists through another is less than that, through which all things are, and which alone exists through itself. Therefore, that which exists through itself exists in the greatest degree of all things.

There is, then, some one being which alone exists in the greatest and the highest degree of all. But that which is greatest of all, and through which exists whatever is good or great, and, in short, whatever has any existence—that must be supremely good, and supremely great, and the highest of all existing beings.

The Critique of Pure Reason

IMMANUEL KANT

Immanuel Kant (1724–1804) summarized the classical arguments against the traditional proofs for the existence of the gods. The German philosopher contended that all speculative proofs were based on an illegitimate extension of pure reason and thus were fallacious.

There are only three kinds of proofs of the existence of God from speculative reason.

All the paths that can be followed to this end begin either from definite experience and the peculiar nature of the world of sense, known to us through experience, and ascend from it, according to the laws of causality, to the highest cause, existing outside the world; or they rest on indefinite experience only, that is, on any existence which is empirically given; or lastly, they leave all experience out of account, and conclude, entirely *a priori* from mere concepts, the existence of a supreme cause. The first proof is the *physico-theological,* the second the *cosmological,* the third the *ontological* proof. There are no more, and there can be no more.

I shall show that neither on the one path, the empirical, nor on the other, the transcendental, can reason achieve anything, and that it stretches its wings in vain, if it tries to soar beyond the world of sense by the mere power of speculation. With regard to the order in which these three arguments should be examined, it will be the opposite of that, followed by reason in its gradual development, in which we placed them also at first ourselves. For we shall be able to show that, although experience gives the first impulse, it is the transcendental concept only which guides reason in its endeavours, and fixes the last goal which reason wishes to retain. I shall therefore begin with the examination of the transcendental proof, and see afterwards how far it may be strengthened by the addition of empirical elements.

Of the Impossibility of an Ontological Proof of the Existence of God

It is easily perceived, from what has been said before, that the concept of an absolutely necessary Being is a concept of pure reason, that is, a mere idea, the objective reality of which is by no means proved by the fact that reason requires it. That idea does no more than point to a

From "The Transcendental Dialectic," Book II, Chapter III, Sections 3–6, in *The Critique of Pure Reason.* The translation is by F. Max Müller.

certain but unattainable completeness, and serves rather to limit the understanding, than to extend its sphere. It seems strange and absurd, however, that a conclusion of an absolutely necessary existence from a given existence in general should seem urgent and correct, and that yet all the conditions under which the understanding can form a concept of such a necessity should be entirely against us.

People have at all times been talking of an *absolutely necessary* Being, but they have tried, not so much to understand whether and how a thing of that kind could even be conceived, as rather to prove its existence. No doubt a verbal definition of that concept is quite easy, if we say that it is something the non-existence of which is impossible. This, however, does not make us much wiser with reference to the conditions that make it necessary to consider the non-existence of a thing as absolutely inconceivable. It is these conditions which we want to know, and whether by that concept we are thinking anything or not. For to use the word *unconditioned,* in order to get rid of all the conditions which the understanding always requires, when wishing to conceive something as necessary, does not render·it clear to us in the least whether, after that, we are still thinking anything or perhaps, nothing, by the concept of the unconditionally necessary.

Nay, more than this, people have imagined that by a number of examples they had explained this concept, at first risked at haphazard, and afterwards become quite familiar, and that therefore all further inquiry regarding its intelligibility were unnecessary. It was said that every proposition of geometry, such as, for instance, that a triangle has three angles, is absolutely necessary, and people began to talk of an object entirely outside the sphere of our understanding, as if they understood perfectly well what, by that concept, they wished to predicate of it.

But all these pretended examples are taken without exception from *judgments* only, not from *things,* and their existence. Now the unconditioned necessity of judgments is not the same thing as an absolute necessity of things. The absolute necessity of a judgment is only a conditioned necessity of the thing, or of the predicate in the judgment. The above proposition did not say that three angles were absolutely necessary, but that under the condition of the existence of a triangle, three angles are given (in it) by necessity. Nevertheless, this pure logical necessity has exerted so powerful an illusion, that, after having formed of a thing a concept a *priori* so constituted that it seemed to include existence in its sphere, people thought they could conclude with certainty that, because existence necessarily belongs to the object of that concept, provided always that I accept the thing as given (existing), its existence also must necessarily be accepted (according to the rule of identity), and that the Being therefore must itself be absolutely necessary, because its existence is implied in a concept, which is accepted voluntarily only, and always under the condition that I accept the object of it as given.

If in an identical judgment I reject the predicate and retain the subject, there arises a contradiction, and hence, I say, that the former belongs to the latter necessarily. But if I reject the subject as well as the predicate, there is no contradiction, because there is nothing left that can be contradicted. To accept a triangle and yet to reject its three angles is contradictory, but there is no contradiction at all in admitting the non-existence of the triangle and of its three angles. The same applies to the concept of an absolutely necessary Being. Remove its existence, and you remove the thing itself, with all its predicates, so that a contradiction becomes impossible. There is nothing external to which the contradiction could apply, because the thing is not meant to be externally necessary; nor is there anything internal that could be contradicted, for in removing the thing out of existence, you have removed at the same time all its internal qualities. If you say, God is almighty, that is a necessary judgment, because almightiness cannot be removed, if you accept a deity, that is, an infinite Being, with the concept of which that other concept is identical. But if you say, God is not, then neither his almightiness, nor any other of his predicates is given; they are all, together with the subject, removed out of existence, and therefore there is not the slightest contradiction in that sentence.

We have seen therefore that, if I remove the predicate of a judgment together with its subject, there can never be an internal contradiction, whatever the predicate may be. The only way of evading this conclusion would be to say that there are subjects which cannot be removed out of existence, but must always remain. But this would be the same as to say that there exist absolutely necessary subjects, an assumption the correctness of which I have called in question, and the possibility of which you had undertaken to prove. For I cannot form to myself the smallest concept of a thing which, if it had been removed together with all its predicates, should leave behind a contradiction; and except contradiction, I have no other test of impossibility by pure concepts *a priori*. Against all these general arguments (which no one can object to) you challenge me with a case, which you represent as a proof by a fact, namely, that there is one, and this one concept only, in which the non-existence or the removal of its object would be self-contradictory, namely, the concept of the most real Being (*ens realissimum*). You say that it possesses all reality, and you are no doubt justified in accepting such a Being as possible. This for the present I may admit, though the ab-

sence of self-contradictoriness in a concept is far from proving the possibility of its object.[1] Now reality comprehends existence, and therefore existence is contained in the concept of a thing possible. If that thing is removed, the internal possibility of the thing would be removed, and this is self-contradictory.

I answer:—Even in introducing into the concept of a thing, which you wish to think in its possibility only, the concept of its existence, under whatever disguise it may be, you have been guilty of a contradiction. If you were allowed to do this, you would apparently have carried your point; but in reality you have achieved nothing, but have only committed a tautology. I simply ask you, whether the proposition, that *this or that thing* (which, whatever it may be, I grant you as possible) *exists,* is an analytical or a synthetical proposition? If the former, then by its existence you add nothing to your thought of the thing; but in that case, either the thought within you would be the thing itself, or you have presupposed existence, as belonging to possibility, and have according to your own showing deduced existence from internal possibility, which is nothing but a miserable tautology. The mere word *reality,* which in the concept of a thing sounds different from existence in the concept of the predicate, can make no difference. For if you call all accepting or positing (without determining what it is) reality, you have placed a thing, with

---

[1] A concept is always possible, if it is not self-contradictory. This is the logical characteristic of possibility, and by it the object of the concept is distinguished from the *nihil negativum*. But it may nevertheless be an empty concept, unless the objective reality of the synthesis, by which the concept is generated, has been distinctly shown. This, however, as shown above, must always rest on principles of possible experience, and not on the principle of analysis (the principle of contradiction). This is a warning against inferring at once from the possibility of concepts (logical) the possibility of things (real).

all its predicates, within the concept of the subject, and accepted it as real, and you do nothing but repeat it in the predicate. If, on the contrary, you admit, as every sensible man must do, that every proposition involving existence is synthetical, how can you say that the predicate of existence does not admit of removal without contradiction, a distinguishing property which is peculiar to analytical propositions only, the very character of which depends on it?

I might have hoped to put an end to this subtle argumentation, without many words, and simply by an accurate definition of the concept of existence, if I had not seen that the illusion, in mistaking a logical predicate for a real one (that is the predicate which determines a thing), resists all correction. Everything can become a *logical predicate,* even the subject itself may be predicated of itself, because logic takes no account of any contents of concepts. *Determination,* however, is a predicate, added to the concept of the subject, and enlarging it, and it must not therefore be contained in it.

Being is evidently not a real predicate, or a concept of something that can be added to the concept of a thing. It is merely the admission of a thing, and of certain determinations in it. Logically, it is merely the copula of a judgment. The proposition, *God is almighty,* contains two concepts, each having its object, namely, God and almightiness. The small word *is,* is not an additional predicate, but only serves to put the predicate *in relation* to the subject. If, then, I take the subject (God) with all its predicates (including that of almightiness), and say, *God is,* or there is a God, I do not put a new predicate to the concept of God, but I only put the subject by itself, with all its predicates, in relation to my concept, as its object. Both must contain exactly the same kind of thing, and nothing can have been added to the concept, which expresses possibility

only, by my thinking its object as simply given and saying, it is. And thus the real does not contain more than the possible. A hundred real dollars do not contain a penny more than a hundred possible dollars. For as the latter signify the concept, the former the object and its position by itself, it is clear that, in case the former contained more than the latter, my concept would not express the whole object, and would not therefore be its adequate concept. In my financial position no doubt there exists more by one hundred real dollars, than by their concept only (that is their possibility), because in reality the object is not only contained analytically in my concept, but is added to my concept (which is a determination of my state), synthetically; but the conceived hundred dollars are not in the least increased through the existence which is outside my concept.

By whatever and by however many predicates I may think a thing (even in completely determining it) nothing is really added to it, if I add that the thing exists. Otherwise, it would not be the same that exists, but something more than was contained in the concept, and I could not say that the exact object of my concept existed. Nay, even if I were to think in a thing all reality, except one, that one missing reality would not be supplied by my saying that so defective a thing exists, but it would exist with the same defect with which I thought it; or what exists would be different from what I thought. If, then, I try to conceive a being, as the highest reality (without any defect), the question still remains, whether it exists or not. For though in my concept there may be wanting nothing of the possible real content of a thing in general, something is wanting in its relation to my whole state of thinking, namely, that the knowledge of that object should be possible *a posteriori* also. And here we perceive the cause of our difficulty. If we were concerned with an object of our senses, I could not mistake the existence of a thing for the mere concept of it; for by the concept the object is thought as only in harmony with the general conditions of a possible empirical knowledge, while by its existence it is thought as contained in the whole content of experience. Through this connection with the content of the whole experience, the concept of an object is not in the least increased; our thought has only received through it one more possible perception. If, however, we are thinking existence through the pure category alone, we need not wonder that we cannot find any characteristic to distinguish it from mere possibility.

Whatever, therefore, our concept of an object may contain, we must always step outside it, in order to attribute to it existence. With objects of the senses, this takes place through their connection with any one of my perceptions, according to empirical laws; with objects of pure thought, however, there is no means of knowing their existence, because it would have to be known entirely *a priori*, while our consciousness of every kind of existence, whether immediately by perception, or by conclusions which connect something with perception, belongs entirely to the unity of experience, and any existence outside that field, though it cannot be declared to be absolutely impossible, is a presupposition that cannot be justified by anything.

The concept of a Supreme Being is, in many respects, a very useful idea, but, being an idea only, it is quite incapable of increasing, by itself alone, our knowledge with regard to what exists. It cannot even do so much as to inform us any further as to its possibility. The analytical characteristic of possibility, which consists in the absence of contradiction in mere positions (realities), cannot be denied to it; but the connection of all real properties in one and the same thing is a synthesis the possibility of which we cannot judge *a priori*

because these realities are not given to us as such, and because, even if this were so, no judgment whatever takes place, it being necessary to look for the characteristic of the possibility of synthetical knowledge in experience only, to which the object of an idea can never belong. Thus we see that the celebrated Leibniz is far from having achieved what he thought he had, namely, to understand *a priori* the possibility of so sublime an ideal Being.

Time and labour therefore are lost on the famous ontological (Cartesian) proof of the existence of a Supreme Being from mere concepts; and a man might as well imagine that he could become richer in knowledge by mere ideas, as a merchant in capital, if, in order to improve his position, he were to add a few noughts to his cash account.

Of the Impossibility of a Cosmological Proof of the Existence of God

It was something quite unnatural, and a mere innovation of scholastic wisdom, to attempt to pick out of an entirely arbitrary idea the existence of the object corresponding to it. Such an attempt would never have been made, if there had not existed beforehand a need of our reason of admitting for existence in general something necessary, to which we may ascend and in which we may rest; and if, as that necessity must be unconditioned and *a priori* certain, reason had not been forced to seek a concept which, if possible, should satisfy such a demand and give us a knowledge of an existence entirely *a priori*. Such a concept was supposed to exist in the idea of an *ens realissimum*, and that idea was therefore used for a more definite knowledge of that, the existence of which one had admitted or been persuaded of independently, namely, of the necessary Being. This very natural procedure of reason was carefully concealed, and instead of ending with that concept, an attempt was made to begin with it, and thus to derive from it the necessity of existence, which it was only meant to supplement. Hence arose that unfortunate ontological proof, which satisfies neither the demands of our natural and healthy understanding, nor the requirements of the schools.

The *cosmological proof,* which we have now to examine, retains the connection of absolute necessity with the highest reality, but instead of concluding, like the former, from the highest reality necessity in existence, it concludes from the given unconditioned necessity of any being, its unlimited reality. It thus brings everything at least into the groove of a natural, though I know not whether of a really or only apparently rational syllogism, which carries the greatest conviction, not only for the common, but also for the speculative understanding, and has evidently drawn the first outline of all proofs of natural theology, which have been followed at all times, and will be followed in future also, however much they may be hidden and disguised. We shall now proceed to exhibit and to examine this cosmological proof which Leibniz calls also the proof *a contingentia mundi.*

It runs as follows: If there exists anything, there must exist an absolutely necessary Being also. Now I, at least, exist; therefore there exists an absolutely necessary Being. The minor contains an experience, the major the conclusion from experience in general to the existence of the necessary.[2] This proof therefore begins with experience, and is not entirely *a priori,* or ontological; and, as the object of

all possible experience is called the world, this proof is called the *cosmological proof.* As it takes no account of any peculiar property of the objects of experience, by which this world of ours may differ from any other possible world, it is distinguished, in its name also, from the physico-theological proof, which employs as arguments, observations of the peculiar property of this our world of sense.

The proof then proceeds as follows: The necessary Being can be determined in one way only, that is, by one only of all possible opposite predicates; it must therefore be determined completely by its own concept. Now, there is only one concept of a thing possible, which *a priori* completely determines it, namely, that of the *ens realissimum.* It follows, therefore, that the concept of the *ens realissimum* is the only one by which a necessary Being can be thought, and therefore it is concluded that a highest Being exists by necessity.

There are so many sophistical propositions in this cosmological argument, that it really seems as if speculative reason had spent all her dialectical skill in order to produce the greatest possible transcendental illusion. Before examining it, we shall draw up a list of them, by which reason has put forward an old argument disguised as a new one, in order to appeal to the agreement of two witnesses, one supplied by pure reason, the other by experience, while in reality there is only one, namely, the first, who changes his dress and voice in order to be taken for a second. In order to have a secure foundation, this proof takes its stand on experience, and pretends to be different from the ontological proof, which places its whole confidence in pure concepts *a priori* only. The cosmological proof, however, uses that experience only in order to make one step, namely, to the existence of a necessary Being in general. What properties that Being may have, can never be learnt from the empirical argument, and for that

___

2 This conclusion is too well known to require detailed exposition. It rests on the apparently transcendental law of causality in nature, that everything *contingent* has its cause, which, if contingent again, must likewise have a cause, till the series of subordinate causes ends in an absolutely necessary cause, without which it could not be complete.

purpose reason takes leave of it altogether, and tries to find out, from among concepts only, what properties an absolutely necessary Being ought to possess, i.e. which among all possible things contains in itself the requisite conditions (*requisita*) of absolute necessity. This requisite is believed by reason to exist in the concept of an *ens realissimum* only, and reason concludes at once that this must be the absolutely necessary Being. In this conclusion it is simply assumed that the concept of a being of the highest reality is perfectly adequate to the concept of absolute necessity in existence; so that the latter might be concluded from the former. This is the same proposition as that maintained in the ontological argument, and is simply taken over into the cosmological proof, nay, made its foundation, although the intention was to avoid it. For it is clear that absolute necessity is an existence from mere concepts. If, then, I say that the concept of the *ens realissimum* is such a concept, and is the only concept adequate to necessary existence, I am bound to admit that the latter may be deduced from the former. The whole conclusive strength of the so-called cosmological proof rests therefore in reality on the ontological proof from mere concepts, while the appeal to experience is quite superfluous, and, though it may lead us on to the concept of absolute necessity, it cannot demonstrate it with any definite object. For as soon as we intend to do this, we must at once abandon all experience, and try to find out which among the pure concepts may contain the conditions of the possibility of an absolutely necessary Being. But if in this way the possibility of such a Being has been perceived, its existence also has been proved: for what we are really saying is this, that under all possible things there is one which carries with it absolute necessity, or that this Being exists with absolute necessity.

Sophisms in arguments are most easily discovered, if they are put forward in a correct scholastic form. This we shall now proceed to do.

If the proposition is right, that every absolutely necessary Being is, at the same time, the most real Being (and this is the *nervus probandi* of the cosmological proof), it must, like all affirmative judgments, be capable of conversion, at least *per accidens*. This would give us the proposition that some *entia realissima* are at the same time absolutely necessary beings. One *ens realissimum*, however, does not differ from any other on any point, and what applies to one, applies also to all. In this case, therefore, I may employ absolute conversion, and say, that every *ens realissimum* is a necessary Being. As this proposition is determined by its concepts *a priori* only, it follows that the mere concept of the *ens realissimum* must carry with it its absolute necessity; and this, which was maintained by the ontological proof, and not recognised by the cosmological, forms really the foundation of the conclusions of the latter, though in a disguised form.

We thus see that the second road taken by speculative reason, in order to prove the existence of the highest Being, is not only as illusory as the first, but commits in addition an *ignoratio elenchi,* promising to lead us by a new path, but after a short circuit bringing us back to the old one, which we had abandoned for its sake.

I said before that a whole nest of dialectical assumptions was hidden in that cosmological proof, and that transcendental criticism might easily detect and destroy it. I shall here enumerate them only, leaving it to the experience of the reader to follow up the fallacies and remove them.

We find, first, the transcendental principle of inferring a cause from the accidental. This principle, that everything contingent must have a cause, is valid in the world of sense only, and has not even a meaning outside it. For the purely intellectual concept of the contingent cannot produce a synthetical proposition like that of causality, and the principle of causality has no meaning and no criterion of its use, except in the world of sense, while here it is meant to help us beyond the world of sense.

Secondly. The inference of a first cause, based on the impossibility of an infinite ascending series of given causes in this world of sense,—an inference which the principles of the use of reason do not allow us to draw even in experience, while here we extend that principle beyond experience, whither that series can never be prolonged.

Thirdly. The false self-satisfaction of reason with regard to the completion of that series, brought about by removing in the end every kind of condition, without which, nevertheless, no concept of necessity is possible, and by then, when any definite concepts have become impossible, accepting this as a completion of our concept.

Fourthly. The mistaking the logical possibility of a concept of all united reality (without any internal contradiction) for the transcendental, which requires a principle for the practicability of such a synthesis, such principle however being applicable to the field of possible experience only, etc.

The trick of the cosmological proof consists only in trying to avoid the proof of the existence of a necessary Being *a priori* by mere concepts. Such a proof would have to be ontological, and of this we feel ourselves quite incapable. For this reason we take a real existence (of any experience whatever), and conclude from it, as well as may be, some absolutely necessary condition of it. In that case there is no necessity for explaining its possibility, because, if it has been proved that it exists, the question as to its possibility is unnecessary.

If then we want to determine that necessary Being more accurately, according to its nature, we do not seek what is sufficient to make us understand from its concept the necessity of its existence. If we could do this, no empirical presupposition would be necessary. No, we only seek the negative condition (*conditio sine qua non*), without which a Being would not be absolutely necessary. Now, in every other kind of syllogisms leading from a given effect to its cause, this might well be feasible. In our case, however, it happens unfortunately that the condition which is required for absolute necessity exists in one single Being only, which, therefore, would have to contain in its concept all that is required for absolute necessity, and that renders a conclusion *a priori,* with regard to such necessity, possible. I ought therefore to be able to reason conversely, namely, that everything is absolutely necessary, if that concept (of the highest reality) belongs to it. If I cannot do this (and I must confess that I cannot, if I wish to avoid the ontological proof), I have suffered shipwreck on my new course, and have come back again from where I started. The concept of the highest Being may satisfy all questions *a priori* which can be asked regarding the internal determinations of a thing, and it is therefore an ideal, without an equal, because the general concept distinguishes it at the same time as an individual being among all possible things. But it does not satisfy the really important question regarding its own existence; and if some one who admitted the existence of a necessary Being were to ask us which of all things in the world could be regarded as such, we could not answer: This here is the necessary Being.

It may be allowable to *admit* the existence of a Being entirely sufficient to serve as the cause of all possible effects, simply in order to assist reason in her search for unity of causes. But to go so far as to say that *such a Being exists necessarily,* is no longer the modest language of an admissible hypothesis, but the bold assurance of apodictic certainty; for the knowledge of that which is absolutely necessary must itself possess absolute necessity.

The whole problem of the transcendental Ideal is this, either to find a concept compatible with absolute necessity, or to find the absolute necessity compatible with the concept of anything. If the one is possible, the other must be so also, for reason recognises that only as absolutely necessary which is necessary according to its concept. Both these tasks baffle our attempts at *satisfying* our understanding on this point, and likewise our endeavours to comfort it with regard to its impotence.

That unconditioned necessity, which we require as the last support of all things, is the true abyss of human reason. Eternity itself, however terrible and sublime it may have been depicted by Haller, is far from producing the same giddy impression, for it only *measures* the duration of things, but does not *support* them. We cannot put off the thought, nor can we support it, that a Being, which we represent to ourselves as the highest among all possible beings, should say to himself, I am from eternity to eternity, there is nothing beside me, except that which is something through my will,—*but whence am I?* Here all sinks away from under us, and the highest perfection, like the smallest, passes without support before the eyes of speculative reason, which finds no difficulty in making the one as well as the other to disappear without the slightest impediment.

Many powers of nature, which manifest their existence by certain effects, remain perfectly inscrutable to us, because we cannot follow them up far enough by observation. The transcendental object, which forms the foundation of all phenomena, and with it the ground of our sensibility having this rather than any other supreme conditions, is and always

will be inscrutable. The thing no doubt is given, but it is incomprehensible. An ideal of pure reason, however, cannot be called inscrutable, because it cannot produce any credentials of its reality beyond the requirement of reason to perfect all synthetical unity by means of it. As, therefore, it is not even given as an object that can be thought, it cannot be said to be, as such, inscrutable; but, being a mere idea, it must find in the nature of reason its place and its solution, and in that sense be capable of scrutiny. For it is the very essence of reason that we are able to give an account of all our concepts, opinions, and assertions either on objective or, if they are a mere illusion, on subjective grounds.

Discovery and Explanation of the Dialectical Illusion in all Transcendental Proofs of the Existence of a Necessary Being

Both proofs, hitherto attempted, were transcendental, that is, independent of empirical principles. For although the cosmological proof assumes for its foundation an experience in general, it does not rest on any particular quality of it, but on pure principles of reason, with reference to an existence given by the empirical consciousness in general, and abandons even that guidance in order to derive its support from pure concepts only. What then in these transcendental proofs is the cause of the dialectical, but natural, illusion which connects the concepts of necessity and of the highest reality, and realises and hypostasises that which can only be an idea? What is the cause that renders it inevitable to admit something as necessary in itself among existing things, and yet makes us shrink back from the existence of such a Being as from an abyss? What is to be done that reason should understand itself on this point, and, escaping from the wavering state of hesitatingly approving or disapproving, acquire a calm insight into the matter?

It is surely extremely strange that, as soon as we suppose that something exists, we cannot avoid the conclusion that something exists necessarily. On this quite natural, though by no means, therefore, certain conclusion, rests the whole cosmological argument. On the other side, I may take any concept of anything, and I find that its existence has never to be represented by me as absolutely necessary, nay, that nothing prevents me, whatever may exist, from thinking its non-existence. I may, therefore, have to admit something necessary as the condition of existing things in general, but I need not think any single thing as necessary in itself. In other words I can never *complete* the regressus to the conditions of existence without admitting a necessary Being, but I can never *begin* with such a Being.

If, therefore, I am obliged to think something necessary for all existing things, and at the same time am not justified in thinking of anything as in itself necessary, the conclusion is inevitable: that necessity and contingency do not concern things themselves, for otherwise there would be a contradiction, and that therefore neither of the two principles can be objective; but that they may possibly be subjective principles of reason only, according to which, on one side, we have to find for all that is given as existing, something that is necessary, and thus never to stop except when we have reached an *a priori* complete explanation; while on the other we must never hope for that completion, that is, never admit anything empirical as unconditioned, and thus dispense with its further derivation. In that sense both principles as purely heuristic and *regulative,* and affecting the formal interests of reason only, may well stand side by side. For the one tells us that we ought to philosophise on nature as if there was a necessary first cause for everything that exists, if only in order to introduce systematical unity into our knowledge, by always looking for such an idea as an imagined highest cause. The other warns us against mistaking any single determination concerning the existence of things for such a highest cause, i.e. for something absolutely necessary, and bids us to keep the way always open for further derivation, and to treat it always as conditioned. If, then, everything that is perceived in things has to be considered by us as only conditionally necessary, nothing that is empirically given can ever be considered as absolutely necessary.

It follows from this that the absolutely necessary must be accepted as *outside the world,* because it is only meant to serve as a principle of the greatest possible unity of phenomena, of which it is the highest cause, and that it can never be reached *in the world,* because the second rule bids you always to consider all empirical causes of that unity as derived.

The philosophers of antiquity considered all form in nature as contingent, but matter, according to the judgment of common reason, as primitive and necessary. If, however, they had considered matter, not relatively as the substratum of phenomena, but as existing *by itself,* the idea of absolute necessity would have vanished at once, for there is nothing that binds reason absolutely to that existence, but reason can at any time and without contradiction remove it in thought, and it was in thought only that it could claim absolute necessity. The ground of this persuasion must therefore have been a certain regulative principle. And so it is; for extension and impermeability (which together constitute the concept of matter) furnish the highest empirical principle of the unity of phenomena, and possess, so far as this principle is empirically unconditioned, the character of a regulative principle. Nevertheless, as every determination of matter, which constitutes its reality, and hence the impermeability of matter also, is an effect (action) which must have a cause, and therefore be itself derived, matter is not adequate to the idea of a necessary Being, as a principle of all derived unity, because every one of its real qualities is derived and, therefore, conditionally necessary only, so that it could be removed, and with it would be removed the whole existence of matter. If this were not so, we should have reached the highest cause of unity, empirically, which is forbidden by the second regulative principle. It follows from all this that matter and everything in general that belongs to the world are not fit for the idea of a necessary original Being, as a mere principle of the greatest empirical unity, but that we must place it outside the world. In that case there is no reason why we should not simply derive the phenomena of the world and their existence from other phenomena, as if there were no necessary Being at all, while at the same time we might always strive towards the completeness of that derivation, just as if such a Being, as the highest cause, were presupposed.

The ideal of the Supreme Being is therefore, according to these remarks, nothing but a *regulative principle* of reason, which obliges us to consider all connection in the world as if it arose from an all-sufficient necessary cause, in order to found on it the rule of a systematical unity necessary according to general laws for the explanation of the world; it does not involve the assertion of an existence necessary by itself. It is impossible, however, at the same time, to escape from a transcendental *subreptio,* which leads us to represent that formal principle as constitutive, and to think that unity as hypostasised. It is the same with space. Space, though it is only a principle of sensibility, yet serves originally to make all forms possible, these being only limitations of it. For that very reason, however, it is mistaken for something absolutely necessary and independent, nay, for an object *a priori* existing in itself. It is the same here, and as this systematical unity of nature can in no wise become the principle of the empirical use of our reason, unless we base it on the idea of an *ens realissimum* as the highest cause, it happens quite naturally that we thus represent that idea as a real object, and that object again, as it is the highest condition, as necessary. Thus a *regulative* principle has been changed into a *constitutive* principle, which substitution becomes evident at once because, as soon as I consider that highest Being, which with regard to the world was absolutely (unconditionally) necessary, as a thing by itself, that necessity cannot be conceived, and can therefore have existed in my reason as a formal condition of thought only, and not as a material and substantial condition of existence.

Of the Impossibility of the Physico-theological Proof

If, then, neither the concept of things in general, nor the experience of any *existence in general,* can satisfy our demands, there still remains one way open, namely, to try whether any *definite experience,* and consequently that of things in the world as it is, their constitution and disposition, may not supply a proof which could give us the certain conviction of the existence of a Supreme Being. Such a proof we should call *physico-theological.* If that, however, should prove impossible too, then it is clear that no satisfactory proof whatever, from merely speculative reason, is possible, in support of the existence of a Being, corresponding to our transcendental idea.

After what has been said already, it will be easily understood that we may expect an easy and complete answer to this question. For how could there ever be an experience that should be adequate to an idea? It is the very nature of an idea that no experience can ever be adequate to it.

The transcendental idea of a necessary and all-sufficient original Being is so overwhelming, so high above everything empirical, which is always conditioned, that we can never find in experience enough material to fill such a concept, and can only grope about among things conditioned, looking in vain for the unconditioned, of which no rule of any empirical synthesis can ever give us an example, or even show the way towards it.

If the highest Being should stand itself in that chain of conditions, it would be a link in the series, and would, exactly like the lower links, above which it is placed, require further investigation with regard to its own still higher cause. If, on the contrary, we mean to separate it from that chain, and, as a purely intelligible Being, not comprehend it in the series of natural causes, what bridge is then open for reason to reach it, considering that all rules determining the transition from effect to cause, nay, all synthesis and extension of our knowledge in general, refer to nothing but possible experience, and therefore to the objects of the world of sense only, and are valid nowhere else?

This present world presents to us so immeasurable a stage of variety, order, fitness, and beauty, whether we follow it up in the infinity of space or in its unlimited division, that even with the little knowledge which our poor understanding has been able to gather, all language, with regard to so many and inconceivable wonders, loses its vigour, all numbers their power of measuring, and all our thoughts their necessary determination; so that our judgment of the whole is lost in a speechless, but all the more eloquent astonishment. Everywhere we see a chain of causes and effects, of means and ends, of order in birth and death, and as nothing has entered by itself into the state in which we find it, all points to another thing as its cause. As that cause necessitates the same further enquiry, the whole universe would

thus be lost in the abyss of nothing, unless we admitted something which, existing by itself, original and independent, outside the chain of infinite contingencies, should support it, and, as the cause of its origin, secure to it at the same time its permanence. Looking at all the things in the world, what greatness shall we attribute to that highest cause? We do not know the whole contents of the world, still less can we measure its magnitude by a comparison with all that is possible. But, as with regard to causality, we cannot do without a last and highest Being, why should we not fix the degree of its perfection *beyond everything else that is possible?* This we can easily do, though only in the faint outline of an abstract concept, if we represent to ourselves all possible perfections united in it as in one substance. Such a concept would agree with the demand of our reason, which requires parsimony in the number of principles; it would have no contradictions in itself, would be favourable to the extension of the employment of reason in the midst of experience, by guiding it towards order and system, and lastly, would never be decidedly opposed to any experience.

This proof will always deserve to be treated with respect. It is the oldest, the clearest, and most in conformity with human reason. It gives life to the study of nature, deriving its own existence from it, and thus constantly acquiring new vigour.

It reveals aims and intention, where our own observation would not by itself have discovered them, and enlarges our knowledge of nature by leading us towards that peculiar unity the principle of which exists outside nature. This knowledge reacts again on its cause, namely, the transcendental idea, and thus increases the belief in a supreme Author to an irresistible conviction.

It would therefore be not only extremely sad, but utterly vain to attempt to diminish the authority of that proof. Reason, constantly strengthened by the powerful arguments that come to hand by themselves, though they are no doubt empirical only, cannot be discouraged by any doubts of subtle and abstract speculation. Roused from every inquisitive indecision, as from a dream, by one glance at the wonders of nature and the majesty of the cosmos, reason soars from height to height till it reaches the highest, from the conditioned to conditions, till it reaches the supreme and unconditioned Author of all.

But although we have nothing to say against the reasonableness and utility of this line of argument, but wish, on the contrary, to commend and encourage it, we cannot approve of the claims which this proof advances to apodictic certainty, and to an approval on its own merits, requiring no favour, and no help from any other quarter. It cannot injure the good cause, if the dogmatical language of the overweening sophist is toned down to the moderate and modest statements of a faith which does not require unconditioned submission, yet is sufficient to give rest and comfort. I therefore maintain that the physico-theological proof can never establish by itself alone the existence of a Supreme Being, but must always leave it to the ontological proof (to which it serves only as an introduction), to supply its deficiency; so that, after all, it is the ontological proof which contains the *only possible argument* (supposing always that any speculative proof is possible), and human reason can never do without it.

The principal points of the physico-theological proof are the following. 1st. There are everywhere in the world clear indications of an intentional arrangement carried out with great wisdom, and forming a whole indescribably varied in its contents and infinite in extent.

2ndly. The fitness of this arrangement is entirely foreign to the things existing in the world, and belongs to them contingently only; that is, the nature of different things could never spontaneously, by the combination of so many means, co-operate towards definite aims, if these means had not been selected and arranged on purpose by a rational disposing principle, according to certain fundamental ideas.

3rdly. There exists, therefore, a sublime and wise cause (or many), which must be the cause of the world, not only as a blind and all-powerful nature, by means of unconscious *fecundity,* but as an intelligence, by *freedom.*

4thly. The unity of that cause may be inferred with certainty from the unity of the reciprocal relation of the parts of the world, as portions of a skilful edifice, so far as our experience reaches, and beyond it, with plausibility, according to the principles of analogy.

Without wishing to argue, for the sake of argument only, with natural reason, as to its conclusion in inferring from the analogy of certain products of nature with the works of human art, in which man does violence to nature, and forces it not to follow its own aims, but to adapt itself to ours (that is, from the similarity of certain products of nature with houses, ships, and watches), in inferring from this, I say, that a similar causality, namely, understanding and will, must be at the bottom of nature, and in deriving the internal possibility of a freely acting nature (which, it may be, renders all human art and even human reason possible) from another though superhuman art—a kind of reasoning, which probably could not stand the severest test of transcendental criticism; we are willing to admit, nevertheless, that if we have to name such a cause, we cannot do better than to follow the analogy of such products of human design, which are the only ones of which we know completely both cause and effect. There would be no excuse, if reason were to surrender a causality which it knows, and have recourse to obscure and indemonstrable principles of explanation, which it does not know.

According to this argument, the fitness and harmony existing in so many works of nature might prove the contingency of the form, but not of the matter, that is, the substance in the world, because, for the latter purpose, it would be necessary to prove in addition, that the things of the world were in themselves incapable of such order and harmony, according to general laws, unless there existed, even in their *substance,* the product of a supreme wisdom. For this purpose, very different arguments would be required from those derived from the analogy of human art. The utmost, therefore, that could be established by such a proof would be an *architect of the world,* always very much hampered by the quality of the material with which he has to work, not a *creator,* to whose idea everything is subject. This would by no means suffice for the purposed aim of proving an all-sufficient original Being. If we wished to prove the contingency of matter itself, we must have recourse to a transcendental argument, and this is the very thing which was to be avoided.

The inference, therefore, really proceeds from the order and design that can everywhere be observed in the world, as an entirely contingent arrangement, to the existence of a cause, *proportionate to it.* The concept of that cause must therefore teach us something quite *definite* about it, and can therefore be no other concept but that of a Being which possesses all might, wisdom, etc., in one word, all perfection of an all-sufficient Being. The predicates of a *very great,* of an astounding, of an immeasurable might and virtue give us no definite concept, and never tell us really what the thing is by itself. They are only relative representations of the magnitude of an object, which the observer (of the world) compares with

himself and his own power of comprehension, and which would be equally grand, whether we magnify the object, or reduce the observing subject to smaller proportions in reference to it. Where we are concerned with the magnitude (of the perfection) of a thing in general, there exists no definite concept, except that which comprehends all possible perfection, and only the all (*omnitudo*) of reality is thoroughly determined in the concept.

Now I hope that no one would dare to comprehend the relation of that part of the world which he has observed (in its extent as well as in its contents) to omnipotence, the relation of the order of the world to the highest wisdom, and the relation of the unity of the world to the absolute unity of its author, etc. Physico-theology, therefore, can never give a definite concept of the highest cause of the world, and is insufficient, therefore, as a principle of theology, which is itself to form the basis of religion.

The step leading to absolute totality is entirely impossible on the empirical road. Nevertheless, that step is taken in the physico-theological proof. How then has this broad abyss been bridged over?

The fact is that, after having reached the stage of admiration of the greatness, the wisdom, the power, etc. of the Author of the world, and seeing no further advance possible, one suddenly leaves the argument carried on by empirical proofs, and lays hold of that contingency which, from the very first, was inferred from the order and design of the world. The next step from that contingency leads, by means of transcendental concepts only, to the existence of something absolutely necessary, and another step from the absolute necessity of the first cause to its completely determined or determining concept, namely, that of an all-embracing reality. Thus we see that the physico-theological proof, baffled in its own undertaking, takes suddenly refuge in the cosmological proof, and as this is only the ontological proof in disguise, it really carries out its original intention by means of pure reason only; though it so strongly disclaimed in the beginning all connection with it, and professed to base everything on clear proofs from experience.

Those who adopt the physico-theological argument have no reason to be so very coy towards the transcendental mode of argument, and with the conceit of enlightened observers of nature to look down upon them as the cobwebs of dark speculators. If they would only examine themselves, they would find that, after they had advanced a good way on the soil of nature and experience, and found themselves nevertheless as much removed as ever from the object revealed to their reason, they suddenly leave that soil, to enter into the realm of pure possibilities, where on the wings of ideas they hope to reach that which had withdrawn itself from all their empirical investigations. Imagining themselves to be on firm ground after that desperate leap, they now proceed to expand the definite concept which they have acquired, they do not know how, over the whole field of creation; and they explain the ideal, which was merely a product of pure reason, by experience, though in a very poor way, and totally beneath the dignity of the object, refusing all the while to admit that they have arrived at that knowledge or supposition by a very different road from that of experience.

Thus we have seen that the physico-theological proof rests on the cosmological, and the cosmological on the ontological proof of the existence of one original Being as the Supreme Being; and, as besides these three, there is no other path open to speculative reason, the ontological proof, based exclusively on pure concepts of reason, is the only possible one, always supposing that any proof of a proposition, so far transcending the empirical use of the understanding, is possible at all.

THE NATURE
OF THE GODS

It is not enough for religious men to know that the gods exist; it is at least as important to know the nature of the divine power. But immediately the philosopher asks whether or not a theory of the nature of the gods makes sense. It clearly does in a polytheism where, through a division of divine labor, each god can assume a specific role. Zeus rules the earth, Poseidon the sea, and Hades the underworld. It is only in jurisdictional disputes, for example at the ocean's edge, that a polytheism raises interesting philosophic problems. Similarly, in theological dualisms, for example Zoroastrianism, a doctrine of the divine nature is not difficult. The divine Ahura Mazda is wholly good, the demonic Angra Mainyu thoroughly evil. Where religious thinking is largely anthropomorphic, it may well be that philosophers have nothing to say.

It is in those religious movements which hold that divine power is in some sense a unity that interesting philosophic puzzles arise. Most of them arise from the following question: How is it possible to describe the nature of divine power in such a way as to avoid suggesting that it is limited? The queston can take this form: If God is here, doesn't it follow that He is not over there? Or it may appear in a more subtle form: If God transcends historical time, then how can He act *in* history? In short, if the process of describing is essentially a process of delimiting, then any description of God will limit Him.[1]

---

[1] Again, this problem does not arise in describing the individual gods of a polytheism, for the division of their labor is intended as a limitation. However, one might want to consider whether or not the problem would arise when the polytheism is considered as a whole, i.e., does the full council table of the gods have a nature?

Although theologians have admitted that this is a problem, they have refused to concede that it is insoluble. The following selections represent four attempts at describing the divine nature without limiting it.

The Muslim *Bahr al-Kalām* seeks to interpret those verses from the Koran where a literal reading suggests that Allah is limited in time and space. The selected passages are an attempted refutation of the anthropomorphism that threatens every theism in which the god is seen as personal. Fundamentally, the refutation consists in charging that the heterodox have brought to the description of the divine, habits of thought appropriate to more commonplace analysis. However, you might wish to ask whether or not the orthodox claim that Allah existed *before* space and time makes philosophic nonsense out of the word "existed."

St. Athanasius is concerned to justify the Christian claim that God was present in Jesus. The doctrine of the Incarnation and its corollary, the doctrine of the Trinity, have always been at the heart of the Christian tradition. The Greek philosophers (in this selection, "the Gentiles") had argued that the Christian claim of an incarnation was absurd. Anthanasius' reply is that on the philosophers' own admission there is a Universal Law, or Word, governing all things. But if the Word governs the whole, it surely must govern the parts. What then is odd in suggesting that this Word appeared in history as a fellow man, sacrificing himself for the sake of the rest of us? To suggest that the Word might better have appeared as a meteor or comet is mere theatrics: to say that He came as a man is to recognize the depth of human need. In brief, though God is beyond man, He makes Himself less that man might become more.

In the view of Śaṁkara, such a claim would not escape anthropomorphism. In his commentary on the *Vedānta Sūtra*, this greatest of Indian philosophers holds that man's highest spiritual state reveals a quality-less Ground that is beyond any specific nature. Even though this Ground may be apprehended as having qualities (Saguṇa Brahman), such an apprehension is fundamentally mistaken. Higher spiritual insight reveals it to be beyond qualification (Nirguṇa Brahman). It is that One that is the Self that is All. If so, It is beyond all distinctions, and the attribution of any qualities to It is false.

Several centuries later, Rāmānuja, also commenting on the *Vedānta Sūtra,* urges a modification of *Śaṁkara's* doctrine. Though it is the case that All is One, it does not follow that all plurality is unreal. Rather, in the high state of mystical realization, the saint comes to enjoy that pure self which is the Ground. Thus, difference persists within unity.

ABU 'L-MU'ĪN AN-NASAFĪ

The Bahr al-Kalām fī 'Ilm at-Tawhīd *was composed by Abū 'l-Mu'īn an-Nasafī, who died in 1114. The Roman numerals indicate Koranic chapters and the Arabic numerals Koranic verses.*

The Karrāmites teach that Allah sat at rest upon the Throne so that it was filled with Him. Their evidence for this is the saying of Allah (XX, 5/4): "The Merciful has taken His seat upon the Throne." Our reply to them is that some of the Commentators say that *istawā* (took seat) means *istawlā*, i.e., "assumed authority," as in Persian one says: *bar 'arsh pādshāh ast* (the sovereign is on the throne). An indication of this meaning is also given by the words of the poet:

A man has taken his seat over 'Irāq,
Without sword, and without blood being shed,

where *istawā* (has taken his seat) clearly means *istawlā*, i.e., "assumed authority." From Mālik b. Anas,[1] the Imām of al-Madīna, is recorded the saying: "The taking of the seat is not a matter of which we are ignorant, though how it comes about is a matter we do not understand. Belief in it is incumbent upon us, and questioning about it is heretical innovation." He said to the one who was asking the question: "All I can see is that you are far astray [in error]." He ordered enquiry to be made, and lo! it was Jahm b. Ṣafwān[2] [who asked the question]. Since Allah existed before He created the Throne and it is not permissible to say that He was transferred to the Throne, because [being subject to] transference [from place to place] is an attribute of creatures and one of the signs of things that are contingent, whereas Allah is far removed from that; and since anyone who affirms the sitting [of Allah] at rest upon the Throne must teach either that He is the same size as the Throne, or that the Throne is bigger than He is, or that He is bigger than the Throne. Whichever way you take it the one who says such things is an unbeliever for he has made Him a limited being.

It is related that 'Alī b. Abī Tālib—

---

[1] Abū 'Abdallah Mālik b. Anas (d. 795 A.D.), was the founder of the second of the four orthodox rites among Sunni Muslims.

[2] Jahm b. Ṣafwān (d. 746 A.D.), the founder of the heretical group of the Jahmites. He was put to death in 746.

From *A Reader on Islam*, Arthur Jeffery, ed.; S-Gravenhage, Mouton & Co., 1962; pp. 393–99, 402. Reprinted by permission of Mouton & Co.

with whom may Allah be pleased—was asked: "Where was our Lord before the Throne was created?" He—with whom may Allah be pleased—said: "How is it that there is such a question about place, seeing that Allah existed when there was as yet neither space nor time, and He is at the present time just as He was then." So it is related that Ja'far aṣ-Ṣādiq [3]—with whom may Allah be pleased—said: "The doctrine of the Divine unity involves three points, viz., that you should recognize that He is not *from* a thing nor *in* a thing, nor *on* a thing, for whosoever describes Him as *from* a thing has described Him as something created, which is unbelief and has no basis; and whoso describes Him as *in* a thing has described Him as limited, which is unbelief; and whoso describes Him as being *on* a thing has described Him as being in need of being upborne, and that too is unbelief."

What is happening is that the Assimilationists are seizing upon the surface meanings of verses such as (XXVIII, 88): "Everything will perish save His face," and (LV, 27): "but the face of thy Lord, majestic and glorious, will remain," and of obscure Traditions, such as the Prophet's saying that Allah created Adam with His hand, wrote the Torah with His hand, created the Garden of Eden with His hand, planted the tree ṭūbā [4] with His hand, and one line of transmission [of this Tradition] adds that He created the camel with His hand. It is related of Muḥammad b. al-Ḥasan [5]—on whom may Allah have

mercy—that he used to say: "We believe in Allah, and in what has come from Allah, according as Allah desired, and as the Apostle of Allah—upon whom be Allah's blessing and peace—desired. We do not concern ourselves with how Allah intended it, or with [the reason for] what the Apostle of Allah brought [to us]." This statement is the one preferred by many of the leaders of the community and the theologians of [our] school.

The Jahmites [6]—whom may Allah curse—teach that Allah is in every place, basing their teaching on such verses as (XLIII, 84): "He it is Who is God in the heavens and God on the earth," and (XVI, 128): "Allah is indeed with those who show piety, and with those who are doers of good," and (LVII, 4): "and He is with you wherever ye may be," and (LVIII, 7/8): "No three are ever in private conference but Allah is the fourth of them, nor five but He is their sixth . . . wherever they may be He is with them." The answer [to them] is that the reference in such verses as: "He it is Who is God in the heaven and God on the earth," is to His decreeing and arranging [things in heaven and on earth]. So also His words in (LXVII, 16): "Or are ye safe from Him Who is in the heaven making the earth sink beneath you? so that lo! it is quaking," mean: [are ye safe] from Him the traces of Whose power show in the heavens? Likewise the verse about three not being in secret talk without His being the fourth, refers to His knowledge, and that about His being with you wherever ye may be, also refers to [His] knowledge. If we speak of Him as being in a place, that [teaching] leads to an evil situation, for needs must it be either that all of Him is in each place, or that He is in each place, being split up to

---

[3] The sixth of the Shī'ite Imāms, who died in 765 A.D.

[4] This is a tree in Paradise of enormous size and miraculous qualities. It is the Islamic equivalent of the commonly found Oriental conception of a "World Tree." The word ṭūbā "blessedness," occurs in Sūra XIII, 29/28, and many of the Commentators insist that the reference there is to this tree in Paradise.

[5] He means ash-Shaibānī (d. 805), the famous Ḥanafite jurist who is one of our best sources for a knowledge of the teaching of Abū Ḥanīfa.

[6] They are the followers of that Jahm b. Ṣafwān mentioned above. They are to be cursed because their teacher was critical of both Muḥammad and the Qur'ān, and taught doctrines regarded as heretical.

this end, or [that He is] in one place as against another. Now that all of Him should be in each place is put out of court by the fact that it would be teaching that there is more than one God and not that there is but one God, yet He is One. That He should be in each place, being Himself partitioned to that intent, is put out of court by the fact that anyone who describes Allah as separated out [into parts] is in unbelief. And that He should be in one place rather than another is put out of court by the fact that it would mean the need of being transferred [from place to place], which is one of the attributes of creatures and a sign of contingent things, whereas Allah is far removed from that.

The Mu'tazilites teach that any vision of the Creator—exalted be He—by the sight is impossible. The orthodox people teach that it is possible. Their (i.e., the Mu'tazilites) proof is Allah's own statement in the story about Moses—on whom be peace —(VII, 143/139): "O my Lord, shew [Thyself to] me that I may look upon Thee. Said He: 'Thou shalt never see Me,'" where the particle *lan*, [say the Mu'tazilites], means "not for ever." Similar is the verse (VI, 103): "Vision does not perceive Him, but He perceives vision." It is related that 'A'isha—may Allah be pleased with her—said: "I asked the Apostle of Allah—on whom be Allah's blessing and peace—'Did you see your Lord on the night of the Mi'raj?,' and he answered: 'No.'" They, (i.e., the Mu'tazilites) also have an intellectual proof, viz., that if we say that He may be seen, that is equivalent to affirming [that He is in a] place, whereas place cannot be predicated of Allah—may He be exalted.

Our proof [for our view] is that same verse in the story about Moses—upon whom be peace—[where it says]: "O my Lord, shew [Thyself to] me that I may look upon Thee," for had not Moses known that a vision of the Creator was

possible he would not have made the request, since Prophets are immune from making impossible requests. There are also such verses as (LXXV, 22, 23): "On that Day [some] faces will be beaming, looking towards their Lord," and (XVIII, 110): "Let whosover hopes to meet his Lord work a righteous work and associate no one in the worship of his Lord," likewise the verse (XLIII, 71): "Therein for you is whatever the souls desire and will delight the eyes," so did the inhabitants of Paradise desire the vision [of Allah] but could not see Him, that would be equivalent to a contradiction of the word of Allah and [a going back on] His promise. Also it is related of the Prophet—upon whom be Allah's blessing and peace—that he said: "Ye shall see your Lord as ye see the moon on the night of its fullness, and ye shall not be crowded—i.e., not pressed together in a crowd—at the vision of Him." There is also the verse (X, 26/27): "For those who do good there shall be goodness and an increase," where by the "increase" is meant the vision of Allah—may He be exalted.

It is related from Ibn Mas'ud—with whom and with whose father may Allah be pleased—that he said: "I asked the Apostle of Allah—upon whom be Allah's blessing and peace—'Did you see your Lord on the night of the Mi'raj?,' and he answered: 'Yes.'" So the answer to their (i.e., the Mu'tazilites) confused opinions is [as follows]:

In the matter of Allah's saying: "Thou shalt never see me," we do not agree that the particle *lan* means "not for ever," but assert that here it is a particle of time determination. We base this [assertion] on the fact that in II, 95/89 Allah informs [us] that unbelievers will not desire death in this world, by saying: "Never (*lan*) will they wish for it, because of what their hands have sent forward," and then informs us that they will desire death in the next world, by saying (XLIII, 77): "And they will cry: 'O Mālik, would that thy Lord would make an end of us'; but he will say: 'You are to remain.' " From these verses it may be deduced that the particle *lan* [in the passage about Moses] is not used to mean "never at any time." This is clear also [from its use] in the Qur'ānic story about Mary [the mother of Jesus]— upon whom be Allah's blessing and His peace— [where she says] (XIX, 26/27): "Truly, I have vowed to the Merciful a fast, so I shall not *(lan)* speak today to any man," which shows that it does not necessarily mean "not for ever."

In the matter of the verse: "Vision does not perceive Him, but He perceives vision," our teaching is that the text demands the denial of perceiving but does not demand the denial of the vision *(ru'ya)*. As concerns the Tradition from 'Ā'isha— with whom may Allah be pleased—our teaching is that the Prophet—upon whom be Allah's blessing and peace—was informing [her] about His not being seen in this world, so what basis is that for teaching that He will not be seen in the next? With regard to the argument that if we say He may be seen that is equivalent to saying that He is in a place, we reply [by asking the question]: "When is this [the case]?" [The answer is: "Only] if the thing looked at is in a place." So if it (i.e., the thing looked at) is not in a place, then the former [view] is sound, and it is the latter which is to be rejected. Here the One looked at is not in a place, so the necessity of denying place with regard to Him does not involve a denial of the vision *(ru'ya)*. The situation here is much the same as that which we taught with regard to knowledge.

The Qur'ān is Allah's speaking, which is one of His attributes. Now Allah in all His attributes is One, and with all His attributes is eternal, not contingent, [so His speaking is] without letters and with-

out sounds, not broken up into syllables nor into paragraphs. It is not He, nor is it other than He. He caused Gabriel [7] to hear it as sound and letters, for He created sound and letters and caused him to hear it by that sound and by those letters. Gabriel—upon whom be peace—memorized it, stored it [in his mind], and transmitted it to the Prophet—upon whom be Allah's blessing and peace—by bringing down revelation *(waḥy)* and message *(risāla)*, which is not the bringing down of a corporeal object *(shakhṣ)* and a form *(ṣūra)*. He recited it to the Prophet—upon whom be Allah's blessing and peace—the Prophet memorized it, storing it up [in his mind], and then recited it to his Companions, who memorized it and recited it to the Followers, the Followers [handed it on] to the upright, and so on until it has reached us. It is recited by the tongues, memorized by hearts, written in Codices, though it is not contained by the Codices. It may be neither added to nor taken from. Should one burn up the Codices the Qur'ān would not be burned up; just as Allah is mentioned by tongues, recognized by hearts, worshipped in places, yet He is not confined to existence in those places nor in the hearts. It is as He said (VII, 157/156): "Those who follow the Messenger, the *ummī* Prophet, whom they find mentioned in the Torah and the Gospel which they have," [8] for they found [there] only his picture, his description, not his

----

[7] In Muḥammad's thought Gabriel is the angel of Revelation, so that it is always Gabriel who receives the message from Allah and transmits it to the human messenger who is to transmit it to the community to whom he is sent.

[8] This is Muḥammad's claim that his coming was foretold in the Scriptures of both Jews and Christians. Later Muslims have selected a variety of passages in the Old and New Testaments which they suggest are such prophecies. The two favourite passages are the promise of a coming Prophet in Deut. XVIII, 15, and the promise of the Paraclete in the Gospel of John chapters XV and XVI.

person. Similarly Paradise and Hell are mentioned but they are not actually amongst us. All this [that we have set forth] is according to the school of the truly orthodox.

Moreover we teach that Allah spoke with Gabriel from behind the veil (*ḥijāb*). Gabriel heard the speech of Allah from behind the veil, and the Apostle of Allah—upon whom be Allah's blessing and peace—on the night of the Mi'rāj, heard the speech of Allah from behind the veil. He spoke to Adam and to Moses—on both of whom be peace—from behind the veil. Each time that Gabriel came to the Prophet—upon whom be Allah's blessing and peace—that was by command of Allah. Allah taught the Qur'ān to Gabriel—on whom be peace—and then commanded him to take down to Muḥammad such and such a verse or such and such a Sūra. Whenever He bade Gabriel—upon whom be peace—bring down to Muḥammad—on whom be peace—a verse of the Qur'ān, or even a word, that was a reference to His eternal speaking, which is not contingent, for the speech of Allah is not contingent. . . .

The question may be raised: "Did not the Prophet—upon whom be Allah's blessing and peace—say: 'Verily Allah has ninety-nine names and whosoever recounts them will enter Paradise?' Were the name and the named one there would in that case be ninety-nine gods, which is impossible. In like manner, if the name and the named are one, then were a man to say 'fire' his mouth would be burned, and were a man to write the name of Allah on an unclean thing, the essence of Allah would be present on an unclean thing, which is impossible"—we reply that the name points to the individuality of that thing and the meaning of the [above mentioned] Tradition is that the Prophet intended thereby [to recommend] the reciting of the names (*tasmiya*). The difference between the name and the recital of names is obvious, for the people of each language name Him according to their language, whether it be the folk of Sindh, the Hindus, the Turks, the Arabs or the Persians. In this recital of names there are varieties, and there are various expressions, but Allah is One, just as it is the same person though he may be called [by the various names] Zaid, a learned man, an ascetic, a virtuous fellow, a pious man, a jurist. So is it here, for by whatever name you call Him He is Allah. As for your argument about the fire, our answer is that his mouth is not burned because it is a matter of the naming (*tasmiya*) of the fire, not of the real fire. Similarly with regard to the writing of Allah's name on an unclean substance, our answer is that there it is a matter of writing and naming, so that the essence of Allah is not present on the unclean substance.

On the Incarnation of the Word

St. Athanasius

St. Athanasius (c. 296–373), Bishop of Alexandria, is best known for his defense of Christian orthodoxy against the Arian heresy. However, his treatise "On the Incarnation of the Word" dates from several years before the development of that controversy. This selection from that treatise is Athanasius' attempt to meet the philosophic objections to the Christian doctrine of the Incarnation.

41. But one cannot but be utterly astonished at the Gentiles, who, while they laugh at what is no matter for jesting, are themselves insensible to their own disgrace, which they do not see that they have set up in the shape of stocks and stones. Only, as our argument is not lacking in demonstrative proof, come let us put them also to shame on reasonable grounds—mainly from what we ourselves also see. For what is there on our side that is absurd, or worthy of derision? Is it merely our saying that the Word has been made manifest in the body? But this even they will join in owning to have happened without any absurdity, if they show themselves friends of truth. If, then, they deny that there is a Word of God at all, they do so gratuitously, jesting at what they know not. But if they confess that there is a Word of God, and he ruler of the universe, and that in him the Father has produced the creation, and that by his providence the whole receives light and

life and being, and that he reigns over all, so that from the works of his providence he is known, and through him the Father—consider, I pray you, whether they be not unwittingly raising the jest against themselves. The philosophers of the Greeks say that the universe is a great body; and rightly so. For we see it and its parts as objects of our senses. If, then, the Word of God is in the universe, which is a body, and has united himself with the whole and with all its parts, what is there surprising or absurd if we say that he has united himself with man also. For if it were absurd for him to have been in a body at all, it would be absurd for him to be united with the whole either, and to be giving light and movement to all things by his providence. For the whole also is a body. But if it beseems him to unite himself with the universe, and to be made known in the whole, it must beseem him also to appear in a human body, and that by him it should be illumined and work.

From *Christology of the Later Fathers, LCC,* Vol. III of *The Library of Christian Classics,* eds. Edward Rochie Hardy and Cyril C. Richardson. Published in the U.S.A. by The Westminster Press, 1954. Used by permission.

For mankind is part of the whole as well as the rest. And if it be unseemly for a part to have been adopted as his instrument to teach men of his Godhead, it must be most absurd that he should be made known even by the whole universe.

42. For just as, while the whole body is quickened and illumined by man, supposing one said it were absurd that man's power should also be in the toe, he would be thought foolish; because, while granting that he pervades and works in the whole, he demurs to his being in the part also; thus he who grants and believes that the Word of God is in the whole universe, and that the whole is illumined and moved by him, should not think it absurd that a single human body also should receive movement and light from him. But if it is because the human race is a thing created and has been made out of nothing, that they regard that manifestation of the Saviour in man, which we speak of, as not seemly, it is high time for them to eject him from creation also; for it too has been brought into existence by the Word out of nothing. But if, even though creation be a thing made, it is not absurd that the Word should be in it, then neither is it absurd that he should be in man. For whatever idea they form of the whole, they must necessarily apply the like idea to the part. For man also, as I said before, is a part of the whole. Thus it is not at all unseemly that the Word should be in man, while all things are deriving from him their light and movement and light, as also their authors say, "In him we live and move and have our being."[1] So, then, what is there to scoff at in what we say, if the Word has used that wherein he is as an instrument to manifest himself? For were he not in it, neither could he have used it; but if we have previously allowed that he is in the whole and in its parts, what is there

[1] Acts 17:28.

incredible in his manifesting himself in that wherein he is? For by his own power he is united wholly with each and all, and orders all things without stint, so that no one could have called it out of place for him to speak, and make known himself and his Father, by means of sun, if he so willed, or moon, or heaven, or earth, or waters, or fire; inasmuch as he holds in one all things at once, and is in fact not only in all, but also in the part in question, and there invisibly manifests himself. In like manner, it cannot be absurd if, ordering as he does the whole, and giving life to all things, and having willed to make himself known through men, he has used as his instrument a human body to manifest the truth and knowledge of the Father. For humanity too is an actual part of the whole. And as mind, pervading man all through, is interpreted by a part of the body—I mean the tongue—without anyone saying, I suppose, that the essence of the mind is on that account lowered, so if the Word, pervading all things, has used a human instrument, this cannot appear unseemly. For, as I have said previously, if it be unseemly to have used a body as an instrument, it is unseemly also for him to be in the whole.

43. Now, if they ask, Why, then, did he not appear by means of other and nobler parts of creation, and use some nobler instrument, as the sun, or moon, or stars, or fire, or air, instead of man merely? let them know that the Lord came not to make a display, but to heal and teach those who were suffering. For the way for one aiming at display would be, just to appear, and to dazzle the beholders; but for one seeking to heal and teach the way is, not simply to sojourn here, but to give himself to the aid of those in want, and to appear as they who need him can bear it; that he may not, by exceeding the requirements of the sufferers, trouble the very persons that need

him, rendering God's appearance useless to them. Now, nothing in creation had gone astray with regard to their notions of God, save man only. Why, neither sun, nor moon, nor heaven, nor the stars, nor water, nor air had swerved from their order; but knowing their artificer and sovereign, the Word, they remain as they were made. But men alone, having rejected what was good, then devised things of nought instead of the truth, and have ascribed the honor due to God, and their knowledge of him, to demons and men in the shape of stones. With reason, then, since it were unworthy of the divine goodness to overlook so grave a matter, while yet men were not able to recognize him as ordering and guiding the whole, he takes to himself as an instrument a part of the whole, his human body, and unites himself with that, in order that since men could not recognize him in the whole, they should not fail to know him in the part; and since they could not look up to his invisible power, might be able, at any rate, from what resembled themselves to reason to him and to contemplate him. For, men as they are, they will be able to know his Father more quickly and directly by a body of like nature and by the divine works wrought through it, judging by comparison that they are not human but the works of God which are done by him. And if it were absurd, as they say, for the Word to be known through the works of the body, it would likewise be absurd for him to be known through the works of the universe. For just as he is in creation, and yet does not partake of its nature in the least degree, but rather all things partake of his power, so, while he used the body as his instrument, he partook of no corporeal property, but, on the contrary, himself sanctified even the body. For if even Plato, who is in such repute among the Greeks, says that its author, beholding the universe tempest-tossed, and in peril of going down to the

place of chaos, takes his seat at the helm of the soul and comes to the rescue and corrects all its calamities,[2] what is there incredible in what we say, that, mankind being in error, the Word lighted down upon it and appeared as man, that he might save it in its tempest by his guidance and goodness?

44. But perhaps, shamed into agreeing with this, they will choose to say that God, if he wished to reform and to save mankind, ought to have done so by a mere fiat, without his Word taking a body, in just the same way as he did formerly, when he produced them out of nothing. To this objection of theirs a reasonable answer would be: that formerly, nothing being in existence at all, what was needed to make everything was a fiat and the bare will to do so. But when man had once been made, and necessity demanded a cure, not for things that were not, but for things that had come to be, it was naturally consequent that the physician and Saviour should appear in what had come to be, in order also to cure the things that were. For this cause, then, he has become man, and used his body as a human instrument. For if this were not the right way, how was the Word, choosing to use an instrument, to appear? or whence was he to take it, save from those already in being, and in need of his Godhead by means of one like themselves? For it was not things without being that needed salvation, so that a bare command should suffice, but man, already in existence, was going to corruption and ruin. It was then natural and right that the Word should use a human instrument and reveal himself everywhither. Secondly, you must know this also, that the corruption which had set in was not external to the body, but had become attached to it; and it was required that, instead of corruption, life should cleave

2 Politicus 273 D.

to it; so that, just as death has been engendered in the body, so life may be engendered in it also. Now if death were external to the body, it would be proper for life also to have been engendered externally to it. But if death was wound closely to the body and was ruling over it as though united to it, it was required that life also should be wound closely to the body, that so the body, by putting on life in its stead, should cast off corruption. Besides, even supposing that the Word had come outside the body, and not in it, death would indeed have been defeated by him, in perfect accordance with nature, inasmuch as death has no power against the life; but the corruption attached to the body would have remained in it none the less. For this cause the Saviour reasonably put on him a body, in order that the body, becoming bound closely to the Life, should no longer, as mortal, abide in death, but, as having put on immortality, should thenceforth rise again and remain immortal. For, once it had put on corruption, it could not have risen again unless it had put on life. And death likewise could not, from its very nature, appear save in the body. Therefore he put on a body that he might find death in the body and blot it out. For how could the Lord have been proved at all to be the Life, had he not quickened what was mortal? And just as, whereas stubble is naturally destructible by fire, supposing [firstly] a man keeps fire away from the stubble, though it is not burned, yet the stubble remains, for all that, merely stubble, fearing the threat of the fire—for fire has the natural property of consuming it; while if a man [secondly] encloses it with a quantity of asbestos, the substance said to be an antidote to fire, the stubble no longer dreads the fire, being secured by its enclosure in incombustible matter; in this very way one may say, with regard to the body and death, that if death had been kept from the body by a mere

command on his part, it would none the less have been mortal and corruptible, according to the nature of bodies; but, that this should not be, it put on the incorporeal Word of God, and thus no longer fears either death or corruption, for it has life as a garment, and corruption is done away in it.

45. Consistently, therefore, the Word of God took a body and has made use of a human instrument, in order to quicken the body also, and as he is known in creation by his works so to work in man as well, and to show himself everywhere, leaving nothing void of his own divinity and of the knowledge of him. For I resume, and repeat what I said before, that the Saviour did this in order that, as he fills all things on all sides by his presence, so also he might fill all things with the knowledge of him, as the divine Scripture also says, "The whole earth was filled with the knowledge of the Lord." [3] For if a man will but look up to heaven, he sees its order, or if he cannot raise his face to heaven, but only to man, he sees his power, beyond comparison with that of men, shown by his works, and learns that he alone among men is God the Word. Or if a man is gone astray among demons, and is in fear of them, he may see this man drive them out, and make up his mind that he is their master. Or if a man has sunk to the waters, and thinks that they are God—as the Egyptians, for instance, reverence the water—he may see its nature changed by him, and learn that the Lord is Creator of the waters. But if a man is gone down even to Hades, and stands in awe of the heroes who have descended thither, regarding them as gods, yet he may see the fact of Christ's resurrection and victory over death, and infer that among them also Christ alone is true God and Lord. For the Lord touched all parts of creation, and freed and undeceived all

[3] Isa. 11:9.

of them from every illusion; as Paul says, "Having put off from himself the principalities and the powers, he triumphed on the cross"; that no one might by any possibility be any longer deceived, but everywhere might find the true Word of God. For thus man, shut in on every side, and beholding the divinity of the Word unfolded everywhere, that is, in heaven, in Hades, in man, upon earth, is no longer exposed to deceit concerning God, but is to worship Christ alone, and through him come rightly to know the Father. By these arguments, then, on grounds of reason, the Gentiles in their turn will fairly be put to shame by us. But if they deem the arguments insufficient to shame them, let them be assured of what we are saying at any rate by facts obvious to the sight of all.

46. When did men begin to desert the worshiping of idols, save since God, the true Word of God, has come among men? Or when have the oracles among the Greeks, and everywhere, ceased and become empty, save when the Saviour has manifested himself upon earth? Or when did those who are called gods and heroes in the poets begin to be convicted of being merely mortal men, save since the Lord effected his conquest of death, and preserved incorruptible the body he had taken, raising it from the dead? Or when did the deceitfulness and madness of demons fall into contempt, save when the power of God, the Word, the master of all these as well, condescending because of man's weakness, appeared on earth? Or when did the art and the schools of magic begin to be trodden down, save when the divine manifestation of the Word took place among men? And, in a word, at what time has the wisdom of the Greeks become foolish, save when the true Wisdom of God manifested itself on earth? For formerly the whole world and every place was led astray by the worshiping of idols, and men regarded nothing else but the idols as gods. But now, all the world over, men are deserting the superstition of the idols, and taking refuge with Christ; and, worshiping him as God, are by his means coming to know that Father also whom they knew not. And, marvelous fact, whereas the objects of worship were various and of vast number, and each place had its own idol, and he who was accounted a god among them had no power to pass over to the neighboring place, so as to persuade those of neighboring peoples to worship him, but was barely served even among his own people; for no one else worshiped his neighbor's god—on the contrary, each man kept to his own idol, thinking it to be lord of all—Christ alone is worshiped as one and the same among all peoples; and what the weakness of the idols could not do—to persuade, namely, even those dwelling close at hand—this Christ has done, persuading not only those close at hand, but simply the entire world, to worship one and the same Lord, and through him God, even his Father.

Commentary on the Vedānta Sūtras

ŚAṀKARA

The Vedānta Sūtras *(also called the "Brahma Sūtras") were one- or two-line scriptural passages composed between 500 and 200 B.C. Because these aphoristic and tightly compacted teachings are nearly unintelligible without a commentary, it is to the commentaries on the* Vedānta Sūtras *that one must turn in order to grasp the central message of Indian Vedāntic thought.*

Śaṁkara (pronounced "Shongkara") (c. 788–820) has written the most famous of the commentaries on the Vedānta Sūtras. *He argues strenuously in his commentaries for the philosophical position called "advaita Vedānta." Advaita means literally "nondual," and the holders of* advaita *argue that ultimately, only Brahman, the Supreme Power, is real, that Brahman is one and without a second. Thus advaita Vedānta is a kind of monistic philosophy which denies the realty of any plurality of entities or substances and upholds the reality of the One.*

BOOK ONE

Chapter 4

21. (The initial statement identifies the individual soul and the highest Self) because the soul when it will depart (from the body) is such (i.e., one with the highest Self); thus Audulomi thinks.*

The individual soul which is inquinated by the contact with its different limiting adjuncts, viz., body, senses, and mind (mano-buddhi), attains through the instrumentality of knowledge, meditation,

* This is the text; now comes the commentary by Śaṁkara—EDS.

and so on, a state of complete serenity, and thus enables itself, when passing at some future time out of the body, to become one with the highest Self; hence the initial statement in which it is represented as non-different from the highest Self. This is the opinion of the teacher Audulomi. Thus Scripture says, "That serene being arising from this body appears in its own form as soon as it has approached the highest light" (Kh. Up. VIII, 12, 3). In another place Scripture intimates, by means of the simile of the rivers, that name and form abide in the individual soul, "As the flowing rivers disappear in the sea, having lost their name and their form, thus a wise man freed from name

From *The Vedānta Sūtras with the Commentary by Śaṅkarācārya*, transl. George Thibaut, in *Sacred Books of the East*, F. Max Müller, ed., Vol. XXXIV; London, Oxford University Press, 1890.

and form goes to the divine Person who is greater than the great" (Mu. Up. III, 2, 8). I.e., as the rivers losing the names and forms abiding in them disappear in the sea, so the individual soul also losing the name and form abiding in it becomes united with the highest person. That the latter half of the passage has the meaning here assigned to it, follows from the parallelism which we must assume to exist between the two members of the comparison.

BOOK TWO

Chapter I

7. If (it is said that the effect is) non-existent (before its origination); we do not allow that because it is a mere negation (without an object).

If Brahman, which is intelligent, pure, and devoid of qualities such as sound, and so on, is supposed to be the cause of an effect which is of an opposite nature, i.e., non-intelligent, impure, possessing the qualities of sound, etc., it follows that the effect has to be considered as non-existing before its actual origination. But this consequence cannot be acceptable to you—the Vedāntin—who maintain the doctrine of the effect existing in the cause already.

This objection of yours, we reply, is without any force, on account of its being a mere negation. If you negative the existence of the effect previous to its actual origination, your negation is a mere negation without an object to be negatived. The negation (implied in "non-existent") can certainly not have for its object the existence of the effect previous to its origination, since the effect must be viewed as "existent," through and in the Self of the cause, before its origination as well as after it; for at the present moment also this effect does not exist independently, apart from the cause; according to such

scriptural passages as, "Whosoever looks for anything elsewhere than in the Self is abandoned by everything" (*Bri.* Up. II, 4, 6). In so far, on the other hand, as the effect exists through the Self of the cause, its existence is the same before the actual beginning of the effect (as after it). But Brahman, which is devoid of qualities such as sound, etc., is the cause of this world (possessing all those qualities)! True, but the effect with all its qualities does not exist without the Self of the cause either now or before the actual beginning (of the effect); hence it cannot be said that (according to our doctrine) the effect is non-existing before its actual beginning. This point will be elucidated in detail in the section treating of the non-difference of cause and effect.

8. On account of such consequences at the time of reabsorption (the doctrine maintained hitherto) is objectionable.

The pūrvapakshin raises further objections. If an effect which is distinguished by the qualities of grossness, consisting of parts, absence of intelligence, limitation, impurity, etc., is admitted to have Brahman for its cause, it follows that at the time of reabsorption (of the world into Brahman), the effect, by entering into the state of non-division from its cause, inquinates the latter with its properties. As therefore—on your doctrine—the cause (i.e., Brahman) as well as the effect is, at the time of reabsorption, characterised by impurity and similar qualities, the doctrine of the Upanishads, according to which an omniscient Brahman is the cause of the world, cannot be upheld. Another objection to that doctrine is that in consequence of all distinctions passing at the time of reabsorption into the state of non-distinction there would be no special causes left at the time of a new beginning of the world, and consequently the new world could not arise with all the distinctions of enjoying souls, objects to be enjoyed and so on (which are actually observed to exist). A third objection is that, if we assume the origin of a new world even after the annihilation of all works, etc. (which are the causes of a new world arising) of the enjoying souls which enter into the state of non-difference from the highest Brahman, we are led to the conclusion that also those (souls) which have obtained final release again appear in the new world. If you finally say, "Well, let this world remain distinct from the highest Brahman even at the time of reabsorption," we reply that in that case a reabsorption will not take place at all, and that, moreover, the effect's existing separate from the cause is not possible. For all these reasons the Vedānta doctrine is objectionable.

To this the next Sūtra replies.

9. Not so; as there are parallel instances.

There is nothing objectionable in our system. The objection that the effect when being reabsorbed into its cause would inquinate the latter with its qualities does not damage our position "because there are parallel instances," i.e., because there are instances of effects not inquinating with their qualities the causes into which they are reabsorbed. Things, for instance, made of clay, such as pots, etc., which in their state of separate existence are of various descriptions, do not, when they are reabsorbed into their original matter (i.e., clay), impart to the latter their individual qualities; nor do golden ornaments impart their individual qualities to their elementary material, i.e., gold, into which they may finally be reabsorbed. Nor does the fourfold complex of organic beings which springs from earth impart its qualities to the latter at the time of reabsorption. You (i.e., the pūrvapakshin), on the other hand, have not any instances to quote in your favour. For reabsorption could not take place at all if the effect when passing back into its causal substance continued to subsist there with all its individual properties.

And that in spite of the non-difference of cause and effect the effect has its Self in the cause, but not the cause in the effect, is a point which we shall render clear later on, under II, 1, 14.

Moreover, the objection that the effect would impart its qualities to the cause at the time of reabsorption is formulated too narrowly because, the identity of cause and effect being admitted, the same would take place during the time of the subsistence (of the effect, previous to its reabsorption). That the identity of cause and effect (of Brahman and the world) holds good indiscriminately with regard to all time (not only the time of reabsorption), is declared in many scriptural passages, as, for instance, "This everything is that Self" (Bri. Up. II, 4, 6); "The Self is all this" (Kh. Up. VII, 25, 2); "The immortal Brahman is this before" (Mu. Up. II, 2, 11); "All this is Brahman" (Kh. Up. III, 14, 1).

With regard to the case referred to in the Śruti-passages we refute the assertion of the cause being affected by the effect and its qualities by showing that the latter are the mere fallacious superimpositions of nescience, and the very same argument holds good with reference to reabsorption also. We can quote other examples in favour of our doctrine. As the magician is not at any time affected by the magical illusion produced by himself, because it is unreal, so the highest Self is not affected by the world-illusion. And as one dreaming person is not affected by the illusory visions of his dream because they do not accompany the waking state and the state of dreamless sleep; so the one permanent witness of the three states (viz., the highest Self which is the one unchanging witness of the creation, subsistence, and reabsorption of the world) is not touched by the mutually exclusive three states. For that the highest Self appears in those three states, is a mere illusion, not more substantial than the snake for which the rope is mistaken in the twilight. With reference to this point teachers knowing the true tradition of the Vedānta have made the following declaration, "When the individual soul which is héld in the bonds of slumber by the beginningless Māyā awakes, then it knows the eternal, sleepless dreamless non-duality" (Gaudap. Kār. I, 16).

So far we have shown that—on our doctrine—there is no danger of the cause being affected at the time of reabsorption by the qualities of the effect, such as grossness and the like. With regard to the second objection, viz., that if we assume all distinctions to pass (at the time of reabsorption) into the state of non-distinction there would be no special reason for the origin of a new world affected with distinctions, we likewise refer to the "existence of parallel instances." For the case is parallel to that of deep sleep and trance. In those states also the soul enters into an essential condition of non-distinction; nevertheless, wrong knowledge being not yet finally overcome, the old state of distinction re-establishes itself as soon as the soul awakes from its sleep or trance. Compare the scriptural passage, "All these creatures when they have become merged in the True, know not that they are merged in the True. Whatever these creatures are here, whether a lion, or a wolf, or a boar, or a worm, or a midge, or a gnat, or a mosquito, that they become again" (Kh. Up. VI, 9, 2; 3). For just as during the subsistence of the world the phenomenon of multifarious distinct existence, based on wrong knowledge, proceeds unimpeded like the vision of a dream, although there is only one highest Self devoid of all distinction; so, we conclude, there remains, even after reabsorption, the power of distinction (potential distinction) founded on wrong knowledge. Herewith the objection that—according to our doctrine—even the finally released souls would be born again is already disposed of. They will not be born again because in their

case wrong knowledge has been entirely discarded by perfect knowledge. The last alternative finally (which the pūrvapakshin had represented as open to the Vedāntin), viz., that even at the time of reabsorption the world should remain distinct from Brahman, precludes itself because it is not admitted by the Vedāntins themselves. Hence the system founded on the Upanishads is in every way unobjectionable. [Śaṁkara continues the argument in a commentary to Book Two, Chapter 1, Section 14—EDS.]

Other objections are stated. If we acquiesce in the doctrine of absolute unity, the ordinary means of right knowledge, perception, etc., become invalid because the absence of manifoldness deprives them of their objects; just as the idea of a man becomes invalid after the right idea of the post (which at first had been mistaken for a man) has presented itself. Moreover, all the texts embodying injunctions and prohibitions will lose their purport if the distinction on which their validity depends does not really exist. And further, the entire body of doctrine which refers to final release will collapse, if the distinction of teacher and pupil on which it depends is not real. And if the doctrine of release is untrue, how can we maintain the truth of the absolute unity of the Self, which forms an item of that doctrine?

These objections, we reply, do not damage our position because the entire complex of phenomenal existence is considered as true as long as the knowledge of Brahman being the Self of all has not arisen; just as the phantoms of a dream are considered to be true until the sleeper wakes. For as long as a person has not reached the true knowledge of the unity of the Self, so long it does not enter his mind that the world of effects with its means and objects of right knowledge and its results of actions is untrue; he rather, in consequence of his ignorance, looks on mere effects (such as body, offspring, wealth, etc.) as forming part of and belonging to his Self, forgetful of Brahman being in reality the Self of all. Hence, as long as true knowledge does not present itself, there is no reason why the ordinary course of secular and religious activity should not hold on undisturbed. The case is analogous to that of a dreaming man who in his dream sees manifold things, and, up to the moment of waking, is convinced that his ideas are produced by real perception without suspecting the perception to be a merely apparent one. But how (to restate an objection raised above) can the Vedānta-texts if untrue convey information about the true being of Brahman? We certainly do not observe that a man bitten by a rope-snake (i.e., a snake falsely imagined in a rope) dies, nor is the water appearing in a mirage used for drinking or bathing. This objection, we reply, is without force (because as a matter of fact we do see real effects to result from unreal causes), for we observe that death sometimes takes place from imaginary venom, (when a man imagines himself to have been bitten by a venomous snake,) and effects (of what is perceived in a dream) such as the bite of a snake or bathing in a river take place with regard to a dreaming person. But, it will be said, these effects themselves are unreal! These effects themselves, we reply, are unreal indeed; but not so the consciousness which the dreaming person has of them. This consciousness is a real result; for it is not sublated by the waking consciousness. The man who has risen from sleep does indeed consider the effects perceived by him in his dream such as being bitten by a snake, bathing in a river, etc., to be unreal, but he does not on that account consider the consciousness he had of them to be unreal likewise. (We remark in passing that) by this fact of the consciousness of the dreaming person not being sublated (by the waking consciousness) the doctrine of the body being our true Self is to be con-

sidered as refuted. Scripture also (in the passage, "If a man who is engaged in some sacrifice undertaken for some special wish sees in his dream a woman, he is to infer therefrom success in his work") declares that by the unreal phantom of a dream a real result such as prosperity may be obtained. And, again, another scriptural passage, after having declared that from the observation of certain unfavorable omens a man is to conclude that he will not live long, continues "if somebody sees in his dream a black man with black teeth and that man kills him," intimating thereby that by the unreal dream-phantom a real fact, viz., death, is notified. It is, moreover, known from the experience of persons who carefully observe positive and negative instances that such and such dreams are auspicious omens, others the reverse. And (to quote another example that something true can result from or be known through something untrue) we see that the knowledge of the real sounds A. etc., is reached by means of the unreal written letters. Moreover, the reasons which establish the unity of the Self are altogether final, so that subsequently to them nothing more is required for full satisfaction. An injunction as, for instance, "He is to sacrifice" at once renders us desirous of knowing what is to be effected, and by what means and in what manner it is to be effected; but passages such as, "Thou art that," "I am Brahman," leave nothing to be desired because the state of consciousness produced by them has for its object the unity of the universal Self. For as long as something else remains a desire is possible; but there is nothing else which could be desired in addition to the absolute unity of Brahman. Nor can it be maintained that such states of consciousness do not actually arise; for scriptural passages such as, "He understood what he said" (Kh. Up. VII, 18, 2), declare them to occur, and certain means are enjoined to bring them about, such as the hearing (of the Veda from a teacher) and the recital of the sacred texts. Nor, again, can such consciousness be objected to on the ground either of uselessness or of erroneousness, because, firstly, it is seen to have for its result the cessation of ignorance, and because, secondly, there is no other kind of knowledge by which it could be sublated. And that before the knowledge of the unity of the Self has been reached the whole real-unreal course of ordinary life, worldly as well as religious, goes on unimpeded, we have already explained. When, however, final authority having intimated the unity of the Self, the entire course of the world which was founded on the previous distinction is sublated, then there is no longer any opportunity for assuming a Brahman comprising in itself various elements.

Commentary on the Vedānta Sūtras

RĀMĀNUJA

Rāmānuja (11th century A.D.), like his predecessor Śaṁkara, wrote a commentary on the aphoristic Vedānta Sūtras. But Rāmānuja denies the monistic philosophy of advaita and argues instead that the world, the self, and God are all real. Thus the one Brahman has two forms, selves and matter, and while the latter are nothing without Brahman, they are, nonetheless, real. We have in Rāmānuja then a qualified form of Śaṁkara's strict nondualism.

Plurality is not unreal.

Next as to the assertion that all difference presented in our cognition—as of jars, pieces of cloth and the like—is unreal because such difference does not persist. This view, we maintain, is altogether erroneous, springs in fact from the neglect of distinguishing between persistence and non-persistence on the one hand, and the relation between what sublates and what is sublated on the other hand. Where two cognitions are mutually contradictory, there the latter relation holds good, and there is non-persistence of what is sublated. But jars, pieces of cloth and the like, do not contradict one another, since they are separate in place and time. If on the other hand the non-existence of a thing is cognised at the same time and the same place where and when its existence is cognised, we have a mutual contradiction of two cognitions, and then the stronger one sublates the other cognition which thus comes to an end. But when of a thing that is perceived in connexion with some place and time, the non-exis-

From *The Vedānta Sūtras with the Commentary of Rāmānuja*, transl. George Thibaut; in *The Sacred Books of the East*, Vol. XLVIII, F. Max Müller, ed.; Oxford, Oxford University Press, 1904.

tence is perceived in connexion with some other place and time, there arises no contradiction; how then should the one cognition sublate the other? or how can it be said that of a thing absent at one time and place there is absence at other times and places also? In the case of the snake-rope, there arises a cognition of non-existence in connexion with the given place and time; hence there is contradiction, one judgment sublates the other and the sublated cognition comes to an end. But the circumstance of something which is seen at one time and in one place not persisting at another time and in another place is not observed to be invariably accompanied by falsehood, and hence mere non-persistence of this kind does not constitute a reason for unreality. To say, on the other hand, that what is is real because it persists, is to prove what is proved already, and requires no further proof.

Being and Consciousness are not one.

Hence mere Being does not alone constitute reality. And as the distinction between consciousness and its objects—which rests just on this relation of object and that for which the object is—is proved by perception, the assertion that only consciousness has real existence is also disposed of.

* * *

The conscious subject persists in the state of release.

To maintain that the consciousness of the "I" does not persist in the state of final release is again altogether inappropriate. It in fact amounts to the doctrine—only expressed in somewhat different words—that final release is the annihilation of the Self. The "I" is not a mere attribute of the Self so that even after its destruction the essential nature of the Self might persist—as it persists on the cessation of ignorance; but it constitutes the very nature of the Self. Such judgments as "I know," "Knowledge has arisen in me," show, on the other hand, that we are conscious of knowledge as a mere attribute of the Self. Moreover, a man who suffering pain, mental or of other kind—whether such pain be real or due to error only—puts himself in relation to pain—"I am suffering pain"—naturally begins to reflect how he may once for all free himself from all these manifold afflictions and enjoy a state of untroubled ease; the desire of final release thus having arisen in him he at once sets to work to accomplish it. If, on the other hand, he were to realise that the effect of such activity would be the loss of personal existence, he surely would turn away as soon as somebody began to tell him about "release." And the result of this would be that, in the absence of willing and qualified pupils, the whole scriptural teaching as to final release would lose its authoritative character. Nor must you maintain against this that even in the state of release there persists pure consciousness; for this by no means improves your case. No sensible person exerts himself under the influence of the idea that after he himself has perished there will remain some entity termed "pure light!"—What constitutes the "inward" Self thus is the "I," the knowing subject.

This "inward" Self shines forth in the state of final release also as an "I"; for it appears to itself. The general principle is that whatever being appears to itself appears as an "I"; both parties in the present dispute establish the existence of the transmigrating Self on such appearance. On the contrary, whatever does not appear as an "I," does not appear to itself; as jars and the like. Now the emancipated Self does thus appear to itself, and therefore it appears as an "I." Nor does this appearance as an "I" imply in any way that the released Self is subject to Nescience and implicated in the Samsāra; for this would contradict the nature of final release, and moreover the consciousness of the "I" cannot be the cause of Nescience and so on. Nescience (ignorance) is either ignorance as to essential nature, or the cognition of something under an aspect different from the real one (as when a person suffering from jaundice sees all things yellow); or cognition of what is altogether opposite in nature (as when mother o' pearl is mistaken for silver). Now the "I" constitutes the essential nature of the Self; how then can the consciousness of the "I," i.e., the consciousness of its own true nature, implicate the released Self in Nescience, or, in the Samsāra? The fact rather is that such consciousness destroys Nescience, and so on, because it is essentially opposed to them. . . .

No scriptural texts teach a Brahman devoid of all difference.

We now turn to the assertion that certain scriptural texts, as e.g., "Being only was this in the beginning," are meant to teach that there truly exists only one homogeneous substance, viz. Intelligence free from all difference. This we cannot allow. For the section in which the quoted text occurs, in order to make good the initial declaration that by the knowledge of one thing all things are known, shows that the highest Brahman which is denoted by the term "Being" is the substantial and also the operative cause of the world; that it is all-knowing, endowed with all powers; that its purposes come true; that it is the inward principle, the support and the ruler of everything; and that distinguished by these and other good qualities it constitutes the Self of the entire world; and then finally proceeds to instruct Svetaketu that this Brahman constitutes his Self also ("Thou art that"). We have fully set forth this point in the Vedārtha-samgraha, and shall establish it in greater detail in the present work also, in the so-called ārambhana-adhikarana. In the same way the passage "the higher knowledge is that by

which the Indestructible is apprehended, etc." (Mu. Up. I, ɪ, 5) first denies of Brahman all the evil qualities connected with Prakriti, and then teaches that to it there belong eternity, all-pervadingness, subtilty, omnipresence, omniscience, imperishableness, creativeness with regard to all beings, and other auspicious qualities. Now we maintain that also the text "True, knowledge, infinite is Brahman," does not prove a substance devoid of all difference, for the reason that the co-ordination of the terms of which it consists explains itself in so far only as denoting one thing distinguished by several attributes. For "co-ordination" (sāmānādhikaranya, lit., "the abiding of several things in a common substrate") means the reference (of several terms) to one thing, there being a difference of reason for the application (of several terms to one thing). Now whether we take the several terms, "True," "Knowledge," "Infinite," in their primary sense, i.e., as denoting qualities, or as denoting modes of being opposed to whatever is contrary to those qualities; in either case we must needs admit a plurality of causes for the application of those several terms to one thing. There is however that difference between the two alternatives that in the former case the terms preserve their primary meaning, while in the latter case their denotative power depends on so-called "implication" (lakshanā). Nor can it be said that the opposition in nature to non-knowledge, etc. (which is the purport of the terms on the hypothesis of lakshanā), constitutes nothing more than the essential nature (of one non-differenced substance; the three terms thus having one purport only); for as such essential nature would be sufficiently apprehended through one term, the employment of further terms would be purposeless. This view would moreover be in conflict with co-ordination, as it would not allow of difference of motive for several terms applied to one thing. On the other hand it cannot be urged against the former alternative that the distinction of several attributes predicated of one thing implies a distinction in the thing to which the attributes belong, and that from this it follows that the several terms denote several things—a result which also could not be reconciled with "co-ordination"; for what "co-ordination" aims at is just to convey the idea of one thing being qualified by several attributes. For the grammarians define "co-ordination" as the application, to one thing, of several words, for the application of each of which there is a different motive.

You have further maintained the following view: In the text "one only without a second," the phrase "without a second" negatives all duality on Brahman's part even in so far as qualities are concerned. We must therefore, according to the principle that all Sākhās convey the same doctrine, assume that all texts which speak of Brahman as cause, aim at setting forth an absolutely non-dual substance. Of Brahman thus indirectly defined as a cause, the text "The True, knowledge, infinite is Brahman," contains a direct definition; the Brahman here meant to be defined must thus be devoid of all qualities. Otherwise, moreover, the text would be in conflict with those other texts which declare Brahman to be without qualities and blemish. But this also cannot be admitted. What the phrase "without a second" really aims at intimating is that Brahman possesses manifold powers, and this it does by denying the existence of another ruling principle different from Brahman. That Brahman actually possesses manifold powers the text shows further on, "It thought, may I be many, may I grow forth," and "it sent forth fire," and so on. But how are we to know that the mere phrase "without a second" is meant to negative the existence of all other causes in general? As follows, we reply. The clause "Being only this was in the beginning, one only," teaches that Brah-

man when about to create constitutes the substantial cause of the world. Here the idea of some further operative cause capable of giving rise to the effect naturally presents itself to the mind, and hence we understand that the added clause "without a second" is meant to negative such an additional cause. If it were meant absolutely to deny all duality, it would deny also the eternity and other attributes of Brahman which you yourself assume. You in this case make just the wrong use of the principle of all the Sākhās containing the same doctrine; what this principle demands is that the qualities attributed in all Sākhās to Brahman as cause should be taken over into the passage under discussion also. The same consideration teaches us that also the text "True, knowledge," etc., teaches Brahman to possess attributes; for this passage has to be interpreted in agreement with the texts referring to Brahman as a cause. Nor does this imply a conflict with the texts which declare Brahman to be without qualities; for those texts are meant to negative the evil qualities depending on Prakriti. Those texts again which refer to mere knowledge declare indeed that knowledge is the essential nature of Brahman, but this does not mean that mere knowledge constitutes the fundamental reality. For knowledge constitutes the essential nature of a knowing subject only which is the substrate of knowledge, in the same way as the sun, lamps, and gems are the substrate of Light. . . .

We now turn to the numerous texts which, according to the view of our opponent, negative the existence of plurality. "Where there is duality as it were" (Bri. Up. IV, 5, 15); "There is not any plurality here; from death to death goes he who sees here any plurality" (Bri. Up. IV, 4, 19); "But when for him the Self alone has become all, by what means, and whom, should he see?" (Bri. Up. IV, 5, 15) etc., But what all these texts deny is only plurality in so far as contradicting that unity of the world which depends on its being in its entirety an effect of Brahman, and having Brahman for its inward ruling principle and its true Self. They do not, on the other hand, deny that plurality on Brahman's part which depends on its intention to become manifold—a plurality proved by the text "May I be many, may I grow forth" (Kh. Up. VI, 2, 3). Nor can our opponent urge against this that, owing to the denial of plurality contained in other passages this last text refers to something not real; for it is an altogether laughable assertion that Scripture should at first teach the doctrine, difficult to comprehend, that plurality as suggested by Perception and the other means of Knowledge belongs to Brahman also, and should afterwards negative this very doctrine! . . .

THE GODS
AND HUMAN AFFAIRS

What difference does the existence of the gods make for the conduct of human affairs? One can easily locate a traditional answer to this question: If the gods exist, if they do take an interest in human affairs, and if they do provide rewards and punishments, both in this life and hereafter, then surely the prudent man will obey the divine commands. To act otherwise would be foolish. But if this is the sum of divine-human relations (and no doubt for many people it is), then the question is philosophically uninteresting; more than that, the answer would seem to be less than honorable. When they are at their best, men do not even treat each other in such a commercial manner; to say that our relations with the gods are simply legalistic is to debase both gods and men. To have philosophic merit, the question must involve more than a simple egoism of reward and punishment.

That the issue is not at all simple is surely the case in the first of the following selections. This passage is a transcript, in somewhat condensed form, of hearings held in 1959–1960 by the Japanese Constitution Investigation Council. The discussion concerns Article 89 of the postwar Japanese Constitution:

> ARTICLE 89. No public money or other property shall be expended or appropriated for the use, benefit or maintenance of any religious institution or association, or for any charitable, educational or benevolent enterprises not under the control of public authority.

Japan had long had at least written guarantees of religious liberty. But after the experience of the Pacific War the framers of the new Constitution, with the encouragement of the occupation forces, held that their new document should make specific provisions against government aid to any religion. There seem to have been two major reasons for this belief. To many, political secularism seemed an essential part of an advanced society. More interestingly, although perhaps a corollary to the first reason, the manipulation of State Shinto in the 1920s and 1930s by the military party seemed tied to the nation's involvement in World War II—thus, Article 89.

However, as the discussion before the Investigation Council indicates, the problem is not so easily solved. Is Shinto really a religion in the sense in which Japanese Buddhism and Japanese Christianity clearly are? To be sure, Shinto does speak of spiritual forces at work in the universe, and particularly in the Japanese islands. These spiritual forces do command an attitude of respect and awe. Thus far, Shinto would seem to be a kind of animism. But it is also claimed that the spiritual forces, the *kami,* have a peculiar relation to the land of Japan and to its society. If the Emperor is the symbol, although no longer the divine leader, of that society, is it not fitting that he should represent the nation at the major Shinto shrines? Further, shouldn't these shrines receive public support, inasmuch as they are essential to the sense of national identity? This is the claim, then—that Shinto, at least at the major shrines (for example, the shrine to the war dead), is a national folkway, not a religion at all, and thus not subject to Article 89.

What is at issue, of course, is the nature of religion. More specifically, it is religious behavior, not theology, which must be defined. In seeking a definition you would do well to consider not only constitutional provisions, but the use of chaplains in legislative houses and military forces, the institution of national cemeteries, and the swearing of oaths.

In the second selection, Reinhold Niebuhr argues that religious conviction justifies our "bearing witness" against the illusions of secular society. The religious man has been granted an insight into the nature of the pride which governs human affairs. He should speak out the divine judgment against the self-righteous, and the message of mercy to the defeated. In short, the religious man is a prophet and a light to the nations, preaching that all human affairs are subject to the divine judgment.

In the view of Sri Ramana Maharshi, the goal of the spiritual life is self-realization. The pluralism of everyday life—when we think we are different from our work, our projects, and our goals—is precisely what binds us physically to them and retards the realization of the self. This is not to say that we should abandon work, but that we should realize our true relation to it. Human affairs are not an "other" opposed to the self. There is but the Self and we are that Self. Viewed in this way, work in the world is no hindrance to self-realization.

The Japanese Constitution and Religion

THE JAPANESE CONSTITUTION INVESTIGATION COUNCIL

The present Japanese Constitution was promulgated under the guidance of the Allied occupation forces and went into effect on May 3, 1947. Although the Constitution has met with wide approval, the departure of the occupation forces encouraged some Japanese to suggest constitutional revision, particularly with respect to the role of Shinto in the national life. What is at issue in this section of the condensed transcript of hearings before the Constitution Investigation Council is the scope of Article 89, quoted in the introduction to this section. Of the participants in the discussion, Takata, Hirose, Oishi, Takayanagi, Tagami, and Kuroda are committeemen; Iinuma, Takao, Fukudo, and Kishimoto are witnesses. Special attention should be given to the remarks of the late Hideo Kishimoto, the most distinguished of Japan's religious scholars.

IINUMA: I think that the present Constitution is all right, if it is the state policy that the Grand Shrine and other shrines are not religion. Anyhow when the Emperor observes the festivals of the Grand Shrine as the chief worshipper, on the one hand, or presides at the rites at the Three Palace Shrines, on the other hand, he becomes for the first time the symbol of the state and of the unity of the people in its true meaning. At least this is the way I think about it.

HIROSE: In relation to Article 89, the Imperial Family and so forth . . .

IINUMA: I think there is no problem, because I do not consider Shrine worship as religion.

TAKAYANAGI: This is a very simple question. I asked the question a little while ago as to whether or not Shinto is a religion. If the Emperor decided to convert to Christianity, for example, would not there be opposition on the part of Shinto? Or would they agree to it? If it is not religion, he would be free to do so.

KISHIMOTO: It would be very shocking, at least for the Shintoists.

TAKAYANAGI: If so, then Shinto has a very strong religious element.

KISHIMOTO: To my understanding, except in special cases, about 70% of Shinto is religion. Therefore, what you have just said naturally follows.

TAKAYANAGI: In case the Emperor be-

From *Contemporary Religions in Japan*, Vol. IV, No. 2, June, 1963, pp. 134–44. Reprinted by permission of the International Institute for the Study of Religions.

came a Christian, would they feel that this was a good thing? Or would they feel like opposing it as unpardonable?

IINUMA: Who do you mean? Persons concerned with shrines?

TAKAYANAGI: Shinto priests?

IINUMA: I think that it would be opposed. It would be very shocking.

TAKAYANAGI: If so it is inevitable that Shinto be recognized as something very religious.

IINUMA: Shrines?

TAKAYANAGI: Because of religious freedom, conversion to Christianity should be all right, if Shinto is not a religion . . .

IINUMA: Do you mean from a legal viewpoint?

TAKAYANAGI: No, as a social phenomenon.

IINUMA: If such a matter arose as a social phenomenon, undoubtedly opposition would occur . . .

TAKAYANAGI: Therefore Shinto priests seem to have a strong feeling that Shrine worship is religion.

IINUMA: Those persons who voluntarily reorganized shrines as religious juridical persons and joined the Association of Shinto Shrines after the issuance of the Directive may think of shrines as religion. As for me, however, Shinto is not religion.

TAKAYANAGI: In case of testifying as to whether or not Shinto is religion, from the standpoint of social psychology or something like that, is the idea acceptable that even the Emperor is personally free to believe in any religion? For example, Christianity or Islam? Or is the feeling strong that the Emperor should not be a believer of any of these religions? This question is very naive, but it seems to touch the point.

IINUMA: From a legal standpoint he may believe in any religion. As a matter of fact, however, if the people concerned with the shrines heard about this they would be opposed to it.

OISHI: I would like to ask Mr. Takao

something. I have heard that the actual administration of the relationship between the Grand Shrine and the Imperial Household has been conducted on the basis of the fundamental human rights of the Emperor as a private individual. However, according to Mr. Ogane's personal opinion, it seems to be doubtful whether even under the present Constitution it is possible to administer the Shrine on the basis of his individual, fundamental human rights. I agree with him. Under the present Constitution the Emperor is the symbol of the state, which constitutes a right belonging exclusively to him in interpreting the Constitution. Therefore, there is no room to consider the Emperor as a private person but only as the symbol of the state. If so, even in regard to his relation to the Grand Shrine, the festivals under the sponsorship of the Emperor in his capacity as a symbol are those of a person having a public capacity recognized by the Constitution. Therefore, according to a strict interpretation of the Constitution, the execution of administrative business on the basis of the fundamental human rights of the Emperor and not as a symbol—the principle may be understood to be an expedient method of defending the tradition against the oppression of the Occupation Forces—does not seem to be right from a logical viewpoint. What does Mr. Takao think about this?

TAKAO: When I spoke about the Emperor observing the rites at the Three Palace Shrines as a personal, fundamental right, I meant that it was done for the reason that there was no other way under postwar conditions. What is done today in the administration of the Imperial Household depends solely upon the provision of Article 89 of the Constitution, which not only strictly prohibits their maintenance by public funds but also forbids giving any aid to them. No other course can be taken under Article 89. We don't say that it is paid out of the private funds of the Court because of the problem of his fundamental human right. We are dealing with it solely as a problem of Article 89.

OISHI: You say that the interpretation of Article 89 is being very strictly applied. Do you mean that the interpretation by the Occupation Force and the legislation enforced during the Occupation are still continuing today?

TAKAO: If the functions of the Grand Shrine are clearly explained as not religion, Article 89 is not a question. However there has not been any definite view about this, even in this meeting. If Article 89 prohibits even the giving of aid, in other words, if it does not permit the disbursement of public money under any circumstances, we think that we should observe the limitations of the law.

OISHI: The chairman has taken up the problem of what would happen if the Emperor converted to Christianity. I think it is simple from the standpoint of Mr. Iinuma. The Emperor is not in a position to be partial to a part of the people. He always stands over and above all people. The Emperor should have no private life in the field of religion or any other individual life, because he is the symbol. From this viewpoint, it is undesirable for him to participate in any particular religion; for example, Ōmoto or Islam. It is desirable for him to be as indifferent as possible to any separate religion. Isn't this the opinion which can be derived from your point of view?

IINUMA: As a matter of fact, I have never thought of the question the chairman has just asked. I did not know how to answer. I don't know whether the Emperor has or has not such an individual human right. Of course I don't think that it is desirable.

OISHI: As for me I thought it a simple question, but you seem to think it is very complicated.

IINUMA: I do not desire such a thing, nor do I think that it will happen.

KURODA: I'd like to ask Dr. Kishimoto a question. I have the impression that you are discussing the problem of whether or not shrines are religion, centering in the shrines or the Grand Shrine as they were developed in line with the national policy of the Meiji Government. The problems since the Meiji era have arisen in a very short period in comparison with the history of shrines from the beginning of Japanese history. In this short period it seems that the shrines were unfavorably influenced by the Meiji Government policy. When we consider such a problem, we should look further back to the shrines as being more historic and traditional. Otherwise, we cannot adequately understand these constitutional problems. What is Dr. Kishimoto's opinion regarding this point?

KISHIMOTO: We normally consider Japanese religion from the time prior to the introduction of Buddhism. In this long history there have been various changes in Shrine Shinto. I think that the form of State Shinto since the Meiji era is nothing but one aspect of the changes. It may be safely said that it is the common sense of scholars of the science of religion that Shinto as a whole is regarded as a religion, though it has a very peculiar character. I consider that Shinto was differentiated from religion by thoughtful Shintoists at the beginning of the Meiji era for a special purpose.

In the years prior to the Meiji era, that is, until the end of Tokugawa period, the shrines had a strong tendency to adhere to common beliefs such as seeking worldly divine favors or incantations and prayers. Many unrefined elements, such as divine inspiration [*kami gakari*], were to be found in them. Therefore, in the early years of Meiji, there occurred a movement to remove such vulgar elements and to make Shinto refined and suitable as the guiding principle of the Meiji Restoration. I think that this was a very pious and idealistic point of view. For this reason these people called this refined thing Shinto, and called the others religion. Therefore the people in Shinto circles after Meiji regarded religion as vulgar beliefs. When a Shinto priest was said to be engaged in religious practices, this meant that he was employing charms or something like that. He was looked down upon by others and he felt great shame. This tradition has continued. Therefore almost all Shinto priests have not considered that among religions there are refined ones, such as Zen, for example. It should be recognized that there is, as a matter of fact, a great difference between the word religion, as it has been used by Shinto priests since Meiji, and as it is being used by us.

TAGAMI: Mr. Fukuda referred a little while ago to public funerals. You said that the observance of religious exercises in government facilities was prohibited. I am doubtful, however, whether the separation of religion and state requires such strict separation. I think that in regard to the strict observance of the separation of religion and state, the Japanese Constitution is modelled after the American system. In the case of America, however, I wonder if an administrative policy which denies the use of Christian elements is possible. For example, the Presidential oath at the time of his inauguration. There seems to be no room for argument here. It would be too formalistic logic to say that any religious color should be wiped out of all national events. Furthermore, there seems to me to be no ground for saying that the Constitution of Japan requires the separation of religion and state in the way that France took in the past and the Soviet Union is taking now in regard to its religious policy. Needless to say there are some countries that do not recognize this separation. The manner of interpreting the Constitution that was adopted by the Government in this regard seems to be too formalistic. On what basis and with reference to what, have you interpreted it in such a way?

FUKUDA: I indeed felt confined in attending to my official duties, just as Mr. Tagami stated. The prohibition of public funerals was derived from the Shinto Directive. Therefore, in order to thoroughly enforce the Directive, this seems to have been a very delicate point. In the postwar days many public funerals were held, mainly for the war-dead. The Occupation paid much attention to the funerals for the war-dead, in case something militaristic might occur. Public funerals were especially watched for this reason.

It was said, however, that a public funeral could be held, if it was in the form of a memorial service for the deceased civilians without a religious ceremony. Therefore it was not intended that public organs should not hold any services but that memorial services or something like that was to a certain extent permissible. However, public funerals in a Shinto form were strictly watched.

The ceremony of setting up the ridge pole is observed in the Shinto manner according to Japanese custom when a house is being built. However, when a government building was under construction, it was prohibited to observe a ceremony for setting up the ridge pole in a Shinto manner. Such religious ceremonies were thus strictly prohibited as well as public funerals.

I think that in America and elsewhere, such ceremonies are observed in a Christian manner. We objected to the policy on this ground. Shouldering a portable shrine in a village festival, for example, falls under this case. At present, however, the Shinto Directive is no more; and a relaxed attitude seems to prevail that past customs or something in accordance with social commonsense should be allowed.

TAGAMI: I'd like to ask another question of Dr. Kishimoto in regard to this point. Is the separation of the state and religion so strict? I would like to follow the view of Roger Williams of America. In his view, if the state was connected with a certain specific religion, it oppressed the other religions. This is the principle. From this viewpoint, I think there is no need to observe a ceremony in such a strict way with no religious color, unless this has an injurious effect on freedom of religion in general.

I think that America is representative of countries where the system of the separation of state and religion prevails. And yet it does not seem to be completely so. Therefore I think that the attitude of postwar Japan in adopting the system was a little extreme. What is your opinion in this regard?

KISHIMOTO: To state my conclusion, it seems to be extreme in regard to the strictness of its enforcement. As to the reason for this strictness, I have my own interpretation. I think that this was caused by a combination of the following two reasons.

One is that the General Headquarters policy generally had its original pattern in America. This seems to be because the General Headquarters authorities had no other model in their mind. The separation of state and religion is the pattern prevailing in America, so it was brought to Japan. This is one of the reasons for stressing the separation of state and religion.

However, there happened to be another reason for strengthening the power of this principle. What was regarded with disapproval by America during the war was that the power of the state and the power of Shinto were connected. They had to be separated by all means. However separating only Shinto was not reasonable. If separation of the state and religion in general was strictly enforced, Shinto as a religion would be automatically separated from the state. Such an idea was active.

These two reasons were combined to work very strictly. As I think that Mr. Fukuda testified, many people in Shinto circles and connected with primary schools were punished by General Headquarters. They were scolded by General Headquarters in performing traditional Shinto practices. Thereafter the Japanese people seem to have accustomed themselves to maintain the extreme strictness mentioned above.

TAKATA: Any other question?

Mr. Fujikashi is also present who wrote about the human declaration of the Emperor. Any questions? If you have no more question, today's meeting is closed.

The Christian Witness in the Social and National Order

REINHOLD NIEBUHR

Reinhold Niebuhr (1892–1971) was the most famous social philosopher of American Protestantism. His social liberalism finds its roots in a "neo-orthodox" interpretation of the Biblical tradition. In 1948 the substance of this selection was given as an address before the First General Assembly of the World Council of Churches.

The natural inclination of the convinced Christian, when viewing the tragic realities of our contemporary world, is to bear witness to the truth in Christ against the secular substitutes for the Christian faith which failed to anticipate, and which may have helped to create the tragic world in which we now live. Did they not destroy the sense of a divine sovereignty to which we are all subject? And did they not invent schemes of redemption from evil which made repentance unnecessary?

This inclination may also define our responsibility. But I doubt whether it is our primary responsibility. It is also our opportunity to bring the truth of the Word of God to bear upon the secular roots of our present predicament because our current history is actually a remarkable illustration of the way Nemesis overtakes the pride of man and how divine judgment is visited upon men and nations who exalt themselves above measure.

The liberal part of our culture thought that the Christian idea of sinfulness of all men was outmoded. In its place it put the idea of a harmless egotism, rendered innocuous either by a prudent self-interest or by a balance of all social forces which would transmute the selfishness of all into a higher social harmony. The vanity of that idea was proved by the ever more dynamic disproportions of power in our society and the ever greater destruction of community in a technical society. Sometimes the liberal part of our culture conceived the idea of redemption through growth and development. Men suffered (so it was argued) not from sin but from impotence. But fortunately the whole historical process was itself redemptive. It translated man from impotence to power, from ignorance to intelligence, from being the victim to becoming the master of historical destiny. This illusion proved as tragic as the first one. Since the sin of man lies in the corruption of his will and not in his weakness, the possibilities of evil grow with the development of the very freedom and power which were supposed to emancipate man.

The obvious illusions of the liberal world prompted a Marxist rebellion against the whole liberal culture. In place of confidence in a simple harmony of all social forces it proclaimed confidence in a new harmony of society through a revolutionary destruction of property, thus making a social institution the root of evil in man and promising redemption through its destruction. In place of the idea of redemption through endless growth and development it promised redemption through the death of an old order and the rise of a new one. But this was not redemption through the perpetual dying to self of the Christian Gospel. It was the promise of a new life for us through the death of our foes.

The tragedy of our age has been deepened by the fact that (1) this alternative to secular liberalism proved in many respects even more illusory and erroneous (2) the two forms of error have involved the world in a bitter civil war which rends society asunder from the national to the international community.

It proved even more erroneous because the prophets of this new religion turned into tyrannical priest-kings who, having lost all sense of the contingent character of all human interests and ideas, filled the world with the cruelty of their self-righteousness. It proved more erroneous because the doctrine of the socialization of property when raised to a doctrine of religious redemption, rather than followed pragmatically, merely combines economic and political power in the hands of one oligarchy and produces tyranny. The obvious evils and cruelties of this alternative have given the proponents of the old order good pretexts for not repenting of their own

sins but to be content with calling attention to the perils of the alternative.

Perhaps it is because there is a little truth and so much error in both secular alternatives to the Christian faith that they involved the world in such a hopeless civil war in which each side had enough truth to preserve its sense of high mission and enough error to frighten the other side with the possible consequences of its victory.

We must undoubtedly bear witness against both types of secular illusion from the standpoint of the truth which we have not of ourselves but from the Gospel. In such a witness the contemporary situation offers the Gospel truth a powerful support. We must preach the Gospel in the day in which the modern man who was so confident that he could control his own destiny is hopelessly caught in an historic fate in which the human will seems to have become completely impotent and frustrated. The vaunted virtues of each side are vices from the standpoint of the other side and sins in the sight of God. The word of the Psalmist fits our situation exactly: "The heathen have raged and the people have imagined vain things. But he who sitteth in the heavens shall laugh."

But let us not presume to laugh with God. God's derisive laughter is the justified divine judgment upon this new and yet very old pride of modern man. We must not laugh, lest we forget that His judgment is upon us, as well as upon them. We are too deeply implicated in the disaster of our day to permit ourselves more than provisional testimony against a so-called secular society. That society in both its liberal and Marxist variety came into being, partly because of the deep involvement of Christianity in the social sins of our day and in the stubbornness of the social injustices. A brief catalog of the sins of the Church proves the depth of our involvement. (1) There is no social evil, no form of injustice whether of the feudal or the capitalist order which has not been sanctified in some way or other by religious sentiment and thereby rendered more impervious to change. In a sense the word of Marx is true: "The beginning of all criticism is the criticism of religion. For it is on this ultimate level that the pretensions of men reach their most absurd form. The final sin is always committed in the name of religion." (2) A part of the Church, fearing involvement in the ambiguities of politics, has declared the problems of politics to be irrelevant to the Christian life. It has abandoned modern men in the perplexities of the modern community and has seen brotherhood destroyed in a technical society without a qualm. Usually this neutrality has not even been honestly neutral. The neutral Church is usually an ally of the established social forces. (3) A part of the Church, facing the complexities of the political order, has been content with an insufferable sentimentality. These problems would not arise, it has declared, if only men would love one another. It has insisted that the law of love is a simple possibility when every experience proves that the real problem of our existence lies in the fact that we ought to love one another, but do not. And how do we establish tolerable community in view of the fact that all men, including Christians, are inclined to take advantage of each other? Even now many Christians fatuously hope that Christian conference will speak some simple moral word which will resolve by love the tragic conflict in the world community. The most opportunistic statesman, who recognizes the complexities which this sentimentality obscures, is a publican who may enter the Kingdom of God before the Phariseeism which imagines that we can lift ourselves above the tragic moral ambiguities of our existence by a simple act of the will. (4) A part of the Church, conscious of these perplexities, has been ready to elaborate detailed schemes of justice and of law for the regulation of the political and social life of mankind, below the level of love and of grace. But it has involved itself in a graceless and inflexible legalism. It does not know that all law can easily be the instrument of sin; that inflexible propositions of justice, particularly in the rapidly shifting circumstances of modern technical development, may hinder rather than help the achievement of true justice. One contribution which Christianity certainly ought to make to the problem of political justice is to set all propositions of justice under the law of love, resolving the fruitless debate between pragmatists and legalists and creating the freedom and maneuverability necessary to achieve a tolerable accord between men and nations in ever more complex human relations. We need a pragmatic attitude toward every institution of property and of government, recognizing that none of them are as sacrosanct as some supposedly Christian or secular system of law has made them, that all of them are subject to corruption and that their abolition is also subject to corruption. This freedom need not degenerate into lawlessness, if it is held in the knowledge that "all things are yours, and ye are Christ's and Christ is God's."

We have spoken negatively. The Christian Church must bear witness against every form of pride and vain-glory, whether in the secular or in the Christian culture, and be particularly intent upon our own sins lest we make Christ the judge of the other but not of ourselves. But the experience of repentance does not stand alone. It is a part of a total experience of redemption. Positively our task is to present the Gospel of redemption in Christ to nations as well as to individuals. According to our faith we are always involved in sin and in death because we try too desperately to live, to preserve our pride, to maintain our prestige. Yet it is possible to live truly if we die to self, if the vainglory of man is broken by divine judgment that life may be truly reformed by divine grace. This promise of new life is for individuals; yet who can deny its relevance for nations and empires, for civilizations and cultures also, even though these collective forms of life do not have the exact integrity of the individual soul; nor do they have as direct an access to divine judgment and grace?

The situation in the collective life of mankind today is that we have made shipwreck of our common life through the new powers and freedom which a technical civilization has placed at our disposal. The shipwreck, manifested in the misery and insecurity of the whole world, is an objective historical judgment. It is the death which has followed upon a vainglorious life of the nations. Without faith it is nothing but death. Without faith it generates the sorrow of the world, which is despair. Without faith this confusion is the mark of meaninglessness which follows the destruction of the simple systems of life's meaning which have had ourselves, our nation and our culture at its center. It is by faith in the God revealed in One who died and rose again that death can become the basis of new life, that meaninglessness turns into meaning, that judgment is experienced as grace. Our business is so to mediate the divine judgment and grace that nations, classes, states and cultures, as well as individuals, may discern the divine author of their wounds, that they may also know the possibility of a new and whole life. In a day of complacency and security the Christian Church must anticipate the judgment which is to come and declare that the day of the Lord will be darkness and not light. In the day of judgment and catastrophe the Christian Gospel has a message of hope for those who truly repent.

It is true that the human situation is such that repentance is always required

even as evil always flourishes. But it is wrong to preach this Gospel *sub specie aeternitatis* as if there were no history with its time and seasons and with its particular occasions. Nor is our preaching of any avail if we only persuade men and nations to acknowledge the original sin which infects us all but not the particular sins of which we are guilty. Not the least of our tasks is to expound a judgment and a mercy which tempers the wind to the shorn sheep. Must we not warn victorious nations that they are wrong in regarding their victory as a proof of their virtue, lest they engulf the world in a new chain of evil by their vindictiveness which is nothing else than the fury of their self-righteousness? And is our word to the defeated nations not of a different order, reminding them that their warfare is accomplished seeing that they have received at the Lord's hand double for all their sins, and that the punishment is really at the Lord's hand even though it is not nicely proportioned to the evil committed? Must we not warn powerful and secure nations and classes that they have an idolatrous idea of their own importance and that as surely as they say, "I sit as a queen and shall never know sorrow," so surely shall "in one moment her sorrow come?" And must we not remind those who are weak and defrauded and despised that God will avenge the cruelties from which they suffer but will also not bear the cruel resentment which corrupts their hearts? Must we not say to the rich and secure classes of society that their vaunted devotion to the laws and structures of society which guarantee their privileges is tainted with self-interest; and must we not say to the poor that their dream of a propertyless society of perfect justice turns into a nightmare of new injustice because it is based only upon the recognition of the sin which the other commits and knows nothing of the sin which the poor man commits when he is no longer poor but has become a commissar? Everywhere life is delivered unto death because it is ensnared in self-delusion and practices every evasion rather than meet the true God. And everywhere the Church is caught in this dance of death because it allows the accents of national pride and of racial prejudice, the notes of self-esteem and complacency to color its message, so that the whole business of religion in our day could seem to the cynical observer (even as it must appear to the righteous God) as a vast effort to lobby in the courts of the Almighty to gain a special advantage for our cause in the divine adjudication. If the slogan that the Church should be the Church is to have a meaning other than its withdrawal from the world, must it not mean that by prayer and fasting it has at least extricated itself in some degree from its embarrassing alliances with this or that class, race and nation so that it may speak the word of God more purely, and more forthrightly to each man and nation, but also to each generation according to the peculiar needs of the person and the hour?

A new life is possible for those who die to the old self, whether nations or individuals, at any time and in any situation. But on the positive side there are also special words to be spoken to an age beside timeless words. The new life which we require collectively in our age is a community wide enough to make the world-wide interdependence of nations in a technical age sufferable; and a justice carefully enough balanced to make the dynamic forces of a technical society yield a tolerable justice rather than an alternation of intolerable anarchy and intolerable tyranny. To accomplish this purpose some of our own preconceptions must go and the same law of love which is no simple possibility for man or society must be enthroned as yet the final standard of every institution, structure and system of justice. To those who exalt freedom we must declare that freedom without community is not love

but leads to man making himself his own end. To those who exalt community we must declare that no historic community deserves the final devotion of man, since his stature and structure is such that only God can be the end of his life. Against those who make the state sacrosanct we must insist that the state is always tempted to set its majesty in rebellious opposition to the divine majesty. To those who fear the extension of the state for the regulation of modern economic life we must point out that their fears are frequently prompted not by a concern for justice but by a jealous desire to maintain their own power. A tolerable community under modern conditions cannot be easily established; it can be established at all only if much of what has been regarded as absolute is recognized to be relative; and if everywhere men seek to separate the precious from the vile and sharply distinguish between their interests and the demands which God and the neighbor make upon them.

Perhaps our generation will fail. Perhaps we lack the humility and charity for the task. There are ominous signs of our possible and even probable failure. There is the promise of a new life for man and nations in the Gospel; but there is no guarantee of historic success. There is no way of transmuting the Christian Gospel into a system of historical optimism. The final victory over man's disorder is God's and not ours; but we do have responsibility for proximate victories. Christian life without a high sense of responsibility for the health of our communities, our nations and our cultures degenerates into an intolerable other-worldliness. We can neither renounce this earthly home of ours nor yet claim that its victories and defeats give the final meaning to our existence.

Jesus wept over Jerusalem and regretted that it did not know the things that belonged to its peace. In the Old Testament we have the touching story of Abraham bargaining with God about the size of the saving remnant which would be needed to redeem the city. Would fifty or forty or thirty be required? He and the Lord finally settled for twenty. Only a small leaven is needed, only a little center of health can become the means of convalescence for a whole community. That fact measures the awful responsibility of the people of God in the world's cities of destruction.

But there is a climax in this story which is frequently disregarded. It is a terrible climax which has relevance for our own day. However small the saving remnant which God requires for the reconstruction of our communities, it was not forthcoming in Sodom and Gomorrah. Perhaps it is valid to express the surmise that the leavening minority in Sodom may have been quantitatively adequate but that its righteousness was irrelevant for saving Sodom and Gomorrah. One has the uneasy feeling that we are in that position. There is so little health in the whole of our modern civilization that one cannot find the island of order from which to proceed against disorder. Our choices have become terribly circumscribed. Must we finally choose between atomic annihilation or subjection to universal tyranny? If such a day should come we will remember that the mystery of God's sovereignty and mercy transcends the fate of empires and civilizations. He will be exalted though they perish. However, He does not desire their perdition but rather that they turn from their evil ways and live. From us He demands that we work while it is day, since the night cometh when no man can work.

Maharshi's Gospel

SRI RAMANA MAHARSHI

Sri Ramana Maharshi (1879–1950) was a South Indian saint widely respected for his learning and his extraordinary ability to communicate that learning to his disciples. The selection is a transcript of a discussion between the Maharshi and one of those disciples.

WORK AND RENUNCIATION

DISCIPLE: What is the highest goal of spiritual experience for man?
MAHARSHI: Self-realization.

DISCIPLE: Can a married man realize the Self?
MAHARSHI: Certainly. Married or unmarried, a man can realize the Self; because That is here and now. If it were

From *Maharshi's Gospel;* Tiruvannamalai, Sri Ramanasramam, 1949. Reprinted by permission of Sri Ramanasramam.

not so, but attainable by some effort at some time, and if it were new and had to be acquired, it would not be worth pursuit. Because, what is not natural is not permanent either. But what I say is that the Self is here and now, and alone.

DISCIPLE: A salt-doll diving into the sea will not be protected by a water-proof coat. This world in which we have to toil day in and day out is like the ocean.

MAHARSHI: Yes, the mind is the water-proof coat.

DISCIPLE: So then, one may be engaged in work and, free from desire, keep up one's solitude? But life's duties allow little time to sit in meditation or even to pray.

MAHARSHI: Yes. Work performed with attachment is a shackle, whereas work performed with detachment does not affect the doer. He is, even while working, in solitude. To engage in your duty is the true *Namaskar* . . . and abiding in God is the only true *Asan*.

DISCIPLE: Should I not renounce my home?

MAHARSHI: If that had been your destiny the question would not have arisen.

DISCIPLE: Why then did you leave your home in your youth?

MAHARSHI: Nothing happens except by Divine dispensation. One's course of conduct in this life is determined by one's *prarabdha*.

DISCIPLE: Is it good to devote all my time to the search for the Self? If that is impossible, should I merely keep quiet?

MAHARSHI: If you can keep quiet, without engaging in any other pursuit, it is very good. If that cannot be done, where is the use of being quiet so far as Realization is concerned? So long as a person is obliged to be active, let him not give up attempts to realize the Self.

DISCIPLE: Do not one's actions affect one in after-births?

MAHARSHI: Are you born now? Why do you think of other births? The fact is, there is neither birth nor death. Let him who is born think of death and the palliative thereof!

DISCIPLE: Can you show us the dead?

MAHARSHI: Did you know your kinsmen before their birth that you should seek to know them after their death?

DISCIPLE: How does a *Grihastha* fare in the scheme of *Moksha?* Should he not necessarily become a mendicant in order to attain Liberation?

MAHARSHI: Why do you think you are a *Grihastha?* Similar thoughts that you are a *Sannyasin* will haunt you, even if you go out as a *Sannyasin*. Whether you continue in the household or renounce it and go to the forest, your mind haunts you. The ego is the source of thought. It creates the body and the world, and it makes you think of being the *Grihastha*. If you renounce, it will only substitute the thought of *Sannyasa* for that of *Grihastha,* and the environment of the forest for that of the household. But the mental obstacles are always there for you. They even increase greatly in the new surroundings. It is no help to change the environment. The one obstacle is the mind; it must be got over whether in the home or in the forest. If you can do it in the forest, why not in the home? Therefore, why change the environment? Your efforts can be made even now, whatever be the environment.

DISCIPLE: Is it possible to enjoy *Samadhi* while busy in worldly work?

MAHARSHI: The feeling "I work" is the hindrance. Ask yourself "Who works?" Remember who you are. Then the work will not bind you; it will go on automatically. Make no effort either to work or to renounce; your effort is the bondage. What is destined to happen will happen. If you are destined not to work, work cannot be had even if you hunt for it; if you are destined to work, you will not be able to avoid it; you will be forced to engage yourself in it. So, leave it to the Higher Power; you cannot renounce or retain as you choose.

DISCIPLE: Bhagavan said yesterday that while one is engaged in search of God "within," "outer" work would go on automatically. In the life of Sri Chaitanya it is said that during his lectures to students he was really seeking Krishna (Self) within, forgot all about his body and went on talking of Krishna only. This raises a doubt whether work can safely be left to itself. Should one keep part-attention on the physical work?

MAHARSHI: The Self is all. Are you apart from the Self? Or can the work go on without the Self? The Self is universal: so, all actions will go on whether you strain yourself to be engaged in them or not. The work will go on of itself. Thus Krishna told Arjuna that he need not trouble to kill the Kouravas; they were already slain by God. It was not for him to resolve to work and worry himself about it, but to allow his own nature to carry out the will of the Higher Power.

DISCIPLE: But the work may suffer if I do not attend to it.

MAHARSHI: Attending to the Self means attending to the work. Because you identify yourself with the body, you think that work is done by you. But the body and its activities, including that work, are not apart from the Self. What does it matter whether you attend to the work or not? Suppose you walk from one place to another: you do not attend to the steps you take. Yet you find yourself after a time at your goal. You see how the business of walking goes on without your attending to it. So also with other kinds of work.

DISCIPLE: It is then *like* sleep-walking.

MAHARSHI: *Like* somnambulism? Quite so. When a child is fast asleep, his mother feeds him; the child eats the food just as well as when he is fully awake. But the next morning he says to the mother, "Mother, I did not take food last night." The mother and others know that he did, but he says that he did not; he was not aware. Still the action had gone on.

A traveller in a cart has fallen asleep. The bulls move, stand still or are unyoked during the journey. He does not know these events but finds himself in a different place after he wakes up. He has been blissfully ignorant of the occurrences on the way, but the journey has been finished. Similarly with the Self of a person. The ever-wakeful Self is compared to the traveller asleep in the cart. The waking state is the moving of the bulls; *Samadhi* is their standing still (because *Samadhi* means *Jagrat-Sushupti*, that is to say, the person is aware but not concerned in the action; the bulls are yoked but do not move); sleep is the unyoking of the bulls, for there is complete stopping of activity corresponding to the relief of the bulls from the yoke.

Or again, take the instance of the cinema. Scenes are projected on the screen in the cinema-show, but the moving pictures do not affect or alter the screen. The spectator pays attention to them, not to the screen. They cannot exist apart from the screen, yet the screen is ignored. So also, the Self is the screen where the pictures, activities, etc., are seen going on. The man is aware of the latter but not aware of the essential former. All the same the world of pictures is not apart from the Self. Whether he is aware of the screen or unaware, the actions will continue.

DISCIPLE: But there is an operator in the cinema!

MAHARSHI: The cinema-show is made out of insentient materials. The lamp, the pictures, the screen etc., are all insentient and so they need an operator, the sentient agent. On the other hand, the Self is absolute Consciousness, and therefore self-contained. There cannot be an operator apart from the Self.

DISCIPLE: I am not confusing the body with the operator; rather, I am referring to Krishna's words in the 61st verse, Chapter XVIII of the *Gita*.

"The Lord, O Arjuna, dwells in the Heart of every being, and He by His delusive power spins round all beings set as if on a machine."

MAHARSHI: The functions of the body involving the need for an operator, are kept in mind, since the body is *jada* or insentient, a sentient operator is necessary. Because people think that they are *jivas*, Krishna said that God resides in the Heart as the Operator of the *jivas*. In fact, there are no *jivas* and no Operator, as it were, outside them; the Self comprises all. It is the screen, the pictures, the seer, the actors, the operator, the light, the theatre and all else. Your confounding the Self with the body and imagining yourself the actor, is like the seer representing himself as an actor in the cinema-show. *Imagine the actor asking if he can enact a scene without the screen!* Such is the case of the man who thinks of his actions apart from the Self.

DISCIPLE: On the other hand, it *is like asking the spectator to act in the cinema-picture.* So, we must learn sleep-waking!

MAHARSHI: Actions and states are according to one's point of view. A crow, an elephant, a snake, each makes use of one limb for two alternate purposes. With one eye the crow looks on either side; for the elephant the trunk serves the purpose of both a hand and a nose, and the serpent sees as well as hears with its eyes. Whether you say the crow has an eye or eyes, or refer to the trunk of the elephant as "hand" or "nose" or call the eyes of the serpent its ears, it means all the same. Similarly in the case of the *Jnani*, sleep-waking or waking-sleep or dream-sleep or dreaming-wakefulness, are all much the same thing.

DISCIPLE: But we have to deal with a physical body in a physical, waking world! If we sleep while work is going on, or try to work while asleep, the work will go wrong.

MAHARSHI: Sleep is not ignorance, it is one's pure state; wakefulness is not knowledge, it is ignorance. There is full awareness in sleep and total ignorance in waking. Your real nature covers both and extends beyond. The Self is beyond both knowledge and ignorance. Sleep, dream and waking states are only modes passing before the Self: they proceed whether you are aware of them or not. This is the state of the *Jnani,* in whom pass the states of *Samadhi,* waking, dream and deep sleep, like the bulls moving, standing, or being unyoked, while the passenger is asleep. These answers are from the point of view of the *ajnani;* otherwise such questions would not arise.

DISCIPLE: Of course, they cannot arise for the Self. Who would be there to ask? But unfortunately, I have not yet realized the Self!

MAHARSHI: That is just the obstacle in your way. You must get rid of the idea that you are an *ajnani* and have yet to realize the Self. You *are* the Self. Was there ever a time when you were not aware of that Self?

DISCIPLE: So, we must experiment in sleep-waking . . . or in day-dreaming?

MAHARSHI: *(Laughs.)*

DISCIPLE: I maintain that the physical body of the man immersed in *Samadhi* as a result of the unbroken "contemplation" * of the Self, may become motionless for that reason. It may be active or inactive. The mind established in such "contemplation" will not be affected by the movements of the body or the senses; nor is disturbance of the mind the forerunner of physical activity. Whereas another person asserts that physical activity certainly presents *Samadhi* or unbroken "contem-

---

* *Note*—The word, contemplation, is often used loosely as referring to a forced mental process, whereas *Samadhi* lies beyond effort. However, in the language of Christian Mysticism "contemplation" is the synonym invariably used for *Samadhi,* and it is in this sense the word is used above.

plation." What is Bhagavan's opinion? You are the abiding proof of my statement.

MAHARSHI: Both of you are right: you refer to *Sahaja Nirvikalpa Samadhi* and the other refers to *Kevala Nirvikalpa Samadhi*. In the latter case the mind lies immersed in the Light of the Self (whereas the same, *i.e.,* the mind, lies in the darkness of ignorance in deep sleep); and the subject makes a distinction between *Samadhi* and activity after waking up from *Samadhi*. Moreover, activity of the body, of the sight, of the vital forces and of the mind and the cognizance of objects, all these are obstructions for one who seeks to realize *Kevala Nirvikalpa Samadhi*.

In *Sahaja Samadhi*, however, the mind has resolved into the Self and has been lost. The differences and obstructions mentioned above do not, therefore, exist here. The activities of such a Being are like the feeding of a somnolent boy, perceptible to the on-looker but not to the subject. The traveller sleeping in the moving cart is not aware of the motion of the cart, because his mind is sunk in darkness. Whereas, the *Sahaja Jnani* remains unaware of his bodily activities because his mind is dead, having been resolved into the ecstasy of *Chidananda* [Bliss of the Self].

Note—The distinction between sleep, *Kevala Nirvikalpa Samadhi* and *Sahaja Nirvikalpa Samadhi* can be clearly put in a tabular form by Sri Bhagavan:

Sleep	Kevala Nirvikalpa Samadhi	Sahaja Nirvikalpa Samadhi
(1) mind alive	(1) mind alive	(1) mind dead
(2) sunk in oblivion	(2) sunk in Light	(2) resolved into the Self
	(3) like a bucket tied to a rope and left lying in the water in a well	(3) like a river discharged into the ocean and its identity lost;
	(4) to be drawn out by the other end of the rope.	(4) a river cannot be redirected from the ocean.

The mind of the Sage who has realized the Self is wholly destroyed. It is dead. But to the on-looker, he may seem to possess a mind just like the layman. Hence the "I" in the Sage has merely an apparent "objective reality"; in fact, however, it has neither a subjective existence nor an objective reality.

Part 4

PROBLEMS OF ETHICS

INTRODUCTION: WHAT IS ETHICS?

Suppose that the social club you belong to is having an election of officers and your best friend is running for president against a person whom you know to be better qualified for the job. Suppose that you decide to vote against your friend and for the more qualified candidate. Then your friend asks you, "How are you going to vote in the club's election for president?" What should you do?

No one will know how you are going to vote unless you tell him. But if you tell your best friend the truth about your intention to vote against him you will run the risk of alienating him. If you lie and say you are going to vote for him it would seem you could save your friendship. But suppose you're the kind of person who believes that lying is generally bad; perhaps you've been reared that way by your parents, or perhaps your society or your religion condemns lying. Or suppose you personally object to deception, and particularly deception between friends. Thus if you were to lie under any of these conditions your conscience would bother you, or you might vaguely feel that you had let someone down—your parents, your society, your religion, or even your friend or yourself. The problem then is simply that if you tell the truth to your friend, you run the risk of ending a fine friendship; if you lie to your friend, you have betrayed your principles or code of behavior. No matter what you do you'll feel miserable. Now, your friend has asked you "How are you going to vote?" What should you do? [1]

[1] To tell your friend "I haven't decided yet" is tantamount to lying, since, *ex hypothesi*, you have decided; and such an attempted evasion is no solution to the problem. (The problem mentioned, incidentally, is taken from an experience of one of our students. The "best friend" was the student's roommate and the student elected to tell the truth. The upshot was that the roommates are no longer best friends.)

The problem above constitutes a moral dilemma.[2] No matter what you do, the results prove to be unfortunate, and unfortunate for you. Problems of conduct that involve the questions "What should I do?" or "What ought I to do?" belong to that area of philosophy called "ethics." It would seem to follow that the solutions to such moral problems would also be found within ethics as well, but this is only partially true. It would indeed be a happy world if we could solve all of our moral problems by turning to the philosophy of ethics. But people who study ethics are far from freed from the agonizing problem of making a correct or right moral choice, else it would follow that professors of ethics must be the most moral of all human beings. No one, particularly those professors, would want to make such a claim.

But though the study of ethics will not necessarily make you into a person who always makes the best moral choice, it can do something else. It can help you to focus your attention on moral situations by making you aware of the kinds of problems called "moral problems"; in so focusing your attention it can make you more sensitive to the fact that moral choices do not admit of easy and simple solution. Thus although ethics cannot directly answer the question, "What ought I to do in this moral situation?" it can provide you with the tools for finding a solution.

NORMATIVE ETHICS AND META-ETHICS

Ethics can be divided into two rather distinct parts. One part of ethics is concerned with providing general principles of conduct on which our actions can be based if those actions are to called "right." It is interested, consequently, in providing answers to such general questions as, "Is it always right to tell the truth?" or "Which is to be more highly valued, truth-telling or friendship?" or "In a moral dilemma in which the issue is that between truth-telling and saving a friendship, which is the choice that is to be made, and why is that particular choice to be made?" We can call this part of ethics "normative ethics." Normative ethics is concerned with general principles of conduct and the justification of these principles.

A second part of ethics is concerned with examining the meanings of the ethical terms used in normative ethics. It states, for example, that before we can accept the principle that whenever truth-telling and the possible loss of friendship conflict we should always save the friendship, we ought first to inquire into the meanings of words like "truth-telling" and "conflict" as they occur in this moral principle. We can call this part of ethics "meta-ethics." "Meta-ethics,"[3] then, is concerned with the meanings of the concepts and judgments of normative ethics; e.g., such concepts as "right,"

---

[2] A dilemma is an argument that forces you to choose one of two unfavorable alternatives. Our dilemma is a *moral* dilemma because the choices are concerned with conduct affecting human beings, yourself or others.

[3] *Meta*-ethics because it comes "after" the normative ethical discussion and is dependent in some sense on that discussion. Thus, if normative ethics is talk about principles of conduct, meta-ethics is talk about normative ethics.

"ought," "good," and their opposites, and such judgments as, "It is always *right* to tell the truth," "Men *ought* to preserve friendship above all else," "The results of telling the truth are always *good*," and their opposites.

In general, then, we may say that ethics is that subdiscipline of philosophy that is concerned with problems of human conduct; particularly those problems that arise in human intercourse—personal, social, political, etc.— in which alternatives of action are presented and justified or condemned by principles which make those alternatives "right" or "wrong," respectively. These principles of conduct are such that they can, in some sense, be justified—i.e., good and compelling reasons can be given to support them. Furthermore, ethics is concerned with *all* principles of conduct and their justifications, and seeks to analyze both the moral language of the principles and the justifications of those principles.

If ethics is concerned then with problems of human conduct, how does it differ from other disciplines which are similarly concerned? For example, psychology, sociology, and economics are certainly concerned with human behavior. Aren't they then in the same business as ethics? There is a vitally important sense in which they differ from ethics, though this is not to say that ethics may not pervade these disciplines as it does so many others. The differences between ethics and these social sciences are of two sorts: First the concepts that ethics uses and the judgments in which it is interested are not the concepts and judgments *per se* with which the social sciences are concerned.[4] The language of obligation, rightness and goodness, and the judgments incorporating these concepts do not appear, except in an ancillary way, in the social sciences. The language of the social sciences is *descriptive;* it is about the way people *are,* the way society *is,* or the way *homo economicus behaves.* The language of normative ethics is *prescriptive;* it is about the way people *ought* to be, the way society *ought* to be, or the way *homo economicus ought* to behave. Ethics is concerned with rules which prescribe a certain sort of conduct. The social sciences are concerned with laws which may describe or be used to predict conduct, and there lies the difference. Second, the problems and questions raised by ethics differ markedly from the problems and questions raised by social science. The problems that ethics examines are directly related to the language of ethics, and this language, we have already seen, differs from the language of social science.[5] These ethical problems may be concerned with

---

[4] *Per se* because the social sciences, though interested in the moral behavior of man for the sake of their sciences, are not interested in his behavior as moral behavior; that is to say, because the social sciences are concerned with particular aspects of human behavior, it would follow that because moral behavior is part of human behavior, it would necessarily be included as subject matter in their disciplines. But it appears only as subject matter, hence descriptively, as we argue below, and is not studied for itself alone, but only to lead the scientist to descriptive and predictive general statements called "laws."

[5] It can be argued that what applies to social science also applies to natural science. Whether or not the discipline of ethics as we have described it differs from the discipline of theology is a matter the reader may ponder. Immanuel Kant has summed up the differences and similarities as follows:

Practical philosophy (that is, the science of how man ought to behave)

the meanings of the concepts "right," "ought," and "good" already mentioned, or they may be concerned with the conditions under which an act is called "right," or "obligatory." The methods for solving these puzzles are not the methods of the social scientist. If the student of ethics wishes to know whether or not he is morally responsible for having told a lie while being tortured, he cannot find the answer by polling torturers and the tortured, nor by referring to an empirical law of nature, nor by appealing to a generalization based upon an empirical sampling from the laboratory or the community. How then can he discover if his lie uttered under torture is an act for which he is morally responsible? Is there some ethical principle to which he can turn for an answer? Is the principle justified in all cases? What justifies the principle? and is the justification legitimate, that is, is it itself justifiable? These are a few of the questions which the student of ethics must consider if he is to provide himself with an answer to the question, "Am I responsible for actions performed under duress?"

THE PROBLEMS OF ETHICS

If one of the distinguishing characteristics of ethics is to be found in the kinds of problems and questions it is concerned with, what are some of these questions or problems?

The selections that follow attempt to deal with four perennial problems of ethics. Ethics, like philosophy in general, cannot provide final and absolute solutions to these problems, nor to any problem with which it deals; we wouldn't expect it to, and that is what makes these problems perennial. As Bertrand Russell, commenting on the nature of philosophy, has said:

> There are many questions—and among them those that are of the profoundest interest to our spiritual life—which, so far as we can see, must remain insoluble to the human intellect unless its powers become of quite a different order from what they are now. Has the universe any unity of plan or purpose, or is it a fortuitous concourse of atoms? Is consciousness a permanent part of the universe, giving hope of indefinite growth in wisdom, or is it a transitory accident on a small planet on which life must ultimately become impossible? Are good and evil of importance to the universe or only to man? (*The Problems of Philosophy;* London, Oxford University Press, 1959, p. 155.)

---

and anthropology (that is, the science of man's actual behavior) are closely connected, and the former cannot subsist without the latter: for we cannot tell whether the subject to which our consideration applies is capable of what is demanded of him unless we have knowledge of that subject. It is true that we can pursue the study of practical philosophy without anthropology, that is, without the knowledge of the subject. But our philosophy is then merely speculative, and an Idea. We therefore have to make at least some study of man. (Immanuel Kant, *Lectures on Ethics*, transl. Louis Infield, New York, Harper & Brothers, 1930, in *Approaches to Ethics*, W. T. Jones et al., eds.; New York, McGraw-Hill Book Co., Inc., 1962, p. 248.)

The questions with which we shall be concerned, questions which, following Russell, admit of no final or certain answers, relate to four basic problems of ethics. These problems may be summarized as follows:

HUMAN FREEDOM AND FATALISM. Suppose, to return to the question with which this section began, that you were going to alienate your friend who was running for club president by telling him you were not going to vote for him in the club election. Suppose, furthermore, it was just *fated:* No matter what you did the alienation was bound to come about and in the way indicated. The question then arises, If you are not free but compelled by fate to act in this way, and if you are then not free to do otherwise, are you responsible if your friend hates you as a result of your decision?

More generally, if all our actions are compelled, are we responsible for our actions? If we are not, and most persons would argue that we are not responsible when we act under compulsion, natural or supernatural, then can we be justly praised or blamed, rewarded or punished, if things turn out as they had to? If we cannot be justly applauded or condemned for acts we are not responsible for, and most persons would argue that we cannot, then are words like "moral" or "immoral" applicable to our acts?

WHAT MAKES AN ACTION RIGHT OR WRONG? Suppose that you lie to your friend by saying that you are going to vote for him in the club election; but suppose that you also believe that the results of lying, the consequences of your act, will produce far better results than the act of telling him the truth. Does the fact that lying leads to better general consequences justify your telling a lie? Suppose that he is the kind of person who might attempt suicide if he thought that you were not going to vote for him. Would the consideration of such probable consequences lead you to lie? Would such probable painful consequences justify your lying? Suppose you intended to make a better man of him by telling the truth, believing that if he saw himself as you see him he would thereby become a wiser and better person. Suppose that you told him the truth, that you were not going to vote for him, and suppose that he killed himself. Would you have done something wrong? Was your action immoral? Your intention was a good intention, and you told the truth; it just happened to produce bad consequences. Who would blame you?

More generally, what is it in an action that makes or determines its rightness or wrongness? The motive? But what if the consequences are bad? The act? But is truth-telling always right? The consequences? But suppose your motive is vicious? Or is the criterion of rightness or wrongness of an action a combination of these three elements rather than any single one?

IS THE UNIVERSE MORAL? Suppose that you lie to your friend and tell him that you are going to vote for him. Suppose also that you believe lying is wrong. Does it follow that you will be punished for your lying? Is it the case that all wrong acts done by men are eventually discovered and the men punished? If this were a just universe then it might be argued that not only will all evil men be punished but, further, all good men will be rewarded for their goodness.

If this were a universe in which every man gets his just desserts (if not in this life, then perhaps in a life beyond this one) and this were known by all men, would our behavior be altered? Would we all try to do "the right thing"? What would "the right thing" be? Would you, out of respect for this eventual justice, tell your friend the truth? Would you tell him the truth if you also believed that it would destroy him?

Would it be a just universe if good men were punished along with men who were not good? Obviously not; it would not be just if you were rewarded for telling a lie and someone else were not rewarded for telling the truth. But if there is some sort of universal justice there must be criteria for its application to the actions of men. What sort of criteria are there? What or who metes out this justice? What is the mechanism of distribution of rightful desserts?

If there is no justice in the universe, then does moral action, or even life itself, make sense? Is it sufficient that political or communal justice be operative? And this brings us to our final problem.

JUSTICE AND SOCIETY. Suppose, again, that you tell your friend the truth: You are not going to vote for him. Suppose, further, that you know that he is unstable and that your admission could very well endanger his mental and physical equilibrium. What if he falls to pieces as a result and you are called before the Student Affairs Committee? Would you consider it just if they reprimanded you for your behavior? Imagine yourself sitting on that committee judging another similar action. Would you, if all the facts were known, consider such an action reprehensible? On what grounds? Should the college community have the right to punish students for such conduct?

More generally, does the state have a mandate for punishing wrong actions and for rewarding right actions? If so, where does the mandate come from? Can we, by studying the origin of governments and nation-states, discover the grounds for justice? Can the criteria for justice in the state be found by looking to history for the foundations of the state? Or does the ground of state justice rest outside history, outside the natural world?

HUMAN FREEDOM
AND FATALISM

WHAT IS FATALISM?

Gilbert Ryle, a contemporary British philosopher, has said, "No philosopher of the first or second rank has defended fatalism or been at great pains to attack it." [1] In the selections that follow, Ryle's remark will be put to the test. Fatalism may be odd, but that it has exercised many great minds cannot be doubted. Let us begin by giving a meaning to "fatalism" and then go on to explore the form it takes in plaguing moral philosophy. Suppose we take fatalism to be that doctrine which holds that there is some force or power in the universe that has fore-ordained or preplanned each event so that those events happen no matter what. Another way of saying this is to state that fatalism is the belief that everything will happen according to a plan, and there is nothing you can do to hinder or help the carrying out of that plan. Fatalism is thus a kind of theory about marionettes where the strings are pulled by some powerful force, and man, the puppet, dangles helplessly. Whether that force works for good or ill, with reason or without, is beside the point: It is there, and It moves you, and you cannot influence It. Edward Fitzgerald's *Rubaiyat,* a famous Victorian paraphrase of the work of Omar Khayyam, puts the matter thus:

> The ball no question makes of Ayes and Noes.
> But here or there as strikes the Player goes:
> And he that toss'd you down into the Field.
> He knows about it all—HE knows—HE knows!

(LXX, Fitzgerald's fourth edition)

[1] *Dilemmas* (Cambridge: University Press, 1960), p. 28.

THE PROBLEM FOR ETHICS

Although the theory of fatalism may be absurd, the fact still remains that philosophers and theologians of the first rank have been concerned about fatalism or variants of it. As noted in the introduction to this section, words like "moral" and "immoral" are meaningful as applied to persons only when those persons are responsible for what they do. Thus, if I am not free, I cannot be responsible; if I am not responsible then neither I nor my actions can be called "moral," "immoral," "right," or "wrong."

One variant of the doctrine of fatalism is predestination. Where fatalism seems to argue that all events in the life of a man are fixed and unalterable, and fixed by some superpower, predestination puts the stress on *major* life events such as the time of your birth, death, and where your soul will spend eternity. It states that these major events are eternally fixed and unalterable. Predestination further stipulates that these momentous life events are known beforehand by a personal God. Further, He may or may not be a causal agent in the chain of events leading up to the particular momentous event.

It is not always easy to distinguish fatalism from predestination. Both, it has been argued, give trouble to ethics because both limit free will. But one theory that does not limit free will is determinism. It is important not to confuse determinism with predestination. Determinism merely holds that all events are caused. "Caused by what?" it might be asked. "Why, caused by preceding events." But if the question is "Caused by whom?" and the answer is "An impersonal force," or even "A personal God," then we may have either fatalism or predestination. But both these philosophies hold that determinism is true. And, it can be argued, even those philosophers who decry fatalism or its variants hold that determinism is true—i.e., they hold that all events are caused: In other words, there are no uncaused events. Determinism is no bar to free will; it just happens that when I am acting freely I am one of the causes of my actions. John Hospers has stated these points rather well when he asks and then replies:

> "But if everything is caused, aren't our own actions caused?" Certainly, the determinist replies, they are; one may indeed be grateful that they are, else we would be stuck with the indeterminist's causeless actions. Indeed, the determinist says, our actions *are* caused—*by us*. "I caused my actions" (active voice) and "My acts are caused by *me*" (passive voice) say the same thing. "I caused my actions" is the motto of freedom; "My actions are caused by me" is that of determinism. Determinism is not only compatible with human freedom, but human freedom is possible only on the assumption that determinism is true. (*An Introduction to Philosophical Analysis;* Englewood Cliffs, N.J., Prentice-Hall, Inc., 2nd ed., 1967, p. 330.)

In the selections that follow, the case for fatalism and predestination is presented in the early Christian and Muslim traditions. St. Paul and Calvin raise the problem which theologians are still debating: If God knows the future, then in some sense or other what is going to happen in that future is already set. This view is closer, it might be argued, to predestination than to fatalism.

Predestination and the problems it entails are taken up in two selections from the Muslim tradition. Jalalu'l-Din Rūmī, the Persian mystic, embraces the consequences of God's foreknowledge, while the author of the *Bahr al-Kalām* is disturbed by its implications; Orthodox Muslims hold that man has free will, and both of these selections try to give voice to that doctrine.

The Christians and the Muslims are not the only ones who have had problems with fatalistic considerations. Earlier, the Hindus also considered the consequences of a doctrine of inscrutable fate. For example, the Hindu *Laws of Manu*, codified perhaps 1000 years before the Christian era, claims that

> All undertakings [in] this [world] depend both on the ordering of fate and on human exertion; but among these two [the ways of] fate are unfathomable. (*The Laws of Manu*, transl. G. Buhler, in *The Sacred Books of the East*, Vol. XXV, F. Max Müller, ed.; Oxford, The Clarendon Press, 1886.)

The great Hindu epic of the fourth or third century B.C., *Bhagavad Gītā*, is also fatalistic when it speaks of the God in the heart of all men Who causes men to do His bidding by the exercise of His power "as if they were mounted on a machine." [2]

The machine is like that used in a marionette's play (the suggestion is Śaṁkara's), which brings us once more to the theme with which we began; the question raised then was "If man is a marionette, does morality make sense?" Thus the fatalistic-predestinarian theme is not found only in the Christian-Muslim tradition, but in the Hindu tradition as well.

Predestination is discussed in a more formal way by Benedict Spinoza, the seventeenth-century Jewish philosopher. However, the predestination discussed by Spinoza faces in two directions. On the one hand, it faces backward to the subject of God's divine foreknowledge, what we have called "predestination," and on the other, forward, by stating that there are no accidental causes ("That which has no cause to exist cannot possibly exist"). Spinoza, by careful argument, then establishes two views: The view called "determinism," i.e., the view that all events are caused; and the view called "predestination," i.e., the view that God is the cause of all events.

Leo Tolstoi considers the implications for free will if causal laws are true. The virtue of this selection from Tolstoi lies more in the questions he raises than in any solution he finds. He gives voice to the fears that many men have that the laws of science and scientific determinism have now nullified free will and shown it to be an empty dream. Tolstoi summarizes the fear as follows:

> If there be a single law governing the actions of men, free will cannot exist, for then man's will is subject to that law.

2 *Bhagavad Gītā* 18.61.

That these fears are groundless is argued in the final selection by a contemporary American philosopher, John Hospers. Hospers shows that free will cannot properly be juxtaposed to determinism, nor does determinism imply compulsion: The laws of science and scientific determinism, far from threatening free will and ethics, actually make the latter possible.

St. Paul's Letter to the Romans

The doctrine of predestination finds its Christian roots in St. Paul's Letter to the Romans. *The letter dates from about 65* A.D. *when St. Paul was probably in Corinth. Of this predestination (Romans 8.29) it has been said, "Predestination or foreordination may be defined as that act of God by which the salvation of man is effected in accordance with the will of God."*

Chapter 8

26 Likewise the Spirit helps us in our weakness; for we do not know how to pray as we ought, but the Spirit himself intercedes for us with sighs too deep for words. ²⁷ And he who searches the hearts of men knows what is the mind of the Spirit, because the Spirit intercedes for the saints according to the will of God.

28 We know that in everything God works for good with those who love him, who are called according to his purpose. ²⁹ For those whom he foreknew he also predestined to be conformed to the image of his Son, in order that he might be the first-born among many brethren. ³⁰ And those whom he predestined he also called; and those whom he called he also justified; and those whom he justified he also glorified.

31 What then shall we say to this? If God is for us, who is against us? ³² He who did not spare his own Son but gave him up for us all, will he not also give us all things with him? ³³ Who shall bring any charge against God's elect? It is God who justifies; ³⁴ who is to condemn? Is it Christ Jesus, who died, yes, who was raised from the dead, who is at the right hand of God, who indeed intercedes for us? ³⁵ Who shall separate us from the love of Christ? Shall tribulation, or distress, or persecution, or famine, or nakedness, or peril, or sword? ³⁶ As it is written,

"For thy sake we are being killed all
 the day long;
we are regarded as sheep to be slaugh-
 tered."

37 No, in all these things we are more than conquerors through him who loved us. ³⁸ For I am sure that neither death, nor life, nor angels, nor principalities, nor things present, nor things to come, nor powers, ³⁹ nor height, nor depth, nor anything else in all creation, will be able to separate us from the love of God in Christ Jesus our Lord.

The selections that follow are from the Revised Standard Version Bible and are used by permission.

Chapter 9

I am speaking the truth in Christ, I am not lying; my conscience bears me witness in the Holy Spirit, 2 that I have great sorrow and unceasing anguish in my heart. 3 For I could wish that I myself were accursed and cut off from Christ for the sake of my brethren, my kinsmen by race. 4 They are Israelites, and to them belong the sonship, the glory, the covenants, the giving of the law, the worship, and the promises; 5 to them belong the patriarchs, and of their race, according to the flesh, is the Christ. God who is over all be blessed for ever. Amen.

6 But it is not as though the word of God had failed. For not all who are descended from Israel belong to Israel, 7 and not all are children of Abraham because they are his descendants; but "Through Isaac shall your descendants be named." 8 This means that it is not the children of the flesh who are the children of God, but the children of the promise are reckoned as descendants. 9 For this is what the promise said, "About this time I will return and Sarah shall have a son." 10 And not only so, but also when Rebecca had conceived children by one man, our forefather Isaac, 11 though they were not yet born and had done nothing either good or bad, in order that God's purpose of election might continue, not because of works but because of his call, 12 she was told, "The elder will serve the younger." 13 As it is written, "Jacob I loved, but Esau I hated."

14 What shall we say then? Is there injustice on God's part? By no means! 15 For he says to Moses, "I will have mercy on whom I have mercy, and I will have compassion on whom I have compassion." 16 So it depends not upon man's will or exertion, but upon God's mercy. 17 For the scripture says to Pharaoh, "I have raised you up for the very purpose of showing my power in you, so that my name may be proclaimed in all the earth." 18 So then he has mercy upon whomever he wills, and he hardens the heart of whomever he wills.

19 You will say to me then, "Why does he still find fault? For who can resist his will?" 20 But, who are you, a man, to answer back to God? Will what is molded say to its molder, "Why have you made me thus?" 21 Has the potter no right over the clay, to make out of the same lump one vessel for beauty and another for menial use? 22 What if God, desiring to show his wrath and to make known his power, has endured with much patience the vessels of wrath made for destruction, 23 in order to make known the riches of his glory for the vessels of mercy, which he has prepared beforehand for glory, 24 even us whom he has called, not from the Jews only but also from the Gentiles? 25 As indeed he says in Hosea,

"Those who were not my people
I will call 'my people,'
and her who was not beloved
I will call 'my beloved.' "
26 "And in the very place where it was
said to them, 'You are not my
people,'
they will be called 'sons of the living
God.' "   (RSV)

On the Christian Faith

JOHN CALVIN

*John Calvin (1509–1564) was one of the great leaders of the Protestant Reforma-
tion of the sixteenth century. This selection, from his* Institutes of the Christian
Religion, *expresses his views on the doctrine enunciated by St. Paul and then
developed by Calvin's own spiritual mentor, St. Augustine (354–430).*

The Eternal Decree of God

Predestination, by which God adopts
some to the hope of life and adjudges
others to eternal death, no one, desirous
of the credit of piety, dares absolutely to
deny. But it is involved in many cavils,
especially by those who make foreknowledge the cause of it. We maintain that
both belong to God; but it is preposterous
to represent one as dependent on the
other. When we attribute foreknowledge
to God, we mean that all things have ever
been, and perpetually remain, before his
eyes, so that to his knowledge nothing is
future or past, but all things are present;
and present in such a manner that he
does not merely conceive of them from
ideas formed in his mind, as things remembered by us appear present to our
minds, but really beholds and sees them
as if actually placed before him. And this
foreknowledge extends to the whole world
and to all the creatures. Predestination we
call the eternal decree of God by which

he has determined in himself what he
would have to become of every individual
of mankind. For they are not all created
with a similar destiny, but eternal life is
foreordained for some and eternal damna-
tion for others. Every man, therefore, being created for one or the other of these
ends, we say he is predestined either to
life or to death. This God has not only
testified in particular persons, but has
given a specimen of it in the whole posterity of Abraham, which should evidently
show the future condition of every nation
to depend upon his decision. "When the
Most High divided the nations, when he
separated the sons of Adam, the Lord's
portion was his people; Jacob was the lot
of his inheritance." [1] The separation is
before the eyes of all: in the person of
Abraham, as in the dry trunk of a tree,
one people is peculiarly chosen to the rejection of others; no reason for this appears, except that Moses, to deprive their

[1] *Deut.* 32. 8, 9.

From John Calvin *On the Christian Faith*, ed. John T. McNeill, copyright © 1957 by
The Liberal Arts Press, Inc., reprinted by permission of the publisher, The Bobbs-
Merrill Company, Inc.

posterity of all occasion of glorying, teaches them that their exaltation is wholly from God's gratuitous love. . . .

Augustine on the Preaching of Predestination

This doctrine is maliciously and impudently calumniated by others as subversive of all exhortations to piety of life. This formerly brought great odium upon Augustine, which he removed by his treatise *On Correction and Grace,* addressed to Valentine, the perusal of which will easily satisfy all pious and teachable persons. Yet I will touch on a few things which I hope will convince such as are honest and not contentious. How openly and loudly gratuitous election was preached by Paul we have already seen; was he therefore cold in admonitions and exhortations? Let these good zealots compare his vehemence with theirs; theirs will be found ice itself in comparison with his incredible fervor. And certainly every scruple is removed by this principle, that "God hath not called us to uncleanness, but that everyone should know how to possess his vessel in sanctification and honor"; [2] and again, that "we are his workmanship, created in Christ Jesus unto good works, which God hath before ordained, that we should walk in them." [3] Indeed, a slight acquaintance with Paul will enable anyone to understand, without tedious arguments, how easily he reconciles things which they pretend to be repugnant to each other. Christ commands men to believe in him. Yet his limitation is neither false nor contrary to his command when he says, "No man can come unto me, except it were given unto him of my Father." [4] Let preaching therefore have its course to bring men to faith, and

by a continual progress to promote their perseverance. Nor let the knowledge of predestination be prevented, that the obedient may not be proud as of anything of their own but may glory in the Lord. Christ had some particular meaning in saying, "Who hath ears to hear, let him hear." [5] Therefore when we exhort and preach, persons endowed with ears readily obey; and those who are destitute of them exhibit an accomplishment of the Scripture, that hearing they hear not.[6] "But why," says Augustine, "should some have ears, and others not? 'Who hath known the mind of the Lord?' [7] Must that which is evident be denied, because that which is concealed cannot be comprehended?" [8] These observations I have faithfully borrowed from Augustine; but as his words will perhaps have more authority than mine, I will proceed to an exact quotation of them. "If, on hearing this, some persons become torpid and slothful, and, exchanging labor for lawless desire, pursue the various objects of concupiscence, must what is declared concerning the foreknowledge of God be therefore accounted false? If God foreknew that they would be good, will they not be so, in whatever wickedness they now live? And if he foreknew that they would be wicked, will they not be so, in whatever goodness they now appear? Are these, then, sufficient causes why the truths which are declared concerning the foreknowledge of God should be either denied or passed over in silence, especially when the consequence of silence respecting these would be the adoption of other errors? The reason of concealing the truth," he says, "is one thing, and the necessity of declaring it is another. It would be tedious to inquire after all the

2 I Thess. 4. 4, 7.
3 Eph. 2. 10.
4 John 6. 65.

5 Matt. 13. 9.
6 Isa. 6. 9.
7 Rom. 11. 34.
8 Augustine, *De dono perseverantiae* XIV. 37; in Migne, *PL,* XLV, 1016; Eng. tr. in *The Nicene and Post-Nicene Fathers,* Vol. V, p. 540.

reasons for passing the truth over in silence, but this is one of them: lest those who understand it not should become worse, while we wish to make those who understand it better informed—who, indeed, are not made wiser by our declaring any such thing, nor are they rendered worse. But since the truth is of such a nature that, when we speak of it, he becomes worse who cannot understand it, and when we are silent about it, he who can understand it becomes worse, what do we think ought to be done? Should not the truth rather be spoken, that he who is capable may understand it, than buried in silence; the consequence of which would be, not only that neither would know it, but even the more intelligent of the two would become worse, who, if he heard and understood it, would also teach it to many others? And we are unwilling to say what we are authorized to say by the testimony of Scripture. For we are afraid, indeed, lest by speaking we may offend him who cannot understand, but are not afraid lest, in consequence of our silence, he who is capable of understanding the truth may be deceived by falsehood." And condensing this sentiment afterwards into a smaller compass, he places it in a still stronger light. "Wherefore, if the apostles and the succeeding teachers of the Church both piously treated of God's eternal election, and held believers under the discipline of a pious life, what reason have these our opponents, when silenced by the invincible force of truth, to suppose themselves right in maintaining that what is spoken of predestination, although it be true, ought not to be preached to the people? But it must by all means be preached, that he who has ears to hear may hear. But who has them, unless he receives them from him who has promised to bestow them? Certainly he who receives not may reject, provided he who receives takes and drinks, drinks and lives. For as piety must be preached that God may be rightly worshiped, so also must predestination, that he who has ears to hear of the grace of God may glory in God and not in himself." [9]

[9] Augustine, *op. cit.*, XV, XVI, XX; Migne, *PL*, XLV, 1016–1018, 1026 f.; *NPNF*, V, 541, 546–547.

Mathnawī

JALALU'L-DIN RŪMĪ

Jalalu'l-Din Rūmī (1207–1273) has been called the greatest mystical poet of Persia. The following selection is from his longest work, the Mathnawī, *which consists of six books and 25,000 rhyming couplets.*

MORAL RESPONSIBILITY [1]

If we let fly an arrow, the action is not ours: we are only the bow, the shooter of the arrow is God.

This is not compulsion [*jabr*]: it is Al-mightiness [*jabbāri*] proclaimed for the purpose of making us humble.[2]

Our humbleness is evidence of Necessity, but our sense of guilt is evidence of Free-will.

If we are not free, why this shame? Why this sorrow and guilty confusion and abashment?

Why do masters chide their pupils? Why do minds change and form new resolutions?

You may argue that the asserter of Free-will ignores God's Compulsion, which is hidden like the moon in a cloud;

But there is a good answer to that: hearken, renounce unbelief, and cleave to the Faith!

When you fall ill and suffer pain, your conscience is awakened, you are stricken with remorse and pray God to forgive your trespasses.

The foulness of your sin is shown to you, you resolve to come back to the right way;

You promise and vow that henceforth your chosen course of action will be obedience.

Note, then, this principle, O seeker: pain and suffering make one aware of God; and the more aware one is, the greater his passion.[3]

[1] *Math.* I, 616. Rūmī defends the orthodox Moslem doctrine that "the creature does not create his actions and is not forced: God creates these actions together with the creature's having a free choice [*ikhtiyār*] in them."

[2] God calls Himself the Compeller [*ai-Fabbār*] in order to remind us that we are His slaves and entirely subject to His Will.

[3] Suffering causes the sinner to repent, and true penitence implies self-abandonment, *i.e.*, knowledge and love of God. Hence the Necessitarian, if he were really conscious of being "compelled," would turn to God in anguish and supplication like a distraught lover.

The text and the notes are from *Rūmī, Poet and Mystic,* by Reynold A. Nicholson; London, George Allen and Unwin, Ltd., 1956; Reprinted by permission of George Allen and Unwin, Ltd.

If you are conscious of God's Compulsion, why are you not heart-broken? Where is the sign of your feeling the chains with which you are loaded?

How should one make merry who is bound in chains? Does the prisoner behave like the man who is free?

Whatever you feel inclined to do, you know very well that you can do it;

But in the case of actions that you dislike, you have become a Necessitarian, saying, "Such is God's Decree."

The prophets are Necessitarians as regards the works of this world; the infidels are Necessitarians as regards the works of the world hereafter.

PREDESTINATION AND FREE-WILL [4]

A Moslem called a Magian to accept the Faith of the Prophet. He replied, "I shall do so, if God will."

"God wills it," said the Moslem; "but your carnal soul and the wicked Devil are dragging you to infidelity and the fire-temple."

"Well," he answered, "if they are the stronger, must not I go in the direction whither they pull me?

You say that God desires me to profess Islam: what is the use of His Desire when He cannot fulfil it?

According to you, the Flesh and the Devil have carried their will to success, while the gracious Divine Purpose has been defeated and pulverized.[5]

God forbid! Whatsoever He wills shall come to pass. He is the Ruler over the worlds of space and spacelessness.

Without His Command no one in His Kingdom shall add so much as the tip of a single hair.

The Kingdom is His, the Command is His: that Devil of His is the meanest dog at His door."

"Beyond doubt," replied the Moslem, "we possess a certain power of choice: you cannot deny the plain evidence of the inward sense.

There is such a power of choice in regard to injustice and wrong-doing: that is what I meant when I spoke of the Flesh and the Devil.[6]

The instinct to choose is latent in the soul, and sight of the desired object brings it into action.

When Iblīs shows to you an object of desire, the sleeping power awakes and moves towards it,

While, on the other hand, the Angel sets before you good objects of desire and commends them to your heart,

In order that the power to resist evil and choose good may be stimulated."

In the eyes of reason, Necessitarianism [jabr] is worse than the doctrine of absolute free-will [qadar], because the Necessitarian is denying his own consciousness.[7]

---

[4] Math. V, 2912. In the long-drawn debate from which a few extracts are given here, the Magian upholds absolute necessitarianism, while the Moslem declares such a doctrine to be absurd.

[5] The same argument was used by an eminent Sūfī, Abū Sulaymān Dārānī (ob. A.D. 830), against the Qadarites and Muʿtazilites: "they have made themselves and the Devil stronger than God; for they say that He created His creatures to obey Him and that Iblīs converted them to disobedience. Thus they maintain that when they will a thing it comes to pass, but when God wills a thing it does not come to pass."

[6] Although the Moslem, speaking the language of religion, attributed the Magian's infidelity to these evil forces, he did not mean that their operation is irresistible: on the contrary, it is limited by a faculty in man which enables him to choose whether or no he will accept the temptation offered to him.

[7] The existence of that which is beyond perception can more reasonably be denied than the existence of that which is perceived by the out-

The other does not deny this, he denies
the action of the Almighty: he says,
"There is smoke, but no fire." [8]

The Necessitarian sees the fire plainly: it
burns his raiment, and like the sceptic
he argues that it is naught.[9]

"If none but God has the power of choice,
why are you angry with a thief who
steals your property?

Even animals recognize this inward sense:
a camel, cruelly beaten, attacks the
driver; his fury is not directed against
the cudgel.

The entire *Qur'ān* consists of commands
and prohibitions and threats of punishment: are these addressed to stones and
brickbats?

You have removed from God the possibility of impotence, but you have virtually
called Him ignorant and stupid.

The doctrine of Free-will does not imply
Divine impotence; and even if it did,
ignorance is worse than impotence.

God's universal power of choice brought
our individual power into existence:
His Power is like a horseman hidden
by the dust which he raises;

But His control of our acts of free-will
does not deprive them of that quality.

Declare that God's Will is exercised in a
complete manner, yet without imputing
to Him compulsion [*jabr*] and responsibility for disobedience to His Commands.

You say your unbelief is willed by Him:
know that it is also willed by yourself;

For without your will it cannot exist at
all: involuntary unbelief is a self-contradiction.

Endeavour to gain inspiration from God's
cup of love: then you will become self-
less and without volition.

Then all volition will belong to that
Wine, and you will be absolutely ex-
cusable."

---

ward or inward senses. Consequently, from this
point of view, the Jabrī, who denies his manifest
power of choice (*ikhtiyār*) is worse than the
Qadarī (Mu'tazilite), who denies the invisible
Divine action.

[8] *I.e.*, he perceives the effect (*athar*), namely his
free-will, but imputes it to himself. ignoring the
Creator and Producer of the effect (*Mu'aththir*),
on Whose Will his choice of good or evil ultimately depends.

[9] The Jabrī is a thorough-going sceptic, for he
contradicts a universal fact of human consciousness.

Bahr al-Kalām

ABŪ 'L-MU'ĪN AN-NASAFĪ

The Bahr al-Kalām fī 'Ilm at-Tawhīd [*Sea of discussion on the science of theology*] *was composed by Abū 'l-Mu'īn an-Nasafī, who died in 1114. The* Bahr al-Kalām *has had considerable popularity as an analysis of the implication for man of God's foreknowledge.*

The Mu'tazilites and the Mortifiers (*al-mutaqashifa*) teach that both the instruction (*ta'rif*) and the understanding (*ma'rifa*) [of the matter of instruction] are created things, while the Voiders (*al-mafrūghiyya*) teach that both of them are uncreated. According to the truly orthodox, however, the *ta'rīf* is from Allah and so is uncreated, while the *ma'rifa* and the *ta'arruf* (i.e. the matter of instruction and the process of being instructed therein), being on the side of man, are created.

Should it be asked: "How Faith is to be described, and what its conditions are?"—we reply that Faith is that you should believe in Allah, in His angels, His Books, His Apostles, in the Last Day, in the resurrection after death, and that the decreeing of both good and evil are from Allah. This is according to the truly orthodox.

The Mu'tazilites teach that evil is wholly from man, for Allah does not decree evil, nor determine it, nor will it, for did He determine evil and then punish men for it, that would be tyranny (*ẓulm*) on His part and injustice (*jawr*), but Allah is far removed from tyranny or injustice. For this reason they (i.e. the Mu'tazilites) call themselves the people of equity and unity (*al-'adl wa't-tawḥīd*). We, on the other hand, teach that man is given the option and is capable, that the determining does not compel men to disobedience, just as is the case with knowledge, for determining is an attribute of the Determiner, and the attribute does not compel anyone to action, just as knowledge of tailoring or carpentering does not compel the tailor or carpenter to do [any tailoring or carpentering]. Man has the option and the ability, and in this sense deserves punishment [if he does wrong]. It is as though a master were to say to his slave: "If you enter the house you are free," and he enters the house and is free—a similar case is that of divorce, when divorce takes place, yet no one says that it

From *A Reader on Islam*, Arthur Jeffery, ed.; S-Gravenhage, Mouton & Co., 1962, pp. 380–83. Reprinted by permission of Mouton & Co.

was because the oath indicated that he might enter, that, therefore, compelled him to enter. So is it here. Even if the action is by the determination of Allah, no one may say that such determining compelled anyone to act. Another answer is that the determining is one of Allah's secret matters which He has kept hidden from creatures, whereas command and prohibition are Allah's clear proof against His creatures, so that if one ignores His revealed commands when he has the ability [to act], then in that sense he deserves punishment.

The question may be raised: "If we say that Allah determines evil, and man is unable to flee from the determining of Allah, that would mean that the evil is to be attributed to Allah, [would it not?]" —to this we reply that man's action is to be distinguished from Allah's determining. Do you not see that Allah created the instrument for fornication yet the fornication is not to be attributed to Allah? This indicates that though Allah created movement and power in man's soul and man is able [to act] by this capacity of his soul and his will, the movement and the power [when they are activated] are not to be attributed to Allah, even though that was by His determining and by His will. This points to the soundness of our teaching that if Allah did not will unbelief and evil and disobedience and did not determine it, whereas man wills it and does it, then man's will would be predominant over Allah's will, and this [in turn] would mean that a deficiency is to be attributed to Allah, which is unbelief, seeing that all wills are under the will of Allah, and under His desire. Allah has said (LXXVI, 30 = LXXXI, 29): "But ye will not save as Allah wills." It is also pointed to by the fact that were one to say: "My will and desire are other than the will of Allah and His desire," that would be making a claim to Lordship along with Allah, which

is unbelief, as 'Alī b. Abū Tālib [1]—may Allah honour his face—has said.

So it stands assured that every will comes under the will of Allah. Because Allah knew that Pharaoh and Iblīs [2] would be in unbelief He cursed them. Should we say that He did not desire their unbelief nor did he produce it [that would be saying that] His desire is in contradiction with His knowledge, and this cannot be, for if knowledge is reduced to nothing there remains but foolishness and ignorance, but Allah is far removed from foolishness and ignorance. This [desire], however, is quite distinct from a command, for there is a verse given textually from Allah [declaring] that He does not command evil. Allah has said (VII, 28/27): "Verily Allah does not command evil deeds (or what is blameworthy)," [3] where the reference is to fornication. Allah has also said (II, 205/201): "and Allah loves not corruption." Here we have a deviation from the rule, because it is possible for Allah to command one with regard to a matter which He does not desire. A case is that of Iblīs—on whom be the curse [of Allah]. He ordered him to do obeisance to Adam,[4] but He

[1] The fourth Caliph, and the first Imām of the Shī'a. He was the cousin and son-in-law of the Prophet, having married the Prophet's daughter Fātima. His father Abū Tālib had been Muhammad's protector when he was left an orphan.

[2] In the Qur'ān this is the personal name of Satan. It is derived from the Greek word *diabolos*.

[3] This latter clause is not in VII, 28/27, but is from a similar passage in XXIV, 1.

[4] The Qur'ān in several passages refers to this legend of the angels doing obeisance to the newly created Adam. In Muhammad's version of the story it was Allah who commanded the angels to do obeisance, but Iblīs refused, and for that reason he was cast out and became the enemy of mankind. Muslim theologians have always been much exercised to explain why Allah should command the angels to do such obeisance to Adam, when obeisance should be tendered to none save Himself.

did not desire from him any act of obeisance. Also He forbade Adam—on whom be Allah's blessings—to eat from the tree, but He did not desire from him any refraining, nay rather He desired that he eat from the tree. And with Allah is success.

Be it known that Allah created all creatures when He brought them forth from the loins of Adam—on whom be peace—on the day of the Covenant.[5] They were not believers nor were they unbelievers but they were creatures. Then He set before them Faith and Unbelief. Each one who chose Faith and accepted it as belief became a believer, and each one who did not choose Faith became an unbeliever, while each one who responded with words instead of belief became a hypocrite. This was as Allah has said (VII, 172/171): "When thy Lord took from the sons of Adam, from their backs, their progeny, and took their witness against themselves, [saying]: 'Am I not your Lord?,' they answered: 'Surely.'" That He said: "Am I not your Lord?" and that they answered: "Surely," would indicate that Allah created them with bodies as well as souls just as they are now, for question and answer are for bodies along with souls. Then He put them back into the loins of their parents, [and little by little] drew out the children of Adam from him, then the children of his children from his children, and so on till the Resurrection Day, because Allah said: "From their backs."

The Jabarites teach that Allah created the believers as believers and the unbe-

lievers as unbelievers. Therefore Iblīs— upon whom be the curse—ceases not to be an unbeliever as he was [from the beginning], and Abū Bakr and 'Umar [6] were believers before there was any Islam. Likewise the Prophets were prophets before any revelation had been given. In that case, curiously enough, the brethren of Joseph must have been prophets at the time of their rebelliousness.[7] The truly orthodox—whom may Allah increase, and among whom we, praise be to Allah, are —teach that they became prophets after that [revelation had been given], and that Iblīs became rebellious by refusing the act of obeisance, and so became an unbeliever by not recognizing that Allah was wise in what He commanded. According to them unbelievers are constrained to unbelief and rebelliousness, and are punished, whereas believers are constrained to obedience and faith. We, however, teach that man is given the option and is capable of either obedience or rebelliousness, being under no constraint, but the aiding or the abandoning (tawfīq wa khidhlān) are from Allah, and the decreeing of good and evil are from Allah. This question will be fully discussed in the latter part of this book.

The truth of our position is indicated by Allah's saying (IV, 136/135): "Believe in Allah and in His Apostle." Had they been [already] believers He would not have given them such a command, nor indeed would He have addressed them about the Faith. Had they not had the

---

[5] This event of the Covenant (mīthāq), also known as "the first creation," is the Islamic version of an ancient Oriental notion. It says that after Adam's creation Allah stroked his loins and drew out all his progeny who should be till the end of time, making the division then as to which of them should be believers and which unbelievers, which should inherit Paradise and which go to the Fire.

[6] Abū Bakr was the first Caliph in succession to Muḥammad, and 'Umar was the second Caliph.

[7] The point here is that four times in the Qur'ān "the Tribes" are referred to as the recipients of revelation, and thus belong to the prophetic succession. Some have thought that there was a confusion in Muḥammad's mind between the Twelve meaning the twelve tribes, and the Twelve meaning the Minor Prophets, but it is more likely that he is reproducing the old Rabbinic notion that the Patriarchs were all recipients of revelation.

possibility of choosing there would have been no point to the command. It is also pointed to by the saying of him on whom be Allah's blessing and peace: "I have been bidden make war on the people till they say: 'There is no deity but Allah, and Muḥammad is the Apostle of Allah.' If they say this they will preserve their blood from me and their property, save what is due therefrom,[8] while their accounting is with Allah," for he did not make war on any believer.

[8] The reference is to the fact that though they became Muslims they still had to pay out of their property the dues demanded by the religious law for the upkeep of the Muslim social and political order.

Short Treatise on God, Man, and His Well-Being

BENEDICT SPINOZA

Benedict Spinoza (1632–1677) finished the Short Treatise *in 1660–1661, and it was published posthumously in 1677. The work is not an ordered whole but a collection of diverse themes written over a long period of time. For a fascinating description of the detective work involved in the discovery of the manuscript, together with an account of the relation of the parts to one another and to Spinoza's other work, the reader should consult the introduction to the text from which the selection is taken.*

ON DIVINE PREDESTINATION

The third attribute, we say, is divine predestination.

1. We proved before that God cannot omit to do what he does; that he has, namely, made everything so perfect that it cannot be more perfect.

2. And, at the same time, that without him no thing can be, or be conceived.

It remains to be seen now whether there are in Nature any accidental things, that is to say, whether there are any things which may happen and may also not happen. Secondly, whether there is any thing concerning which we cannot ask why it is.

Now that there are no accidental things we prove thus: That which has no cause to exist cannot possibly exist; that which is accidental has no cause: therefore . . .

The first is beyond all dispute; the second we prove thus: If any thing that

From *Spinoza's Short Treatise on God, Man, and His Well-Being*, transl. and ed., with introduction, commentary, and a life of Spinoza by A. Wolf; Adam and Charles Black: London, 1910.

is accidental has a definite and certain cause why it should exist, then it must necessarily exist; but that it should be both accidental and necessary at the same time, is self-contradictory; Therefore . . .

Perhaps some one will say, that *an accidental thing* has indeed no definite and certain cause, but an accidental one. If this should be so, it must be so either *in sensu diviso* or *in sensu composito,* that is to say, either the existence of the cause is accidental, and not its being a cause; or it is accidental that a certain thing (which indeed must necessarily exist in Nature) should be the cause of the occurrence of that accidental thing. However, both the one and the other are false.

For, as regards the first, if the accidental something is accidental because [the existence of] its cause is accidental, then that cause must also be accidental, because the cause which has produced it is also accidental, *et sic in infinitum.*

And since it has already been proved, *that all things depend on one single cause,* this cause would therefore also have to be accidental: which is manifestly false.

As regards the second: if the cause were no more compelled to produce one thing than another, that is, [if the cause were no more compelled] to produce this something than not to produce it, then it would be impossible at once both that it should produce it and that it should not produce it, which is quite contradictory.

Concerning the second [question raised] above, *whether there is no thing in Nature about which one cannot ask why it is,* this remark of ours shows that we have to inquire through what cause a thing is real; for if this [cause] did not exist it were impossible that the thing should exist. Now, we must look for this cause either in the thing or outside the thing. If, however, any one should ask for a rule whereby to conduct this inquiry, we say that none whatever seems necessary. For if existence pertains to the nature of a

thing, then it is certain that we must not look outside it for its cause; but if such is not the case, we must always look outside the thing for its cause. Since, however, the first pertains to God alone, it is thereby proved (as we have already also proved before) that God alone is the first cause of all things. From this it is also evident that this or that will of man (since the existence of the will does not pertain to its essence) must also have an external cause, by which it is necessarily caused; that this is so is also evident from all that we have said in this chapter; and it will be still more evident when, in the second part, we come to consider and discuss the freedom of man.

Against all this others object: how is it possible that God, who is said to be supremely perfect, and the sole cause, disposer, and provider of all, nevertheless permits such *confusion* to be seen everywhere in Nature? Also, why has he not *made man so as not to be able to sin?*

Now, in the first place, it cannot be rightly said that there is *confusion in Nature,* since nobody knows all the causes of things so as to be able to judge accordingly. This objection, however, originates in this kind of ignorance, namely, that they have set up general Ideas, with which, they think, particular things must agree if they are to be perfect. These *Ideas,* they state, are in the understanding of God, as many of *Plato's* followers have said, namely, that these *general Ideas* (such as Rational, Animal, and the like) *have been created by God;* and although those who follow *Aristotle* say, indeed, that these things are not *real* things, only things of Reason, they nevertheless regard them frequently as [real] things, since they have clearly said that his providence does not extend to particular things, but only to kinds; for example, God has never exercised his providence over Bucephalus, etc., but only over the whole genus Horse. They say also that God has no knowledge of particular and transient things, but only of the general, which, in their opinion, are imperishable. We have, however, rightly considered this to be due to their ignorance. For it is precisely the particular things, and they alone, that have a cause, and not the general, because they are nothing.

God then is the cause of, and providence over, particular things only. If particular things had to conform to some other Nature, then they could not conform to their own, and consequently could not be what they truly are. For example, if God had made all human beings like Adam before the fall, then indeed he would only have created Adam, and no Paul nor Peter; but no, it is just perfection in God, that he gives to all things, from the greatest to the least, their essence, or, to express it better, that he has all things perfectly in himself.

As regards the other [objection], *why God has not made mankind so that they should not sin,* to this it may serve [as an answer], that whatever is said about sin is only said with reference to us, that is, as when we compare two things with each other, or [consider one thing] from different points of view. For instance, if some one has made a clock precisely in order to strike and to show the hours, and the mechanism quite fulfils the aims of its maker, then we say that it is good, but if it does not do so, then we say that it is bad, notwithstanding that even then it might still be good if only it had been his intention to make it irregular and to strike at wrong times.

We say then, in conclusion, that Peter must, as is necessary, conform to the Idea of Peter, and not to the Idea of *Man;* good and evil, or sin, these are only modes of thought, and by no means things, or any thing that has reality, as we shall very likely show yet more fully in what follows. For all things and works which are in Nature are perfect.

War and Peace

LEO TOLSTOI

Leo Tolstoi (1828–1910) wrote his great novel, War and Peace, *in 1869. This selection gives his views on the nature of history, law, and human freedom. Tolstoi is concerned primarily with the problem of the relationship between man's freedom and the new scientific determinism.*

Chapter VIII

If history dealt only with external phenomena, the establishment of this simple and obvious law would suffice and we should have finished our argument. But the law of history relates to man. A particle of matter cannot tell us that it does not feel the law of attraction or repulsion and that the law is untrue, but man, who is the subject of history, says plainly: I am free and am therefore not subject to the law.

The presence of the problem of man's free will, though unexpressed, is felt at every step of history.

All seriously thinking historians have involuntarily encountered this question. All the contradictions and obscurities of history and the false path historical science has followed are due solely to the lack of a solution of that question.

If the will of every man were free, that is, if each man could act as he pleased, all history would be a series of disconnected incidents.

If in a thousand years even one man in a million could act freely, that is, as he chose, it is evident that one single free act of that man's in violation of the laws governing human action would destroy the possibility of the existence of any laws for the whole of humanity.

If there be a single law governing the actions of men, free will cannot exist, for then man's will is subject to that law.

In this contradiction lies the problem of free will, which from most ancient times has occupied the best human minds and from most ancient times has been presented in its whole tremendous significance.

The problem is that regarding man as a subject of observation from whatever point of view—theological, historical, ethical, or philosophic—we find a general law of necessity to which he (like all that exists) is subject. But regarding him from within ourselves as what we are conscious of, we feel ourselves to be free.

This consciousness is a source of self-cognition quite apart from and independent of reason. Through his reason man observes himself, but only through consciousness does he know himself.

Apart from consciousness of self no observation or application of reason is conceivable.

To understand, observe, and draw conclusions, man must first of all be conscious of himself as living. A man is only conscious of himself as a living being by the fact that he wills, that is, is conscious of his volition. But his will—which forms the essence of his life—man recognizes (and can but recognize) as free.

If, observing himself, man sees that his will is always directed by one and the same law (whether he observes the necessity of taking food, using his brain, or anything else) he cannot recognize this never-varying direction of his will otherwise than as a limitation of it. Were it not free it could not be limited. A man's will seems to him to be limited just because he is not conscious of it except as free.

You say: I am not free. But I have lifted my hand and let it fall. Everyone understands that this illogical reply is an irrefutable demonstration of freedom.

That reply is the expression of a consciousness that is not subject to reason.

If the consciousness of freedom were not a separate and independent source of self-consciousness it would be subject to reasoning and to experience, but in fact such subjection does not exist and is inconceivable.

A series of experiments and arguments proves to every man that he, as an object of observation, is subject to certain laws, and man submits to them and never resists the laws of gravity or impermeability once he has become acquainted with them. But the same series of experiments and arguments proves to him that the complete freedom of which he is conscious in himself is impossible, and that his every action depends on his organization, his character, and the motives acting upon him: yet man never submits to the deductions of these experiments and arguments. Having learned from experiment and argument that a stone falls downwards, a man indubitably believes this and always expects the law that he has learned to be fulfilled.

But learning just as certainly that his will is subject to laws, he does not and cannot believe this.

However often experiment and reasoning may show a man that under the same conditions and with the same character he will do the same thing as before, yet when under the same conditions and with the same character he approaches for the thousandth time the action that always ends in the same way, he feels as certainly convinced as before the experiment that he can act as he pleases. Every man, savage or sage, however incontestably reason and experiment may prove to him that it is impossible to imagine two different courses of action in precisely the same conditions, feels that without this irrational conception (which constitutes the essence of freedom) he cannot imagine life. He feels that however impossible it may be, it is so, for without this conception of freedom not only would he be unable to understand life, but he would be unable to live for a single moment.

He could not live, because all man's efforts, all his impulses to life, are only efforts to increase freedom. Wealth and poverty, fame and obscurity, power and subordination, strength and weakness, health and disease, culture and ignorance, work and leisure, repletion and hunger, virtue and vice, are only greater or lesser degrees of freedom.

A man having no freedom cannot be conceived of except as deprived of life.

If the conception of freedom appears to reason to be a senseless contradiction like the possibility of performing two actions at one and the same instant of time, or of an effect without a cause, that only proves that consciousness is not subject to reason.

This unshakable, irrefutable consciousness of freedom, uncontrolled by experiment or argument, recognized by all thinkers and felt by everyone without exception, this consciousness without which no conception of man is possible constitutes the other side of the question.

Man is the creation of an all-powerful, all-good, and all-seeing God. What is sin, the conception of which arises from the consciousness of man's freedom? That is a question for theology.

The actions of men are subject to general immutable laws expressed in statistics. What is man's responsibility to society, the conception of which results from the conception of freedom? That is a question for jurisprudence.

Man's actions proceed from his innate character and the motives acting upon him. What is conscience and the perception of right and wrong in actions that follows from the consciousness of freedom? That is a question for ethics.

Man in connection with the general life of humanity appears subject to laws which determine that life. But the same man apart from that connection appears to be free. How should the past life of nations and of humanity be regarded—as the result of the free, or as the result of the constrained, activity of man? That is a question for history.

Only in our self-confident day of the popularization of knowledge—thanks to that most powerful engine of ignorance, the diffusion of printed matter—has the question of the freedom of will been put on a level on which the question itself cannot exist. In our time the majority of so-called advanced people—that is, the crowd of ignoramuses—have taken the work of the naturalists who deal with one side of the question for a solution of the whole problem.

They say and write and print that the soul and freedom do not exist, for the life of man is expressed by muscular movements and muscular movements are conditioned by the activity of the nerves; the soul and free will do not exist because at an unknown period of time we sprang from the apes. They say this, not at all suspecting that thousands of years ago that same law of necessity which with such ardor they are now trying to prove by physiology and comparative zoology was not merely acknowledged by all the religions and all the thinkers, but has never been denied. They do not see that the role of the natural sciences in this matter is merely to serve as an instrument for the illumination of one side of it. For the fact that, from the point of view of observation, reason and the will are merely secretions of the brain, and that man following the general law may have developed from lower animals at some unknown period of time, only explains from a fresh side the truth admitted thousands of years ago by all the religious and philosophic theories—that from the point of view of reason man is subject to the law of necessity; but it does not advance by a hair's breadth the solution of the question, which has another, opposite, side, based on the consciousness of freedom.

If men descended from the apes at an unknown period of time, that is as comprehensible as that they were made from a handful of earth at a certain period of time (in the first case the unknown quantity is the time, in the second case it is the origin); and the question of how man's consciousness of freedom is to be reconciled with the law of necessity to which he is subject cannot be solved by comparative physiology and zoology, for in a frog, a rabbit, or an ape, we can observe only the muscular nervous activity, but in man we observe consciousness as well as the muscular and nervous activity.

The naturalists and their followers, thinking they can solve this question, are like plasterers set to plaster one side of the walls of a church who, availing themselves of the absence of the chief superintendent of the work, should in an access of zeal plaster over the windows, icons, woodwork, and still unbuttressed walls, and should be delighted that from their point of view as plasterers, everything is now so smooth and regular.

Chapter IX

For the solution of the question of free will or inevitability, history has this advantage over other branches of knowledge in which the question is dealt with, that for history this question does not refer to the essence of man's free will but to its manifestation in the past and under certain conditions.

In regard to this question, history stands to the other sciences as experimental science stands to abstract science.

The subject for history is not man's will itself but our presentation of it.

And so for history, the insoluble mystery presented by the incompatibility of free will and inevitability does not exist as it does for theology, ethics, and philosophy. History surveys a presentation of man's life in which the union of these two contradictions has already taken place.

In actual life each historic event, each human action, is very clearly and definitely understood without any sense of contradiction, although each event presents itself as partly free and partly compulsory.

To solve the question of how freedom and necessity are combined and what constitutes the essence of these two conceptions, the philosophy of history can and should follow a path contrary to that taken by other sciences. Instead of first defining the conceptions of freedom and inevitability in themselves, and then ranging the phenomena of life under those definitions, history should deduce a definition of the conceptions of freedom and inevitability themselves from the immense quantity of phenomena of which it is cognizant and that always appear dependent on these two elements.

Whatever presentation of the activity of many men or of an individual we may consider, we always regard it as the result partly of man's free will and partly of the law of inevitability.

Whether we speak of the migration of the peoples and the incursions of the barbarians, or of the decrees of Napoleon III, or of someone's action an hour ago in choosing one direction out of several for his walk, we are unconscious of any contradiction. The degree of freedom and inevitability governing the actions of these people is clearly defined for us.

Our conception of the degree of freedom often varies according to differences in the point of view from which we regard the event, but every human action appears to us as a certain combination of freedom and inevitability. In every action we examine we see a certain measure of freedom and a certain measure of inevitability. And always the more freedom we see in any action the less inevitability do we perceive, and the more inevitability the less freedom.

The proportion of freedom to inevitability decreases and increases according to the point of view from which the action is regarded, but their relation is always one of inverse proportion.

A sinking man who clutches at another and drowns him; or a hungry mother exhausted by feeding her baby, who steals some food; or a man trained to discipline who on duty at the word of command kills a defenseless man—seem less guilty, that is, less free and more subject to the law of necessity, to one who knows the circumstances in which these people were placed, and more free to one who does not know that the man was himself drowning, that the mother was hungry, that the soldier was in the ranks, and so on. Similarly a man who committed a murder twenty years ago and has since lived peaceably and harmlessly in society seems less guilty and his action more due to the law of inevitability, to someone who considers his action after twenty years have elapsed than to one who examined it the day after it was committed. And in the same way every action of an insane, intoxicated, or highly excited man appears less free and more inevitable to one who knows the mental condition of him who committed the action, and seems more free and less inevitable to one who does not know it. In all these cases the conception of freedom is increased or diminished and the conception of compulsion is correspondingly decreased or increased, according to the point of view from which the action is regarded. So that the greater the conception of necessity the smaller the conception of freedom and vice versa.

Religion, the common sense of mankind, the science of jurisprudence, and history itself understand alike this relation between necessity and freedom.

All cases without exception in which our conception of freedom and necessity is increased and diminished depend on three considerations:

1. The relation to the external world of the man who commits the deeds.

2. His relation to time.

3. His relation to the causes leading to the action.

The first consideration is the clearness of our perception of the man's relation to the external world and the greater or lesser clearness of our understanding of the definite position occupied by the man in relation to everything coexisting with him. This is what makes it evident that a drowning man is less free and more subject to necessity than one standing on dry ground, and that makes the actions of a man closely connected with others in a thickly populated district, or of one bound by family, official, or business duties, seem certainly less free and more subject to necessity than those of a man living in solitude and seclusion.

If we consider a man alone, apart from his relation to everything around him, each action of his seems to us free. But if we see his relation to anything around him, if we see his connection with anything whatever—with a man who speaks to him, a book he reads, the work on which he is engaged, even with the air he breathes or the light that falls on the things about him—we see that each of these circumstances has an influence on him and controls at least some side of his activity. And the more we perceive of these influences the more our conception of his freedom diminishes and the more our conception of the necessity that weighs on him increases.

The second consideration is the more or less evident time relation of the man to the world and the clearness of our perception of the place the man's action occupies in time. That is the ground which makes the fall of the first man, resulting in the production of the human race, appear evidently less free than a man's entry into marriage today. It is the reason why the life and activity of people who lived centuries ago and are connected with me in time cannot seem to me as free as the life of a contemporary, the consequences of which are still unknown to me.

The degree of our conception of freedom or inevitability depends in this respect on the greater or lesser lapse of time between the performance of the action and our judgment of it.

If I examine an act I performed a moment ago in approximately the same circumstances as those I am in now, my action appears to me undoubtedly free. But if I examine an act performed a month ago, then being in different circumstances, I cannot help recognizing that if that act had not been committed much that resulted from it—good, agreeable, and even essential—would not have taken place. If I reflect on an action still more remote, ten years ago or more, then the consequences of my action are still plainer to me and I find it hard to imagine what would have happened had that action not been performed. The farther I go back in memory, or what is the same thing the farther I go forward in my judgment, the more doubtful becomes my belief in the freedom of my action.

In history we find a very similar progress of conviction concerning the part played by free will in the general affairs of humanity. A contemporary event seems to us to be indubitably the doing of all the known participants, but with a more remote event we already see its inevitable results which prevent our considering anything else possible. And the farther we go back in examining events the less arbitrary do they appear.

The Austro-Prussian war appears to us undoubtedly the result of the crafty conduct of Bismarck, and so on. The Napoleonic wars still seem to us, though already questionably, to be the outcome of their heroes' will. But in the Crusades we already see an event occupying its définite place in history and without which we cannot imagine the modern history of Europe, though to the chroniclers of the Crusades that event appeared as merely due to the will of certain people. In regard to the migration of the peoples it does not enter anyone's head today to suppose that the renovation of the European world depended on Attila's caprice. The farther back in history the object of our observation lies, the more doubtful does the free will of those concerned in the event become and the more manifest the law of inevitability.

The third consideration is the degree to which we apprehend that endless chain of causation inevitably demanded by reason, in which each phenomenon comprehended, and therefore man's every action, must have its definite place as a result of what has gone before and as a cause of what will follow.

The better we are acquainted with the physiological, psychological, and historical laws deduced by observation and by which man is controlled, and the more correctly we perceive the physiological, psychological, and historical causes of the action, and the simpler the action we are observing and the less complex the character and mind of the man in question, the more subject to inevitability and the less free do our actions and those of others appear.

When we do not at all understand the cause of an action, whether a crime, a good action, or even one that is simply nonmoral, we ascribe a greater amount of freedom to it. In the case of a crime we most urgently demand the punishment for such an act; in the case of a virtuous act we rate its merit most highly. In an indifferent case we recognize in it more individuality, originality, and independence. But if even one of the innumerable causes of the act is known to us we recognize a certain element of necessity and are less insistent on punishment for the crime, or the acknowledgment of the merit of the virtuous act, or the freedom of the apparently original action. That a criminal was reared among malefactors mitigates his fault in our eyes. The self-sacrifice of a father or mother, or self-sacrifice with the possibility of a reward, is more comprehensible than gratuitous self-sacrifice, and therefore seems less deserving of sympathy and less the result of free will. The founder of a sect or party, or an inventor, impresses us less when we know how or by what the way was prepared for his activity. If we have a large range of examples, if our observation is constantly directed to seeking the correlation of cause and effect in people's actions, their actions appear to us more under compulsion and less free the more correctly we connect the effects with the causes. If we examined simple actions and had a vast number of such actions under observation, our conception of their inevitability would be still greater. The dishonest conduct of the son of a dishonest father, the misconduct of a woman who had fallen into bad company, a drunkard's relapse into drunkenness, and so on are actions that seem to us less free the better we understand their cause. If the man whose actions we are considering is on a very low stage of mental development, like a child, a madman, or a simpleton—then, knowing the causes of the act and the simplicity of the character and intelligence in question, we see so large an element of necessity and so little free will that as soon as we know the cause prompting the action we can foretell the result.

On these three considerations alone is based the conception of irresponsibility for crimes and the extenuating circumstances admitted by all legislative codes. The responsibility appears greater or less according to our greater or lesser knowledge of the circumstances in which the man was placed whose action is being judged, and according to the greater or lesser interval of time between the commission of the action and its investigation, and according to the greater or lesser understanding of the causes that led to the action.

Chapter X

Thus our conception of free will and inevitability gradually diminishes or increases according to the greater or lesser connection with the external world, the greater or lesser remoteness of time, and the greater or lesser dependence on the causes in relation to which we contemplate a man's life.

So that if we examine the case of a man whose connection with the external world is well known, where the time between the action and its examination is great, and where the causes of the action are most accessible, we get the conception of a maximum of inevitability and a minimum of free will. If we examine a man little dependent on external conditions, whose action was performed very recently, and the causes of whose action are beyond our ken, we get the conception of a minimum of inevitability and a maximum of freedom.

In neither case—however we may change our point of view, however plain we may make to ourselves the connection between the man and the external world, however inaccessible it may be to us, however long or short the period of time, however intelligible or incomprehensible the causes of the action may be—can we ever conceive either complete freedom or complete necessity.

1. To whatever degree we may imagine a man to be exempt from the influence of the external world, we never get a conception of freedom in space. Every human action is inevitably conditioned by what surrounds him and by his own body. I lift my arm and let it fall. My action seems to me free; but asking myself whether I could raise my arm in every direction, I see that I raised it in the direction in which there was least obstruction to that action either from things around me or from the construction of my own body. I chose one out of all the possible directions because in it there were fewest obstacles. For my action to be free it was necessary that it should encounter no obstacles. To conceive of a man being free we must imagine him outside space, which is evidently impossible.

2. However much we approximate the time of judgment to the time of the deed, we never get a conception of freedom in time. For if I examine an action committed a second ago I must still recognize it as not being free, for it is irrevocably linked to the moment at which it was committed. Can I lift my arm? I lift it, but ask myself: could I have abstained from lifting my arm at the moment that has already passed? To convince myself of this I do not lift it the next moment. But I am

not now abstaining from doing so at the first moment when I asked the question. Time has gone by which I could not detain, the arm I then lifted is no longer the same as the arm I now refrain from lifting, nor is the air in which I lifted it the same that now surrounds me. The moment in which the first movement was made is irrevocable, and at that moment I could make only one movement, and whatever movement I made would be the only one. That I did not lift my arm a moment later does not prove that I could have abstained from lifting it then. And since I could make only one movement at that single moment of time, it could not have been any other. To imagine it as free, it is necessary to imagine it in the present, on the boundary between the past and the future —that is, outside time, which is impossible.

3. However much the difficulty of understanding the causes may be increased, we never reach a conception of complete freedom, that is, an absence of cause. However inaccessible to us may be the cause of the expression of will in any action, our own or another's, the first demand of reason is the assumption of and search for a cause, for without a cause no phenomenon is conceivable. I raise my arm to perform an action independently of any cause, but my wish to perform an action without a cause is the cause of my action.

But even if—imagining a man quite exempt from all influences, examining only his momentary action in the present, unevoked by any cause—we were to admit so infinitely small a remainder of inevitability as equaled zero, we should even then not have arrived at the conception of complete freedom in man, for a being uninfluenced by the external world, standing outside of time and independent of cause, is no longer a man.

In the same way we can never imagine the action of a man quite devoid of freedom and entirely subject to the law of inevitability.

1. However we may increase our knowledge of the conditions of space in which man is situated, that knowledge can never be complete, for the number of those conditions is as infinite as the infinity of space. And therefore so long as not *all* the conditions influencing men are defined, there is no complete inevitability but a certain measure of freedom remains.

2. However we may prolong the period of time between the action we are examining and the judgment upon it, that period will be finite, while time is infinite, and so in this respect too there can never be absolute inevitability.

3. However accessible may be the chain of causation of any action, we shall never know the whole chain since it is endless, and so again we never reach absolute inevitability.

But besides this, even if, admitting the remaining minimum of freedom to equal zero, we assumed in some given case—as for instance in that of a dying man, an unborn babe, or an idiot—complete absence of freedom, by so doing we should destroy the very conception of man in the case we are examining, for as soon as there is no freedom there is also no man. And so the conception of the action of a man subject solely to the law of inevitability without any element of freedom is just as impossible as the conception of a man's completely free action.

And so to imagine the action of a man entirely subject to the law of inevitability without any freedom, we must assume the knowledge of an *infinite* number of space relations, an *infinitely* long period of time, and an *infinite* series of causes.

To imagine a man perfectly free and not subject to the law of inevitability, we must imagine him all alone, *beyond space, beyond time,* and *free from dependence on cause.*

In the first case, if inevitability were possible without freedom we should have reached a definition of inevitability by the laws of inevitability itself, that is, a mere form without content.

In the second case, if freedom were possible without inevitability we should have arrived at unconditioned freedom beyond space, time, and cause, which by the fact of its being unconditioned and unlimited would be nothing, or mere content without form.

We should in fact have reached those two fundamentals of which man's whole outlook on the universe is constructed—the incomprehensible essence of life, and the laws defining that essence.

Reason says: (1) space with all the forms of matter that give it visibility is infinite, and cannot be imagined otherwise. (2) Time is infinite motion without a moment of rest and is unthinkable otherwise. (3) The connection between cause and effect has no beginning and can have no end.

Consciousness says: (1) I alone am, and all that exists is but me, consequently I include space. (2) I measure flowing time by the fixed moment of the present in which alone I am conscious of myself as living, consequently I am outside time. (3) I am beyond cause, for I feel myself to be the cause of every manifestation of my life.

Reason gives expression to the laws of inevitability. Consciousness gives expression to the essence of freedom.

Freedom not limited by anything is the essence of life, in man's consciousness. Inevitability without content is man's reason in its three forms.

Freedom is the thing examined. Inevitability is what examines. Freedom is the content. Inevitability is the form.

Only by separating the two sources of cognition, related to one another as form to content, do we get the mutually exclu-sive and separately incomprehensible conceptions of freedom and inevitability.

Only by uniting them do we get a clear conception of man's life.

Apart from these two concepts which in their union mutually define one another as form and content, no conception of life is possible.

All that we know of the life of man is merely a certain relation of free will to inevitability, that is, of consciousness to the laws of reason.

All that we know of the external world of nature is only a certain relation of the forces of nature to inevitability, or of the essence of life to the laws of reason.

The great natural forces lie outside us and we are not conscious of them; we call those forces gravitation, inertia, electricity, animal force, and so on, but we are conscious of the force of life in man and we call that freedom.

But just as the force of gravitation, incomprehensible in itself but felt by every man, is understood by us only to the extent to which we know the laws of inevitability to which it is subject (from the first knowledge that all bodies have weight, up to Newton's law), so too the force of free will, incomprehensible in itself but of which everyone is conscious, is intelligible to us only in as far as we know the laws of inevitability to which it is subject (from the fact that every man dies, up to the knowledge of the most complex economic and historic laws).

All knowledge is merely a bringing of this essence of life under the laws of reason.

Man's free will differs from every other force in that man is directly conscious of it, but in the eyes of reason it in no way differs from any other force. The forces of gravitation, electricity, or chemical affinity are only distinguished from one another in that they are differently defined by reason. Just so the force of man's free will is distinguished by reason from the other forces of nature only by the definition reason gives it. Freedom, apart from necessity, that is, apart from the laws of reason that define it, differs in no way from gravitation, or heat, or the force that makes things grow; for reason, it is only a momentary undefinable sensation of life.

And as the undefinable essence of the force moving the heavenly bodies, the undefinable essence of the forces of heat and electricity, or of chemical affinity, or of the vital force, forms the content of astronomy, physics, chemistry, botany, zoology, and so on, just in the same way does the force of free will form the content of history. But just as the subject of every science is the manifestation of this unknown essence of life while that essence itself can only be the subject of metaphysics, even so the manifestation of the force of free will in human beings in space, in time, and in dependence on cause forms the subject of history, while free will itself is the subject of metaphysics.

In the experimental sciences what we know we call the laws of inevitability, what is unknown to us we call vital force. Vital force is only an expression for the unknown remainder over and above what we know of the essence of life.

So also in history what is known to us we call laws of inevitability, what is unknown we call free will. Free will is for history only an expression for the unknown remainder of what we know about the laws of human life.

Chapter XI

History examines the manifestations of man's free will in connection with the external world in time and in dependence on cause, that is, it defines this freedom by the laws of reason, and so history is a science only in so far as this free will is defined by those laws.

The recognition of man's free will as something capable of influencing historical events, that is, as not subject to laws, is the same for history as the recognition of a free force moving the heavenly bodies would be for astronomy.

That assumption would destroy the possibility of the existence of laws, that is, of any science whatever. If there is even a single body moving freely, then the laws of Kepler and Newton are negatived and no conception of the movement of the heavenly bodies any longer exists. If any single action is due to free will, then not a single historical law can exist, nor any conception of historical events.

For history, lines exist of the movement of human wills, one end of which is hidden in the unknown but at the other end of which a consciousness of man's will in the present moves in space, time, and dependence on cause.

The more this field of motion spreads out before our eyes, the more evident are the laws of that movement. To discover and define those laws is the problem of history.

From the standpoint from which the science of history now regards its subject on the path it now follows, seeking the causes of events in man's free will, a scientific enunciation of those laws is impossible, for however man's free will may be restricted, as soon as we recognize it as a force not subject to law, the existence of law becomes impossible.

Only by reducing this element of free will to the infinitesimal, that is, by regarding it as an infinitely small quantity, can we convince ourselves of the absolute inaccessibility of the causes, and then instead of seeking causes, history will take the discovery of laws as its problem.

The search for these laws has long been begun and the new methods of thought which history must adopt are being worked out simultaneously with the self-destruction toward which—ever dissecting and dissecting the causes of phenomena—the old method of history is moving.

All human sciences have traveled along that path. Arriving at infinitesimals, mathematics, the most exact of sciences, abandons the process of analysis and enters on the new process of the integration of unknown, infinitely small, quantities. Abandoning the conception of cause, mathematics seeks law, that is, the property common to all unknown, infinitely small, elements.

In another form but along the same path of reflection the other sciences have proceeded. When Newton enunciated the law of gravity he did not say that the sun or the earth had a property of attraction; he said that all bodies from the largest to the smallest have the property of attracting one another, that is, leaving aside the question of the cause of the movement of the bodies, he expressed the property common to all bodies from the infinitely large to the infinitely small. The same is done by the natural sciences: leaving aside the question of cause, they seek for laws. History stands on the same path. And if history has for its object the study of the movement of the nations and of humanity and not the narration of episodes in the lives of individuals, it too, setting aside the conception of cause, should seek the laws common to all the inseparably interconnected infinitesimal elements of free will.

Chapter XII

From the time the law of Copernicus was discovered and proved, the mere recognition of the fact that it was not the sun but the earth that moves sufficed to destroy the whole cosmography of the ancients. By disproving that law it might have been possible to retain the old conception of the movement of the bodies, but without disproving it, it would seem impossible to continue studying the Ptolemaic worlds. But even after the discovery of the law of Copernicus the Ptolemaic worlds were still studied for a long time.

From the time the first person said and proved that the number of births or of crimes is subject to mathematical laws, and that this or that mode of government is determined by certain geographical and economic conditions, and that certain relations of population to soil produce migrations of peoples, the foundations on which history had been built were destroyed in their essence.

By refuting these new laws the former view of history might have been retained; but without refuting them it would seem impossible to continue studying historic events as the results of man's free will. For if a certain mode of government was established or certain migrations of peoples took place in consequence of such and such geographic, ethnographic, or economic conditions, then the free will of those individuals who appear to us to have established that mode of government or occasioned the migrations can no longer be regarded as the cause.

And yet the former history continues to be studied side by side with laws of statistics, geography, political economy, comparative philology, and geology, which directly contradict its assumptions.

The struggle between the old views and the new was long and stubbornly fought out in physical philosophy. Theology stood on guard for the old views and accused the new of violating revelation. But when truth conquered, theology established itself just as firmly on the new foundation.

Just as prolonged and stubborn is the struggle now proceeding between the old and the new conception of history, and theology in the same way stands on guard for the old view, and accuses the new view of subverting revelation.

In the one case as in the other, on both sides the struggle provokes passion and stifles truth. On the one hand there is fear and regret for the loss of the whole edifice constructed through the ages, on the other is the passion for destruction.

To the men who fought against the rising truths of physical philosophy, it seemed that if they admitted that truth it would destroy faith in God, in the creation of the firmament, and in the miracle of Joshua the son of Nun. To the defenders of the laws of Copernicus and Newton, to Voltaire for example, it seemed that the laws of astronomy destroyed religion, and he utilized the law of gravitation as a weapon against religion.

Just so it now seems as if we have only to admit the law of inevitability, to destroy the conception of the soul, of good and evil, and all the institutions of state and church that have been built up on those conceptions.

So too, like Voltaire in his time, uninvited defenders of the law of inevitability today use that law as a weapon against religion, though the law of inevitability in history, like the law of Copernicus in astronomy, far from destroying, even strengthens the foundation on which the institutions of state and church are erected.

As in the question of astronomy then, so in the question of history now, the whole difference of opinion is based on the recognition or nonrecognition of something absolute, serving as the measure of visible phenomena. In astronomy it was the immovability of the earth, in history it is the independence of personality—free will.

As with astronomy the difficulty of recognizing the motion of the earth lay in abandoning the immediate sensation of the earth's fixity and of the motion of the planets, so in history the difficulty of recognizing the subjection of personality to the laws of space, time, and cause lies in renouncing the direct feeling of the independence of one's own personality. But as in astronomy the new view said: "It is true that we do not feel the movement of the earth, but by admitting its immobility we arrive at absurdity, while by admitting its motion (which we do not feel) we arrive at laws," so also in history the new view says: "It is true that we are not conscious of our dependence, but by admitting our free will we arrive at absurdity, while by admitting our dependence on the external world, on time, and on cause, we arrive at laws."

In the first case it was necessary to renounce the consciousness of an unreal immobility in space and to recognize a motion we did not feel; in the present case it is similarly necessary to renounce a freedom that does not exist, and to recognize a dependence of which we are not conscious.

An Introduction to Philosophical Analysis

JOHN HOSPERS

John Hospers (b. 1918) is Professor of Philosophy at the University of Southern California. The selection that follows represents a contemporary attempt to meet the so-called problem of fatalism, determinism, and freedom. Hospers' program begins by clarifying the concepts involved in the problem and ends by drawing inferences from the analysis of these concepts.

DETERMINISM AND FREEDOM

Discussions of causality usually go hand in hand with discussions of determinism and freedom. The connection among these three concepts is not always made clear, but as a rule it is conceived in this way: If everything that happens has a cause, then we live in a deterministic universe, or in other words, *determinism* is true; and if determinism is true, then there is no room for freedom of the human will. Having arrived at this point, people commonly take one of two views: either "There is freedom, and therefore determinism is false," or "Determinism is true, and therefore there is no freedom."

Consider the following argument:

With every day that passes, science is able to tell us more about the causes of things—the *determining* factors which *make* things happen the way they do. This includes human actions as well as events

in the physical world: we know more than ever before about what makes people behave as they do.

Consequently, more and more people's actions are becoming predictable. Once eclipses were not predictable; now we can predict their occurrence to within a tenth of a second ten thousand years in advance. Once the path of a projectile could not be predicted; now it can be mapped out with such precision that we know how to make it hit a certain distant target at just the right moment. Even when we don't know exactly what a thing will do, for instance just how a stone will roll downhill, this isn't because its path is not completely determined by the forces acting upon it, but because we don't know what all those forces are: just where the stone will hit this crevice, whether the slippery side of the stone in rolling down the hill will be against the smooth part of the ground on this part of its journey downward, and so on. We know the laws, but

From *An Introduction to Philosophical Analysis* by John Hospers; Englewood Cliffs, N.J.: Prentice-Hall, Inc., 1953. Reprinted by permission of Prentice-Hall, Inc.

not all the initial conditions. But nobody imagines—at least, no one who has the slightest acquaintance with science—that its path *couldn't* be calculated if we knew, or bothered to acquaint ourselves with, all the million and one factors that would have to be considered in computing its course down the slope.

Now, nobody ever pretended that stones have freedom, or free-will. But it *has* been contended that human beings have, and science is gradually showing up this claim for what it is—a mere superstition. We know far more today than ever before about people's hereditary constitution and environmental conditions, the laws of how people behave, all the factors that make people act as they do. The person is becoming more and more like the stone. He may fancy that he is free, but this is a delusion: he is no more free than the stone is. The forces acting on him are more *complex,* and therefore far more difficult to discover, than those acting on the stone, but they are there just the same. Whether he knows what they are or not, they are there, and they inevitably make him what he is and make him do what he does. Anyone who had knowledge of the laws and of his total state at any given moment would be able to predict everything that he would do in response to every future situation; he would, in short, be able to show how every moment of the person's life is determined.

The above argument is an imaginary one, but it closely resembles many arguments that take place around us every day. If anything, it is probably more clearly outlined than most of them are. Yet it is full of confusions. (Before reading further, you will do well to spot as many errors in it as you can.) For example, three of the concepts used in it—causality, compulsion, and predictability—are treated as if they were the same. Let us, then, endeavor to see what can be said

about human freedom in the light of the preceding sections. This task will consist chiefly of trying to dispel confusions which are almost always made in discussions of this issue. We shall begin, as it were, at the bottom of the ladder of clarity, beginning with a rather uncritical use of the animistically tinged language of ordinary life, but making the distinctions that bear upon the topic at hand, until we have cleared up the whole issue as much as we can.

Determinism and Fatalism

DETERMINISM. The word "determinism" usually stands for the view that everything that happens is determined. The word "determined," however, is not very clear. In the context of everyday usage "to be determined" usually means "to be resolved," as in "I was determined to arrive there on time no matter what the cost." But in the context of the problem of freedom, "to be determined" usually means "to be caused." Determinism, then, is the view that everything that happens has a cause. The determinist argues: "Everything that happens has a cause; we may not know what it is, but there *is* one all the same. Whenever you do something, there is some cause for your doing that rather than something else. Every event that occurs, whether in your history or that of a stone, is a link in an unbreakable chain of cause and effect. There are no 'loose ends,' no 'gaps' or breaks, in the constitution of the universe; there are no broken links in the iron chain." When asked how he knows that everything has a cause, the determinist replies, "I don't; but more causes are being discovered all the time. I don't claim that we'll ever discover all the causes that there are, but at any rate when I have found the causes of events A, B, and C, I know that *they* at any rate have causes; whereas my opponent can never prove even of one event in the whole universe that it is causeless. At best he can only say that we haven't yet *found* a cause for it."

The determinist is not always as crude as this, nor does he always fall victim to the animistic language used here. At his clearest, the determinist is simply the person who holds to the Causal Principle in one or another of the forms discussed in the preceding section.

INDETERMINISM. The indeterminist denies that everything has a cause. Indeterminism, like determinism, can be either a confused, animistically tinged view like determinism at its cloudiest, or it can be a denial of the Causal Principle in one of the forms stated in the preceding section. No matter which version he takes, however, he is at a disadvantage from the start; he cannot point to any causeless events, but only to events for which no cause has been found. With regard to these, he can say, "Not all of them are determined. For many events we have found determining causes, but not for all; may it not be that the reason for this is that they (some of them, at any rate) *have* no causes? If you can't find gold, this may be because it has escaped your scrutiny, but it may also be because there is none there to be found."

As for the events in inorganic nature, the indeterminist is likely to leave these entirely to the determinist, without a battle. "Maybe the path of projectiles and planets is determined," he says, "but with events on a higher level it is otherwise. This is particularly true of human behavior. There is surely no conclusive evidence for determinism in the realm of human actions. We have never found any exceptionless generalizations about human actions, and those we have formulated are so vague and general that almost any kind of behavior could occur without falsifying them. Human behavior is predictable to only a very small degree. The

99.99 per cent we can't predict *may,* as the determinist says, be due to the complexity of the causes, but it may also be due to a genuine indeterminism in human beings themselves. If this is true, then even a *complete* knowledge of the causal factors influencing a person would not enable us to predict whether, in a situation of choice, he would choose A or B. That decision remains free."

One might object that if there is no conclusive evidence for determinism in the realm of human actions, neither is there evidence against it. Why then does the indeterminist hold to his position? The chief motive underlying this conviction, in almost every case, is the belief that human beings have freedom of choice—"free-will" is the usual term for it—and that if determinism were true they would not have this freedom. Not all human actions are free, of course, but (according to the indeterminist) some are. You are faced with a difficult moral choice, between two alternatives, A and B. Morality makes no sense unless you are really *free* to choose between them. Freedom of choice is the most precious of human possessions. Determinism, if it were true, would make freedom impossible. Determinism, then, is false, for free-will does exist.

(Sometimes the determinist points to the occurrence of *chance* events as evidence for his view. But ordinarily when we speak of events occurring "by chance" we do not mean that they are uncaused; or, if we ever do, there could be no evidence in favor of our view, for, as we saw in the preceding section, there could be no evidence for uncaused events. We do speak of events as occurring by chance, and by speaking in this way, we may mean any of several different things, none of which implies the absence of cause. (1) We may mean that an occurrence was unplanned or unintentional, as when we say, "We met by chance downtown this morning." We do not deny that there were causes for our respective trips downtown, but only that we planned the meeting. (2) We may mean to refer simply to our ignorance of the causal factors, either because they are so complex or simply because we do not consider it worth while to track them down. "I don't know what will happen," we say; "it's all a matter of chance." (3) We may mean to refer to *probability:* "There's a 50-50 chance that when you toss the coin it will turn out to be heads." Again, we are not denying that either outcome would be caused by something, principally by the way we tossed the coin.)

FATALISM. At this point, another distinction becomes important: the distinction between determinism and fatalism. Determinists do not declare that all events are beyond human control, or that things will happen in a certain way regardless of what we do. This belief is *fatalism.* Seizing upon some future event, the fatalist says, "If it's going to happen, it's going to happen"—which he does not intend as a tautology; he wants to say that all human efforts are futile, that the event will happen (or fail to happen, as the case may be) regardless of what he or other human beings may try to do about it. The determinist says nothing of this kind; he insists only that if the event does occur, there will be causes leading up to it, and that if it does not occur, its failure to occur will also be caused. He will not for a moment deny that human beings themselves are often causal influences which help to determine whether events will or will not occur.

The members of a certain congregation were opposed to having a liquor store brought into their small town, but decided that if it was fated to happen (in this case, if God so willed it), it would happen regardless of human efforts; accordingly they decided that there was nothing they could do. The thing they

feared came to pass. Their efforts might have prevented it; but they made no effort, and as a result, the thing they disapproved of occurred. They were fatalists about the matter. Had they been merely determinists, they would not have been committed to such a policy; they could then have said, "Whichever way it turns out will be the result of determining causes; but *we* can be a part of those determining causes; because of the causal influences *we* exert, we may be able to bring about the event or prevent it, as we wish." Determinism merely says that all events have determining causes; fatalism says that all events have causes *outside of ourselves,* in other words, that everything that happens does so regardless of what we do.

Probably no one is a fatalist with regard to every event that occurs; at least, such a view could not be put into practice. Nobody says, "If I'm fated to have my lunch today, it will be given to me, regardless of what I do or don't do," and then take no steps to prepare lunch or go to a restaurant. People know well enough that there are *some* things they can do which will make a difference to what happens later. Thus the doctrine that what we do *never* makes a difference is as manifestly false as any doctrine can be. Determinism is, at least, not easily refutable; fatalism is refuted by hundreds of events we all observe and take part in every day.

FREEDOM. Having now eliminated the confusion between his own view and fatalism, the determinist asserts that he is in as good a position to believe in freedom as anyone else. "Doesn't my view," he asks, "leave human beings as much freedom as they would ever want? You are free to do something when you can do it *if* you want to: more precisely, when your willing to do it is actually followed by the thing's occurring. I am free to move my arm (if I don't get a paralytic stroke), because I can do it if I will to; but I am not free to lift the house, for no amount of willing or wanting can enable me to achieve this result. We are not free to do *everything;* no human being is free in this way; but we *are* free to do a vast number of things. Our volitions, in other words, can make a considerable difference in the world; they act as causes as well as do the forces of nature. What more freedom than this can anyone ask for?

Indeed, the determinist carries the battle into the enemy's camp; he will say to the indeterminist, "Not only will my view permit freedom; yours will not! Freedom, in my opinion, is possible only to the extent that determinism is true. Suppose that some act of yours were causeless; it would not be affected by your character, your habits up to now, in short by *you.* Don't you want your acts to be determined *by you?* Can you really call them free if they are determined by *nothing*—are cut off from all roots whatever? In that case how could they even be called *your* acts? Suppose you had a friend whom you had known for years and trusted implicitly; if he were to be cut off from all causal conditions, in other words if he were seized with an attack of indeterministic free-will, there would be nothing to determine his action, and no grounds whatever for trusting him. Education, reformation, advice, reward, and punishment would be useless, for, in the absence of causality, there would be no chance that they might *cause* a change in the person's character and determine his future actions. In education and reformation, do we not assme the truth of of determinism? What would be the use of these things if they could have no influence in determining subsequent behavior?"

The indeterminist, on the other hand, will reply: "Don't make my position absurd. No indeterminist believes that all events are uncaused. If there were only a small amount of indeterminism in the universe, say in a small range of human behavior, this would not interfere with the regularity and uniformity in the universe to any appreciable degree. Nor would it interfere with our powers of prediction: there are enough things that are unpredictable now, and always will be. Human behavior, in particular, is notoriously unpredictable; the causal factors here are so infinitely complex that they will surely never all be known, and the introduction of a bit of indeterminism here would not be noticeable any more than a drop of water in the sea. You need not feel that all is lost if the universe is not rigidly deterministic. There are still plenty of causal factors for the sciences to unearth."

"Nevertheless," comes the determinist's reply, *"to the extent* that we do admit indeterminism, to that extent we admit chaos. It is simply a mistake to admit it at all. You admit that your position is without evidence in its favor; your sole motive for introducing it is to give grounds for freedom. I hold that this is unnecessary, for freedom occurs without it."

But neither do you have evidence for your view. You have found causes for some events, but not all. You simply assume that the rest have."

"No, I say it is probable on the basis of evidence. The area of events known to be caused constantly increases as scientists discover more causes. But there is no area of events *known not* to be caused; there is merely an area of events *not known* to be caused, and that area is constantly diminishing in size."

Thus, at this level, rests the controversy between determinism and indeterminism. The proponents of each view hold that they make room for free-will. However, we have scarcely yet begun to examine the confusions that beset this controversy.

WHAT MAKES
ACTIONS RIGHT?

ACTIONS AND RIGHTNESS

Suppose someone said to you, "What you have just done was the right thing to do." You might, if you're curious, ask him why he thought so. Your question and his answer launch us into this new section in ethics, a section that will deal primarily with the question, What criteria justify us in calling an action "good" or "right"? Philosophers and laymen who have been concerned about this question have answered it in many ways. The selections that follow illustrate three criteria that men have employed to justify calling actions "right" or "wrong."

Let us begin by distinguishing *act* from *action,* and *good* from *right.* Although the distinctions are not universally recognized, it will make the discussion simpler if we can begin by defining and clarifying our technical vocabulary. An action will be defined as a complex entity consisting of three parts: the *motive,* the *act,* and the *consequences.* These three components of an action can be distinguished in various ways: First, in a temporal sense, the motive precedes the other two, and it is followed in time by the act which precedes and is followed by the consequences of the act. Second, the motive is not public in the same sense as the consequences or the act; motive is mind-related and private, while act and consequence need not be. Third, motive is usually regarded as an envisioned future state in the mind of the actor such that the actor wishes or desires that that state be brought about. The act is the means by which this desire is satisfied, and the consequences are the envisioned state manifested in the world. We usually say that the act is "successful" if there is some close approximation between motive and consequences.

Suppose again that your best friend is running for the office of club president. He is not the most qualified man and so you have decided not to vote for him. Then he asks you who you are going to vote for in the club election. You don't want to hurt his feelings, but you must answer him honestly. What do you do? Suppose you answer cryptically, "I'm going to vote for the best-qualified man." Surely one of the motives you have here is not to hurt your friend's feelings. There may be other motives, as there are in most moral situations (we do speak of "mixed motives" for precisely this reason). The primary *motive* here might simply be described as the wish or desire that your friend not be alienated. The *act* is the behavior you exhibit, your speaking, which follows after your motive. Finally, the *consequence* in this case is the effect the act has on your friend. He may be furious at your subterfuge or placated by your seeming flattery. If he is indeed placated then we might call the action "successful"; if he is angered then your motive is frustrated and we could say the action is "unsuccessful." But however we decide to label the action, the point remains that we can distinguish these three parts of an action: motive, act, and consequence.[1]

A second distinction can now be made. Philosophers often note the difference between "right" and "good": "right" is applied to acts, "good" is applied to consequences; thus we seldom speak of "right consequences," and it is odd to speak of "good acts." The reason for this distinction is that it is often expedient to be able to use "right" alone and know we are talking about acts, and to use "good" alone and know we are talking about consequences. Motives, however, may be indifferently labeled either "right" or "good."

What we are left with then is a distinction between the three parts of an action: motive, act, and consequence; and a way of labeling these three as "right" (motive and act) and "good" (motive and consequence). Now we can go on to put our distinctions to some philosophic use in preparation for the readings that follow.

MORAL PROBLEMS

Suppose that while standing on a busy street corner you notice an elderly woman standing on another corner across the street. It seems to you that she wants to cross the street. You thread your way through the noisy traffic to her side of the street, take her by the arm, and steer her briskly to your side of the street. You deposit her on the curb, where she promptly drops dead of a heart attack. Is the action right or wrong? Is what you did right

[1] The matter is more complicated than it appears here. Plausible arguments can be constructed to show that such a trichotomy is quite frivolous, and that motive, act, and consequence are logical, but not real, distinctions. Thus, act and motive play back and forth into each other so much that a separation between the two becomes an illusion. The same can be said of consequence and act, especially where act is defined as "that which is done." For one "does" the consequence just as surely as one "does" the act and the motive. But ordinarily, and for purposes of exposing three moral views about rightness, the trichotomy can be accepted as real.

or wrong? Return now to the judgment with which we began this discussion. If the person who said, "What you have just done was the right thing to do," were talking about this example, then he would have to be talking about the motive or the act. i.e., either desiring to help or actually helping an elderly woman cross a busy street. Thus "what" in his judgment is ambiguous. For though we can indeed say that the motive and the act are right, we could not say that the consequence of the act is good: After all, the woman dropped dead.

Suppose you hate people who wear green ties. You see a man with a green tie coming toward you and you lash out with your foot, kicking him in the leg. He falls to the ground with a cry of pain. At that moment a police car draws up and several policemen leap out and grab the fallen man, who happens to be a notorious counterfeiter. You receive a reward, your picture in the paper, and the thanks of the Treasury Department. Is what you did right or good? Is the action right? We have seen that it all depends now on where you put your attention. What carries the burden of rightness? The motive (good or right)? The act (right)? Or the consequences (good)? In this example we can admit that the motive is bad, the act is wrong, but the long-run consequences are good (capturing a green-tied counterfeiter) even though the immediate consequences are bad (causing pain to a green-tied man).

In the following table we can list all the possible combinations of rightness (wrongness) or goodness (badness) under the three components of an action. From this list we can then determine whether the action is to be called "right" or "wrong." At this point philosophers and also laymen

	Motive	Act	Consequences	Verdict on Action
1.	good	right	good	?
2.	good	right	bad	?
3.	good	wrong	good	?
4.	good	wrong	bad	?
5.	bad	right	good	?
6.	bad	right	bad	?
7.	bad	wrong	good	?
8.	bad	wrong	bad	?

begin to disagree; some put the stress on one component and others put it on another. It is obvious that we would all agree on action 1 and action 8. If we could all agree that the adjectives "good" and "bad," "right" and "wrong" can be used descriptively of motive, act and, consequence in just the way we have used them here, then it can be safely argued that no one would object to our holding that action 1 is patently right and action 8 is patently wrong.

In the elderly woman illustration and the green tie illustration, the former could be represented by action 2 and the latter by action 7. But again, whether actions 2 and 7 are right or wrong is a question to be answered according to one's own moral theory.[2]

[2] One might also ask which actions would be called "successful" and which not.

THREE MORAL THEORIES

The selections that follow are divided according to the views of rightness taken by three groups of philosophers. Following the outline of our previous discussion, the first group holds that motives are the chief determinant in characterizing an action as "right" or "wrong." Immanuel Kant can be interpreted as representative of this view of action. C. D. Broad, a British philosopher, on the other hand, believes that talk about motives is misleading and mistaken.

The second view holds that rightness depends on the nature of the act itself and not on the motives. This view is illustrated in a theory of natural law found in St. Thomas Aquinas, in the work of Sir David Ross, and in the ancient Indian laws of Manu. It is interesting to note that both Ross and Manu provide an ordering for right acts, Ross calling them *prima facie* duties, and Manu referring to the sources of the laws.

The third and final view holds that rightness depends on the consequences; this view is generally called "utilitarianism." This theory is found in the works of the Chinese philosopher Motse, and in the European tradition in the writings of John Stuart Mill.

Lectures on Ethics

Immanuel Kant

Immanuel Kant (1724–1804) was born, educated, taught, and finally died in Königsberg, East Prussia. The following selection is taken from an extremely popular course of lectures on ethics. It illustrates the way in which Kant stressed the importance of motives in ethics.

THE GENERAL PRINCIPLE OF MORALITY

Having considered the ideal of the highest moral perfection, we must now see wherein the general principle of morality consists. So far we have said no more than that it rests upon the goodness of free will. We must now investigate what it essentially is. To establish the general principle of science is by no means easy, particularly if the sciences have already reached a certain stage of development. Thus, for instance, it is difficult to establish the general principle of law or of mechanics. But as we all need a basis for our moral judgments, a principle by which to judge with unanimity what is morally good and what bad, we apprehend that there must exist a single principle having its source in our will. We must therefore set ourselves to discover this principle, upon which we establish morality, and through which we are able to discriminate between what is moral and what immoral. However capable and tal-

ented a man may be, we still ask about his character. However great his qualities, we still ask about his moral quality. What then is the one principle of morality, the criterion by which to judge everything and in which lies the distinction between moral goodness and all other goodness? Before we decide these questions we must cite and classify the various points of view which lead to the definition of this principle in various ways.

The theoretical concept (not yet a theory, but merely a concept from which a theory can be constructed) is that morality has either an empirical or an intellectual basis, and that it must be derived either from empirical or from intellectual principles. Empirical grounds are derived from the senses, in so far as the senses find satisfaction in them. Intellectual grounds are those in which all morality is derived from the conformity of our actions to the laws of reason. Accordingly, *systema morale est vel empiricum vel intellectuale.*

If an ethical system is based upon empirical grounds, those may be either inner

From *Lectures on Ethics,* transl. Louis Infield; London, Methuen & Co., Ltd., 1930. Reprinted by permission of Methuen & Co., Ltd.

or outer grounds, as they are drawn from the objects of the inner or of the outer sense. The ethics derived from inner grounds gives us the first part of the empirical system; ethics derived from outer grounds, the second part. Those who derive ethics from the inner grounds of the empirical principle, presuppose a feeling, either physical or ethical.

The physical feeling which they take is self-love, which has two constituents, vanity and self-interest. Its aim is advantage to self; it is selfish and aims at satisfying our senses. It is a principle of prudence. Writers who follow the principle of self-love are, among the ancients, Epicurus (who grounds his philosophy in general upon an intuitional principle), and, among the moderns, Helvetius and Mandeville.

The second principle of the inner ground of the empirical system appears when the ground is placed in the ethical feeling whereby we discriminate between good and evil. Among those who build on this basis the foremost are Shaftesbury and Hutcheson.

To the empirical system of the theoretical concept of ethics belong, in the second place, outer grounds. Philosophers who base ethics on these argue that all morality rests upon two things, education and government, which in turn are a matter of custom; we judge all actions in a customary way by what we have been taught or by what the law tells us. Example or legal precept are thus the sources of the moral judgment. While Hobbes takes precept as his thesis and argues that the sovereign power may permit or prohibit any act, Montaigne bases himself on example and points out that in matters of morality men differ with environment, and that the morality of one locality is not that of another. He quotes as instances the permission of theft in Africa, that in China parents may desert their children with impunity, that the Eskimos strangle them,

and that in Brazil children are buried alive.

On these grounds it is not permissible for reason to pass ethical judgments on actions. Instead, we act by reference to customary example and the commands of authority, from which it follows that there is no ethical principle, unless it be one borrowed from experience.

But now, in the empirical system, the first principle of ethics is based upon contingent grounds. In the case of self-love, contingent circumstances decide the nature of the action which will advantage or harm us. Where ethical feeling is the basis, and we judge actions by liking or disliking, by repugnance, or in general by taste, the grounds of judgment are again contingent, for what may please one individual may disgust another. (Thus a savage will turn from wine with abhorrence, while we drink it with pleasure.) It is the same with the outer grounds of education and government.

In the second *Systema morale*, which is the intellectual, the philosopher judges that the ethical principle has its ground in the understanding and can be completely apprehended a priori. We say, for instance: "Thou shalt not lie." On the principle of self-love this would mean: "Thou shalt not lie if it harm thee; if it advantage thee then thou mayest lie." If ethical feeling were the basis, then a person so devoid of a refined ethical feeling, that in him lying evoked no disgust, would be at liberty to lie. If it depended on upbringing and government, then, if we were brought up to telling lies and if the Government so ordained, it would be open to us to tell lies. But if the principle lies in the understanding we say simply: "Thou shalt not lie, be the circumstances what they may." This, if I look into my free will, expresses the consistency of my free will with itself and with that of others; it is a necessary law of the free will. Such principles, which are universal, constant and necessary, have their source in pure reason; they cannot be derived from experience. Every ethical law expresses a categorical necessity, not one drawn from experience, and as every necessary rule must be established a priori, the principles of morality must be intellectual. The moral judgment never occurs at all in virtue of sensuous or empirical principles, for the ethical is never an object of the senses, but purely of the understanding.

The intellectual principle may be of two kinds:

1. Internal—if it depends on the inner nature of the action as apprehended by the understanding.

2. External—where our actions bear some relation to an external being.

But just as we have an ethical theology, so we have theological ethics, and the external intellectual principle is of that kind; but it is false, because discrimination between moral good and evil does not depend on any relation to another being. It follows, therefore, that the basic moral principle is of the first (i.e., the internal) of the above two kinds of intellectual principle. *Principium morale est intellectuale internum.* Our aim in what follows will be to discern and determine its constitution; but this can only be done gradually.

All imperatives are formulae of a practical necessitation. Practical necessitation is the necessitating of a free action. But all our free actions may be necessitated in two ways. They may be necessary in accordance with laws of the free will, when their necessity is practical; or of our sensuous inclination, when their necessity is pathological. Accordingly, our actions are determined either practically, i.e. in accordance with laws of freedom, or pathologically, in accordance with laws of our sensuous nature. Practical determination is an objective determination of the free act, while pathological determination is subjective. Accordingly, all objective laws of action are practically and not pathologically necessary.

Every imperative is a formula of practical necessitation, and only that. It expresses a determination of our actions, assuming their goodness. The formula of practical necessitation is that of the *causa impulsiva* of a free act, and because it necessitates objectively it is called a *motivum.* The formula of pathological necessitation is that of the *causa impulsiva per stimulos* because it necessitates subjectively. Thus all subjective *necessitationes* are *necessitationes per stimulos.*

To each of the three types of imperative there is a corresponding type of good, the objective determination of which is in each case expressed in the corresponding imperative:

1. *Bonitas problematica.* This follows from the *Imperativus problematicus* which says that a thing is good as a means to some optional end.

2. *Bonitas pragmatica.* This corresponds to the pragmatic imperative, the imperative of the judgment of prudence, which expresses the necessity of an action as a means to our happiness. Here the end is determinate, and therefore, although the determination of action is conditional, the condition is of absolute and of universal validity.

3. *Bonitas moralis.* This is expressed in the ethical imperative, which asserts the goodness of an action in and for itself. Ethical necessitation is therefore categorical and not hypothetical, constituted as it is by the absolute goodness of the free act.

The three types of imperative lead to the following deductions.

Moral necessitation constitutes an Obligation; but pragmatic necessitation, the consequence of an action from rules of prudence, does not. The obligation, being moral, is practical. Every obligation is either one of duty or one of compulsion, of which much more anon.

An obligation implies not that an action is necessary merely, but that it is made necessary; it is not a question of *necessitas,* but of *necessitatio.* Thus, while the divine will is, as regards morality, a necessary will, the human will is not necessary, but necessitated. It follows that, in the case of the Highest Being, practical necessity does not constitute an Obligation. God's acts are necessarily moral, but not from obligation. We do not say that God is obliged to be true and holy. Further, moral necessity is objective; if it happens to be also subjective it ceases to imply necessitation. Moral necessity, then, makes an action necessary objectively, and constitutes an Obligation if the subjective necessity is contingent. Every imperative expresses the objective necessitation of actions which are subjectively contingent. Suppose, for example, that I say, "You must eat when you are hungry and you have something to eat." Here we have both an objective and a subjective necessity; consequently necessitation falls away and there is no Obligation. In the case, therefore, of a perfect will, for which the moral necessity is not only objective but is also subjective, there is no room for necessitation or Obligation; but in the case of an imperfect will, for which the ethical good is objectively necessary, we have a place for necessitation and so also for obligation. Moral actions must therefore be contingent if they are to be determined, and human beings, whose wills are ethical, but imperfect, are subject to obligation.

Every obligation is a *necessitatio practica,* not *pathologica*—an objective, not a subjective determination. We have pathological necessitation where the impulse comes from the senses, or from the feeling of what is pleasant or unpleasant. The man who does a thing because it is pleasant is pathologically determined; he who does it because it is good, and because it is good in and for itself, acts on Motives and is practically determined. In so far, therefore, as *causae impulsivae* proceed from what is good, they are of the understanding; in so far as they proceed from what is pleasant, they are of the senses. He who is impelled to action by the former acts *per motiva;* he who is impelled by the latter acts *per stimulos.*

It follows from this argument that all Obligation is not pathological or pragmatic, but moral necessitation. As for the Motives, these have either a pragmatic basis, or else the moral basis of intrinsic goodness.

Pragmatic Motives are conditioned solely by the consideration that actions must be a means to happiness. Actions, being thus a means, do not contain their ground in themselves, and it follows that all *imperativi pragmatici hypothetice necessitant et non absolute.*

Imperativi morales, however, *necessitant absolute* and express a *bonitas absoluta,* just as *imperativi pragmatici* express a *bonitas hypothetica.* Thus honesty may possess a mediated goodness on grounds of prudence, as in commerce, where it is as good as ready money. But from an absolute point of view, to be honest is good in itself, good whatever the end in view, and dishonesty is in itself pernicious. Thus moral necessitation is absolute and the *motivum morale* expresses *bonitas absoluta.* We cannot at this stage explain how it is possible that an action should have *bonitas absoluta;* we must first interpolate the following remarks. If the will is subordinated to the dictate of ends universally valid, it will be in harmony with all human purposes, and herein is to be found its inherent goodness and absolute perfection. To exemplify this is not easy, but truthfulness, for instance, conforms to all my rules; it is in accord with every purpose; it is in harmony with the will of others, and every one can guide his conduct by it; one truth is consistent with another. On the other hand, lies contradict each other and are inconsistent with my purposes and with those of others. Moral goodness consists, therefore, in the submission of our will to rules whereby all our voluntary actions are brought into a harmony which is universally valid. Such a rule, which forms the first principle of the possibility of the harmony of all free wills, is the moral rule. Neither nature nor the laws determine a free action; and freedom, leaving our actions, as it does, quite undetermined, is a terrible thing. Our actions must be regulated if they are to harmonize, and their regulation is effected by the moral law. A pragmatic rule cannot do this. Pragmatic rules may make our actions consistent with our own will, but they will not bring them into harmony with the wills of others: in point of fact they may not even make them consistent with our own will; for the source of such rules is our well-being, and this cannot be determined a priori; rules of prudence can thus be laid down only a posteriori, and they cannot, therefore, apply to all actions, for in order to do that they would have to be a priori rules. Pragmatic rules are not, therefore, consistent with the wills of others and may not be consistent even with our own. But we must have rules to give our actions universal validity and to mould them into a general harmony. These rules are derived from the universal ends of mankind, and they are the moral rules.

The morality of an action is a quite peculiar thing: there is a distinct difference between a moral act and any pragmatic or pathological action; morality is subtle and pure and calls for special consideration on its own. There are actions for which moral Motives are not sufficient to produce moral goodness and for which pragmatic, or even pathological, *causae impulsivae* are wanted in addition; but when considering the goodness of an ac-

tion we are not concerned with that which moves us to that goodness, but merely with what constitutes the goodness in and for itself.

The *motivum morale* must, therefore, be considered purely in and for itself, as something apart and distinct from other Motives, whether of prudence or of the senses. Nature has implanted in us the faculty of drawing a subtle but very definite distinction betwen moral goodness and problematic and pragmatic goodness, and action which has a moral goodness is as pure as if it came from heaven itself. A pure moral ground is a more potent impulse than one intermingled with pathological and pragmatic Motives. These latter have a greater effect on our sensuous nature, but the motive power to which the understanding looks is one of universal validity. It is true that morality is not very impressive: it is not particularly pleasing, but it refers to a pleasure of universal validity: as such it must please the Supreme Being, and this constitutes the strongest motive force.

Prudence requires a good understanding, morality a good will. If our conduct as free agents is to have moral goodness, it must proceed solely from a good will. The will can, therefore, be good in itself. In the case of prudence everything depends, not on the end, since the end is always the same, namely happiness, but on the understanding which apprehends the end and the means to attain it; one individual may be a greater adept at this than another. But while a sound undertaking is requisite to prudence, to morality what is requisite is a will which is simply good in itself. Thus, for instance, the will to be rich is good in reference to its end, but not in itself.

We now proceed to examine what exactly constitutes that will, simply good in itself, on which moral goodness depends.

There is not only a clear distinction

between a moral and a pragmatic Motive, but the one is not in the least comparable to the other. This statement requires some explanation.

All ethical Motives are either merely *obligandi* or *obligantia*. *Motiva obligandi* constitute grounds for an Obligation: if the grounds are adequate they become *obligantia,* binding. Not all grounds of obligation are also binding grounds. *Motiva moralia non sufficientia non obligant, sed motiva sufficientia obligant.* There are, therefore, ethical rules which impose a plain obligation and render the action obligatory—as, for instance, "Thou shalt not lie." But if we combine *motiva pragmatica* with *motiva moralia* are they *homogenia?* No more than lack of candour in a person can be compensated by his possession of money; no more than a deficiency of good looks can be made good by wealth, which cannot turn ugliness into beauty. No more can we suppose that *motiva pragmatica* are of the same order as *motiva moralia,* or comparable to them. But their determining force can be compared. We get the illusion that it is advisable, on the judgment of the understanding, to prefer advantage to virtue. Nevertheless, moral perfection and advantage cannot be compared, for they are essentially different. How, then, is it that we actually fall into this confusion? We may say, for instance, when we meet a person in distress, that we should relieve his want and affliction, but only in so far as we can do it without detriment to ourselves. Judged by the understanding, though there is a difference here between moral and pragmatic action, there is no distinction between moral and pragmatic Motive, because both prudence and morality tell me to study my interest. I ought not to give to the poor wretch more than I can spare, for if I were to give away what I cannot spare I should myself be in want, I should myself have to seek the charity of others, and I should cease to be in a position to act morally. Objectively, therefore, moral and pragmatic motives cannot be set in opposition, for they are unlike.

Some of the Main Problems of Ethics

C. D. BROAD

C. D. Broad (1887–1971) was a British scholar whose interests in philosophy ranged over a wide variety of topics from science to psychical research. In this selection Broad examines the importance of motives to moral situations and concludes that it is expedient to exclude all reference to motives from our judgments regarding actions.

Intention and Rightness

When a person performs a deliberate action he does so in view of his knowledge and beliefs about the present situation and with certain expectations about the consequences which will ensue. These two factors are closely connected; for his expectations about the consequences are in part determined by his knowledge or beliefs about the present situation. I shall say that an act is *intentional* in respect of (1) all those features and only those which the agent knows or believes to be present in the initial situation, and (2) all those consequences and only those which he expects to follow. Now a person's information on both these matters will always be incomplete and it may be in part mistaken. No man can foresee the very remote consequences of an action; and anyone may be mistaken about some of its immediate consequences, either through miscalculation or through inadequate or inaccurate information about present circumstances. Suppose, e.g., that a person receives a letter purporting to come from his old nurse and that he is moved to send her a postal-order in the belief that she is in want and with the expectation that it will enable her to buy comforts. It may be that in fact the nurse has died, that the letter has been written in her name by a dishonest relative, and that the money will be spent by him on drink. What this man intended to do was to bring relief to his old nurse; what he in fact did was to enable a dishonest stranger to get drunk.

Now, if we consider the agent's intention in this example, we are inclined to say that he acted rightly. But, if we consider the actual facts of the situation and the consequences, we are inclined to say that he acted wrongly and that the right action would have been to refuse to send money and to have reported the matter

From *Philosophy*, Vol. XXI, No. 79, July, 1946; pp. 108–13. Reprinted with the permission of the executors of the estate of C. D. Broad.

to the police. Thus we are faced with the problem of the relation between intention and rightness or wrongness.

This question may be approached in the following way. Any act which can be called "right" or "wrong" can be viewed from two standpoints, viz., that of the agent who does it and that of the patient who is affected by it. In general these will be different persons, though there are special cases in which the agent and the patient are the same person at an earlier and a later stage of his life. Now in considering whether an act is right or wrong we must view it, so to speak, from both ends, i.e., in relation to the patient and in relation to the agent. In relation to the patient an act is right if and only if it fulfils his claims on the agent, or, as we say, "gives the patient his rights in the matter concerned." From this standpoint the agent's intention is irrelevant. In relation to the agent an act is right if and only if it is done with the intention of fulfilling the patient's claim and giving him his rights in the matter. From this standpoint anything in the actual consequences which is outside or contrary to the agent's intention is irrelevant.

I propose to call any act which in fact fulfils the claims of the patient upon the agent *materially right,* regardless of whether the agent intended it to have this consequence or not. I propose to call any act which was intended by the agent to bring about the fulfilment of the patient's claims *formally right,* regardless of whether it does in fact have that result or not. A *perfectly right* act in a given situation would be one that was both formally and materially right. It would be an act which was intended by the agent to give to the patient his rights and which did in fact do so. Owing to incomplete or incorrect information on the part of the agent, or to defects in his powers of inference, it may happen that an act which is formally right is materially wrong, or

that one which is formally indifferent or wrong is materially right. It should be noticed that the notion of material rightness is, in a certain sense, more fundamental than that of formal rightness. For what is formally right for the agent to do is to try to secure to the patient what is materially right for him to have done to him.

There remains, however, a further serious complication to be considered. So far I have supposed that the agent makes no *ethical* mistakes. I have supposed only that he may have incomplete or inaccurate information about *matters of fact* and may make mistaken inferences on such matters from his information. I have assumed that he knows what ought to happen to the patient if his factual information were adequate and accurate. But of course the agent *may* be ignorant or mistaken about *ethical* matters too.

Suppose, e.g., that a person is brought up in a community in which it is held to be a duty to carry on a family vendetta, and that he accepts that opinion. Let us assume, for the sake of argument, that it is mistaken, and that it is wrong to kill a member of another family simply because one of his ancestors killed one of one's own. Suppose that this person is in a situation in which he can either kill a certain member of the other family or let him escape. Whichever alternative he chooses we are inclined to say that he acts rightly, and we are about equally inclined to say that he acts wrongly. If he kills the patient, he intentionally does to him what he believes ought to be done to him, but this is in fact what ought not to be done to him. If he lets the patient escape, he intentionally does to him what he believes ought not to be done to him, but this is in fact what ought to be done to him.

It is plain that we are here concerned with yet another sense of "right" and "wrong." I propose to call it *subjective* rightness and wrongness. An act is sub-

jectively right if and only if the effects
which the agent expected it to have on
the patient are those which he believed
that the patient is entitled to have produced in him.

The relations between the various
senses of "right" which I have distinguished may be summarized as follows.
(1) A person could be sure of doing a *perfectly right* act only if both his relevant
factual and his relevant ethical beliefs
were complete and correct and if he had
made no mistakes in his inferences. It is
therefore plain that, if a person ever does
a perfectly right act, it is largely a matter
of luck that he does so. (2) A person could
be sure of doing a *formally right* act, even
if his factual information were incomplete
or inaccurate and he made mistakes in his
inferences, provided that the effects which
he *thinks* his act would have upon the
patient are such as the latter *really would*
be entitled to if his nature and situation
were as the agent *believes* them to be.
Therefore when an agent's relevant ethical
information is incomplete or incorrect it
is a matter of luck if he performs a formally right act. (3) A person could be sure
of doing a *subjectively right* act, no matter
how inadequate or inaccurate his factual
and his ethical beliefs might be or how
mistaken he may be in his inferences, provided only that the effects which he *thinks*
his act will have on the patient are such
as he *thinks* that the latter would be entitled to if his nature and situation were
as the agent *believes* them to be. It is
therefore plain that a person who is ignorant, stupid, and misinformed about facts,
who is incapable of drawing reasonable
inferences, and who is insensitive or crazy
in his opinions about what is materially
right and wrong, may perform acts that
are subjectively right. So it is not surprising that such acts may inflict the most
terrible wrongs on those whom they affect.

The problems which we have been discussing arise because we fail to distinguish

these three senses of "right" and "wrong,"
and use these words in a vague way to
include them all, sometimes having one
meaning predominantly before our minds
and sometimes another.

Motives and their Ethical Function

Among the characteristics which an
agent believes an action to have, and
among the consequences which he expects
to follow from it, some will attract him
towards doing it, some will repel him from
doing it, and others will leave him indifferent. Suppose, e.g., that a person contemplates throwing a bomb at a ruler in a
public procession. He may expect that
the effects will include the death of the
ruler, the death or injury of a number of
innocent bystanders, and the breakage of
a number of windows in the neighbour-
hood. The first part of the expected consequences may attract him, the second may
repel him, and the third may leave him
indifferent. A person's total motive *in* doing a certain action consists of all that he
believes about the action itself and all that
he expects about its consequences, which
either attracts him towards or repels him
from doing it. The former constitutes his
total motive *for* doing it, and the latter
his total motive *against* doing it. If, in
fact, he does it, he does it *because of* his
motives for doing it and *in spite of* his
motives against doing it. Suppose, e.g.,
that the anarchist in my example is in
general a humane man and that he decides to throw the bomb at the ruler. Then
his motive for doing so is the attractive
belief that it will kill the ruler; his motive
against doing so is the repellant belief that
it will kill or injure innocent bystanders;
and he acts because of the former and in
spite of the latter motive.

It is plain that there are two aspects to
any motive, viz., a cognitive and a cona-
tive-emotional aspect. The cognitive aspect of a motive is the fact that it is a

belief about the nature of the action or an *expectation* about its consequences. The conative aspect is the fact that the agent has a certain disposition to be *attracted or repelled* which is excited by this belief.

When we know what was a person's intention in doing an action and what consequences in fact followed from it we are in a position to judge whether it was subjectively right, or formally right, or perfectly right, without needing to know anything about his motives in doing the action. But it is quite obvious that a man's motives in doing an action have a very important bearing on *some* kind of moral judgment which we make either on the agent or on the action. This fact is indicated in ordinary speech by such phrases as, "He did the right thing from the wrong motive."

Suppose, e.g., that a man performs an act which is intended to secure the just punishment of a criminal. He will foresee that the criminal will suffer directly and his family and friends indirectly, so this must be included as part of his intention. Now it may be that the belief that the law will be vindicated, that other men will be deterred from committing similar crimes, and that the criminal may be reformed is an attracting one; that the belief that the criminal and his family will suffer is a repelling one; and that the agent acts because of the former and in spite of the latter. If so, we should be inclined to say, not only that his action was right, but also that his motives in doing it were good. But it may be that the belief that the law would be vindicated, other men deterred, and the criminal perhaps reformed, exercised no attraction on the agent. He had, perhaps, had a quarrel with the criminal or was jealous of him; and what attracted him was his belief that the criminal and his family would suffer. If so, the action would still be right in any of the senses which we have considered, but we should certainly say that the agent's motive in doing it was bad.

I have no doubt that the words "right" and "wrong" have, in addition to the ambiguities which we have already cleared up, the further ambiguity that they are sometimes used to include a reference to the agent's motives and sometimes used without such a reference. I think that it is on the whole more convenient explicitly to exclude reference to motives from our description of right and wrong action. One important reason for drawing the line at this point is the following. A person can choose which of several alternative possible actions he will do. But he cannot, in the same sense, choose which of several alternative motives shall attract him towards or repel him from doing a certain action. Now the predicates "right" and "wrong" are commonly understood to be confined to that which is directly dependent on a person's volition, in the sense in which his actions are so and his motives in acting are not.

Summa Theologica

St. Thomas Aquinas

St. Thomas Aquinas (1224–1274) wrote what has become the most widely read and famous document in the Christian philosophy of the Middle Ages, the Summa Theologica *(called "the great* Summa*" by many, to distinguish it from his second work, the* Summa Contra Gentiles*). St. Thomas employs a kind of scholastic dialectic, presenting an objection to a question, followed by three kinds of replies to the objection. The answer to the question, What makes an action right? is simply that certain laws have in themselves been declared to be right, and declared so by God.*

QUESTION XC: ON THE ESSENCE OF LAW
(In Four Articles)

First Article: Whether Law Is Something Pertaining To Reason?

We proceed thus to the First Article:
Objection 1. It would seem that law is not something pertaining to reason. For the Apostle says (Rom. vii., 23): *I see another law in my members,* etc. But nothing pertaining to reason is in the members, since the reason does not make use of a bodily organ. Therefore law is not something pertaining to reason.

Obj. 2. Further, in the reason there is nothing else but power, habit and act. But law is not the power itself of reason. In like manner, neither is it a habit of reason, because the habits of reason are the intellectual virtues, of which we have spoken above. Nor again is it an act of reason, because then law would cease when the act of reason ceases, for instance, while we are asleep. Therefore law is nothing pertaining to reason.

Obj. 3. Further, the law moves those who are subject to it to act rightly. But it belongs properly to the will to move to act, as is evident from what has been said above. Therefore law pertains, not to the reason, but to the will, according to the words of the Jurist: *Whatsoever pleaseth the sovereign has the force of law.*

On the contrary, It belongs to the law to command and to forbid. But it belongs to reason to command, as was stated above. Therefore law is something pertaining to reason.

I answer that, Law is a rule and measure of acts, whereby man is induced to act or is restrained from acting; for *lex* [*law*] is derived from *ligare* [*to bind*], be-

From *Basic Writings of Saint Thomas Aquinas,* Vol. II, Anton C. Pegis, ed.; New York, Random House, 1945. Reprinted by permission of Random House, Inc.

cause it binds one to act. Now the rule and measure of human acts is the reason, which is the first principle of human acts, as is evident from what has been stated above. For it belongs to the reason to direct to the end, which is the first principle in all matters of action, according to the Philosopher. Now that which is the principle in any genus is the rule and measure of that genus: for instance, unity in the genus of numbers, and the first movement in the genus of movements. Consequently, it follows that law is something pertaining to reason.

Reply Obj. 1. Since law is a kind of rule and measure, it may be in something in two ways. First, as in that which measures and rules; and since this is proper to reason, it follows that, in this way, law is in the reason alone. Secondly, as in that which is measured and ruled. In this way, law is in all those things that are inclined to something because of some law; so that any inclination arising from a law may be called a law, not essentially, but by participation as it were. And thus the inclination of the members to concupiscence is called *the law of the members.*

Reply Obj. 2. Just as, in external acts, we may consider the work and the work done, for instance, the work of building and the house built, so in the acts of reason, we may consider the act itself of reason, *i.e.,* to understand and to reason, and something produced by this act. With regard to the speculative reason, this is first of all the definition; secondly, the proposition; thirdly, the syllogism or argument. And since the practical reason also makes use of the syllogism in operable matters, as we have stated above and as the Philosopher teaches, hence we find in the practical reason something that holds the same position in regard to operations as, in the speculative reason, the proposition holds in regard to conclusions. Such universal propositions of the practical reason that are directed to operations

have the nature of law. And these propositions are sometimes under our actual consideration, while sometimes they are retained in the reason by means of a habit.

Reply Obj. 3. Reason has its power of moving from the will, as was stated above; for it is due to the fact that one wills the end, that the reason issues its commands as regards things ordained to the end. But in order that the volition of what is commanded may have the nature of law, it needs to be in accord with some rule of reason. And in this sense is to be understood the saying that the will of the sovereign has the force of law; or otherwise the sovereign's will would savor of lawlessness rather than of law.

Second Article: Whether Law Is Always Directed To The Common Good?

We proceed thus to the Second Article:

Objection 1. It would seem that law is not always directed to the common good as to its end. For it belongs to law to command and to forbid. But commands are directed to certain individual goods. Therefore the end of law is not always the common good.

Obj. 2. Further, law directs man in his actions. But human actions are concerned with particular matters. Therefore law is directed to some particular good.

Obj. 3. Further, Isidore says: *If law is based on reason, whatever is based on reason will be a law.* But reason is the foundation not only of what is ordained to the common good, but also of that which is directed to private good. Therefore law is not directed only to the good of all, but also to the private good of an individual.

On the contrary, Isidore says that *laws are enacted for no private profit, but for the common benefit of the citizens.*

I answer that, As we have stated above, law belongs to that which is a principle of human acts, because it is their rule and measure. Now as reason is a principle of human acts, so in reason itself there is something which is the principle in respect of all the rest. Hence to this principle chiefly and mainly law must needs be referred. Now the first principle in practical matters, which are the object of the practical reason, is the last end: and the last end of human life is happiness or beatitude, as we have stated above. Consequently, law must needs concern itself mainly with the order that is in beatitude. Moreover, since every part is ordained to the whole as the imperfect to the perfect, and since one man is a part of the perfect community, law must needs concern itself properly with the order directed to universal happiness. Therefore the Philosopher, in the above definition of legal matters, mentions both happiness and the body politic, since he says that we call those legal matters *just which are adapted to produce and preserve happiness and its parts for the body politic*. For the state is a perfect community, as he says in *Politics* i.

Now, in every genus, that which belongs to it chiefly is the principle of the others, and the others belong to that genus according to some order towards that thing. Thus fire, which is chief among hot things, is the cause of heat in mixed bodies, and these are said to be hot in so far as they have a share of fire. Consequently, since law is chiefly ordained to the common good, any other precept in regard to some individual work must needs be devoid of the nature of a law, save in so far as it regards the common good. Therefore every law is ordained to the common good.

Reply Obj. 1. A command denotes the application of a law to matters regulated by law. Now the order to the common good, at which law aims, is applicable to particular ends. And in this way commands are given even concerning particular matters.

Reply Obj. 2. Actions are indeed concerned with particular matters, but those particular matters are referable to the common good, not as to a common genus or species, but as to a common final cause, according as the common good is said to be the common end.

Reply Obj. 3. Just as nothing stands firm with regard to the speculative reason except that which is traced back to the first indemonstrable principles, so nothing stands firm with regard to the practical reason, unless it be directed to the last end which is the common good. Now whatever stands to reason in this sense has the nature of a law.

Third Article: Whether The Reason Of Any Man Is Competent To Make Laws?

We proceed thus to the Third Article:
Objection 1. It would seem that the reason of any man is competent to make laws. For the Apostle says (Rom. ii. 14) that *when the Gentiles, who have not the law, do by nature those things that are of the law, . . . they are a law to themselves.* Now he says this of all in general. Therefore anyone can make a law for himself.

Obj. 2. Further, as the Philosopher says, *the intention of the lawgiver is to lead men to virtue.* But every man can lead another to virtue. Therefore the reason of any man is competent to make laws.

Obj. 3. Further, just as the sovereign of a state governs the state, so every father of a family governs his household. But the sovereign of a state can make laws for the state. Therefore every father of a family can make laws for his household.

On the contrary, Isidore says, and the *Decretals* repeat: *A law is an ordinance of the people, whereby something is sanctioned by the Elders together with the Commonalty.* Therefore not everyone can make laws.

I answer that, A law, properly speaking, regards first and foremost the order to the common good. Now to order anything to the common good belongs either to the whole people, or to someone who is the vicegerent of the whole people. Hence the making of a law belongs either to the whole people or to a public personage who has care of the whole people; for in all other matters the directing of anything to the end concerns him to whom the end belongs.

Reply Obj. 1. As was stated above, a law is in a person not only as in one that rules, but also, by participation, as in one that is ruled. In the latter way, each one is a law to himself, in so far as he shares the direction that he receives from one who rules him. Hence the same text goes on: *Who show the work of the law written in their hearts* (Rom. ii. 15).

Reply Obj. 2. A private person cannot lead another to virtue efficaciously; for he can only advise, and if his advice be not taken, it has no coercive power, such as the law should have, in order to prove an efficacious inducement to virtue, as the Philosopher says. But this coercive power is vested in the whole people or in some public personage, to whom it belongs to inflict penalties, as we shall state further on. Therefore the framing of laws belongs to him alone.

Reply Obj. 3. As one man is a part of the household, so a household is a part of the state; and the state is a perfect community, according to *Politics* i. Therefore, just as the good of one man is not the last end, but is ordained to the common good, so too the good of one household is ordained to the good of a single state, which is a perfect community. Consequently, he that governs a family can indeed make certain commands or ordinances, but not such as to have properly the nature of law.

Fourth Article: Whether Promulgation Is Essential To Law?

We proceed thus to the Fourth Article:
Objection 1. It would seem that promulgation is not essential to law. For the natural law, above all, has the character of law. But the natural law needs no promulgation. Therefore it is not essential to law that it be promulgated.

Obj. 2. Further, it belongs properly to law to bind one to do or not to do something. But the obligation of fulfilling a law touches not only those in whose presence it is promulgated, but also others. Therefore promulgation is not essential to law.

Obj. 3. Further, the binding force of law extends even to the future, since *laws are binding in matters of the future,* as the jurists say. But promulgation concerns those who are present. Therefore it is not essential to law.

On the contrary, It is laid down in the *Decretals* that *laws are established when they are promulgated.*

I answer that, As was stated above, a law is imposed on others as a rule and measure. Now a rule or measure is imposed by being applied to those who are to be ruled and measured by it. Therefore, in order that a law obtain the binding force which is proper to a law, it must needs be applied to the men who have to be ruled by it. But such application is made by its being made known to them by promulgation. Therefore promulgation is necessary for law to obtain its force.

Thus, from the four preceding articles, the definition of law may be gathered. Law is nothing else than an ordinance of reason for the common good, promulgated by him who has the care of the community.

Reply Obj. I. The natural law is promulgated by the very fact that God instilled it into man's mind so as to be known by him naturally.

Reply Obj. 2. Those who are not present when a law is promulgated are bound to observe the law, in so far as it is made known or can be made known to them by others, after it has been promulgated.

Reply Obj. 3. The promulgation that takes place in the present extends to future time by reason of the durability of written characters, by which means it is continually promulgated. Hence Isidore says that *lex* [*law*] *is derived from legere* [*to read*] *because it is written*.

QUESTION XCI: ON THE VARIOUS KINDS OF LAW
(In Six Articles)

First Article: Whether There Is An Eternal Law?

We proceed thus to the First Article: Objection 1. It would seem that there is no eternal law. For every law is imposed on someone. But there was not someone from eternity on whom a law could be imposed, since God alone was from eternity. Therefore no law is eternal.

Obj. 2. Further, promulgation is essential to law. But promulgation could not be from eternity, because there was no one to whom it could be promulgated from eternity. Therefore no law can be eternal.

Obj. 3. Further, law implies order to an end. But nothing ordained to an end is eternal, for the last end alone is eternal. Therefore no law is eternal.

On the contrary, Augustine says: *That Law which is the Supreme Reason cannot be understood to be otherwise than unchangeable and eternal.*

I answer that, As we have stated above, law is nothing else but a dictate of practical reason emanating from the ruler who governs a perfect community. Now it is evident, granted that the world is ruled by divine providence, as was stated in the First Part, that the whole community of the universe is governed by the divine reason. Therefore the very notion of the government of things in God, the ruler of the universe, has the nature of a law. And since the divine reason's conception of things is not subject to time, but is eternal, according to Prov. viii. 23, therefore it is that this kind of law must be called eternal.

Reply Obj. 1. Those things that do not exist in themselves exist in God, inasmuch as they are known and preordained by Him, according to Rom. iv. 17: *Who calls those things that are not, as those that are.* Accordingly, the eternal concept of the divine law bears the character of an eternal law in so far as it is ordained by God to the government of things foreknown by Him.

Reply Obj. 2. Promulgation is made by word of mouth or in writing, and in both ways the eternal law is promulgated, because both the divine Word and the writing of the Book of Life are eternal. But the promulgation cannot be from eternity on the part of the creature that hears or reads.

Reply Obj. 3. Law implies order to the end actively, namely, in so far as it directs certain things to the end; but not passively—that is to say, the law itself is not ordained to the end, except accidentally, in a governor whose end is extrinsic to him, and to which end his law must needs be ordained. But the end of the divine government is God Himself, and His law is not something other than Himself. Therefore the eternal law is not ordained to another end.

Second Article: Whether There Is In Us A Natural Law?

We proceed thus to the Second Article: Objection 1. It would seem there is no natural law in us. For man is governed sufficiently by the eternal law, since Augustine says that *the eternal law is that by which it is right that all things should be most orderly.* But nature does not abound in superfluities as neither does she fail in necessaries. Therefore man has no natural law.

Obj. 2. Further, by the law man is directed, in his acts, to the end, as was stated above. But the directing of human acts to their end is not a function of nature, as is the case in irrational creatures, which act for an end solely by their natural appetite; whereas man acts for an end by his reason and will. Therefore man has no natural law.

Obj. 3. Further, the more a man is free, the less is he under the law. But man is freer than all the animals because of his free choice, with which he is endowed in distinction from all other animals. Since, therefore, other animals are not subject to a natural law, neither is man subject to a natural law.

On the contrary, the Gloss on Rom. ii. 14 *(When the Gentiles, who have not the law, do by nature those things that are of the law)* comments as follows: *Although they have no written law, yet they have the natural law, whereby each one knows, and is conscious of, what is good and what is evil.*

I answer that, As we have stated above, law, being a rule and measure, can be in a person in two ways: in one way, as in him that rules and measures; in another way, as in that which is ruled and measured, since a thing is ruled and measured in so far as it partakes of the rule or measure. Therefore, since all things subject to divine providence are ruled and measured by the eternal law, as was stated above, it is evident that all things partake in some way in the eternal law, in so far as, namely, from its being imprinted on them, they derive their respective inclinations to their proper acts and ends. Now among all others, the rational creature is subject to divine providence in a more excellent way, in so far as it itself partakes of a share of providence, by being provident both for itself and for others. Therefore it has a share of the eternal reason, whereby it has a natural inclination to its proper act and end; and this participation of the eternal law in the rational creature is called the natural law. Hence the Psalmist, after saying (Ps. iv. 6): *Offer up the sacrifice of justice,* as though someone asked what the works of justice are, adds: *Many say, Who showeth us good things?*

in answer to which question he says: *The light of Thy countenance, O Lord, is signed upon us.* He thus implies that the light of natural reason, whereby we discern what is good and what is evil, which is the function of the natural law, is nothing else than an imprint on us of the divine light. It is therefore evident that the natural law is nothing else than the rational creature's participation of the eternal law.

Reply Obj. 1. This argument would hold if the natural law were something different from the eternal law; whereas it is nothing but a participation thereof, as we have stated above.

Reply Obj. 2. Every act of reason and will in us is based on that which is according to nature, as was stated above. For every act of reasoning is based on principles that are known naturally, and every act of appetite in respect of the means is derived from the natural appetite in respect of the last end. Accordingly, the first direction of our acts to their end must needs be through the natural law.

Reply Obj. 3. Even irrational animals partake in their own way of the eternal reason, just as the rational creature does. But because the rational creature partakes thereof in an intellectual and rational manner, therefore the participation of the eternal law in the rational creature is properly called a law, since a law is something pertaining to reason, as was stated above. Irrational creatures, however, do not partake thereof in a rational manner, and therefore there is no participation of the eternal law in them, except by way of likeness.

Third Article: Whether There Is A Human Law?

We proceed thus to the Third Article:
Objection 1. It would seem that there is not a human law. For the natural law is a participation of the eternal law, as was stated above. Now through the eternal law

all things are most orderly, as Augustine states. Therefore the natural law suffices for the ordering of all human affairs. Consequently there is no need for a human law.

Obj. 2. Further, law has the character of a measure, as was stated above. But human reason is not a measure of things, but *vice versa,* as is stated in *Metaph.* x. Therefore no law can emanate from the human reason.

Obj. 3. Further, a measure should be most certain, as is stated in *Metaph.* x. But the dictates of the human reason in matters of conduct are uncertain, according to *Wis.* ix. 14: *The thoughts of mortal men are fearful, and our counsels uncertain.* Therefore no law can emanate from the human reason.

On the contrary, Augustine distinguishes two kinds of law, the one eternal, the other temporal, which he calls human.

I answer that, As we have stated above, a law is a dictate of the practical reason. Now it is to be observed that the same procedure takes place in the practical and in the speculative reason, for each proceeds from principles to conclusions, as was stated above. Accordingly, we conclude that, just as in the speculative reason, from naturally known indemonstrable principles we draw the conclusions of the various sciences, the knowledge of which is not imparted to us by nature, but acquired by the efforts of reason, so too it is that from the precepts of the natural law, as from common and indemonstrable principles, the human reason needs to proceed to the more particular determination of certain matters. These particular determinations, devised by human reason, are called human laws, provided that the other essential conditions of law be observed, as was stated above. Therefore Tully says in his *Rhetoric* that *justice has its source in nature; thence certain things came into custom by reason of their utility; afterwards these things which ema-*

nated from nature, and were approved by custom, were sanctioned by fear and reverence for the law.

Reply Obj. 1. The human reason cannot have a full participation of the dictate of the divine reason, but according to its own mode, and imperfectly. Consequently, just as on the part of the speculative reason, by a natural participation of divine wisdom, there is in us the knowledge of certain common principles, but not a proper knowledge of each single truth, such as that contained in the divine wisdom, so, too, on the part of the practical reason, man has a natural participation of the eternal law, according to certain common principles, but not as regards the particular determinations of individual cases, which are, however, contained in the eternal law. Hence the need for human reason to proceed further to sanction them by law.

Reply Obj. 2. Human reason is not, of itself, the rule of things. But the principles impressed on it by nature are the general rules and measures of all things relating to human conduct, of which the natural reason is the rule and measure, although it is not the measure of things that are from nature.

Reply Obj. 3. The practical reason is concerned with operable matters, which are singular and contingent, but not with necessary things, with which the speculative reason is concerned. Therefore human laws cannot have that inerrancy that belongs to the demonstrated conclusions of the sciences. Nor is it necessary for every measure to be altogether unerring and certain, but according as it is possible in its own particular genus.

Fourth Article: Whether There Was Any Need For A Divine Law?

We proceed thus to the Fourth Article:
Objection 1. It would seem that there was no need for a divine law. For, as was

stated above, the natural law is a participation in us of the eternal law. But the eternal law is the divine law, as was stated above. Therefore there is no need for a divine law in addition to the natural law and to human laws derived therefrom.

Obj. 2. Further, it is written (*Ecclus.* xv. 14) that *God left man in the hand of his own counsel.* Now counsel is an act of reason, as was stated above. Therefore man was left to the direction of his reason. But a dictate of human reason is a human law, as was stated above. Therefore there is no need for man to be governed also by a divine law.

Obj. 3. Further, human nature is more self-sufficing than irrational creatures. But irrational creatures have no divine law besides the natural inclination impressed on them. Much less, therefore, should the rational creature have a divine law in addition to the natural law.

On the contrary, David prayed God to set His law before him, saying (*Ps.* cxviii. 33): *Set before me for a law the way of Thy justifications, O Lord.*

I answer that, Besides the natural and the human law it was necessary for the directing of human conduct to have a divine law. And this for four reasons. First, because it is by law that man is directed how to perform his proper acts in view of his last end. Now if man were ordained to no other end than that which is proportionate to his natural ability, there would be no need for man to have any further direction, on the part of his reason, in addition to the natural law and humanly devised law which is derived from it. But since man is ordained to an end of eternal happiness which exceeds man's natural ability, as we have stated above, therefore it was necessary that, in addition to the natural and the human law, man should be directed to his end by a law given by God.

Secondly, because, by reason of the uncertainty of human judgment, especially on contingent and particular matters, different people form different judgments on human acts; whence also different and contrary laws result. In order, therefore, that man may know without any doubt what he ought to do and what he ought to avoid, it was necessary for man to be directed in his proper acts by a law given by God, for it is certain that such a law cannot err.

Thirdly, because man can make laws in those matters of which he is competent to judge. But man is not competent to judge of interior movements, that are hidden, but only of exterior acts which are observable; and yet for the perfection of virtue it is necessary for man to conduct himself rightly in both kinds of acts. Consequently, human law could not sufficiently curb and direct interior acts, and it was necessary for this purpose that a divine law should supervene.

Fourthly, because, as Augustine says, human law cannot punish or forbid all evil deeds, since, while aiming at doing away with all evils, it would do away with many good things, and would hinder the advance of the common good, which is necessary for human living. In order, therefore, that no evil might remain unforbidden and unpunished, it was necessary for the divine law to supervene, whereby all sins are forbidden.

And these four causes are touched upon in *Ps.* cxviii. 8, where it is said: *The law of the Lord is unspotted, i.e.,* allowing no foulness of sin: *converting souls,* because it directs not only exterior, but also interior, acts; *the testimony of the Lord is faithful,* because of the certainty of what is true and right; *giving wisdom to little ones,* by directing man to an end supernatural and divine.

Reply Obj. 1. By the natural law the eternal law is participated proportionately to the caacity of human nature. But to his supernatural end man needs to be directed in a yet higher way. Hence the additional law given by God, whereby man shares more perfectly in the eternal law.

Reply Obj. 2. Counsel is a kind of inquiry, and hence must proceed from some principles. Nor is it enough for it to proceed from principles imparted by nature, which are the precepts of the natural law,

for the reasons given above; but there is need for certain additional principles, namely, the precepts of the divine law.

Reply Obj. 3. Irrational creatures are not ordained to an end higher than that which is proportionate to their natural powers. Consequently the comparison fails.

The Right and the Good

W. D. Ross

W. D. Ross *(1877–1940) is widely known as an Aristotelian scholar and as the editor of the Oxford edition of Aristotle's complete works. He is also recognized as an authority in ethical theory and as the British champion of the view known as "deontological ethics."*

WHAT MAKES RIGHT ACTS RIGHT?

The real point at issue between hedonism and utilitarianism on the one hand and their opponents on the other is not whether "right" means "productive of so and so"; for it cannot with any plausibility be maintained that it does. The point at issue is that to which we now pass, viz., whether there is any general character which makes right acts right, and if so, what it is. Among the main historical attempts to state a single characteristic of all right actions which is the foundation of their rightness are those made by egoism and utilitarianism. But I do not propose to discuss these, not because the subject is unimportant, but because it has been dealt with so often and so well already, and because there has come to be so much agreement among moral philosophers that neither of these theories is satisfactory. A much more attractive theory has been put forward by Professor Moore: that what makes actions right is that they are productive of more *good* than could have been produced by any other action open to the agent.[1]

This theory is in fact the culmination

[1] I take the theory which, as I have tried to show, seems to be put forward in *Ethics* rather than the earlier and less plausible theory put forward in *Principia Ethica*.

From *The Right and the Good;* Oxford, Clarendon Press, 1930. Reprinted by permission of the Clarendon Press, Oxford.

of all the attempts to base rightness on productivity of some sort of result. The first form this attempt takes is the attempt to base rightness on conduciveness to the advantage or pleasure of the agent. This theory comes to grief over the fact, which stares us in the face, that a great part of duty consists in an observance of the rights and a furtherance of the interests of others, whatever the cost to ourselves may be. Plato and others may be right in holding that a regard for the rights of others never in the long run involves a loss of happiness for the agent, that "the just life profits a man." But this, even if true, is irrelevant to the rightness of the act. As soon as a man does an action *because* he thinks he will promote his own interests thereby, he is acting not from a sense of its rightness but from self-interest.

To the egoistic theory hedonistic utilitarianism supplies a much-needed amendment. It points out correctly that the fact that a certain pleasure will be enjoyed by the agent is no reason why he *ought* to bring it into being rather than an equal or greater pleasure to be enjoyed by another, though, human nature being what it is, it makes it not unlikely that he *will* try to bring it into being. But hedonistic utilitarianism in its turn needs a correction. On reflection it seems clear that pleasure is not the only thing in life that we think good in itself, that for instance we think the possession of a good character, or an intelligent understanding of the world, as good or better. A great advance is made by the substitution of "productive of the greatest good" for "productive of the greatest pleasure."

Not only is this theory more attractive than hedonistic utilitarianism, but its logical relation to that theory is such that the latter could not be true unless *it* were true, while it might be true though hedonistic utilitarianism were not. It is in fact one of the logical bases of hedonistic utilitarianism. For the view that what produces the maximum pleasure is right has for its bases the views (1) that what produces the maximum good is right, and (2) that pleasure is the only thing good in itself. If they were not assuming that what produces the maximum *good* is right, the utilitarians' attempt to show that pleasure is the only thing good in itself, which is in fact the point they take most pains to establish, would have been quite irrelevant to their attempt to prove that only what produces the maximum *pleasure* is right. If, therefore, it can be shown that productivity of the maximum good is not what makes all right actions right, we shall *a fortiori* have refuted hedonistic utilitarianism.

When a plain man fulfils a promise because he thinks he ought to do so, it seems clear that he does so with no thought of its total consequences, still less with any opinion that these are likely to be the best possible. He thinks in fact much more of the past than of the future. What makes him think it right to act in a certain way is the fact that he has promised to do so —that and, usually, nothing more. That his act will produce the best possible consequences is not his reason for calling it right. What lends colour to the theory we are examining, then, is not the actions (which form probably a great majority of our actions) in which some such reflection as "I have promised" is the only reason we give ourselves for thinking a certain action right, but the exceptional cases in which the consequences of fulfilling a promise (for instance) would be so disastrous to others that we judge it right not to do so. It must of course be admitted that such cases exist. If I have promised to meet a friend at a particular time for some trivial purpose, I should certainly think myself justified in breaking my engagement if by doing so I could prevent a serious accident or bring relief to the victims of one. And the supporters of the view we are examining hold that my thinking so is due to my thinking that I shall bring more good into existence by the one action than by the other. A different account may, however, be given of the matter, an account which will, I believe, show itself to be the true one. It may be said that besides the duty of fulfilling promises I have and recognize a duty of relieving distress,[2] and that when I think it right to do the latter at the cost of not doing the former, it is not because I think I shall produce more good thereby but because I think it the duty which is in the circumstances more of a duty. This account surely corresponds much more closely with what we really think in such a situation. If, so far as I can see, I could bring equal amounts of good into being by fulfilling my promise and by helping some one to whom I had made no promise, I should not hesitate to regard the former as my duty. Yet on the view that what is right is right because it is productive of the most good I should not so regard it.

There are two theories, each in its way simple, that offer a solution of such cases of conscience. One is the view of Kant, that there are certain duties of perfect obligation, such as those of fulfilling promises, of paying debts, of telling the truth, which admit of no exception whatever in favour of duties of imperfect obligation, such as that of relieving distress. The other is the view of, for instance, Professor Moore and Dr. Rashdall, that there is only the duty of producing good, and that all "conflicts of duties" should be resolved by asking "by which action will most good be produced?" But it is more important that our theory fit the facts than that it be simple, and the account we have given above corresponds (it seems to me) better than either of the simpler theories with what we really think, viz., that normally promise-keeping, for example, should

come from benevolence, but that when and only when the good to be produced by the benevolent act is very great and the promise comparatively trivial, the act of benevolence becomes our duty.

In fact the theory of "ideal utilitarianism," if I may for brevity refer so to the theory of Professor Moore, seems to simplify unduly our relations to our fellows. It says, in effect, that the only morally significant relation in which my neighbours stand to me is that of being possible beneficiaries by my action.[3] They do stand in this relation to me, and this relation is morally significant. But they may also stand to me in the relation of promisee to promiser, of creditor to debtor, of wife to husband, of child to parent, of friend to friend, of fellow countryman to fellow countryman, and the like; and each of these relations is the foundation of a *prima facie* duty, which is more or less incumbent on me according to the circumstances of the case. When I am in a situation, as perhaps I always am, in which more than one of these *prima facie* duties is incumbent on me, what I have to do is to study the situation as fully as I can until I form the considered opinion (it is never more) that in the circumstances one of them is more incumbent than any other; then I am bound to think that to do this *prima facie* duty is my duty *sans phrase* in the situation.

I suggest "*prima facie* duty" or "conditional duty" as a brief way of referring to the characteristic (quite distinct from that of being a duty proper) which an act has, in virtue of being of a certain kind (e.g., the keeping of a promise), of being an act which would be a duty proper if it were not at the same time of another kind which is morally significant. Whether an act is

---

[2] These are not strictly speaking duties, but things that tend to be our duty, or *prima facie* duties.

[3] Some will think it, apart from other considerations, a sufficient refutation of this view to point out that I also stand in that relation to myself, so that for this view the distinction of oneself from others is morally insignificant.

a duty proper or actual duty depends on *all* the morally significant kinds it is an instance of. The phrase *"prima facie* duty" must be apologized for, since (1) it suggests that what we are speaking of is a certain kind of duty, whereas it is in fact not a duty, but something related in a special way to duty. Strictly speaking, we want not a phrase in which duty is qualified by an adjective, but a separate noun. (2) *"Prima" facie* suggests that one is speaking only of an appearance which a moral situation presents at first sight, and which may turn out to be illusory; whereas what I am speaking of is an objective fact involved in the nature of the situation, or more strictly in an element of its nature, though not, as duty proper does, arising from its *whole* nature. I can, however, think of no term which fully meets the case. "Claim" has been suggested by Professor Prichard. The word "claim" has the advantage of being quite a familiar one in this connexion, and its seems to cover much of the ground. It would be quite natural to say, "a person to whom I have made a promise has a claim on me," and also, "a person whose distress I could relieve (at the cost of breaking the promise) has a claim on me." But (1) while "claim" is appropriate from *their* point of view, we want a word to express the corresponding fact from the agent's point of view— the fact of his being subject to claims that can be made against him; and ordinary language provides us with no such correlative to "claim." And (2) (what is more important) "claim" seems inevitably to suggest two persons, one of whom might make a claim on the other; and while this covers the ground of social duty, it is inappropriate in the case of that important part of duty which is the duty of cultivating a certain kind of character in oneself. It would be artificial, I think, and at any rate metaphorical, to say that one's character has a claim on oneself.

There is nothing arbitrary about these *prima facie* duties. Each rests on a definite circumstance which cannot seriously be held to be without moral significance. Of *prima facie* duties I suggest, without claiming completeness or finality for it, the following division.[4]

(1) Some duties rest on previous acts of my own. These duties seem to include two kinds, (*a*) those resting on a promise or what may fairly be called an implicit promise, such as the implicit undertaking not to tell lies which seems to be implied in the act of entering into conversation (at any rate by civilized men), or of writing books that purport to be history and not fiction. These may be called the duties of fidelity. (*b*) Those resting on a previous wrongful act. These may be called the duties of reparation. (2) Some rest on previous acts of other men, i.e. services done by them to me. These may be loosely described as the duties of gratitude. (3) Some rest on the fact or possibility of a distribution of pleasure or happiness (or of the means thereto) which is not in accordance with the merit of the persons concerned; in such cases there arises a duty to upset or prevent such a distribution. These are the duties of justice. (4) Some rest on the mere fact that there are other beings in

[4] I should make it plain at this stage that I am *assuming* the correctness of some of our main convictions as to *prima facie* duties, or, more strictly, am claiming that we *know* them to be true. To me it seems as self-evident as anything could be, that to make a promise, for instance, is to create a moral claim on us in someone else. Many readers will perhaps say that they do *not* know this to be true. If so, I certainly cannot prove it to them; I can only ask them to reflect again, in the hope that they will ultimately agree that they also know it to be true. The main moral convictions of the plain man seem to me to be, not opinions which it is for philosophy to prove or disprove, but knowledge from the start; and in my own case I seem to find little difficulty in distinguishing these essential convictions from other moral convictions which I also have, which are merely fallible opinions based on an imperfect study of the working for good or evil of certain institutions or types of action.

the world whose condition we can make better in respect of virtue, or of intelligence, or of pleasure. These are the duties of beneficence. (5) Some rest on the fact that we can improve our own condition in respect of virtue or of intelligence. These are the duties of self-improvement. (6) I think that we should distinguish from (4) the duties that may be summed up under the title of "not injuring others." No doubt to injure others is incidentally to fail to do them good; but it seems to me clear that non-maleficence is apprehended as a duty distinct from that of beneficence, and as a duty of a more stringent character. It will be noticed that this alone among the types of duty has been stated in a negative way. An attempt might no doubt be made to state this duty, like the others, in a positive way. It might be said that it is really the duty to prevent ourselves from acting either from an inclination to seek our own pleasure, in doing which we should incidentally harm them. But on reflection it seems clear that the primary duty here is the duty not to harm others, this being a duty whether or not we have an inclination that if followed would lead to our harming them; and that when we have such an inclination the primary duty not to harm others gives rise to a consequential duty to resist the inclination. The recognition of this duty of non-maleficence is the first step on the way to the recognition of the duty of beneficence; and that accounts for the prominence of the commands "thou shalt not kill," "thou shalt not commit adultery," "thou shalt not steal," "thou shalt not bear false witness," in so early a code as the Decalogue. But even when we have come to recognize the duty of beneficence, it appears to me that the duty of non-maleficence is recognized as a distinct one, and as *prima facie* more binding. We should not in general consider it justifiable to kill one person in order to keep another alive, or to steal from one in order to give alms to another.

The essential defect of the "ideal utilitarian" theory is that it ignores, or at least does not do full justice to, the highly personal character of duty. If the only duty is to produce the maximum of good, the question who is to have the good—whether it is myself, or my benefactor, or a person to whom I have made a promise to confer that good on him, or a mere fellow man to whom I stand in no such special relation—should make no difference to my having a duty to produce that good. But we are all in fact sure that it makes a vast difference. . . .

An attempt may be made to arrange in a more systematic way the main types of duty which we have indicated. In the first place it seems self-evident that if there are things that are intrinsically good, it is *prima facie* a duty to bring them into existence rather than not to do so, and to bring as much of them into existence as possible. It will be argued in our fifth chapter that there are three main things that are intrinsically good—virtue, knowledge, and, with certain limitations, pleasure. And since a given virtuous disposition, for instance, is equally good whether it is realized in myself or in another, it seems to be my duty to bring it into existence whether in myself or in another. So too with a given piece of knowledge.

The case of pleasure is difficult; for while we clearly recognize a duty to produce pleasure for others, it is by no means so clear that we recognize a duty to produce pleasure for ourselves. This appears to arise from the following facts. The thought of an act as our duty is one that presupposes a certain amount of reflection about the act; and for that reason does not normally arise in connexion with acts towards which we are already impelled by another strong impulse. So far, the cause of our not thinking of the promotion of our own pleasure as a duty is analogous to the cause which usually prevents a highly sympathetic person from thinking of the promotion of the pleasure of others as a duty. He is impelled so strongly by direct interest in the well-being of others towards promoting their pleasure that he does not stop to ask whether it is his duty to promote it; and we are impelled so strongly towards the promotion of our own pleasure that we do not stop to ask whether it is a duty or not. But there is a further reason why even when we stop to think about the matter it does not usually present itself as a duty: viz., that, since the performance of most of our duties involves the giving up of some pleasure that we desire, the doing of duty and the getting of pleasure for ourselves come by a natural association of ideas to be thought of as incompatible things. This association of ideas is in the main salutary in its operation, since it puts a check on what but for it would be much too strong, the tendency to pursue one's own pleasure without thought of other considerations. Yet if pleasure is good, it seems in the long run clear that it is right to get it for ourselves as well as to produce it for others, when this does not involve the failure to discharge some more stringent *prima facie* duty. The question is a very difficult one, but it seems that this conclusion can be denied only on one or other of three grounds: (1) that pleasure is not *prima facie* good (i.e., good when it is neither the actualization of a bad disposition nor undeserved), (2) that there is no *prima facie* duty to produce as much that is good as we can, or (3) that though there is a *prima facie* duty to produce other things that are good, there is no *prima facie* duty to produce pleasure which will be enjoyed by ourselves. I give reasons later for not accepting the first contention. The second hardly admits of argument but seems to me plainly false. The third seems plausible only if we hold that an act that is pleasant or brings pleasure to ourselves must for that reason not be a duty; and this would lead to paradoxical consequences, such as that if a man enjoys giving pleasure to others or working for their moral improvement, it cannot be his duty to do so. Yet it seems to be a very stubborn fact, that in our ordinary consciousness we are not aware of a duty to get pleasure for ourselves; and by way of partial explanation of this I may add that though, as I think, one's own pleasure is a good and there is a duty to produce it, it is only if we *think* of our own pleasure not as simply our own pleasure, but as an objective good, something that an impartial spectator would approve, that we can think of the getting it as a duty; and we do not habitually think of it in this way.

If these contentions are right, what we have called the duty of beneficence and the duty of self-improvement rest on the same ground. No different principles of duty are involved in the two cases. If we feel a special responsibility for improving our own character rather than that of others, it is not because a special principle is involved, but because we are aware that the one is more under our control than the other. It was on this ground that Kant expressed the practical law of duty in the form "seek to make yourself good and other people happy." He was so persuaded of the internality of virtue that he regarded any attempt by one person to produce virtue in another as bound to produce, at most, only a counterfeit of virtue, the doing of externally rights acts not from the true principle of virtuous action but out of regard to another person. It must be admitted that one man cannot compel another to be virtuous; compulsory virtue would just not be virtue. But experience clearly shows that Kant overshoots the mark when he contends that one man cannot do anything to *promote* virtue in another, to bring such influences to bear upon him that his own response to them is more likely to be virtuous than his response to other influences would have been. And our duty to do this is not different in kind from our duty to improve our own characters.

It is equally clear, and clear at an earlier stage of moral development, that if there are things that are bad in themselves we ought, *prima facie*, not to bring them upon others; and on this fact rests the duty of non-maleficence.

The duty of justice is particularly complicated, and the word is used to cover things which are really very different—things such as the payment of debts, the reparation of injuries done by oneself to another, and the bringing about of a distribution of happiness between other people in proportion to merit. I use the word to denote only the last of these three. [Later] I shall try to show that besides the three (comparatively) simple goods, virtue, knowledge, and pleasure, there is a more complex good, not reducible to these, consisting in the proportionment of happiness to virtue. The bringing of this about is a duty which we owe to all men alike, though it may be reinforced by special responsibilities that we have undertaken to particular men. This, therefore, with beneficence and self-improvement, comes under the general principle that we should produce as much good as possible, though the good here involved is different in kind from any other.

But besides this general obligation, there are special obligations. These may arise, in the first place, incidentally, from acts which were not essentially meant to create such an obligation, but which nevertheless create it. From the nature of the case such acts may be of two kinds —the infliction of injuries on others, and the acceptance of benefits from them. It seems clear that these put us under a special obligation to other men, and that only these acts can do so incidentally. From these arise the twin duties of reparation and gratitude.

And finally there are special obligations arising from acts the very intention of which, when they were done, was to put us under such an obligation. The name for such acts is "promises"; the name is wide enough if we are willing to include under it implicit promises, i.e., modes of behaviour in which without explicit verbal promise we intentionally create an expectation that we can be counted on to behave in a certain way in the interest of another person.

These seem to be, in principle, all the ways in which *prima facie* duties arise. In actual experience they are compounded together in highly complex ways. Thus, for example, the duty of obeying the laws of one's country arises partly (as Socrates contends in the *Crito*) from the duty of gratitude for the benefits one has received from it; partly from the implicit promise to obey which seems to be involved in permanent residence in a country whose laws we know we are *expected* to obey, and still more clearly involved when we ourselves invoke the protection of its laws (this is the truth underlying the doctrine of the social contract); and partly (if we are fortunate in our country) from the fact that its laws are potent instruments for the general good.

The Laws of Manu

Manu, according to the Indian tradition, was the first man, a sort of primordial Noah. He is looked upon as the progenitor of mankind and the founder of the political and moral codes of society. The Laws of Manu (c. 800–500 B.C.) continue to be held in high esteem by all Hindus.

Chapter II

1. Learn that sacred law which is followed by men learned [in the Veda] and assented to in their hearts by the virtuous, who are ever exempted from hatred and inordinate affection.

2. To act solely from a desire for rewards is not laudable, yet an exemption from that desire is not [to be found] in this [world]: for on [that] desire is grounded the study of the Veda and the performance of the actions, prescribed by the Veda.

3. The desire [for rewards], indeed, has its root in the conception that an act can yield them, and in consequence of [that] conception sacrifices are performed; vows and the laws prescribing restraints are all stated to be kept through the idea that they will bear fruit.

4. Not a single act here [below] appears ever to be done by a man free from desire; for whatever [man] does, it is [the result of] the impulse of desire.

5. He who persists in discharging these [prescribed duties] in the right manner, reaches the deathless state and even in this [life] obtains [the fulfilment of] all the desires that he may have conceived.

6. The whole Veda is the [first] source of the sacred law, next the tradition and the virtuous conduct of those who know the [Veda further], also the customs of holy men, and [finally] self-satisfaction.

7. Whatever law has been ordained for any [person] by Manu, that has been fully declared in the Veda: for that [sage was] omniscient.

8. But a learned man after fully scrutinising all this with the eye of knowledge, should, in accordance with the authority of the revealed texts, be intent on [the performance of] his duties.

9. For that man who obeys the law prescribed in the revealed texts and in the sacred tradition, gains fame in this [world] and after death unsurpassable bliss.

10. But by Śruti [revelation] is meant the Veda, and by Smriti [tradition] the Institutes of the sacred law: those two must not be called into question in any

From "The Laws of Manu," transl. G. Bühler, in *The Sacred Books of the East*, Vol. XXV, F. Max Müller, ed.

matter, since from those two the sacred law shone forth.

11. Every twice-born man, who, relying on the Institutes of dialectics, treats with contempt those two sources [of the law], must be cast out by the virtuous, as an atheist and a scorner of the Veda.

12. The Veda, the sacred tradition, the customs of virtuous men, and one's own pleasure, they declare to be visibly the fourfold means of defining the sacred law.

13. The knowledge of the sacred law is prescribed for those who are not given to the acquisition of wealth and to the gratification of their desires; to those who seek the knowledge of the sacred law the supreme authority is the revelation [Sruti].

14. But when two sacred texts [Sruti] are conflicting, both are held to be law; for both are pronounced by the wise [to be] valid law.

15. [Thus] the [Agnihotra] sacrifice may be [optionally] performed, at any time after the sun has risen, before he has risen, or when neither sun nor stars are visible; that [is declared] by Vedic texts.

16. Know that he for whom [the performance of] the ceremonies beginning with the rite of impregnation [Garbhâdhâna] and ending with the funeral rite [Antyeshti] is prescribed, while sacred formulas are being recited, is entitled [to study] these Institutes, but no other man whatsoever.

17. That land, created by the gods, which lies between the two divine rivers Sarasvatî and Drishadvatî, the [sages] call Brahmâvarta.

18. The custom handed down in regular succession [since time immemorial] among the [four chief] castes [varna] and the mixed [races] of that country, is called the conduct of virtuous men.

19. The plain of the Kurus, the [country of the] Matsyas, Pañkâlas, and Sûrasenakas, these [form], indeed, the country of the Brahmarshis [Brâhmanical sages, which ranks] immediately after Brahmâvarta.

20. From a Brâhmana, born in that country, let all men on earth learn their several usages.

21. That [country] which [lies] between the Himavat and the Vindhya [mountains] to the east of Prayâga and to the west of Vinasana [the place where the river Sarasvatî disappears] is called Madhyadesa [the central region].

22. But [the tract] between those two mountains [just mentioned], which [extends] as far as the eastern and the western oceans, the wise call Âryâvarta [the country of the Âryans].

23. That land where the black antelope naturally roams, one must know to be fit for the performance of sacrifices; [the tract] different from that [is] the country of the Mlekkhas [barbarians].

24. Let twice-born men seek to dwell in those [above-mentioned countries]; but a Sûdra, distressed for subsistence, may reside anywhere.

25. Thus has the origin of the sacred law been succinctly described to you and the origin of this universe; learn [now] the duties of the castes [varna].

Universal Love

MOTSE

Motse (or Mo Tzu) (fl. 479–438 B.C.), as has been mentioned, was the founder of the Moist school of Chinese philosophy. His doctrine of universal love is certainly one of the earliest forms of utilitarian ethics.

Mo Tzu said: It is the business of the benevolent man to try to promote what is beneficial to the world and to eliminate what is harmful. Now at the present time, what brings the greatest harm to the world? Great states attacking small ones, great families overthrowing small ones, the strong oppressing the weak, the many harrying the few, the cunning deceiving the stupid, the eminent lording it over the humble—these are harmful to the world. So too are rulers who are not generous, ministers who are not loyal, fathers who are without kindness, and sons who are unfilial, as well as those mean men who, with weapons, knives, poison, fire, and water, seek to injure and undo each other.

When we inquire into the cause of these various harms, what do we find has produced them? Do they come about from loving others and trying to benefit them? Surely not! They come rather from hating others and trying to injure them. And when we set out to classify and describe those men who hate and injure others, shall we say that their actions are motivated by universality or partiality? Surely we must answer, by partiality, and it is this partiality in their dealings with one another that gives rise to all the great harms in the world. Therefore we know that partiality is wrong.

Mo Tzu said: Whoever criticizes others must have some alternative to offer them. To criticize and yet offer no alternative is like trying to stop flood with flood or put out fire with fire. It will surely have no effect. Therefore Mo Tzu said: Partiality should be replaced by universality.

But how can partiality be replaced by universality? If men were to regard the states of others as they regard their own, then who would raise up his state to attack the state of another? It would be like attacking his own. If men were to regard the cities of others as they regard their own, then who would raise up his city to attack the city of another? It would be like attacking his own. If men were to regard the families of others as they regard their own, then who would raise up his

From *Mo Tzu, Basic Writings*, transl. Burton Watson; New York and London, Columbia University Press, 1963. Reprinted by permission of The Columbia University Press and Burton Watson.

family to overthrow that of another? It would be like overthrowing his own. Now when states and cities do not attack and make war on each other and families and individuals do not overthrow or injure one another, is this a harm or a benefit to the world? Surely it is a benefit.

When we inquire into the cause of such benefits, what do we find has produced them? Do they come about from hating others and trying to injure them? Surely not! They come rather from loving others and trying to benefit them. And when we set out to classify and describe those men who love and benefit others, shall we say that their actions are motivated by partiality or by universality? Surely we must answer, by universality, and it is this universality in their dealings with one another that gives rise to all the great benefits in the world. Therefore Mo Tzu has said that universality is right.

I have said previously that it is the business of the benevolent man to try to promote what is beneficial to the world and to eliminate what is harmful. Now I have demonstrated that universality is the source of all the great benefits in the world and partiality is the source of all the great harm. It is for this reason that Mo Tzu has said that partiality is wrong and universality is right.

Now if we seek to benefit the world by taking universality as our standard, those with sharp ears and clear eyes will see and hear for others, those with sturdy limbs will work for others, and those with a knowledge of the Way will endeavor to teach others. Those who are old and without wives or children will find means of support and be able to live out their days; the young and orphaned who have no parents will find someone to care for them and look after their needs. When all these benefits may be secured merely by taking universality as our standard, I cannot understand how the men of the world can hear about this doctrine of universality and still criticize it!

And yet the men of the world continue to criticize it, saying, "It may be a good thing, but how can it be put to use?"

Mo Tzu said: If it cannot be put to use, even I would criticize it. But how can there be a good thing that still cannot be put to use? Let us try considering both sides of the question. Suppose there are two men, one of them holding to partiality, the other to universality. The believer in partiality says, "How could I possibly regard my friend the same as myself, or my friend's father the same as my own?" Because he views his friend in this way, he will not feed him when he is hungry, clothe him when he is cold, nourish him when he is sick, or bury him when he dies. Such are the words of the partial man, and such his actions. But the words and actions of the universal-minded man are not like these. He will say, "I have heard that the truly superior man of the world regards his friend the same as himself, and his friend's father the same as his own. Only if he does this can he be considered a truly superior man." Because he views his friend in this way, he will feed him when he is hungry, clothe him when he is cold, nourish him when he is sick, and bury him when he dies. Such are the words and actions of the universal-minded man.

So the words of these two men disagree and their actions are diametrically opposed. Yet let us suppose that both of them are determined to carry out their words in action, so that word and deed agree like the two parts of a tally and nothing they say is not put into action. Then let us venture to inquire further. Suppose that here is a broad plain, a vast wilderness, and a man is buckling on his armor and donning his helmet to set out for the field of battle, where the fortunes of life and death are unknown; or he is setting out in his lord's name upon a distant mission to Pa or Yüeh, Ch'i or Ching, and his return is uncertain. Now let us ask, to whom would he entrust the support of his parents and the care of his wife and children? Would it be to the universal-minded man, or to the partial man? It seems to me that, on occasions like these, there are no fools in the world. Though one may disapprove of universality himself, he would surely think it best to entrust his family to the universal-minded man. Thus people condemn universality in words but adopt it in practice, and word and deed belie each other. I cannot understand how the men of the world can hear about this doctrine of universality and still criticize it!

And yet the men of the world continue to criticize, saying, "Such a principle may be all right as a basis in choosing among ordinary men, but it cannot be used in selecting a ruler."

Let us try considering both sides of the question. Suppose there are two rulers, one of them holding to universality, the other to partiality. The partial ruler says, "How could I possibly regard my countless subjects the same as I regard myself? That would be completely at variance with human nature! Man's life on earth is as brief as the passing of a team of horses glimpsed through a crack in the wall." Because he views his subjects in this way, he will not feed them when they are hungry, clothe them when they are cold, nourish them when they are sick, or bury them when they die. Such are the words of the partial ruler, and such his actions. But the words and actions of the universal-minded ruler are not like these. He will say, "I have heard that the truly enlightened ruler must think of his subjects first, and of himself last. Only then can he be considered a truly enlightened ruler." Because he views his subjects in this way, he will feed them when they are hungry, clothe them when they are cold, nourish them when they are sick,

and bury them when they die. Such are the words and actions of the universal-minded ruler.

So the words of these two rulers disagree and their actions are diametrically opposed. Yet let us suppose that both of them speak in good faith and are determined to carry out their words in action, so that word and deed agree like the two parts of a tally and nothing they say is not put into action. Then let us venture to inquire further. Suppose this year there is plague and disease, many of the people are suffering from hardship and hunger, and the corpses of countless victims lie tumbled in the ditches. If the people could choose between these two types of ruler, which would they follow? It seems to me that, on occasions like this, there are no fools in the world. Though one may disapprove of universality himself, he would surely think it best to follow the universal-minded ruler. Thus people condemn universality in words but adopt it in practice, and word and deed belie each other. I cannot understand how the men of the world can hear about this doctrine of universality and still criticize it!

And yet the men of the world continue to criticize, saying, "This doctrine of universality is benevolent and righteous. And yet how can it be carried out? As we see it, one can no more put it into practice than one can pick up Mount T'ai and leap over a river with it! Thus universality is only something to be longed for, not something that can be put into practice."

Mo Tzu said: As for picking up Mount T'ai and leaping over rivers with it, no one from ancient times to the present, from the beginning of mankind to now, has ever succeeded in doing that! But universal love and mutual aid were actually practiced by four sage kings of antiquity. How do we know that they practiced these?

Mo Tzu said: I did not live at the same time as they did, nor have I in person heard their voices or seen their faces. Yet I know it because of what is written on the bamboo and silk that has been handed down to posterity, what is engraved on metal and stone, and what is inscribed on bowls and basins.

The "Great Oath" says: "King Wen was like the sun or moon, shedding his bright light in the four quarters and over the western land." That is to say, the universal love of King Wen was so broad that it embraced the whole world, as the universal light of the sun and the moon shines upon the whole world without partiality. Such was the universality of King Wen, and the universality which Mo Tzu has been telling you about is patterned after that of King Wen.

Not only the "Great Oath" but the "Oath of Yü" also expresses this idea. Yü said: "All you teeming multitudes, listen to my words! It is not that I, the little child, would dare to act in a disorderly way. But this ruler of the Miao, with his unyielding ways, deserves Heaven's punishment. So I shall lead you, the lords of the various states, to conquer the ruler of the Miao." When Yü went to conquer the ruler of the Miao, it was not that he sought to increase his wealth or eminence, to win fortune or blessing, or to delight his ears and eyes. It was only that he sought to promote what was beneficial to the world and to eliminate what was harmful. Such was the universality of Yü, and the universality which Mo Tzu has been telling you about is patterned after that of Yü.

And not only the "Oath of Yü" but the "Speech of T'ang" also expresses this idea. T'ang said: "I, the little child, Lü, dare to sacrifice a dark beast and make this announcement to the Heavenly Lord above, saying, 'Now Heaven has sent a great drought and it has fallen upon me, Lü. But I do not know what fault I have committed against high or low. If there is good, I dare not conceal it; if there is evil, I dare not pardon it. Judgment resides with the mind of God. If the myriad regions have any fault, may it rest upon my person; but if I have any fault, may it not extend to the myriad regions.'" This shows that, though T'ang was honored as the Son of Heaven and possessed all the riches of the world, he did not hesitate to offer himself as a sacrifice in his prayers and entreaties to the Lord on High and the spirits. Such was the universality of T'ang, and the universality which Mo Tzu has been telling you about is patterned after that of T'ang.

This idea is expressed not only in the "Speech of T'ang" but in the odes of Chou as well. In the odes of Chou it says:

Broad, broad is the way of the king,
Neither partial nor partisan.
Fair, fair is the way of the king,
Neither partisan nor partial.

It is straight like an arrow,
Smooth like a whetstone.
The superior man treads it;
The small man looks upon it.

So what I have been speaking about is no mere theory of action. In ancient times, when Kings Wen and Wu administered the government and assigned each person his just share, they rewarded the worthy and punished the wicked without showing any favoritism toward their own kin or brothers. Such was the universality of Kings Wen and Wu, and the universality which Mo Tzu has been telling you about is patterned after that of Wen and Wu. I cannot understand how the men of the world can hear about this doctrine of universality and still criticize it!

And yet the men of the world continue to criticize, saying, "If one takes no thought for what is beneficial or harmful to one's parents, how can one be called filial?"

Mo Tzu said: Let us examine for a moment the way in which a filial son plans for the welfare of his parents. When a filial son plans for his parents, does he wish others to love and benefit them, or does he wish others to hate and injure them? It stands to reason that he wishes others to love and benefit his parents. Now if I am a filial son, how do I go about accomplishing this? Do I first make it a point to love and benefit other men's parents, so that they in return will love and benefit my parents? Or do I first make it a point to hate and injure other men's parents, so that they in return will love and benefit my parents? Obviously, I must first make it a point to love and benefit other men's parents, so that they in return will love and benefit my parents. So if all of us are to be filial sons, can we set about it any other way than by first making a point of loving and benefiting other men's parents? And are we to suppose that the filial sons of the world are all too stupid to be capable of doing what is right?

Let us examine further. Among the books of the former kings, in the "Greater Odes" of the *Book of Odes,* it says:

There are no words that are not
    answered,
No kindness that is not requited.
Throw me a peach,
I'll requite you a plum.

The meaning is that one who loves will be loved by others, and one who hates will be hated by others. So I cannot understand how the men of the world can hear about this doctrine of universality and still criticize it!

Do they believe that it is too difficult to carry out? Yet there are much more difficult things that have been carried out. In the past King Ling of the state of Ching loved slender waists. During his reign, the people of Ching ate no more than one meal a day, until they were too weak to stand up without a cane, or to walk without leaning against the wall.

Now reducing one's diet is a difficult thing to do, and yet people did it because it pleased King Ling. So within the space of a single generation the ways of the people can be changed, for they will strive to ingratiate themselves with their superiors.

Again in the past King Kou-chien of Yüeh admired bravery and for three years trained his soldiers and subjects to be brave. But he was not sure whether they had understood the true meaning of bravery, and so he set fire to his warships and then sounded the drum to advance. The soldiers trampled each other down in their haste to go forward, and countless numbers of them perished in the fire and water. At that time, even though he ceased to drum them forward, they did not retreat. The soldiers of Yüeh were truly astonishing. Now consigning one's body to the flames is a difficult thing to do, and yet they did it because it pleased the king of Yüeh. So within the space of a single generation the ways of the people can be changed, for they will strive to ingratiate themselves with their superiors.

Duke Wen of Chin liked coarse clothing, and so during his reign the men of the state of Chin wore robes of coarse cloth, wraps of sheepskin, hats of plain silk, and big rough shoes, whether they were appearing before the duke in the inner chamber or walking about in the outer halls of the court. Now bringing oneself to wear coarse clothing is a difficult thing to do, and yet people did it because it pleased Duke Wen. So within the space of a single generation the ways of the people can be changed, for they will strive to ingratiate themselves with their superiors.

To reduce one's diet, consign one's body to the flames, or wear coarse clothing are among the most difficult things in the world to do. And yet people will do them because they know their superiors will be pleased. So within the space of a single generation the ways of the people can be changed. Why? Because they will strive to ingratiate themselves with their superiors.

Now universal love and mutual benefit are both profitable and easy beyond all measure. The only trouble, as I see it, is that no ruler takes any delight in them. If the rulers really delighted in them, promoted them with rewards and praise, and prevented neglect of them by punishments, then I believe that people would turn to universal love and mutual benefit as naturally as fire turns upward or water turns downward, and nothing in the world could stop them.

The principle of universality is the way of the sage kings, the means of bringing safety to the rulers and officials and of assuring ample food and clothing to the people. Therefore the superior man can do no better than to examine it carefully and strive to put it into practice. If he does, then as a ruler he will be generous, as a subject loyal, as a father kind, as a son filial, as an older brother comradely, and as a younger brother respectful. So if the superior man wishes to be a generous ruler, a loyal subject, a kind father, a filial son, a comradely older brother, and a respectful younger brother, he must put into practice this principle of universality. It is the way of the sage kings and a great benefit to the people.

Utilitarianism

JOHN STUART MILL

John Stuart Mill (1806–1873) published his Utilitarianism *in 1861. The work has done more than any other single volume to popularize and spread the philosophy of universal ethical hedonism (the view that the rightness of an action is determined by the amount of pleasure produced for all those persons affected by the action).*

The creed which accepts as the foundation of morals Utility, or the Greatest Happiness Principle, holds that actions are right in proportion as they tend to promote happiness, wrong as they tend to produce the reverse of happiness. By "happiness" is intended pleasure, and the absence of pain; by "unhappiness," pain, and the privation of pleasure. To give a clear view of the moral standard set up by the theory, much more requires to be said; in particular, what things it includes in the ideas of pain and pleasure; and to what extent this is left an open question. But these supplementary explanations do not affect the theory of life on which this theory of morality is grounded—namely, that pleasure, and freedom from pain, are

---

From *Utilitarianism, Liberty and Representative Government;* New York, E. P. Dutton & Co., 1910.

the only things desirable as ends; and that all desirable things (which are as numerous in the utilitarian as in any other scheme) are desirable either for the pleasure inherent in themselves, or as means to the promotion of pleasure and the prevention of pain.

Now such a theory of life excites in many minds, and among them in some of the most estimable in feeling and purpose, inveterate dislike. To suppose that life has (as they express it) no higher end than pleasure—no better and nobler object of desire and pursuit—they designate as utterly mean and groveling; as a doctrine worthy only of swine, to whom the followers of Epicurus were, at a very early period, contemptuously likened; and modern holders of the doctrine are occasionally made the subject of equally polite comparisons by its German, French, and English assailants.

When thus attacked, the Epicureans have always answered that it is not they but their accusers who represent human nature in a degrading light; since the accusation supposes human beings to be capable of no pleasures except those of which swine are capable. If this supposition were true, the charge could not be gainsaid, but would then be no longer an imputation; for if the sources of pleasure were precisely the same to human beings and to swine, the rule of life which is good enough for the one would be good enough for the other. The comparison of the Epicurean life to that of beasts is felt as degrading, precisely because a beast's pleasures do not satisfy a human being's conceptions of happiness. Human beings have faculties more elevated than the animal appetites, and when once made conscious of them, do not regard anything as happiness which does not include their gratification. I do not, indeed, consider the Epicureans to have been by any means faultless in drawing out their scheme of consequences from the utilitarian prin-

ciple. To do this in any sufficient manner, many Stoic, as well as Christian elements require to be included. But there is no known Epicurean theory of life which does not assign to the pleasures of the intellect, of the feelings and imagination, and of the moral sentiments, a much higher value as pleasures than to those of mere sensation. It must be admitted, however, that utilitarian writers in general have placed the superiority of mental over bodily pleasures chiefly in the greater permanency, safety, uncostliness, etc., of the former—that is, in their circumstantial advantages rather than in their intrinsic nature. And on all these points utilitarians have fully proved their case; but they might have taken the other, and, as it may be called, higher ground, with entire consistency. It is quite compatible with the principle of utility to recognize the fact, that some *kinds* of pleasure are more desirable and more valuable than others. It would be absurd that while, in estimating all other things, quality is considered as well as quantity, the estimation of pleasures should be supposed to depend on quantity alone.

If I am asked what I mean by difference of quality in pleasures, or what makes one pleasure more valuable than another merely as a pleasure, except its being greater in amount, there is but one possible answer. Of two pleasures, if there be one to which all or almost all who have experience of both give a decided preference, irrespective of any feeling of moral obligation to prefer it, that is the more desirable pleasure. If one of the two is, by those who are competently acquainted with both, placed so far above the other that they prefer it, even though knowing it to be attended with a greater amount of discontent, and would not resign it for any quantity of the other pleasure which their nature is capable of, we are justified in ascribing to the preferred enjoyment a superiority in quality, so far outweighing quantity as to render it, in comparison, of small account.

Now it is an unquestionable fact that those who are equally acquainted with, and equally capable of appreciating and enjoying, both, do give a most marked preference to the manner of existence which employs their higher faculties. Few human creatures would consent to be changed into any of the lower animals, for a promise of the fullest allowance of a beast's pleasures; no intelligent human being would consent to be a fool, no instructed person would be an ignoramus, no person of feeling and conscience would be selfish and base, even though they should be persuaded that the fool, the dunce, or the rascal is better satisfied with his lot than they are with theirs. They would not resign what they possess more than he for the most complete satisfaction of all the desires which they have in common with him. If they ever fancy they would, it is only in cases of unhappiness so extreme, that to escape from it they would exchange their lot for almost any other, however undesirable in their own eyes. A being of higher faculties requires more to make him happy, is capable probably of more acute suffering, and certainly accessible to it at more points, than one of an inferior type; but in spite of these liabilities, he can never really wish to sink into what he feels to be a lower grade of existence. We may give what explanation we please of this unwillingness: we may attribute it to pride, a name which is given indiscriminately to some of the most and to some of the least estimable feelings of which mankind are capable; we may refer it to the love of liberty and personal independence, an appeal to which was with the Stoics one of the most effective means for the inculcation of it; to the love of power, or to the love of excitement, both of which do really enter into and contribute to it: but its most appropriate appellation is a sense of dignity, which all human beings possess in one form or other, and in some, though by no means in exact, proportion to their higher faculties, and which is so essential a part of the happiness of those in whom it is strong, that nothing which conflicts with it could be, otherwise than momentarily, an object of desire to them. Whoever supposes that this preference takes place at a sacrifice of happiness—that the superior being, in anything like equal circumstances, is not happier than the inferior—confounds the two very different ideas, of happiness and content. It is indisputable that the being whose capacities of enjoyment are low, has the greatest chance of having them fully satisfied; and a highly endowed being will always feel that any happiness which he can look for, as the world is constituted, is imperfect. But he can learn to bear its imperfections, if they are at all bearable; and they will not make him envy the being who is indeed unconscious of the imperfections, but only because he feels not at all the good which those imperfections qualify. It is better to be a human being dissatisfied than a pig satisfied; better to be Socrates dissatisfied than a fool satisfied. And if the fool, or the pig, are of a different opinion, it is because they only know their own side of the question. The other party to the comparison knows both sides.

It may be objected that many who are capable of the higher pleasures, occasionally, under the influence of temptation, postpone them to the lower. But this is quite compatible with a full appreciation of the intrinsic superiority of the higher. Men often, from infirmity of character, make their election for the nearer good, though they know it to be the less valuable; and this no less when the choice is between two bodily pleasures, than when it is between bodily and mental. They pursue sensual indulgences to the injury of health, though perfectly aware that health is the greater good. It may be further objected that many who begin with youthful enthusiasm for everything noble, as they advance in years sink into indolence and selfishness. But I do not believe that those who undergo this very common change, voluntarily choose the lower description of pleasures in preference to the higher. I believe that before they devote themselves exclusively to the one, they have already become incapable of the other. Capacity for the nobler feelings is in most natures a very tender plant, easily killed, not only by hostile influences, but by mere want of sustenance; and in the majority of young persons it speedily dies away if the occupations to which their position in life has devoted them, and the society into which it has thrown them, are not favorable to keeping that higher capacity in exercise. Men lose their high aspirations as they lose their intellectual tastes, because they have not time or opportunity for indulging them; and they addict themselves to inferior pleasures not because they deliberately prefer them, but because they are either the only ones to which they have access or the only ones which they are any longer capable of enjoying. It may be questioned whether anyone who has remained equally susceptible to both classes of pleasures, ever knowingly and calmly preferred the lower; though many, in all ages, have broken down in an ineffectual attempt to combine both.

From this verdict of the only competent judges I apprehend there can be no appeal. On a question which is the best worth having of two pleasures, or which of two modes of existence is the most grateful to the feelings, apart from its moral attributes and from its consequences, the judgment of those who are qualified by knowledge of both, or, if they differ, that of the majority among them, must be admitted as final. And there need be the less hesitation to accept this judgment respecting the quality of pleasures, since there is no other tribunal to be referred to even

on the question of quantity. What means are there of determining which is the acutest of two pains, or the intensest of two pleasurable sensations, except the general suffrage of those who are familiar with both? Neither pains nor pleasures are homogeneous, and pain is always heterogeneous with pleasure. What is there to decide whether a particular pleasure is worth purchasing at the cost of a particular pain, except the feelings and judgment of the experienced? When, therefore, those feelings and judgment declare the pleasures derived from the higher faculties to be preferable in kind, apart from the question of intensity, to those of which the animal nature, disjoined from the higher faculties, is suspectible, they are entitled on this subject to the same regard.

I have dwelt on this point, as being a necessary part of a perfectly just conception of utility, or happiness, considered as the directive rule of human conduct. But it is by no means an indispensable condition to the acceptance of the utilitarian standard; for that standard is not the agent's own greatest happiness, but the greatest amount of happiness altogether; and if it may possibly be doubted whether a noble character is always the happier for its nobleness, there can be no doubt that it makes other people happier, and that the world in general is immensely a gainer by it. Utilitarianism, therefore, could only attain its end by the general cultivation of nobleness of character, even if each individual were only benefited by the nobleness of others, and his own, so far as happiness is concerned, were a sheer deduction from the benefit. But the bare enunciation of such an absurdity as this last renders refutation superfluous.

According to the Greatest Happiness Principle as above explained, the ultimate end, with reference to and for the sake of which all other things are desirable (whether we are considering our own good or that of other people), is an existence exempt as far as possible from pain, and as rich as possible in enjoyments, both in point of quantity and quality; the test of quality, and the rule for measuring it against quantity, being the preference felt by those who in their opportunities of experience, to which must be added their habits of self-consciousness and self-observation, are best furnished with the means of comparison. This, being, according to the utilitarian opinion, the end of human action, is necessarily also the standard of morality; which may accordingly be defined, the rules and precepts for human conduct, by the observance of which an existence such as has been described might be, to the greatest extent possible, secured to all mankind; and not to them only, but, so far as the nature of things admits, to the whole sentient creation. . . .

Though it is only in a very imperfect state of the world's arrangements that anyone can best serve the happiness of others by the absolute sacrifice of his own, yet so long as the world is in that imperfect state, I fully acknowledge that the readiness to make such a sacrifice is the highest virtue which can be found in man. I will add that in this condition of the world, paradoxical as the assertion may be, the conscious ability to do without happiness gives the best prospect of realizing such happiness as is attainable. For nothing except that consciousness can raise a person above the chances of life, by making him feel that, let fate and fortune do their worst, they have not power to subdue him; which, once felt, frees him from excess of anxiety concerning the evils of life, and enables him, like many a Stoic in the worst times of the Roman Empire, to cultivate in tranquillity the sources of satisfaction accessible to him, without concerning himself about the uncertainty of their duration, any more than about their inevitable end.

Meanwhile, let utilitarians never cease to claim the morality of self-devotion as a possession which belongs by as good a right to them, as either to the Stoic or to the Transcendentalist. The utilitarian morality does recognize in human beings the power of sacrificing their own greatest good for the good of others. It only refuses to admit that the sacrifice is itself a good. A sacrifice which does not increase, or tend to increase, the sum total of happiness, it considers as wasted. The only self-renunciation which it applauds, is devotion to the happiness, or to some of the means of happiness, of others; either of mankind collectively, or of individuals within the limits imposed by the collective interests of mankind.

I must again repeat, what the assailants of utilitarianism seldom have the justice to acknowledge, that the happiness which forms the utilitarian standard of what is right in conduct, is not the agent's own happiness, but that of all concerned. As between his own happiness and that of others, utilitarianism requires him to be as strictly impartial as a disinterested and benevolent spectator. In the golden rule of Jesus of Nazareth, we read the complete spirit of the ethics of utility. To do as you would be done by, and to love your neighbor as yourself, constitute the ideal perfection of utilitarian morality. As the means of making the nearest approach to this ideal, utility would enjoin, first, that laws and social arrangements should place the happiness, or (as speaking practically it may be called) the interest, of every individual, as nearly as possible in harmony with the interest of the whole; and secondly, that education and opinion, which have so vast a power over human character, should so use that power as to establish in the mind of every individual an indissoluble association between his own happiness and the good of the whole—especially between his own happiness and the practice of such modes of conduct, negative and positive, as regard for the universal happiness prescribes; so that not only he may be unable to conceive the possibility of happiness to himself, consistently with conduct opposed to the general good, but also that a direct impulse to promote the general good may be in every individual one of the habitual motives of action, and the sentiments connected therewith may fill a large and prominent place in every human being's sentient existence. If the impugners of the utilitarian morality represented it to their own minds in this its true character, I know not what recommendation possessed by any other morality they could possibly affirm to be wanting to it; what more beautiful or more exalted developments of human nature any other ethical system can be supposed to foster, or what springs of action, not accessible to the utilitarian, such systems rely on for giving effect to their mandates.

The objectors to utilitarianism cannot always be charged with representing it in a discreditable light. On the contrary, those among them who entertain anything like a just idea of its disinterested character sometimes find fault with its standard as being too high for humanity. They say it is exacting too much to require that people shall always act from the inducement of promoting the general interests of society. But this is to mistake the very meaning of a standard of morals, and confound the rule of action with the motive of it. It is the business of ethics to tell us what are our duties, or by what test we may know them; but no system of ethics requires that the sole motive of all we do shall be a feeling of duty; on the contrary, ninety-nine hundredths of all our actions are done from other motives, and rightly so done, if the rule of duty does not condemn them. It is the more unjust to utilitarianism that this particular misapprehension should be made a ground of objection to it, inasmuch as utilitarian moralists have gone beyond al-most all others in affirming that the motive has nothing to do with the morality of the action, though much with the worth of the agent. He who saves a fellow creature from drowning does what is morally right, whether his motive be duty, or the hope of being paid for his trouble; he who betrays the friend that trusts him, is guilty of a crime, even if his object be to serve another friend to whom he is under greater obligations. But to speak only of actions done from the motive of duty, and in direct obedience to principle: it is a misapprehension of the utilitarian mode of thought, to conceive it as implying that people should fix their minds upon so wide a generality as the world, or society at large. The great majority of good actions are intended not for the benefit of the world, but for that of individuals, of which the good of the world is made up; and the thoughts of the most virtuous man need not on these occasions travel beyond the particular persons concerned, except so far as is necessary to assure himself that in benefiting them he is not violating the rights, that is, the legitimate and authorized expectations, of anyone else. The multiplication of happiness is, according to the utilitarian ethics, the object of virtue: the occasions on which any person (except one in a thousand) has it in his power to do this on an extended scale, in other words to be a public benefactor, are but exceptional, and on these occasions alone is he called on to consider public utility; in every other case, private utility, the interest or happiness of some few persons, is all he has to attend to. Those alone the influence of whose actions extends to society in general, need concern themselves habitually about so large an object. In the case of abstinences indeed—of things which people forbear to do from moral considerations, though the consequences in the particular case might be beneficial—it would be unworthy of an intelligent agent not to be consciously aware that the action is of a class which, if practiced generally, would be generally injurious, and that this is the ground of the obligation to abstain from it. The amount of regard for the public interest implied in this recognition is no greater than is demanded by every system of morals, for they all enjoin to abstain from whatever is manifestly pernicious to society.

The same considerations dispose of another reproach against the doctrine of utility, founded on a still grosser misconception of the purpose of a standard of morality, and of the very meaning of the words right and wrong. It is often affirmed that utilitarianism renders men cold and unsympathizing; that it chills their moral feelings towards individuals; that it makes them regard only the dry and hard consideration of the consequences of actions, not taking into their moral estimate the qualities from which those actions emanate. If the assertion means that they do not allow their judgment respecting the rightness or wrongness of an action to be influenced by their opinion of the qualities of the person who does it, this is a complaint not against utilitarianism, but against having any standard of morality at all; for certainly no known ethical standard decides an action to be good or bad because it is done by a good or a bad man, still less because done by an amiable, a brave, or a benevolent man, or the contrary. These considerations are relevant, not to the estimation of actions, but of persons; and there is nothing in the utilitarian theory inconsistent with the fact that there are other things which interest us in persons besides the rightness and wrongness of their actions. The Stoics, indeed, with the paradoxical misuse of language which was part of their system, and by which they strove to raise themselves above all concern about anything but virtue, were fond of saying that he who has that has everything; that he, and

only he, is rich, is beautiful, is a king. But no claim of this description is made for the virtuous man by the utilitarian doctrine. Utilitarians are quite aware that there are other desirable possessions and qualities besides virtue, and are perfectly willing to allow to all of them their full worth. They are also aware that a right action does not necessarily indicate a virtuous character, and that actions which are blamable, often proceed from qualities entitled to praise. When this is apparent in any particular case, it modifies their estimation, not certainly of the act, but of the agent. I grant that they are, notwithstanding, of opinion that in the long run the best proof of a good character is good actions; and resolutely refuse to consider any mental disposition as good, of which the predominant tendency is to produce bad conduct. This makes them unpopular with many people; but it is an unpopularity which they must share with everyone who regards the distinction between right and wrong in a serious light; and the reproach is not one which a conscientious utilitarian need be anxious to repel.

If no more be meant by the objection than that many utilitarians look on the morality of actions, as measured by the utilitarian standard, with too exclusive a regard, and do not lay sufficient stress upon the other beauties of character which go towards making a human being lovable or admirable, this may be admitted. Utilitarians who have cultivated their moral feelings, but not their sympathies nor their artistic perceptions, do fall into this mistake; and so do all other moralists under the same conditions. What can be said in excuse for other moralists is equally available for them, namely, that if there is to be any error, it is better that it should be on that side. As a matter of fact, we may affirm that among utilitarians as among adherents of other systems, there is every imaginable degree of rigidity and of laxity in the application of their standard: some are even puritanically rigorous, while others are as indulgent as can possibly be desired by sinner or by sentimentalist. But on the whole, a doctrine which brings prominently forward the interest that mankind have in the repression and prevention of conduct which violates the moral law, is likely to be inferior to no other in turning the sanctions of opinion against such violations. It is true, the question, "What does violate the moral law?" is one on which those who recognize different standards of morality are likely now and then to differ. But difference of opinion on moral questions was not first introduced into the world by utilitarianism, while that doctrine does supply. if not always an easy, at all events a tangible and intelligible mode of deciding such differences.

IS THE UNIVERSE
MORAL?

For many men the felt fact of moral imperatives (e.g., imperatives like "You ought always to keep your promises," and "You should never kill another human being") has forced consideration of the morality of the universe. Although some philosophers have not considered this a legitimate question, many have, contending that an answer to the question, Is this a moral or just universe? is implicit or explicit in every fully developed ethic.

The following selections contain four important answers to the question. Fundamental to both Hinduism and Buddhism, the doctrine of *karma* maintains that meritorious behavior is always appropriately rewarded and vicious behavior always appropriately punished. Just as every event in the universe stands as the effect of a prior cause and is, in turn, the cause of a future effect, so, it is argued, there must be a sufficient reason why the relative advantages and disadvantages of our existence are the way they are. In his miserliness the greedy man builds for himself the conditions and causes of his own misery; the industrious man builds through his industry the conditions and causes of his own success and happiness. It is contended that to argue otherwise is to concede that there are events which have no justifiable causes and which do not stand as reasonable causes of future events, and to admit finally that the program of morality makes no sense.

Much of the recent literature of secular existentialism claims that this is clearly not a moral universe. The righteous often suffer and the evil often prosper; yet it is not the case that the absurdity of our situation frees us from the moral responsibility of our acts. Although the absurd hero is surely an absurd man living in an absurd world, he is nonetheless a hero. The retelling of the myth of Sisyphus by the French existentialist writer Albert

Camus suggests to the reader that the program of morality makes sense precisely because this is not a moral universe, that the heroic character of the moral man depends on his recognition that his "whole being is exerted toward accomplishing nothing."

The "meliorism" advanced by William James is neither so optimistic as the Indian's *karma* nor so pessimistic as the existentialist's theory of the absurd. The tragedies of this life are obvious enough to show the optimist's confidence to be unfounded; yet the possibilities of historical existence are great enough to prove the pessimist equally wrong-headed. "The salvation of the world" is neither a certainty nor an impossibility but a program for human action. If this is not at present a moral universe, it can at least be made more moral than it is. Just as the evils of smallpox can be eliminated from human experience by human effort, so the morality or "moralization" of the universe is a possibility, neither a fact nor a fraud.

The Doctrine of Karma

SARVEPALLI RADHAKRISHNAN

Sarvepalli Radhakrishnan (b. 1888) has been president of India and is a philosopher with an international reputation. The first selection describes the doctrine of karma *as it is found in the Upanishads; the second describes* karma *as interpreted by the Buddhists.*

KARMA

The law of karma is the counter-part in the moral world of the physical law of uniformity. It is the law of the conservation of moral energy. The vision of law and order is revealed in the Ṛta of the Ṛg-Veda. According to the principle of karma there is nothing uncertain or capricious in the moral world.[1] We reap what we sow. The good seed brings a harvest of good, the evil of evil. Every little action has its effect on character. Man knows that some of the tendencies to action which now exist in him are the result of conscious or intelligent choice on his part. Conscious actions tend to be-

[1] Carlyle puts this principle thus: "Fool! thinkest thou that because no Boswell is there to note thy jargon, it therefore dies and is buried? Nothing dies, nothing can die. The idlest word thou speakest is a seed cast into time, which brings forth fruit to all eternity." "Be not deceived; God is not mocked: for whatsoever a man soweth, that shall he also reap" (Gal. vi. 7).

come unconscious habits, and not unnaturally the unconscious tendencies we find in ourselves were regarded as the result of past conscious actions. We cannot arrest the process of moral evolution any more than we can stay the sweep of the tides or the course of the stars. The attempt to overleap the law of karma is as futile as the attempt to leap over one's shadow. It is the psychological principle that our life carries within it a record that time cannot blur or death erase. To remedy the defects of the old Vedic idea, that redemption from sin could be had by sacrifices to gods, great emphasis is laid on the law of karma. It proclaims the awful doom, the soul that sinneth, it shall die. Not through sacrifices, but through good deeds does a man become good. "A man becomes good by good deeds and bad by bad deeds." Again, "Man is a creature of will. According as he believes in this world, so will he be when he is departed." So we are asked to will the good and do the good. "Whatever world he covets by his

From *Indian Philosophy*, Vol. I; George Allen & Unwin, London; Macmillan Co., New York, 1929. Reprinted by permission of George Allen & Unwin, Ltd., and Humanities Press.

mind, and whatever objects he wishes, for the man of pure mind, he gains those worlds and those objects; therefore let him who longs for bhūti, manifested power, worship him who knows the Ātman." The requital of action makes saṁsāra with birth and death, beginningless and endless. The karma theory embraces in its sweep men and gods, animals and plants.

Since the sense of individual responsibility is emphasised there are critics who think that the karma doctrine is inconsistent with social service. It is said that there is no emphasis on the bearing of one another's burdens. As a matter of fact, the Upaniṣads hold that we can be free from karma only by social service. So long as we perform selfish work we are subject to the law of bondage. When we perform disinterested work we reach freedom. "While thus you live there is no way by which karma clings to you." What binds us to the chain of birth and death is not action as such but selfish action. In an age when the individual was ever ready to shirk responsibility for what he did by throwing the burden on providence or stars or some other being than his own self, the doctrine of karma urged that a man "fetters himself by himself, like a bird by its nest." What looms over us is no dark fate but our own past. We are not the victims of a driving doom. Suffering is the wages of sin. There is no question that such an idea is a great incentive to good conduct. It only says that there are some limiting conditions of human action. We did not make ourselves. When we come up against the impossible, we realise that we cannot do anything we please. Karma rightly understood does not discourage moral effort, does not fetter the mind or chain the will. It only says that every act is the inevitable outcome of the preceding conditions. There is a tendency of the cause to pass into the effect. If the spirit, which is on a higher

plane than nature, does not assert its freedom, past conduct and present environment will account completely for the actions of man. Man is not a mere product of nature. He is mightier than his karma. If the law is all, then there is no real freedom possible. Man's life is not the working of merely mechanical relations. There are different levels—the mechanical, the vital, the sentient, the intellectual and the spiritual—these currents cross and recross and inter-penetrate each other. The law of karma, which rules the lower nature of man, has nothing to do with the spiritual in him. The infinite in man helps him to transcend the limitations of the finite. The essence of spirit is freedom. By its exercise man can check and control his natural impulses. That is why his life is something more than a succession of mechanically determined states. His acts to be free must not be expressive of the mere force of habit or shock of circumstance, but of the freedom of the inner soul. The spiritual nature is the basis of his initiative and endeavour. The mechanical part is under constraint. Were man merely the sum of natural conditions, he would be completely subject to the law of karma. But there is a soul in him which is the master. Nothing external can compel it. We are sure that the material forces of the world must bend to the spiritual rule, and so can the law of karma be subjected to the freedom of spirit. Man can have the highest freedom only when he becomes one with God. "He who departs from this world, without having known the soul or those true desires, his part in all worlds is a life of constraint. But he who departs from this world after having known the soul and those true desires, his part in all worlds is a life of freedom." Becoming one with God is the attainment of the highest freedom. The more we live in the presence of God, the more we assert the rights of spirit, the more free we are; the more we lose our grip on the whole to which we belong, the more selfish we are, the more is our bondage to karma. Man oscillates between nature and spirit, and so is subject to both freedom and necessity.

Karma has a cosmic as well as a psychological aspect. Every deed must produce its natural effect in the world; at the same time it leaves an impression on or forms a tendency in the mind of man. It is this tendency or saṁsāra or vāsana that inclines us to repeat the deed we have once done. So all deeds have their fruits in the world and effects on the mind. So far as the former are concerned, we cannot escape them, however much we may try. But in regard to mental tendencies we can control them. Our future conduct holds all possibilities. By self-discipline we can strengthen the good impulses and weaken the bad ones.

The actions of men are capable of prediction and precalculation. If rational, they will show certain properties: we shall detect in them an inward coherence, an unselfish purpose, and so on. But from that we cannot assume that the acts are determined in any mechanical sense. Every living soul is potentially free. His acts are not a mere unwinding of the thread from a reel. Man possesses freedom as the focus of spiritual life. God has not granted him freedom from outside. He possesses freedom because he is rooted in God. The more he realises his true divine nature, the more free is he.

It is sometimes argued that the law of karma is inconsistent with theism. Karma is a blind unconscious principle governing the whole universe. It is not subject to the control even of God. We do not require a judge to administer a mechanical law. The principle of karma is not inconsistent with the reality of the absolute Brahman. The moral law of karma is the expression of the nature of the absolute. Anthropomorphically we can say a divine power controls the process. Ṛta is the law

in the Vedas. Varuṇa is the lord of Ṛta. Karma refers to the unchanging action of the gods. It is an expression of the nature of reality. It renders impossible any arbitrary interference with moral evolution. The same conclusion is arrived at by modern theories of scientific law and habit, which are irreconcilable with capricious interference. If miracles are necessary to prove God, then science has killed God for all time. Divine interference is regulated by laws. God does not act by private volitions, as Malebranche would say. Only the karma theory can give us a just conception of the spiritual universe. It brings out the living rational nature of the whole. It is the mechanism by which spirit works. The freedom of the spiritual world is expressed in the world of nature by the iron law of mechanical necessity.[2] Freedom and karma are the two aspects of the same reality. If God is immanent in the cosmos, then His spirit resides in the machine. The divine expresses itself in law, but law is not God. The Greek fate, the Stoic reason, and the Chinese Tao, are different names for the primary necessity of law.

There is no doctrine that is so valuable in life and conduct as the karma theory. Whatever happens to us in this life we have to submit in meek resignation, for it is the result of our past doings. Yet the

[2] We need not oppose the law of karma to the will of God as conceived in the Upaniṣads. The two are not exclusive of each other. Should there be many gods as in the Vedic theory, the gods themselves will be subject to karma. "The Gods cannot save even a man whom they love when the dread fate of death lays hold upon him. Zeus himself laments that it is 'fate' that his son Sarpedon, dearest to him of all men, must die at the hands of Patroclus. He 'does not venture to undo what fate decrees.' It is impossible even for a God to avoid the fate that is ordained. 'What is ordained,' says Athena in Euripides, using Anaximander's word, 'is master of the Gods and thee.'" Francis M. Cornford, *From Religion to Philosophy;* New York, Longmans, Green and Co., pp. 12, 13.

future is in our power, and we can work with hope and confidence. Karma inspires hope for the future and resignation to the past. It makes men feel that the things of the world, its fortunes and failures, do not touch the dignity of the soul. Virtue alone is good, not rank or riches, not race or nationality. Nothing but goodness is good.

KARMA AND REBIRTH

The law of karma is not imposed from without, but is worked into our very nature. The formation of mental habits, the increasing proneness to evil, the hardening influence of repetition which undermines the effective freedom of the self, whether we know it or not, are comprehended under the law of karma. We cannot escape from the effects of our acts. The past in a real sense produces the present and the future. The law of karma is the principle working out justice in human relations. "It is through a difference in their karma that men are not all alike. But some are long lived, some short lived, some healthy, and some sickly, etc." Without this explanation men would feel themselves to be the victims of an immense injustice. It also helps to make the sufferer resigned, because he feels that through suffering he is wiping out an old debt. It makes the enjoyer courteous, for he must do good again to deserve it. When a persecuted disciple came to Buddha with broken head and streaming wounds, Buddha told him: "Suffer it to be so, O Arhat . . . you are now feeling results of your karma that might have cost you centuries of suffering in purgatory." It insists on individual responsibility and the reality of a future life. It recognises that the retribution of sin depends on the status of the sinner. If a man weak in mind and morals does an evil deed, it may lead him to the inferno. If a good man does it he

may escape with a small pain in this life. "It is as if a man were to put a lump of salt into a small cup of water, the water would be made salt and undrinkable. But if the same lump of salt were put into the river Ganges, the water of the Ganges would not be perceptibly tainted."

The theory of karma is much older than Buddhism, though it gets a logical justification in the philosophy of becoming. Men are temporary links in a long chain of causes and effects where no link is independent of the rest. The history of an individual does not begin at his birth, but has been for ages in the making.

When karma becomes the supreme principle superior to gods and men, it is difficult to assign any place to the initiative and endeavour of man. If everything that happens is determined by it, it is hard to see why the individual should take thought of what he does. He cannot but act in harmony with the law. Salvation is another name for acquiescence in the course of things. Such a conception again and again crops up in the history of thought. The Greek held that there was an inexorable destiny higher than man or god which could not be altered by effort or prayer. The same dread fate appears in the faith of the Calvinists and the Kismet of the Muslims. Nobody can learn even from Buddha if he has not already been destined for it or done enough merit to deserve it. We admit that Buddha did not give a straight answer to the question of freedom, but put it aside as a problem of speculation. Yet his system allows the possibility of free action and ultimate conquest over the whole law of karma. His insistence on energy and endeavour and struggle against hate and error is not consistent with a denial of freedom. His scheme has a place for repentance, or saṁvega. The following suggestions may enable us to reconcile the Buddhist emphasis on karma with freedom. The chief argument in support of determination even in modern thought is that from causation. Karma, according to Buddhism, is not a mechanical principle, but is organic in character. The self grows and expands. There is no self, but only an evolving consciousness which may be spread out in a series of states. Though the present is determined by the past, the future remains open and depends on the direction of our will. The determination of the present by the past is not, however, a merely mechanical one. The law of karma tells us that there is continuity between the past and the present, that the present accords with the past. This does not mean that the present is the only possible outcome of the past. "O priests, if anyone says that a man must reap according to his deeds, in that case there is no religious life, nor is any opportunity offered for the entire extinction of misery. But if anyone says, O priests, that a reward a man reaps accords with his deeds, in that case, O priests, there is a religious life, and opportunity is afforded for the entire extinction of misery." A mechanical misinterpretation of the law of karma conflicts with the claims of ethics and religion.

The Myth of Sisyphus

ALBERT CAMUS

Albert Camus (1913–1960) wrote philosophic essays, plays, novels, and edited Combat, *the paper of the French Resistance.*

The gods had condemned Sisyphus to ceaselessly rolling a rock to the top of a mountain, whence the stone would fall back of its own weight. They had thought with some reason that there is no more dreadful punishment than futile and hopeless labor.

If one believes Homer, Sisyphus was the wisest and most prudent of mortals. According to another tradition, however, he was disposed to practice the profession of highwayman. I see no contradiction in this. Opinions differ as to the reasons why he became the futile laborer of the underworld. To begin with, he is accused of a certain levity in regard to the gods. He stole their secrets. Aegina, the daughter of Aesopus, was carried off by Jupiter. The father was shocked by that disappearance and complained to Sisyphus. He, who knew of the abduction, offered to tell about it on condition that Aesopus would give water to the citadel of Corinth. To the celestial thunderbolts he preferred the benediction of water. He was punished for this in the underworld. Homer tells us also that Sisyphus had put Death in chains. Pluto could not endure the sight of his deserted, silent empire. He dispatched the god of war, who liberated Death from the hands of her conqueror.

It is said also that Sisyphus, being near to death, rashly wanted to test his wife's love. He ordered her to cast his unburied body into the middle of the public square. Sisyphus woke up in the underworld. And there, annoyed by an obedience so contrary to human love, he obtained from Pluto permission to return to earth in order to chastise his wife. But when he had seen again the face of this world, enjoyed water and sun, warm stones and the sea, he no longer wanted to go back to the infernal darkness. Recalls, signs of anger, warnings were of no avail. Many years more he lived facing the curve of the gulf, the sparkling sea, and the smiles of earth. A decree of the gods was necessary. Mercury came and seized the impudent man by the collar and, snatching him from his joys, led him forcibly back to the underworld, where his rock was ready for him.

You have already grasped that Sisyphus is the absurd hero. He *is*, as much through his passions as through his torture. His scorn of the gods, his hatred of death, and his passion for life won him that unspeakable penalty in which the whole being is extended toward accomplishing nothing. This is the price that must be paid for the passions of this earth. Nothing is told us about Sisyphus in the underworld. Myths are made for the imagination to breathe life into them. As for this myth, one sees merely the whole effort of a body straining to raise the huge stone, to roll it and push it up a slope a hundred times over; one sees the face screwed up, the cheek tight against the stone, the shoulder bracing the clay-covered mass, the foot wedging it, the fresh start with arms outstretched, the wholly human security of

two earth-clotted hands. At the very end of his long effort measured by skyless space and time without depth, the purpose is achieved. Then Sisyphus watches the stone rush down in a few moments toward that lower world whence he will have to push it up again toward the summit. He goes back down to the plain.

It is during that return, that pause, that Sisyphus interests me. A face that toils so close to stones is already stone itself! I see that man going back down with a heavy yet measured step toward the torment of which he will never know the end. That hour like a breathing-space which returns as surely as his suffering, that is the hour of consciousness. At each of those moments when he leaves the heights and gradually sinks toward the lairs of the gods, he is superior to his fate. He is stronger than his rock.

If this myth is tragic, that is because its hero is conscious. Where would his torture be, indeed, if at every step the hope of succeeding upheld him? The workman of today works every day in his life at the same tasks, and this fate is no less absurd. But it is tragic only at the rare moments when it becomes conscious. Sisyphus, proletarian of the gods, powerless and rebellious, knows the whole extent of his wretched condition: it is what he thinks of during his descent. The lucidity that was to constitute his torture at the same time crowns his victory. There is no fate that cannot be surmounted by scorn.

If the descent is thus sometimes performed in sorrow, it can also take place in joy. This word is not too much. Again I fancy Sisyphus returning toward his rock, and the sorrow was in the beginning. When the images of earth cling too tightly to memory, when the call of happiness becomes too insistent, it happens that melancholy rises in man's heart: this is the rock's victory, this is the rock itself. The boundless grief is too heavy to bear. These are our nights of Gethsemane. But crushing truths perish from being acknowledged. Thus, Oedipus at the outset obeys fate without knowing it. But from the moment he knows, his tragedy begins. Yet at the same moment, blind and desperate, he realizes that the only bond linking him to the world is the cool hand of a girl. Then a tremendous remark rings out: "Despite so many ordeals, my advanced age and the nobility of my soul make me conclude that all is well." Sophocles' Oedipus, like Dostoevsky's Kirilov, thus gives the recipe for the absurd story. Ancient wisdom confirms modern heroism.

One does not discover the absurd without being tempted to write a manual of happiness. "What! by such narrow ways—?" There is but one world, however. Happiness and the absurd are two sons of the same earth. They are inseparable. It would be a mistake to say that happiness necessarily springs from the absurd discovery. It happens as well that the feeling of the absurd springs from happiness. "I conclude that all is well," says Oedipus, and that remark is sacred. It echoes in the wild and limited universe of man. It teaches that all is not, has not been, exhausted. It drives out of this world a god who had come into it with dissatisfaction and a preference for futile sufferings. It makes of fate a human matter, which must be settled among men.

All Sisyphus' silent joy is contained therein. His fate belongs to him. His rock is his thing. Likewise, the absurd man, when he contemplates his torment, silences all the idols. In the universe suddenly restored to its silence, the myriad wondering little voices of the earth rise up. Unconscious, secret calls, invitations from all the faces, they are the necessary reverse and price of victory. There is no sun without shadow, and it is essential to know the night. The absurd man says yes and his effort will henceforth be unceasing. If there is a personal fate, there is no higher destiny, or at least there is but one which he concludes is inevitable and despicable. For the rest, he knows himself to be the master of his days. At that subtle moment when man glances backward over his life, Sisyphus returning toward his rock, in that slight pivoting he contemplates that series of unrelated actions which becomes his fate, created by him, combined under his memory's eye and soon scaled by his death. Thus, convinced of the wholly human origin of all that is human, a blind man eager to see who knows that the night has no end, he is still on the go. The rock is still rolling.

I leave Sisyphus at the foot of the mountain! One always finds one's burden again. But Sisyphus teaches the higher fidelity that negates the gods and raises rocks. He too concludes that all is well. This universe henceforth without a master seems to him neither sterile nor futile. Each atom of that stone, each mineral flake of that night-filled mountain, in itself forms a world. The struggle itself toward the heights is enough to fill a man's heart. One must imagine Sisyphus happy.

Pragmatism and Religion

WILLIAM JAMES

William James (1842–1910) was one of the founders of the philosophic school of American Pragmatism. This selection was the last of a series of lectures delivered in Boston and New York in 1906 and 1907.

At the close of the last lecture I reminded you of the first one, in which I had opposed tough-mindedness to tender-mindedness and recommended pragmatism as their mediator. Tough-mindedness positively rejects tender-mindedness's hypothesis of an eternal perfect edition of the universe coexisting with our finite experience.

On pragmatic principles we can not reject any hypothesis if consequences useful to life flow from it. Universal conceptions, as things to take account of, may be as real for pragmatism as particular sensations are. They have, indeed, no meaning and no reality if they have no use. But if they have any use they have that amount of meaning. And the meaning will be true if the use squares well with life's other uses.

Well, the use of the Absolute is proved by the whole course of men's religious history. The eternal arms are then beneath. Remember Vivekanda's use of the Atman: it is indeed not a scientific use, for we can make no particular deductions from it. It is emotional and spiritual altogether.

It is always best to discuss things by the help of concrete examples. Let me read therefore some of those verses entitled "To You" by Walt Whitman—"You" of course meaning the reader or hearer of the poem whosoever he or she may be.

Whoever you are, now I place my hand
    upon you that you be my poem;
I whisper with my lips close to your ear,
I have loved many women and men,
    but I love none better than you.

O I have been dilatory and dumb;
I should have made my way to you long
    ago;
I should have blabbed nothing but you,
    I should have chanted nothing but
    you.

I will leave all and come and make the
    hymns of you;
None have understood you, but I understand you;
None have done justice to you—you
    have not done justice to yourself;
None but have found you imperfect—
    I only find no imperfection in you.

O I could sing such glories and grandeurs about you;

From *Pragmatism;* New York, Longmans, Green, and Co., 1907.

You have not known what you are—
you have slumbered upon yourself
all your life;
What you have done returns already in
mockeries.

But the mockeries are not you;
Underneath them and within them, I
see you lurk;
I pursue you where none else has pur-
sued you.
Silence, the desk, the flippant expression, the night, the accustomed routine, if these conceal you from others,
or from yourself, they do not conceal
you from me;
The shaved face, the unsteady eye, the
impure complexion, if these balk
others, they do not balk me;
The pert apparel, the deformed attitude, drunkenness, greed, premature
death, all these I part aside.

There is no endowment in man or
woman that is not tallied in you;
There is no virtue, no beauty, in man
or woman, but as good is in you;
No pluck nor endurance in others, but
as good is in you;
No pleasure waiting for others, but an
equal pleasure waits for you.

Whoever you are! claim your own at
any hazard!
These shows of the east and west are
tame, compared with you;
These immense meadows—these interminable rivers—you are immense and
interminable as they;
You are he or she who is master or
mistress over them,
Master or mistress in your own right
over Nature, elements, pain, passion,
dissolution.

The hopples fall from your ankles—
you find an unfailing sufficiency;
Old or young, male or female, rude,
low, rejected by the rest whatever
you are promulges itself;

Through birth, life, death, burial, the
means are provided, nothing is
scanted;
Through angers, losses, ambition, ignorance, ennui, what you are picks its
way.

Verily a fine and moving poem, in any
case, but there are two ways of taking it,
both useful.

One is the monistic way, the mystical
way of pure cosmic emotion. The glories
and grandeurs, they are yours absolutely,
even in the midst of your defacements.
Whatever may happen to you, whatever
you may appear to be, inwardly you are
safe. Look back, *lie* back, on your true
principle of being! This is the famous way
of quietism, of indifferentism. Its enemies
compare it to a spiritual opium. Yet pragmatism must respect this way, for it has
massive historic vindication.

But pragmatism sees another way to
be respected also, the pluralistic way of
interpreting the poem. The you so glorified, to which the hymn is sung, may mean
your better possibilities phenomenally
taken, or the specific redemptive effects
even of your failures, upon yourself or
others. It may mean your loyalty to the
possibilities of others whom you admire
and love so that you are willing to accept
your own poor life, for it is that glory's
partner. You can at least appreciate, ap-
plaud, furnish the audience, of so brave
a total world. Forget the low in yourself,
then, think only of the high. Identify your
life therewith; then, through angers, losses,
ignorance, ennui, whatever you thus make
yourself, whatever you thus most deeply
are, picks its way.

In either way of taking the poem, it
encourages fidelity to ourselves. Both ways
satisfy; both sanctify the human flux. Both
paint the portrait of the *you* on a gold
background. But the background of the
first way is the static One, while in
the second way it means possibles in the

plural, genuine possibles, and it has all the restlessness of that conception.

Noble enough is either way of reading the poem; but plainly the pluralistic way agrees with the pragmatic temper best, for it immediately suggests an infinitely larger number of the details of future experience to our mind. It sets definite activities in us at work. Altho this second way seems prosaic and earth-born in comparison with the first way, yet no one can accuse it of tough-mindedness in any brutal sense of the term. Yet if, as pragmatists, you should positively set up the second way *against* the first way, you would very likely be misunderstood. You would be accused of denying nobler conceptions, and of being an ally of tough-mindedness in the worst sense.

You remember the letter from a member of this audience from which I read some extracts at our previous meeting. Let me read you an additional extract now. It shows a vagueness in realizing the alternatives before us which I think is very widespread.

"I believe," writes my friend and correspondent, "in pluralism; I believe that in our search for truth we leap from one floating cake of ice to another, on an infinite sea, and that by each of our acts we make new truths possible and old ones impossible; I believe that each man is responsible for making the universe better, and that if he does not do this it will be in so far left undone.

"Yet at the same time I am willing to endure that my children should be incurably sick and suffering (as they are not) and I myself stupid and yet with brains enough to see my stupidity, only on one condition, namely, that through the construction, in imagination and by reasoning, of a *rational unity of all things*, I can conceive my acts and my thoughts and my troubles as *supplemented by all the other phenomena of the world, and as forming—when thus supplemented—a* scheme which I approve and adopt as my own; and for my part I refuse to be persuaded that we can not look beyond the obvious pluralism of the naturalist and pragmatist to a logical unity in which they take no interest or stock."

Such a fine expression of personal faith warms the heart of the hearer. But how much does it clear his philosophic head? Does the writer consistently favor the monistic, or the pluralistic, interpretation of the world's poem? His troubles become atoned for *when thus supplemented,* he says, supplemented, that is, by all the remedies that *the other phenomena* may supply. Obviously here the writer faces forward into the particulars of experience, which he interprets in a pluralistic-melioristic way.

But he believes himself to face backward. He speaks of what he calls the rational *unity* of things, when all the while he really means their possible empirical *unification*. He supposes at the same time that the pragmatist, because he criticises rationalism's abstract One, is cut off from the consolation of believing in the saving possibilities of the concrete many. He fails in short to distinguish between taking the world's perfection as a necessary principle, and taking it only as a possible *terminus ad quem*.

I regard the writer of the letter as a genuine pragmatist, but as a pragmatist *sans le savoir*. He appears to me as one of that numerous class of philosophic amateurs whom I spoke of in my first lecture, as wishing to have all the good things going, without being too careful as to how they agree or disagree. "Rational unity of all things" is so inspiring a formula, that he brandishes it off-hand, and abstractly accuses pluralism of conflicting with it (for the bare names do conflict), altho concretely he means by it just the pragmatistically unified and ameliorated world. Most of us remain in this essential vagueness, and it is well that we should;

but in the interest of clearheadedness it is well that some of us should go farther, so I will try now to focus a little more discriminatingly on this particular religious point.

Is then this you of yous, this absolutely real world, this unity that yields the moral inspiration and has the religious value, to be taken monistically or pluralistically? Is it *ante rem* or *in rebus*? Is it a principle or an end, an absolute or an ultimate, a first or a last? Does it make you look forward or lie back? It is certainly worth while not to clump the two things together, for if discriminated, they have decidedly diverse meanings for life.

Please observe that the whole dilemma revolves pragmatically about the notion of the world's possibilities. Intellectually, rationalism invokes its absolute principle of unity, as a ground of possibility for the many facts. Emotionally, it sees it as a container and limiter of possibilities, a guarantee that the upshot shall be good. Taken in this way, the absolute makes all good things certain, and all bad things impossible (in the eternal, namely), and may be said to transmute the entire category of possibility into categories more secure. One sees at this point that the great religious difference lies between the men who insist that the world *must and shall be,* and those who are contented with believing that the world *may be,* saved. The whole clash of rationalistic and empiricist religion is thus over the validity of possibility. It is necessary therefore to begin by focusing upon that word. What may the word "possible" definitely mean? To unreflecting men it means a sort of third estate of being, less real than existence, more real that non-existence, a twilight realm, a hybrid status, a limbo into which and out of which realities ever and anon are made to pass.

Such a conception is of course too vague and nondescript to satisfy us. Here, as elsewhere, the only way to extract a term's meaning is to use the pragmatic method on it. When you say that a thing is possible, what difference does it make? It makes at least this difference that if any one calls it impossible you can contradict him, if any one calls it actual you can contradict *him,* and if any one calls it necessary you can contradict him too.

But these privileges of contradiction don't amount to much. When you say a thing is possible, does not that make some farther difference in terms of actual fact?

It makes at least this negative difference that if the statement be true, it follows that *there is nothing extant capable of preventing* the possible thing. The absence of real grounds of interference may thus be said to make things *not impossible,* possible therefore in the *bare* or *abstract* sense.

But most possibles are not bare, they are concretely grounded, or well-grounded, as we say. What does this mean pragmatically? It means not only that there are no preventive conditions present, but that some of the conditions of production of the possible thing actually are here. Thus a concretely possible chicken means: (1) that the idea of chicken contains no essential self-contradiction; (2) that no boys, skunks, or other enemies are about; and (3) that at least an actual egg exists. Possible chicken means actual egg—plus actual sitting hen, or incubator, or what not. As the actual conditions approach completeness the chicken becomes a better-and-better-grounded possibility. When the conditions are entirely complete, it ceases to be a possibility, and turns into an actual fact.

Let us apply this notion to the salvation of the world. What does it pragmatically mean to say that this is possible? It means that some of the conditions of the world's deliverance do actually exist. The more of them there are existent, the fewer preventing conditions you can find, the better-grounded is the salvation's possibility, the more *probable* does the fact of the deliverance become.

So much for our preliminary look at possibility.

Now it would contradict the very spirit of life to say that our minds must be indifferent and neutral in questions like that of the world's salvation. Any one who pretends to be neutral writes himself down here as a fool and a sham. We all do wish to minimize the insecurity of the universe; we are and ought to be unhappy when we regard it as exposed to every enemy and open to every life-destroying draft. Nevertheless there are unhappy men who think the salvation of the world impossible. Theirs is the doctrine known as pessimism.

Optimism in turn would be the doctrine that thinks the world's salvation necessary.

Midway between the two there stands what may be called the doctrine of meliorism, tho it has hitherto figured less as a doctrine than as an attitude in human affairs. Optimism has always been the regnant *doctrine in European* philosophy. Pessimism was only recently introduced by Schopenhauer and counts few systematic defenders as yet. Meliorism treats salvation as neither necessary nor impossible. It treats it as a possibility, which becomes more and more of a probability the more numerous the actual conditions of salvation become.

It is clear that pragmatism must incline towards meliorism. Some conditions of the world's salvation are actually extant, and she can not possibly close her eyes to this fact: and should the residual conditions come, salvation would become an accomplished reality. Naturally the terms I use here are exceedingly summary. You may interpret the word "salvation" in any way you like, and make it as diffuse and

distributive, or as climacteric and integral a phenomenon as you please.

Take, for example, any one of us in this room with the ideals which he cherishes and is willing to live and work for. Every such ideal realized will be one moment in the world's salvation. But these particular ideals are not bare abstract possibilities. They are grounded, they are *live* possibilities, for we are their live champions and pledges, and if the complementary conditions come and add themselves, our ideals will become actual things. What now are the complementary conditions? They are first such a mixture of things as will in the fulness of time give us a chance, a gap that we can spring into, and, finally, *our act*.

Does our act then *create* the world's salvation so far as it makes room for itself, so far as it leaps into the gap? Does it create, not the whole world's salvation of course, but just so much of this as itself covers of the world's extent?

Here I take the bull by the horns, and in spite of the whole crew of rationalists and monists, of whatever brand they be, I ask *why not?* Our acts, our turning-places, where we seem to ourselves to make ourselves and grow, are the parts of the world to which we are closest, the parts of which our knowledge is the most intimate and complete. Why should we not take them at their face-value? Why may they not be the actual turning-places and growing-places which they seem to be, of the world—why not the workshop of being, where we catch fact in the making, so that nowhere may the world grow in any other kind of way than this?

Irrational! we are told. How can new being come in local spots and patches which add themselves or stay away at random, independently of the rest? There must be a reason for our acts, and where in the last resort can any reason be looked for save in the material pressure or the logical compulsion of the total nature of the world? There can be but one real agent of growth, or seeming growth, anywhere, and that agent is the integral world itself. It may grow all-over, if growth there be, but that single parts should grow *per se* is irrational.

But if one talks of rationality—and of reasons for things, and insists that they can't just come in spots, what *kind* of a reason can there ultimately be why anything should come at all? Talk of logic and necessity and categories and the absolute and the contents of the whole philosophical machine-shop as you will, the only *real* reason I can think of why anything should ever come is that *some one wishes it to be here.* It is *demanded*—demanded, it may be, to give relief to no matter how small a fraction of the world's mass. This is *living reason,* and compared with it material causes and logical necessities are spectral things.

In short the only fully rational world would be the world of wishing-caps, the world of telepathy, where every desire is fulfilled instanter, without having to consider or placate surrounding or intermediate powers. This is the Absolute's own world. He calls upon the phenomenal world to be, and it *is,* exactly as he calls for it, no other condition being required. In our world, the wishes of the individual are only one condition. Other individuals are there with other wishes and they must be propitiated first. So Being grows under all sorts of resistances in this world of the many, and, from compromise to compromise, only gets organized gradually into what may be called secondarily rational shape. We approach the wishing-cap type of organization only in a few departments of life. We want water and we turn a faucet. We want a kodak-picture and we press a button. We want information and we telephone. We want to travel and we buy a ticket. In these and similar cases, we hardly need to do more than the wishing—the world is rationally organized to do the rest.

But this talk of rationality is a parenthesis and a digression. What we were discussing was the idea of a world growing not integrally but piecemeal by the contributions of its several parts. Take the hypothesis seriously and as a live one. Suppose that the world's author put the case to you before creation, saying: "I am going to make a world not certain to be saved, a world the perfection of which shall be conditional merely, the condition being that each several agent does its own "level best." I offer you the chance of taking part in such a world. Its safety, you see, is unwarranted. It is a real adventure, with real danger, yet it may win through. It is a social scheme of co-operative work genuinely to be done. Will you join the procession? Will you trust yourself and trust the other agents enough to face the risk?"

Should you in all seriousness, if participation in such a world were proposed to you, feel bound to reject it as not safe enough? Would you say that, rather than be part and parcel of so fundamentally pluralistic and irrational a universe, you preferred to relapse into the slumber of nonentity from which you had been momentarily aroused by the tempter's voice?

Of course if you are normally constituted, you would do nothing of the sort. There is a healthy-minded buoyancy in most of us which such a universe would exactly fit. We would therefore accept the offer—"Top! und schlag auf schlag!" It would be just like the world we practically live in; and loyalty to our old nurse Nature would forbid us to say no. The world proposed would seem "rational" to us in the most living way.

Most of us, I say, would therefore welcome the proposition and add our *fiat* to the *fiat* of the creator. Yet perhaps some would not; for there are morbid minds in every human collection, and to them the prospect of a universe with only a fighting chance of safety would probably make no appeal. There are moments of discouragement in us all, when we are sick of self and tired of vainly striving. Our own life breaks down, and we fall into the attitude of the prodigal son. We mistrust the chances of things. We want a universe where we can just give up, fall on our father's neck, and be absorbed into the absolute life as a drop of water melts into the river or the sea.

The peace and rest, the security desiderated at such moments is security against the bewildering accidents of so much finite experience. Nirvana means safety from this everlasting round of adventures of which the world of sense consists. The hindoo and the buddhist, for this is essentially their attitude, are simply afraid, afraid of more experience, afraid of life.

And to men of this complexion, religious monism comes with its consoling words: "All is needed and essential—even you with your sick soul and heart. All are one with God, and with God all is well. The everlasting arms are beneath, whether in the world of finite appearance you seem to fail or to succeed." There can be no doubt that when men are reduced to their last sick extremity absolutism is the only saving scheme. Pluralistic moralism simply makes their teeth chatter, it refrigerates the very heart within their breast.

So we see concretely two types of religion in sharp contrast. Using our old terms of comparison, we may say that the absolutistic scheme appeals to the tender-minded while the pluralistic scheme appeals to the tough. Many persons would refuse to call the pluralistic scheme religious at all. They would call it moralistic, and would apply the word religious to the monistic scheme alone. Religion in the sense of self-surrender, and moralism in the sense of self-sufficingness, have been pitted against each other as incompatibles frequently enough in the history of human thought.

We stand here before the final question of philosophy. I said in my fourth lecture that I believed the monistic-pluralistic alternative to be the deepest and most pregnant question that our minds can frame. Can it be that the disjunction is a final one? that only one side can be true? Are a pluralism and monism genuine incompatibles? So that, if the world were really pluralistically constituted, if it really existed distributively and were made up of a lot of eaches, it could only be saved piecemeal and *de facto* as the result of their behavior, and its epic history in no wise short-circuited by some essential oneness in which the severalness were already "taken up" beforehand and eternally "overcome"? If this were so, we should have to choose one philosophy or the other. We could not say "yes, yes" to both alternatives. There would have to be a "no" in our relations with the possible. We should confess an ultimate disappointment: we could not remain healthy-minded and sick-minded in one indivisible act.

Of course as human beings we can be healthy minds on one day and sick souls on the next; and as amateur dabblers in philosophy we may perhaps be allowed to call ourselves monistic pluralists, or free-will determinists, or whatever else may occur to us of a reconciling kind. But as philosophers aiming at clearness and consistency, and feeling the pragmatistic need of squaring truth with truth, the question is forced upon us of frankly adopting either the tender or the robustious type of thought. In particular *this* query has always come home to me: May not the claims of tender-mindedness go too far? May not the notion of a world already saved *in toto* anyhow, be too saccharine to stand? May not religious optimism be too idyllic? Must *all* be saved? Is *no* price to be paid in the work of salvation? Is the last word sweet? Is all "yes, yes" in the universe? Doesn't the fact of "no" stand at the very core of life? Doesn't the very "seriousness" that we attribute to life mean that ineluctable noes and losses form a part of it, that there are genuine sacrifices somewhere, and that something permanently drastic and bitter always remains at the bottom of its cup?

I can not speak officially as a pragmatist here; all I can say is that my own pragmatism offers no objection to my taking sides with this more moralistic view, and giving up the claim of total reconciliation. The possibility of this is involved in the pragmatistic willingness to treat pluralism as a serious hypothesis. In the end it is our faith and not our logic that decides such questions, and I deny the right of any pretended logic to veto my own faith. I find myself willing to take the universe to be really dangerous and adventurous, without therefore backing out and crying "no play." I am willing to think that the prodigal-son attitude, open to us as it is in many vicissitudes, is not the right and final attitude towards the whole of life. I am willing that there should be real losses and real losers, and no total preservation of all that is. I can believe in the ideal as an ultimate, not as an origin, and as an extract, not the whole. When the cup is poured off, the dregs are left behind for ever, but the possibility of what is poured off is sweet enough to accept.

As a matter of fact countless human imaginations live in this moralistic and epic kind of a universe, and find its disseminated and strung-along successes sufficient for their rational needs. There is a finely translated epigram in the Greek anthology which admirably expresses this state of mind, this acceptance of loss as

unatoned for, even though the lost element might be one's self:

"A shipwrecked sailor, buried on this coast,
   Bids you set sail.
Full many a gallant bark, when we were lost,
   Weathered the gale."

Those puritans who answered "yes" to the question: Are you willing to be damned for God's glory? were in this objective and magnanimous condition of mind. The way of escape from evil on this system is *not* by getting it "aufgehoben," or preserved in the whole as an element essential but "overcome." *It is by dropping it out altogether, throwing it overboard and getting beyond it, helping to make a universe that shall forget its very place and name.*

It is then perfectly possible to accept sincerely a drastic kind of a universe from which the element of "seriousness" is not to be expelled. Whoso does so is, it seems to me, a genuine pragmatist. He is willing to live on a scheme of uncertified possibilities which he trusts; willing to pay with his own person, if need be, for the realization of the ideals which he frames.

What now actually *are* the other forces which he trusts to co-operate with him, in a universe of such a type? They are at least his fellow men, in the stage of being which our actual universe has reached. But are there not superhuman forces also, such as religious men of the pluralistic type we have been considering have always believed in? Their words may have sounded monistic when they said "there is no God but God"; but the original polytheism of mankind has only imperfectly and vaguely sublimated itself into monotheism, and monotheism itself, so far as it was religious and not a scheme of classroom instruction for the metaphysicians, has always viewed God as but one helper, *primus inter pares,* in the midst of all the shapers of the great world's fate.

I fear that my previous lectures, confined as they have been to human and humanistic aspects, may have left the impression on many of you that pragmatism means methodically to leave the superhuman out. I have shown small respect indeed for the Absolute, and I have until this moment spoken of no other superhuman hypothesis but that. But I trust that you see sufficiently that the Absolute has nothing but its superhumanness in common with the theistic God. On pragmatistic principles, if the hypothesis of God works satisfactorily in the widest sense of the word, it is true. Now whatever its residual difficulties may be, experience shows that it certainly does work, and that the problem is to build it out and determine it so that it will combine satisfactorily with all the other working truths. I can not start upon a whole theology at the end of this last lecture; but when I tell you that I have written a book on men's religious experience, which on the whole has been regarded as making for the reality of God, you will perhaps exempt my own pragmatism from the charge of being an atheistic system. I firmly disbelieve, myself, that our human experience is the highest form of experience extant in the universe. I believe rather that we stand in much the same relation to the whole of the universe as our canine and feline pets do to the whole of human life. They inhabit our drawing-rooms and libraries. They take part in scenes of whose significance they have no inkling. They are merely tangent to curves of history the beginnings and ends and forms of which pass wholly beyond their ken. So we are tangent to the wider life of things. But, just as many of the dog's and cat's ideals coincide with our ideals, and the dogs and cats have daily living proof of the fact, so we may well believe, on the proofs that religious experience affords, that higher powers exist and are at work to save the world on ideal lines similar to our own.

You see that pragmatism can be called religious, if you allow that religion can be pluralistic or merely melioristic in type. But whether you will finally put up with that type of religion or not is a question that only you yourself can decide. Pragmatism has to postpone dogmatic answer, for we do not yet know certainly which type of religion is going to work best in the long run. The various overbeliefs of men, their several faith-ventures, are in fact what are needed to bring the evidence in. You will probably make your own ventures severally. If radically tough, the hurly-burly of the sensible facts of nature will be enough for you, and you will need no religion at all. If radically tender, you will take up with the more monistic form of religion: the pluralistic form, with its reliance on possibilities that are not necessities, will not seem to afford you security enough.

But if you are neither tough nor tender in an extreme and radical sense, but mixed as most of us are, it may seem to you that the type of pluralistic and moralistic religion that I have offered is as good a religious synthesis as you are likely to find. Between the two extremes of crude naturalism on the one hand and transcendental absolutism on the other, you may find that what I take the liberty of calling the pragmatistic or melioristic type of theism is exactly what you require.

JUSTICE AND SOCIETY

One very practical way in which ethical problems arise is in the relation of the individual to the group, particularly the political group. What do I owe to the State? What does the State owe me? Although political relations are in large part power relations, most moral philosophers will not let the problem drop with the aphorism that might makes right. The moral philosopher seeks to find what it is that authorizes or authenticates the use of public power. If he can find that, it is relatively easy to decide what it is he owes to the State and what the State owes him.

Invariably, State power is exercised in the name of justice. Whatever else may be offered in explanation of the origin of wars and tax assessments, they are all advertised under the banner of justice, either social or economic. But if the State acts in the name of justice, what could ever justify a man's refusal to obey State edicts? Surely only an appeal to that very justice which the State offers as authentication of its own action. And it is here that the moral conflict arises. That is to say, in justifying his civil disobedience or his revolution, the reformer will have to explain not only his own action but what it is that he conceives to be the authority of the State against which he protests. Nowhere is the logic of political protest clearer than in the argument of the American Declaration of Independence.[1] But the familiar

[1] "When in the course of human events, it becomes necessary for one people to dissolve the political bonds which have connected them with another, and to assume among the powers of the earth the separate and equal station to which the laws of nature and nature's God entitle them, a decent respect to the opinions of mankind requires that they should declare the causes which impel them to the separation.

We hold these truths to be self-evident; that all men are created equal; that they are

Lockean-Jeffersonian theory need not be the only justification of revolution and its corollary, the authentication of State power.

The four selections that follow argue the complicated relations between the individual and the State—all in the name of justice. St. Paul's letter to the Romans, although not perhaps fully consistent with other statements of Christian belief, contends that political obedience is religiously grounded. If social hisory is the arena of God's action, then social power and authority must derive from God's power and authority. Although it is surely implied that God's servants, the political authorities, are answerable to God in carrying out their commissions, it is equally clear that the subject cannot invoke God's name in support of revolution.

A similar appeal to cosmic power in justification of social power is contained in the selection from Hsüntze. Drawing on the ancient Chinese belief in the existence of an overarching cosmic pattern and the Confucian doctrine of the five stable, social relationships, Hsüntze holds that to put oneself in accord with the government is to put oneself in accord with the very principles of Being. As in St. Paul, it is clear that the emperor would do well to guide his actions by Heaven's decree. And the social revolutionary is encouraged to believe that in his protest he opposes not only a human power, but Heaven itself.

In Plato's *Crito,* however, the justification of State action against the individual is offered not so much in terms of a cosmic sanction as in an implied contract between the citizen and the laws which have guarded, even reared, him in happier times. Unjustly, although legally, sentenced to death, Socrates is offered the opportunity to escape his prison cell. In the dialogue with his friend Crito, and in imagined conversation with the Laws of Athens, Socrates wrestles with the delicate balance between momentary injustice and the lasting demands of civil obedience. If his conclusion offers little that is pleasing to the revolutionary activist, it has given much solace to the quiet martyr.

Thoreau's essay on civil disobedience follows by a year and a half his brief imprisonment for failure to pay the poll tax. His concern is not so much with the Mexican War and the institution of slavery as it is with the inertia which encourages good men to obey unjust laws. The contrast with

---

endowed by their creator with inherent and inalienable rights; that among these are life, liberty, and the pursuit of happiness; that to secure these rights, governments are instituted among men, deriving their just powers from the consent of the governed; that whenever any form of government becomes destructive of these ends, it is the right of the people to alter or to abolish it, and to institute new government, laying its foundation on such principles, and organizing its powers in such form, as to them shall seem most likely to effect their safety and happiness. Prudence, indeed, will dictate that governments long established should not be changed for light and transient causes; and accordingly all experience hath shown that mankind are more disposed to suffer while evils are sufferable, than to right themselves by abolishing the forms to which they are accustomed. But when a long train of abuses and usurpations begun at a distinguished period and pursuing invariably the same object, evinces a design to reduce them under absolute despotism, it is their right, it is their duty, to throw off such government, and to provide new guards for their future security."

Socrates is far from perfect,[2] but Thoreau does call into question the validity of Socrates' loyalty to laws that have treated him unjustly. It may be that Thoreau too would have refused escape from Socrates' prison (indeed, there is evidence that he was angry when prematurely released, after only one day, from Concord jail), but it seems unlikely that his reasons would have been the same as those given to Socrates by the Laws.

[2] See also Thoreau's view that "under a government which imprisons unjustly, the true place for a just man is also a prison."

St. Paul's Letter to the Romans

St. Paul's Letter to the Romans 12:1–15:13 was intended to provide guidance to a struggling Christian community in a world that had declared its faith illegal.

Chapter 12

I appeal to you therefore, brethren, by the mercies of God, to present your bodies as a living sacrifice, holy and acceptable to God, which is your spiritual worship. 2 Do not be conformed to this world but be transformed by the renewal of your mind, that you may prove what is the will of God, what is good and acceptable and perfect.

3 For by the grace given to me I bid every one among you not to think of himself more highly than he ought to think, but to think with sober judgment, each according to the measure of faith which God has assigned him. 4 For as in one body we have many members, and all the members do not have the same function, 5 so we, though many, are one body in Christ, and individually members one of another. 6 Having gifts that differ according to the grace given to us, let us use them: if prophecy, in proportion to our faith; 7 if service, in our serving; he who teaches, in his teaching; 8 he who exhorts, in his exhortation; he who contributes, in liberality; he who gives aid, with zeal; he who does acts of mercy, with cheerfulness.

9 Let love be genuine; hate what is evil, hold fast to what is good; 10 love one another with brotherly affection; outdo one another in showing honor. 11 Never flag in zeal, be aglow with the Spirit, serve the Lord. 12 Rejoice in your hope, be patient in tribulation, be constant in prayer. 13 Contribute to the needs of the saints, practice hospitality.

14 Bless those who persecute you; bless and do not curse them. 15 Rejoice with those who rejoice, weep with those who weep. 16 Live in harmony with one another; do not be haughty, but associate with the lowly; never be conceited. 17 Repay no one evil for evil, but take thought for what is noble in the sight of all. 18 If possible, so far as it depends upon you, live peaceably with all. 19 Beloved, never avenge yourselves, but leave it to the wrath of God; for it is written, "Vengeance is mine, I will repay, says the Lord." 20 No, "if your enemy is hungry, feed him; if he is thirsty, give him drink; for by so doing you will heap burning coals upon his head." 21 Do not be overcome by evil, but overcome evil with good.

The selection is from the Revised Standard Version Bible and is used by permission.

Chapter 13

Let every person be subject to the governing authorities. For there is no authority except from God, and those that exist have been instituted by God. ² Therefore he who resists the authorities resists what God has appointed, and those who resist will incur judgment. ³ For rulers are not a terror to good conduct, but to bad. Would you have no fear of him who is in authority? Then do what is good, and you will receive his approval, ⁴ for he is God's servant for your good. But if you do wrong, be afraid, for he does not bear the sword in vain; he is the servant of God to execute his wrath on the wrongdoer. ⁵ Therefore one must be subject, not only to avoid God's wrath but also for the sake of conscience. ⁶ For the same reason you also pay taxes, for the authorities are ministers of God, attending to this very thing. ⁷ Pay all of them their dues, taxes to whom taxes are due, revenue to whom revenue is due, respect to whom respect is due, honor to whom honor is due.

8 Owe no one anything, except to love one another; for he who loves his neighbor has fulfilled the law. ⁹ The commandments, "You shall not commit adultery, You shall not kill, You shall not steal, You shall not covet," and any other commandment, are summed up in this sentence, "You shall love your neighbor as yourself." ¹⁰ Love does no wrong to a neighbor; therefore love is the fulfilling of the law.

11 Besides this you know what hour it is, how it is full time now for you to wake from sleep. For salvation is nearer to us now than when we first believed; ¹² the night is far gone, the day is at hand. Let us then cast off the works of darkness and put on the armor of light; ¹³ let us conduct ourselves becomingly as in the day, not in reveling and drunkenness, not in debauchery and licentiousness, not in quarreling and jealousy. ¹⁴ But put on the Lord Jesus Christ, and make no provision for the flesh, to gratify its desires.

Chapter 14

As for the man who is weak in faith, welcome him, but not for disputes over opinions. ² One believes he may eat anything, while the weak man eats only vegetables. ³ Let not him who eats despise him who abstains, and let not him who abstains pass judgment on him who eats; for God has welcomed him. ⁴ Who are you to pass judgment on the servant of another? It is before his own master that he stands or falls. And he will be upheld, for the Master is able to make him stand.

5 One man esteems one day as better than another, while another man esteems all days alike. Let every one be fully convinced in his own mind. ⁶ He who observes the day, observes it in honor of the Lord. He also who eats, eats in honor of the Lord, since he gives thanks to God; while he who abstains, abstains in honor of the Lord and gives thanks to God. ⁷ None of us lives to himself, and none of us dies to himself. ⁸ If we live, we live to the Lord, and if we die, we die to the Lord; so then, whether we live or whether we die, we are the Lord's. ⁹ For to this end Christ died and lived again, that he might be Lord both of the dead and of the living.

10 Why do you pass judgment on your brother? Or you, why do you despise your brother? For we shall all stand before the judgment seat of God; ¹¹ for it is written,

"As I live, says the Lord, every knee shall bow to me,
and every tongue shall give praise to God."

¹² So each of us shall give account of himself to God.

13 Then let us no more pass judgment on one another, but rather decide never to put a stumbling-block or hindrance in the way of a brother. ¹⁴ I know and am

persuaded in the Lord Jesus that nothing is unclean in itself; but it is unclean for any one who thinks it unclean. [15] If your brother is being injured by what you eat, you are no longer walking in love. Do not let what you eat cause the ruin of one for whom Christ died. [16] So do not let what is good to you be spoken of as evil. [17] For the kingdom of God does not mean food and drink but righteousness and peace and joy in the Holy Spirit; [18] he who thus serves Christ is acceptable to God and approved by men. [19] Let us then pursue what makes for peace and for mutual upbuilding. [20] Do not, for the sake of food, destroy the work of God. Everything is indeed clean, but it is wrong for any one to make others fall by what he eats; [21] it is right not to eat meat or drink wine or do anything that makes your brother stumble. [22] The faith that you have, keep between yourself and God; happy is he who has no reason to judge himself for what he approves. [23] But he who has doubts is condemned, if he eats, because he does not act from faith; for whatever does not proceed from faith is sin.

Chapter 15

We who are strong ought to bear with the failings of the weak, and not to please ourselves; [2] let each of us please his neighbor for his good, to edify him. [3] For Christ did not please himself; but, as it is written, "The reproaches of those who reproached thee fell on me." [4] For whatever was written in former days was written for our instruction, that by steadfastness and by the encouragement of the scriptures we might have hope. [5] May the God of steadfastness and encouragement grant you to live in such harmony with one another, in accord with Christ Jesus, [6] that together you may with one voice glorify the God and Father of our Lord Jesus Christ.

7 Welcome one another, therefore, as Christ has welcomed you, for the glory of God. [8] For I tell you that Christ became a servant to the circumcised to show God's truthfulness, in order to confirm the promises given to the patriarchs, [9] and in order that the Gentiles might glorify God for his mercy. As it is written,

"Therefore I will praise thee among
  the Gentiles,
and sing to thy name";
[10] and again it is said,
"Rejoice, O Gentiles, with his people";
[11] and again,
"Praise the Lord, all Gentiles,
and let all the peoples praise him";
[12] and further Isaiah says,
"The root of Jesse shall come,
he who rises to rule the Gentiles;
in him shall the Gentiles hope."

[13] May the God of hope fill you with all joy and peace in believing, so that by the power of the Holy Spirit you may abound in hope.

Kingly Government

Hsüntze (fl. 298–238 B.C.) is the leading representative of ancient Confucian naturalism.

Heaven and Earth are the source of life. The rules of proper conduct (*Li*) and justice (*Yi*) are the source of good government; the superior man is the source of the rules of proper conduct (*Li*) and justice (*Yi*). To carry them out, to practise them, to study them much, and to love them greatly is the source of being a superior man. For Heaven and Earth give birth to the superior man; the superior man brings Heaven and Earth into order; the superior man forms a triad with Heaven and Earth; he is the controller of all things, the father and mother of the people. Without the superior man Heaven and Earth are not ordered, the rules of proper conduct (*Li*) and justice (*Yi*) have no control. When on the one hand there is no prince and leader, on the other hand there cannot be the distinction of father and son—this is what is called extreme disorder. The prince and minister, the father and son, the older and younger brother, husband and wife—here we have a beginning and end, an end and a beginning; this social structure exhibits the same principles as Heaven and Earth; it is of equal permanence with the universe—this is called the great foundation. Hence mourning rites, sacrificial rites, court ceremonies, and methods of courtesy are governed by one principle. Promotion, degradation, condemnation to death, permission to live [1] giving and taking away are governed by the same principle. That the prince should be treated as prince, the minister should be treated as minister, the father should be treated as father, the son as son, the older brother as older brother, the younger brother as younger brother, is following the same pinciple. That the farmer should be treated as farmer, the scholar as scholar, the labourer as labourer and the merchant as merchant is the same principle.

Water and fire have essences, but not life; herbs and trees have life, but no

[1] The opposite of condemnation to death, i.e., acquitting an accused man and allowing him to live. We must remember that in Hsüntze's time government was not by law, but by the ruler, who was and is yet the law-maker, prosecutor, and judge. The acquittal of an accused man was solely dependent upon his word.

From *The Works of Hsüntze*, transl. Homer H. Dubs; London, Arthur Probsthain, 1928. Reprinted by permission of Arthur Probsthain, London.

knowledge; birds and beasts have knowledge but no sense of what are rights (*Yi*). Man has an essence, life, knowledge, and in addition has a sense of human rights (*Yi*); hence he is the highest being on earth. His strength is not equal to that of the bull; his running is not equal to that of the horse; yet the bull and horse are used by him. How is that? Men are able to form social organizations, the former are not able to form social organizations. How is it that men are able to form social organizations? Because of their distinctions. How is it that distinctions can be carried out? Through rights (*Yi*). For class rights (*Yi*) are harmonized through social distinctions. When people are harmonious, they can unite; when united, they have greater strength; when they have great strength, they become strong; when strong, they can dominate nature. Hence they can have palaces and houses for habitation. Hence they can order their actions according to the four seasons and control all things. Hence they can enjoy the goodness of the whole world. They gain this for no other reason than that they have social distinctions and class rights (*Yi*). Hence, if men are to live, they cannot get along without forming a social organization. If they form a social organization, but have no social distinctions, then they will quarrel; if they quarrel, there will be disorder; if there is disorder, people will fail to co-operate; if they fail to co-operate, then they will be weak; if they are weak, then they will not be able to dominate nature. Hence they could not have palaces or houses for habitation. All of which means that people cannot abandon the rules of proper conduct (*Li*) or class rights (*Yi*) for an instant. He who is able thereby to serve his parents, is said to have filial piety; he who is able thereby to serve his older brother is said to have brotherly respect; he who is able thereby to serve his superior is said be obedient; he who is able thereby to utilize his inferiors is said to

have the virtues of a prince. A prince is one who is good at social organization.

If this doctrine (*Tao*) of forming a social organization is carried out as it should be, then all things will fulfil their appropriate function; the six kinds of domestic animals will all thrive; all living beings will fulfil their destiny. For if their nourishment and growth is at the proper season, then the six kinds of domestic animals will develop and increase; if killing and saving alive are at the proper season, then grass and trees will flourish. If government decrees are timely, the people will be united, the worthy and the good will serve the ruler; it will be the rule of a Sage-King. When shrubs and trees are in bloom and leaf, the axe must not enter the forest, people must not cut short the life of the trees or shrubs when young, nor stop their growth; when sea tortoises, water lizards, fish, turtles, eels, and sturgeons, are full of roe or have spawned, nets or poison must not enter the marshes or pools, people must not cut short the life of these water creatures when young nor stop their growth. The springtime ploughing, the summertime weeding, the fall harvesting, and the winter storing away of the grain—these four things must not be out of season. Hence the five cereals will not fail, and the people will have an abundance of food. Ponds, pools, streams, and marshes should be strictly closed at the proper time; hence fish and turtles will be very plentiful, and the people will have a surplus for use. The cutting down and growth of timber should not be at the wrong season; then the mountains and forests will not be bare, and the people will have a surplus of timber. This is the way the Sage-King uses the country's resources. On the one hand, he observes the heavens, and on the other he applies it to the earth. He fills up what is lacking in heaven and earth, and diffuses it upon all things. He makes plain that which was obscure; he makes long that which was too short; he enlarges that which was too narrow. Although he is as wise and great as the gods, yet he is very simple. Hence it is said: By one principle he unifies the whole. The man who acts in this way is called a Sage.

Crito

PLATO

Plato (428-7–348-7 B.C.) has been one of the most influential philosophers in the Western tradition. The Apology, Crito, *and* Phaedo *are his record of the trial, imprisonment, and death of his mentor Socrates.*

Scene: *The Prison of Socrates*

SOCRATES: Why have you come at this hour, Crito? it must be quite early?

CRITO: Yes, certainly.

SOCRATES: What is the exact time?

CRITO: The dawn is breaking.

SOCRATES: I wonder that the keeper of the prison would let you in.

CRITO: He knows me, because I often come, Socrates; moreover, I have done him a kindness.

SOCRATES: And are you only just arrived?

CRITO: No, I came some time ago.

SOCRATES: Then why did you sit and say nothing, instead of at once awakening me?

CRITO: I should not have liked myself, Socrates, to be in such great trouble and unrest as you are—indeed I should not: I have been watching with amazement your peaceful slumbers; and for that reason I did not awake you, because I wished to minimize the pain. I have always thought you to be of a happy disposition; but never did I see anything like the easy, tranquil manner in which you bear this calamity.

SOCRATES: Why, Crito, when a man has reached my age he ought not to be repining at the approach of death.

CRITO: And yet other men find themselves in similar misfortunes, and age does not prevent them from repining.

SOCRATES: That is true. But you have not told me why you come at this early hour.

CRITO: I come to bring you a message which is sad and painful; not, as I believe, to yourself, but to all of us who are your friends, and saddest of all to me.

SOCRATES: What? Has the ship come from Delos, on the arrival of which I am to die?

CRITO: No, the ship has not actually arrived, but she will probably be here to-day, as persons who have come from

---

This translation of the *Crito* was made by Benjamin Jowett.

Sunium tell me that they left her there; and therefore to-morrow, Socrates, will be the last day of your life.

SOCRATES: Very well, Crito; if such is the will of God, I am willing; but my belief is that there will be a delay of a day.

CRITO: Why do you think so?

SOCRATES: I will tell you. I am to die on the day after the arrival of the ship.

CRITO: Yes; that is what the authorities say.

SOCRATES: But I do not think that the ship will be here until to-morrow; this I infer from a vision which I had last night, or rather only just now, when you fortunately allowed me to sleep.

CRITO: And what was the nature of the vision?

SOCRATES: There appeared to me the likeness of a woman, fair and comely, clothed in bright raiment, who called to me and said: O Socrates,

"The third day hence to fertile Phthia
    shalt thou go."

CRITO: What a singular dream, Socrates!

SOCRATES: There can be no doubt about the meaning, Crito, I think.

CRITO: Yes; the meaning is only too clear. But, oh! my beloved Socrates, let me entreat you once more to take my advice and escape. For if you die I shall not only lose a friend who can never be replaced, but there is another evil: people who do not know you and me will believe that I might have saved you if I had been willing to give money, but that I did not care. Now, can there be a worse disgrace than this—that I should be thought to value money more than the life of a friend? For the many will not be persuaded that I wanted you to escape, and that you refused.

SOCRATES: But why, my dear Crito, should we care about the opinion of the many? Good men, and they are the only persons who are worth considering, will think of these things truly as they occurred.

CRITO: But you see, Socrates, that the opinion of the many must be regarded, for what is now happening shows that they can do the greatest evil to any one who has lost their good opinion.

SOCRATES: I only wish it were so, Crito; and that the many could do the greatest evil; for then they would also be able to do the greatest good—and what a fine thing this would be! But in reality they can do neither; for they cannot make a man either wise or foolish; and whatever they do is the result of chance.

CRITO: Well, I will not dispute with you; but please to tell me, Socrates, whether you are not acting out of regard to me and your other friends: are you not afraid that if you escape from prison we may get into trouble with the informers for having stolen you away, and lose either the whole or a great part of our property; or that even a worse evil may happen to us? Now, if you fear on our account, be at ease; for in order to save you, we ought surely to run this, or even a greater risk; be persuaded, then, and do as I say.

SOCRATES: Yes, Crito, that is one fear which you mention, but by no means the only one.

CRITO: Fear not—there are persons who are willing to get you out of prison at no great cost; and as for the informers, they are far from being exorbitant in their demands—a little money will satisfy them. My means, which are certainly ample, are at your service, and if you have a scruple about spending all mine, here are strangers who will give you the use of theirs; and one of them, Simmias the Theban, has brought a large sum of money for this very purpose; and Cebes and many others are prepared to spend their money in helping you to escape. I say, therefore, do not hesitate on our account, and do not say, as you did in the court, that you will have a difficulty in knowing what to do with yourself anywhere else. For men will love you in other places to which you may go, and not in Athens only; there are friends of mine in Thessaly, if you like to go to them, who will value and protect you, and no Thessalian will give you any trouble. Nor can I think that you are at all justified, Socrates, in betraying your own life when you might be saved; in acting thus you are playing into the hands of your enemies, who are hurrying on your destruction. And further I should say that you are deserting your own children; for you might bring them up and educate them; instead of which you go away and leave them, and they will have to take their chance; and if they do not meet with the usual fate of orphans, there will be small thanks to you. No man should bring children into the world who is unwilling to persevere to the end in their nurture and education. But you appear to be choosing the easier part, not the better and man-lier, which would have been more becoming in one who professes to care for virtue in all his actions, like yourself. And indeed, I am ashamed not only of you, but of us who are your friends, when I reflect that the whole business will be attributed entirely to our want of courage. The trial need never have come on, or might have been managed differently; and this last act, or crowning folly, will seem to have occurred through our negligence and cowardice, who might have saved you, if we had been good for anything; and you might have saved yourself, for there was no difficulty at all. See now, Socrates, how sad and discreditable are the consequences, both to us and you. Make up your mind then, or rather have your mind already made up, for the time of deliberation is over, and there is only one thing to be done, which must be done this very night,

and if we delay at all will be no longer practicable or possible; I beseech you therefore, Socrates, be persuaded by me, and do as I say.

SOCRATES: Dear Crito, your zeal is invaluable, if a right one; but if wrong, the greater the zeal the greater the danger; and therefore we ought to consider whether I shall or shall not do as you say. For I am and always have been one of those natures who must be guided by reason, whatever the reason may be which upon reflection appears to me to be the best; and now that this chance has befallen me, I cannot repudiate my own words: the principles which I have hitherto honoured and revered I still honour, and unless we can at once find other and better principles, I am certain not to agree with you; no, not even if the power of the multitude could inflict many more imprisonments, confiscations, deaths, frightening us like children with hobgoblin terrors. What will be the fairest way of considering the question? Shall I return to your old argument about the opinions of men?—we were saying that some of them are to be regarded, and others not. Now were we right in maintaining this before I was condemned? And has the argument which was once good now proved to be talk for the sake of talking—mere childish nonsense? That is what I want to consider with your help, Crito: whether, under my present circumstances, the argument appears to be in any way different or not; and is to be allowed by me or disallowed. That argument, which, as I believe, is maintained by many persons of authority, was to the effect, as I was saying, that the opinions of some men are to be regarded, and of other men not to be regarded. Now you, Crito, are not going to die to-morrow—at least, there is no human probability of this—and therefore you are disinterested and not liable to be deceived by the circumstances in which you are placed. Tell me then, whether I am right in saying that some opinions, and the opinions of some men only, are to be valued, and that other opinions, and the opinions of other men, are not to be valued. I ask you whether I was right in maintaining this?

CRITO: Certainly.

SOCRATES: The good are to be regarded, and not the bad?

CRITO: Yes.

SOCRATES: And the opinions of the wise are good, and the opinions of the unwise are evil?

CRITO: Certainly.

SOCRATES: And what was said about another matter? Is the pupil who devotes himself to the practice of gymnastics supposed to attend to the praise and blame and opinion of every man, or of one man only—his physician or trainer, whoever he may be?

CRITO: Of one man only.

SOCRATES: And he ought to fear the censure and welcome the praise of that one only, and not of the many?

CRITO: Clearly so.

SOCRATES: And he ought to act and train, and eat and drink in the way which seems good to his single master who has understanding, rather than according to the opinion of all other men put together?

CRITO: True.

SOCRATES: And if he disobeys and disregards the opinion and approval of the one, and regards the opinion of the many who have no understanding, will he not suffer evil?

CRITO: Certainly he will.

SOCRATES: And what will the evil be, whither tending and what affecting, in the disobedient person?

CRITO: Clearly, affecting the body; that is what is destroyed by the evil.

SOCRATES: Very good; and is not this true, Crito, of other things which we need not separately enumerate? In questions of just and unjust, fair and foul, good and

evil, which are the subjects of our present consultation, ought we to follow the opinion of the many and to fear them; or the opinion of the one man who has understanding? Ought we not to fear and reverence him more than all the rest of the world: and if we desert him shall we not destroy and injure that principle in us which may be assumed to be improved by justice and deteriorated by injustice; there is such a principle?

CRITO: Certainly there is, Socrates.

SOCRATES: Take a parallel instance: if, acting under the advice of those who have no understanding, we destroy that which is improved by health and is deteriorated by disease, would life be worth having? And that which has been destroyed is—the body?

CRITO: Yes.

SOCRATES: Could we live, having an evil and corrupted body?

CRITO: Certainly not.

SOCRATES: And will life be worth having, if that higher part of man be destroyed, which is improved by justice and depraved by injustice? Do we suppose that principle, whatever it may be in man, which has to do with justice and injustice, to be inferior to the body?

CRITO: Certainly not.

SOCRATES: More honourable than the body?

CRITO: Far more.

SOCRATES: Then, my friend, we must not regard what the many say of us: but what he, the one man who has understanding of just and unjust, will say, and what the truth will say. And therefore you begin in error when you advise that we should regard the opinion of the many about just and unjust, good and evil, honourable and dishonourable. "Well," some one will say, "but the many can kill us."

CRITO: Yes, Socrates; that will clearly be the answer.

SOCRATES: And it is true: but still I

find with surprise that the old argument is unshaken as ever. And I should like to know whether I may say the same of another proposition—that not life, but a good life, is to be chiefly valued?

CRITO: Yes, that also remains unshaken.

SOCRATES: And a good life is equivalent to a just and honourable one—that holds also?

CRITO: Yes, it does.

SOCRATES: From these premisses I proceed to argue the question whether I ought or ought not to try and escape without the consent of the Athenians: and if I am clearly right in escaping, then I will make the attempt; but if not, I will abstain. The other considerations which you mention, of money and loss of character and the duty of educating one's children, are, I fear, only the doctrines of the multitude, who would be as ready to restore people to life, if they were able, as they are to put them to death—and with as little reason. But now, since the argument has thus far prevailed, the only question which remains to be considered is, whether we shall do rightly either in escaping or in suffering others to aid in our escape and paying them in money and thanks, or whether in reality we shall not do rightly; and if the latter, then death or any other calamity which may ensue on my remaining here must not be allowed to enter into the calculation.

CRITO: I think that you are right, Socrates; how then shall we proceed?

SOCRATES: Let us consider the matter together, and do you either refute me if you can, and I will be convinced; or else cease, my dear friend, from repeating to me that I ought to escape against the wishes of the Athenians: for I highly value your attempts to persuade me to do so, but I may not be persuaded against my own better judgment. And now please to consider my first position, and try how you can best answer me.

CRITO: I will.

SOCRATES: Are we to say that we are never intentionally to do wrong, or that in one way we ought and in another we ought not to do wrong, or is doing wrong always evil and dishonourable, as I was just now saying, and as has been already acknowledged by us? Are all our former admissions which were made within a few days to be thrown away? And have we, at our age, been earnestly discoursing with one another all our life long only to discover that we are no better than children? Or, in spite of the opinion of the many, and in spite of consequences whether better or worse, shall we insist on the truth of what was then said, that injustice is always an evil and dishonour to him who acts unjustly? Shall we say so or not?

CRITO: Yes.

SOCRATES: Then we must do no wrong?

CRITO: Certainly not.

SOCRATES: Nor when injured injure in return, as the many imagine; for we must injure no one at all?

CRITO: Clearly not.

SOCRATES: Again, Crito, may we do evil?

CRITO: Surely not, Socrates.

SOCRATES: And what of doing evil in return for evil, which is the morality of the many—is that just or not?

CRITO: Not just.

SOCRATES: For doing evil to another is the same as injuring him?

CRITO: Very true.

SOCRATES: Then we ought not to retaliate or render evil for evil to any one, whatever evil we may have suffered from him. But I would have you consider, Crito, whether you really mean what you are saying. For this opinion has never been held, and never will be held, by any considerable number of persons; and those who are agreed and those who are not agreed upon this point have no common ground, and can only despise one another when they see how widely they differ. Tell me, then, whether you agree with and assent to my first principle, that neither injury nor retaliation nor warding off evil by evil is ever right. And shall that be the premiss of our argument? Or do you decline and dissent from this? For so I have ever thought, and continue to think; but, if you are of another opinion, let me hear what you have to say. If, however, you remain of the same mind as formerly, I will proceed to the next step.

CRITO: You may proceed, for I have not changed my mind.

SOCRATES: Then I will go on to the next point, which may be put in the form of a question: Ought a man to do what he admits to be right, or ought he to betray the right?

CRITO: He ought to do what he thinks right.

SOCRATES: But if this is true, what is the application? In leaving the prison against the will of the Athenians, do I wrong any? or rather do I wrong those whom I ought least to wrong? Do I not desert the principles which were acknowledged by us to be just—what do you say?

CRITO: I cannot tell, Socrates; for I do not know.

SOCRATES: Then consider the matter in this way: Imagine that I am about to play truant (you may call the proceeding by any name which you like), and the laws and the government come and interrogate me: "Tell us, Socrates," they say; "what are you about? are you not going by an act of yours to overturn us—the laws, and the whole state, as far as in you lies? Do you imagine that a state can subsist and not be overthrown, in which the decisions of law have no power, but are set aside and trampled upon by individuals?" What will be our answer, Crito, to these and the like words? Any one, and especially a rhetorician, will have a good deal to say on behalf of the law which requires a sentence to be carried out. He will argue that this law should not be set aside; and

shall we reply, "Yes; but the state has injured us and given an unjust sentence." Suppose I say that?

CRITO: Very good, Socrates.

SOCRATES: "And was that our agreement with you?" the law would answer; "or were you to abide by the sentence of the state?" And if I were to express my astonishment at their words, the law would probably add: "Answer, Socrates, instead of opening your eyes—you are in the habit of asking and answering questions. Tell us—What complaint have you to make against us which justifies you in attempting to destroy us and the state? In the first place did we not bring you into existence? Your father married your mother by our aid and begat you. Say whether you have any objection to urge against those of us who regulate marriage?" None, I should reply. "Or against those of us who after birth regulate the nurture and education of children, in which you also were trained? Were not the laws, which have the charge of education, right in commanding your father to train you in music and gymnastic?" Right, I should reply. "Well then, since you were brought into the world and nurtured and educated by us, can you deny in the first place that you are our child and slave, as your fathers were before you? And if this is true you are not on equal terms with us; nor can you think that you have a right to do to us what we are doing to you. Would you have any right to strike or revile or do any other evil to your father or your master, if you had one, because you have been struck or reviled by him, or received some other evil at his hands?—you would not say this? And because we think right to destroy you, do you think that you have any right to destroy us in return, and your country as far as in you lies? Will you, O professor of true virtue, pretend that you are justified in this? Has a philosopher like you failed to discover that our country is more to be valued and higher and holier far than mother or father or any ancestor, and more to be regarded in the eyes of the gods and of men of understanding? also to be soothed, and gently and reverently entreated when angry, even more than a father, and either to be persuaded, or if not persuaded, to be obeyed? And when we are punished by her, whether with imprisonment or stripes, the punishment is to be endured in silence; and if she leads us to wounds or death in battle, thither we follow as is right; neither may any one yield or retreat or leave his rank, but whether in battle or in a court of law, or in any other place, he must do what his city and his country order him; or he must change their view of what is just: and if he may do no violence to his father or mother, much less may he do violence to his country." What answer shall we make to this, Crito? Do the laws speak truly, or do they not?

CRITO: I think that they do.

SOCRATES: Then the laws will say, "Consider, Socrates, if we are speaking truly that in your present attempt you are going to do us an injury. For, having brought you into the world, and nurtured and educated you, and given you and every other citizen a share in every good which we had to give, we further proclaim to any Athenian by the liberty which we allow him, that if he does not like us when he has become of age and has seen the ways of the city, and made our acquaintance, he may go where he pleases and take his goods with him. None of us laws will forbid him or interfere with him. Any one who does not like us and the city, and who wants to emigrate to a colony or to any other city, may go where he likes, retaining his property. But he who has experience of the manner in which we order justice and administer the state, and still remains, has entered into an implied contract that he will do as we command him. And he who disobeys us is, as we

maintain, thrice wrong; first, because in disobeying us he is disobeying his parents; secondly, because we are the authors of his education; thirdly, because he has made an agreement with us that he will duly obey our commands; and he neither obeys them nor convinces us that our commands are unjust; and we do not rudely impose them, but give him the alternative of obeying or convincing us; that is what we offer, and he does neither.

"These are the sort of accusations to which, as we were saying, you, Socrates, will be exposed if you accomplish your intentions; you, above all other Athenians." Suppose now I ask, why I rather than anybody else? they will justly retort upon me that I above all other men have acknowledged the agreement. "There is clear proof," they will say, "Socrates, that we and the city were not displeasing to you. Of all Athenians you have been the most constant resident in the city, which, as you never leave, you may be supposed to love. For you never went out of the city either to see the games, except once when you went to the Isthmus, or to any other place unless when you were on military service; nor did you travel as other men do. Nor had you any curiosity to know other states or their laws: your affections did not go beyond us and our state; we were your special favourites, and you acquiesced in our government of you; and here in this city you begat your children, which is a proof of your satisfaction. Moreover, you might in the course of the trial, if you had liked, have fixed the penalty at banishment; the state which refuses to let you go now would have let you go then. But you pretended that you preferred death to exile, and that you were not unwilling to die. And now you have forgotten these fine sentiments, and pay no respect to us the laws, of whom you are the destroyer; and are doing what only a miserable slave would do, running away and turning your back upon the compacts and agreements which you made as a citizen. And first of all answer this very question: Are we right in saying that you agreed to be governed according to us in deed, and not in word only? Is that true or not?" How shall we answer, Crito? Must we not assent?

CRITO: We cannot help it, Socrates.

SOCRATES: Then will they not say: "You, Socrates, are breaking the covenants and agreements which you made with us at your leisure, not in any haste or under any compulsion or deception, but after you have had seventy years to think of them, during which time you were at liberty to leave the city, if we were not to your mind, or if our covenants appeared to you to be unfair. You had your choice, and might have gone either to Lacedaemon or Crete, both which states are often praised by you for their good government, or to some other Hellenic or foreign state. Whereas you, above all other Athenians, seemed to be so fond of the state, or, in other words, of us her laws (and who would care about a state which has no laws?), that you never stirred out of her; the halt, the blind, the maimed were not more stationary in her than you were. And now you run away and forsake your agreements. Not so, Socrates, if you will take our advice; do not make yourself ridiculous by escaping out of the city.

"For just consider, if you transgress and err in this sort of way, what good will you do either to yourself or to your friends? That your friends will be driven into exile and deprived of citizenship, or will lose their property, is tolerably certain; and you yourself, if you fly to one of the neighbouring cities, as, for example, Thebes or Megara, both of which are well governed, will come to them as an enemy, Socrates, and their government will be against you, and all patriotic citizens will cast an evil eye upon you as a subverter of the laws, and you will confirm in the minds of the judges the justice of their own condemnation of you. For he who is a corrupter of the laws is more than likely to be a corrupter of the young and foolish portion of mankind. Will you then flee from well-ordered cities and virtuous men? and is existence worth having on these terms? Or will you go to them without shame, and talk to them, Socrates? And what will you say to them? What you say here about virtue and justice and institutions and laws being the best things among men? Would that be decent of you? Surely not. But if you go away from well-governed states to Crito's friends in Thessaly, where there is great disorder and license, they will be charmed to hear the tale of your escape from prison, set off with ludicrous particulars of the manner in which you were wrapped in a goatskin or some other disguise, and metamorphosed as the manner is of runaways; but will there be no one to remind you that in your old age you were not ashamed to violate the most sacred laws from a miserable desire of a little more life? Perhaps not, if you keep them in a good temper; but if they are out of temper you will hear many degrading things; you will live, but how?—as the flatterer of all men, and the servant of all men; and doing what?—eating and drinking in Thessaly, having gone abroad in order that you may get a dinner. And where will be your fine sentiments about justice and virtue? Say that you wish to live for the sake of your children—you want to bring them up and educate them—will you take them into Thessaly and deprive them of Athenian citizenship? Is this the benefit which you will confer upon them? Or are you under the impression that they will be better cared for and educated here if you are still alive, although absent from them; for your friends will take care of them? Do you fancy that if you are an inhabitant of Thessaly they will take care of them, and if you are an inhabitant of the other world that they will not take care of them?

Nay; but if they who call themselves friends are good for anything, they will—to be sure they will.

"Listen, then, Socrates, to us who have brought you up. Think not of life and children first, and of justice afterwards, but of justice first, that you may be justified before the princes of the world below. For neither will you nor any that belong to you be happier or holier or juster in this life, or happier in another, if you do as Crito bids. Now you depart in innocence, a sufferer and not a doer of evil; a victim, not of the laws but of men. But if you go forth, returning evil for evil, and injury for injury, breaking the covenants and agreements which you have made with us, and wronging those whom you ought least of all to wrong, that is to say, yourself, your friends, your country, and us, we shall be angry with you while you live, and our brethren, the laws in the world below, will receive you as an enemy; for they will know that you have done your best to destroy us. Listen, then, to us and not to Crito."

This, dear Crito, is the voice which I seem to hear murmuring in my ears, like the sound of the flute in the ears of the mystic; that voice, I say, is humming in my ears, and prevents me from hearing any other. And I know that anything more which you may say will be vain. Yet speak, if you have anything to say.

CRITO: I have nothing to say, Socrates.

SOCRATES: Leave me then, Crito, to fulfil the will of God, and to follow whither he leads.

Civil Disobedience

HENRY DAVID THOREAU

Henry David Thoreau (1817–1862), an American Transcendentalist, spent most of his life in Concord, Massachusetts. The essay "Civil Disobedience," part of which is printed below, was first delivered January 26, 1848, and first published in Aesthetic Papers, No. 1, Boston, 1849.

Unjust laws exist: shall we be content to obey them, or shall we endeavor to amend them, and obey them until we have succeeded, or shall we transgress them at once? Men generally, under such a government as this, think that they ought to wait until they have persuaded the majority to alter them. They think that, if they should resist, the remedy would be worse than the evil. But it is the fault of the government itself that the remedy *is* worse than the evil. *It* makes it worse. Why is it not more apt to anticipate and provide for reform? Why does it

From *A Yankee in Canada;* Boston, Houghton Mifflin and Company, 1881.

not cherish its wise minority? Why does it cry and resist before it is hurt? Why does it not encourage its citizens to be on the alert to point out its faults, and *do* better than it would have them? Why does it always crucify Christ, and excommunicate Copernicus and Luther, and pronounce Washington and Franklin rebels?

One would think, that a deliberate and practical denial of its authority was the only offence never contemplated by government; else, why has it not assigned its definite, its suitable and proportionate penalty? If a man who has no property refuses but once to earn nine shillings for the State, he is put in prison for a period unlimited by any law that I know, and determined only by the discretion of those who placed him there; but if he should steal ninety times nine shillings from the State, he is soon permitted to go at large again.

If the injustice is part of the necessary friction of the machine of government, let it go, let it go: perchance it will wear smooth—certainly the machine will wear out. If the injustice has a spring, or a pulley, or a rope, or a crank, exclusively for itself, then perhaps you may consider whether the remedy will not be worse than the evil; but if it is of such a nature that it requires you to be the agent of injustice to another, then, I say, break the law. Let your life be a counter friction to stop the machine. What I have to do is to see, at any rate, that I do not lend myself to the wrong which I condemn.

As for adopting the ways which the State has provided for remedying the evil, I know not of such ways. They take too much time, and a man's life will be gone. I have other affairs to attend to. I came into this world, not chiefly to make this a good place to live in, but to live in it, be it good or bad. A man has not everything to do, but something; and because he cannot do *everything*, it is not neces-

sary that he should do *something* wrong. It is not my business to be petitioning the Governor or the Legislature any more than it is theirs to petition me; and, if they should not hear my petition, what should I do then? But in this case the State has provided no way: its very Constitution is the evil. This may seem to be harsh and stubborn and unconciliatory; but it is to treat with the utmost kindness and consideration the only spirit that can appreciate or deserves it. So is all change for the better, like birth and death, which convulse the body.

I do not hesitate to say, that those who call themselves Abolitionists should at once effectually withdraw their support, both in person and property, from the government of Massachusetts, and not wait till they constitute a majority of one, before they suffer the right to prevail through them. I think that it is enough if they have God on their side, without waiting for that other one. Moreover, any man more right than his neighbors constitutes a majority of one already.

I meet this American government, or its representative, the State government, directly, and face to face, once a year—no more—in the person of its tax-gatherer; this is the only mode in which a man situated as I am necessarily meets it; and it then says distinctly, Recognize me; and the simplest, the most effectual, and, in the present posture of affairs, the indispensablest mode of treating with it on this head, of expressing your little satisfaction with and love for it, is to deny it then. My civil neighbor, the tax-gatherer, is the very man I have to deal with—for it is, after all, with men and not with parchment that I quarrel—and he has voluntarily chosen to be an agent of the government. How shall he ever know well what he is and does as an officer of the government, or as a man, until he is obliged to consider whether he shall treat me, his neighbor, for whom he has respect, as a neighbor and well-disposed man, or as a maniac and disturber of the peace, and see if he can get over this obstruction to his neighborliness without a ruder and more impetuous thought or speech corresponding with his action. I know this well, that if one thousand, if one hundred, if ten men whom I could name—if ten *honest* men only—ay, if *one* HONEST man, in this State of Massachusetts, *ceasing to hold slaves,* were actually to withdraw from this co-partnership, and be locked up in the county jail therefor, it would be the abolition of slavery in America. For it matters not how small the beginning may seem to be: what is once well done is done forever. But we love better to talk about it: that we say is our mission. Reform keeps many scores of newspapers in its service, but not one man. If my esteemed neighbor, the State's ambassador, who will devote his days to the settlement of the question of human rights in the Council Chamber, instead of being threatened with the prisons of Carolina, were to sit down the prisoner of Massachusetts, that State which is so anxious to foist the sin of slavery upon her sister—though at present she can discover only an act of inhospitality to be the ground of a quarrel with her—the Legislature would not wholly waive the subject the following winter.

Under a government which imprisons any unjustly, the true place for a just man is also a prison. The proper place to-day, the only place which Massachusetts has provided for her freer and less desponding spirits, is in her prisons, to be put out and locked out of the State by her own act, as they have already put themselves out by their principles. It is there that the fugitive slave, and the Mexican prisoner on parole, and the Indian come to plead the wrongs of his race, should find them; on that separate, but more free and honorable ground, where the State places those who are not *with* her, but *against* her—the only house in a slave State in which a free man can abide with honor. If any think that their influence would be lost there, and their voices no longer afflict the ear of the State, that they would not be as an enemy within its walls, they do not know by how much truth is stronger than error, nor how much more eloquently and effectively he can combat injustice who has experienced a little in his own person. Cast your whole vote, not a strip of paper merely, but your whole influence. A minority is powerless while it conforms to the majority; it is not even a minority then; but it is irresistible when it clogs by its whole weight. If the alternative is to keep all just men in prison, or give up war and slavery, the State will not hesitate which to choose. If a thousand men were not to pay their tax-bills this year, that would not be a violent and bloody measure, as it would be to pay them, and enable the State to commit violence and shed innocent blood. This is, in fact, the definition of a peaceable revolution, if any such is possible. If the tax-gatherer, or any other public officer, asks me, as one has done, "But what shall I do?" my answer is, "If you really wish to do anything, resign your office." When the subject has refused allegiance, and the officer has resigned his office, then the revolution is accomplished. But even suppose blood should flow. Is there not a sort of blood shed when the conscience is wounded? Through this wound a man's real manhood and immortality flow out, and he bleeds to an everlasting death. I see this blood flowing now.

I have contemplated the imprisonment of the offender, rather than the seizure of his goods—though both will serve the same purpose—because they who assert the purest right, and consequently are most dangerous to a corrupt State, commonly have not spent much time in accumulating property. To such the State renders comparatively small service, and a slight tax is wont to appear exorbitant, particularly if they are obliged to earn it by special labor with their hands. If there were one who lived wholly without the use of money, the State itself would hesitate to demand it of him. But the rich man—not to make any invidious comparison—is always sold to the institution which makes him rich. Absolutely speaking, the more money, the less virtue; for money comes between a man and his objects, and obtains them for him; and it was certainly no great virtue to obtain it. It puts to rest many questions which he would otherwise be taxed to answer; while the only new question which it puts is the hard but superfluous one, how to spend it. Thus his moral ground is taken from under his feet. The opportunities of living are diminished in proportion as what are called the "means" are increased. The best thing a man can do for his culture when he is rich is to endeavor to carry out those schemes which he entertained when he was poor. Christ answered the Herodians according to their condition. "Show me the tribute-money," said he—and one took a penny out of his pocket—if you use money which has the image of Caesar on it, and which he has made current and valuable, that is, *if you are men of the State,* and gladly enjoy the advantages of Caesar's government, then pay him back some of his own when he demands it; "Render therefore to Caesar that which is Caesar's, and to God those things which are God's"—leaving them no wiser than before as to which was which; for they did not wish to know.

When I converse with the freest of my neighbors, I perceive that, whatever they may say about the magnitude and seriousness of the question, and their regard for the public tranquillity, the long and the short of the matter is, that they cannot spare the protection of the existing government, and they dread the consequences to their property and families of disobedience to it. For my own part, I should not like to think that I ever rely on the protection of the State. But, if I deny the authority of the State when it presents its tax-bill, it will soon take and waste all my property, and so harass me and my children without end. This is hard. This makes it impossible for a man to live honestly, and at the same time comfortably, in outward respects. It will not be worth the while to accumulate property; that would be sure to go again. You must hire or squat somewhere, and raise but a small crop, and eat that soon. You must live within yourself, and depend upon yourself always tucked up and ready for a start, and not have many affairs. A man may grow rich in Turkey even, if he will be in all respects a good subject of the Turkish government. Confucius said: "If a state is governed by the principles of reason, poverty and misery are subjects of shame; if a state is not governed by the principles of reason, riches and honors are the subjects of shame." No: until I want the protection of Massachusetts to be extended to me in some distant Southern port, where my liberty is endangered, or until I am bent solely on building up an estate at home by peaceful enterprise, I can afford to refuse allegiance to Massachusetts, and her right to my property and life. It costs me less in every sense to incur the penalty of disobedience to the State, than it would to obey. I should feel as if I were worth less in that case.

Some years ago, the State met me in behalf of the Church, and commanded me to pay a certain sum toward the support of a clergyman whose preaching my father attended, but never I myself. "Pay," it said, "or be locked up in the jail." I declined to pay. But, unfortunately, another man saw fit to pay it. I did not see why the schoolmaster should be taxed to support the priest, and not the priest the schoolmaster; for I was not the State's schoolmaster, but I supported myself by voluntary subscription. I did not see why the lyceum should not present its tax-bill, and have the State to back its demand, as well as the Church. However, at the request of the selectmen, I condescended to make some such statement as this in writing: "Know all men by these presents, that I, Henry Thoreau, do not wish to be regarded as a member of any incorporated society which I have not joined." This I gave to the town clerk; and he has it. The State, having thus learned that I did not wish to be regarded as a member of that church, has never made a like demand on me since; though it said that it must adhere to its original presumption that time. If I had known how to name them, I should then have signed off in detail from all the societies which I never signed on to; but I did not know where to find a complete list.

I have paid no poll-tax for six years. I was put into a jail once on this account, for one night; and, as I stood considering the walls of solid stone, two or three feet thick, the door of wood and iron, a foot thick, and the iron grating which strained the light, I could not help being struck with the foolishness of that institution which treated me as if I were mere flesh and blood and bones, to be locked up. I wondered that it should have concluded at length that this was the best use it could put me to, and had never thought to avail itself of my services in some way. I saw that, if there was a wall of stone between me and my townsmen, there was a still more difficult one to climb or break through, before they could get to be as free as I was. I did not for a moment feel confined, and the walls seemed a great waste of stone and mortar. I felt as if I alone of all my townsmen had paid my tax. They plainly did not know how to treat me, but behaved like persons who are underbred. In every threat and in every compliment there was a blunder; for they thought that my chief desire was to stand the other side of that stone wall. I could not but smile to see how industriously they locked the door on my meditations, which followed them out again without let or hindrance, and *they* were really all that was dangerous. As they could not reach me, they had resolved to punish my body; just as boys, if they cannot come at some person against whom they have a spite, will abuse his dog. I saw that the State was half-witted, that it was timid as a lone woman with her silver spoons, and that it did not know its friends from its foes, and I lost all my remaining respect for it, and pitied it.

Thus the State never intentionally confronts a man's sense, intellectual or moral, but only his body, his senses. It is not armed with superior wit or honesty, but with superior physical strength. I was not born to be forced. I will breathe after my own fashion. Let us see who is the strongest. What force has a multitude? They only can force me who obey a higher law than I. They force me to become like themselves. I do not hear of *men* being *forced* to live this way or that by masses of men. What sort of life were that to live? When I meet a government which says to me, "Your money or your life," why should I be in haste to give it my money? It may be in a great strait, and not know what to do: I cannot help that. It must help itself; do as I do. It is not worth the while to snivel about it. I am not responsible for the successful working of the machinery of society. I am not the son of the engineer. I perceive that, when an acorn and a chestnut fall side by side, the one does not remain inert to make way for the other, but both obey their own laws, and spring and grow and flourish as best they can, till one, perchance, overshadows and destroys the other. If a plant cannot live according to its nature, it dies; and so a man. . . .